DESIGN OF ON-LINE COMPUTER SYSTEMS

DESIGN OF ON-LINE COMPUTER SYSTEMS

EDWARD YOURDON

President, YOURDON inc.

PRENTICE-HALL, INC.
Englewood Cliffs, New Jersey

to Jennifer

© 1972 by
PRENTICE-HALL, INC.
Englewood Cliffs, N.J.

10 9 8 7

ISBN: 0-13-201301-0

Library of Congress Catalog Card Number: 76-39497

Printed in the United States of America

PRENTICE-HALL INTERNATIONAL, INC., London
PRENTICE-HALL OF AUSTRALIA, PTY. LTD., Sydney
PRENTICE-HALL OF CANADA, LTD., Toronto
PRENTICE-HALL OF INDIA PRIVATE LIMITED, New Delhi
PRENTICE-HALL OF JAPAN, INC., Tokyo

CONTENTS

PART II
Designing The System, 73

PART III
Application Programs
For On-Line Systems, 169

PREFACE

As recently as 1965, one prominent writer in the computer field defined a "very large program" as one "sufficiently complex structurally to require more than ten coders for implementation". At present, it seems that even the most modest systems require more than ten programmers, and one often has the feeling that none of them really know how the entire system fits together. On the more complex real-time systems, it becomes apparent that even the most experienced and talented systems analysts do not *really* know what is happening "inside" the system.

I personally feel that much of the blame for this state of affairs lies in our mistaken impression that the field of computer programming is a science; it would be more appropriate to think of it as a *craft*, much like carpentry or tailoring. While programming may draw upon various scientific disciplines, the finished product reflects the idiosyncrasies, the talent and the blunders of an individual. In any trade, one learns by serving an apprenticeship under someone older and wiser; this certainly seems to be true of the computer field. It follows that if the apprentices of the computer field are to learn their trade well, they should be supplied with books that demonstrate practical *techniques* of programming, program design and systems design.

These thoughts formed the background of DESIGN OF ON-LINE COMPUTER SYSTEMS. The major purpose of this book is to present an integrated design guideline for on-line computer systems, focusing on hardware, software, testing, debugging and user considerations. The emphasis is on techniques and approaches that one might take, with an attempt to present trade-offs and alternatives at all levels of design.

I am primarily concerned with the *technical* aspects of such systems (e.g. how to write a good application program, how to devise a good scheduling algorithm), rather than with the management aspects of the system. This does not in any way represent an attempt to minimize the role of good management and good planning in any on-line system. I have found, though, that many of the bad decisions that have been made in *any* large computer system stemmed from the manager's lack of understanding of the technical aspects (and pitfalls) of the system. While it is pointless to ask the manager to keep up with *all* of the developments in the computer field, it is perhaps not unreasonable to ask that he be enough of a generalist to have a fundamental understanding of what his programmers and analysts are up to. Hopefully, this book can serve that function, too.

It is assumed throughout the book that the reader has been exposed to computers and computer programming. Aside from this restriction, no special knowledge of any particular computer, or any particular computer language is assumed. Thus, DESIGN OF ON-LINE COMPUTER SYSTEMS should be relevant to the undergraduate or graduate college student, as well as the programmer or analyst in the business world.

The book is divided into six parts, each of which is basically independent of the others. Part I discusses a number of introductory concepts for those who may be approaching the subject of on-line computer systems for the first time. Included in this section are chapters on terms and concepts, a discussion of the characteristics of common on-line computer systems, and a review of hardware requirements for on-line systems.

Part II of the book is devoted to the planning and analysis required to build an on-line system. The purpose of this section is to present a basic design "methodology" for on-line systems. Also included are chapters on the general feasibility of on-line systems, bottlenecks, empirical design formulas (otherwise known as "rules of thumb"), simulation, modelling and performance measurements.

Parts III and IV are intended for the application programmer and analyst. In this section, we assume that the reader has been presented with a machine and an operating system, and that his job is to design an efficient set of application programs and file organization techniques. Accordingly, various chapters in this section discuss the structure of application programs, command languages, programming languages, file accessing techniques, file security techniques and file recovery considerations. I expect that this part of the book will be of most use to the business-oriented computer professional.

Part V of the book is devoted to a discussion of operating systems for on-line computers. In this section, we assume that the reader is in a position to design his own operating system as well as the application programs. The structure of a generalized operating system is discussed, and each of the major components (scheduler, IO routines, priority control) is discussed at greater length. We also discuss the various ways in which a system can fail, and the various techniques of preventing and minimizing the failure.

Part VI is concerned with one of the more pragmatic aspects of the design of an on-line system—testing and debugging. Since a large number of the system failures mentioned above are due to program errors, or "bugs", it seems reasonable to include a discussion of testing techniques and useful utility programs for checking out on-line systems. Finally, we discuss an on-line debugging program known as DDT.

This book has evolved slowly, over the past few years. In 1967, Larry Constantine, a college class-mate and recognized authority in the field of program design, invited me to develop an intensive seminar entitled *Real-Time Systems Design*. The original 5-page outline for that seminar slowly grew into a set of handwritten notes; these were extensively modified and re-written in 1969 for a seminar entitled *Design of On-Line Computer Systems*, which has been sponsored on a regular basis by the Institute for Advanced Technology, a directorate of the Control Data Corporation. The handwritten notes have since undergone two more revisions, the latest of which was the basis for this book.

The present form of the book represents the influence of over 1000 students—many of whom are far more knowledgeable in this field than I—in my seminars. I shudder, as I am sure most teachers do, when I think back to the woefully inadequate storehouse of knowledge that I had at my command for my first seminar. Whatever merits this book may have are largely due to the comments, suggestions and new insights given to me, over a period of several years, by my students. Through their eyes, I have been able to see the common principles of program design and systems design that are valid on any kind of computer and any kind of on-line system.

In keeping with the theme of this book—that the computer field is a craft in which one's own handiwork is as important as any scientific principles—it is only fitting and proper to acknowledge the skill and artistry of the veterans who tutored me so unselfishly. To Larry Portner of the Digital Equipment Corporation, I owe heartfelt thanks for helping me begin my career in the computer field. Tom Hastings and Dit Morse have probably taught me more about the subjects of operating systems and program design than anyone else, and their friendship and assistance over the years is gratefully acknowledged. In the presence of such experienced masters of the trade, one learns as much through osmosis as through verbal communication. Jerry Wiener of Mandate Systems and Pal Schmelzer of E.L.I. Computer Time-Sharing also deserve thanks for having broadened my experience to include new machines, new techniques and new ways of looking at computer systems.

EDWARD YOURDON

PART

I

INTRODUCTORY CONCEPTS

TERMS AND CONCEPTS

INTRODUCTION

Once upon a time a sailor was shipwrecked on the shores of a deserted island. He had no food, no weapons or tools, and, worst of all, no clothing. Being a somewhat organized fellow, he sat down in the sand and tried to decide which of his basic needs—namely food, clothing, and shelter—he should worry about first. Since food was uppermost in his mind, he decided that his first project should be to hunt one of the animals in the nearby forests. However, after a little more thought, he decided that he could not do any hunting, since, without clothing, his skin would be scratched and torn by the thorns and bushes. Similarly, he reasoned that while it would be nice to build himself a shelter, his nakedness prevented him from going into the forest to chop down trees for a house. Finally, he considered clothing—but since he had no way of sewing anything, his only alternative was to go into the forest and hunt an animal, from whose skin he could make a leather garment. Once again, he was foiled, for he could not go into the forest without any clothing. After several more hours of thought, he decided that there simply was no solution to the problem, so he sat on the beach and waited to be rescued.

The moral, of course, is that it is often very easy to be overwhelmed by difficulties when embarking upon a new project—especially if one does not have a backlog of knowledge or experience to serve as a guide. This situation is often true in the computer field, and the result is that an indefinite amount of time is spent in planning, with each new plan being rejected because it poses new problems or does not solve existing ones. In the end, the project may never get done.

The purpose of this book is to provide enough information and enough of a guideline that the dilemma posed above may be avoided. In order to accomplish this, we must first solve the problem that our shipwrecked sailor was unable to solve: that of deciding where to *begin*.

Since the digital computer has been in existence for almost a generation already, we may safely assume that the reader has had at least some exposure to the basic hardware and software aspects of computers. However, this book is aimed at only one segment of the computer field—the area of on-line systems. Any detailed discussion of on-line systems may introduce terms and concepts that are unfamiliar or confusing to one whose background has been in another area of the computer field. Thus, it seems that a logical way of beginning our discussion is to agree on some common definitions of terms.

There are several other good reasons for emphasizing these definitions— the main one being that, in many cases, there are no definitions that have been documented and agreed upon. Since the computer field is so "glamor"-oriented, many technical terms, such as "time-sharing," have different connotations in different industries, in different areas of the country, or among different manufacturers of computer equipment. While it is perhaps too much to ask that everyone use all of the technical jargon in exactly the same way, it is important for us to at least have a feeling for the manner in which the terms are used.

On-Line

An obvious choice of a term with which to begin our discussion is that of "on-line," as illustrated in Figure A1. Let us begin by giving a fairly loose, but formal, definition:

> An *on-line* system is one which accepts input directly from the area where it is created. It is also a system in which the output, or results of computation, are returned directly to the area where they are required.

It should be noted that this definition is not very restrictive; a number of computer systems might fit this definition even though we would ordinarily not think of them as "on-line." In fact, the normal use of the word "on-line" assumes a few additional conditions:

1 *Remote access*

The formal definition above implies that the input is delivered to the computer from a *remote* area (i.e. *not* by means of a card reader, magnetic tape, or paper tape reader located in the computer room). This is felt by some to be a *necessary* condition for on-line computer systems.

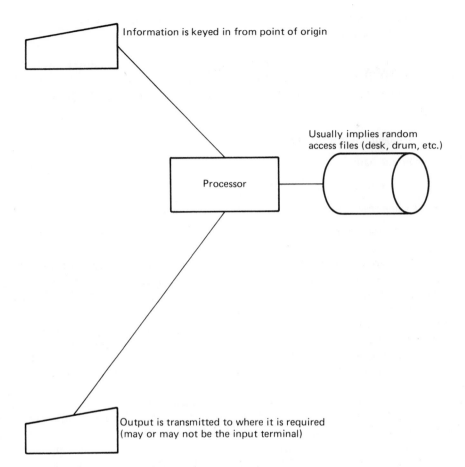

Fig. A1 On-line computer systems

2   *Files and data maintained on-line*

Another characteristic that is common (and, according to some, necessary) among on-line systems is a data base maintained in core memory, or on a random access device—disk, drum, data cell, etc. An on-line system is rarely characterized by large serially-accessed files on magnetic tape or cards.

3   *A "people-orientation"*

The current use of the word "on-line" throughout the computer industry suggests that on-line systems are "people-oriented" systems. That is, "on-line" usually has the connotation of teletypewriter terminals or cathode-ray tubes (CRTs), with which people interact to obtain inventory information, results of scientific calculations, and so forth. This is an important point, for it means that many computer people would prefer not to refer to a *process control* system as "on-line," but rather as "real-time." This is a good example of the kind of confusion that sometimes arises in the use of these closely-related technical terms.

Many of the on-line systems that are being designed today are business-oriented systems, and the list of examples that one might cite is almost endless. Some of the more common types of on-line systems are the following:

1   Management information systems

2   On-line banking systems

3   Medical information systems

4   Airline reservation systems

5   Sales order entry systems

Finally, we should point out that while it is extremely common for on-line systems to include a number of other characteristics—time-sharing, multiprogramming, real-time, and multiprocessing, for example—these are not *necessary* characteristics. For example, a number of sales order entry systems will allow a salesman to input the details of a sale from a remote terminal in his sales office. However, for reasons of simplicity and greater reliability, input transactions may be stored, *without processing*, on disk or tape. A batch program, often on a different machine, will later examine the transactions, update the appropriate files, and create a tape of output transactions to be sent back to the salesman the next morning. Such a system might not be considered "real-time," since it does not give the salesman immediate information on depleted inventory or poor credit risk; in its simplest form, it may not even involve time-sharing, multi-programming or multiprocessing. Yet it *is* an on-line system: the salesman *is* sending input to the computer from his remote sales office, and the output *is* returned to the sales office the next morning.

Real-Time

Another important term in the on-line computer field is the word "real-time," illustrated in Figure A2. Perhaps the best definition is that given by James Martin in *Design of Real-Time Computer Systems:*†

> A real time computer system may be defined as one which controls an environment by receiving data, processing them, and returning the results sufficiently quickly to affect the environment at that time.

---

† James Martin *Design of Real-Time Computer Systems* (Englewood Cliffs, N.J.: Prentice-Hall, 1967)

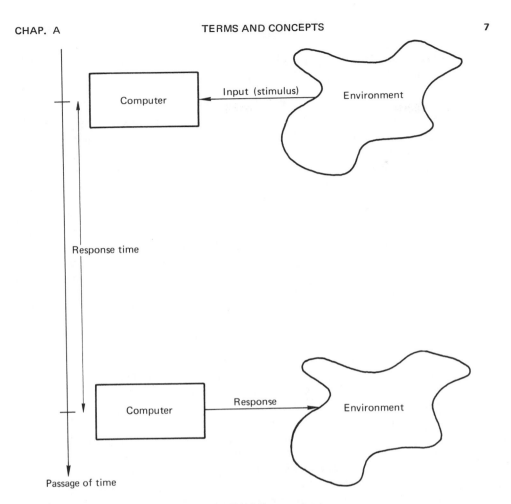

Fig. A2 Real-time systems

Once again, we have a definition that is fairly loose and non-restrictive. Presumably, a computer system that interacted with the shop foreman to control a manufacturing process might be considered "real-time" if it responded within five or ten minutes—because that would be fast enough to keep up with the typical manufacturing process. We could use the same argument for systems that might take hours, or even days to respond on the theory that the computer was actually keeping up with the environment.

However, it is usually not reasonable to speak of a system as being "real-time" if it requires more than 30 minutes or so to respond to some form of input. At this point, the computer system will probably begin to take on more and more of the characteristics of a typical batch system, and will bear no *internal* resemblance to a fast real-time system. In fact, most people associate the notion of "real-time" with systems whose response times are on the order of microseconds or milliseconds.

In some cases, it may be desirable to distinguish between systems that *accept data* in real time, and those that actually *process data* in real time. To illustrate the difference, let us briefly consider a few different "real-time" systems:

1 Authorities at the U.S. Panama Canal Zone are currently planning a real-time system that will help predict the occurrence of dangerous fog conditions within the Canal Zone. The system is to gather atmospheric data every 15 minutes, and, after analyzing the data, print the results on a terminal. Since weather conditions usually do not change extremely rapidly, the system designers feel that it is sufficient for the system to report its results within "an hour or two" after the data are received.

It is obvious that the data are not being *processed* under tight real-time conditions. Once the data have been gathered, one could almost have a 2nd generation batch computer perform the analysis. If necessary, the results could be printed on a high-speed printer and a courier could deliver the output to the appropriate location. Note also that the *data collection* requirements are not really very severe. It is reasonable to assume that the atmospheric data will be *continuously* available, and if the computer gets too busy to sample the weather data at precisely 9:00 AM, no great harm will be done if it samples the data 30 seconds late.

2 Next, consider an automated laboratory system. An on-line, real-time computer allows scientists to perform various experiments (e.g. chemical analysis, stress and strain measurements, etc.) with the data being collected and analyzed by the system.

In this case, there *is* a real-time requirement for data collection. Depending on the particular laboratory instrument and the type of experiment being conducted, the computer may have to sample as little as one and as many as 100,000 data points per second. If the computer reacts too slowly and misses some data, the resulting analysis may be significantly inaccurate.

On the other hand, there may not be a requirement to *process* the data in real time. It would be nice, of course, to return the results of the analysis to the scientist within a few minutes after the end of the experiment (and in some cases, it may actually be necessary—the scientist may want to use the results of one experiment to determine the nature of the next one). However, in many cases, it is reasonable to ask the scientist to wait 30 minutes or an hour or even a day for the results. The processing could then be done in batch mode, on another machine, if desired. This might prove advantageous to some installations, for it would allow the data to be collected on a relatively small mini-computer (e.g. a PDP-8 or a Honeywell 516), and processed by a relatively large scientific computer (e.g. a Univac 1108 or a CDC 6600).

3 Finally, consider the case of the on-line "customer inquiry" systems. A variety of business organizations have implemented computer systems that make it possible for customers to inquire into the status of their account. Since there may be several terminals sending inquiries to the system, there is certainly a real-time requirement to collect input; since often an irritable customer is

waiting impatiently for the results, there is also a real-time requirement to process the input.

Some common examples of real-time systems are the following:

1   Process control systems

2   Military command and control systems

3   Some air traffic control systems

Time-Sharing

The word "time-sharing" is perhaps one of the most ill-defined and poorly-used words in the computer field today. It currently has (at least) the following three meanings:

1   *A method of scheduling jobs in the computer* (see Figure A3)

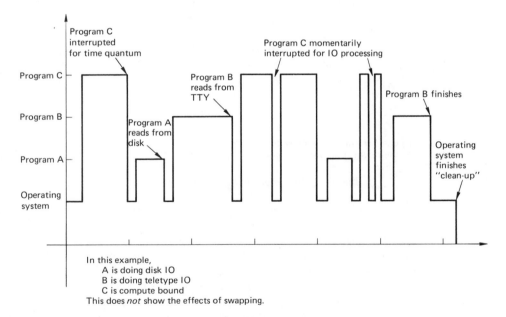

Fig. A3   Time-sharing as a scheduling algorithm

"Time-sharing" or "time-slicing" is often used to identify a particular kind of scheduling algorithm inside the computer. With this type of algorithm, a job (or "application program" or "user program," depending on the context of the system) is given full access to the central processor for a limited period of time (usually less than one second). Then, whether the job has completed its processing or not, control is passed on to the next job. The period of time during which the job is allowed to use the processor may be fixed or variable, depending on the nature of the job and the nature of the scheduling algorithm.

It should be remembered that this type of time-sharing is an *internal* characteristic of the system (one that the user rarely, if ever, is aware of), and one that may be independent of a number of the other characteristics of the system. That is, a computer system with a time-sharing scheduling algorithm may or may not involve multiprogramming, on-line processing, or real-time processing.

2 *A type of commercially offered computer service* (see Figure A4)

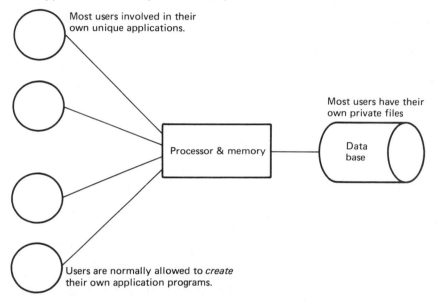

Fig. A4 Time-sharing as a type of service

The term "time-sharing system" sometimes refers to service bureaus and data centers that offer a variety of programming languages and application programs to engineers and scientists as a means of on-line problem-solving. To avoid confusion, we shall refer to this type of time-sharing system as a "scientific-engineering time-sharing system," or SETSS.

Most such systems allow the engineer to program in FORTRAN IV, BASIC, PL/I, or any one of a number of specialized problem-solving languages. While we shall examine the characteristics of time-sharing systems in more detail in Chapter B, we may point out here that SETSS differ from many other types of on-line computer systems in that each person using the system is fairly independent of other users. Thus, each user has his own programs and files (although there usually are provisions for sharing them among other users), and may decide to edit, compile, or execute his application programs regardless of the activities of others on the system.

3   *A general type of computer system*

Finally, we often see the term "time-sharing" used almost as a synonym for "on-line." That is, a time-sharing system is often thought of simply as any computer system to which terminals are attached, and with which users may communicate for various purposes. In this context, we often see the phrase "time-*shared*" system.

To summarize, there are a variety of meanings which might be attached to the phrase "time-sharing." To avoid confusion, we shall always identify which of the three major meanings are intended, by using the phrase "time-slicing" when a scheduling connotation is intended; the term "scientific-engineering time-sharing system," or SETSS, will be used when a service bureau or data center connotation is intended; and "time-shared" system when a more general connotation is intended.

Multiprogramming

The term "multiprogramming" is often closely linked with time-sharing systems, but is also found on most current third generation batch operating systems. It is interesting that a few computer manufacturers either purposely or inadvertently confuse multiprogramming with multiprocessing—a term which we shall discuss next.

We may define multiprogramming very simply as follows: "Multiprogramming is a mode of operation in a computer system in which more than one partially completed task is processed concurrently." Note that this definition does not imply that tasks are processed *simultaneously*—that would involve multiprocessing. In a multiprogramming system, only *one* task is actually being executed at any instant of time, but within a larger time frame (i.e. several seconds or minutes), *several* tasks may be alternating between using the central processor (i.e. executing), and waiting for input/output events to finish.

It is usually implied that the multiprogramming system is capable of keeping more than one job *in core memory at the same time*. There are many computer systems that have only enough memory for one job; other jobs are kept on a swapping disk or drum, and the entire computer is generally idle while one job is being "swapped" out and another "swapped" into core.

Once again, it should be emphasized that the words "time-sharing," "multiprogramming," and "on-line" need not be linked together. For example,

1   There are still some SETSS that are not multiprogrammed. The most dramatic example was the original time-sharing system developed at MIT's Project MAC, in which one job was executed for a "slice" of time in an IBM 7094, after

which the next job was brought into core memory. Several small SETSS, on minicomputers, also tend to be "uniprogramming" systems because of lack of sufficient core memory.

2   Many multiprogramming systems need not be on-line systems. For example, the following operating systems may be used as multiprogramming *batch* systems:

Burroughs B5500 MCP

IBM System/360 OS MVT and MFT

CDC 6600 Scope

GE-635 GECOS III

Univac 1108 EXEC II

3   It is quite possible to build an on-line system that does not include multiprogramming. In a small on-line banking system, for example, one bank teller's IO need not necessarily be overlapped with processing for another bank teller.

Multiprogramming usually implies much more about the implementation of the system than any external characteristics that a user of the system might see. That is, the user is normally not aware that the system is operating in a multiprogramming mode, except possibly in terms of a delayed response from the system (there are exceptions, of course—some multiprogramming systems require the user to restrict the amount of core memory he uses, so that more jobs may be placed in memory at the same time). Because it is an *internal* characteristic of the system, it is possible to have various *degrees* of multiprogramming without the user ever being aware of it. There are two dimensions to this variability:

1   The number of jobs which the system is keeping track of may vary. Some systems can handle two jobs, some four, and some can handle a variable number of jobs. Generally, the more jobs in the system, the more overhead is involved in keeping track of what the system is doing at any point. Also, as shown in Figure A5, multiprogramming has a tendency to be similar to juggling—the more balls one has up in the air, the more chance that one will be dropped. A sophisticated multiprogramming system is much more prone to software errors than a simple uniprogramming system.

2   The conditions under which the system may switch control from one job to another may vary. On some systems, the operating system can switch control from one application program to another only when the application program itself signals that it wishes to relinquish control; on other systems, the operating system itself can take control away from an application program whenever an

IO call is issued; on still others, the system can take control away from an application program at any arbitrary time. As we shall see in Chapter H, this can greatly influence the efficiency of the application program.

Multiprogramming is somewhat
similar to juggling——the more balls
one has in the air, the more chances
that one will be dropped.

Fig. A5 The dangers of multiprogramming

Multiprocessing and Multiple-Computer Processing

Multiprocessing is another technical term that conjures up different images in different people's minds. While most programmers have a general feeling for what the word means, there are so many types and applications of multiprocessing that confusion is inevitable.

We may define *multiprocessing* in the following way: "A multiprocessing system is one in which more than one central processor *of the same type* operate in parallel." Thus, in a multiprocessing system, the two (or more) central processors are executing the same instructions simultaneously, whereas in a multiprogramming system, one processor executes the instructions of different programs *concurrently*, but not *simultaneously*.

Multiple-computer-processing, on the other hand, may be defined as follows:

"A multiple-computer-processing system is one in which more than one central processor, not necessarily of the same type, operate in parallel."

Thus, the distinction between multiprocessing and multiple-computer-processing has to do with the similarity of the processors involved.

There are four basic configurations in which multiple-computer-processing and multiprocessing are involved, as illustrated by Figures A6a, A6b, A6c, and A6d. Figures A6a and A6b are examples of multiprocessing systems, since the processors involved are of the same type. Figures A6c and A6d, on the other hand, are examples of multiple-computer-processing systems, since different types of processors are involved.

It is interesting to note that, in the American computer field, there are few examples of multiple-computer-processing systems in which all of the processors are "large." That is, it is very rare to find a system in which a large Univac computer is connected to a large IBM computer, or one in which a large Control Data computer is connected to a large Honeywell machine. This is probably due to the virtually non-existent software interfaces between computers, and because American industry tends to buy large processors from the *same* vendor. In many foreign countries, however, it is a little more common for independent companies, each with their own large processor, to hook up together to form a multiple-computer processing network. The same situation also exists in a few government agencies in this country, much to the dismay of a number of private citizens.

It is also interesting to note that more and more of the major computer manufacturers are beginning to *combine* the basic types of multiprocessing and multiple-computer-processing configurations shown in Figures A6a-A6d.

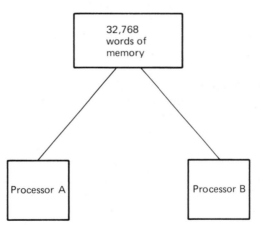

Example: Burroughs B5500 computer.

Fig. A6a   Examples of multiprocessing: processors sharing main memory

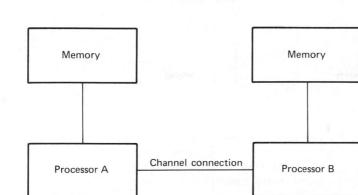

Examples: some IBM 360/65 configurations
GE-635 configurations

**Fig. A6b   Examples of multiprocessing: processors with independent
memory**

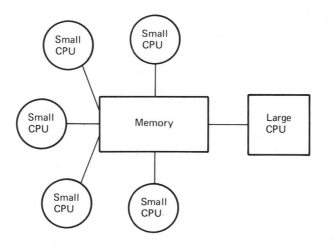

Example: Control Data 6400

**Fig. A6c   Examples of multiple computer processing: dissimilar processors
processors sharing main memory**

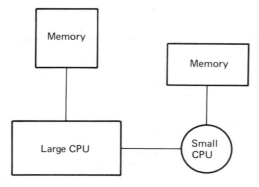

Examples: GE-635 and Datanet-30
           IBM 360/50 and PDP-8
           Univac 1108 and PDP-8

Fig. A6d **Examples of multiple computer processing: dissimilar processors with independent memories**

A good example is the Control Data 6500 computer shown in Figure A6e—here we have ten small peripheral processors, each with 4096 words of "private" memory, as well as the capability of sharing the memory of the two large processors.

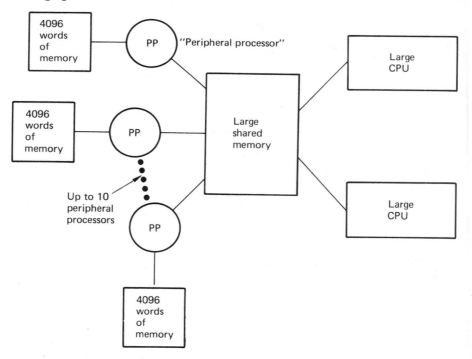

Fig. A6e **The Control Data 6500 computer**

A similar approach has been taken by a number of other manufacturers. The "peripheral processors" are often dedicated to such tasks as IO control or diagnostics programming. In many cases, the processors are extremely small and limited in power, being either hard-wired or microprogrammed.

There appear to be three major ways in which multiprocessing and multiple-computer-processing are used:

load-sharing

separation of functions

reliability considerations

Load-sharing simply refers to the approach of allowing any one of a "pool" of processors to execute a job or an application program. This is not yet a common technique, but it involves no conceptual difficulties if all of the processors have easy access to the queue of tasks or jobs. In many such configurations, it is necessary for one computer to be considered the "master," and all other processors to be considered "slaves." On the Burroughs B5500 computer system, for example, one of the central processors is capable only of operating on application programs. It relies on the other central processor to handle all IO activities, and to tell it which job to work on. On the Burroughs B6500 computer, on the other hand, *either* processor is free to perform applications-oriented processing or operating system functions.

Another approach to multiprocessing and multiple-computer-processing is to isolate the various functions within the system, and make different processors responsible for each of these functions. Perhaps the most common example of this approach is the idea of having a separate programmable (or microprogrammable) computer handle the data communications processing within an on-line system. In a general-purpose on-line system, it might be feasible to have different applications (or different parts of the same application) executed by separate processors.

As we mentioned above, there seems to be a growing trend among the computer manufacturers to separate IO functions into separate processors. For high-speed IO devices like printers, disks, and drums, a small processor might be used to handle the following types of functions:

buffering

queueing of requests

optimization of the device

code conversion and editing

error handling

The most dramatic use of a separate processor in the IO area is that of *random access file handling.* As we shall see in Part IV of this book, there is often a great deal of bookkeeping associated with random access files. A small processor can be kept quite busy maintaining directories and indexes; checking file security codes; maintaining a log of all updates to the data base; resolving problems of simultaneous access to the data base; and so forth.

Still another way of separating functions within a computer system is on a geographical basis. This appears to be the goal of the "computer utility" concept that some computer companies have introduced in the past few years. That is, it is possible to build a multiple computer system in which all of the Chicago users are serviced by one machine, all of the Boston users by another machine, and so forth. The major problem seems to be that of common access to a centralized data base. If the data base is physically centralized, as shown in Figure A7a, inefficiencies might result if large volumes of data have to be transferred from one machine to another, and from the user to the data base. If, on the other hand, the data base is logically centralized, but physically distributed, as shown in Figure A7b, then a failure at any one of the computer centers could make that part of the data base inaccessbile.

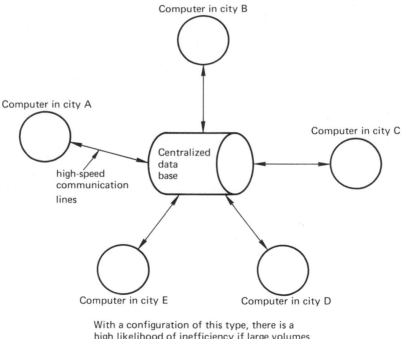

With a configuration of this type, there is a
high likelihood of inefficiency if large volumes
of data must be transferred back and forth.

Fig. A7a   Multiple computer network with a physically centralized data base

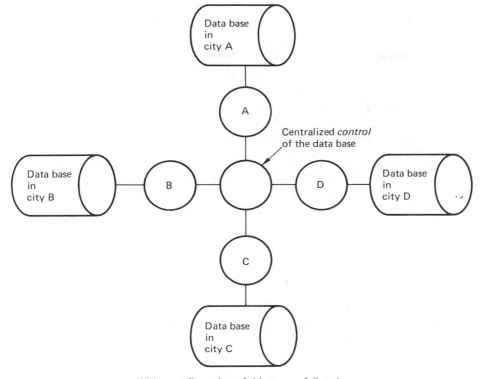

With a configuration of this type, a failure in
any one of the computers may make key parts
of the data base inaccessible.

Fig. A7b Multiple computer network with a logically centralized, but
physically distributed data base

Still another common use of the concept of multiprocessing and
multiple-computer processing is to gain added reliability in the system. The
two most common methods of providing this extra reliability are *duplexed
systems* and *dual systems.*

A duplexed system is one in which one or more hardware components
have a "back-up," or "stand-by," that may be called into play in the event of
a failure or malfunction. As applied to multiprocessing, this means that we
might build a system with a backup central processor that can take over
when the main processor fails. During normal processing of the system, the
backup processor may suffer any one of the following fates:

it may stand idle

it may be used for debugging and testing of new systems

it may be used for background batch processing (payroll, etc.)

it may be used to share the load of the main processor

A dual computer system is one in which two central processors are simultaneously processing the same application, periodically checking each other to ensure the validity of their results. There are few, if any, examples of dual systems in American business. This type of redundancy can be justified only in cases where reliable performance is of critical importance.

Sometimes the "separation of functions" approach to multiple computer processing can also be used to add reliability to the system. For example, an on-line system in which the data communications processing is handled by a separate computer can continue to function even when the main processor fails and is out of service. Transactions can be stored on magnetic tape for later processing when the main processor is brought into service again, and users can be informed as to the current level of service.

Interactive Computer Systems (see Figure A8)

The adjective "interactive" is normally applied to those systems in which there is a high degree of man-machine interaction. On most such systems, a typical sequence of activity is as follows:

computer asks a question

user thinks about the question for a little while

user types in a reply (an answer to the question)

computer does a small amount of processing

computer asks another question

etc.

The degree of interactiveness is determined by the rapidity with which these exchanges take place, and by the amount of processing that must be performed by the system during each interaction.

The interactiveness of a computer system—and here we are almost always talking of a real-time, on-line computer system—can have an important effect on the throughput and efficiency of the system. It is common for highly interactive systems to involve a large amount of system overhead, because each new interaction may require an application program to be "swapped" from drum or disk into core memory. Once the application program has been brought into core, though, it may only execute for a few milliseconds before finishing—at which time another application program may be brought into core to service the next interaction.

Some examples of an interactive system are the following:

management information systems

sales order entry systems

library information retrieval systems

some aspects of scientific-engineering time-sharing systems

```
          hello
          HELLO. THIS LIBRARY HAS BOOKS ON THE FOLLOWING
          AREAS. TYPE THE NUMBER OF THE AREA YOU WISH:
              1. SCIENCE
              2. LITERATURE-FICTION
              3. HISTORY
              4. ART
              5. BUSINESS ADMINISTRATION
          1
          UNDER "SCIENCE," WE HAVE
              1. PHYSICS
              2. COMPUTER SCIENCES
              3. ASTROLOGY
              4. CHEMISTRY
              5. MATHEMATICS
          PLEASE TYPE THE NUMBER OF THE SUBJECT YOU
          WISH TO EXPLORE
          2
          UNDER COMPUTER SCIENCES WE HAVE
              1. GENERAL TOPICS AND EDUCATION
              2. COMPUTING MILIEU
              3. APPLICATIONS
              4. PROGRAMMING
              5. MATHEMATICS OF COMPUTATION
              6. DESIGN AND CONSTRUCTION
              7. ANALOG COMPUTERS
          PLEASE TYPE THE NUMBER OF THE AREA YOU
          WISH TO EXPLORE
              etc.
              etc.
              etc.
               .
               .
               .
```

Fig. A8 Example of a dialogue with an interactive system: a library
information retrieval system (user in lower case, COMPUTER IN
UPPER CASE)

Dedicated Computer Systems

A dedicated computer system is one which is devoted to one application, or one function, or one programming language (in a SETSS). This may be contrasted with a general-purpose system in which a variety of applications may be processed simultaneously.

An example of a dedicated system is an airline reservation system that cannot be used for anything else. It is not possible for a COBOL programmer to type his program into the system from an airline ticket agent's terminal, nor is it possible (either by system design or administrative fiat) for him to execute his COBOL job by loading a deck of cards into the card reader at the central site. In the SETSS world, an example of a dedicated system would be any of the following:

the original Dartmouth GE-265 BASIC time-sharing system

the Digital Equipment Corporation TIME-SHARE-8 system

the Hewlett-Packard HP200A BASIC Time-Sharing System

the original IBM System/360 CALL/360:BASIC system

In contrast, a *general-purpose* system allows the concurrent or simultaneous execution of a number of different applications, usually in a multiprogramming or multiprocessing mode. For example, the operating system on the IBM System/360, known as OS, allows on-line applications to run at the same time that background batch jobs are being processed. Burroughs, XDS, General Electric, and most of the other major computer manufacturers provide the same facility in the standard operating systems they provide with their medium-scale and large-scale computers. In the scientific-engineering time-sharing world, examples of general-purpose systems would be the following:

the SDS-940 time-sharing system, as implemented by XDS and modified by several service bureau companies.

the Applied Logic ALCOM time-sharing system, implemented on a Digital Equipment PDP-10 computer.

more recent versions of IBM's CALL/360 system.

There are usually very serious consequences in terms of throughput, efficiency, and overhead when one uses a general-purpose system. A system that is "tuned" and "adjusted" for a special application is usually much more efficient, if one accepts as a criterion of efficiency the number of simultaneously active terminals the system is able to support. On the other hand, a dedicated system is often much less efficient in terms of utilization, since the special application may not provide enough of a load to make full use of the system.

Fall-Back

There are now a large number of terms in the computer industry which refer to a variety of hardware and/or software schemes to prevent a complete loss of service after a hardware or software malfunction. Some of the common synonyms for "fall-back" are:

fail-soft

graceful degradation

planned down-time

In some cases, it is not so much the interruption of service that may annoy the users of the system, but rather the loss of files and data. Fall-back schemes may thus involve a number of techniques to ensure the safety of the data base.

Sometimes, the fall-back schemes are completely automatic—that is, completely under the control of the computer system. More often than not, though, the computer operator is involved in some way. For example, a number of fall-back schemes maintain back-up copies of records in the data base as they are modified; after a failure, the fall-back routines may request the computer operator to mount the recovery tape and participate in the data base recovery procedure.

In almost all cases, the fall-back schemes involve *redundancy*—either a duplexing of peripheral IO units, file storage devices or central processors, and/or redundancy in the software and the data base. A number of "reasonableness" or validity checks may be built into the software, and the data base may be protected by maintaining a log of input transactions, by maintaining frequent dumps of the data base, by keeping redundant directories, or with a variety of "audit trail" techniques. These will all be discussed at greater length in Chapter N and Chapter U.

On some systems, the fall-back schemes may be extremely simple. One of the most interesting examples involves a process control system that was used to control the mixing of ingredients for cookies in a large plant. The computer controlled the mixing of flour, chocolate, sugar, milk, and all of the other ingredients that go into the cookies that keep our dentists so prosperous. In this case, the fall-back routine was very simple: if something went wrong, control was transferred to the chocolate routine, for, as any cook knows, chocolate covers any mistake. As one wit was heard to comment, "It was a smart cookie that designed *that* fall-back scheme!"

Response Time

Depending on the type of on-line or real-time system that is being discussed, "response time" may have an entirely different meaning. For most "people-oriented" on-line computer systems, response time may be defined in the manner illustrated by Figure A9:

> Response time may be defined as the interval of time between the last character of input typed by the user of the system, and the first character of output typed by the computer system.

For process control systems and other types of real-time systems, this definition obviously does not apply. However, the following, more general, definition will usually suffice:

Response time, in the general case, may be defined as the period of time for a computer system to react to an external stimulus with an appropriate action.

For some types of "periodic" systems, where the inputs to the systems are well-known, and the processing performed by the system is also well-known,

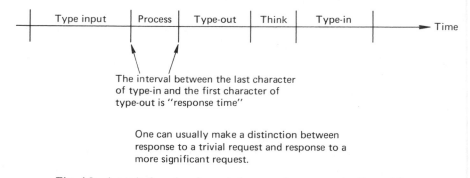

Fig. A9　A typical cycle of events in a user's communication with an on-line system

it may very well be possible for the system analyst to accurately predict the response time for the system. On most systems, though, the response time is a function of how many people are using the system, and *how* they are using the system. At best, response time may be predicted as a probability distribution using queueing theory techniques, but many of these techniques assume that the *arrival rate* of input from users is independent of the *service rate*, or the rate at which that input is processed by the system. For most on-line systems, this is not the case—a user cannot type his next line of input until the system has responded to the current line of input.

Operating System

The term "operating system" has already been used to describe a number of other terms above—in the hope that the reader is already familiar with its meaning. In any type of contemporary computer system, there is a conglomeration of software that controls the computer's environment—that is, this conglomeration of software controls the hardware and the application programs that perform the logical processing of the system.

On some types of on-line or real-time computer systems, it may be difficult to distinguish the operating system from the application programs. This is especially true in process control systems and some data acquisition systems, in which *all* of the software is likely to be of a supervisory nature—and it is also true of some dedicated systems that are so highly "tuned" for the on-line application that the operating system and the application programs become closely entwined. Usually, though, it is possible to make *some* distinction between the two types of programs.

Occasionally, it may be meaningful to speak of different *levels* of operating systems, as illustrated by Figure A10. In a simple example, we might imagine the most basic level of operating system to be a set of input/output handling routines provided by the computer manufacturer. The next level of operating system might be provided by the customer, and might include a scheduling and core allocation package. Another level might be concerned with the allocation of such resources as peripheral devices or the data base.

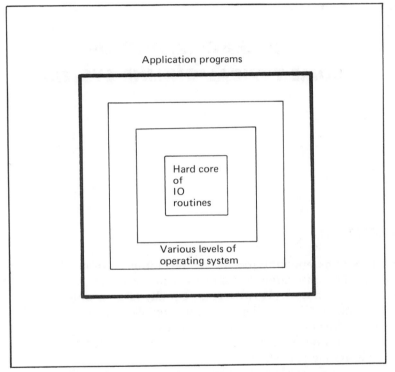

Fig. A10   Levels of operating system

Perhaps because of the possibility of so many levels of operating systems, and perhaps because each computer manufacturer likes to give his own trade-name to their operating systems, there are a large number of synonyms with which we should be familiar:

monitor

executive program

control program

supervisor program

For reasons of consistency, we will refer to this type of program as an *operating system* throughout the remainder of the book.

CHARACTERISTICS OF
SOME TYPICAL ON-LINE SYSTEMS

INTRODUCTION

The problems encountered in the development of an on-line system—or, for that matter, *any* large system—are usually partly technical and partly administrative in nature. However, an equally large problem is that we often don't understand the problem, or the application, well enough. In many cases, this is because the system designer is not aware of the common categories of on-line systems that have evolved in industry, and consequently ends up redesigning the wheel.

However, the problem goes even deeper: we are usually not even in a position to tell whether a given computer project has even succeeded in what it was supposed to do. Other industries seem to have a much clearer notion of success and failure in their projects, even though they may have the same degree of problems in achieving that success or failure. A newly-designed airplane, for example, usually either flies or crashes into the nearest hillside. A newly-designed on-line computer system, on the other hand, often behaves in a manner analagous to an airplane taxiing from New York to Los Angeles. The system that was supposed to handle 200 terminals seems to get bogged down whenever more than 20 people are using it; the information retrieval system that was supposed to provide a 2-second response time seems to take 5 seconds or longer; the system that was supposed to run in 4000 words of storage ends up requiring 16,000 words and still doesn't seem to run efficiently.

Perhaps if we have a better way of measuring and classifying the systems we have, we will be in a better position to judge the success or failure of our ventures. To do a complete job, we should also be able to perform a cost-effectiveness analysis of our system, a subject which is beyond the realm of this book; and we should also be able to measure the performance of a system, once it has been implemented, a subject which is discussed in Chapter G. However, our first job should be that of properly identifying the basic type of system we are building. To draw another analogy, it is not always meaningful to compare one automobile with another—but if we can identify certain types of automobiles, such as "sports cars" or "station wagons," we will be in a better position to make a comparison.

We can classify on-line computer systems from two different points of view: from an *applications* point of view, or from a *functional* viewpoint. In the first case, we are more interested in what the systems are doing; in the second, we are more concerned with the "black boxes," or functional components, that make up the system. From an applications point of view, we can identify five different types of systems, and from a functional point of view, we can identify seven or eight different systems. Each of these will be described below.

ON-LINE SYSTEMS FROM AN APPLICATIONS VIEWPOINT

On-line computer systems are beginning to invade laboratories, factories, banks, and every conceivable kind of business. In addition, massive systems are being planned and built for a variety of government and military applications. Yet, even with this diversity, we can identify five major categories of systems:

1 Process control systems

2 Business-oriented "information" systems

3 Scientific-engineering time-sharing systems (SETSS)

4 Remote batch systems

5 Data acquisition systems

The reader should be able to identify one of these categories as the one in which his present (or planned) system fits—but it *is* possible for more than one of these categories to be combined in one general-purpose on-line system. For example, it is becoming increasingly common to find a SETSS combined with a business-oriented "information" system, or with a remote batch system.

Our purpose in this chapter is to describe the general characteristics of each system. More detail on these systems will be found in later sections of this book. Parts III and IV, on Application Programs and Data Bases, will probably be most relevant to those interested in business-oriented "information" systems, while Part V, on Operating Systems, will probably be more relevant to those interested in process control systems, scientific-engineering time-sharing systems, remote batch systems, and data acquisition systems.

PROCESS CONTROL SYSTEMS

There are an ever-increasing number of computer systems that are loosely referred to as *process control systems*, or *real-time control systems*, or sometimes "command and control" systems. These include systems that control petroleum refineries, oil wells, and steel mills, as well as the military control systems of the SAGE variety. The basic elements of the system are illustrated in Figure B1, in which the box labelled "environment" may be a steel mill, a manufacturing process, or an entire air-defense system.

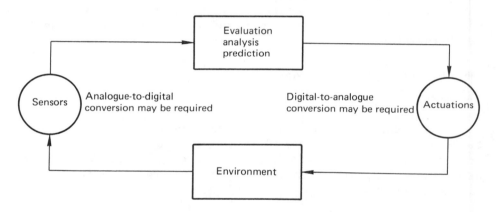

Fig. B1   A process control system

In a process control system, information about the state of the outside world is received from various forms of "sensors"—strain gauges, thermostats, radar units, or any of a number of analog devices (in which case a conversion to a digital form of input is required). After some evaluation of the input, and/or a prediction of future activity of the "outside world," the process control computer exerts its *control* by activating a switch, shutting a valve, or perhaps signalling an "alarm" condition.

Our interest here is in the *characteristics* of a process control system, and perhaps the most important characteristic is the short response time of most process control systems. The response time is usually a direct function of the frequency of interrupts from external devices, or, in some cases, the frequency with which the status of some device must be interrogated. Rarely is there a process control system whose response times are greater than one second; many have response times of 10-100 milliseconds, corresponding to external interrupts at the rate of 10 to 100 per second. As we mentioned in Chapter A, process control systems often have such short response times that the average computer professional prefers to call them "real-time" systems, and not "on-line" systems. The major point to be remembered is that the response time can occasionally be a little longer for most business-oriented and SETSS systems, because the only damage is that of the patience of the user. In a process control system, a delayed response may result in disaster: a chemical reaction may get out of control, or a jet engine might fly off its test stand.

This requirement for a *guaranteed* response time is usually not possible in other types of on-line systems because, as was mentioned in Chapter A, the response time is a function of the number of users on the system, and the type of input that each user is typing into the system. If there are only a few people using a system, and if they are only calling for relatively trivial types of processing, the response time will probably be good for all users; on the other hand, if there are a large number of users, some of whom are asking for complex information retrieval functions or complex scientific calculations, then the response time is likely to be somewhat uneven and unpredictable.

Such is not the case in most process control systems. The algorithms for controlling the process in question may be complex, but they are usually very well-defined. That is, differential or integral equations may be involved, but at least we know *what* the equations are, and we can calculate the "worst-case" response time with some precision. Thus, a specified response time is much easier to guarantee than on a scientific-engineering time-sharing system.

Another important characteristic of most process control systems is the lack of any significant files or data base. There may be some tables or data maintained in core memory or on a high-speed drum or disk, but these are definitely not data-base-oriented systems. This is an important point, for it eliminates all of the overhead associated with file management, file security and file recovery software found in other types of on-line systems.

Similarly, one finds, in most cases, that all of the necessary programs fit within the computer's main memory. While there are some exceptions to this, there is almost never any large amount of overlaying and "swapping" in a process control system. This, too, can be important, for a large amount of system overhead is usually associated with program overlaying and swapping.

One usually finds limited numbers and types of terminals attached to process control systems. On some systems, it may be meaningful to speak of numerical control machines or jet engine test stands as "terminals." On other systems, there may only be *one* terminal—an operator's control panel. At any rate, one usually does *not* find 50-100 terminals attached to the system, as is common on many of the other types of on-line systems.

Another important characteristic of the process control system is the requirement for high reliability of the system. This is usually necessary for two reasons:

the systems are often left unattended for long periods of time, so there would be no computer operator to witness a failure.

the *cost* of a failure, in lost production time or human lives, is often immediate and high.

Hence, a process control system might have to insist on a Mean Time Between Failures (MTBF) of 2000 hours, and a Mean Time To Repair (MTTR) of 10 minutes. This may be contrasted with many business-oriented and SETSS systems, whose MTBF ranges from 4 hours to 40 hours, and whose MTTR ranges from 10-60 minutes.

Most of the process control systems are developed on small machines. Some of the more common computers that are currently being used in this area are the following:

Digital Equipment PDP-8, PDP-9, and PDP-11

Honeywell 516

Control Data 1700

IBM 1800

Data General Corporation NOVA

Xerox Data Systems Sigma-2 and Sigma-5

There is a growing number of machines available on the market today, and the list above will certainly be obsolete in the very near future. However, all of the computers of this class—the so-called "mini-computers"—are characterized by

low price (usually between $10,000 and $100,000)

fast cycle time (one microsecond or less)

high reliability

good priority interrupt hardware structure

word length of 12 to 18 bits

In many cases, the user writes *all* of his own software, including the operating system and application packages. Some of the computer manufacturers are attempting to provide "standard" process control packages (often referred to as "real-time operating systems"), but most users feel that their needs are so unique, their response time requirements so stringent, and their available core space so cramped that they prefer to write their own software.

Response time requirements and core restrictions usually force all software for process control systems to be written in assembly language.

FORTRAN is occasionally used, but, at the present time, this is the exception rather than the rule.

Summary of Characteristics of Process Control Systems

extremely fast response time

guaranteed response time

no significant data base

no significant "swapping" or overlaying

limited numbers and types of terminals

high reliability requirements

small, fast, cheap computers

most software written in assembly language

BUSINESS-ORIENTED "INFORMATION" SYSTEMS *(see Figure B2)*

Although real-time and on-line computer systems have been in existence since the late 1950's, there have been distinct *phases* of development which have seen significant advances in one type of system, then in another. The very first such systems were the large command-and-control systems such as the Air Force SAGE system and the American Airlines SABRE system. Beginning in the early 1960's, a number of universities began developing

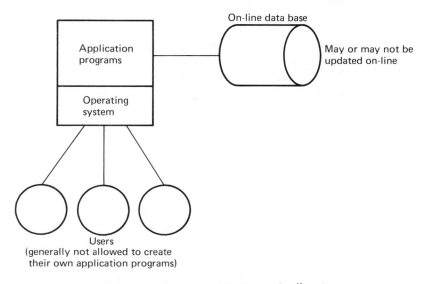

Fig. B2 Business-oriented "information" systems

general-purpose scientific-engineering time-sharing systems, MIT's Project MAC and Dartmouth's BASIC system being among the most notable. Development of this type of system continued throughout the 1960's, and a number of commercial service bureaus were formed with the idea of providing the services of SETSS's to a variety of engineering customers.

However, it has only been in the past few years that the business community has become involved in on-line systems. A few of the very large American corporations began building *message-switching systems* to help relay information among their branch offices around the country, and a very few actually built some on-line inventory control or sales order entry computer systems. The lack of available systems software and the high cost of on-line systems were probably the two main factors that prevented medium-sized and small-sized companies from experimenting with systems of their own. These factors seem to have been overcome, and we are now beginning to see a proliferation of systems in the following areas:

inventory control systems

credit-checking systems

banking systems

sales order entry systems

medical information systems

library information retrieval systems

computer-assisted instruction systems (CAI)

management information systems

These systems differ from the process control systems in that they provide *information* rather than *control*. The inputs to the system are usually inquiries to a data base or updates to the data base; the output from the system is either information or an acknowledgment of input. Because each line of input is often referred to as a *transaction*, these systems are also referred to as *transaction-oriented* systems.

Most of the business-oriented systems have a small vocabulary, and are often dedicated. For example, on an airline reservation system, an airline ticket agent has a relatively limited number of capabilities she can draw upon (make a reservation, cancel a reservation, check for available space, etc.); she does not have access to other types of computational services (i.e. she cannot compose a FORTRAN program from her terminal).

In contrast to the process control systems, the system designer rarely is concerned with the operating system, and devotes most of his attention to the applications area. The operating system is provided, in most cases, as part of the standard software on the computer, and often represents a simple evolution from a multiprogramming batch operating system. In this type of environment, the operating system may be capable of handling several concurrent jobs, of which *one* is the on-line application. The other jobs may be "background" processing associated with the on-line application, or may be an entirely different type of processing, such as a payroll job.

Because of the type of operating system, there is almost always a much higher amount of *overhead* in a business-oriented on-line system—that is, time spent either performing "house-keeping" processing within the operating system or time spent idle while waiting for input/output or "swapping" to finish. If the system is dedicated to only one on-line application, this overhead can often be greatly reduced, since all of the application programs can be kept in core.

The manner in which the operating system handles the on-line application program is interesting, for it differs sharply from the remote batch systems, which we shall describe presently. In most of the business-oriented "information" systems, the application program is *started* at the beginning of the day, and is not *terminated* until the system is shut down at the end of the day. When there is no terminal input to be processed, the application program is idle, and the operating system switches control to other "background" jobs, if there are any. On many such systems, the application program is "locked" into core, so that when a new transaction arrives, the operating system merely has to give it to the program for processing. On the other hand, the core memory occupied by the application program is being wasted during periods when there are no transactions to be processed.

In contrast to this approach, the application program in most remote batch systems is *started* when a transaction arrives in the system, and is *terminated* when the processing of that transaction is complete. Thus, during periods when there are no transactions arriving in the system, the application program does not tie up any core storage, and the remote batch operating system is completely free to perform other types of processing. On the other hand, there is usually a significant amount of overhead required to initiate and terminate an application program—several hundred milliseconds of processor time and several disk accesses to update the operating system's accounting files. This overhead can obviously become quite excessive if transactions arrive frequently during the day, especially if the processing of the transaction itself only takes a few hundred milliseconds of processor time.

One other important characteristic of the business-oriented "information" system is the type of reliability that is required. In most cases, there is no need for the stringent MTBF requirement that exists for process control systems. The users may grumble a bit if the system breaks down, but it is not likely to result in a catastrophe. However, it usually *is* important to restore the system to its normal level of operation as quickly as possible after a failure. If the system remains out of service for more than five or ten minutes, users may begin to fall behind in their work, or, in the case of a commercial service bureau, the users may attempt to find a more reliable system. In any case, the users normally become extremely annoyed at prolonged periods of "down-time."

Much more important than MTBF or MTTR, however, is the protection of the data base. For an increasingly large number of business-oriented systems, the data base represents the records of the company—financial records, production records, personnel records, etc. If the data base is lost, the company may be totally unable to carry on its business; if a day's transactions and data base updates are lost because of a system failure, a great financial loss may result. Accordingly, there is often great emphasis on the two different aspects of data base reliability:

> protection of the data base itself
>
> avoiding confusion on the part of the users, so that transactions are not missed or duplicated.

The techniques of data base reliability are discussed at length in Chapter N.

As an example of the need for reliability, the reader is invited to visit any of the branch offices of the New York Department of Motor Vehicles. An on-line computer system is used to process and print registration certificates and driver's licenses; several hundred terminals in the branch offices all over the State of New York are connected to a central computer system in Albany. Whenever the system fails (which, as one harried clerk explained, "is guaranteed to happen twice a day"), the long lines of people begin fidgeting and growing impatient. If the computer stays "down" more than five or ten minutes, utter pandemonium reigns: some of the customers are told to turn in their forms and applications, and then go home and wait for the license or automobile registration to arrive in the mail; other customers are told that they must wait, since the computer will have to check its files for arrests or traffic violations before issuing the license. If the entire Motor Vehicle Bureau data base was lost, New York's 16 million residents would probably drive their automobiles into the ocean and return to the happier days of horses and carriages.

Summary of Characteristics of Business-Oriented On-Line Systems

> supply information rather than control
>
> limited capabilities provided to users
>
> systems are often dedicated
>
> operating system is usually provided by the computer vendor
>
> operating system starts the application program only once, then puts it into a "wait" state when there are no more transactions
>
> data base reliability is usually more important than MTTR or MTBF.

SCIENTIFIC-ENGINEERING TIME-SHARING SYSTEMS

What began as an experiment at MIT and Dartmouth College in the early 1960's has become one of the most glamorous segments of the computer industry. As of mid-1969, some sixty independent service bureaus were offering time-sharing services to a variety of customers, on a variety of types of computers. Development has taken place in two widely divergent directions: the large "utility" approach to time-sharing, favored by universities and large companies; and the small systems which allow eight or ten users to program in BASIC or a subset of FORTRAN.

The primary difference between the business-oriented on-line system and the SETSS is that the SETSS offers *raw machine time* to its users, while the business-oriented system usually provides a *service*, or an application package. While it is true that most scientific time-sharing systems offer a variety of programming languages and a library of engineering and mathematical packages, the charges are usually based on such factors as

central processing time

input/output time

terminal "connect" time

file storage costs

Business-oriented systems, on the other hand, charge their customers according to the number of *transactions* that have been typed in.

Most time-sharing systems can accommodate fairly large numbers of terminals—ranging from 30 to 200, depending on the machine. However, it is usually true that a dedicated business-oriented system can accommodate far *more* on-line users, since all users are executing the same application program. In the case of a SETSS, each user is, to a large extent, independent of all other users on the machine. Thus, as illustrated in Figure B3, each user is likely to have his own application programs and his own set of files. As a result, a much larger amount of system overhead time is spent "swapping" application programs between a drum (or disk) and main memory.

Because of the variety of application programs that may be running at any time, it is usually extremely difficult to predict response times at the user's terminals. As we shall see later in this chapter, certain functional configurations make it easier for the system to respond to "trivial" requests (such as editing a program, logging in to the system, carrying on terminal-to-terminal communications, and so on) immediately. The scheduling algorithms in most time-sharing systems are built to "discriminate" against compute-bound jobs, and to favor the short, interactive jobs—and as a result, large, slow programs usually receive very poor service.

In terms of reliability, the emphasis in a SETSS is usually on MTTR. A simple system failure is usually not catastrophic, but it is imperative to get the system "on the air" again as quickly as possible, in order to avoid the wrath

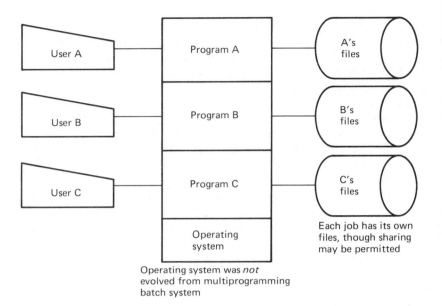

Fig. B3   Scientific-engineering time-sharing systems

of impatient users. While the business-oriented system must be concerned with *any* loss of data after a failure, the SETSS is usually only concerned about *total* losses of data. It has come to be accepted among time-sharing users that a system failure may require the last ten minutes' worth of work to be repeated—it is only if they are told that *all* of their files have disappeared that they complain. Consequently, the average SETSS does not bother with the audit trail that most business-oriented systems find so necessary, but rather dumps the data base to magnetic tape on a daily basis.

It is interesting to note that most of the earlier scientific-engineering time-sharing systems were not written by the computer manufacturers (the Digital Equipment Corporation PDP-6 time-sharing system being the only known exception). Most of the original time-sharing systems were written at universities (witness the GE-265 system written at Dartmouth and the SDS-940 system written at Berkeley) or outside service bureaus. By 1967 or 1968, however, the manufacturers had begun to catch up, and it is now possible to obtain a time-sharing operating system with many of the current third generation computers. As a result, interest in developing time-sharing operating systems has begun to fall off, and more attention is being given to the problem of developing application programs to run in a time-sharing environment.

The SETSS is normally most useful for short computations, "interactive problem-solving," and so forth. Because of the scheduling algorithms, it is not economical to run large, compute-bound programs on a production basis. For similar reasons, it is not usually economical to put large data bases or files on these systems.

REMOTE BATCH COMPUTER SYSTEMS *(see Figure B4)*

As the potentials of remote-access computers and data communications became more apparent to the computer manufacturers, there began to be a movement to develop computer systems that would allow jobs to be submitted for execution from remote locations. Most of these systems have evolved from earlier multiprogramming batch systems, and simply allow the jobs that are running concurrently to interact with a terminal in a relatively non-interactive fashion, or allow the operating system to gather input from high-speed communication lines.

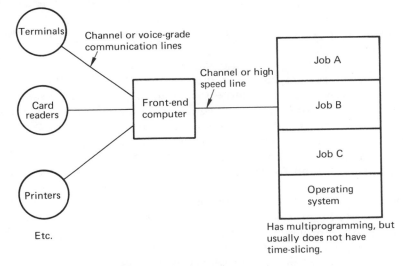

Fig. B4   Remote batch computer systems

The purpose of the remote batch systems is to combine the advantages of high-throughput batch processing with the convenience of remote terminals. One tends to see fairly large computers used as the main CPU in this kind of system. Some of the more common computers used in remote batch processing are:

Univac 1108

Burroughs B5500 and B6500

Control Data 6600

IBM 360/65, 360/75, and larger models

This approach becomes more and more feasible with the advent of machines like the Honeywell 516 and the PDP-8 to handle the communications processing involved.

Programs and jobs are batched at the remote facility, thus relieving the programmer of the delay caused by mailing or transporting decks of cards to the central facility. One often finds various peripheral devices at the remote facility—card readers, printers, card punches, magnetic tapes, etc. Once the job has been transmitted to the central facility, it is usually processed in a multiprogrammed *batch* fashion. To reduce operating system overhead and "swapping," time-slicing is normally not employed in the scheduling algorithms, or if it is, the time quantum is much longer than one would find on most scientific-engineering time-sharing systems.

One of the most significant differences between the remote batch computer system and the three previous types of systems is a lack of a tight response time requirement. Since users are not interacting in a "conversational" manner (with the exception of a few systems that allow programmers to type and edit their programs on-line, but this activity is often handled by a "front-end" processor), the system does not have to sacrifice throughput for responsiveness.

As we mentioned earlier, application programs are handled differently in a remote batch system than in an on-line business information system. When some input arrives from a remote terminal, the operating system *initiates a job*, which then processes the data and terminates. This is a very natural outgrowth of earlier batch systems, where the computer operator placed a deck of cards in the card reader, and the operating system executed the appropriate program (e.g. the FORTRAN compiler, the payroll program, etc.) and then waited for the next deck of cards to be inserted into the card reader.

There are two variations of the standard remote batch system that are of some interest. Some scientific time-sharing systems allow the user to begin execution of a program, and then disconnect his terminal. Although the program may not run as efficiently as it would in a true remote batch system (because it is being time-sliced and "swapped" more often), this arrangement takes on the appearance of an ordinary remote batch system to the unsuspecting user. Conversely, there are some remote batch systems that allow one of the jobs to handle "conversational" users. Such an arrangement is normally only useful if the number of conversational users is very small—less than eight or ten.

DATA ACQUISITION SYSTEMS *(see Figure B5)*

Data acquisition systems are very similar to process control systems, and, in fact, many people prefer to think of data acquisition as a subset of process control. However, the difference is that sometimes there is no known *control* algorithm for a process. This is true of weather systems, some medical systems, nuclear experiments, and so forth.

In such cases, the system is designed to collect raw data, then format them, perform any necessary data reduction, and then record the data for later analysis. In some cases, the recording process may consist of an on-line CRT display—thus allowing the research scientist to "watch" an experiment in progress. In most cases, though, the data are recorded for later *off-line* analysis.

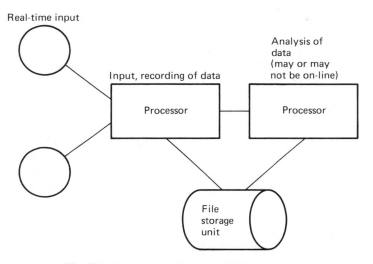

Fig. B5   A common data acquisition system

What makes most data acquisition systems "real-time" is the high data rate of the input being gathered. Even if the data are to be analyzed off-line, they must still be gathered, reduced, and stored away quickly enough to receive the next piece of input.

An example will help illustrate the essential differences and similarities between process control and data acquisition systems. For a process control example, let us consider a major oil company whose oil wells are scattered over vast expanses of land in Texas and Oklahoma. Once the wells are in production, they can run in an automatic, unattended fashion. While this is a desirable mode of operation, it means that nobody is on hand to watch for the occurrence of fire. Until recently, one man would ride from one oil well to the next, visiting each one about once a week, to ensure that everything was functioning properly. The wells are as much as 500 miles apart, and completely isolated from civilization; thus, it would be possible for a fire to break out and burn unnoticed for a week. A small PDP-8 computer is now used to maintain a *continuous* watch over all of the wells; an alarm is sounded at the central computer site if a fire or other malfunction is noticed.

The same kind of computer—a small PDP-8—is being used by a major lumber company to gather data from an experimental, prefabricated house recently constructed by the company. Every 15 minutes the computer measures temperature, humidity, and air circulation in each room of the house; meanwhile, the engineers experiment with various aspects of the house's construction by artificially raising and lowering the temperature and humidity. The data are gathered on magnetic tape, and the engineers are then free to display the data with a plotter, or analyze them with a FORTRAN program.

In both cases, the PDP-8 is gathering data on a regular basis, but the oil well system is obviously exerting some *control*. In this case, the system would be referred to as an *open-loop system*, since a human is obviously involved once the fire alarm has been sounded; if the PDP-8 had the capability to trigger a mechanical fire-extinguishing device at the first hint of fire, we would consider it a *closed-loop* control system. In the case of the experimental house, it is clear that no control is being exerted at all; the engineers are merely *experimenting*.

Aside from the absence of control, data acquisition systems are very similar to process control systems. They are usually built with small computers, and the operating system software is usually written by the system designer, in assembly language. One rather subtle difference, though, is that there *are* application programs in the data acquisition system, while in the process control system, all of the programs are considered part of the operating system. The application programs are usually written in FORTRAN to analyze the input being gathered by the operating system, and may either run in real-time (in which case, a larger, faster computer is required), or off-line, perhaps on a different computer.

ON-LINE SYSTEMS FROM A FUNCTIONAL VIEWPOINT

Instead of looking at on-line systems from an applications point of view, we can look at the functional components, or "black boxes," that make up the system. Here, there are seven or eight different types of systems, and there will probably be many more as new hardware developments occur over the next few years.

Again, our interest here is not in the detailed technical intricacies of each type of functional configuration. We are only concerned with the general characteristics of each configuration, so that the reader will be more familiar with the alternatives available to him as he designs his own system.

THE SIMPLEX SYSTEM

Probably the most common configuration in the computer field today is that illustrated by Figure B6. The terminals are connected directly to the main central processor, which, in turn, is connected directly to the file storage unit. While the name "simplex" implies that the system is either simple or small, this is not always the case: the processor can be large and powerful, and the file storage unit may consist of rows and rows of disk packs. The point is that, from a *functional* point of view, the configuration is simple.

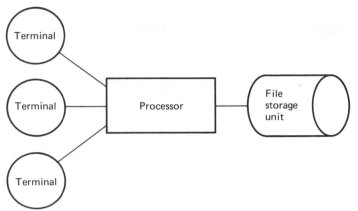

Fig. B6 A simplex system

In many cases, this simplicity is an advantage. The simplex configuration is often the least expensive to lease or purchase, because there are no redundant hardware units—no backup disk packs, no backup processor, etc. It is also usually true that the operating systems for this type of configuration are much simpler, smaller, and easier to write.

On the negative side, the simplex configuration makes no provision for failures or preventive maintenance. In either case, the entire system must be shut down. This can be tolerated in some cases, especially when the processor is a small, highly-reliable "mini-computer" that is expected to run 24 hours a day. On the other hand, there are many large business-oriented on-line systems with this configuration, in which case a hardware, software, or human failure may put the system out of service for several hours.

Another disadvantage of the simplex system is that the central processor is required to handle *all* of the functions of the system. On many such configurations, the central processor is interrupted each time a character of input is received from any one of the terminals. Similarly, a large amount of overhead is often expended in the area of file management, and the result of all of this overhead is ragged and uneven response at the terminals. Even in a dedicated system, the central processor is behaving almost as if it were a general-purpose system: handling communications processing, applications programs, data base management, and various forms of IO processing.

While it is not *necessary* for a simplex system to be small and simple, it would seem, from the characteristics we have just described, that the simplex configuration is perhaps best suited to a relatively small and simple application. It is applicable to a small or medium-sized SETSS or business-oriented system, in which the number of terminals is less than thirty or so. It is also applicable to many process control and data acquisition systems in which reliability is important, but not utterly imperative.

SIMPLEX SYSTEMS WITH A COMMUNICATIONS "FRONT-END"

Another common functional configuration is illustrated by Figure B7, in which a new "black box" has been added to the simplex configuration. The purpose of the new box is to handle the *function* of communications processing, and it may either be a simple hardware box, or a programmable computer. One of the more common hardware front-ends is IBM's 2703. A large variety of mini-computers have been successfully used as programmable front-ends.

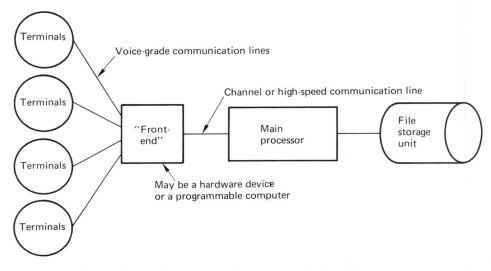

Fig. B7   Simplex system with a communications "front-end"

There are a number of advantages to this type of configuration, most of which are due to the increased modularity of the system. The small computer can control the communication lines, buffer input and output, perform error-checking, editing and formatting functions, thus allowing the main processor to concentrate its efforts on the application programs. The result is often a much "smoother" and more consistent response time at the terminals, since the trivial requests can be handled immediately by the front-end computer, and the more complicated requests can be scheduled to be sent to the larger computer.

In many cases, the necessary software for the front-end computer is provided by the vendor. However, this software usually only includes the basic functions of line control, error checking, and buffering of messages. If the system designer wishes to add more "intelligence" to the front-end—by including such functions as formatting, editing, and so forth—he will probably have to write the necessary programs himself.

One of the disadvantages of this type of configuration is the possibility of lower reliability. There are two computers which can fail, and two operating systems which might have bugs in them. However, experience has shown that the reliability of the front-end device is so much greater than the main computer complex that its effect on overall system reliability can virtually be ignored. Similarly, the software in the front-end tends to be more reliable—probably because it is not changed as often as the software in the main computer. The only significant reliability problem occurs when the front-end is located somewhere remote from the main computer. Then, if there *is* a failure in the front-end, there may not be any sufficiently trained personnel nearby to repair it.

Another commonly mentioned disadvantage of the "front-end" configuration is an increase in the cost of the system. However, it is precisely because of economic considerations that many system designers favor this configuration. The two factors which may make the front-end system more economical than the simplex configuration are:

1   Communication costs

   If terminals are located at a great distance from the main computer, it is much cheaper to place a small front-end computer (or perhaps only a simple hardware multiplexer) near the remote terminals, and connect the front-end to the main computer with a high-speed communication line.

2   Terminal interface units

   In the simplex configuration, each terminal is connected directly to the main computer—but the vendor usually requires a hardware interface unit to connect each modem, data-set, or direct wire connection to the computer. When the number of terminals exceeds sixteen or twenty, it is often cheaper to replace these interface units with one front-end device.

Perhaps the only significant disadvantage of the front-end configuration is the difficulty of getting it to work in the first place. If the system designer elects to write his own software in the front-end computer, he must have programmers who are fluent in two different assembly languages. The testing problems are more complex than in the simplex system, since computer-to-computer communication is involved. Restart problems may be somewhat difficult: if one machine fails, the other should continue operating and should later be able to "synchronize" itself when the other machine becomes operational again.

SIMPLEX SYSTEMS WITH COMMUNICATIONS AND DATA BASE MANAGEMENT COMPUTERS *(see Figure B8)*

The philosophy behind the "front-end" configuration was to identify a *function* in the on-line system, isolate it, and place it in a separate computer. This same philosophy can be extended to another common area in most on-line systems: the management of the files and the data base. The following functions could easily be placed in a separate computer:

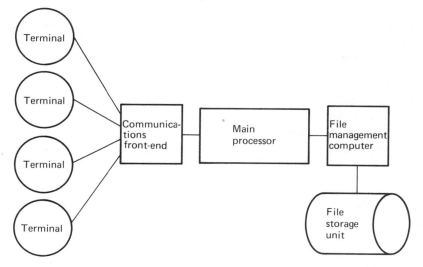

Fig. B8 Simplex with communications and data base management computers

optimizing of reads and writes on disks or drum

file security (checking of pass words and access keys)

file recovery (maintaining an audit trail, etc.)

file accessing (locating a particular record or file from a symbolic identification).

At present, the only function that has been relegated to a separate computer is the optimization of reads and writes. However, as more and more systems begin handling large, sensitive data bases, this type of configuration should gain more popularity.

The characteristics of this configuration are much the same as the "front-end" configuration. The system is likely to be more expensive, since more hardware is involved; and less reliable, since there are more components that might fail. However, we should expect such a system to be more efficient, since the three major functions of the system have been separated.

MASTER-SLAVE SYSTEM

In the three configurations described above, the large computer was generally in control of the environment. In the master-slave configuration, all of the "house-keeping," scheduling and control are carried out by the smaller "front-end," which is referred to as the *master* computer. The large processor, which handles the applications programs, is called the *slave* computer because it works on a specific application program only at the direction of the master computer.

The philosophy of putting the "house-keeping" and control in the smaller computer is based on the feeling that the larger computer, which is usually a powerful scientific-oriented processor, could better spend its time on applications processing. In addition, many requests made by users may not require the power of the large processor, so the small master computer can improve response time by handling the request itself. This capability is improved if the master and the slave computers *both* have access to the file storage units, as shown in Figure B9.

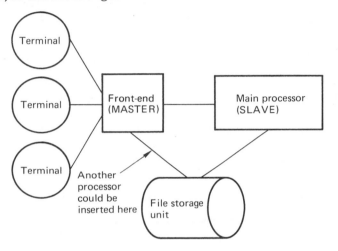

Fig. B9   Master-slave system

SHARED FILE SYSTEM

A less common configuration is shown in Figure B10 and involves two separate and independent computers which communicate through a common disk or drum. The configuration is similar to the master-slave system, except the computers have no means of direct communication.

The configuration can be used in the same fashion as the master-slave system, with one computer controlling the workload and sequence of jobs handled by the other computer. The only major disadvantage is that a longer response time might be involved: the access time on most disks ranges from 30 to 250 milliseconds, so it would take 60 to 500 milliseconds for one computer to place a message on the common disk and the other computer to read it.

DUPLEXED AND DUAL SYSTEMS

Still another type of configuration involves redundant processors, as shown in Figure B11. As was described in Chapter A, a dual system is one in which the processing is performed by both machines, with occasional checks to see that the results are the same. A duplexed system, on the other hand, involves a backup computer which may or may not be idle while the system is functioning normally.

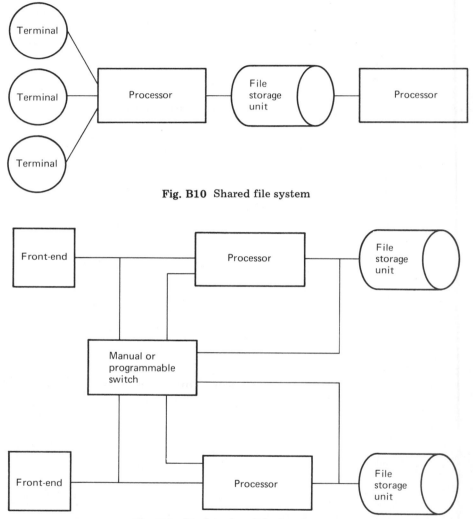

Fig. B10 Shared file system

Fig. B11 Duplexed and dual systems

The major goal of the duplexed and dual systems is, of course, increased reliability and availability of the system; these configurations do *not* make any attempt to improve the efficiency or the throughput of the system. In a dual system, recovery is essentially *immediate*, since both processors are always performing the same functions at the same time; the faulty processor merely drops out of the picture, and the other processor continues with its work.

In a duplexed system, though, switch-over is not immediate. We can identify three basic types of recovery using duplexed systems:

1 Completely manual recovery

2 Partially automatic recovery

3 Completely automatic recovery

With a completely manual recovery scheme, the backup processor is completely divorced from the primary processor. The recovery depends entirely on the computer operator, who must, in the event of a failure, perform the following actions:

1 Shut down the primary system as gracefully as possible.

2 Shut down any background processing that may have been taking place on the backup machine.

3 Perform any necessary file recovery.

4 Reload the on-line operating system and any necessary application programs on the backup machine.

5 Start the system up on the backup machine.

Depending on the nature of the failure, the complexity of the system, and the skill of the computer operator, this kind of recovery may take as little as 5 minutes and as much as an hour.

Much of this recovery activity is straightforward and could be accomplished by the computer itself—especially when the failure occurs in a peripheral device instead of a processor. Thus, it is possible to arrange a computer system so that the computer operator is requested to switch disks, drums, tape drives, or even processors manually from the backup system to the primary system. The computer itself could then perform any necessary file recovery, reloading of programs, etc.; the entire recovery process could easily take place within 30-60 seconds.

If the switch shown in Figure B11 can be activated under program control, then it is possible for the duplexed computer system to effect fully automatic recovery. Recovery from an IO device error is rather straightforward; recovery from a processor error requires that the backup processor periodically check to see that the primary processor is still "healthy." If it detects a failure on the part of the primary processor, the backup processor can then switch all of the peripheral devices and continue the operation of the system.

From a functional point of view, the most important characteristic of the duplexed and dual systems is their complexity. The operating system and error recovery routines are more difficult to write and much more difficult to test. Obviously, the system is more expensive because of the added equipment, and this must be justified by the greater reliability and availability of the system.

MULTIPROCESSING SYSTEMS

Many of the functional configurations described above are *multiple-computer systems*, but not multiprocessing systems. This final configuration, illustrated in Figure B12, may involve both multiprocessing and multiple-computer processing. As we discussed in Chapter A, processing may be distributed on a geographic, functional, or load basis, and the data base may be centralized or distributed, both from a logical point of view and a physical point of view.

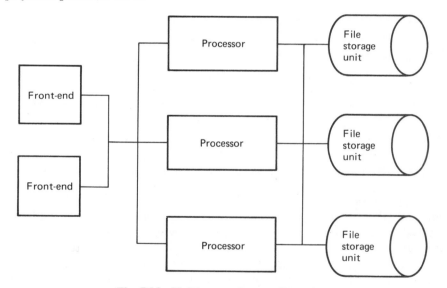

Fig. B12 Multiprocessing configuration

Relatively simple multiprocessing systems and multiple-computer processing systems are in existence today, and are supported by the computer manufacturers. Thus, General Electric supports a multiprocessing GE-635 configuration, which can be combined with a Datanet-30 for communications processing; Burroughs supports its B5500 and B6500 configurations, both of which involve multiprocessing; IBM supports multiprocessing versions of its larger System/360 computers; Control Data features multiprocessing on its CDC-6600 and CDC-7600 computers.

A number of organizations are planning to build "networks" of computers on a far grander scale than those in existence today. Thus, General Electric has been planning a time-sharing *network* of GE-635 computers, and various independent time-sharing service bureaus have been planning time-sharing networks on machines like the Univac 1108. Research agencies and universities supported by the federal Advanced Research Projects Agency (ARPA) have already begun linking together in what is known as the "ARPA network."

The objectives of these large network systems are many: greater reliability, greater availability, sharing of data bases and processing power, and greater efficiency and throughput. It is reasonable to assume that these goals will be achieved only after extended periods of difficult testing and debugging, for these systems are *much* more complex than any of the systems described earlier.

Chapter C

A REVIEW OF HARDWARE REQUIREMENTS
FOR ON-LINE SYSTEMS

INTRODUCTION

Computer hardware is certainly a very significant part of any on-line system, and it obviously cannot be ignored during the design phase of the project. However, a thorough discussion of hardware selection criteria could fill an entire book, and that is not what we are attempting to accomplish here. For the purposes of this book, it is probably best to assume that the reader has already chosen his hardware, or is at least leaning strongly toward one vendor or another.

Nevertheless, we should remember that hardware is not always chosen for the best of reasons: the system designer is often constrained by financial and political considerations, and ends up with a machine that he knows is not best for the job. Even worse, the system designer is occasionally ignorant of the hardware features that are important for on-line systems, and ends up using a good batch COBOL machine for a data acquisition system.

In the hope of forestalling some of these calamities, it might be wise for us to review some of the more critical elements of hardware for on-line systems. As we pointed out in Chapter A, an on-line system usually involves random-access data bases and short bursts of computation; we are usually *not* terribly concerned with large serial-access files or large compute-bound batch programs, except possibly in remote batch systems.

For the most part, then, we can ignore most of the standard serial-access IO devices—the card readers, magnetic tape drives, high-speed printers, etc.—and concentrate our attention on the three most critical parts of the typical on-line system:

> the central processor
>
> the file storage devices, specifically disks
>
> terminals

THE CENTRAL PROCESSOR

If a system designer had unlimited amounts of time, money, and talent, he might well attempt to design the hardware and software simultaneously. In most real-life situations, though, we do *not* have unlimited time or money, and as we pointed out above, the system designer is often severely limited by financial or political considerations in his choice of hardware.

While it is true that most system designers do not have the freedom or the inclination to build their own hardware, it is *not* always true that they are limited solely to a choice between IBM, GE, or one of the other computer manufacturers. In fact, the system designer must first choose one of the following *philosophies:*

> up-grading an older machine for use as an "on-line" computer
>
> using a current, "off-the-shelf" machine designed for on-line use
>
> using a machine which greatly advances the state of the art

For most on-line projects, the second approach is the safest and the most practical. Still, a number of organizations have attempted the first approach to save money, or to save an obsolete product line (the GE-265 is an excellent example of this). Those that choose the third approach usually do so out of a sense of desperation, because the "off-the-shelf" equipment seems totally inadequate for the job; sometimes the third approach is chosen out of a sense of adventure or for research purposes.

As a cynic once said, experience helps us recognize our errors when we make them again. Thus, it is only fitting that we point out some of the problems that have plagued those who have attempted to build on-line systems from up-graded antiques or extremely advanced machines. This discussion may not prevent the reader from making the same mistake on his own system, but it may help him recognize the mistake once he has made it!

If an older machine is modified to make it capable of operating in an on-line fashion, there will almost certainly be some new hardware bugs introduced. It has been quite common, for example, to add real-time clocks, master mode/slave mode, memory protection and relocation hardware, and an improved interrupt scheme to 2nd generation or early 3rd generation machines; paging and virtual memory have been added to a few machines, such as the GE-435 and the PDP-10; a few organizations are even considering adding a microprogramming capability to their existing computers.

All of these additions and "enhancements" are worthwhile and useful; a number of them, as we shall see later, are utterly imperative if one is to have a decent on-line machine. However, hardware changes of this magnitude cannot be made to *any* computer without some problems, and the system designer should plan on spending 6-12 months exorcising the hardware bugs from his new machine.

These hardware bugs have a tremendously bad effect on the development of the on-line software. With hardware changes of the magnitude described above, it is almost certain that a new operating system will have to be developed, and the debugging of the new operating system will have to take place while hardware bugs are still being removed. It is bad enough debugging application programs on a faulty piece of equipment; debugging operating systems under these conditions is enough to bring out suicidal tendencies in all but the most stout-hearted of programmers!

To make matters worse, it is possible that the standard application packages (e.g. the compilers, assemblers, loaders, payroll packages, and so forth) may not execute properly on the modified hardware. This can happen as a result of a change in the nature of the machine's "program status word" or a change in the hardware interrupt structure, or in the timing characteristics of some of the IO equipment, or anything else that might significantly affect the environment in which the application program runs. In many cases, the problem is due to poor programming practices on the part of the original programmer, but this does not help the on-line system designer.

Furthermore, if the original machine was built from an older circuit technology (such as transistors), the system designer may find that it does not run reliably under the long and demanding hours of an on-line environment.

Similar problems can occur with an extremely advanced piece of hardware. A machine that runs well in the laboratory may not run well at all in a "production" environment. The laboratory prototypes are usually not wired and soldered in the same way as the production line machines; they do not have as much core memory or as many IO devices; they are not used as heavily and under the demanding conditions of temperature, humidity, dust, and doughnut crumbs that one finds in the field.

Perhaps the most dangerous aspect of the advanced machine is that it either forces or tempts the programmer to use entirely new programming techniques or to take advantage of totally new hardware features. One of the more dramatic examples of this type of problem occurred when *paging* and *virtual memory* were introduced; it is questionable whether software designers on machines like the GE-645 and the IBM 360/67 have yet recovered from these advanced hardware techniques. When general-purpose, user-accessible, read/write microprogramming is introduced, a similar debacle will no doubt occur.

This does not mean that we should discourage advanced hardware and software development. However, as one highly successful computer executive remarked, "You can always tell the pioneers by the arrows in their backs!" If possible, it is best to let someone *else* suffer the pain of those arrows; it is best to be the second (or the third or even the fourth) person to try paging, microprogramming, and all of the other techniques.

The main objective of the system designer should be to build an on-line system that will fulfill the functional requirements with the *minimum possible risk.* With the exception of legitimate research activities and deliberate entrepreneurial gambles, this means that the system designer should make the strongest possible effort to use current, "off-the-shelf" computers. They may not be the most economical, and they may not be the best suited for the application from a purely technical point of view, *but at least they are known quantities.*

Necessary Features for an On-Line Central Processor

Regardless of the type or model computer that the system designer chooses, there are certain hardware capabilities that must be present. Virtually all third and fourth generation computers have these features, so the following discussion is for review purposes only.

Real-Time Clock or Interval Timer

By a "real-time" clock, we mean a hardware device that signals the processor at some convenient interval of time; we are *not* talking about a "time-of-day" clock that tells the computer that it is 5:15 PM.

Most real-time clocks measure time in intervals of 1/60 second, since that corresponds to ordinary line frequency. It is not at all unusual, though, to find computers that can measure intervals on one millisecond; a few computers allow the programmer to measure time at the internal clock rate of the machine, which can range from one microsecond to as little as 50 nanoseconds.

A common way of implementing the real-time clock is to use one of the memory locations (in the area occupied by the operating system) or a special hardware register to act as a *counter.* This counter can be set to a negative number by the operating system, and is incremented by the hardware at the end of each "interval" of time. When the counter reaches zero, a hardware interrupt is generated.

One use of the real-time clock is to aid in the scheduling process. A number of operating systems use "time-slicing" algorithms—that is, they take control away from one application program and turn it over to another application program at convenient intervals of, say, 1/4 second. When used for this purpose, it is convenient to have a real-time clock that measures time on a millisecond basis rather than 1/60 of a second. One sixtieth of a second is, of course, 16 2/3 milliseconds, and a lot can happen during that period of time. During a 16 2/3 millisecond period of time allotted to an application program, the operating system may have to interrupt and spend a few milliseconds handling an IO operation. Since the smallest unit of time that can be measured is 16 2/3 milliseconds, there is no way for the operating system to separate its own processing time from that of the application program—in effect, the operating system is "stealing" time from the application program. Under ideal circumstances, this would be balanced by situations when the application program stole time from the operating system—but most systems are far from ideal. In any case, the extent of this theft is much smaller with a one-millisecond clock.

Another important use of the real-time clock is as an "alarm clock" to prevent any part of the software from sitting in a loop forever. This is useful for "timing out" an application program in a batch environment as well as timing out the processing of a transaction in an on-line environment. In some cases, it may even be used to "time out" the operating system; the "time out" routine would then initiate some kind of recovery process.

One of the more common examples of a "time out" routine has to do with input/output. When the operating system issues an IO command to a device like a disk or a terminal, it knows that it should get a response within some reasonable period of time, usually less than one second. The real-time clock is then used to tell the operating system whether the IO device has responded in time; if it does not, the operating system can type a message to the computer operator and inform him that the device is not functioning properly.

Memory Protection and Relocation Features

Memory protection and relocation hardware can take a variety of forms—"bounds" registers, "base" registers, "paging" registers, and so forth. The hardware registers that control memory protection are usually closely related with the ones that control memory relocation.

One of the more common forms of memory protection is the so-called "memory protect mask" or "memory protect key." In its simplest form, one bit in the mask is used to describe the memory protection associated with a convenient-sized block of memory (e.g. 1,024 words, 4,096 bytes, etc.). Thus, if the bit is a zero, the currently running application program is not allowed to write into the corresponding block of memory; if the bit is a one, the program *is* allowed to write into the block. On more sophisticated computers, we may have an *access code* associated with each block of memory; thus, a two-bit access code might have the following meanings:

0   no access is allowed at all

1   execute-only access is allowed

2   read-only access

3   read/write access

Memory protection registers have two important uses: they allow the operating system to protect the application programs from each other; they also allow the operating system to protect *itself* against the application programs. The registers are usually set in such a way that an illegal attempt by the application program to reference an area outside its own "domain" is trapped by the operating system.

It should be pointed out that memory protection hardware is not always necessary on process control systems, data acquisition systems, or, for that matter, any on-line system being developed by a small team (i.e. three to five people) of competent programmers. On a large time-sharing system or business-oriented system, or any other system implemented by large groups of programmers, this kind of hardware protection is imperative. Only a few small mini-computers fail to offer memory protection as either a standard feature or an option.

Memory relocation is usually implemented with the aid of "base" registers, whose contents are arithmetically added to the effective address of an instruction just prior to its execution. The relocation register aligns the application program at the beginning of one of the convenient-sized blocks of memory we mentioned above; that is, the number contained in the memory relocation register is a multiple of 1,024 or 2,048 or whatever the "block size" may happen to be. An exception to this approach is found on the Burroughs B5500 and B6500 computers: on these machines, the operating system can relocate an application program to *any* address in the machine.

Memory relocation registers allow the operating system to execute an application program from *any* area of memory (or, to be more precise, from the beginning of any "page" boundary or "block" boundary). A common sequence of events is shown in Figure C1, in which the operating system is constantly "swapping" application programs between disk or drum and main memory.

It is highly desirable that the memory relocation registers not be accessible to the application program; that is, the memory relocation registers should be set only by the operating system, and should be used as part of the *hardware* sequence of effective address calculation. If the application program is allowed to access the memory relocation registers, or to circumvent the relocation scheme, then it is capable of calculating an *absolute address*. This means that the operating system is no longer capable of arbitrarily relocating the program to a different area of memory.

As an example, consider the IBM System/360, in which relocatability is accomplished by using one of the sixteen general registers. Since the base registers can be accessed by the application program, it follows that absolute addresses can be calculated. We must conclude that relocatability on the

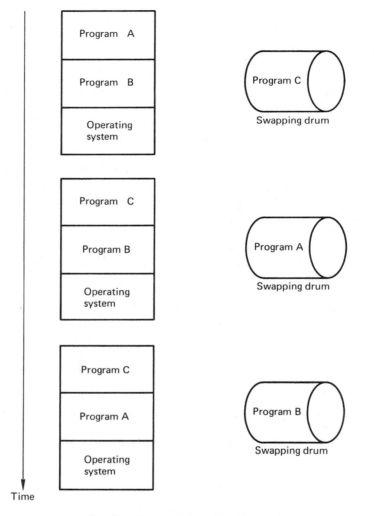

Fig. C1 The need for relocation registers

System/360 depends on the good will and intelligence of the application programmer, qualities which are in rare supply these days.

On some machines, like the GE-435, the GE-635, and earlier models of the PDP-10, there is only *one* memory relocation register. This means that the operating system must relocate the entire application program, and that it cannot separate the executable code from the data. Many of the more recent machines, such as the XDS Sigma 7, the IBM 360, the GE-645, and later models of the PDP-10, have two or more relocation registers. This allows the operating system to relocate the executable code and the data independently; even more important, it allows for the implementation of *reentrant programs*, since the operating system can make the application program switch from one data area to another merely by changing the contents of the appropriate relocation registers.

If we carry this idea to its logical conclusion, we can have a separate relocation register for each of the "blocks" or "pages" of memory that is protected by our memory protection scheme. The resulting configuration is known as "paging," and is discussed later in this chapter.

Master Mode/Slave Mode

Most of the features we have described above are intended to be used *only* by the operating system, and not by the application programs, Thus, it could be a catastrophe if the application programs were allowed to

halt the machine

set the memory protection and relocation registers

reset the real-time clock

execute machine language IO instructions

The standard way of avoiding this problem is to have two *modes* of operation: *master* mode and *slave* mode. In master mode (sometimes referred to as "control mode" or "executive mode") all of the instructions and capabilities of the machine are considered legal; in slave mode, some of the instructions are considered illegal, and, if executed, cause a "trap" to the operating system.

Once again, this feature is not absolutely necessary on small process control systems and data acquisition systems. For any on-line system with a large number of potentially un-debugged programs, though, it is extremely important.

Hardware Interrupts

On all third-generation computers, and especially on on-line computers, input/output is performed simultaneously with computation. Typically, the operating system will begin several input/output operations on various IO devices and will then commence execution of an application programming task. The application program will be allowed to continue its execution until the input/output operation (e.g. the reading of a record from disk, the punching of a card, the printing of a line on the high-speed printer, etc.) has been completed; the only question is *how* to inform the central processor that the IO operation has finished.

Earlier computers typically tended to check a hardware flag periodically to see if the IO operation had finished; the programmer still has the option of using this approach on several current minicomputers, including the

PDP-8. However, most current machines, with very few exceptions, use an *interrupt* to take control away from the currently-executing application program (or perhaps from an operating system subroutine) and turn control over to an IO routine in the operating system.

The only significant example of a machine which does not have some form of interrupt structure is the Control Data 6600. On this machine, the small peripheral processors are capable of initiating an IO activity, but must then periodically check a hardware flag to see whether the IO operation has finished; in most CDC-6600 systems, the peripheral processor does not attempt to do any other computations while waiting for the completion of IO. Since there are ten peripheral processors available on a CDC-6600 configuration, and since the two large processors can continue processing while the peripheral processors are waiting for IO, this approach is not as inefficient as it obviously would be on a non-multiprocessing machine.

Various types of hardware interrupt structures are discussed in more detail in Chapter Q.

Input/Output Channels

By input/output channels, we simply mean an independent path from an IO device to the computer's memory, thus avoiding the necessity of doing input/output through the accumulator or the general registers of the machine. There are various types of IO channels, and each of the computer manufacturers seems to have a different terminology for describing the nature of his IO channels.

Despite all the variations and different trade names, there are only three different kinds of channels with which we need be concerned. *Dedicated* channels represent a permanent connection between an input/output device and the computer and are usually desirable for high-speed devices like disks and drums. *Floating* channels (to use one manufacturer's terminology) are connected to an IO device only for the duration of the IO transfer; at the completion of the IO activity, the channel is available for use by other devices. *Multiplexor* channels allow for the simultaneous transfer of data from several low-speed devices and represent the most inexpensive way of connecting several low-speed devices to the on-line computer system.

The most interesting development in the area of IO channels has been the appearance of the "intelligent" channel. At the moment, all of these devices are either hard-wired or microprogrammable; nevertheless, they *can* be modified by an enterprising programmer. An intelligent channel can, in addition to transferring data from the IO device to memory, perform "scatter-gather" IO, code translation, error-checking, and various other functions. There will undoubtedly be a trend towards more "intelligence" of this type in the future; at this point, though, our only concern is that there be *some* kind of IO channel on the machine.

Desirable Features for On-Line Processors

As we have already noted, most of the hardware features that have been described above are available on almost all current computers—with the possible exception of some of the small mini-computers.

There are a number of additional features, though, which, while not absolutely necessary, make the on-line system more flexible, more efficient, and easier to build. Some of these features are found on many current 3rd generation computers; other features will become "standard" in the computers of the 4th generation only after their value has been proven by a few fearless pioneers.

A Sophisticated Multilevel Hardware
Priority Interrupt Scheme

The hardware interrupt structure we discussed above can be implemented in a number of different ways, some of which are quite primitive. A number of the more recent third generation computers, however, allow different IO devices to be assigned to different hardware *priority levels*. The number of priority levels ranges from as few as three or four on some machines to as many as 128 or more on other machines.

This kind of sophisticated hardware interrupt structure makes it possible for a low-speed IO device to interrupt an application program; more important, it allows a critical, high-speed, real-time IO device to interrupt the processing of the low priority IO processing. This can be of great value in process control and data acquisition systems, where it is utterly imperative that a critical external interrupt be able to wrest control away from a less urgent interrupt routine.

The alternative to the sophisticated hardware is, in some cases, a sophisticated *software* priority interrupt scheme, which we shall discuss at length in Chapter Q.

Paging and Virtual Memory

Earlier in this chapter, we introduced the notion of *relocation registers;* the reader will recall that the effect of the relocation register was to *offset* every effective address by the amount contained in the register. Thus, if the relocation register contained the octal number 2000, then the instruction

ADD 1234

would be executed with an *absolute* address of 1234+2000, or 3234. Note that this relocation affects *every* effective address calculation, including both data accesses and instruction accesses. Thus, if the programmer writes the instruction

JMP 1234

the instruction will, when executed, cause a transfer of control to *absolute* location 3234 in the machine.

We also noted that it would be possible to have more than one relocation register in the machine. The IBM System/360 provides this capability to the application programmer by including a *base register field* in every machine language instruction; thus, the programmer can relocate (or index) the address of one instruction by the contents of general register 15, and the next instruction by the contents of general register 14. The PDP-10 provides a similar capability by using one relocation register (which is *not* accessible to the application program) for instruction references, such as the JMP instruction mentioned above; and another relocation register (also not directly accessible by the application programmer) for data references.

Suppose we carried this idea one step further, and provided *several* relocation registers for our computer. Instead of having just one relocation register for the instruction references and one for the data references, we would associate a relocation register with every 512-word block of memory (or every 1024-word block of memory, or any other convenient size; some of the more common arrangements are listed in Table H1 of Chapter H) available to the application programmer.

The memory that is available to the application programmer is usually referred to as *virtual memory*, and the hardware process of independently relocating 512-word blocks or "pages" or memory is known as *paging* (it is also referred to as "remapping," "relabelling," and a variety of other obscure terms). As an example, consider the following two instructions in memory locations 777 octal and 1000 octal:

777   ADD 3456

1000   STORE 4567

When the ADD instruction is executed, it references *virtual* memory location 3456. We must remember that, in this hypothetical example, virtual memory locations 0-777 octal are affected by relocation register (or "paging" register) 0; virtual memory locations 1000-1777 are affected by the contents of paging register 1; and so forth. Thus, when the ADD instruction is executed, the virtual address of 3456 is relocated (or "remapped," or "translated," or "relabelled," to use terminology currently in vogue) by the contents of paging register 3.

After the ADD instruction has been executed, the program presumably proceeds to the instruction at *virtual* location 1000. This address also requires relocation, in this case by the contents of paging register 1. Thus, we see that it is possible for a *virtually contiguous* program to be *physically non-contiguous*. This is illustrated in Figure C2.

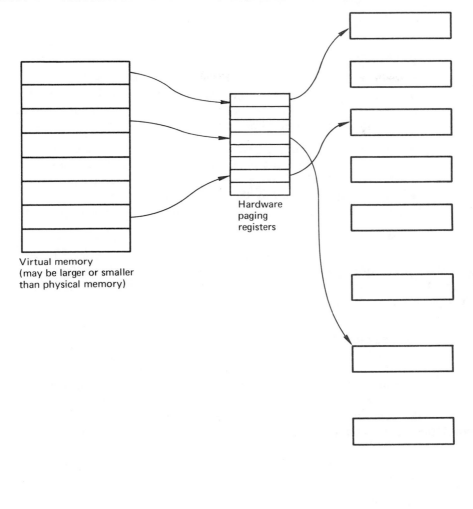

Fig. C2 Hardware paging

This description of paging and virtual memory is somewhat over-simplified, but it does illustrate the general principles involved. There are various forms of paging available on a number of third generation computers; if used properly, paging has a number of advantages on these machines:

1   Many different jobs can share one physical copy of a program, providing, of course, that the program was written in a reentrant fashion. Each different

execution of the program has its own separate data pages, and the operating system switches from one execution of the program to another merely by changing the contents of the appropriate paging registers.

2   "Demand paging" is possible—i.e. only that part of the application program which is actually referenced (i.e. "demanded") is brought into physical memory. This can result in considerable savings of memory for programs which spend most of their time in a small loop.

3   Less swapping is required, assuming that the programs are written in a reentrant fashion. Since the program does not modify itself, the operating system does not need to store a copy of the partially-executed program; it can *overlay* the pages occupied by the reentrant program, and merely read an old copy of the program from disk or drum when it wants to resume its execution.

While paging is a potentially powerful hardware feature, it requires a tremendous amount of intelligent programming in both the operating system and the application programs. Some of the paging problems faced by the application programmer are discussed in Chapter H; the problems faced by the operating system are discussed in Chapter T.

Ability to Add Large Amounts of Directly Addressable Memory

It is obviously desirable to have the ability to add more memory to one's computer. As we will see in Chapter D, one of the more common bottlenecks in an on-line system is an insufficient amount of memory. This can happen for a variety of reasons, but the three most common ones are:

the operating system grows so large that it takes up a significant amount of available memory.

the application programs grow to take up more room than expected.

the application programs are so *interactive* that they can only execute for a short amount of time before having to wait for some input/output to finish. In such cases, it is desirable to have room for a large number of application programs, so that the operating system will always be able to find at least one executable application program.

A number of currently available third generation computers will support as much as 8-16 million bytes of memory. Unfortunately, the cost of reasonably fast memory (i.e. one microsecond or less) is so high that most installations must use the less expensive "large core storage" which generally has a memory cycle time of about 8 microseconds. It is hoped that the 1970's will see the development of large, fast, low-cost memories for the on-line systems of the future.

Fast Index Registers, Fast Accumulators,
"Scratch-Pad" Memory, Etc.

There are often a number of application-oriented operations, such as matrix multiplications, that can be programmed into a tight loop. This could be speeded up tremendously if it could be executed in fast registers with a cycle time of 100 nanoseconds or less.

Also, much of the processing in the typical operating system consists of indexing into tables, which point to other tables, and so forth. Fast indexing can thus reduce the amount of operating system overhead to some extent.

Rapid Context-Switching

Whenever the operating system switches control from one application program to another, all of the accumulators, index registers, program status words, etc. must be saved; similarly, all of these registers must be *restored* for the new application program that is to be started up or resumed from its last point of interruption. This can be a very lengthy process if the saving and restoring of registers requires the repeated execution of an instruction for each register saved. On the other hand, the process can be very efficient if there is *one* machine language instruction called "save the state of the machine," and another one called "restore the state of the machine."

The savings that can be achieved with an instruction of this type can be tremendous. On one on-line system on a GE-435 computer, for example, it took approximately 500 microseconds to save and restore the state of the machine; on the XDS Sigma series computers, on the other hand, the vendor claims to be able to save and restore the state of the machine in 6 microseconds. Since the operating system may switch from one application program to another (or from one operating system subroutine to another) several times a second, this savings can be very important, especially in process control and data acquisition systems.

Ability to Upgrade to a Larger Machine

A number of the computer manufacturers are beginning to stress the idea of "modular" computers, and the idea of compatible "families" of computers. This has always been desirable, and is even more desirable when designing an on-line system. As we shall see in Part II of this book, it is often extremely difficult to calculate the hardware requirements for an on-line system; one always ends up wanting more memory, a larger processor, a more powerful instruction set, and so forth.

The possibility of upgrading to a larger machine is increased somewhat if the applications are written in a higher level language, and if the system designer has not incorporated any special changes into the vendor's operating system.

Microprogramming

Until recently, there have been only two levels of programming available to the programmer. Languages like FORTRAN and COBOL provide a *high level* of programming; assembly languages provide a *low level* of programming. Microprogramming provides an even lower level of programming, allowing the programmer to directly address and manipulate the adders, shifters, flip-flops, and other internal hardware registers.

Microprogramming is certainly not a new concept. The term was first introduced by Professor M.V. Wilkes of Cambridge University in 1951, and machines like the IBM System/360 have utilized microprogramming for a number of years. Until recently, though, microprogramming was not generally accessible to the average programmer at a computer installation. Machines like the IBM System/370, the Standard Computer Corporation IC-4000, IC-6000, and MLP-900, and the Interdata-3 have begun what may be a trend towards user-accessible microprogramming machines.

Microprogramming offers a number of advantages to the computer manufacturer. For one thing, it allows him to delay the final specification of the instruction set of the machine until late in the hardware development effort. Once the machine has been designed and built, microprogramming allows the vendor to *change* the instruction set—as was the case in 1968, when IBM changed the operation of their floating point instructions on the IBM System/360. Microprogramming also makes it easier to build a *compatible* machine, and makes possible the *emulation* of other machines on one processor.

For the on-line system designer, microprogramming may offer advantages above and beyond the ones mentioned above. It is quite possible that the system designer might design microprogrammed instructions to perform the following types of functions:

sophisticated interrupt handling

complex IO handling of the type handled by "intelligent" channels

file searching and file optimization

list manipulation

string handling and symbol manipulation

mathematical functions, such as square root and exponential

In an extreme case, one might even imagine an entire operating system or compiler written as a microprogram.

At the moment, a number of vendors seem rather hesitant about making microprogramming operations available to users of the equipment. There is some justification to this fear, since an undebugged microprogram might cause the machine to fail. We may very well see the development of "master mode" and "slave mode" microprograms, so that the entire system will not be at the mercy of the careless programmer; there are those who feel, though, that the very nature of microprogramming precludes this kind of protection. As a result, we are probably more likely to see user-accessible microprogramming on the minicomputers, where the user is more likely to build a *dedicated* microprogramming system.

FACTORS IN CHOOSING A TERMINAL FOR AN ON-LINE SYSTEM

Because of the increasing number of on-line systems, the terminal industry is probably the fastest-growing segment of the computer industry. Because most systems will accept a wide variety of terminals, the system designer has a wide choice of terminals available to him. The following is a partial list of factors that should be kept in mind in the choice of a terminal:

1 *The speed of the terminal*

Most teletypewriter terminals operate at 10-15 characters per second, although some of the new ones, with thermal printing mechanisms, may achieve speeds of 20-40 characters per second. Speed can be an important factor in some of the business-oriented on-line systems, in which each transaction may involve a large amount of terminal IO.

The cathode ray tube terminal is often a more suitable alternative in situations of this kind, but it may be inconvenient if hard-copy output is required. Most manufacturers allow a low-speed printer or a teletypewriter device to be attached to the CRT control unit, but this involves extra expense for the system designer.

In some applications, where an especially high volume of terminal IO is expected, a low-speed remote printer (operating at speeds of 200-300 lines per minute) may be required.

2 *Reliability of the terminals*

Some teletypewriter terminals are specified by their manufacturer as a "light duty" terminal, and are intended to be used no more than 100 hours per month. If the terminal is to be used eight hours a day, five days a week, it might be better to invest in a more rugged terminal.

Reliability can be an especially important factor if the on-line system's terminals are distributed over a large geographical area.

3 *Acoustical noise level*

In some applications, it is desirable to have a reasonably quiet terminal. For on-line medical information systems, library information retrieval systems, and certain types of office-oriented systems, a quiet CRT might be preferable to the clatter of a teletypewriter device.

4   *Electrical noise level*

A factor that is usually of interest only to military users is the susceptibility of the terminal to electronic "eavesdropping."

5   *Security devices*

Half of the problem of security on an on-line system is to identify the individual using the system. This can sometimes be accomplished with the aid of hardware devices on the terminal. Examples are the standard answer-back drums on many teletypes; badge reader devices; fingerprint-reading devices; and voiceprint devices.

An answer-back drum is a small, cylindrical device which can accept a message of up to 20 characters. When interrogated by the computer, the message on the answer-back drum will be transmitted as an identification of the terminal. Its drawback is that it can be tampered with quite easily on most terminals.

A badge reader device requires the user to slip a small plastic card, much like the current credit cards, into a slot on the terminal. The user's identification is encoded on the card, and on some systems, if the identification is not proper, the terminal will gobble up the card and refuse to give it back!

The fingerprint and voiceprint devices are, for the most part, still in the development stage and will probably be far too expensive for the average system. They do offer the advantage of greater security—it is somewhat more difficult to forge a fingerprint or imitate a voice than it is to steal or forge a plastic identification badge.

There have been reports of a security device that allows the user of the system to insert his hand in a large slot on the side of the terminal. The terminal then measures the length and width of the five fingers for identification purposes, and if dissatisfied, presumably gobbles up the user's hand and refuses to give it back.

6   *Cost of the terminal*

This is a self-explanatory item, but one to which the reader should probably give his attention for the next few years. At the present time, most of the simple teletypewriter devices lease for $50-100 per month, and most of the CRT devices lease for $100-300 per month. There are a number of terminal companies, and it should be possible, by 1975, to obtain teletypewriter terminals for $25-50 per month, and CRT terminals for approximately $50-75 per month.

7   *Ability to poll the terminal*

For the systems designer and the communications specialist, it is important to know how the terminal signals that it has a message to send to the computer. Many terminals work on a "contention" basis, attempting to interrupt the processor whenever a character or a message has been typed in by the terminal user. On other terminals, it is possible for the processor to "poll" the terminal, that is, specifically *ask* it if there is any input ready to be sent.

8 *Ability to address the terminal on a multi-drop line*

A large number of the on-line systems currently in existence dedicate a communications line to each terminal on the system. While this is a reasonable approach on medium-sized systems, it is very uneconomical for systems with many hundreds of terminals. It is desirable to attach many terminals to a communication line, in which case it is necessary for the processor to be able to indicate *which* terminal is to receive an output message. This is illustrated in Figure C3.

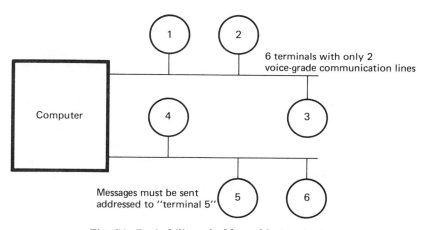

Fig. **C3** Desirability of addressable terminals

9 *Ability to attach the terminal to a voice-grade communication line*

Most teletypewriter devices transmit at a sufficiently low speed that they can be attached to the same communication lines that are used for voice communications. Many CRT devices, on the other hand, require medium-speed communication lines (on the order of 2400 bits per second). This can be an important consideration for reasons of economy and convenience. Not only are the voice-grade lines cheaper, they are more plentiful.

10 *Character set of the terminal*

Most current terminals either transmit characters in the ASCII character set or some variation of the BCD character set. It is desirable to have a terminal whose character set is compatible with the rest of the system, so that time-consuming translations from one character set to another can be avoided.

11 *Buffering at the terminal*

It is desirable, though not common, to be able to transmit and receive an entire message from the terminal. Buffering in the front-end computer or at the main processor is now rather common, but a buffer at the terminal can cut down on the overhead required at the processor, and can also help make more efficient use of communication lines.

One of the developments that may make terminal buffering more common in the near future is the *mag tape cassette memory* that some manufacturers provide with their terminals. This allows one or more messages to be stored up at the terminal while the user is preparing them for the computer; or, in the reverse direction, it allows the computer to transmit a burst of messages to the terminal, whereupon the terminal can type out the message one character at a time.

12 *Ability of the terminal to transmit in half duplex and/or full duplex*

A terminal operating in a half-duplex mode can either transmit messages to the computer or receive them from the computer—but not both simultaneously. A full-duplex terminal, on the other hand, can transmit in both directions at the same time. There are advantages and disadvantages to both arrangements, and in most cases, it is possible to obtain a terminal that can operate in *either* mode with a flip of a switch.

13 *Ability to have multiple printers and keyboards on the terminal*

On many business-oriented on-line systems, it is desirable to have one printing mechanism and keyboard for communication with the system, and another for printing special forms (i.e. invoices, order forms, etc.). This is not possible on most of the current terminals, and the user is faced with the alternative of using two terminals (and thus two communication lines) or changing forms at various times during his dialogue with the system.

14 *Ability of the terminal to check for errors*

Most current terminals check for transmission errors with a simple *parity bit* associated with each error. While this mechanism is suitable for single-bit errors, many of the data transmission errors are due to bursts of noise on the transmission line—in which two, three, or ten bits may be lost.

One of the advantages of full-duplex transmission is that it allows the user to check for transmission errors—for the character that he strikes on his keyboard is not printed locally, but sent to the computer and "echoed" back to the terminal. What the full-duplex scheme does not allow for, though, is some way for the computer to verify that a message was sent to the terminal properly.

Two things are needed in this area, and they are available on some terminals: an error-checking code associated with an entire message, rather than a simple parity bit on each character; and an *acknowledgement* of receipt of message at both ends of the transmission line. The error-checking code can be derived mathematically in order to ensure an arbitrarily low probability of an undetected error, and can be built into the hardware very easily and cheaply.

15 *"Intelligence" of the terminal*

There is a growing feeling among systems people that the "intelligence" of the system should be distributed farther and farther away from the large central processor. The "front-end" computer is one example of this move. The next step is to have a processing unit and programmable memory in the terminal itself. The terminal could then perform such functions as:

formatting of input and output

syntax-checking

complex buffering and polling

editing

pre-processing of input

16 *Compatibility with other terminals*

An interesting point is that it would be desirable to have different types of terminals on the same on-line system, or even on the same communication line. The problem is that many terminals have different baud rates (i.e. transmission speeds), character sets, and polling techniques.

Even if each terminal has its own dedicated communication line, it may be difficult to mix different combinations on the same system. It is usually impossible to place different types of terminals on the same communication line.

FACTORS IN CHOOSING A DISK STORAGE DEVICE

One of the most important characteristics of an on-line computer system is *random-access data.* Many of today's on-line systems have data bases that are huge by the standards of three or four years ago, and the data bases are growing each day. There are a few on-line systems currently being designed with billion-character data bases; at least one is being planned, at the Air Force Logistics Command, with a 20-billion character data base. For this reason, the choice of a good disk storage device is important (even though we are probably not too far away from some technological breakthrough which will permit *huge* data bases). Some of the more important considerations for choosing a disk are:

1 *Expandability of the disk*

How many disk "modules" or storage units can be added? It is important to remember that disk-packs do *not* represent an infinite storage capacity—we are interested in the amount of *on-line accessible* storage.

2 *Speed of the disk*

The speed of the disk can be a critical bottleneck for some types of on-line applications. We are primarily concerned here with *seek time;* latency time and transfer rates are usually not such critical factors. Seek times can vary by as much as a factor of ten, as noted below:

fixed-head disks:	20-40 milliseconds
disk-packs:	30-60 milliseconds
older movable-head disks:	180-250 milliseconds

3   *Reliability of the disk*

The reliability of a disk often is a subjective matter—some vendors seem to have a better reputation than others. It is very common for a computer manufacturer to obtain a disk from another vendor and include it in his own system. Maintenance of the disk may then be a rather difficult task.

4   *Maintenance of the disk*

Regardless of the reliability of the disk, it will certainly fail sooner or later. Thus, it is important to know whether it is possible to set aside spare platters, or tracks, or file units for maintenance while the rest of the system keeps running.

5   *Ability to have many simultaneous seeks*

On almost all disk-pack configurations, it is possible to perform independent seeks on each disk, as illustrated by Figure C4. On other disks, however, it may only be possible to perform one seek at a time—and this represents a potential bottleneck in the system.

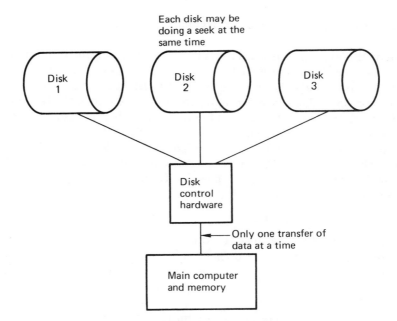

Fig. C4   Multiple "seeks" on disk

Because the hardware is *capable* of operating multiple seeks is no guarantee, of course, that the system will be capable of taking advantage of it. The operating system may not be capable of performing many disk IO operations concurrently, and the data base may be structured in such a way that most of the reads and writes are confined to one of the disks.

PART

II

DESIGNING THE SYSTEM

Chapter D

A DESIGN GUIDELINE FOR ON-LINE SYSTEMS

INTRODUCTION

In earlier chapters, we have assumed that the reader was being exposed to on-line systems for the first time; in subsequent chapters, we will proceed on the assumption that the reader is deeply involved in the implementation of his system, and will be interested in discussions of file accessing techniques, operating systems, and so forth.

However, there must be an intermediate step. It is not reasonable to jump immediately from an introduction to on-line systems into a discussion of scheduling algorithms and file access techniques, nor is it reasonable for the reader of this book to jump from an initial decision to build an on-line system to a decision about the finer details of the system. In fact, one might even argue that it is not reasonable to begin the design of an on-line system by discussing the hardware to be used.

How, then, do we begin the design of an on-line system? It is the underlying theme of this book that the "design" activity is not so much a *science* as it is a trade or a craft. Thus, it is difficult to verbalize some of the aspects of the design and organization of a system, for they are skills that are either intuitive or inherited. Nevertheless, there are some basic design decisions that must be made at the beginning of any system project, and it is the purpose of this chapter to identify and discuss them as completely as possible.

Basic Design Decisions

In far too many computer systems, the designers become engrossed in the details and the paperwork of their system before answering some very basic questions about the nature and purpose of their system. For most on-line systems, there are five questions to be answered:

1　What are the goals of the system?

2　What basic type of on-line system best meets those needs?

3　What hardware configuration can be used to realize those goals?

4　What kind of operating system should be used?

5　What kind of application programs should be written?

To some extent, these questions are "circular" in nature. That is, in order to decide what hardware configuration should be used, one must know something about the nature of the application programs that are going to be written; conversely, in order for the application programs to be designed efficiently, the system architect must know something about the hardware configuration. However, this is common for many types of systems, and one can usually proceed by "assuming" the answer to one question and then adjusting the assumptions in a series of successive approximations as the design process becomes more detailed.

THE GOALS OF AN ON-LINE SYSTEM

The most basic of all decisions should be that of determining what the system is to do. This is usually done in great detail in a *functional specification*, but the system designers should be able to provide, in written form, a description of the benefits and advantages of the proposed system. The basic goal of any on-line system should be either to *solve a problem that cannot reasonably be solved in any other way* or to *attempt a better solution to a problem than the current approach.*

It is important that these goals be as *specific* as possible, so that everyone in the project will know what he is working towards. A common danger in any large project is "sub-optimization," which occurs when individuals or small groups within the project attempt to optimize their own part of the system—at the expense of the overall performance of the system. This becomes much more of a danger when the goals are stated in a "fuzzy" manner that can be interpreted differently by each member of the project.

For example, consider a "total management information" system being designed for a typical business. The stated goal of the system is usually simply to provide "more information" or "more timely information" to the manager. The data processing department usually interprets this as a mandate to eliminate the voluminous batch reports that they suspect nobody reads; management, on the other hand, expects a complex information retrieval system that will allow them to ask questions such as "tell me how many salesmen in the Northeastern region sold more than X dollars of product Y during the spring season." In addition, the manager still wants all of his batch reports, for he simply doesn't feel secure without them.

Similarly, a general-purpose scientific-engineering time-sharing system might have a stated goal of providing "on-line computational facilities" to programmers and scientists within an organization. One group might interpret this as a specification for a system with an easy-to-learn language like BASIC; another group might see the need for extensive development of an incremental FORTRAN IV compiler; still another group might be more concerned with the file structure of the system, feeling that the sharing of programs and files was of paramount importance.

Whatever the goals of the system are, they should be as tangible as possible, so that the success of the end product can be measured. An on-line inventory system whose goal is simply to provide "more up-to-date inventory information" to its users is not easy to justify from a financial point of view. How many orders will not be lost as a result of the manager or salesman having real-time information about the availability of his stock items? How much of a reduction in inventory levels can be achieved by having more up-to-date information? In a scientific-engineering time-sharing system, we might ask how much time will be saved as a result of engineers obtaining "instant" turnaround time, and how much will be gained by making the system accessible to non-programmers as well as the programmers.

It is often said that some of the benefits of on-line systems cannot be measured. How does one measure the increase in creativity in a scientist when he has an interactive, conversational problem-solving computer at his side? Similarly, how does one measure the improvement in a manager's decision-making ability that results from a real-time management information system? In most cases, we are talking about such qualitative factors as "convenience," "flexibility," "availability," and so forth, and we are simply at a loss when it comes to quantifying them.

The important point is that the system designer should be *aware* of these goals, and should make the customer, or user of the system, equally aware of them. If the goal can be stated in a quantitative fashion, so much the better: both the designer and the user will be able to tell whether the system lived up to expectations. If, on the other hand, the benefits and goals of the system are purely qualitative in nature, that too should be made known to all parties.

In many cases, an on-line computer system is built as an alternative to, or a replacement for, a batch computer system. Using such arguments as "greater convenience," "more up-to-date information," and "greater flexibility," the designer proceeds with his on-line system, only to find that it is more difficult, and more expensive than the batch system it replaced, and that the supposed benefits were not forthcoming. The system designer might be well advised to consider the following questions before deciding to build an on-line system, rather than a simple batch system:

1   *Requirement for "real time" versus "relevant time" processing*

There are a large number of situations in which "real time," "conversational," "instant response" systems are a convenience (or even a status symbol!) but not really a necessity. We might introduce the phrase "relevant time" systems to describe those systems which may not be "real time" (e.g. they may be batch systems), but which still provide information fast enough to be of value to the user.

Many business organizations, for instance, currently operate with inventory, sales, or accounts receivable information that is days, weeks, or even months old. The company may very well want to computerize its inventory and accounts receivables so as to have more up-to-date information; this does *not* necessarily imply that the company requires a real-time system. An efficient batch system might be able to provide information only one day old, and this might be just as acceptable as information that is only one second old.

Similarly, the system designer might consider providing an on-line system that allows clerks and managers to type in transactions from a remote terminal, but which does not perform any real-time updating of the data base. On-line data base inquiries might be allowed, but the data base would be one day old; all of the updates to the data base could be collected on a magnetic tape or a "transaction file," and merged into the data base at night.

The main point we are trying to make here is that the user may not *need* real-time processing; he may even be able to do without the convenience of on-line processing. This is especially true of many organizations considering a move from a manual or EAM system to an on-line, real-time system.

2   *Number of records accessed in the data base each day*

If only a small part of the data base is accessed each day, the need for a random-access, on-line data base is probably very great. One certainly does not want to make a serial search through a magnetic tape file to access only one or two records.

There are, however, situations where a large part of the data base is accessed during the course of the day. Similarly, there are situations where one data base record is accessed repeatedly during the processing of several transactions; this might be the case, for example, in an on-line order entry system, where one inventory record is repeatedly updated as orders arrive from the remote sales offices.

In these cases, the overhead associated with random-access file retrieval techniques may be prohibitive. As we shall see in Chapter K, the accessing of one data base record might require *several* disk accesses to read in the appropriate directories or perform the necessary "hash-code" search.

The system designer might prefer to "batch" his on-line transactions for five or ten minutes; that is, he might collect *several* transactions before actually processing any of them. Thus, if several transactions required access to the same data base record, it would only have to be read once. Data base records could be blocked to further reduce the number of disk accesses.

Similarly, the system designer could allow the on-line system to collect transactions all day long. At the end of the day, the transactions could be sorted and processed with a serial tape file on a batch computer.

3 The cost of a system failure

There are *many* ways for an on-line system to fail, including power failures, processor errors, program bugs, and operator errors. Since on-line systems tend to be so much more complicated than batch systems, the possibilities for system failures are often much greater. The various types of system failures and the relative frequency of their occurrence are discussed in more detail in Chapter U.

More important than the frequency of on-line system failures is their *visibility*. In the case of a time-sharing system or a business-oriented information system, the users literally have their fingers on the pulse of the system; if there is a failure, they are *immediately* aware of it. Similarly, a failure in a process control system can have immediate and catastrophic consequences.

Prevention of system failures and recovery from system failures *are* possible, but it is both expensive and difficult; backup hardware may be required, and extremely thorough testing is a must. In some cases, this extra cost (both hardware and software) is so great that it might be better to stay with a batch or manual system.

4 Remoteness of users

One of the important factors in some systems is the geographical distribution of the users of the system. If the users are spread all over the country, as in the case of an airline reservation system or a corporate-wide order entry system, there may not be any alternative to an on-line system.

On the other hand, the users may all be in the same building or in the same city. Even so, there is no doubt that an on-line system is convenient, and many an engineer and manager would dearly love to have a terminal in his office. The system designer must weigh the conveniences of an interactive on-line system against the lower cost of a fast-turnaround batch system or a remote batch system.

5 Cost of an on-line data base

Batch computer systems have traditionally used magnetic tape as the storage medium for their large data bases. A 2400-foot reel of magnetic tape costs approximately $10-15, and can easily hold 15-20 million characters of data (depending, of course, on the recording density and the blocking factor). On-line disk storage can easily cost 50-100 times more than magnetic tape, depending on the vendor and the type of disk storage used.

When one realizes that many batch systems have data bases consisting of several *hundred* reels of tape, it is obvious that the cost of on-line storage might become outrageously high.

6   *Difficulty of implementation*

As we shall attempt to demonstrate in various parts of this book, on-line systems can be *extremely* complicated. In spite of this (or perhaps in total ignorance of this), an alarming number of organizations make a brave, but often futile, effort to jump from a manual or EAM system directly to a third generation, real-time, on-line system. It is not sufficient to have programmers on the staff; nor is it sufficient to have analysts who are familiar with third-generation computer systems. One requires the following type of talent, preferably within the organization, but perhaps from the computer vendor or a consulting organization:

familiarity with third generation computer systems

familiarity with the application being implemented

familiarity with on-line or real-time systems *of the type being implemented;* that is, a scientific time-sharing system expert is not necessarily adequate talent to build a management information system.

If this type of talent is not readily available, then it might be best to avoid building the on-line system; it might be better to use the services of a service bureau, or perhaps just stay with a batch system.

7   *System overhead associated with an on-line system*

Swapping, overlaying, time-slicing, and multiprogramming are among the internal characteristics of an on-line system that add significantly to the overhead required to process a given number of transactions or a specified application program. On many batch systems, one can count on 75% of the available computer time being spent actually processing application programs; on on-line systems, this figure often drops to as low as 33-50%. Thus, in simple economic terms, it may be prohibitively expensive to go on-line.

WHAT BASIC TYPE OF SYSTEM SHOULD BE BUILT?

As we indicated at the beginning of this chapter, there are five basic questions that the system designer should ask at the beginning of the project. After determining the goals of the system, he should attempt to choose the *type* of on-line system that best meets the requirements. As we described in Chapter B, there are five different types of on-line systems, if one looks at them from an *applications* point of view:

process control systems

on-line business-oriented systems

scientific-engineering time-sharing systems

remote batch systems

data acquisition systems

While the choice of the type of system is usually an obvious one because of the application, the system designer occasionally has some freedom. He may decide, for example, to implement his business-oriented application on a scientific-engineering system. Similarly, he might decide to provide scientific time-sharing services on a remote batch system for reasons of throughput. We shall have more to say about different application-oriented systems in Chapter I.

WHAT TYPE OF HARDWARE CONFIGURATION SHOULD BE USED?

In addition to classifying systems by their application, Chapter B presented a number of hardware configurations which can be used by the system designer. In choosing between such configurations as the simplex system, the master-slave system, and the multiprocessing system, the designer should attempt to balance several factors.

The first, and most obvious, factor is the *cost* of the configuration. Generally speaking, the cost of the hardware configuration increases as it becomes larger and more complex. However, there are cases where this might not be true, as in the example of the simplex system with a front-end communications computer; in any case, the cost of the computer generally only increases as the square root of the power of the computer. The system designer should also remember that there may be a higher software cost associated with the more complex hardware configurations, since the hardware manufacturer may not provide a standard operating system.

A second factor is the *throughput and efficiency* of the system. As we pointed out in Chapter B, the philosophy of many of the more complex configurations was to separate the various functions performed in the on-line system, and to relegate each of the functions to a separate processor. This philosophy normally leads to a more efficient system, and while it may be more expensive, the cost per unit of work may actually decrease.

The system designer should also remember that many of the applications-oriented on-line systems might be inefficient if used for the *wrong* type of application. Thus, a scientific time-sharing system might be very efficient in a university environment, where most of the jobs are very short; it might be very inefficient for some engineering applications involving heavily compute-bound jobs. As we will see in Chapter I, a scientific time-sharing system is also very inefficient for business-oriented applications where all of the users are typing in the same type of transactions and using the same application programs.

Still another factor is the *availability* of the system. Some of the more complex configurations may make it possible for the system designer to keep the system operational on a 24-hour-a-day basis. On the other hand, the simplex configuration must be shut down for maintenance and repairs, except for isolated peripheral devices like the magnetic tape drives. If the on-line system is only needed for one shift during the day, then a simplex configuration will probably be adequate.

Finally, the system designer should keep in mind the *reliability* requirements of the system when he chooses a hardware configuration. If reliability is not a critical matter, he might be able to use a simplex system, or one of the other less complex configurations. If it is necessary to be able to recover from a system failure within two or three minutes, the system designer may decide upon a *duplexed* configuration, in which the backup computer is used for batch processing or testing except during periods when the primary system is not functioning. If immediate recovery is necessary, the system designer will probably have to use a *dual* system, in which both computers are doing the same processing at the same time.

WHAT TYPE OF OPERATING SYSTEM SHOULD BE USED?

In most cases, the system designer builds his on-line system with an operating system provided by the computer manufacturer. On many machines, there is a choice of two or three different operating systems, the difference being one of sophistication and flexibility offered to the application programmer. Table D1 lists some of the common operating systems on a number of contemporary third generation computers.

TABLE D1 *Operating Systems Available on Common Third Generation Computers*

General Electric GE-635	GECOS II
	MARK III
IBM System/360	BOS
	TOS
	DOS
	OS-MFT
	OS-MVT
Burroughs B5500	BATCH MCP
	DATACOM MCP
	TIME-SHARING MCP
Xerox Data Systems	BTM
	UTS
Univac 1108	EXEC II
	EXEC 8
Control Data 6600	SCOPE III

In the event that the system designer decides to write his own operating system, he must also decide on the complexity and sophistication of the operating system. The following types of decisions must be made:

should the operating system be dedicated to the on-line application, or should it possible to perform "background" processing as well?

which programming languages should the operating system support?

what kind of multiprogramming capabilities should be made available to the application programmer?

what types of file handling capabilities should be provided?

how much overhead can be tolerated in the operating system?

how much memory should the operating system be allowed to occupy?

how difficult will it be for the application programmers to become proficient in their use of the operating system?

WHAT TYPE OF APPLICATION PROGRAMS WILL BE NEEDED?

For most on-line systems, the major part of the programming effort will be in the area of the application programs. On the one hand, the system designer may take a very straightforward approach, and write all of his programs in COBOL or FORTRAN; in some cases, though, he may have to write highly modular, reentrant application programs in assembly language. Thus, some of the questions that have to be answered at this point are as follows:

1   *What programming language is best suited to the application?*

We shall discuss various programming languages in Chapter I of this book; it will become apparent that each of the major programming languages—FORTRAN, COBOL, PL/I, and assembly language—have their advantages and disadvantages, their strengths and their weaknesses. The system designer's choice of a programming language may take into account the strengths of the language, the talents of his programmers, the political climate of his organization, the support of the language by the computer vendor, and so forth.

2   *Should the application be written in only one programming language?*

The system designer may decide that it would be best to write the entire application in one language, such as COBOL, FORTRAN, or assembly language. This might have the advantage of decreasing the problem of training new programmers; it would make the on-line system easier to transfer to a different machine; it would also lessen the testing problems. On the other hand, the system designer might decide that certain parts of the application would be best handled by COBOL, while the IO portions of the application would be most efficiently programmed in assembly language. If scientific or mathematical calculations were involved, it would be natural to write that portion of the application in FORTRAN or PL/I.

3 *Should the application programs be made reentrant?*

There are often great advantages to be gained from writing the application programs in a reentrant fashion. It allows the application program to be shared by many users; it cuts down on overlaying and swapping, since the operating system always has a good copy of the program on disk or drum; it may also prevent the program from "clobbering" itself, since the reentrant program can be executed in read-only memory.

On the other hand, the choice of reentrant programming limits the choice of a programming language: COBOL and FORTRAN generally do not support reentrant application programming. It may even limit the choice of an operating system or a machine—not all vendors support the notion of reentrancy. It might also require more training of new application programmers, since reentrant programming is a concept with which they are not likely to be familiar.

4 *Should the application program be segmented?*

If the application program is written as one large core-resident program, there will be no lost "swapping" time or overlaying time. In addition, the program will be relatively simple to write. On the other hand, the program may needlessly waste a large amount of core memory.

A segmented application program might make much more efficient use of core memory, since only that portion of the program which is actually being used will be kept in core. This approach is necessary on some systems where there is an artificial limit to the size of the application programs; it may also be necessary if the application programs are simply too large to fit in the machine at one time.

Unfortunately, there are some disadvantages to segmented programs. It makes the programming job more difficult, and requires the application programmer to be more proficient. Some of the programming languages on some computers may not provide good segmenting capabilities. Highly segmented programs will probably lead to a great deal of overhead, since the operating system will have to perform much more reading of application programs from disk or drum.

5 *Should the application program attempt concurrent processing of transactions?*

With a small, simple on-line system, it is preferable to allow the application program to process transactions in a sequential fashion. From a programming point of view, this is the simplest approach; from a testing and debugging point of view, it is also simpler.

However, on large on-line systems, where a large number of transactions are arriving in the machine each second, the application program may have to process several different transactions concurrently. In some cases, this might be handled entirely by the operating system, with the use of reentrant application programs. In most cases, though, it will be the application program that controls the concurrent processing of transactions. The application programmer will have to keep all the data associated with a transaction in a separate area, so that his program can easily switch from one transaction to another; he will have to make sure that there are no conflicts in the area of file accessing as he processes the transactions (a subject which is discussed in more detail in Chapter L); he will have to be much more thorough in his testing and debugging.

A Summary of the Basic Design Decisions

The reader may well argue that we have not presented any *answers* to the questions listed above. This is true, and deliberately so. At this point, we are merely pointing out the basic decisions that must be made at the very *beginning* of the project. As we mentioned above, many of these decisions are circular, and many of them are made in a subjective manner. It is the purpose of mathematical models, simulations, and some simple paper-and-pencil arithmetic calculations discussed in Chapter F to verify the appropriateness of the answers to questions posed in this chapter.

While the decisions may be somewhat subjective in nature, there are many *constraints* and *design trade-offs* which may strongly influence the system designer. Some of the more important constraints are listed below:

1 *Time*

Only the most modest of on-line systems can be designed and implemented in less than a year. To do so, the designer must choose an existing computer, with a working operating system. His application programs must be coded as quickly and simply as possible, probably in a higher-level language, and probably by programming talent already in his organization.

If the system designer elects to write his own operating system, or if he undertakes a *complex* real-time, on-line system on an existing system, he should probably plan on two to three years for design and implementation.

One further time constraint that the system designer must take into account is the *test time* required to thoroughly check out the system. A good "rule of thumb" on most on-line systems is that 1/3 to 1/2 of the total project time will be spent testing the system. Thus, it is unreasonable to expect that a system requiring two years to design and code can be checked out in one month.

2 *Money*

As mentioned above, economics can be an important factor in the choice of a hardware configuration. With a restricted budget, the system designer may be forced to implement the system on a much simpler and less efficient hardware configuration than he would have preferred.

The programming and administrative costs of an on-line programming project are much less well known, but the system designer should be aware of two more "rules of thumb" that have been employed on a number of systems:

the programming and administrative costs of many programming projects are approximately equal to the hardware costs.

the utility routines, maintenance routines and testing routines are likely to comprise 50-80% of the total programming effort in an on-line system.

3   *Personnel*

For a variety of reasons, on-line computer projects require a much higher level of talent than a comparable batch computer system. The application and its impact on the user of the system are more complex than in the batch or manual system; the interactions with the operating system are more complicated; the sheer size of the programming effort is usually larger than on earlier systems.

As was mentioned above, it is not sufficient to simply have good programmers on one's staff. It is just as important to have people who understand the problem to be solved, who understand the user's problems and needs. While there is still a great deal of controversy in this area, it is generally agreed that it is better to take a person who understands the application and teach him the rudiments of programming and systems analysis—rather than taking a computer specialist and trying to teach him the application.

What makes this area a constraint for the system designer is the fact that there are often not a sufficient number of sufficiently talented people. Many organizations are forced to take on junior people, or experienced people whose experience is in a different area. While these people can be introduced to the system by working on utility routines, there must be a hard core of knowledgeable and experienced analysts and programmers to hold the project together.

4   *Expandability of the system*

The system designer's job is often made more difficult if he is forced to design an open-ended system. Unfortunately, most systems are (or should be) open-ended, and the system designer might modify his basic decisions in light of the following possibilities:

will the system have to be available to more users in the future? That is, will the system have to support 50 terminals instead of its initial 25?

will more memory be required on the system as the number and size of the application programs grow?

will the files and data base grow? In a scientific-engineering system, this will occur as more users join the system, and/or as each user adds more programs and files to their libraries. In a business-oriented system, a growing data base is also a natural phenomenon.

will the applications themselves grow? That is, will new commands, new capabilities or new application languages be added to the system?

5 *Reliability*

In Chapter A, three different aspects of "reliability" were described: MTBF (Mean Time Between Failures), MTTR (Mean Time To Repair), and protection of the data base. Any of these requirements for reliability will add to the complexity of the on-line system, and certainly represent a constraint and a factor which the system designer must take into account.

If the primary emphasis is on MTBF, the designer will probably choose a hardware configuration involving a duplexed processor or file storage unit; if the emphasis is on MTTR, the system designer may or may not duplex his equipment, but will almost certainly stress the simplification of operating procedures and restart procedures; if, on the other hand, the emphasis is on protection of the data base, the system designer will probably devote most of his energies to the design of an adequate audit trail scheme.

6 *Security of files and information*

Many business-oriented systems now contain vital information on their on-line systems—sales and inventory information, personnel records, profit and loss information—all of which must be protected from prying eyes. Similarly, in a scientific-engineering time-sharing system, each user normally wishes to protect his programs and files from other users. This trend will probably increase dramatically in the next few years as more and more sensitive information finds its way into somebody's data base.

As we will discuss in detail in Chapter M, the problem of file security has two major parts: identifying the user of the system, and actually providing the file protection mechanism. Identification of users may either take the form of hardware devices attached to the terminal, or *password* mechanisms built into the software. The file lockout mechanisms are almost always built into the software, and while they are normally fairly straightforward to implement, they involve increasingly more overhead (both in terms of file space *and* processing time) as the file protection mechanisms become implemented on the record or field level.

File security represents still another type of design constraint for the system designer: most computer vendors only provide software to protect an entire file. If the system designer wishes to include protective mechanisms at the record or field level, he must provide them himself.

FUNCTIONAL SPECIFICATIONS FOR ON-LINE SYSTEMS

Thus far, we have been discussing the basic decisions which the system designer must make, and the factors which might influence those decisions.

Once these decisions have been made, a *functional specification* of the system should be drawn up before any more detailed work is done.

The functional specification is probably the single most important document in the entire on-line systems project. While the goals describe *what* the benefits and advantages of the on-line system are, the functional specifications describe *how* to provide them. They should be written in the language of the user of the system, and it is usually immensely helpful to have the user either write the specification or, at the very least, approve the specifications.

Many engineering and computer organizations have developed detailed procedures for writing, reviewing and approving functional specifications. This area is beyond the scope of this text, and the reader is referred to a number of texts at the end of this chapter for information on this aspect of planning. Our concern here is simply that the substance and content of the functional specification be complete. For on-line systems, the specification should include the following areas:

1   *Number and type of terminals on the system*

The user's major interface with an on-line system is his terminal. Thus, it is of paramount importance that they be specified and chosen with care. The system designer must specify whether a teletypewriter terminal or a CRT terminal is to be used. Equally important, the functional specification must state whether the system is to be able to accept more than one type of terminal, and if so, which types.

The functional specification should take into account the tremendous amount of development in the computer terminal field. Thus, it is probably better to specify the terminal in terms of *requirements* (i.e. "the terminal must print at the rate of 15 characters per second," etc.) rather than in terms of a specific terminal. For an excellent discussion of terminal specifications, the reader is referred to Dolotta's article [6].

In addition to the *type* of terminal, the functional specification should also describe the number of terminals to be supported by the system. This is usually done in terms of "active terminals"—that is, the functional specification should state that the system will support N active terminals. It should also indicate whether this number is fixed, or subject to expansion at some later time.

2   *Availability of the system*

The functional specification should indicate whether the system is to be available one, two or three shifts a day. If the system is to be available for more than eight hours a day, there should be a statement about the *continuity* of service—some systems operate from 8 AM to 6 PM, then again from 7 PM to 12 midnight.

There should also be a specification of the time to be allocated to such auxiliary functions as preventive maintenance, software maintenance (i.e. assembling or compiling a new version of the system), accounting, file maintenance, and system debugging.

3   *Response time*

It is important to specify the response time that users will see at their terminal, for a slow or uneven response will make the system a burden for them to use. It is usually best to state the response time as a *range* rather than as a simple average, for the system designer and the user will want a protection against extremely poor response during busy periods of the day. For example, the functional specification should state "90% of the responses will be less than N seconds" rather than "the average response time will be N seconds."

In some cases, it may be meaningful to specify different response times for different functions. In a scientific time-sharing system, for example, the system specification should call for extremely fast response to file maintenance and program editing commands; a slower response will be tolerated for such things as compilation or execution of a program.

Finally, it might be desirable to specify different response time requirements for different terminals or different users. In some cases, it may even be desirable to allow the user to control the priority of his request.

4   *Computational facilities*

In a business-oriented on-line system, the functional specification should indicate what type of commands the users will be able to type from their terminal. While the exact description of this command language may not be available at this time, it is important to specify the types of computational facilities the system will have.

In a scientific time-sharing system, the functional specification should not only state the languages available (i.e. BASIC, FORTRAN, etc.), but should indicate the maximum size of program allowed, and any restrictions in the language itself. On some time-sharing systems, for example, the user is limited to approximately 500 program statements; on other systems, he is allowed to write as large a program as he wants, so long as the compiled object code does not occupy more than 16,384 words. There may also be restrictions on the number of variables, the size of arrays, and so forth.

5   *File storage capabilities*

On many business-oriented on-line systems, the data base is "invisible" to the user—he cannot write programs to alter or update the data base. He must thus use whatever commands have been given to him by the system designer, and his capability of accessing and updating the data base must be described in the functional specification. This is especially important in any kind of "information" system, where the sole point of the system is to provide meaningful information to its users.

On a scientific time-sharing system, it is equally important to describe the type of file manipulation capabilities available to the user. There are three different areas that must be described by the functional specification:

How many files may each user have? What type may they be (ASCII, binary, etc)? How large may they be? How may they be shared among other users?

What capabilities will the user have to modify the files from his terminal? Will he be able to delete files, append to files, edit his source programs, and so forth?

What types of file capabilities will the user program have? How many files may a user program have "open" at any one time? What types of access methods are permitted—serial, random, "update," or "append" mode? What type of blocking is permitted?

On either type of on-line system, it is extremely important for the functional specification to indicate the size of the data base. This may be done conveniently in terms of number of records, or in terms of characters or bytes of storage. Obviously, it is also important to specify whether the data base is expected to grow during the lifetime of the system.

6   Reliability

Many of the common business and scientific systems fail to state an acceptable level of reliability, an omission which government and military systems would find totally intolerable. As an on-line system grows larger and takes on more and more functions in the business or university, the consequences of its failure become more and more serious. The functional specifications should indicate the number of failures that can be tolerated per week, per day or per month, and should also indicate a MTTR for the failures.

It is often meaningful to specify reliability standards for different types of failures. For example, we might define a *simple loss of service* as a failure which can be corrected within two minutes with no significant loss of data or files. A *serious failure* might be defined as one in which there is a significant loss of data and/or a substantially longer time to recover the system. Thus, the functional specification for a scientific time-sharing system might insist on no more than one simple loss of service per day (about average for most current systems) and no more than one serious failure per month; a business-oriented system might be able to tolerate two or three simple failures per day (especially if its users have no alternative systems to use!), but only one serious failure a year.

The reliability specifications should include a number of other aspects of a system failure. For instance, the specifications should indicate the action to be taken if an isolated part of the system breaks down (i.e. one of the disk packs on the system, or one of the printers, etc.). There should also be a description of the manner in which users are informed of failures in the system, and a specification of the role of the computer operator in any recovery procedure.

For on-line business systems, it is extremely important that the user's role in error recovery be specified. There are two classic problems that occur in business systems, both of which are discussed in Chapter N, and both of which should be discussed in the functional specification:

The user may type a transaction into the system, and the system may process it just before failing. If the user receives no acknowledgment at his terminal, he will assume that the transaction was not received by the system. Thus, when the system is restored, he may duplicate his last transaction.

The user may type a transaction, but the system may fail before or during the processing of that transaction. Since he has received no information to the contrary, the user will assume that the transaction *was* processed, and will fail to type it in again.

A Top-Level Systems Design Methodology

Thus far, we have discussed the basic design decisions that must be made in an on-line computer system project and the functional specifications that describe the capabilities of the system. There are a number of additional "design activities" that must be carried out before the system can be implemented. The most important activities are the establishment of schedules and milestones; the establishment of a documentation plan; and the design of a test and debugging package for use in checking out the system. It is suggested that the following sequence of activities be performed, in the order indicated:

1 *Establish the goals of the system*

   It is important to emphasize the difference between goals and functional specifications. The goals of the system indicate *what* the system is to do and *why* it is desirable to build the system; the functional specifications, on the other hand, tell *how* the goals are to be implemented.

2 *Establish functional specifications of the system*

   The functional specifications should be in writing, in order to avoid any later confusion or misinterpretation. In covering the areas described above, they should be as specific as possible.

3 *Choose the hardware configuration*

   By this time, the goals and the functional specifications should have determined such things as:

      the largeness or smallness of the computer

      the number of terminals and the complexity of the communications system

      the type of random access storage

      duplexing of hardware, if any

   However, the functional specifications have *not* determined

      the particular computer manufacturer

the decision to use multiprogramming

the decision to use multiprocessing

4   *Determine the major components of the system*

At this point, it should be possible to figure out what the "big pieces" of the system are. In an on-line business system, one should be able to draw a rough one-page flowchart showing the relationship between such application programs as:

a teleprocessing "handler" program

a preprocessing program

an accounts receivable module

an inventory control module

a data management module

Similarly, in a scientific time-sharing system, one should be able to identify such major components as:

the compilers

the loader

the editing and file maintenance programs

If the operating system is being developed as part of the project, the following major components should have been decided upon:

the priority control mechanism

the scheduler

the IO routines

the file handling routines

5   *Establish documentation and control conventions*

It is reasonable to determine documentation assignments after the basic structure of the system has been decided upon, for most of the documentation will be the responsibility of individual groups. The system designer should describe, in writing, the level and format of documentation in the following areas:

functional specifications of individual programs

documentation of finished programs

data specifications

operating instructions

program maintenance documentation (i.e. assembly, loading, and editing instructions).

6 *Start the design of the test programs*

It is important that the test effort be begun as early in the project as possible, for the testing effort will require as much as half of the total project time and 80% of the total code. At this point, the system designer should know what basic type of system he is dealing with, and should be able to get a fairly good idea of the types of test programs that will be required. If he is building a system with a data base, he will certainly need programs to generate test data bases; if he is building a transaction-oriented business system, he will need programs to generate test transactions.

As functional specifications for more and more detailed parts of the system are developed, the test programmers will have the information they require to develop their programs. In the meantime, the system designer should be available to help guide and instruct the test programmers.

7 *Establish a set of milestones and schedules*

It is important that milestones and schedules be established early, and it is even more important that the milestones be as specific and tangible as possible. A common dodge of many programmers is to report to their supervisor that their program is "90% complete" when there is no basis at all for their statement.

8 *Proceed with more detailed design*

At this point, the system designer can begin deciding *which* machine to use, which scheduling algorithm to use, and so forth. The programmers and analysts on the project should now be in a position to start drawing up more detailed functional specifications, flowcharts, and documentation.

Application programmers often cry out in anguish that they cannot begin to design their data base until they know what machine and what file accessing techniques they will be given; similarly, they cannot begin to design their programs until they know the environment that will be provided to them on the machine they will be using. While this is true, it is also true that the application programmers should not be designing on such a detailed level until the entire team has reached this point in the design effort.

REFERENCES

1 James Martin, *Design of Real-Time Computer Systems* (Englewood Cliffs, N.J.: Prentice-Hall, Inc., 1967)

2 James Martin, *Programming Real-Time Computer Systems* (Englewood Cliffs, N.J.: Prentice-Hall, Inc., 1965)

3 Robert Head, *Real-Time Business Systems* (New York, N.Y.: Holt, Rinehart and Winston, Inc., 1964)

4 Edward Yourdon, editor, *Real-Time Systems Design* (Cambridge, Mass.: Information and Systems Press, 1967)

5 W.H. Desmonde, *Real-Time Data Processing Systems: Introductory Concepts* (Englewood Cliffs, N.J.: Prentice-Hall, Inc., 1964)

6 T.A. Dolotta, *Functional Specifications for Typewriter-like Time-Sharing Terminals*, ACM Computing Surveys, Volume 2, Number 1 (March 1970)

7 Michael Rothstein, *Guide to the Design of Real-Time Systems* (New York, N.Y.: John Wiley and Sons, Inc., 1970)

8 B. Hartman et al., *Management Information Systems Handbook* (New York, N.Y.: McGraw-Hill Book Company, 1968)

Chapter E

A CASE STUDY: THE MEDINET SYSTEM

INTRODUCTION

In Chapter D, we suggested some guidelines for the design of an on-line computer system. Our discussion was rather brief, for, as we have pointed out, our emphasis in this book is on the *technical* aspects of on-line systems. However, we often find that the technical people in an on-line systems project—i.e. the programmers, analysts, and technical project leaders—fail to appreciate the critical need for careful planning and good management; as a result, they often *contribute* to the failure of a project, as much or more so than the top management who initiates the project.

To illustrate that point, this chapter is devoted to a case study of an on-line project that failed: General Electric's MEDINET hospital information system. As we will see, the problems were not caused by any fundamental weakness in General Electric's computer expertise, though GE has encountered similar problems on a number of other on-line projects; nor were the problems the result of the particular computer used, though it did have its weaknesses. *The problem, fundamentally, was that the entire technical staff overestimated its abilities, and thus overcommitted itself.* Having done so, it failed to use any reasonable management or control techniques which would have indicated the immensity of the problems at an early date.

This is sometimes difficult for technically-oriented computer people to appreciate. This project has been used as a case study in over fifty seminars on on-line systems design, and the reaction of the average programmer or analyst has often been, "Well, it's obvious that this case study is obsolete—just look at the ancient machine that was used! Now, if an IBM System/360 or a CDC 6600 had been used, none of these problems would have occurred. Besides, nobody had any experience with on-line systems in 1966, so these problems are only natural—now we all know enough not to make these mistakes." This kind of attitude will lead to precisely the same kind of problems that were encountered at MEDINET.

The question of "obsolescence" is an especially moot one. The computer used in the MEDINET system, a modified GE-435, was originally designed only one or two years before the IBM System/360, which is often mentioned as a "better" machine; the hardware modifications that were made to the GE-435 resulted in a computer that was more advanced than a number of computers in the field today. Also, the argument that "we all know much more about on-line systems than we did in 1966" is largely an illusion: we may know more about some of the technical details, but we seem to have learned very little about planning and control. All this means is that in the 1970's, we can look forward to making the same mistakes with newer computers.

We will begin our discussion of the MEDINET system with a brief sketch of the history and background of the project. This will be followed by a technical discussion, in which we will investigate some of the hardware and software used in the system. We will conclude by enumerating the major problems and mistakes made in the project; to end the chapter on a positive note, we will make some suggestions that will hopefully help the reader avoid similar catastrophes.

It should be pointed out that this entire discussion is based on the personal experiences of the author; as a result, there will undoubtedly be some errors and omissions caused by the author's ignorance, prejudices, or faulty memory. When writing about such an ambitious undertaking, one always has the fear of stirring up old debates, rivalries, and passions (passion was one thing that was not lacking on this project—one would have thought it was being implemented in Peyton Place instead of Watertown, Massachusetts!); however, it is hoped that after five or six years, most of the heated feelings will have died away so that we can discuss the project in a rational way. Again, the views expressed in this chapter are those of the author alone, and should not be construed as any kind of official statement on the merits of General Electric computers or programming systems.

THE HISTORY AND BACKGROUND
OF THE MEDINET PROJECT

The MEDINET project began as a result of experimental work performed by the firm of Bolt, Beranek and Newman (BBN), a long-established consulting company located in Cambridge, Massachusetts. With the cooperation and assistance of the Massachusetts General Hospital and a grant from the National Institute of Health, BBN began investigating the use of a "conversational" time-sharing system in hospitals in late 1962. Their aim was *not* to invade the area of billing, accounting, inventory, or payrolls; nor did BBN intend to enter the politically sensitive (from the hospital's point of view) area of on-line patient monitoring. Their aim was instead to help alleviate the *information flow* problems in the hospital by placing terminals at strategic locations.

One of the primary applications was *hospital admissions* and *bed census reports*. It was hoped that one or more terminals could be placed at the admissions desk of the hospital, so that the admitting nurse could carry on a dialogue with the computer instead of filling out a long form manually. Another application was in the area of *drug orders;* a terminal could be used to ensure that a doctor did not prescribe a harmful medicine, or a lethal dosage of the proper medicine—and it could also check to see that a nurse administered the medicine on schedule. A third project was in the area of *laboratory reports;* it was felt that appropriately placed terminals could reduce the paperwork and delays encountered in the gathering and analysis of such things as blood samples from hospital patients.

The experimental project was implemented on a Digital Equipment Corporation PDP-1 computer, using a time-sharing system and a programming language (called TELCOMP) developed earlier by BBN. Several terminals were installed in one wing of the Massachussetts General Hospital, and development work proceeded over a period of two or three years.

The project was generally successful, and it was apparent that there were commercial possibilities with such a system. In late 1965, negotiations with the General Electric Company resulted in the formation of a relatively autonomous new department—the MEDINET department—and an agreement whereby several key members of the BBN project were given extended leaves of absence to join MEDINET. MEDINET's charter was fairly simple: convert the BBN programs to a General Electric computer, and market it nationally on a commercial basis.

In spite of these limited objectives, the next two years saw the following developments:

1 Extensive hardware modifications, including paging and extended memory, to an existing GE computer.

2 Development of two new operating systems.

3 Development of a new programming language.

4 Development of a completely new set of utility routines, including a macro assembler, loader, debugging routines, etc.

5 Development of a new terminal, new communications controller, and a new disk file controller.

This proved to be too much to cope with—MEDINET had clearly become a massive research and development effort. Two years after the project began, GE wisely decided to abandon this effort and take an entirely new approach. The details of the original system and the reasons for its demise are the subjects of this study.

The current General Electric MEDINET system represents a radically different approach: instead of a real-time "conversational" system, the new system uses on-line data collection to gather transactions from the hospitals. The transactions are batched on tape, and processed in four daily cycles, whereupon the results are batched for eventual transmission to the hospitals. In addition to being much more reliable than the original approach, it has the enviable advantage of *being operational.*

A BRIEF DESCRIPTION OF EVENTS
IN THE MEDINET PROJECT

As we pointed out above, there were a large number of development efforts within the MEDINET project. One of the major problems within the organization was caused by the fact that all of these projects were taking place simultaneously; as a result, there was a tremendous amount of effort expended on projects that were not really critical to MEDINET'S immediate objective—*to convert some working application programs from a PDP-1 computer to a GE computer, and sell them to hospitals.*

In the interest of space, we will not discuss those development efforts which were not critical to the overall project. Thus, the development of a new teletypewriter terminal, which included provisions for a badge reader, carousel projector and other special devices, will not be discussed; the development of a Honeywell-516 communications controller to replace General Electric's Datanet-30 will be omitted; and the development of a Honeywell-516 "intelligent" disk controller will not be mentioned. In the area of software, we will not discuss the development of a new assembler, loader, DDT debugging program (a simple version of which is described in Chapter W), or other utility programs.

The critical efforts within the MEDINET project consisted of hardware development, an operating system, a programming language, and the application programs. Had these four efforts been successful, the other development efforts would have been extremely important; without these four parts of the system, a new terminal, disk controller, communications controller, and assembler were useless.

Figure E1 shows a rather abbreviated time chart of the four major development efforts. Each of them is described in more detail below.

The Hardware Development Effort

Interestingly enough, very few of the early technical members of the MEDINET staff had had previous experience with GE equipment; many had

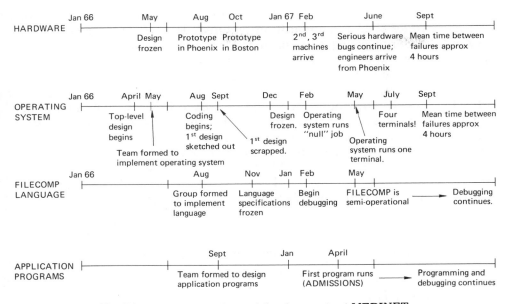

Fig. E1   A brief time chart of developments at MEDINET

come from BBN, from MIT, or from the Digital Equipment Corporation. Thus, there was little initial enthusiasm for the idea of using a General Electric computer, and there were several unsuccessful grass-roots attempts to convince the management to use a Digital Equipment Corporation PDP-10. As one might expect, this sort of thing *does* happen occasionally (e.g. General Electric and Control Data have been known to use IBM computers at various times in the past; Digital Equipment Corporation once used Burroughs computers for their payroll; IBM has, at least once in its magnificent corporate history, considered using DEC equipment for production control), but it does not enhance the corporate image; thus, the MEDINET team was persuaded to use General Electric equipment very early in the game.

However, there were some serious questions about *which* GE computer to use. The GE-265 system did have a working time-sharing system, but it seemed far too slow and far too small to handle any large number of terminals and/or application programs. Similarly, the GE-435 seemed rather small (24-bit word), rather slow (memory speeds ranged from three to six microseconds, depending on the particular configuration), and basically unsuited to real-time applications; at the time the project was begun, there were no operating systems capable of supporting on-line applications. The GE-635, on the other hand, *was* large, *was* fast, and *did* have several time-sharing operating systems in various stages of development and field testing. Thus, as far as most of the programmers and analysts were concerned, if it was necessary to use GE equipment, the GE-635 was the obvious choice.

Unfortunately, economic considerations mitigated against the GE-635: it seemed larger than the application required. The GE-635 is a very large, very powerful processing system, and it did not appear that the hospital applications would require very much computational power. In addition, the GE-635 was much more expensive than the smaller GE-435.

As a result, a basic decision was made in the very early stages of the project that a GE-435 computer would be used as the main computer in the system. However, since everyone realized that the processor lacked hardware features that would make it suitable for on-line applications, an effort was begun to add several new features onto the machine; the modified machine was then referred to as a GE-485. We will discuss the hardware in more detail when we focus on the technical aspects of the system; for now, it is sufficient to indicate that these hardware changes included the following:

virtual memory, or "paging"

memory relocation and protection (built into the paging registers)

extended memory (131,072 words)

floating point hardware

master mode/slave mode

real-time clock

Many of these features are now standard on some of the GE-400 series computers, but they were all quite new at the time.

Work began on the specifications for these hardware changes at the end of 1965, when the project was just beginning. By mid-May of 1966, all of the hardware changes had been documented, and an engineering group in Phoenix, Arizona began to build a prototype machine. The prototype was available for checkout by early August, and a group of MEDINET systems programmers grabbed their tennis rackets, swimming trunks, and coding pads and flew to Phoenix to begin working on it.

It took slightly over a month to satisfy the programmers that the machine was in some semblance of working order; thus, in early September of 1966, the prototype was loaded onto a truck and shipped back to Boston, where the rest of the programmers anxiously awaited its arrival. Unfortunately, the truck driver got lost on the way, and it was almost the beginning of October before the machine was finally unloaded and installed.

The remainder of 1966 was spent working on the prototype machine; a number of hardware bugs were found, but it was still capable of being used for development work. Preliminary work was done on the operating system, the programming language, various utility routines, and some administrative software (i.e. the payroll programs). In February and March of 1967, two more machines arrived from Phoenix; these were "production" machines, in contrast to the first "prototype" machine. The machines were installed in a new computer room, from which it was hoped that several hospitals in the Boston area could be serviced.

Unfortunately, the machines never worked very well. By April of 1967, it had become apparent that the problems were more serious than the usual "post-installation blues" that accompany every machine; it appeared that there might be several rather serious problems resulting from all the modifications that had been made to the original GE-435.

Hardware problems can, of course, plague any computer project; they tend to be much more serious when one works with an experimental machine, or with a "new" machine, i.e. the first machine of any vendor's new product line. Table E1 lists some of the hardware problems that were encountered during a three-month period in the spring of 1967; the on-line systems designer should expect that most of these will happen to him unless he is using a standard "off-the-shelf" computer—in which case only 75% of the hardware problems will occur!

TABLE E1 *A Sample of Some of the Hardware Problems on the MEDINET Project*

04/14/67	Memory parity errors occurred whenever a ROTATE instruction was executed.
04/15/67	Memory parity errors occurred in the upper 32K bank of core.
04/23/67	Card Punch was inoperable.
04/25/67	An "instruction alert" (i.e. an illegal instruction interrupt to the operating system) occurred when the system was first started up in the morning, but not on subsequent startups.
04/26/67	Two high-speed printers inoperable; memory parity errors; hardware that facilitated addressing of "extended" memory wasn't working.
04/27/67	Somebody removed the connections to the modems; air conditioning down all day.
04/28/67	Tape drives down; card reader down; Datanet-30 circuitbreakers bad; telephone lines bad.
04/30/67	Card reader down. Everything else considered, this was a very good day!
05/09/67	Two out of three disks down; no preventative maintenance scheduled for the disks (a slight lack of communication with the field engineers).
05/15/67	Storing in memory location 126000 causes the same data to be stored in memory locations 122000, 132000, and 136000.
05/17/67	A disk causes the system to "hang" (i.e. to be permanently locked up) while waiting for a "seek" operation to finish.
05/21/67	Spurious interrupts from the Datanet-30 cannot be cleared.
05/24/67	Disks left in incorrect operating condition by field engineers.
05/29/67	Indefinite transfers from disk—i.e. the disk began transferring data and never gave an interrupt to signal that it was finished. As a result, the machine somehow got into a state where both the HALT light and the RUN light on the console were off. Also, "transfer timing" errors began to occur on the drum; there were so many accesses to memory by the CPU and other IO devices that data could not be accepted fast enough to keep up with the drum.
06/05/67	One magnetic tape handler begins stretching and creasing tapes.

TABLE E1—*cont.*

06/07/67   Consistent memory parity errors; discovered the three most common "store" instructions do not clear bad parity in memory.

06/14/67   First discovered an interrupt priority problem with the real-time clock.

06/16/67   "Race" problems between drum and disk first noticed. That is, if both the drum and the disk were attempting to transfer data at the same time, it was possible that one of them would not get enough memory accesses.

06/19/67   "Phantom" terminals started appearing on the system—i.e. terminals that did not exist.

06/26/67   "Instruction alert" first noticed on 04/25 discovered to be a hardware bug; console typewriter went wild, and began spewing out endless streams of garbage; drum parity errors occurred repeatedly.

06/29/67   Machine halted when the console was jostled. After a long night of frustrating debugging, one of the programmers threw a chair against the console of the machine, and was surprised to see it halt. He stomped away, muttering that it was the only intelligent thing the machine had done all night.

07/12/67   Discovered that disk IO and drum IO were getting mixed together; that is, disk data mysteriously appeared in the drum buffer, and drum data mysteriously appeared in disk buffer.

By June of 1967, the weather in Boston had improved to the point where the Phoenix hardware engineers could be convinced to pack their golf clubs and come to Boston to fix the hardware. After a couple of weeks, some of the more urgent hardware problems had been fixed, and the hardware engineers returned to the sunny climate of Phoenix.

Despite these efforts, and those of the local MEDINET engineers and field service personnel, the equipment continued to operate unreliably. Throughout the summer and fall of 1967, hardware problems caused an average of two or three failures per day. In most cases, the system could be restarted rather quickly, but as can be seen in Table E1, some of the hardware problems were rather serious.

The effect of such hardware problems on an on-line computer project are almost incalculable. When the system designers ought to be spending their time and energy on other parts of the system, they instead spend long hours wrestling with the hardware; when the operating system stops working, they have no idea of whether to look for hardware bugs or software bugs. Clearly, even if all of the software had already been developed, one could not hope to operate an on-line system with hundreds of terminals—especially in a hospital environment, where reliability would be of utmost importance—if the machine had an average of two or three failures per day.

The Operating System Effort

From the very beginning of the MEDINET project, it was accepted by everyone that an operating system would have to be developed. For one thing, the original GE-435 did not have an operating system capable of supporting on-line applications (a situation which has changed in the last few years); for another thing, the *modified* GE-435 which was used at MEDINET *required* a new operating system—the standard GE operating system could not be expected to take advantage of all the new hardware features.

Thus, a development effort was begun in early 1966; Table E2 gives a slightly more detailed indication of the progress than does the overall time chart in Figure E1. The most important feature of the operating system was that it was designed as a general purpose time-sharing system, in the sense that we defined time-sharing systems in Chapter B. That is, each terminal on the system was considered a separate "job," requiring its own storage area, accounting overhead, etc.

TABLE E2   *The Progress of the Operating System Development Effort*

April, 1966	Top-level design of operating system begins.
May, 1966	Project team formed for development of operating system; design of virtual memory portion of operating system begins.
June, 1966	Personnel for operating system project complete; design begins on preliminary disk routines; design begins on interface with the Datanet-30 communications controller.
July, 1966	Specifications written for priority control program (i.e. the interrupt handler); specifications written for first version of the "page manager" (i.e. that portion of the operating system which allocated and kept track of the pages in virtual memory).
August 1, 1966	Operating system group leaves for Phoenix to check out prototype machine; detailed design of scheduling algorithm begins: coding and debugging of preliminary disk routines.
August 15, 1966	A primitive one-terminal operating system was to have been working now, according to original plans; obviously, it wasn't.
September, 1966	Operating system group returns from Phoenix; preliminary design of disk routines and "page manager" scrapped; coding of routines for interface with Datanet-30 continues; design of magnetic tape IO routines begins.
October, 1966	Design begins on code to handle calls from the application programs to the operating system; completed first version of code for interface with Datanet-30; began redesign of page manager, disk routines, and drum routines.
November, 1966	Design of second operating system begins (to be used only with FILECOMP); coding of new page manager continues; debugging of priority control program continues.
December 25, 1966	Interface between operating system and applications programs frozen. First document appears specifying the interface.
January 30, 1967	All parts of the operating system loaded and "link edited" together; the "idle job" runs successfully; second operating system begins to show signs of life.
May 3, 1967	Started debugging operating system with first real application program from a terminal.
May 4, 1967	User-mode DDT (see Chapter W for a description of this type of debugging program) appears to be working—but full of bugs.
May 10, 1967	User-mode DDT magnetic tape IO begins to work; test application program executes successfully to completion once.

TABLE E2—*cont.*

May 12, 1967	Began attempting to "swap" application programs to the drum when memory filled up.
May 15, 1967	First serious attempt to run more than one *real* application program with the operating system.
May 17, 1967	First serious attempt to test the disk file maintenance routines.
May 23, 1967	Migration from drum to disk showed signs of life; that is, when the drum filled up with virtual memory pages, some of the least active ones would be moved to the disk.
May 25, 1967	First successful attempt to read a disk directory when a program referenced a page that was residing on the disk.
May 26, 1967	First attempt to recover from user-mode errors (illegal instructions); first serious attempt to run application programs from two terminals, switching between programs only on IO "wait" conditions; first attempt to share a reentrant version of DDT; first attempt to execute an application program in read-only mode (all of these experiments were partially successful).
May 29, 1967	Tried running with three terminals, not too successfully.
May 30, 1967	Ran two terminals with "time-slicing."
May 31, 1967	Ran SWAPTEST to completion once—this was an application program that generated a large number of virtual pages and thus caused the operating system to perform a large amount of swapping. The virtual pages were filled with bit patterns, which the test program then read and checked to see that they had not been destroyed by the operating system.
June 2, 1967	Drum storage allocation routines appear to work for the first time.
June 4, 1967	First reasonably "solid" version of DDT.
June 5, 1967	Interrupt handler in program to interface with Datanet-30 works.
June 9, 1967	First difficult "timing" bug in operating system fixed—involved the real-time clock, the drum routines, and the page manager.
June 15, 1967	Simultaneous magnetic tape IO for two application programs appears to work.
June 16, 1967	SWAPTEST started running more than once; it would run to completion about five times before the operating system would self-destruct.
June 20, 1967	Decided to consolidate all operating system error messages in one subroutine.
June 21, 1967	First started making a serious test of swapping to the disk when the drum filled up; first successful attempt of "overlapped," or "double-buffered" IO on the drum (see Chapter S for a more complete description of this type of IO).
June 30, 1967	Agreed on the need to "time-stamp" every message typed on the operator's console typewriter.
July 1, 1967	First noticed the existence of a second major timing problem; the bug was not found and fixed until August!
July 5, 1967	First noticed the existence of a third major timing problem; this bug was not found and fixed until November!
July 7, 1967	Successfully ran two copies of the SWAPTEST program from two terminals.
July 9, 1967	Discovered the need for keeping a sorted list of waiting tasks in the priority control program (see Chapter Q for a more complete description); ran DSKTEST to completion for the first time—this

TABLE E2—*cont.*

	was a test application program that generated so many virtual pages that it overflowed the drum and forced swapping to the disk.
July 11, 1967	First ambitious attempt to run DSKTEST from five terminals—not successful.
July 13, 1967	First of several subtle bugs in the memory allocation routines discovered; several of these bugs are discussed in the section of "bit-map" techniques in Chapter T.
July 16, 1967	Successfully ran DSKTEST five times before the sytem crashed.
July 17, 1967	Ran DSKTEST successfully from two terminals.
July 18, 1967	Routine to type the time of day on console typewriter implemented; first noticed the existence of "thrashing"—the thrashing was so bad that none of the users would get any response from their terminals.
July 20, 1967	Assembled the CALL program and the Segment Librarian for the first time. These were operating system utility routines written as application programs.
July 22, 1967	First attempt to run a FILECOMP program under the operating system with four terminals.
July 23, 1967	Operating system ran unattended for 17 hours; all members of the operating system team had collapsed from exhaustion and were sleeping on the machine room floor.
July 25, 1967	Ran the basic instruction test diagnostic programs under the operating system.
July 27, 1967	System ran for 3.5 hours with three terminals.
July 28, 1967	System ran for 5.5 hours with three terminals.
August 9, 1967	Finally discovered problem with priority control program "underflow" caused by a task going *below* its original level (see Chapter Q for an explanation of this phenomenon).
August 12, 1967	Basic subroutines in Segment Librarian first worked; queueing of disk IO first showed definite signs of life.
August 15, 1967	Adopted a standard method of identifying new versions of the operating system—began with version E01.00.
August 20, 1967	A mysterious halt at location 3 (which had been occurring since debugging first began—see entry for July 1, 1967) was found to be a subtle hardware timing bug.
August 24, 1967	First design of error recovery and "graceful shutdown"; abandoned verison E01.84 of operating system, and reassembled everything to form E02.00.
August 26, 1967	CALL program and Segment Librarian showed signs of working together.
August 27, 1967	Managed to shut down the operating system, and save all user's file directories on the disk for the first time.
August 29, 1967	Drum and disk queueing and disk storage allocation appear to work.
September 6, 1967	Reassembled operating system again—version E03.00; found another major bug in the code handling the interface between the application programs and the operating system.
September 8, 1967	Managed to start up entire system with CALL, Segment Librarian, and DDT resident on the disk.
September 12, 1967	Moved back to the prototype machine.
September 27, 1967	LOGIN program worked for the first time.

October 2, 1967	Reassembled entire operating system—version E04.00.
October 21, 1967	More sophisticated form of LOGIN worked for the first time.
October 25, 1967	Reassembled entire operating system—version E05.00.
October 28, 1967	Segment Librarian seems thoroughly debugged; inserted "debug" mode and "production" mode in the operating system.
November 7, 1967	Reassembled operating system—version E06.00.
November 13, 1967	Reassembled operating system—version E07.00.

There was some hope that the negative effects of this approach would be offset by the paging hardware on the machine. The "page box," as it was called, allowed the operating system to break the application programs into 512-word pages, which could be "swapped" between disk, drum, and core memory without the explicit knowledge of the application programs. This same hardware mechanism allowed *sharing* of common application programs; thus, all nurses and doctors using a common application would require only one copy of the program in memory.

As Table E2 shows, progress on the operating system was rather slow and ill-defined in the early stages; the activity was quite frantic during the spring, summer, and fall of 1967, and it finally died away in late November, as it became apparent that the entire project was about to be reorganized. The original plan was to implement a very primitive version of the operating system by mid-August of 1966; this primitive version would service only one terminal, and would not involve much at all in the way of scheduling, swapping, or job accounting—however, it *would* allow an application programmer to run his program. By October of 1966, it was hoped that a primitive multi-terminal operating system would be running; again, no fancy scheduling, swapping, or accounting was required, as long as it would enable half a dozen application programmers to use the system for their development work. Clearly, these schedules were not met—the operating system was barely able to service half a dozen terminals for three hours before crashing, in the fall of 1967!

The *general-purpose* nature of the operating system had some important consequences on the entire project. It was intended that the application programmers would use the same system for their development work, while nurses and doctors used the system for the actual hospital applications. Thus, many of the application programmers had terminals in their offices, and this was intended to speed up the process of writing the application programs.

All of this depended, of course, on having a working operating system. Thus, the original plan of having a primitive one-terminal system by mid-August, and a primitive multi-terminal by mid-October, was quite critical. Without a working operating system, there was no way for the application programmers to compile, execute, and debug their programs—there was no provision for running test shots of the application programs on an overnight basis, for even that would have required some form of operating system. Because the application programs were written in a non-standard language, namely FILECOMP, there was no chance of running them under the standard batch General Electric operating system, either.

As a result, the application programmers grew increasingly apprehensive during the late fall of 1966, as it became clear that the operating system effort was going to be much larger and more complicated than had originally been anticipated. In November of 1966, it was decided that a second, *special-purpose*, operating system should be designed; this operating system would run *only* FILECOMP programs, whereas the general-purpose operating system was intended to run programs in any language. A team of two talented programmers began coding almost immediately, and by the spring of 1967, their operating system worked sufficiently well that the application programmers were able to use it to execute their FILECOMP programs.

Thus, during most of 1967, two operating system projects were underway; the special-purpose operating system was used almost exclusively by the application programmers, and was enhanced to include swapping, a sophisticated time-slicing algorithm, etc. Meanwhile, debugging continued on the large, general-purpose operating system, hampered by machine problems, inexperience with paging machines, lack of personnel, and an obvious attempt to get too much working too quickly. As early as November of 1966, it had become apparent that the general-purpose operating system was sufficiently complicated that nobody would be able to predict a date for its completion; thus, while schedules and milestones continued to be made, everyone paid less and less attention to them.

The FILECOMP Development Effort

As we mentioned earlier, the original hospital project had been implemented on a Digital Equipment Corporation PDP-1 computer, using a language known as TELCOMP. TELCOMP had been developed by BBN, and bore some resemblance to BASIC and a variety of other relatively simple programming languages; it was a time-sharing language, in the sense that it required the programmer to type his program a line at a time, and then execute it from his terminal.

When the MEDINET project began, it was assumed that TELCOMP would again be used as the programming language with which the application programs would be developed. However, the TELCOMP language did not (and does not currently) exist on the GE-435 computer, so it was apparent that a team would have to be formed to implement the language. As Figure E1 shows, the team was not even formed until mid-summer of 1966—after the hardware design effort had been completed and the operating system effort was underway.

Once the language team began working, it became evident that there were a number of additional features that should be added to the TELCOMP language; this resulted in a long series of design sessions, the end product of which was a *new* language called FILECOMP. FILECOMP was basically a

TELCOMP-like language, with additional features to facilitate scanning and searching of character strings (a desirable feature, since the application programs were dealing with variable-length input from terminals) and more powerful data base features.

The specifications of the language were not finalized until October of 1966; the two-man team immediately began designing and implementing. The first crude version of the language was available in the early spring of 1967; by May of 1967, it was possible to write a FILECOMP program with some hope that it would actually work. The remainder of the summer of 1967 was spent eliminating bugs, adding new features, and generally improving the language.

An interesting feature of FILECOMP was that it was implemented as an *interpreter* instead of a *compiler*. That is, *each* time a FILE COMP program was executed, *source* statements were analyzed and executed by the FILE COMP interpreter; a compiler approach, of course, would have generated executable machine language code. The interpretive approach was chosen because it required less memory for the application program. A source program (after comments, multiple blanks, and other extraneous characters have been removed) is usually much more compact than a compiled program. Unfortunately, the interpretive approach is usually slower than the compiler approach by a factor of 10 to 100, depending on the language; it was hoped that the savings in memory would outweigh the increase in CPU time.

Development of the Application Programs

We finally come to the development effort that was ultimately the key to the entire MEDINET system: the application programs. As we mentioned at the beginning of the chapter, the original purpose of the project was to convert existing programs from BBN's PDP-1 system to a General Electric computer. Since this conversion effort initially seemed so simple, *General Electric was told that within a year and a half, the application programs would be implemented on a GE computer, would be running in a hospital, and would be generating revenue.* Unfortunately, the full impact of this promise was never felt by the systems programmers, as they continued to devote their efforts to new hardware, new operating systems, and new programming languages; by the end of the project, the systems people had finally begun to realize that financial people are like elephants: they never forget promises.

With this background information, it is interesting to note the progress of the application programs, as shown on Figure E1. *The applications group was not even formally organized until October of 1966*, though some application programmers had been hired during the summer. Since the last application programs at BBN had been developed during 1965, almost a year of inactivity had transpired; during that time, many of the original programmers found other jobs, got married, got drafted, or simply disappeared. As a result, most of the application programmers that began work in October of 1966 were completely unfamiliar with the hospital project, and with hospital applications in general.

The result was, of course, predictable: the original BBN application programs were redesigned, and the resulting programs bore little resemblance to the original version. Working with a new machine, a new language, and a new type of data base, the programmers had the opportunity to "improve" upon the original design.

As Figure E1 illustrates, very few recognizable milestones emerged from the applications group. Several programs were under development, and there was much hectic development; however, only one program was actually written with any success: the admissions program. This program, consisting of a few hundred FILECOMP statements, carried on a dialogue with the nurse at the admissions desk of a hospital to admit a patient into a hospital. While some of the other programs worked on a limited basis, none of them was really running in a production environment.

Why not? Aside from some minor difficulties, such as the relative inexperience of the application programmers and the effort to "re-invent" the original BBN programs, the main problem was that the application programmers did not have a working system with which to implement their application programs. On a typical day, the application programmer found that the hardware was inoperable when he arrived for work in the morning. When the hardware was finally fixed, the operating system group spent another hour or two fixing some problems with the operating system; when they were done, the FILECOMP language team spent another hour fixing some bugs in the interpreter. It was often early afternoon by the time the application programmers were able to access the system from their terminals—and after two or three hours of typing their programs and attempting to do some debugging, the system would often crash and destroy all of their files!

A SUMMARY OF THE DEVELOPMENT EFFORTS WITHIN THE MEDINET PROJECT

As we have seen, there were four major efforts simultaneoulsy under development within the MEDINET project. All of them were far too complicated to be successfully accomplished within a year and a half; more important, problems in one area usually had negative effects on the next area. Thus, problems in the hardware area slowed the progress in the operating system area considerably; problems with the operating system made debugging of the FILECOMP language much more difficult; the combination of all of these problems made the job of writing application programs nearly impossible.

By the spring of 1967, it had become obvious that the project was much larger than had been anticipated. The response, on the part of almost all of the technical staff, was simply to work harder. As people began to work 16 and 18 hours a day, seven days a week, it became more difficult to bring them together for meetings in which common problems and strategies could be discussed; as everyone worked harder, tempers grew short. Criticisms and helpful suggestions were ignored or rejected summarily. By the end of the summer, it had become apparent to the top management within GE that the project was in trouble; an investigating team was sent in to evaluate the entire project.

After spending two months studying all phases of the project, the team reported some interesting findings:

1 The GE-485 hardware was interesting, but was not reliable and probably would never be sufficiently reliable for hospitals. In addition, it was too slow.

2 The general-purpose operating system was very advanced, but would probably require another six months of debugging before it could be used; even then, it was probably too big and too inefficient. The special-purpose operating system appeared to be quite capable of handling FILECOMP programs, but it would require some work to modify it for more general applications.

3 The FILECOMP language was quite interesting and quite powerful, as a programming language. However, it was extremely slow, and it was doubtful that anyone would ever want to implement it on any other computer; in addition, there was a *very* limited supply of FILECOMP programmers.

4 The application programmers were working very diligently, but had not accomplished very much. In addition, it seemed that they had not done a very good job of coordinating with the hospitals; it was not really clear whether the application programs would be useful or acceptable in most hospitals.

As a result of this study, and after much political in-fighting, it was decided to reorganize the entire project. All development work was scrapped; a new project was begun to design a simple on-line data collection system, with the application programs written in COBOL. As is common in many projects, the change in direction was accomplished so abruptly that most of the project members left within the next few months; as a result, their experiences, valuable as they might have been, were ultimately lost.

This is, of course, a very brief history of the events that took place during a two-year period; however, it should at least give some indication of the kinds of activities that can and do take place in a large, ambitious on-line project. If, during this discussion, it has seemed that many of the development efforts proceeded in a rather random and haphazard fashion, it is only because that is what really happened.

Management-oriented students are often aghast after hearing this tale of woe. "How could all of this have happened?" they say. "Where were the controls? What kind of organization could have let things get so out of hand? Weren't there any PERT charts, milestones, or deadlines?"

The superficial answer to all of these questions is very simple: *there wasn't any*. The organization, such as it was, is shown in Figure E2; the managers of the various departments met regularly, and the entire project was small enough (approximately 200 people at the height of the project) so that everyone could easily communicate with most other members of the staff. However, the organization chart in Figure E2 is conspicuous for its lack of a "testing," or "quality assurance" group, and for the absence of a "coordination" group to make sure that all of the projects were meshing together properly.

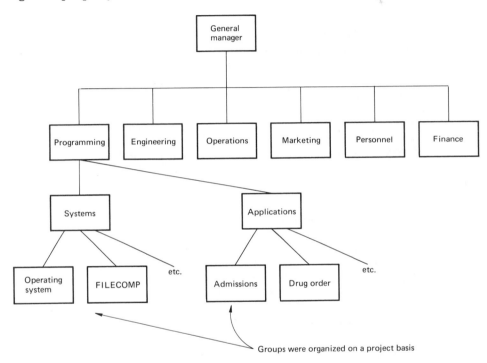

Fig. E2 Organization within the MEDINET department

The organization problem was actually much more fundamental than that. Those who are aghast at the chaotic events of this project usually come from an organization where a *formal* organization of projects is a way of life. Within large banks, insurance companies, computer manufacturers, and aerospace firms, the approach to a computer project is characterized not so much by the organization chart but by the *attitude*, or *approach*, to the project. The project *always* begins with a feasibility study, which must be approved by several levels of management, committees, and innocent bystanders; this is *always* followed by a formal specification of what the system is to do; after this comes a detailed document describing the system design—all of these steps requiring enormous amounts of review, revision, approval, and an abundance of paperwork. At each stage, management theoretically has an opportunity to withdraw support if it appears that the project is becoming too complicated, too expensive, or too unrealistic.

This approach presumably works well within large organizations—at any rate, it seems to be a way of life. However, when one reads of the cost over-runs and dismal failures within the aerospace industry, one begins to wonder about the infallibility of the organized, formal approach. One of the very few "systems" in which this approach *did* work was the American manned spacecraft effort, a project which extended over a decade—and yet one wonders whether, behind all the publicity and fanfare, there might have been a few fiascos.

At any rate, it has been a maxim within the computer industry that a small group of highly talented people can often accomplish what a larger group cannot. Many of the early time-sharing systems, implemented during the mid-1960's, were designed and implemented by a handful of people in 12-18 months; some of the better-known examples include the Dartmouth GE-265 time-sharing system, the DEC PDP-6 time-sharing system, and the IBM Call/360 BASIC time-sharing system. Many of these projects were rather informally organized, and succeeded because of the perserverance and genius of a small group of people working in harmony with one another.

The MEDINET project was simply an attempt to use this philosophy on a larger scale. Everyone "knew" that an operating system could be designed and built by a team of three or four people; everyone knew that a programming language could be implemented by one or two people; the MEDINET group even had the temerity to think they could write a sophisticated macro assembler in one weekend! Thus, one cannot fault the MEDINET group for "poor" organization—they did not think *any* organization was necessary! It is important to point out that this approach works very well for groups of less than ten people, working on a project that requires less than a year or two—MEDINET's mistake was assuming that the same philosophy would hold for two hundred people.

Despite this unorganized approach, one still wonders why it took two years for the project to be terminated—and why that decision had to be made by outsiders. The answer is very simple, and yet very complicated: nobody expected the project to fail, so nobody made any provisions or preparations, either organizationally or psychologically, for the possibility of a failure. While this problem has been noted by management scientists in discussions of the management of R&D projects, it is one that can occur in any computer project—*especially when the project members are implementing a larger version of a system they had previously implemented successfully.* Thus, when one has successfully implemented a batch order entry system, the implementation of a larger, on-line order entry system appears to be relatively simple and straightforward; when one has implemented a small, experimental hospital system, then a larger hospital system should be no problem at all!

There are usually several manifestations of this inability to admit the possibility of failure. Management usually fails to organize the basic design activities (i.e. feasibility study, functional specifications, and the system design itself) in such a way that it can be cancelled gracefully if any of these steps leads to problems. On a personal level, people simply refuse to admit that things might be seriously wrong; their reaction is similar to that of the horse in George Orwell's classic *Animal Farm:* whenever things went wrong, his response was, "I must work harder." Even when it becomes obvious that the project cannot succeed, it is extremely difficult to make the decision to terminate it; after dedicating a year or two of one's life to a project, it becomes emotionally impossible to kill it. In such situations, someone outside the organization is often the *only* one who can make the hard, final decision.

Finally, we should mention one last fundamental problem with such projects: *it is usually impossible to estimate how long it will take to do something that has never been done before.* Accurate schedules and milestones were impossible on the MEDINET system, because nobody had ever attempted anything vaguely resembling a hospital system on a large, virtual memory machine. This is usually acceptable on pure research projects, but *not* on commercial projects that are supposed to make a profit.

A BRIEF SUMMARY OF THE TECHNICAL ASPECTS OF THE MEDINET SYSTEM

In this section, we will give only a brief description of the technical aspects of the MEDINET system. While many of the hardware and software features were quite interesting, a complete description would fill an entire book, and would not serve our purpose—which is to show the problems that can be encountered in a large, ambitious on-line system.

We will begin with a description of the hardware. Figure E3 shows the hardware configuration used in the project; a duplicate of the entire configuration was provided for reliability purposes, though, as we will see below, much more would have been required for any meaningful reliability.

The terminals were, for the most part, simple Model-33 Teletypes. Eventually, all of these would have been replaced (with the possible exception of the terminals in the programmers' offices) with the specially designed MEDINET terminals. However, even the MEDINET terminals used a Model-33 keyboard, and simply added a few extra attachments. No plans were made for using CRT's, though they doubtless would have been incorporated into the system eventually. This is an interesting point, for many hospital-oriented systems designers feel that the type of applications planned by MEDINET could only have succeeded with CRT's—applications such as hospital admissions require the nurse to fill in a "form," which can be very time-consuming with a "conversational" teletype.

The terminals were connected to the system via voice grade lines and standard Bell Telephone data sets. No attempt was made to include multi-drop lines, polling, addressing, or any other "sophisticated" communications facilities. Again, had the system ever worked, most of these sophisticated communications facilities would have been added eventually.

Nevertheless, it is interesting to note that the original plans did not take into account any such sophisticated telecommunications features.

The "concentrators" that are shown in Figure E3 consisted of Datanet-30 computers. The Datanet-30 has a 6.94 microsecond cycle time, 16K of memory, and an 18-bit word; while it has fairly powerful instructions for communications applications, it is relatively expensive compared to many of the minicomputers that were available even in 1966.

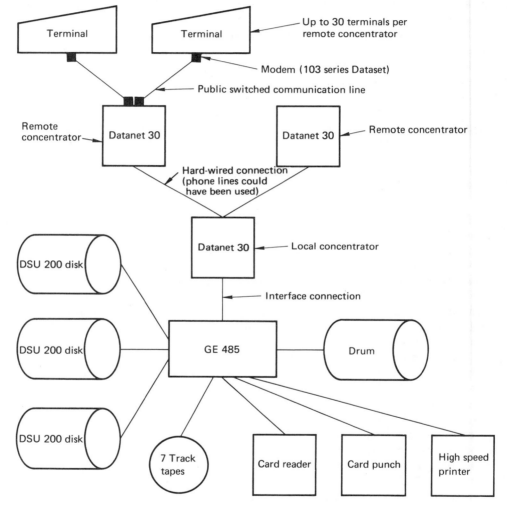

Fig. E3 Hardware configuration for MEDINET project

Though the "remote" concentrators were actually located in the machine room for the duration of the MEDINET project, it was intended that they eventually be located in some remote location—perhaps in the basement of a hospital. Though the Datanet-30 is capable of accommodating a relatively large number of terminals, the plans initially called for attaching only 30 terminals to each remote concentrator; however, it was anticipated that as many as six of the remote concentrators could be attached to a *local concentrator*—the local concentrator getting its name from the fact that it was always intended to be in the computer room, attached to the GE-485 through an interface unit. Thus, we see that the system was intended to handle something on the order of 180 terminals, with two levels of communications controllers.

The main computer, as we have already mentioned, was a GE-485 computer. As part of GE's family of medium-sized computers, it has a 24-bit word, 32K of memory and a 2.7 microsecond cycle time. The memory capacity was extended to 128K with the use of specially designed hardware paging registers. The paging registers also provided memory relocation and protection, and made it possible to write *reentrant* application programs. The machine featured an extremely powerful addressing scheme, and a "movable" accumulator—that is, the programmer could place the computer's accumulator at any location in memory. Many of the instructions were character-oriented, and were quite efficient for business-oriented COBOL applications.

The GE-485 was capable of supporting as many as six movable-head disks, though the MEDINET operating system was only designed to support the three disks shown in Figure E3. Each of the disks had a capacity of 18.8 million characters, and an average access time of 250 milliseconds. The disks were used almost exclusively for file storage, although they were also intended for long-term storage of application programs.

In addition, the machine was provided with a high-speed drum as a secondary storage for application programs and portions of the data base. The drum had a capacity of approximately 3 million characters and an average access time of approximately 17 milliseconds. Because of the "paging" nature of the CPU, information was read and written on the drum in 512-word pages.

As was mentioned above, there was a duplicate of the entire configuration for reliability purposes. A set of manual switches allowed the computer operator to switch any one of the disks, the magnetic tape drives, the high-speed printer, the card reader and the card punch; unfortunately, it was impossible to switch the drum or the local concentrator. In addition, the switches themselves were somewhat unreliable. Much more important was the fact that no *software* error recovery was planned to go along with the *hardware* backup; by the time it was recognized that the operating system would have to include some error recovery routines (see entry for August 24, 1967, in Table E2), it was effectively too late. Thus, while the computer operator could manually switch to a backup subsystem (e.g. one of the peripheral devices) or to a complete backup system (which would have taken ten or fifteen minutes), the system was not protected against such things as power failures (see Chapter U for a description of other types of system failures)—nor were there any provisions for recovering the data base in the event of a failure or switchover (see Chapter N for a description of file recovery techniques). As we point out in Chapter U, error recovery is only possible if it is designed into the system from the very beginning, *and* if the system designers take every possible form of failure into account.

Rather than attempt to describe the operating system, the FILECOMP interpreter, or the application programs in detail, we will simply give an example of the type of processing performed with the *hospital admissions* application. The example can be understood quite easily with the aid of Figure E3, and will serve to illustrate the salient features of the operating system, programming language, and application programs. We will skip over the preliminary actions that are required of the nurse: turning on her terminal, logging in to the system, and asking for the admissions program. These activities caused a tremendous amount of activity and overhead in the system, but they are relatively uninteresting.

Once the operating system had ascertained that the nurse wanted to execute the admissions program, it would cause the program to begin executing in the nurse's virtual memory space. As we have pointed out, the MEDINET system was implemented as a general-purpose time-sharing system; each terminal (and hence each nurse) had its own "job" area, and its own virtual memory. As we saw in Chapter B, an alternative approach would be to have *one* admissions program (and hence one virtual memory) capable of communicating with several terminals; this "transaction-oriented" approach would require the application program to determine the order in which each nurse's admissions transaction would be serviced.

At any rate, the nurse's admissions program would begin executing; specifically, this meant that the FILECOMP interpreter *and* the source version of the admissions program would be called into her virtual memory to begin executing. After some initialization, the admissions program would execute a statement to cause a message to be printed on the nurse's terminal; upon processing the statement, the FILECOMP interpreter would make the appropriate call to the operating system to perform the terminal output.

This request generated a frenzy of activity within the operating system. The terminal-handling routines were called with an indication of the nature of the request made by the application program; the terminal-handling routines checked to see that the request was legal, then entered the output message in a queue of other messages to be sent to the local concentrator. The scheduling algorithm was then called to find some other application program to run, since the admissions program would have to wait until the terminal output was complete. The scheduler program would choose another application program, and would often find that there was insufficient room for it in memory; this necessitated removing at least a portion of some other application program and placing it on the drum. In fact, it was not at all unusual for the admissions program to be "swapped" out of memory while waiting for its terminal output to finish.

Eventually, the local concentrator would receive the output message, and would send an acknowledgment back to the GE-485. The output message would then be placed in a queue of messages to be sent to the remote concentrator, and would eventually be transmitted. In a similar fashion, the remote concentrator would acknowledge the receipt of the message, and would then start typing it on the nurse's terminal. At the end of this lengthy sequence, the nurse would see the following typed on her terminal:

PATIENT'S NAME?

This was the first question of a lengthy dialogue, and the nurse knew that she was supposed to type the name of the patient being admitted to the hospital.

Meanwhile, the remote concentrator sent a short message to the local concentrator, indicating that the requested output message had been completely typed on the terminal. After the appropriate acknowledgment, the local concentrator passed the information on to the GE-485. At this point, the terminal-handling routines in the operating system informed the scheduler that the admissions program was again in a "runnable" state.

Eventually, the scheduler program would decide to execute the admissions program again; however, it would often find that at least a portion of the program was no longer resident in core memory (the FILECOMP interpreter usually remained in memory, but the actual admissions program was more likely to be swapped)—thus, there would be another delay while the appropriate pages of the program were brought in from the drum.

Thus, the admissions program would eventually be given the opportunity to resume its execution at the point where it had last stopped—that is, at the statement just after the terminal output statement. In most cases, this next statement would be a terminal *input* statement—that is, a statement to read in the answer to the PATIENT'S NAME question that had just been typed. Thus, a call would again be made to the operating system, and the same pattern of communication between the GE-485, the local concentrator, and the remote concentrator would ensue. Meanwhile, the admissions program again was "swapped" to the drum.

When the nurse finally typed the name of the patient to be admitted to the hospital, the admissions program would again be retrieved from the drum. At this point, it would perform some computation and open some files (though they were not called files, but rather *segments*, in keeping with the paging nature of the machine). After this brief flurry of activity, the admissions program would execute another terminal output statement, to cause the next question to be typed on the terminal. Thus, the cycle began again—an enormous amount of overhead and swapping and a relatively small amount of application program processing. At one point, the hospital admissions dialogue consisted of approximately fifty questions, and it usually required more time than the manual form with which the nurse had previously worked!

Brief as this discussion has been, it should give some idea of the type of processing that often takes place in a time-sharing "conversational" system of this type. This system was further complicated by the intricate paging algorithms which added even more overhead. Many of the paging algorithms are discussed in Chapter T.

A SUMMARY OF PROBLEMS
ON THE MEDINET SYSTEM

Every on-line computer project has its troubles; the troubles seem to be an exponential function of the size of the project. Thus, while it is interesting and perhaps amusing to read of the miseries suffered by the MEDINET team, it can also be instructive. We should attempt to identify the *fundamental* failures in the MEDINET project, so that the reader may possibly avoid them in his own project.

1 *Too much was attempted by too few in too little time*

This was probably *the* major weakness in the system; the system designers simply bit off more than they could chew. Of course, it is much easier to see this *after* a project has failed (or exceeded its budget or deadline) than *before*. Nevertheless, it should be intuitively obvious that it is well nigh impossible to hire a team of two hundred people, design new hardware, design and implement two operating systems, a programming language, a new terminal, a disk controller, and a multiplexor in a period of two years. In fact, two years would have been just sufficient to write the application programs, install them in a hospital, and get them running on a commercial basis—if none of the other development work had to be done.

2 *The hospitals probably did not need anything so sophisticated*

It is interesting to note that the experimental system upon which the MEDINET system was based had been a *free* experiment: it had been funded by the National Institute of Health, and possibly with research money from other sources. However, it apparently never occurred to anyone that had the MEDINET system succeeded, it would have cost a great deal of money to install terminals and pay for the computer services. This phenomenon was noticed by a number of other vendors who experimented with the hospital field—as long as it was an experiment, the hospitals loved it, but when it began to cost money, they took a very dim view of it.

The fact that the hospitals were reasonably happy with the "new" MEDINET system is very interesting; again, the new system involves on-line data collection with batch processing of transactions. Thus, though they may have liked an on-line, real-time system they were willing to live with a much simpler system—especially when it came time to pay the bill. For those organizations about to embark upon very expensive, ill-defined "management information" systems, this is an interesting point to keep in mind.

3 *There was not enough knowledge of this type of on-line system*

As we pointed out, the MEDINET system was designed as a general-purpose time-sharing system. As we saw in Chapter B, there were many alternative types of systems that could have been built—a *transaction-oriented* on-line system would have been appropriate, and a *remote batch* system may also have served quite well. In Chapter H and Chapter I, we will dwell on some of the reasons that make a time-sharing system undesirable for this type of application.

Considering these inefficiencies, why was a time-sharing system used? The answer is quite simple: most of the key system designers had previously helped design and implement time-sharing systems, in environments where a time-sharing system was appropriate. Hence, MEDINET seemed to them to be just another time-sharing application—just a little larger and more general-purpose. People are always influenced by their past experience—and if a new on-line system is radically different than anything previously designed within the organization, it might be better to hire trained and experienced people.

4   *No design calculations were made*

In the next chapter, we will discuss the types of calculations that one can make when designing an on-line system. In some cases, *mathematical modeling* might be appropriate; in most cases, *simulation* is a good tool for predicting the bottlenecks in a system; in still other cases, there are a number of simple *"rules of thumb"* that can be used. Unfortunately, *none* of these design calculations were made in the MEDINET system.

One small example will show the magnitude of the problem caused by this omission. As we mentioned earlier, the MEDINET system used movable-head disks with an average access time of approximately 250 milliseconds. As we will see in Chapter F, it is reasonable to make an initial estimate of 10-20 disk accesses per transaction. Thus, unless we can count on overlapped disk seeks or some other sophistication (which MEDINET did not have), each transaction requires at least 2.5 seconds of processing time. Another simple throughput formula in Chapter F then shows us that, with the conditions specified above, the system will be able to handle approximately 25 terminals. Since the MEDINET system was designed for *200* terminals, something was obviously wrong!

5   *The "advanced" hardware caused severe reliability problems*

Not many organizations are ambitious enough to design their own hardware; thus, it may seem that MEDINET's problems were rather unique in this area. However, there *are* organizations that take pride in receiving the very first machine in a vendor's new product line. In Chapter C, we outlined some of the problems that are caused by this "pioneering" approach; Table E1 should confirm that discussion.

The moral: if the goal is to get a reasonable on-line system *working* with a minimum of confusion and problems, buy a standard, off-the-shelf computer. Don't let a vendor sell you a "paper tiger": insist on seeing one or two real installations (demonstration computers at the Spring Joint Computer Conference don't count!).

6   *No use was made of standard programming packages*

This was another obvious mistake. Very little use was made of any of the standard General Electric software for the GE-435. While it is true that much of the standard software would not have run on the modified machine, *some* of it could have. Thus, even though the special hardware required a new operating system, some of the IO routines from the standard GE-435 operating system could have been utilized. Other standard GE programming packages, such as the compilers and utility routines, could have been modified so that they would run under the MEDINET operating system.

7   *Adequate recovery was not planned*

As we have seen, file recovery was not even considered until the project was more than 18 months old. *System* recovery was attempted by duplicating the entire hardware configuration, but nobody had thought out the details of switching over to the backup system.

In Chapter U, we will review the various causes of system failures, and the various strategies that can be employed to minimize the extent of a failure. The major point that we want to make here is that recovery must be planned, *in detail*, at the beginning of the project. By the time the project is 18 months old, it is too late—major changes would have to be made to the operating system and/or the application programs.

SOME MORALS AND GUIDELINES
FOR ON-LINE SYSTEMS PROJECTS

To end the chapter on a positive note, we will briefly list some suggestions that may help avoid the problems encountered by MEDINET.

1   *Minimize your commitment and risk*

This is a fairly vague notion, perhaps, but it seems foolish to risk several million dollars in a business venture, only to find out two or three years later that the whole idea was no good. On the assumption that everything goes wrong in the computer business anyway (a corollary to Murphy's Third Law?), the idea is to at least make the failure as small as possible.

Thus, if you are contemplating an on-line system for a completely new application, it might be best to start with a batch system. Alternatively, it is often wise to begin with a system that permits on-line inquiry, with overnight batch updating of the data base. If the simple system works, *then* you can advance to a more sophisticated configuration.

2   *Hire experienced application programmers*

According to a common prejudice, application programmers don't have to be very intelligent or experienced, because the system programmers will take care of everything. On a complex on-line system, it is quite easy for an application programmer to innocently (or maliciously) thwart the cleverest algorithms of the best operating system; no matter how cleverly the system programmer *designs* the system, the application programmer still has to write the programs.

If his program gets into a subtle loop or performs too many disk accesses, the entire system may bog down.

Thus, it is best to find application programmers who have had some experience with on-line systems. Now that on-line systems have been in existence for a few years, it should certainly be possible to find programmers with COBOL, PL/I, or assembly language experience on a business-oriented on-line system. For process control systems and data acquisition systems, it is much more difficult to find an experienced programmer.

3   *Ensure that the application programmers can do most of their coding, compiling, and early debugging on an existing system*

Unless the on-line systems project is fairly small and simple, it is a good idea to have a backup machine that can be used by the application programmers while the systems programmers are working on their operating system; similarly, if the on-line system requires a large hardware configuration and/or a new computer room (taking a long time to order the equipment, prepare the facility, install the machine, and get it working), the application programmers should have some way of continuing to do their work without any disturbances.

4   *Insist on complete, even if not exhaustively detailed, specifications*

We discussed the nature of specifications for on-line systems in Chapter D; however, detailed, comprehensive specifications are sometimes so voluminous that nobody reads them and nobody keeps them up to date. Also, some projects are too small, or lack sufficient time and manpower to do a good job in this area. Still, this is no excuse for not insisting on at least a *broad* specification of the entire system. Many aspects of the MEDINET system, by way of contrast, were *totally* unspecified.

5   *Have review sessions outside the normal working environment*

Many projects get into trouble because the programmers, analysts, and managers are so close to their work that they can't see the problems. By having a formal review session at various stages of the project—in a secluded place, away from the secretaries, telephones, computer time commitments, and other distractions—some of these problems can be brought to light.

6   *Use existing packages, operating systems, programming languages, and hardware wherever possible*

7   *Try to keep the key people from quitting in the middle of the project*

On a project that extends over three or four years, it can be catastrophic if a key man leaves. This is especially a problem with some of the junior people: their market value often increases faster than the company's salary increase schedule. While money is certainly an important motivating force, it is not the only one: recognition by one's colleagues and managers is often almost as important. Good working conditions, a nice office, a title, a promotion, a free Coca-Cola machine, special parking spaces for programmers with motorcycles—all of these "tricks" will go a long way toward keeping the programmers happy.

MEDINET provided free crash helmets to any programmer with a motorcycle (on the theory that the motorcycle saved a valuable parking space, and that the programmer's head deserved to be protected, since he undoubtedly had *not* done any documentation!).

8 *Try not to hire prima donna programmers*

On most on-line systems, each program interacts with a large number of other programs. Thus, a programmer, who disobeys the standard programming conventions or is not available to debug his program, can seriously delay other members of the project. Similarly, a programmer who refuses to document his programs, or frowns on flowcharting ("My programs are so good they don't need to be flowcharted") is to be avoided.

In many cases, there *is* a use for the brilliant, but unsociable, programmer. Use him as a trouble-shooter, an idea man, and a problem-solver. Let him invent clever algorithms, but don't let him code them. Let him devise elaborate, tricky testing sequences for the on-line programs, but don't count on him to carry them out. Give him a portion of the system that is independent of the rest of the system, and then let him attack the problem in his own mysterious fashion.

9 *Plan the implementation schedule in as much detail as possible*

This is obviously not easy to do; in fact, some will argue that it cannot be done at all for any kind of research and development project—for it asks a man to estimate how long it will take him to do something he has never done before.

As a result, many managers have a habit of multiplying the estimates of their programmers by a factor of two; on some of the more complex systems, a "fudge factor" of three or five might be more appropriate. Other managers bear in mind the "rule of thumb" given by James Martin:[†] an average programmer can write approximately 12-15 debugged statements per day, and two to three statements per day for an operating system.

On the subject of scheduling, there is one other thing that we should mention: if the project is behind schedule at the end of the first milestone, then there is good reason to believe that it will continue to fall further behind schedule for the remainder of the project. Thus, if a manager discovers that he is three months behind schedule at the end of the first year, he should expect, unless there is strong evidence to the contrary, that it will be six months behind at the end of the second year.

This suggestion has nothing to do with PERT charts or critical path scheduling; we are simply saying that a manager has an opportunity to review *his own ability to estimate* at the end of each milestone of the project. If he discovers that he has been optimistic, then he should expect that subsequent milestones have been estimated with an equal proportion of unrealistic optimism.

[†] James Martin *Programming Real-Time Computer Systems* Prentice-Hall, 1965, page 348

10   *Retain control of the project in one group*

If control of the on-line system is fragmented between various departments, agencies, or companies, the system itself will reflect that fragmentation.

11   *Let inexperienced people gradually take over the system*

It is unrealistic to assume that the key people will remain with the system forever. As soon as it works fairly well (or sooner, depending on their temperaments), there will be pressure to put the senior men on another project; or, in other cases, the senior people will begin getting bored with routine maintenance work, and will look elsewhere for new projects. In either case, it is a good idea to begin phasing in junior people during the testing phase (or perhaps earlier) to gradually take over the system. This is also an excellent way of training junior people.

12   *The manager should not abdicate his responsibilities to his technical people*

It seems that many managers devote most of their time to *administrative* management, and leave *technical* management to the programmers and analysts. Thus, it is often the technical people who choose the hardware configuration and type of system to be built—and nobody asks them: "Is this the most cost-effective way?", or "Is this the simplest, least risky approach?"

Of course, it is unreasonable to expect that a manager should be aware of the intricacies of operating systems design or data base management routines. However, he *is* the person who should be able to take a hard-nosed attitude toward the system. While he must ultimately trust his technical people to give him the correct answers, it is the manager who must ask the correct questions. As we have seen in the MEDINET project, the abdication of that responsibility can have fatal results.

DESIGN CALCULATIONS FOR ON-LINE SYSTEMS

INTRODUCTION

In Chapter D, we discussed the process of designing a system as a qualitative, subjective process—one which involved such factors as time, availability of talent, and availability of money. By evaluating the goals, or requirements of his system with relation to these many constraints, the system designer should be able to make some preliminary choice of a basic type of on-line system. However, the question remains: *will it do the job?*

Exactly what the system must do is described by the functional specifications that are jointly drawn up by the system designer and the user of the system; whether his design is capable of meeting those specifications is something that only the system designer can tell. There has been a great deal of talk in the computer industry about the application of various *management sciences* to large computer projects (both on-line and otherwise, though the on-line systems tend to predominate because of their size and complexity), and some of this talk is well directed. Management principles *can* help plan for efficient use of manpower, computer time, and other resources; management principles can help avoid errors of omission by reminding the system designer that he must have a well-organized plan for the testing, documentation, conversion, and maintenance of his system; management can suggest proven techniques for budgeting, status reporting, training, liaison with customers, project organization, and project review. However, neither management nor management sciences can help the system designer make technical decisions—especially the more difficult technical decisions regarding hardware configurations or the relative merits of one operating system versus another.

To make such a decision, the system designer must be able to make some *quantitative* statements about his on-line system. There are basically three techniques for doing this, each of which has its advantages and disadvantages:

1   Mathematical modeling

2   Simulation

3   Empirical formulas, "rules of thumb," and "common sense" calculations

As the reader can see from the bibliography at the end of this chapter, there has been a great deal of research in this area, and one worries sometimes that the researchers might have missed the point of their modelling and simulation: to expose the potential bottlenecks in the system, and to verify that the system will indeed do the job it is supposed to do.

The system designer should keep this point uppermost in his mind as he becomes involved with the intricate mathematics of queueing theory or the voluminous printouts from simulation runs. There are a number of potentially critical areas in any on-line system, and an efficient system is one in which these bottlenecks are balanced so that no one of them stands out. Our models and our simulations, then, should point out which areas are critical, and just how critical they are—if they merely predict average response time, the job is only half done.

Our first job, obviously, is to examine these critical areas. Basically, the three major areas where the system can become overloaded are the computer, the input/output area, and the communications area. Each of these three major areas can be broken into smaller pieces, each of which deserves to be discussed individually.

BOTTLENECKS IN THE COMPUTER

The most obvious bottleneck in the computer is the processor itself. It is characteristic of most on-line systems that some semblance of a real-time response be given; this cannot be done if the processor is too slow to finish transactions as quickly as they come into the machine, or if it cannot execute user programs sufficiently quickly in a university time-sharing environment.

In many cases, it is a straightforward task to determine whether or not the processor will cause trouble. If, in a business-oriented system, there are good estimates of the average and peak transaction arrival rates, the system designer should be able to see whether his system is keeping up with that rate. Similarly, in a process control system or a data acquisition system, the system designer should be able to calculate peak arrival rate of data or interrupts.

There are, however, several situations in which it is difficult to determine whether the processor will be fast enough. Chief among these are:

1   *The case where the arrival rate is unknown*

A company contemplating a scientific time-sharing system for its research department might have no way of knowing what types of input will be typed in by the users—i.e. how many compilations per minute, how many executions per minute, and so forth. This is probably true in any case where an on-line system is being introduced in an area where there was no prior system with which to compare it.

Similarly, many on-line business-oriented systems cannot easily estimate the arrival rate of transactions. If their on-line system is replacing a manual or batch system, the system designer will often find that there are no statistics to guide him—the user from whom he tries to elicit such information will give him answers such as "Oh, we have. . . ummm. . . maybe three or four thousand transactions a day. . . I think. . ."

Even when the input arrival rate *is* known with some accuracy, the system designer is often in trouble if he uses it to determine the acceptability of his central processor. On-line systems have a way of growing far beyond the initial plans; managers make more inquiries of an on-line management information system than they did before, because it is more convenient; scientists find more problems to solve on their time-sharing terminal than they had originally intended.

2   *The case where the processing rate is unknown*

There may also be difficulties if the system designer cannot accurately tell how fast the processor actually executes jobs. However, we must admit that this is very often the case when the applications are written in a higher level language. If one is lucky enough to run benchmarks on a similar computer, this problem can be minimized to some extent—but it may not be convenient or practical when the system designer is making his design calculations.

Even if the system designer can tell how fast a COBOL program executes on an XYZ computer, he may not have any way of estimating the size of the application programs being written for his system. Here again, we can draw a distinction between on-line systems that are being built to replace existing batch systems, and on-line systems that are being built from scratch. If the system is a new one, the application programmers will have only the vaguest idea of the nature of their programs when the analyst starts asking them for estimates—and any answers they give him should be disregarded!

There is somewhat of a solution to this dilemma: with mathematical models, simulation, or whatever other magic he may have at his disposal, the system designer can tell how quickly each transaction must be processed. Thus, knowing that each transaction must be processed in N milliseconds if the system is not to be bogged down, and knowing that N milliseconds is equivalent to M COBOL statements, the system designer can ask the application programmers whether it is possible, or reasonable, to write their application programs in M "average" COBOL statements. This is an admittedly primitive technique, but it will expose the cases where the application programmer would have to process an input transaction with three COBOL statements in order not to overload the processor.

In addition to the central processor, the main memory of the machine can be a serious bottleneck. An insufficient amount of memory may be caused by any one of the following reasons:

1   An operating system that is so large that it uses valuable memory that should have been used by application programs.

2   Application programs that were larger than expected. If overlaying (or swapping, or roll-in/roll-out, depending on one's terminology) is not permitted, this is a crucial bottleneck—if the application programs won't fit into core, the system won't run.

3   Application programs that are so interactive that the operating system cannot manage to keep a sufficient number of *runnable* application programs in core.

The first two situations are rather straightforward, and easy to recognize. The third situation is also very common, but is often more obscure. As an example, consider one of the versions of the scientific-engineering time-sharing systems written for the SDS-940 computer. It had the following characteristics:

1   An application program would use an average of 52 milliseconds of CPU time before requiring input or output of some form. Most of this IO was *teletype* IO, and it was a consequence of the extremely interactive nature of most of the application programs on the system.

2   The operating system would "swap" application programs from a high-speed drum to core memory and back again, basing its swapping decisions on a complex algorithm involving the IO wait condition of the application program, the number of people using the application program, the length of time it had been in core, and various other factors. When it did decide to swap a program, though, an average of 175-200 milliseconds were required.

3   Because of the relatively large size of both the operating system and the application programs, an average of only three to four application programs could fit in the machine at any one time.

With these characteristics, even the novice programmer can predict the consequences: the operating system simply could not bring new application programs into core quickly enough to compensate for their interactive nature. The three or four application programs in core would end up in a "wait" condition (waiting for disk IO or terminal IO or mag tape IO to finish) after a total of 150-200 milliseconds—barely enough time for the operating system to bring in *one* application program from drum. As a result, the system spent approximately 35% of its time waiting for new application programs to be brought into core.

Bottlenecks in the Input/Output Area of the Computer

The major IO bottleneck in most on-line computer systems is the speed of the file storage unit. In a business-oriented on-line system, each transaction requires several reads and writes from a data base on disk or drum; on a scientific-engineering time-sharing system, each user program may be accessing its own files and records on a common storage device.

The bottleneck is usually one of *speed:* if data cannot be retrieved from the data base quickly enough, the whole system may bog down. We should be careful to distinguish between three different types of "access times" on file storage units:

1 *Seek time*

This is the time required to move the read/write heads from their current position on a disk to a specified track. This is usually the most significant part of the access time on most disks.

2 *Latency time*

This is the time required for a disk platter or a drum to rotate so that the required record is under the read/write heads. Since most disks and drums rotate at approximately 2400 RPM, the latency time is uniformly distributed between 0 and 25 milliseconds.

3 *Transfer time*

This is the time required to actually transfer the record(s) from the disk or drum to the channel. This is usually very insignificant compared to the latency time and the seek time, since most disks and drums can transfer data at approximately 200,000-300,000 characters per second.

The disk is usually a critical area simply because of the number of reads and writes that might be required to process input from the terminals; occasionally, though, the bottleneck is due to the *nature* of the requests, and the type of file organization employed in the system. For example, the processing of an input transaction in a business-oriented system might require the retrieval of records on the inner track *and* the outer track of the disk. Thus, while the disk might be fast enough, in terms of *average* access times (i.e. average seek time + average latency time + average transfer time), it might not be fast enough in light of the particular file organization.

The one other aspect of a file storage unit which might cause it to be a potential bottleneck is its *storage capacity*. Most disk-packs have a capacity of approximately 30 million characters of storage, and most computer systems have 200-400 million characters in total. However, if the system designer miscalculates the number of records or files in his data base, or the size of the average record, this may not be enough.

Aside from the file storage units, the other major bottleneck in the IO area is the channel that connects the IO device to the computer's memory. On some machines, it is customary to dedicate a channel to one high-speed device—thus virtually eliminating the problem. However, it is very common to share several disks on one channel, or a disk and several magnetic tape drives. With this type of configuration, it is possible for the devices to be able to transmit data faster than the channel can carry them. Thus, a common complaint on the part of some operation managers is that "the computer isn't driving the magnetic tape drives fast enough." Investigation often shows that while the processor is capable of driving the tape drives, the channels are being used for so many other forms of IO that the tape drives sit idle for seconds on end.

Bottlenecks in the Communications Area

There are two areas of the communications sytem that are usually overlooked by the system designer: the front-end computer (or hardware multiplexer) with its buffer storage, and the communication lines themselves. Bottlenecks in the front-end computer may show themselves in a number of ways:

1   If the front-end computer cannot keep up with the flow of traffic from low-speed terminals, it may ask the users at their terminals to temporarily stop typing.

2   If the front-end computer cannot keep up with the flow of messages from the main computer, it may refuse to accept any more until it catches up.

3   If there is insufficient buffer space for messages from low-speed terminals, the front-end computer may send shorter *partial* messages to the main computer, thus causing more interrupts in the main computer and much more overhead.

4   An excessive rate of input from the low-speed terminals (which occasionally happens on scientific-engineering time-sharing terminals when users submit their input on paper tape instead of manually typing it in) may cause the front-end computer actually to lose data by not responding to interrupts fast enough.

5   If the front-end computer is overloaded, it may build up long queues of messages to be sent to the main processor, or to be sent *from* the main processor to the terminals. As a result, the response at the terminals may be sluggish and inconsistent.

Much the same types of bottlenecks can occur in a hardware communications multiplexor, although the reaction to an overload is usually not as "intelligent."

The communication lines are not usually a critical factor in most on-line systems, since it is common practice to dedicate a voice-grade communications line to each terminal on the system. The situations in which the communications lines *can* become a bottleneck are as follows:

1 If several terminals are attached to one voice-grade communications line, excessive traffic on any one or all of the terminals may cause an overload on the line. In that event, terminal users may be restrained from typing input until the traffic has eased. Similarly, output messages from the computer may be delayed in such a situation.

2 If the terminal consists of a CRT, a low-speed or high-speed printer (i.e. 200 lines per minute or greater) or any other high-speed device, the communication line may not be fast enough to transmit data to and from the device at its optimal rate.

3 If the front-end computer transmits input and output messages to the main computer via a medium-speed or high-speed communication line, there is a possibility of a bottleneck in that communication line. This situation rarely occurs.

An aspect of communications that is more likely to be crucial is the terminal itself. As we mentioned in Chapter C, most of the teletypewriter terminals that are currently on the market operate at speeds of 10-15 characters per second. For applications where there are large volumes of data to be typed out on the terminal, this may not be fast enough. It is also possible for the terminal to be a bottleneck in the sense of being difficult to use: if the control keys are awkwardly placed, or if the keyboard itself is not engineered properly, it may be difficult for anything but a double-jointed chimpanzee to use it efficiently.

Speaking of chimpanzees, we should mention the bottleneck that virtually everyone forgets: the user of the system. With the exception of process control systems and data acquisition systems, on-line systems depend on human beings (or reasonable facsimiles) for intelligent input, and yet many systems are designed as if they were intended to be used only by programmers. Difficult log-in procedures, incomprehensible command languages, and cryptic error messages are but three of the insults that most non-technical users must face when they use an on-line system. Even if it is easy to use the system, the analyst should keep in mind that the average user only types at the rate of 1-2 characters per second.

MATHEMATICAL MODELLING

One of the techniques for evaluating an on-line system is a *mathematical model.* There has been a great deal of research in this area since the mid-1960's, but as the references at the end of the chapter indicate, most of the research has been oriented toward the scientific-engineering time-sharing systems, whose properties are often markedly different from other types of on-line systems. The emphasis has been on time-slicing scheduling algorithms, with an attempt to determine average response times at the user terminal, though some papers have investigated the mathematical aspects of scheduling reads and writes for disk and drum [10, 46, 49, 51, 54].

As McKinney points out in his excellent survey [8], most of the time-sharing models can be classified according to the following criteria:

1 The number of terminals on the system.

2 The number of processors performing the work.

3 The arrival rate at which transactions or programs enter the system.

4 The amount of service required by each program or transaction, and the distribution of such service demands.

5 The assumptions made about swapping and overhead in the time-sharing operating system.

6 The size of each "slice" in the time-slicing algorithm—i.e. whether it is to remain finite or approach zero.

7 The service discipline that determines the *order* in which jobs or transactions are processed.

The more common models assume that the system operates with a round-robin service discipline, as illustrated by Figure F1; or a foreground-background scheme, as illustrated by Figures F2 and F3. Typically, the arrival rates are assumed to be Poisson in nature, and the service rates are assumed to be exponential in nature—though, of course, researchers have experimented with several other arrival and service disciplines.

It is not within the scope of this book to delve into a mathematical discussion of modelling. We are more concerned here with the *practical* aspects of modelling—that is, given that all of this research has been done, what use can be made of it by the system designer, whose background and interests are not usually mathematical in nature? To the system designer, modelling should be a *tool*, to be used with various other tools to evaluate the effectiveness of his system. In this context we can envision several possible scenarios in which the mathematical model might be useful:

1 For the system designer building a process control system or a data acquisition system, the arrival rates are often well known. Further, the mathematical description of the arrival rate is often very simple—e.g. a particular real-time device must be sampled exactly 2 times per second, etc. Also, the service rates are often well known and easy to describe—even though they are not always constant.

With such an environment, it is often fairly simple for the system designer to mathematically calculate response times to real-time inputs and interrupts.

2   For the system designer building a scientific-engineering time-sharing system, the situation becomes more difficult. If he is obtaining the time-sharing operating system from the computer vendor, it will be difficult to ascertain the nature of the scheduling algorithm and the extent of swapping overhead without a tremendous amount of tedious research. If he is designing his own operating system, he can, of course, draw upon the findings of the researchers in the field, but as we will see below, there are a number of basic problems inherent in modelling.

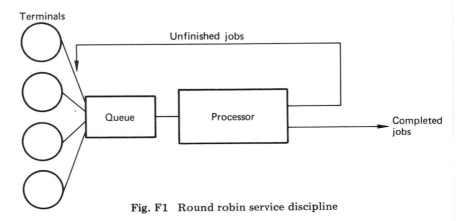

Fig. F1 Round robin service discipline

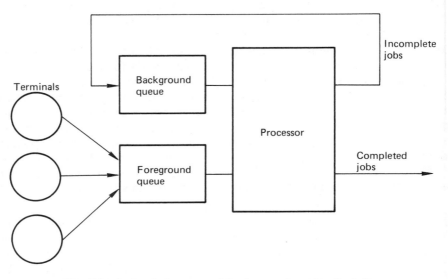

Fig. F2 A simple foreground-background service discipline

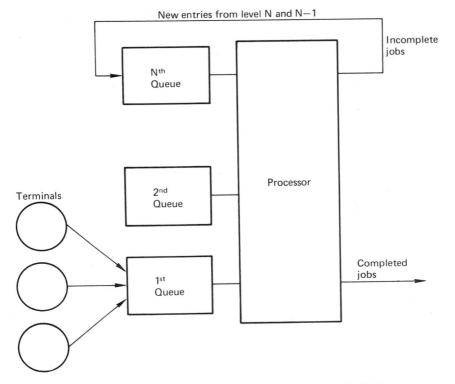

Fig. F3   A complex foreground-background service discipline

3   For the system designer building application programs on a typical business-oriented on-line system, the situation is very different. Many of the multi-programming operating systems offered by vendors do *not* employ time-slicing, and swapping (or overlaying) is often controlled by the application program. While the priority discipline is usually similar to the foreground-background schemes illustrated in Figures F2 and F3, there is not likely to be movement of jobs from one queue to another.

Consequently, many of the results obtained for scientific-time-sharing systems are not applicable for the business-oriented on-line system. However, some of the elements of queueing theory can be applied by completely ignoring the effects of the operating system. That is, the system designer may prefer to assume that the application programs run in an environment where:

there is no swapping.

there is no overlaying of application programs.

the system is dedicated to the application programs, so there are no *priority* considerations—i.e. no background job to which the operating system might give control.

there is no time-slicing; input transactions are processed to completion.

file requests are handled on a first-come-first-serve basis by the operating system, with a known distribution of access times.

With such simplifying assumptions, it is indeed possible for the system designer to formulate a relatively simple model of his application (see, for example, [32]).

It is generally agreed among most of the workers in this area of the computer field that a great deal remains to be done in the way of modelling the generalized on-line system. This is important to bear in mind, for the system designer can easily delude himself with inaccurate models, and the mathematics are often sufficiently formidable to discourage the critic. While the system designer should definitely draw upon the talents of operations research people or mathematicians in his organization, he should also be aware of the following common drawbacks in mathematical models:

1   *The input arrival rates are often not mathematically describable*

Most mathematical models assume that the arrival rate of transactions can be described by a "nice" mathematical function. However, most on-line systems find that the arrival rate is a function of several external factors, and the result is *not* capable of being described with any kind of straightforward mathematical equation. For example, almost every time-sharing service bureau finds that the number of users on the system rises and falls in roughly the manner shown by Figure F4; banks and stock brokerage houses may find that their load is more accurately described by Figure F5; airline reservation systems presumably have peak periods before and after holiday periods. Other on-line systems may be affected by rush-hour traffic, the phase of the moon, the state of the economy, or the outcome of the World Series—and the mathematician will usually be hard pressed to incorporate these factors into his model.

2   *Arrival rates and service rates are usually not independent*

Almost all mathematical models assume that the rate at which transactions or requests enter the system is completely independent of the rate at which they are serviced. Thus, if transactions arrive in the system at a rate that temporarily exceeds the capacity of the system to process them, queues will build up—*but it is assumed that more input will continue arriving, regardless of the size or nature of these queues.* This is simply not true of many on-line systems—a user waits at his terminal for his nth request to be processed before typing in his $n+1$st. If the response time is so long that it offends him, he may simply turn off his terminal and come back later. This possibility is not foreseen by the mathematical model, and it may have serious repercussions on the validity of the results.

3   *Service rates are not always mathematically describable*

The amount of processing time required to service a transaction or a time-sharing job is not always exponential or geometric in nature. The length and type of processing is usually a function of the application, and may also be influenced by external factors. On some systems, users may predominately type in transaction type A in the morning, and transaction type B in the afternoon; on scientific-engineering time-sharing systems, users may spend most of their time editing in the morning and compiling and executing in the afternoon.

For a variety of reasons, then, it is possible for the service rate to be a very complex function. The assumption of exponential service rates may turn out to be extremely inaccurate.

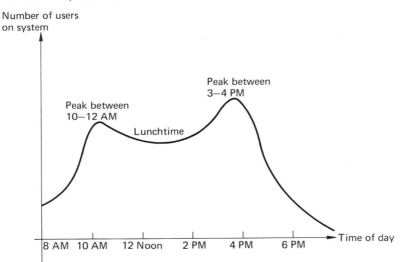

Fig. F4   Load distribution for a scientific-engineering time-sharing system

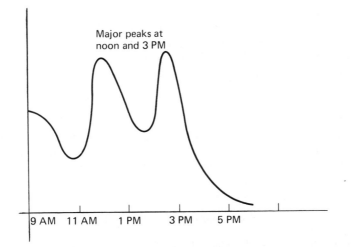

Fig. F5   Load distribution for an on-line banking system

4   *Priority disciplines are rarely simple*

As we mentioned above, most models assume either a round-robin or a foreground-background priority scheme in the operating system's scheduling algorithm. Unfortunately, many operating systems are far more complex. Initial placement of the input may be the result of external priority assignments (i.e. the user *insists* that his input be processed quickly), or the size of the application program, or any of a number of other factors. The time quantum may vary from one queue to another in a foreground-background system; the rules for moving jobs from one queue to another may depend on the amount of processing time consumed, the type of input/output being carried on by the program, and the length of time the job has been in the system. Scheduling decisions are also dependent on swapping considerations on many systems—a job already in core may receive priority over a job that has been swapped out to the drum.

In most cases, the scheduling algorithm represents attempts on the part of those who wrote the operating system to achieve some kind of balance between *throughput* and *interactiveness*. Time-sharing systems have traditionally favored the short, interactive job—but usually at the cost of increased swapping and system overhead. At some point, the system programmer introduces new algorithms to offset this overhead, and the result is a scheduling algorithm that is extremely difficult to represent in a mathematical fashion.

5   *Mathematical models rarely include all of the resources in a system*

Most time-sharing models are concerned with the nature of the time-slicing algorithm, and the priority discipline that decides when a job is allowed to use the central processor. However, there are several other resources that should be included in the model—core allocation, IO channels, file accessing, swapping, use of peripheral devices (magnetic tape, printer, etc.), and the communications network (including the front-end computer, if any). As we noted before, some researchers have considered models for file accessing, but most of the other resources have been ignored. What is really needed is a *unified model*—one that includes arrival rates, service rates, and priority disciplines for each of the resources of the system. At the present time, this seems to be beyond the capabilities of available mathematical models.

6   *The nature of most operating systems and applications programs is unknown*

For the system designer, the worst aspect of mathematical modelling is that it requires him to be able to describe the operation of the application programs and the operating system in detail. Not only are many operating systems difficult to describe mathematically, they are difficult to describe verbally or conceptually. The system designer may not even be able to look at the program listing of the operating system he is using, and the programmers who wrote the operating system may have long since vanished. While he may be able to get a general feeling for the nature of the application programs during the modelling exercise, the system designer should remember that the structure of the programs may change radically once implementation begins.

To conclude, mathematical modelling is a technique which can be used in certain well-defined situations by people who are very sure of what they are doing. For many scientific time-sharing systems, the models oversimplify things to such an extent that they lose their value; in business-oriented on-line systems, on the other hand, this simplification can allow the system designer to make some useful calculations.

SIMULATION

Another common technique for evaluating various aspects of a computer system is that of *simulation*. Though the amount of research in this area is perhaps not as great [4,5 books; 2,4,5,14,22,26,27,28,32,37,55], the use of this technique in the computer field is far greater than the use of mathematical modelling. There are a variety of simulation techniques available, but as in the case of mathematical models, they can be classified into three groups:

1   *The proprietary packages*

There are simulation *packages*, of which SCERT [4] is the most widely known, that allow the programmer to describe various aspects of his on-line system and receive printouts describing the lengths of various queues, the utilization of resources, and so forth. Most of the packages were first written for batch systems, and have only recently been upgraded to include the features of on-line systems.

While the simulation package contains information about the hardware characteristics of various machines (i.e. memory speeds, file access times, and so on), it is up to the system designer to specify the manner in which he intends to use the machine. He must specify arrival rates, service rates, the type of file accessing techniques, and overlay structures he will use.

2   *Simulation languages*

A more common simulation technique involves a higher-level language that allows the system designer to describe the processing techniques in his system. There are a wide variety of simulation languages on different computers, but some of the more popular ones are SIMSCRIPT, GPSS III, and SIMULA. The simulation language then produces reports describing the following aspects of each *facility* in the system:

the utilization of the facility

the average and peak queues for each facility

the amount of core required for the queues

the time required for a transaction to pass from one facility to another

This approach to simulation is by far the easiest, since it affords the system designer the same advantages of any higher-level language: powerful constructions, less need to be aware of the programming of the simulation, and easy modification of the simulation run.

3   *Hand-coded simulation programs*

It is possible to write a simulation program in assembly language, FORTRAN, COBOL, or any other computer language. While this is certainly more difficult than many other approaches to simulation, it may have its advantages. There are many on-line and real-time systems where the system designer is interested in a *visual* (and perhaps visceral) assurance that the system works properly. By writing a simulation program that closely mimics the behavior of the system (but perhaps on a reduced time scale), the system designer can see whether the *user* is overwhelmed by the system, whether outputs are correct, and whether the system gives all other external assurances of behaving properly.

The dangers of simulation are much the same as the dangers of mathematical modelling, and we can sum them up by saying that *the system designer is in trouble if his simulation does not bear a close resemblance to the real world.* It is just as easy to make a simplifying (and disastrously incorrect) assumption about arrival and service rates in a simulation program as it is in a mathematical model. A classic example of this occurred when the city fathers of an anonymous city decided to install a computerized traffic-control system. A simulation was done and the city fathers were assured that the computer had more than enough capacity to handle all the traffic lights during the rush hour. However, when the system was actually installed, the computer became overloaded during the rush hour traffic and ground to a halt. Incensed, the city fathers demanded an explanation of the system analysts, who proceeded to run their simulation *again*. Once again, the simulation proved, beyond a doubt, that the computer could not become overloaded—so the system analysts were vindicated! Meanwhile, the computer was removed, and the project was scrapped.

The major advantage of simulation techniques is the ease with which they can be changed during the implementation of a system. Programmers are universal in their eagerness to invent new and better approaches to a problem in the middle of implementation, and while most of their "improvements" should probably be discouraged, the consequences of some of the changes should be examined with the simulation package. Thus, the system designer might want to employ a simulation program to determine the consequences of such changes as:

a new file accessing technique that would require one less (or one more) disk access per transaction

more memory on the machine

an increase in the amount of processing time required for each transaction

more channels

Empirical Formulas, "Rules of Thumb," and "Common Sense" Calculations

In our discussion of design calculations, we should not omit the formulas and rules of thumb that have been discovered *empirically* by systems designers over the years, and passed on by word of mouth. While some of them have some basis in theory, most have simply been discovered by *watching* on-line systems in action, and are listed below in the hopes that they may be of some use to the reader:

1   *The average typing rate of users of on-line systems*

    On most on-line systems, users type at the rate of one to two characters per second, depending on their typing skill, the difficulty and length of their input, and their familiarity with the system. As we noted before, this "rule of thumb" can be seriously affected if users begin using paper tape input.

2   *The average arrival rate of transactions*

    On most scientific-engineering time-sharing systems and most business-oriented on-line systems, transactions or requests for service usually arrive from each terminal at the rate of one every 30-60 seconds. Scherr [3] has confirmed this on the MIT Project MAC time-sharing system, where the mean typing time was found to be 35.2 seconds, and was apparently independent of the time of day, the number of users on the system, and other external factors.

3   *The average terminal connect time*

    On most scientific-engineering time-sharing systems, it has been found that the average user stays on his terminal for 30-60 minutes. It should be emphasized that this rule of thumb probably does *not* apply to the business-oriented on-line system, where the user may either stay at his terminal all day long; or, at the other extreme, he may only use the system for five minutes to make an inquiry to a management information system.

4   *Average number of disk accesses per transaction*

    Most business-oriented on-line systems require some type of access and/or update to the data base. It is very common to grossly underestimate the number of disk accesses that will be required in the processing of each transaction, and as we discussed earlier in this chapter, the speed of the disk can be a very critical bottleneck in an on-line system. In the average on-line system, the number of disk accesses per transaction varies from a minimum of 8-10 to an average of 15-20. Applications written in a higher level language, using complex data management systems, can expect a much higher number.

5   *Number of people that can be serviced by a time-sharing system*

    It is usually possible to tell, either from a mathematical model or from direct observation, how many active terminals a scientific time-sharing system can support. However, it is also important to know how large a *community of users* can be serviced by the system. This is given by the formula

$$N = 2.5 \cdot n$$

where n is the number of active terminals, and N is the total number of people the system can support. Thus, if a time-sharing system can support 40 active terminals, it can support a community of 100 engineers and scientists without being overloaded.

While this formula is strictly empirical in nature, we can easily see what affects it. The two major factors must be the average terminal connect time, which is 30-60 minutes for most time-sharing systems, and the level of frustration felt by a user when he cannot gain access to the system. One might assume the number of 2.5 might increase as n increases—simply because the probability of the 1000th user getting a busy signal on a 400-user system is smaller than the probability of the 100th user getting a busy signal on a 40-user system. However, the situation often becomes complicated on large systems because of *dedicated communication lines:* the system designer might decide to dedicate 10 lines to New York, 10 to Washington, 10 to Philadelphia, and so forth. It is probably safer to assume that the factor of 2.5 holds for all sizes of systems, though the system designer should certainly attempt to find out for himself.

It should be noted that this formula probably does not hold for the on-line business-oriented system, not only because the terminal connect time is likely to be different, but also because the level of frustration on the part of users is likely to be higher. If a scientist cannot gain access to a time-sharing system, he will probably grumble—but he can always come back and try later. If a manager cannot gain access to his management information system, he may fire the entire data processing department in a fit of pique; if a salesman cannot gain access to an on-line order entry system, he may lose the order.

6   *Number of active terminals on an on-line system*

The number of active terminals that an on-line system can support is given by

$$n = \frac{T}{P} + 1$$

where T is the "think time" defined by Scherr [3] —i.e. the sum of type-in time, type-out time, and time spent thinking about what to do next. Thus, T is the arrival rate of transactions from each terminal. P is the average processing time required for each transaction, and the extra one user in the formula represents the overlap of one user's typing with other users' processing.

This formula has been discussed at length in the literature [3,8], but it is basically a simple *throughput* formula relating the amount of work arriving in the system with the system's capacity for processing it.

Finally, we should mention the technique of simply using paper-and-pencil calculations to examine the possibility that the simulations and models are incorrect. The system designer who is not a mathematician is often at the mercy of analysts, programmers, and computer salesmen—all of whom inundate him with formulas, simulations, and promises. With some simple common-sense calculations, the system designer (or his manager) should be able to see whether there is any truth to their promises. Consider the following example:

EXAMPLE. *The Widget Corporation of America.* The Widget Corporation of America has decided to install an on-line sales order entry system to allow all of its national salesmen to type orders into a computer from terminals in their 200 branch sales offices. The purpose of the system is two-fold: to perform a credit check on prospective customers before approving the sale, and to check on inventory. Widgets are kept in a number of warehouses around the country, and the real-time inventory input will be used to determine when to replenish inventory supplies, and in extreme cases it can be used to ship items from distant warehouses if a local warehouse is unable to meet an order.

Sensing the opportunity to place a very large computer order, a salesman from the XYZ computer company proposes his company's Aardvark 301 computer as a candidate for the on-line system. The price is attractive, and Widget's top management are inclined to go with XYZ because of their reputation for getting the job done. However, Wilbur Goodbody, manager of Data Processing at Widget, is concerned that the Aardvark might not be capable of doing the job—although it is priced competitively with other equipment, it seems somewhat slower, especially in the area of file storage. He repeatedly asks the XYZ salesman whether the system will *really* be capable of handling 200 active terminals. To reassure him, the salesman brings in three systems analysts who study the problem, ask interminable questions, mutter darkly about exponential interarrival rates, and finally *prove mathematically* that the system is capable of handling 500 active terminals. To prove it, they show Wilbur the output from an impressive simulation package that estimates the probability of intolerable delays with 500 terminals of only 0.0002. Wilbur is overwhelmed, and top management is convinced. As is the custom, the salesman takes the top management out for a night on the town on the evening before the order is to be signed, leaving Wilbur at the office.

Late that night, Wilbur pores over the mathematical calculations made by the XYZ analysts, convinced that something is wrong. He looks through the XYZ proposal, and notices that it calls for an inventory file structured as shown in Figure F6, and an Accounts Receivable file structured as shown in Figure F7. Knowing nothing about the precise nature of the application programs that would process and order entry from a salesman at a terminal, Wilbur nonetheless postulates the following basic sequence of activities:

1   When a transaction is received from a terminal, it is written on a Log File on disk. This is a serial file that keeps a record of each transaction for recovery and accounting purposes. *One* disk access is required here.

2   In order to perform the credit check, a Master Customer Index must be read from the disk. This is used to obtain the disk address of the appropriate Regional Customer Index, which in turn contains the disk address of the Accounts Receivable record of the potential customer.

Thus, *two* disk accesses are required just to *locate* the proper Accounts Receivable record.

3   The Accounts Receivable record is read into the machine, and an application program checks to see that the customer's credit rating is in order. If the customer's credit is bad, the transaction is rejected, but Wilbur knows that 95% of the orders will be approved, so he decides to ignore the rejected orders. *One* disk access is required to obtain the Accounts Receivable record, and it is left in core for possible later processing.

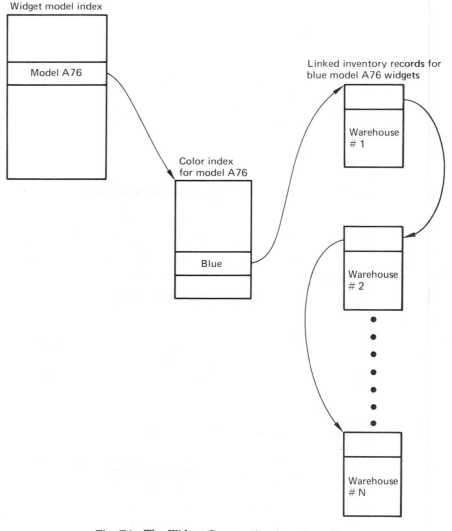

Fig. F6   The Widget Corporation inventory file

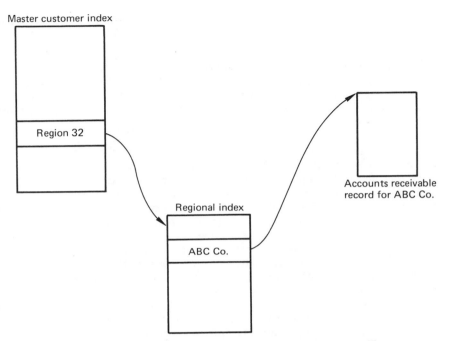

Master customer index

Region 32

Regional index

ABC Co.

Accounts receivable
record for ABC Co.

Fig. F7   The Widget Corporation's accounts receivable file

4   Next, the inventory must be checked. First the application program reads the Widget Model Index, and after locating the entry for the model of widget being ordered, reads in the Widget Color Index for that model. Thus, *two* disk accesses are required to locate the inventory records for the model and color of widgets being ordered.

5   Based on his knowledge of the current manual system, Wilbur estimates that three inventory records will have to be read in order to locate the optimum warehouse to meet the order. That is, each model and color of widget is likely to be stocked in six warehouses, of which three will have to be examined to find one that is close to the customer's location and has sufficient stock to meet the order. Thus, *three* disk accesses are required to locate the inventory record that will be used to fill the order.

6   At this point, the order can be filled. However, the Widget Corporations auditors and accountants are extremely concerned with the possibility of system failures (as is Wilbur), and insist that an Audit Trail be kept whenever inventory files or accounting files are updated. The XYZ Computer salesman has suggested that the Audit Trail be kept on disk, since the Aardvark 301's tape drives are abysmally slow—so Wilbur notes that *two* more disk accesses are required to write an updated Accounts Receivable record to the Audit Trail, and an updated inventory record to the Audit Trail.

7   The updated Accounts Receivable record is then written to the Accounts

Receivable file, and the updated inventory record is written to the inventory file. *Two* more disk accesses are made by the application programs.

8   At this point, the transaction has been processed. As a final gesture, the application programs write another record to the Log File to indicate that the transaction was not only received, but completely processed. This turns out to be useful for recovery purposes, but it requires *one* more disk access.

At this point, Wilbur calculates that 14 disk accesses will be required to service the average transaction. While the number may vary for unusual credit or inventory situations, he feels confident that well over 90% of the transactions will require the eight steps described above. Since the Aardvark 301 has a disk pack with an average access time of 60 milliseconds, it follows that a transaction would require 840 milliseconds of processing time even if there were no computations to be done at all. He realizes that some of the file accessing time can be overlapped with computations, but the extent of overlap depends on the nature of the operating system and the nature of the application programs—both of which are unknown factors at this point. However, there must be *some* unoverlapped applications processing, and there will certainly be some overhead in the operating system, and Wilbur feels that he is being more than generous when he assumes that only 160 milliseconds of computation time will be required for the average transaction. A total of one second is thus required to process the average transaction.

Wilbur and the XYZ analysts have already agreed that the average arrival rate of transactions will be one every 60 seconds from each terminal. It is anticipated that each Widget branch office will have one terminal manned by clerks and/or salesmen, and that there will be a rather steady stream of transactions typed into the terminal. This is further corroborated by the fact that the current mode of operation involves the processing of an average of 450-500 orders per eight-hour day from the average-sized branch office, and the knowledge that the current paper order forms can be filled out by a competent clerk in about a minute.

With this knowledge, Wilbur applies the simple throughput formula

$$n = \frac{t}{p} + 1 = \frac{60}{1} + 1 = 61$$

and is flabbergasted to see that the Aardvark 301 will only be able to handle a maximum of 61 terminals!

When the XYZ salesman appears the next morning to sign the order for the Aardvark 301, Wilbur announces his astonishing discovery to the assembled group of top management. The XYZ salesman first responds by saying that the users won't *always* be typing at the rate of one transaction per sixty seconds, and the computer will have a chance to "catch up" during slow periods. Wilbur responds by reminding him that his calculations involve only *averages*, and that he is not concerned with slow periods and peak periods—the system is simply not capable of handling the load.

Somewhat flustered, the XYZ computer salesman calls in his three analysts, who reject Wilbur's calculations on the grounds that his approach is not mathematical. With pride, they point out that *their* simulations and models are as thorough and exhaustive as possible, and that the results of their simulation cannot be disputed. Wilbur attempts to put the situation into very simple terms: each terminal will send a total of 450-500 transactions to the computer per eight-hour day. For the sake of simplicity, we will assume that each terminal sends 480 transactions per day, and, as we have seen, a *minimum* of one second is required to process the transaction. Thus, each terminal sends in enough transactions to tie up the computer for 480 seconds per day—or eight minutes. Thus, 60 terminals will generate enough work to keep the computer busy for eight hours. There is absolutely no way on earth, says Wilbur, for the Aardvark 301 to process the input from 200 terminals in an eight-hour day, let alone the 500 terminals that the salesman promised.

The analysts make one last feeble attempt to save the situation by pointing out that the file organization could be changed, so that two or three disk accesses could be eliminated. Wilbur agrees, but points out that such a refinement of his calculations would also have to include extra disk accesses caused by the operating system—as well as a more realistic estimate of the processing time required by the application programs. In any event, Wilbur points out, it would take a miracle to improve matters to the point where the number of users could be tripled from 60 to 200.

In utter dismay, the XYZ salesman retreats, saying only that the Widget people are making "a terrible mistake." However, top management has been listening to the entire discussion and has been perfectly capable of understanding the arithmetic involved—as indeed any elementary-school child could. Overjoyed at having avoided a disaster, they offer Wilbur a raise and a promotion. However, *he* is so overjoyed that he quits his job and starts his own consulting company. . . and is bankrupt by the end of the year, for not *all* of life's problems are as simple as the one at the Widget Corporation of America.

REFERENCES

BOOKS

1 James Martin, *Design of Real-Time Computer Systems* (Englewood Cliffs, N.J.: Prentice-Hall, Inc., 1967)

2 L. Takacs, *Introduction to the Theory of Queues* (New York, N.Y.: Oxford University Press, Inc., 1962)

3 Alan Scherr, *An Analysis of Time-Shared Computer Systems* (Cambridge, Mass.: MIT Press, 1967)

4 Theodor D. Sterling and Seymour V. Pollack, *Introduction to Statistical Data Processing* (Englewood Cliffs, N.J.: Prentice-Hall, Inc., 1968)

5 Francis F. Martin, *Computer Modeling and Simulation* (New York, N.Y.: John Wiley & Sons, Inc., 1968)

6 William Feller, *An Introduction to Probability Theory and Its Applications*, Volume 1, Third Edition (New York, N.Y.: John Wiley & Sons, Inc., 1968)

7 T.L. Saaty, *Elements of Queuing Theory* (New York, N.Y.: McGraw-Hill Book Company, 1961)

PAPERS

1   J.H. Katz, *An Experimental Model of System/360*, Communications of the ACM, November, 1967, pages 694-702

2   J.H. Katz, *Simulation of a Multiprocessing Computer System*, Proceedings of the AFIPS 1966 Spring Joint Computer Conference, Volume 28 (New York, N.Y.: Spartan Books, 1966), pages 127-139

3   E.G. Coffman, *Studying Multiprogramming Systems*, Datamation, June, 1967

4   D.J. Hermann, *SCERT: A computer evaluation tool*, Datamation, February, 1967

5   N.R. Nielson, *The Simulation of Time-Sharing Systems*, Communications of the ACM, July, 1967

6   B.W. Lampson, *A Scheduling Philosophy for Multiprocessing Systems*, Communications of the ACM, May, 1968

7   D.J. Lasser, *Productivity of Multiprogrammed Computers—Progress in Developing an Analytic Prediction Method*, Communications of the ACM, December, 1969

8   J.M. McKinney, *A Survey of Analytical Time-Sharing Models*, ACM Computing Surveys, June, 1969, pages 105-116

9   E.G. Coffman, Jr., and R. C. Wood, *Interarrival Statistics for Time-Sharing Systems*, Communications of the ACM, Volume 9, Number 7 (July, 1966), pages 500-502

10   Allen Weingarten, *The Eschenbach Drum Scheme*, Communications of the ACM, Volume 9, Number 7 (July, 1966), pages 509-512

11   B. Krishnamoorthi and R. C. Wood, *Time-Shared Computer Operations with Interarrival and Service Times Exponential*, Document SP-1848, System Development Corporation, Santa Monica, California, 1964; also *Journal of ACM*, Volume 13, Number 3 (July, 1966) pages 317-338

12   E.G. Coffman and B. Krishnamoorthi, *Preliminary Analyses of Time-Shared Computer Operations*, Document SP-1719, System Development Corporation, Santa Monica, California, August, 1964

13   J.I. Schwartz, E. G. Coffman, and C. Weissman, *A General-Purpose Time-Sharing System*, Proceedings of the AFIPS Spring Joint Computer Conference, Volume 25, May, 1964 (New York, N. Y.: Spartan Books), page 397

14   G.H. Fine and P. V. McIsaac, *Simulation of a Time-Sharing System*, Document SP-1909, System Development Corporation, Santa Monica, California, December, 1964

15   N.R. Patel, *Mathematical Analysis of Computer Time-Sharing Systems*, Master's Thesis, Electrical Engineering Department, MIT, Cambridge, Massachusetts, 1965

16   John L. Smith, *An Analysis of Time-Shared Computer Systems Using Markov Models*, Proceedings of AFIPS 1966 Spring Joint Computer Conference, Volume 28 (New York, N.Y.: Spartan Books, 1966), pages 87-95

17   John L. Smith, *Multiprogramming under a Page on Demand Strategy*, Communications of the ACM, Volume 10, Number 10 (October, 1967), pages 636-646

18   G.H. Fine, C. W. Jackson, and P. V. McIsaac, *Dynamic Program Behavior under*

Paging, Proceedings of the 21st ACM National Conference, Washington, D.C., 1966, ACM Publication P-66, pages 223-228

19 Peter J. Denning, *The Working Set Model for Program Behavior,* Communications of the ACM, Volume 11, Number 5 (May, 1968), pages 323-333

20 C.V. Ramamoorthy, *The Analytic Design of a Dynamic Look-Ahead and Program Segmenting System for Multiprogrammed Computers,* Proceedings of the ACM 21st National Conference (Washington, D.C.: Thompson Book Company, 1966), pages 229-239

21 J.H. Saltzer, *Traffic Control in a Multiplexed Computer Environment,* MIT Project MAC Technical Report MAC-TR-30, MIT, Cambridge, Mass., July, 1966

22 L. Varian and E. Coffman, *An Empirical Study of the Behavior of Programs in a Paging Environment,* Proceedings of the ACM Symposium of Operating Systems Principles, Gatlinburg, Tennessee, October, 1967

23 L.A. Belady, *A Study of Replacement Algorithms for a Virtual Storage Computer,* IBM Systems Journal, Volume 5, Number 2 (1966) pages 78-101

24 D.W. Fife, *An Optimization Model for Time-Sharing,* Proceedings of the AFIPS 1966 Spring Joint Computer Conference, Volume 28 (New York, N.Y.: Spartan Books, 1966), pages 97-104

25 Kurt Fuchel and Sidney Heller, *Considerations in the Design of a Multiple Computer System with Extended Core Storage,* Communications of the ACM, Volume 11, Number 5 (May, 1968), pages 334-340

26 T.A. Humphrey, *Large Core Storage Utilization in Theory and in Practice,* Proceedings of the AFIPS 1967 Spring Joint Computer Conference, Volume 30 (Washington, D.C.: Thompson Book Company), page 719

27 M.H. MacDougall, *Simulation of an ECS-based Operating System,* Proceedings of the AFIPS 1967 Spring Joint Computer Conference, Volume 30, (Washington, D.C.: Thompson Book Company), page 735

28 Peter J. Denning, *A Statistical Model for Console Behaviour in Multiuser Computers,* Communications of the ACM, Volume 11, Number 9 (September, 1968), pages 605-612

29 Saul Stimler, *Some Criteria for Time-Sharing System Performance,* Communications of the ACM, Volume 12, Number 1 (January, 1969), pages 47-53

30 Thomas C. Lowe, *Analysis of Boolean Program Models for Time-Shared, Paged Environments,* Communications of the ACM, Volume 12, Number 4 (April, 1969), pages 199-205

31 James D. Foley, *A Markovian Model of the University of Michigan Executive System,* Communications of the ACM, Volume 10, Number 9 (September, 1967), pages 584-588

32 J.H. Katz, *Simulation of Outpatient Appointment Systems,* Communications of the ACM, Volume 12, Number 4 (April, 1969), pages 215-222

33 V.L. Wallace and D.L. Mason, *Degree of Multiprogramming in Page-on-Demand Systems,* Communications of the ACM, Volume 12, Number 6 (June, 1969), pages 305-308

34 L.A. Belady, R.A. Nelson, and G.S. Shedler, *An Anomaly in Space-Time Charac-teristics of Certain Programs Running in a Paging Machine*, Communications of the ACM, Volume 12, Number 6 (June, 1969), pages 349-353

35 B. Randell, *A Note on Storage Fragmentation and Program Segmentation*, Communications of the ACM, Volume 12, Number 7 (July, 1969), pages 365-372

36 L.W. Comeau, *A Study of the Effect of User Program Optimization in a Paging System*, ACM Symposium of Operating System Principles, Gatlinburg, Tennessee, October, 1967

37 R.A. Totschek, *An Empirical Investigation into the Behavior of the SDC Time-Sharing System*, Document SP-2191, System Development Corporation, Santa Monica, California, 1965

38 Alan Batson, Shy-Ming Ju, and David C. Wood, *Measurements of Segment Size*, Communications of the ACM, Volume 13, Number 3 (March, 1970), pages 155-159

39 Wei Chang and Donald J. Wong, *Analysis of Real-Time Multiprogramming*, Journal of the ACM, Volume 12, Number 4 (October, 1965), pages 581-588

40 Leonard Kleinrock, *Time-Sharing Systems: A Theoretical Treatment*, Journal of the ACM, Volume 14, Number 2 (April, 1967), pages 242-261

41 Jack E. Schemer, *Some Mathematical Considerations of Time-Sharing Scheduling Algorithms*, Journal of the ACM, Volume 14, Number 2 (April, 1967), pages 262-272

42 W. Chang, *A queuing model for a simple case of time-sharing*, IBM Systems Journal, Volume 5, Number 2 (1966), pages 115-125

43 D.P. Gaver, Jr., *Probability Models for Multiprogramming Computer Systems*, Journal of the ACM, Volume 14, Number 3 (July, 1967), pages 423-438

44 G.K. Manacher, *Production and Stabilization of Real-Time Task Schedules*, Journal of the ACM, Volume 14, Number 3 (July, 1967), pages 439-465

45 E.G. Coffman, Jr., *Analysis of Two Time-Sharing Algorithms Designed for Limited Swapping*, Journal of the ACM, Volume 15, Number 3 (July, 1968), pages 341-353

46 Thomas C. Lowe, *The Influence of Data Base Characteristics and Usage on Direct-Access File Organization*, Journal of the ACM, Volume 15, Number 4 (October, 1968), pages 535-548

47 Edward G. Coffman and Leonard Kleinrock, *Feedback Queueing Models for Time-Sharing Systems*, Journal of the ACM, Volume 15, Number 4 (October, 1968), pages 549-576

48 E.G. Coffman, *Stochastic Models of Multiple and Time-Shared Computer Operation*, Report Number 66-38, Department of Engineering, University of California at Los Angeles, June, 1966

49 Joseph Abate, Harvey Dubner, and Sheldon B. Weinberg, *Queueing Analysis of the IBM 2314 Disk Storage Facility*, Journal of the ACM, Volume 15, Number 4 (October, 1968), pages 577-589

50 N.R. Nielsen, *The Analysis of General-Purpose Computer Time-Sharing Systems*, Document 40-10-1, Computation Center, Stanford University, Stanford, California, 1966

51 Peter J. Denning, *Effects of Scheduling on File Memory Operations*, Proceedings of the AFIPS 1967 Spring Joint Computer Conference, Volume 30, (Washington, D.C.: Thompson Books), pages 9-21

52 P.H. Seaman, R.A. Lind, and T.L. Wilson, *An Analysis of Auxiliary Storage Activity*, IBM Systems Journal, Volume 5, 1966, pages 158-170

53 Raymond Reiter, *Scheduling Parallel Computations*, Journal of the ACM, Volume 15, Number 4 (October, 1968), pages 590-599

54 E.G. Coffman, Jr., *Analysis of a Drum Input/Output Queue Under Scheduled Operation in a Paged Computer System*, Journal of the ACM, Volume 16, Number 1 (January, 1969), pages 73-90

55 G. Estrin and L. Kleinrock, *Measures, Models and Measurements for Time-Sharing Computer Utilities*, Proceedings of the 22nd National ACM Conference, ACM Publication P-67 (Washington, D.C.: Thompson Book Company, 1967), pages 85-96

56 I. Adiri and B. Avi-Itzhak, *A Time-Sharing Queue with a Finite Number of Customers*, Journal of the ACM, Volume 16, Number 2 (April, 1969), pages 315-323

57 H. Frank, *Analysis and Optimization of Disk Storage Devices for Time-Sharing Systems*, Journal of the ACM, Volume 16, Number 4 (October, 1969), pages 602-620

58 E.G. Coffman, Jr., R.R. Muntz, and H. Trotter, *Waiting Time Distributions for Processor-Sharing Systems*, Journal of the ACM, Volume 17, Number 1 (January, 1970), pages 123-130

59 Philip J. Rasch, *A Queueing Theory Study of Round-Robin Scheduling of Time-Shared Computer Systems*, Journal of the ACM, Volume 17, Number 1 (January, 1970), pages 131-145

60 L.E. Schrage, *Some Queueing Models for a Time-Shared Facility*, Ph.D. Dissertation, Department of Industrial Engineering, Cornell University, Ithaca, New York, February, 1966

61 E.G. Coffman and R.R. Muntz, *Models of Resource Allocation Using Pure Time-Sharing Disciplines*, Proceedings of the 24th ACM National Conference, 1969, pages 217-228

62 P. Rasch, *A Queueing Theory Study of Time-Shared Computer Systems*, Doctoral Dissertation, Southern Methodist University, Dallas, Texas, August, 1967

63 E.G. Coffman, *Studying Multiprogramming Systems with the Queueing Theory*, Datamation, Volume 13, Number 6 (June, 1967), pages 47-54

64 J.D.C. Little, *A Proof of the Queueing Formula L = λW*, Operations Research, 9 (1961), pages 383-387

Chapter G

STATISTICS AND PERFORMANCE MEASUREMENT
FOR ON-LINE SYSTEMS

INTRODUCTION

One of the great difficulties with the mathematical models and computer simulations that were discussed in Chapter F is that of obtaining *good estimates* of various parameters in the system. How many people are going to be using the system? How many transactions will they type per hour? How many FORTRAN executions will be taking place in a scientific time-sharing system, and how long will they execute? How large will the application programs be, and how much overhead will there be in the operating system?

All of these questions are difficult to answer at the beginning of an on-line project, for there is often no experience from which to draw. The on-line system might be replacing a manual system, in which certain throughput requirements may be known—but as we have indicated before, these often prove inaccurate as the users become caught up in the fun and "glamor" of the on-line system. In other cases, the on-line system might have no comparable manual predecessor—such as a scientific time-sharing system.

Thus, one of the most important reasons for gathering statistics about the performance of an on-line system is to *provide feed-back* (either to a mathematical model or a computer simulation program) *for future revisions of the system.* The initial design calculations are almost always in error by 10-20%, and in certain critical areas this could prove to be the difference between a reasonable system and a totally inefficient system. It is important to realize that an on-line system is not likely to be operating at full load when it first becomes operational—and the system designer is in danger of being lulled into a sense of false security. Just because the system runs efficiently with 10 active terminals is no reason to assume that it will run well with 100 terminals. However, the statistics gathered from these first ten users may provide useful input to a simulation program, which can then tell whether the system will still function when the load has built to 100 users.

The emphasis on the *user* of the on-line system is intentional and extremely important. On most on-line systems, it is the user who is the critical factor. He supplies the input, makes the inquiries, calls for the executions of programs, and is the source of all work that is generated in the system. The user is also the largest unknown factor in most systems. We have no idea how fast he will type, how long he will stay on the terminal, what types of commands or application packages he is likely to favor, or how many errors he will make. Thus, the gathering of statistics allows us to gather a *user profile*. With more information about the users, we are in a position to correct an awkward command language, optimize heavily-used application programs, and predict future problem areas in the system.

Thus, statistics help verify that the system is indeed capable of operating in the environment for which it was intended. It can help point out critical areas in the system—disk, drum, amount of memory, and speed of the terminals—before they really become critical, and it can help us to learn more about the users who are the primary reason for building the system in the first place.

Statistics are often gathered from systems as an afterthought, after it has become apparent to the system designer that he really doesn't know what is going on inside the system. The logistics of inserting statistics-gathering codes in the operational programs is often so awkward and cumbersome that the whole idea is abandoned, or done in a very primitive fashion. It is preferable that the system designer keep statistics in mind as he designs and implements the system, so that the appropriate counters and subroutines can be inserted as the system is being built.

HARDWARE TECHNIQUES
FOR GATHERING STATISTICS

One of the techniques of performance measurement is to use hardware devices to capture information about the system as it runs. In most cases, the hardware devices are simple *counters* that increment a count whenever a specified event occurs. Some examples of useful parameters that can be measured in this fashion are:

the number of clock ticks (i.e. sixtieths of a second) during which the processor (or IO channel, or magnetic tape drive, or any other part of the system) is idle.

the number of attempts on the part of users to call the system when all of the communication lines are in use.

the number of disk transfers, disk errors, etc.

Hardware counters are available from computer manufacturers, and from a very few independent organizations; it is often fairly simple for an engineer to jury-rig a counter right at the computer installation.

One of the great advantages of hardware counters is the low amount of overhead they require. It often requires less than one microsecond to increment a counter, and this does not change the characteristics of the phenomenon being measured. This is in sharp contrast to many of the software techniques, in which a relatively large amount of overhead is required to record statistical information.

However, there are a number of areas where hardware counters do not apply. Basically, anything that goes on *inside* the computer is difficult to measure with hardware techniques. Some examples of parameters that are *difficult* to measure with counters are as follows:

the processing time required for a particular application program, especially when it is one of several hundred different application programs, and may be executed from any area of core.

the lengths of various queues in the system, such as the queue of transactions waiting to be processed by a particular application program, or the queue of requests for records to be read from the disk.

the utilization of buffer space or other memory in the machine. What percentage of available buffer space is in use at any moment? How many thousand words of storage are in use by application programs at any moment? In a virtual machine, how many pages of an application program are in core, and how many are non-resident?

Even in the areas where hardware counters are applicable, there is another weakness. Unless there is an effective technique for sampling the counters, the statistics will simply be *time averages* and will give very little information about peaks and loads. Further, there may be cases where the analyst wants to examine a functional relationship other than *time*, as illustrated in the example below:

EXAMPLE. A systems analyst is building an on-line information retrieval system, and has attempted to minimize the number of disk accesses required to process a transaction. Each transaction normally has to read two or three *directories*, or indexes, before it can locate the required record. However, the directories and records are kept in core after they have been read, and subsequent transactions attempt to avoid disk accesses by checking the directories and the records in core to see if they are the right ones.

The analyst could keep a number of such directories and records in core and devise a complex algorithm to determine which directories should be overlayed when there is no more available space [Figure G1]. However, all of this takes both time and memory, and the analyst is not really sure whether the effort is justified. He would like to implement a simple version of his algorithm and gather some statistics to see whether the number of disk accesses has really been decreased at all.

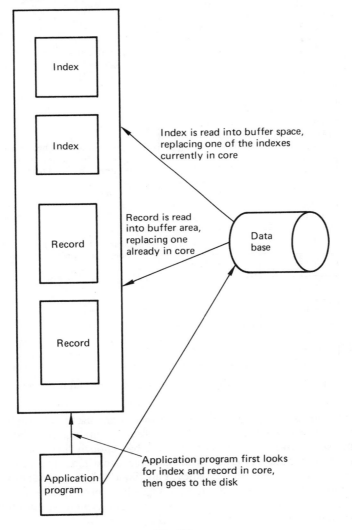

Fig. G1

His first option is to use a hardware counter that counts the number of disk accesses. Unfortunately, the counter cannot be interrogated by the application program, and nobody knows how to modify the operating system to read the counter. As a result, the analyst must rely upon the computer operator to read the counter at various times during the day. This involves opening up one of the cabinets in the disk control unit, and the operator often forgets to take his reading. A typical day's readings are shown in Figure G2.

Time	Disk count	
8:00 AM	0	
8:15	574	
8:30	—	← Operator took a coffee break
8:45	2,612	
9:00	3,597	
9:15	—	
9:30	—	← Operator did not have time to read the counter because a large number of users got on the system
9:45	14,206	
10:00	20,002	
10:15	26,773	
10:30	—	← System failed here. Computer operator restarted the machine
10:45	7,658	
11:00	16,215	
11:15	24,802	
11:30	33,436	

Fig. G2   Sample input form filled in by computer operator

Unfortunately, this does not give the analyst any useful information at all. What he really wants to know is the relationship between the number of disk accesses and the number of transactions processed. It is bad enough that the statistics gathered by the computer are very crude—what is worse is that *time*, as a variable, should not have found its way into the statistics at all. Even if the computer operator had read the counter once a second, the results might have been misleading simply because not many transactions were being processed! The type of relationship that would be meaningful to the analyst is illustrated by Figure G3c.

There are *some* hardware techniques that allow the system designer to gather statistics as a *distribution*, and this is far preferable to the simple counters. If the hardware device can measure the time between events as well as the event itself, and collect these "inter-arrival" statistics as a rough distribution, the resulting statistics will be tremendously more useful. However, even this type of hardware would not have helped the analyst in our example, unless it was combined with other hardware counters.

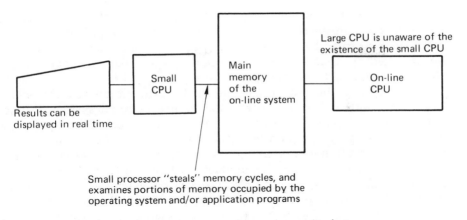

Fig. G3a   Hardware-software performance monitoring

HARDWARE-SOFTWARE TECHNIQUES

Another approach to performance measurement is to use a dedicated computer or "intelligent" hardware box to gather information about the on-line system. This idea has been discussed by Saltzer and Gintell [9]; they describe the use of a small PDP-8 computer to monitor the performance of the large GE-645 Multics system. The basic idea, as shown in Figure G3a, is to allow the small processor to have direct access to the memory of the main on-line system; it thus has the ability to examine queues, tables, buffers, counters, and any other interesting aspect of the operating system and/or the application programs.

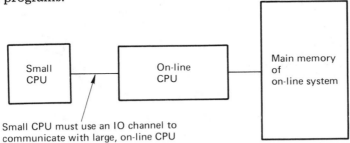

Fig. G3b   A poor configuration for hardware-software performance monitoring

The great advantage of this approach is that it does not represent a significant amount of overhead in the system. While the small processor may steal cycles from the large on-line processor, the on-line system is basically unaware of the existence of the statistics-gathering machine. At the same time, a programmable (or microprogrammable) statistics-gathering computer gives the system designer a flexibility he does not have with a primitive hardware counter. A variety of programs can be written for the small machine, and the statistics can be displayed in real time on a CRT, or recorded on a magnetic tape for later analysis. The performance measurement programs can be changed at will in the small machine, and could even be arranged so that the system designer could decide dynamically which statistics he wanted to gather and observe.

A number of business organizations lack the money and the engineering talent to build the type of performance measurement system described by Saltzer and Gintell. However, the same concept could be applied to any multiprocessing system in which there were a number of small processors able to access the memory of the other processors on the system. Thus, this approach would be ideal for a machine like the CDC-6600, with its ten peripheral processors; it could also be used on machines like the Burroughs B6500. If the trend towards small microprogrammable processors continues, it should be relatively easy for the system designer of the 1970's to build this kind of performance measurement into his system.

Note that we would not want to use this technique on a hardware configuration of the type shown in Figure G3b, since the small processor does not have direct access to the memory of the larger machine. In order to monitor the performance of the large machine, the small machine would have to send it a message, requesting information about the contents of specified tables, queues, buffers, etc. The overhead associated with these messages might easily distort the statistics being gathered by the small machine. Thus, we probably would not want to use this approach on configurations like the GE-635—Datanet-30 time-sharing system.

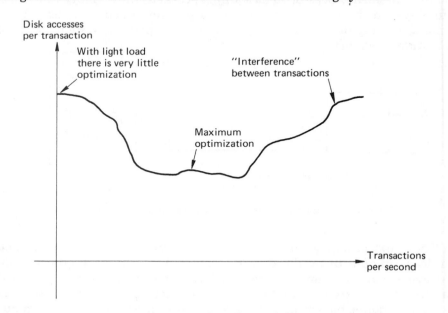

Fig. G3c Useful statistics for disk optimization

SOFTWARE COUNTERS

One of the more common techniques for gathering statistics is to allow the various programs—operating system *and* application programs—to gather their own statistics, and output the results whenever they want to. It is usually implied that the programs perform their own data reduction, i.e. calculate their own averages, distributions, and standard deviations. This is a common approach on many time-sharing systems, where one finds that the statistics are printed on the console typewriter at regular intervals.

The advantage of the software counters is that it allows the system to measure things that simply cannot be measured with hardware "black boxes." Thus, we can use software counters to keep track of the number of entries in a queue, the number of terminals on the system, the number of disk accesses per hour, and so forth.

However, there are a number of disadvantages to the software counter approach. First, there is often a maintenance problem, since the counters and data reduction subroutines are imbedded in the operational routines. If the system designer decides to calculate a new average, he must reassemble or recompile his entire operational program, and introduce the new version into his system—a practice frowned upon by operations managers and quality control people. There may also be a maintenance problem because of the programming language involved: if the application programs are written in COBOL or SNOBOL, it may be inconvenient to build in mathematical data reduction subroutines.

However, the major disadvantage of this technique is that it yields basically the same type of information as the hardware counters: *time averages*. The statistics may show that an average of 43 users were on the system during the day, but often do not show peaks and loads. It is possible to structure the counters in such a way that a *distribution* can be shown, but this involves more space and more processing time.

For example, we could keep *two* software counters to keep track of core allocation; one counter could be used to keep track of the *average* number of free core blocks, and another counter could keep track of the *minimum* number of available core blocks. Similarly, we could keep a number of software counters to record the size of application programs: the first counter would be incremented every time the operating system started up an application program between 0-4000 words long; the second counter would keep track of programs between 4000-8000 words, etc.

SOFTWARE "SAMPLING" PROGRAMS

Another technique is to have the operating system and the application programs gather the statistics in the form of counters, but have a separate program (preferably an independent application program) sample the counters. The sampling program can perform any desired data reduction, and can output the results in any desirable format. This approach is illustrated in Figure G4.

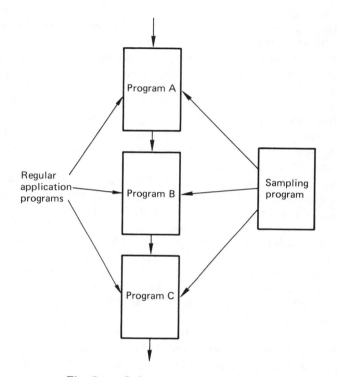

Fig. G4   Software sampling approach

One of the advantages of the sampling approach is that maintenance is much simpler. The data reduction and analysis can be done in one program, and often in a higher-level language that is suited to such work. Thus, the sampling program might be written in FORTRAN, and the application program might be written in COBOL—or the sampling program might gather statistics from an operating system written in assembly language. In either case, it is far simpler to perform the statistical calculations in FORTRAN, and it is convenient to be able to change the FORTRAN program without affecting the rest of the application programs or the operating system.

However, the sampling approach often suffers from the same weakness that we have already described—only crude time averages are calculated by the sampling program. This is because the sampling program is often only executed every hour or so—or whenever the system designer feels like gathering some statistics. If the sampling program can be made to run every second or so, the results will be much more valuable.

In addition, the sampling approach often exhibits a weakness akin to the

Heisenberg uncertainty principle in physics. Simply stated, the Heisenberg principle says that by attempting to measure a phenomenon, one changes the very nature of the phenomenon. This is especially true if the sampling program is large and time-consuming. For example, a scientific time-sharing system had a sampling program that was called into core every 15 minutes to gather statistics and print reports. One of the statistics that was to be gathered was the utilization of core memory—but the sampling program was so large that it took up all of the core memory! Thus, it reported that memory was being completely utilized by itself. The same type of problem occurs if the sampling program requires a significant amount of processor time to perform its calculations.

THE "EVENT STREAM" APPROACH

Still another software technique is the "event stream" approach. Here we gather statistics in much the same way that a simulation program gathers information about the characteristics of a computer system—by recording the occurrence of each and every interesting event that occurs. An "interesting event" can be defined as broadly or as specifically as required. For example, an event might be any one of the following:

a transaction enters a queue to be processed

processing is completed on a transaction

a user logs on to the system

a user signs off and disconnects his terminal

ten words of core are allocated from a dynamic buffer pool to provide a queue entry in which to place a new transaction for processing

a record is read from disk

a record is placed in a queue, eventually to be written to disk

an application program is moved from one scheduling queue to another during execution of the scheduling algorithm in the operating system

It is interesting to note that many batch operating systems currently in existence gather information in this manner. The information so recorded is called a *log*, and it contains separate entries or records for each beginning of a job, for each job termination, for each file opening and file closing. It can also be seen that this is basically the technique followed by the simulation programs—each statement in the simulation language describes something entering a queue, leaving a queue, grabbing a resource, and so forth.

The event stream approach can be fairly simple to implement, especially in an application program where there are relatively few "events" to keep track of. One simply identifies the events that are interesting, and inserts in the application program a subroutine call to a statistics-recording subroutine. The subroutine records the nature of the event and the time at which it occurred on magnetic tape, disk, or cards—and it then returns to the application program. In this way, sufficient information is gathered to plot peaks and loads, since no data are lost. It is also possible, with the event stream approach, to plot various parameters *as a function of each other*, rather than as a function of time.

It is important to realize that the statistics are recorded off-line, and are not lost. Thus, the raw data can be analyzed and reduced off-line, perhaps even on a different machine. One of the more interesting examples of this was a CRT display of the movement of user programs on scheduling queues in the Project MAC time-sharing system at MIT. The same technique can be used to plot graphs, histograms, bar charts, or any other representation of the data. Also, the data can be saved for later analysis. To prove some hypothesis, the system designer may decide to plot the number of users on the system as a function of the Dow-Jones average—and he can do this by retrieving previous statistical data and re-analyzing it.

Unfortunately, there is a tremendous amount of overhead involved in actually recording each event. As we have pointed out, the analysis need not be done on-line, but the data themselves must be recorded on-line, and in real-time. This may require several disk accesses, magnetic tape operations, or other forms of IO—and we have the danger of slowing down the system to keep up with the statistics. The best way of avoiding this problem is by *blocking* several statistical records into one physical record on tape or disk, and use double or triple buffers. However, this may use up an excessive amount of core, and if events occur rapidly, the IO device may be simply incapable of keeping up with the statistical data.

THE TYPES OF STATISTICS
THAT SHOULD BE GATHERED

Basically, all of the parameters which are input to a simulation package are candidates for being measured by one or more of the techniques we have discussed above. This may involve arrival rates of various forms of input to the system; lengths of various queues; service rates for various application programs; and priority disciplines employed both in the operating system and the application programs.

However, there are some types of statistics that are of general usefulness in *any* on-line system. Perhaps the most important type of statistic is the one that describes the *utilization of the system's resources*. The most important resource, in many cases, is the central processor, but such things as disks, drums, tape drives, and IO channels should also be thought of as resources.

Basically, what we want here is a set of statistics that tells us how each of the resources spent its time while the system was in operation. There are four categories of interest:

1   *Idle time*

This is obviously time during which no services are being requested of the system. It includes the periods of time when the system is operational but no users are at their terminals; it also includes the times when users are at their terminals but simply not doing anything; and also the times when the users and the application programs are making use of *other* resources. Thus, there may be long periods of time during which the application programs are using *only* the central processor and the disks—during the period the magnetic tape drives, the high-speed printer, and all of the other resources of the system are obviously idle.

It is desirable to be able to gather these kinds of "idle time" statistics as distributions. That is, it is useful to know that the central processor was idle for 10% of the day; it is *more* useful, though, to know that the idle time consisted of two long idle periods of 30 minutes duration each, and 423 idle periods of 4 milliseconds duration each. The same is obviously true of all the other resources of the system.

2   *Operating system overhead time*

We are also interested in recording the time spent by the operating system. The resource used most heavily by the operating system tends to be the central processor itself; we are interested in keeping track of how much CPU time is spent actually *computing* in the operating system—i.e. scheduling, allocating memory, handling interrupts, and all of the other mysterious things that operating systems are wont to do. It is often difficult to measure this time accurately, as we described in Chapter C, because it occurs in such short bursts. Much of the operating system overhead is associated with the processing of IO interrupts, each of which may require only a few milliseconds of CPU time. Many computers have real-time clocks that "tick" once every sixtieth of a second—or 16 2/3 milliseconds. Thus, it is possible for the operating system to receive an IO interrupt, do its processing, and return to the application program *between* clock ticks—and the entire sixtieth of a second will be charged to the application program. Obviously, one is better off with a millisecond clock.

The same type of statistics should also be kept for the other resources of the system. Thus, we should keep track of the amount of time during which the magnetic tape drives, the IO channels and the disks are used by the operating system for "overhead" activities—reading and writing library programs, "swapping," keeping accounting information, and so forth.

3   *Productive time*

The system designer should gather statistics that record the periods of time during which the resources of the system were used productively. In the case of the central processor, this is the time spent processing in the application programs, otherwise known as "user time" or "useful processing." For those designing operating systems, it is usually sufficient to classify this simply as "application program time"; for those writing application programs, it is probably desirable to have a finer breakdown of this category of CPU time.

Thus, there should be statistics describing each application program, and perhaps individual subroutines within each program.

The same kind of statistics should also be kept for the other resources of the system. The system designer will want to know how frequently the IO channels, the disks, drums, and magnetic tape drives are used. In some cases, it may be desirable to keep track of only those periods of time during which an IO device is in use; in other cases, the application programmer may be able to "reserve" a device like a magnetic tape drive, and it would be useful to keep track of the periods of time during which the device has been "reserved."

4   *Time waiting for other resources to become available*

There are a number of situations in which there is a demand for several resources, some of which may not be immediately available. As a result, some of the available resources may be idle until such time as the other resources are free. As one example, consider a scientific time-sharing system in which a high-speed drum is used as a "swapping" device. There are many cases when the processor is available, but cannot be used because all of the executable programs are currently on the drum; the processor must sit idle until the application programs have been brought into the machine.

Another common example is the combination of disks and processor time. There are many situations where the application programs are placed in a "wait" condition until some disk IO has completed. In an optimum situation, the operating system would always be able to find at least one application program to process while the rest were waiting for the completion of their disk IO; in many real-life situations, though, the operating system cannot find anything else to do, and must let the processor remain unused until the disk IO has completed.

Another example has to do with the allocation of IO devices. An application program may, during its execution, require six magnetic tape drives. If only three are available, the operating system will suspend the operation of the program until three more tape drives become available. In the meantime, there are three idle tape drives.

This is obviously an area where the system designer wants complete and accurate statistics; it is also an area that requires intelligent interpretation by the system designer. The amount of time that a resource is idle while waiting for another resource to be freed is, to some extent, a function of *multiprogramming* on the system; thus, the statistics are basically useless without additional information telling how many jobs and/or users were on the system. For example, if there is only one application program running on the machine, there will be no opportunity for overlapping of disk IO and computation time; thus, whenever the application program calls for disk IO, the processor will be idle.

USER STATISTICS

One of the most important areas of statistics is that of *user-oriented* statistics—i.e. the ones that give us some idea of what the average user on the system is doing. Depending on the type of system, these statistics may be gathered by the operating system or the application programs. Typically, a scientific time-sharing system will gather these statistics in the operating system, while the business-oriented systems gather them in the application programs (for reasons that will become evident in Part III of this book).

Some of the more common types of user statistics are the following:

1   *Number of active terminals on the system*

This is the most common barometer of the load on the system. In a scientific time-sharing system, this statistic is kept by the operating system, since each application program can interact with only one terminal, and since it has no knowledge of any other application programs in the system. However, in a business-oriented system, it is common for one application program to be able to control many terminals—and as a result, the application program keeps its own statistics (occasionally duplicating those kept by the operating system).

There are many cases when it is interesting to record other statistics as a function of the number of terminals on the system. For example, the system designer might want to draw a graph of the operating system overhead as a function of the number of terminals on the system; similarly, it would be interesting to plot, as a function of the number of terminals on the system, the percentage of time that the CPU was forced to be idle while waiting for swapping or disk IO.

This is one of the types of statistics that can be kept much more accurately with the "event stream" approach than with simple counters, though both techniques are easy to implement. With the event stream approach, we merely record the time of day whenever a terminal connects or disconnects from the system. This not only provides an instantaneous picture of the number of terminals on the system, but also tells how long each terminal remains connected to the system.

2   *Terminal connect time for users*

This is also a common statistic for many types of on-line systems. As we discussed in Chapter F, it is an important one, too, for it helps determine how large a community of users will be able to use the system. If a user stays on his terminal for only five or ten minutes, then each terminal, or "port," should be able to support several people. Conversely, if each user stays on his terminal for several hours, a much larger number of terminals will be required.

3   *Processing time per interaction*

As we saw in Chapter F, the number of terminals that the system can support at any one time is a function of the processing time required for each of the user's interactions with the system. In a business-oriented on-line system, it is common to call each interaction with a system a *transaction*, even though it may occasionally require more than one line of input. On a scientific time-sharing system, it is common to call each line of input an *interaction*—it may be a request for a compilation, or a command to an editing program, or input to one of his own programs.

Once again, it is important to gather this type of statistic as a distribution, and not just as an average. Many of the mathematical models assume that the *service rate* (i.e. the time required to process an interaction) is exponentially distributed, and it behooves the system designer to verify that the assumption is true. For the throughput formula

$$n = \frac{t}{p} + 1$$

it is sufficient to use *average* processing time.

For the application programmer, this statistic can be the most important of all of his statistics, since it relates to the efficiency of his application program. He probably cannot control the rate at which users type their transactions, or the length of time they stay on their terminal. However, he *can* control his application program to some extent, and if he sees that certain types of input require a large amount of processing time, he can either attempt to improve the program, or discourage users from using it (by charging more money for its use, or by giving it a lower priority in the scheduling queues, etc.).

4   *Average typing time per interaction*

This statistic is what Scherr calls "think time" [3] —the total time required for type-in, type-out, and thinking. Actually, this represents the length of time *between* interactions, and it is an important part of the mathematical models of time-sharing systems. In the simple throughput formula

$$n = \frac{t}{p} + 1$$

it is sufficient to use the *average* think time, for we are interested only in the average arrival rate of new transactions. However, for calculations of the lengths of various queues, it is necessary to have much better information. The statistics can be kept by recording the time of day when each transaction arrives in the system.

5   *Response time, or wait time for users at their terminals*

In Chapter A, we defined response time as the length of time for the system to respond to input—i.e. the time from the last character of input until the first character of type-out. The response time includes operating system overhead, CPU time in the application programs, time spent waiting for disk accesses, time while the input was in a queue waiting to be processed, and so forth. For the application programmer, it is usually sufficient to record the time of day when a message is sent to the terminal—even though the operating system may delay actually sending the message.

6   *Size of the application programs*

In an on-line system where there are more application programs than can fit into core, it is important to keep track of the utilization of available memory. One of the ways to do this is to record the *size* of the various application programs that are running. In fact, some systems measure the mathematical product of *memory* and *CPU time*, feeling that this gives a more accurate measure of the load that the program places on the system. Large, slow programs are penalized, and small, fast programs are given special preference.

7   *Number of application programs in core*

For the system designer who is building his own operating system, it is important to keep statistics on the number of application programs (or jobs, or user programs) that can be kept in core. This is not only a measure of the throughput of the system, but is also a measure of its ability to multiprogram efficiently. That is, one would expect "drum time not overlapped by computation" and "disk time not overlapped by computation" to decrease as the number of jobs increases. However, operating system overhead and file access times (or to be more specific, the length of time a request for a disk read remains in a queue) can be expected to increase as the number of jobs increase.

INPUT/OUTPUT STATISTICS

A number of statistics should be maintained for the IO devices on the on-line system. We list here only the statistics for three of the more common devices for on-line systems—disk, drum, and terminals.

DISK STATISTICS

As we have noted several times, the disk can be one of the crucial bottlenecks in an on-line system. It is important to gather statistics on the manner in which application programs use the disk. Some of the more important of these statistics are the following:

1   *Number of logical record accesses per transaction*

We are interested in knowing how many reads and writes to the disk are required for each transaction that is processed. For a large number of business-oriented on-line systems, this comprises the major part of the processing time for a transaction. It is important to note that we are only talking about *logical* record accesses—the number of *physical*, or *actual*, disk accesses may be higher or lower, depending on the file organization.

2   *Number of physical disk accesses per logical record access*

It is important to know how much overhead is involved in a particular type of file organization. A "hash-code" technique may turn out to be bad because the keys are not randomly distributed; a directory-structured file may be inefficient, even though it is convenient and flexible. A measure of just how inefficient a file organization is can be made by keeping track of the actual *physical* accesses that are required for each logical access.

This area can be somewhat confusing, for a number of reasons. On some on-line systems, the operating system imposes its own file organization on the application programs. Thus, even when the application program knows exactly which record it wants to read, the operating system may go through several layers of directories to find the specified record. On other systems, logical records may be blocked in such a way that one physical disk access can bring several logical records into core, and this may or may not be done with the knowledge and cooperation of the application programs.

However, there are usually *some* areas in which the application programmer knows that he must invoke a *search* (binary search, hash-code search, etc.) or a *look-up procedure* (directory structure) to access particular logical records. In those cases, it is important for him to keep track of the physical accesses, so that he can tell whether his access technique should be changed.

3   *Number of updates per transaction*

On systems where the data base is updated in real time, it is often important to know how many records are updated, and how many are simply read. The primary reason for keeping track of this information on a business-oriented on-line system is that the data base must be protected. An *audit trail* is normally maintained while the system runs, and each record that is updated on the data base is also written to the audit trail.

4   *Number of bytes, or characters, per record*

On a number of systems, data base records may vary in length. For reasons of buffering, core allocation, and scheduling of disk requests, it is important to know how large the records are.

5   *Disk errors (both recoverable and non-recoverable)*

This statistic is not really needed for optimization or simulation of the system, but it is useful for maintenance and diagnostic purposes. In many cases, catastrophic disk errors (such as a head crash) can be predicted on the basis of the "recoverable" errors. In any event, the maintenance engineer should be kept aware of the status of the disk.

DRUM STATISTICS

Many on-line systems have a high-speed drum for swapping programs and part of the operating system. If the application programs are allowed to read and write records on the drum, it is desirable to keep the same type of statistics as the ones we have specified for the disk. However, the drum is normally only used by the operating system, and the statistics we keep are slightly different:

1   *Drum reads per second and drum writes per second*

Here we are basically interested in the activity of the drum. As the load on the system builds up, the operating system can be expected to do more swapping, for reasons that are often not completely clear. Thus, the system designer may want to investigate the number of drum accesses as a function of the number of users on the system, the number of transactions being processed, the number of application programs in core, or the phase of the moon.

Once again, we see that simple counters do not give us an accurate picture of the drum activity. Ideally, we would like to follow the "event stream" approach and record the time of day when each and every drum read or write was made. However, there are often such a large number of drum operations on a heavily-loaded on-line system, especially on a scientific time-sharing system, that it is difficult to implement the event stream approach.

It is important to separate the drum reads from the drum writes, for this allows us to see the effect of re-entrant and overlayable programs. A drum write implies that the program has changed itself while in memory, and must be written to the drum before the memory can be used for other purposes.

2   *Drum errors (both recoverable and non-recoverable)*

3   *Number of drum "blocks" or "pages" per application program*

This statistic is essentially the same as an earlier user statistic on the size of application programs. However, there may be some differences due to dynamic allocation of core storage: a program may be swapped in from the drum, allocated a large amount of working core storage, and released before being swapped out again.

4   *Total number of drum operations required for a swap*

This is probably the most important drum statistic, since it includes the reads *and* writes required to swap an application program into core. Combined with statistics on the average CPU time per transaction, and the average number of application programs in core, it gives the system designer a feeling for the operating system's ability to multiprogram effectively.

TERMINAL STATISTICS

The most important statistics involving terminals have already been described under "user statistics." However, for buffering and core allocation purposes, it is useful to keep the following special statistics:

1   *Number of input characters per transaction*

2   *Number of output characters per transaction*

3   *Number of terminal errors*

REFERENCES

1   Tad Pinkerton, *Performance Monitoring in a Time-Sharing System*, Communications of the ACM, Volume 12, Number 11 (November, 1969), page 608

2   Edward Yourdon, *The Art of Measuring a Time-Sharing System*, Datamation, April, 1969

3   Alan Scherr, *An Analysis of Time-Shared Computer Systems* (Cambridge, Mass.: MIT Press, 1967)

4   N.R. Nielson, *The Simulation of Time-Sharing Systems*, Communications of the ACM, July, 1967

5   T.A. Humphrey, *Large Core Storage Utilization in Theory and in Practice*, Proceedings of the AFIPS 1967 Spring Joint Computer Conference Volume 30 (Washington, D.C.: Thompson Book Company, 1967)

6   Saul Stimler, *Some Criteria for Time-Sharing System Performance*, Communications of the ACM, Volume 12, Number 1 (January, 1969) pages 47-53

7   Alan Batson, Shy-Ming Ju, and David D. Wood, *Measurements of Segment Size*, Communications of the ACM, Volume 13, Number 3 (March, 1970), pages 155-159

8   G. Estrin and L. Kleinrock, *Measures, Models and Measurements for Time-Sharing Computer Utilities*, Proceedings of the 22nd National ACM Conference, ACM Publication P-67 (Washington, D.C.: Thompson Book Company, 1967), pages 85-96

9   Jerome H. Saltzer and John W. Gintell, *The Instrumentation of Multics*, Communications of the ACM, Volume 13, Number 8 (August 1970), pages 495-500

10   Henry C. Lucas, Jr., *Performance Evaluation and Monitoring*, ACM Computing Surveys, Volume 3, Number 3 (September, 1971) pages 79-92

APPLICATION PROGRAMS
FOR ON-LINE SYSTEMS

Chapter H

CONCEPTS AND PHILOSOPHIES OF WRITING
APPLICATION PROGRAMS
FOR AN ON-LINE COMPUTER SYSTEM

INTRODUCTION

In this section, we begin discussing the many aspects of writing *application programs* for on-line computer systems. However, this is not an easy job, for the design of the application programs is largely determined by the type of system being built. Application programs for a scientific time-sharing system are vastly different from the application programs for on-line airline reservation systems or on-line management information systems.

The design of the application programs is also influenced very greatly by the type of operating system that is provided with the computer. One very dramatic example of this is the fact that some operating systems allow an application program to communicate with only *one* terminal, while others allow access to many terminals. The environment in which the application programs operate is almost completely determined by the operating system, and, as we shall see, this has a great influence on the *design* of the application programs.

Our purpose in this section of the book is to illustrate the basic structure of on-line systems and their application programs. In this chapter, we will introduce some terms and concepts with which the application programmer should be familiar as he writes his programs—concepts that make his job much different than it was on a batch computer system. In the following chapters, we will discuss the nature of application programs for scientific time-sharing systems, and for on-line business-oriented systems. Finally, we will discuss command languages and programming languages for on-line systems.

Definition of Terms

Our first task is to define some of the terms that we will be using in our discussion of application programs. This was much easier in Chapter A, where we were simply discussing *general* terms concerning on-line systems. Here we are forced to define terms for which each computer manufacturer has his own definition. However, the *concepts* that we describe here should be generally applicable to any on-line system.

THE CONCEPT OF A JOB

It is perhaps easier to describe the notion of a job by viewing it in terms of earlier batch systems. In this context, a job could be defined as a *collection of programs, data, and control information* sufficient to describe the sequence and nature of processing to take place. Thus, on second-generation batch computers, one often heard the term "job stream" to describe a sequence of jobs which were *processed to completion*, usually in a sequential manner.

This notion of processing to completion is an important one, and one that was natural for batch computer systems. A programmer would submit a FORTRAN compilation which would require ten minutes of computer time, and would then finish; another programmer might submit a job consisting of a COBOL compilation, followed by execution of the compiled COBOL program. At the completion of the job, the computer operator would record the elapsed time of the job from which accounting charges could later be made. In more recent computer systems, the operating system records the processing time, IO time and elapsed time of each job, and an accounting program can then allocate charges to the job.

In an on-line environment, the notion of a "job" takes on different meanings. It is still useful to think of a job as an *accounting entity*—i.e. the smallest unit of work in the system which can be accounted for by the computer operator or the operating system. However, it is no longer true that a job begins, executes, and finishes within any reasonable period of time. On most scientific time-sharing systems, a job begins when a user logs onto the system, and does not terminate until he logs off the system. On dedicated on-line systems, one or two jobs may be running in the machine as long as the system is operational.

Perhaps another way of thinking of the difference between a batch *job* and an on-line *job* is that a batch job has a fairly well-specified sequence of activities to be performed. There is a compilation to be performed, a program to be executed, and so forth. While the precise nature of the steps that the application program takes may be unknown to the programmer at the time of execution, he is at least aware of the general nature of the program. In an on-line computer system, though, the sequence of activities is usually much less well-specified, and is often random in nature. Processing is based on the nature of input that arrives from terminals—input that usually cannot be predicted in advance. Thus, we note that an on-line job may still be defined as a collection of programs, data, and control information; *however, the data, and perhaps even some of the control information, are not necessarily available when the program begins execution.*

For the application programmer, it is important to note that another characteristic of the *job* is its independence from all other jobs that may be running in the system. This is usually true of batch systems as well as on-line systems, and evolved from a desire on the part of operation systems specialists to make the application programmer totally unaware of the existence of other jobs. As a result, jobs cannot share magnetic tape drives, core memory, or any other resources—with the exception of random access files, where the sharing can become a major problem.

On the more elementary on-line systems, only one job may be running at any one time. On multiprogramming on-line systems and multiprogramming batch systems, a number of jobs may run concurrently. Similarly, a multiprocessing system may allow several jobs to run *simultaneously*. Some systems allow a *fixed* number of jobs to run concurrently, while others allow a variable number—as many as can be packed into the machine.

To summarize, a job is the smallest independent unit of work in a system that the operating system keeps track of for accounting purposes. In an on-line system, jobs tend to run for a long time and perform random, unpredictable processing based on input received from terminals. While most computer vendors agree on this basic notion of a job, some give it different names. On the IBM System/360, for example, there is a notion of a job, but the area in which the job executes in the computer is called a *partition*. On the Control Data 6600, to cite another example, our notion of a job is called a *control point*.

THE NOTION OF A TASK

The astute reader may have wondered why we did not define a job as the smallest unit of work that can allocate resources in the system. This would seem to be a more complete definition, since most jobs do allocate resources (such as memory, processor time, IO devices, and access to random access files), use them, and then get charged for them.

The reason is that, on some computer systems, a job can be broken into several smaller pieces, *each* of which can allocate its own resources. We shall call this small piece of a job a *task: the smallest piece of work within a system that can allocate resources.* It is important to note that a job may consist of several tasks, as shown in Figure H1. Each task may be processing concurrently (or simultaneously in a multiprocessing system) with other tasks in the same job, and with other tasks in other jobs.

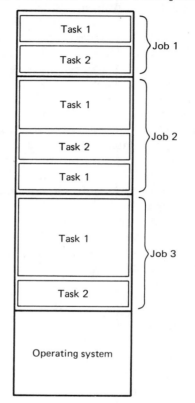

Fig. H1 A job may consist of several tasks

The mechanics of executing several tasks within the same job differ from system to system, ranging from the very complex and sophisticated to the very simple cases where a job can consist of only one task. A task may cause another task to start processing by making the equivalent of a *subroutine call*, as shown in Figure H2. More sophisticated systems allow the application programmer to invoke the *parallel execution* of a task (i.e. concurrent or simultaneous, depending on whether the system multiprograms or multi-processes), in the manner shown by Figure H3. On some systems, it is difficult to invoke parallel tasks in a higher level language; on other systems, independent jobs can take on some of the characteristics of *multitasking*.

Perhaps the most important difference between a task and a job is that tasks are not necessarily independent. Tasks are usually subprograms or subroutines that can share working storage, files, and IO devices. Also, while the operating system may allocate resources independently for each task, it does not usually provide separate accounting for each task—that is done only for jobs.

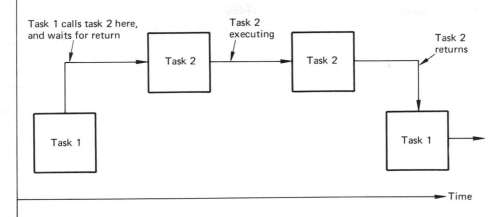

Fig. H2 Task linkage without parallel execution

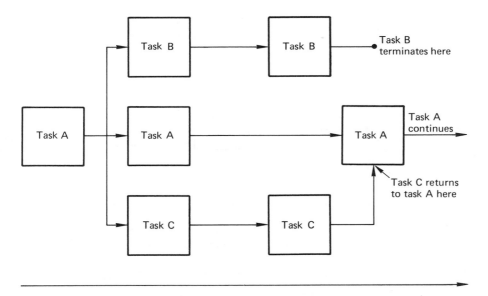

Fig. H3 Task linkage with parallel execution

PAGING, VIRTUAL MEMORY, AND SEGMENTATION

In Chapter C, we discussed paging hardware as a desirable feature to have on one's computer. Most of the details of this hardware are discussed in Chapter C, and are usually not of any concern to the programmer. However, the application programmer should be aware of the *effect* that this paging hardware (whatever its form) may have on his program.

To simplify matters, let us assume that the application programmer writes his program in a one-for-one assembly language, as shown in Figure H4. With the aid of various forms of hardware registers, the operating system is able to chop the application program into "pages," each of which may be dealt with separately. The size of a page may vary from machine to machine, as shown in Table H1, and the total amount of memory which the application programmer may use also varies tremendously. However, the important point here is that the application programmer is not *aware* of the fact that his program is being chopped up into pages.

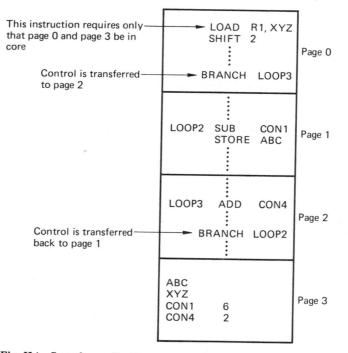

Fig. H4 Sample application program in a paging environment

TABLE H1 *Paging Characteristics of Some Common Third Generation Computers*

Computer	Size of pages	Amount of memory for application programs	Maximum actual memory on machine
SDS-940	2048 words	16,384 words	65,536 words
PDP-10	Variable (2 relocation registers)	131,072 words	262,144 words
GE-485	512 words	32,768 words	131,072 words
GE-645	64 words and 1024 words	16,777,216 words	262,144 words

TABLE H1 *cont.*

Computer	Size of pages	Amount of memory for application programs	Maximum actual memory on machine
Sigma 7	512 words	131,072 words	131,072 words
Burroughs B5500	Variable	Unlimited	32,768 words
Burroughs B6500	Variable	Unlimited	2,000,000 words
IBM 360/67	4096 bytes	16,777,216 bytes (may be made smaller at the whim of the system designer)	16,777,216 bytes

In order to write efficient application programs, it is important to be aware of the type of activities carried on by the operating system, even though the paging mechanisms work without the explicit knowledge of the programmer. The major use of paging is to reduce the number of pages of a program that are actually in the machine, as shown by Figure H5. If the

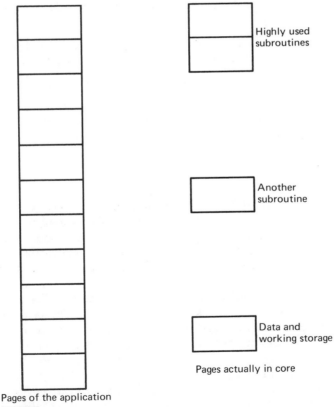

Highly used subroutines

Another subroutine

Data and working storage

Pages actually in core

Pages of the application program

Fig. H5 Paging helps reduce the amount of code that is actually in core application program attempts to reference a part of the program or data that is not currently in core, the operating system intervenes and brings the page in from disk or drum. As a result, an application program may be much larger than the actual amount of memory on the machine—but only that part which is needed at any moment is in core.

However, in order to implement this mechanism, the operating system must have a double-sided algorithm (which is discussed at much greater length in Part V). It must first decide when to bring pages *into* the machine, and once the available memory has been filled up, it must decide when to throw pages *out of* the machine. A number of *page-in* strategies have been discussed and attempted by systems analysts, and it is now generally agreed that the best approach is the *page-on-demand* strategy. Thus, the operating system makes no attempt to *predict* pages that will be required by the application programmers, and simply waits until the application program actually references or *demands* a page before bringing it into the machine.

The *page-throwing* strategies are much more diverse, and there is no general agreement on a "best" algorithm. Some of the more common ones are:

> a page could be removed when the application program decides that it is no longer needed.

> an attempt could be made to remove the page least likely to be needed in the near future—i.e. from the job currently lowest in the scheduling queue.

> the least recently referenced page (i.e. the one referenced longest ago) could be removed first.

> a first-in/first-out strategy could be employed, on the theory that the application program will probably proceed in a straight-line fashion.

> pages could be thrown out when the application program has completely finished its processing.

Almost all of these algorithms have been attempted, with varying degrees of success. The area continues to be one of debate among operating systems specialists, because a faulty algorithm leads to a phenomenon appropriately called "thrashing." Thrashing occurs when the operating system keeps removing pages from an application program just before the application program needs the page.

In most cases, the application programmer has no effective control over the paging activities carried on by the operating system. However, an application program that jumps from page to page in a more or less random fashion will almost always suffer at the hands of the operating system. The page throwing strategies are most efficient when the application program spends most of its time executing in what Denning calls a "working set" of pages—i.e. a few pages in which the highly active subroutines and data reside. Occasionally, the application programmer does have the ability to inform the operating system of the pages which he intends to use, in which case the operating system can be expected to make much more intelligent page-throwing decisions.

Computers with paging hardware are, at the current time, most commonly used for scientific time-sharing systems, and there has been a tremendous amount of research in this area (see, for example, the references at the end of Chapter F, many of which are concerned with paging). However, some of the non-paging machines encounter some of the same problems when they allow the application programs to be broken into *segments*, each of which can be overlayed or swapped. Typically, the tasks that we described above can be controlled in much the same way that pages are controlled in a scientific time-sharing system. However, the control is often carried out by the application programs, with the operating system only playing a subservient role. That is, one of the tasks in the application programmer's job decides which of the other tasks are to be called into core, which ones are to be overlayed, and so forth.

Obviously, there is some difference between this form of segmentation and the paging that we have described. However, the basic principle is the same—only that part of a program which is actually needed is kept in core. If the application program employs this type of segmentation, it must have the double-sided algorithm that is present in time-sharing operating systems: that is, the controlling application task must decide when other tasks should be brought *in*, and when other tasks should be thrown *out*. Hence, it may well behoove the application programmer to read some of the literature on paging, even though it may be oriented towards a different type of processing.

MACROS

There is one last term which we need to define—one to describe the call made from an application program to the operating system. We will call this a *macro*, simply because it seems to be a commonly used term on many systems. This is not to be confused with an *assembly language* macro, with which one assembly language statement is expanded into several machine instructions. The "operating system call" macro is sometimes referred to by one of the names shown in Table H2.

TABLE H2 *Some Common Synonyms for "Macro"*

Machine	Name for "Macro"	Meaning
SDS-940	POP,SYSPOP	Programmed operator
GE-635	MME	Master mode entry
GE-435	GEN	General instruction
PDP-10	UUO	Unused operation code
IBM-360	SVC	Supervisor call

An application program issues a macro whenever it requires some form of service from the operating system. The most common type of call is for input or output—from disk, drum, printer, magnetic tapes, or any other device to which the application program may have access. There are a number of other types of calls that will be described later in this chapter.

Macros have existed ever since there was an operating system, and the only thing unique about macros for on-line systems is that there are more of them. In addition to input and output macros, the application programs can call the operating system to allocate core, to initiate parallel tasks, to type messages on the console typewriter, or to find out how much time has been used in the processing of a transaction.

GOALS AND OBJECTIVE FOR
ON-LINE APPLICATION PROGRAMS

Actually, the concepts that we have discussed above—jobs, tasks, parallel tasks, paging and segmentation, and macros—all exist in most current third generation batch computer systems. Thus, it is likely that the application programmer who has written batch FORTRAN or COBOL programs under multiprogramming operating systems is already familiar with some of these concepts. Thus, the question becomes: what is different about on-line systems? What changes should be made to the application programs in order to make them run more efficiently? What different types of philosophies should be employed?

To answer these questions, it is necessary to remember the truly *random, unpredictable* nature of most on-line systems. Application programs are often larger than the available memory, so the required subroutines are brought into core as they are required. Accesses to the data base cannot be planned in advance, so the files are organized for random access. With all of this, there is likely to be a large amount of overhead—in terms of extra processing in the operating system to control all of the randomness; extra swapping because nobody knows which application programs will be required in core at which time; and extra file accesses because directories must be searched in order to find a required record.

Because of all of the overhead and all of the randomness, it is *extremely* important for the application programmer to worry about the efficiency of his program. No longer can the application programmer write a mammoth COBOL program on the theory that "if it works, that's good enough." No longer can the application programmer write a FORTRAN program with a 100x100 array without worrying about the efficiency of his program. There are four cardinal rules that the application programmer must keep in mind:

programs must be written in a modular fashion

there must be a good overlap of IO and computation

file accesses must be minimized

Yourdon's Paradox must be observed

MODULAR PROGRAMMING

A modular computer program is one in which any logical part of the program can be modified or replaced without affecting the rest of the program. Modularity is probably one of the most important concepts in the programming field, and has long been espoused as one of the primary means of increasing the efficiency, flexibility, and maintainability of a program.

How does one go about writing a modular program? More important, how does one write a modular application program for an on-line computer system? To put it very simply, everyone has an intuitive feeling for modular programs, but nobody has been able to describe, in clear, concise terms, the techniques and approaches that will guarantee a modular program. There *is* some work being done in this area,† and it is hoped that we will eventually see a definitive work on the theory and practice of modular programming— especially as it pertains to on-line and real-time computer systems.

In the meantime, we can only use those guidelines that we have learned on batch computer systems. These guidelines include the following suggestions:

1   *Break the application into small subroutines*

If the on-line application is written as one large, straight-line piece of code, it will certainly not be modular. It will be difficult to debug, difficult to modify, and, very possibly, difficult to fit into core.

Thus, the application should be broken into small, distinct subroutines. In a business-oriented on-line application, each type of transaction should be processed by a separate subroutine, or group of subroutines; in a scientific application, an analagous breakdown is possible. The IO portion of the application should generally be kept in separate subroutines from the computational part of the application.

2   *Parameterize the application*

It is common for the novice programmer to assume that his program will never have to be changed or modified; thus, he incorporates all of the parameters of the application in his program as *constants*. When the inevitable modification to the program is eventually requested, he must laboriously change all of the constants, and perhaps restructure his program entirely.

Obviously, the programmer should define as many aspects of the application as possible as *symbolic parameters*. For an on-line application, some of the things that might be parameterized include:

---

†Larry Constantine, ed., *Concepts in Program Design* (Cambridge, Mass.: Information and Systems Press, 1967)

the size of buffers and data base records

the number of buffers for an IO device

the length of tables and queues

the number of terminals that can be handled by the program

field and bit positions within a buffer or record (COBOL is good at this)

the length of the longest allowable message from a terminal

the ASCII or BCD codes used as delimiters in an input message

the amount of working storage used by the program

In short, any aspect of the program that is referenced or used more than once should be defined as a symbolic parameter.

3 *Avoid programs which modify themselves*

The following kind of programming trick has been a favorite of many novice programmers:

```
LOAD      ABC       ; PICK UP AN INSTRUCTION
ADD       XYZ       ; MODIFY THE ADDRESS FIELD
STORE     * + 1     ; STORE IT INTO THE NEXT LOCATION
**                  ; THIS LOCATION IS MODIFIED
```

There are times when it is convenient to write a program that modifies itself as it runs; there are times when it might actually save a few locations or speed the program up by a few microseconds; the reader may even argue that there are cases when this practice is absolutely necessary.

There can be no doubt, though, that such a program is *not* modular. It is extremely difficult for someone other than the original programmer to understand what the program is doing, and it will probably be rather difficult for the original programmer to debug this kind of program. Even worse, this dubious programming practice destroys whatever chance the program ever had of being reentrant. Thus, it cannot be shared concurrently by other users, and the operating system will have to engage in more IO in order to swap or overlay the program.

4 *Do not share temporary storage among application subroutines*

In many programming projects, it is common to share temporary storage locations. Thus, we might have subroutines A,B,C,D, and E all sharing locations TEMP1 and TEMP2.

This practice normally works as long as the subroutines do not conflict with one another from a logical point of view. That is, subroutines A and B can both use location TEMP1 as long as A does not call B, and B does not call A. On real-time systems, though, it often is necessary to make sure that subroutines A and B do not interfere with one another from an *interrupt* point of view. If subroutine A begins executing and gets interrupted by subroutine B (perhaps because of the devious scheduling algorithms in the operating system), then it is possible that temporary storage location TEMP1 might be destroyed.

In situations like this, it is usually far better to reserve dedicated temporary storage locations for each subroutine. This is a very natural thing to do with languages like ALGOL and PL/I, and also on machines that make pushdown lists easy to implement. Even on a simple minicomputer, though, it is far better to set aside a few dedicated temporary storage locations for each subroutine. Even though some subroutines may be able to safely share temporary storage when the program is first written, there very likely will be trouble later on when the program is changed. Subroutines that were once independent of one another will suddenly begin to conflict in subtle and unrepeatable ways, and will begin to destroy temporary storage locations.

5   *Decision tables, truth tables, and a "state"-oriented approach*

Many business-oriented applications involve a number of complicated logical conditions. For example, consider the following specification of a typical order-processing system:

> **EXAMPLE.** If a customer has placed an order which is less than the minimum shipping quantity, then the order should be rejected and sent to the shipping department manager. However, the computer system should be capable of receiving "exceptions" to this rule, as there will be cases when a customer will insist that his order be shipped, even though it is too small. If the customer's order exceeds his credit limit, then the order should be rejected and sent to the manager of the credit department. However, the order should always be accepted if this one of our special customers—i.e. one who does business with us regularly, and whose credit has been assured.

The average programmer will attack this problem in a variety of ways, the most common of which is to draw a flowchart directly from the specification above. The problem is that the resulting program probably will be rather awkward to deal with. If the customer decides to change his specification (as is almost inevitable), the program will essentially have to be redesigned and rewritten. Also, it is not clear whether the program covers all possible combinations of input; i.e. what happens if an order is received that exceeds the credit limit *and* is too small for shipment?

A better way of attacking this type of problem is to construct a *decision table,* or *truth table.* In the above problem, for example, we can see that there are four possible input conditions:

1   The dollar order amount of the order exceeds the credit limit.

2   This is a customer for whom special approval has been given by the credit department.

3   The size of the order is less than the minimum allowed by the shipping department.

4   The shipping department has approved this order for shipment.

Similarly, we see that there are three possible actions that the program can take:

1   The order can be rejected and sent to the credit department.

2   The order can be rejected and sent to the shipping department.

3   The order can be processed normally.

A decision table, or truth table, can be built to show all combinations of input and output. In this example, there are 2^4 = 16 different combinations of input, and for each of those combinations there should be only one allowable action taken by the program. From a modularity point of view, this approach is good because the programmer can easily arrange his program so that all input combinations leading to action #1 are grouped together, all input conditions leading to action #2 are grouped together, etc.

This kind of approach is extremely useful for *on-line* applications. As we suggested above, the application programmer now has to worry about *real-time* situations, as well as ordinary logical situations. Thus, a decision-table approach might help the programmer enumerate all of the possible real-time situations in his program. This concept is illustrated in Chapter J, which is devoted to an extensive discussion of a state-oriented approach to a typical on-line business-oriented application.

If all of the application programs can be kept in core during execution, then all of these guidelines for modularity are important, but no more important than they are in a batch computer system. However, if the application programs are not all in core—either due to paging or segmentation—then modularity is essential. In fact, it is so essential that it is not sufficient to merely break the application program down into well-defined subroutines. An on-line system could easily be strangled by an application program consisting of one thousand subroutines, three or four of which must be brought into core in order to perform any useful amount of work. Thus, in addition to the type of modularity we have described above, it may also be necessary for the application program to be "modular" in its use of core.

Denning's concept of a "working set"[†] is valid for *any* type of on-line system, even though it was developed with scientific time-sharing systems in mind. What it implies is that the application programmer—either through the grace of the operating system or by his own design—must see to it that enough subroutines, modules, or tasks are in core at any one time that a "useful" amount of work can be done. Our measure of "useful" may vary from system to system: in a business-oriented on-line system, it would be nice to have enough application modules in core to process a transaction completely; in a scientific time-sharing system, there is an analogous intuitive feeling for a "working set."

[†]Peter J. Denning, *The Working Set Model for Program Behaviour*, Communications of the ACM, Volume 11, Number 5 (May, 1968), pages 323-333

Much of the effort of keeping a working set of the application modules in core is properly in the domain of the operating system. However, it is the application programmer's responsibility to see that logically associated modules are in close proximity in his program. This proximity often takes different forms in scientific time-sharing systems and business-oriented on-line systems, as illustrated in the two examples below:

EXAMPLE 1 Application programs for an on-line management information system are structured as shown in Figure H6. Input transactions are received by

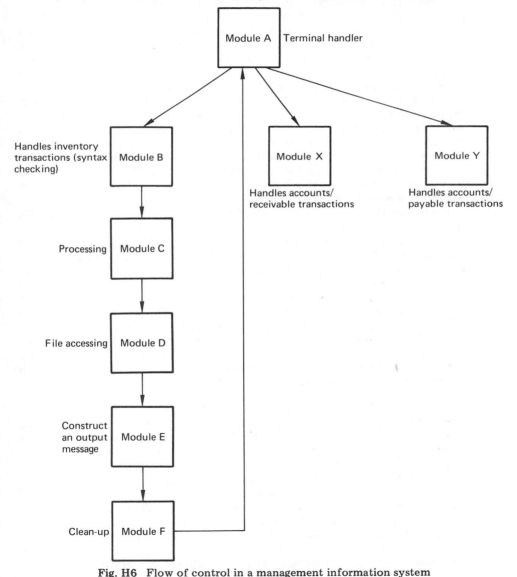

Fig. H6 Flow of control in a management information system

Module A, which decodes the transaction and passes it to the appropriate processing transactions. Thus, inventory transactions are sent to Module B, accounts receivable transactions are sent to Module X, and accounts payable transactions are sent to Module Y.

However, once Module B receives control, it may call upon several other modules. Module B only checks for syntax errors; the transaction is then passed on to Module C for actual processing. Module C always calls Module D to perform file accesses and Module E to construct a reply to be sent back to the terminal. Finally, Module F does any necessary clean-up work, and returns control to Module A.

This type of modularity is commendable, and one assumes that the division of modules was really a division of labor—i.e. one programmer wrote Module A, another wrote Module B, and so forth. However, this commendable modularity becomes very inefficient if it turns out that Modules B, C, D, and E are non-resident. In such a case, each inventory transaction would require at least four disk accesses (or drum accesses) to bring the four inventory modules into core. They would quite likely be overlayed as soon as an accounts receivable transaction was received.

There are two approaches that can be taken to remedy this problem, but both approaches assume that there is enough room in core for all four modules, an assumption which may not be valid. First, the application programmer could arrange for the four inventory modules to be brought into core at the same time. This could be done by placing the modules on neighboring tracks of the disk or the drum, and requesting the operating system to bring them all in with one physical access. This approach has the advantage that each module could also be brought in separately, if desired, for the exceptional cases.

A second approach is to combine all of the modules into one larger module. That is, instead of having four separate inventory modules, they could all be compiled together (or assembled together, or loaded together, depending on the machine), so that they were all part of one logical program. This approach is much more likely to save disk or drum accesses, and often reduces the subroutine-calling overhead. However, there is the danger that modules may be brought into core when they are not really needed. For instance, it may turn out that 30% of the inventory transactions do not require any file accesses (because of syntax errors in the transaction, or because the required information is in core already). Thus, module D is only needed 70% of the time, and there is obviously a need to establish a trade-off between bringing Module D in all of the time, and bringing it in only when required. This is certainly an area where the statistics that were discussed in Chapter G can be of tremendous value.

EXAMPLE 2 A programmer is writing an application program on a scientific time-sharing system that has hardware paging. He has been told that "the operating system will take care of everything," and that his only job is to subroutinize his program as heavily as possible. His application turns out to be similar to that described in Example 1 above: subroutine A reads input from the terminal, and passes it to subroutines B, X, or Y depending on the nature of the input. Assuming that subroutine B receives control, it eventually calls subroutines C, D, and E. The only problem is that the subroutines are scattered through the programmer's virtual memory space in such a random fashion, as we see in Figure H7. Suppose, for example, that each subroutine is only about 100 words long, and that the page size is 512 words. As a result of the programmer's placement of his subroutines, each subroutine call results in a reference to a different page, and probably results in a disk access by the operating system. Even worse is the fact that the "working set" in this case is five subroutines, or some 500 words of memory. However, in order to get those 500 words into the machine, the operating system is forced to read five *pages*, or 2560 words, into core memory.

The problem can only be solved if the programmer is aware of the *size* of his

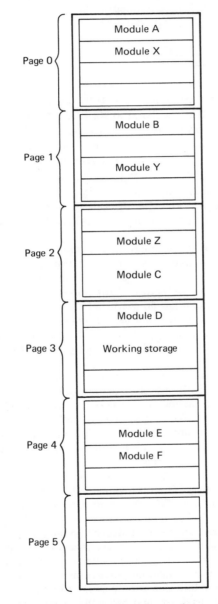

Fig. H7 Modular programming in a paging environment

virtual pages, and only if he makes a concerted effort to arrange his memory in such a way as to make effective use of the pages. This is often a very difficult point to impress upon users of scientific time-sharing systems, where the emphasis is often on ease and convenience of programming, rather than on efficiency and throughput. It can also be a difficult goal to achieve if the application program is written in a higher level language; there is no guarantee that the compiler will arrange the subroutines in an efficient manner.

EFFECTIVE OVERLAP OF
IO AND COMPUTATION

Almost all on-line systems have multiprogramming operating systems, and the efficiency of the resulting system is often largely influenced by the extent to which the application programs are able to make use of this concept of multiprogramming. Here again, we often have operating systems specialists telling the application programmer not to worry about such esoteric things—"the operating system will take care of it." However, the *extent* of multiprogramming is usually a function of the application program's ability to provide the operating system with a sufficient mix of computation and IO. The two examples below demonstrate this point:

EXAMPLE 3 A systems analyst is responsible for designing an inventory control system of the nature described in Example 1. As we indicated before, the system consists of several modules, each of which may or may not receive control—depending on the nature of the input. The analyst has decided to place all of these modules in one job, in the belief that it may occasionally be desirable to run a background job—such as a payroll job or a batch scientific FORTRAN job. However, the analyst has also decided to make all of the application modules part of the same *task*—even though the operating system allows multiple tasks within the same job.

Since there are rarely any background jobs running on the machine, the system ends up doing very little multiprogramming. When Module A calls the operating system to read a transaction from one of the terminals, the entire job is placed in a "wait" state until the operating system has gathered some input. Whenever Module D decides to read a record from disk, the job must again be placed in a "wait" state by the operating system until the record actually arrives in the machine. While the job is in a wait state, *nothing else can take place.* Since the programmer has indicated that the modules are all part of the same task, the operating system cannot assume that they can be scheduled independently.

The reader may complain that this example is unrealistic. On a number of common 3rd generation systems, there *are* background jobs that can receive control whenever the on-line job is waiting for IO. In fact, the on-line job may be only one of a number of jobs running on a large, general-purpose computing system.

Nevertheless, it remains true that whenever the on-line application program is forced into an IO wait condition, it loses control of the central processor. Whether the processor remains idle or works on a background job is irrelevant to the *users* of the on-line system. The fact that the CPU remains fully utilized by working on background jobs is of interest to the system designer, but the only thing that is of interest to the terminal users is their response time. Every time the on-line application program gives up control of the CPU to a background job, the response time of the terminal users suffers.

Whether this is important depends, to a large extent, on the number of users on the system. If there are only five or ten terminals on the system, and if the users are not too vocal in their complaints, then it may not matter whether the on-line application effectively multiprograms or not. On the other hand, if there are 200 terminals on the system, then it matters a great deal what the application program does. Every second that the on-line application program relinquishes control is another second that 200 users have to wait.

It is not always necessary for the on-line application programmer to use *multitasking* capabilities in order to achieve a good overlap between IO and computation. On some computer systems, the application program may be allowed to call the operating system for IO, *and then continue executing.* Thus, while the operating system is actually performing the IO, the application program can continue processing.

To get back to our example, the efficiency and throughput of the system would be increased greatly if the analyst arranged his modules as shown in Figure H8. Task 1 simply consists of Module A, which is solely concerned with gathering input from terminals. Task 2 consists of Modules B, C, D, and E—all of the inventory modules. Task 3 consists of Module X and any other accounts receivable modules; task 4 consists of Module Y and any other accounts payable modules.

Let us see what the effect of this new arrangement is. Whenever Task 1 calls the operating system for more input from a terminal, it must be placed in a "wait" condition by the operating system. However, the operating system can then turn control over to task 2, which can start processing an inventory transaction. Within task 2, it is possible that Module D might receive control, and call the operating system to read a disk record. The operating system would then place task 2 in a wait state, and give control to task 3—or perhaps back to task 1, in the event that a transaction has arrived from a terminal.

It should be pointed out that this arrangement is not always easy to implement. A large number of systems do not allow multiple tasks within the same job, and even if they do, some of the higher level languages may not be able to take advantage of it. On the IBM System/360, for example, PL/I is the only language (other than assembly language) that allows the use of multiple tasks in the same partition. On some types of computer systems, it is feasible to put different functions in different *jobs*—that is, Module A could be in Job 1, while Modules B, C, D, and E could be in Job 2. As we noted earlier in this chapter, the only difficulty is that of communicating between the jobs, and sharing IO devices. We shall have much more to say on the implementation of this type of idea in Chapter J.

EXAMPLE 4 A programmer has decided to build a simple sales order entry system to run on a scientific time-sharing system. As we shall see in Chapter I, two of the more important characteristics of time-sharing systems are the fact that each job can interact with only one terminal, and the fact that it is not usually possible to have multiple tasks within a job.

As a result, the programmer has written his program in a manner shown by Figure H9. A salesman using this system must type several lines of input to specify all of the parameters of a sale—the customer's name and address, the item that was sold, the quantity sold, and so forth. Basically, the program asks for each piece of information, and once it has been typed in by the salesman, any necessary processing (i.e. credit-checking, inventory checking, and so forth) is performed before the next question is typed out.

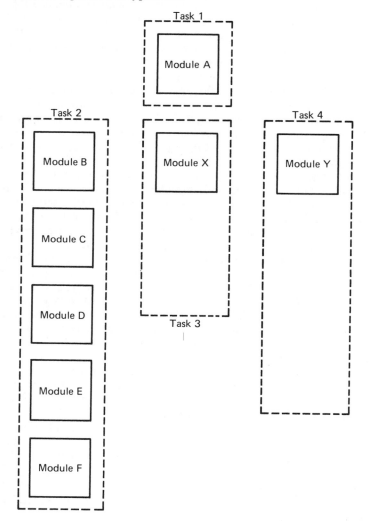

Fig. H8 Effective multiprogramming for application programs

The problem with this approach is that the operating system cannot keep up with such *interactiveness.* When the application program asks the salesman to type, for example, the customer's name, the operating system must then put the program into a "wait state" until the input is complete. Since it is likely to be 30-60 seconds before the input arrives, the application program is likely to be swapped out of core by the operating system. When the salesman finally does type his input, the operating system must swap the program back into core, then wait for the job to reach the top of the scheduling queues before resuming the processing. However, the processing will probably consist of only a very few milliseconds of computation, and one or two disk accesses—then the program will ask the salesman for another line of input. This will go on until the salesman has finally typed all of his input, and the overhead will probably be tremendous. Moreover, the operating system has a difficult time trying to cope with this poor overlap of IO and computation.

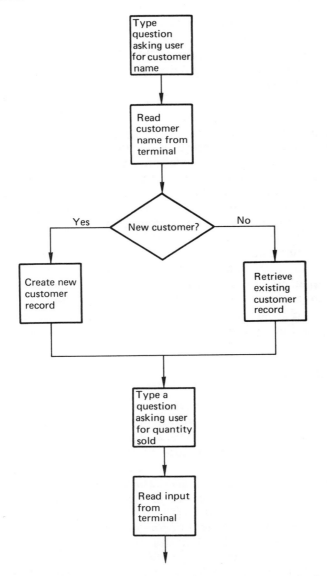

Fig. H9 Partial flowchart for a sales order entry system on a scientific-engineering time sharing system

Although it is often difficult to accomplish on a time-sharing system, a much better approach is to somehow get *all* of the input from the salesman before doing any significant processing. Once the salesman has provided all of the necessary parameters concerning the sale, the application program can perform all of its processing at once. There is less chance of being interrupted by the operating system, and much less chance of being swapped out once the processing has started.

MINIMIZE DISK ACCESSES

As we have pointed out repeatedly, the number of people using an on-line system can be severely limited by the number of disk accesses required for each line of input or each transaction. It is very common for a transaction in a business-oriented on-line system to require 10-20 disk accesses, and the system designer must always be on the lookout for extraneous and unneeded accesses.

Actually, the number of disk accesses per transaction is usually more a function of the data base organization, and the application programmer often does not have much to say about that area of the system. However, the application programmer should try to use his influence to see that all of the data required to process one transaction are contained in one record—or at least in neighboring records, so that "seek" time can be minimized. It is extremely important that the system designer ensure that two different application modules do not reread the same record during processing of a transaction. This often happens when the two modules are written by different people, neither of whom knew that the other fellow intended to read the same record; occasionally, this also happens when the two programmers decide that it is too bothersome to pass data between modules, and that it is simpler to have each module read the record itself.

YOURDON'S PARADOX

Many of the comments we have made above imply that the application programmer should have a good working knowledge of the hardware and the operating system. It is difficult, for example, to write an effectively modular program without knowing the nature of the hardware paging scheme, and the nature of the operating system's overlay and swapping facilities. Multiprogramming is not easy to accomplish without a solid understanding of multitasking features that may or may not be available in the operating system.

Unfortunately, some application programmers try to carry this too far. They are aware, for example, that the scheduling algorithm in a scientific time-sharing system tends to favor the short jobs, so they write their programs in such a way that an IO operation is performed after every quarter of a second of processing. Similarly, an application programmer on a paging machine may have some idea of the algorithm used by the operating system to remove pages, so he may decide to alter the nature of his program to reflect his understanding of the operating system's page-throwing algorithm.

Unfortunately, these tactics often make matters worse. The application programmer attempting to outsmart the operating system's scheduling algorithm is probably not aware of *all* of the parameters that go into the scheduling algorithm. Similarly, if he attempts to outwit the page-throwing algorithm, he may very well find that his application runs more poorly on a paging machine.

All of these contradictory thoughts lead us to *Yourdon's Paradox:*

The more you try to outsmart the operating system, the more it will outsmart you.

In simple terms, we are saying that the application programmer should attempt to minimize his interactions with the operating system, but he should not attempt to outsmart it. Every call to the operating system involves some overhead—either in terms of tables and pointers that must be set up within the operating system, or extra disk accesses and drum swaps. Thus, it behooves the application programmer to ensure somehow that his subroutines are all in core and that they execute with minimum interference from the operating system. On the other hand, the application programmer should not build his application program around the false hopes of a particular scheduling algorithm or core allocation algorithm within the operating system. Two examples from current third generation systems illustrate this point:

EXAMPLE 5 Using the operating system provided with the IBM System/360, OS, it is possible to cause multiple tasks to execute within the same job. There are a number of macros that can help the programmer achieve this multi-tasking capability. The system designer building the inventory control system that we described in Example 1 could also use the ATTACH and DELETE macros, as shown in Figure H10. However, this would involve a tremendous amount of interaction with the operating system, since each inventory transaction entering the system would require a complex table (called a Task Control Block) to be initialized within the operating system before control could pass to Modules B, C, D, and E.

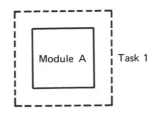

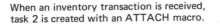

When an inventory transaction is received,
task 2 is created with an ATTACH macro.

Fig. H10a Management information system on the IBM System/360 with the ATTACH and DELETE macros

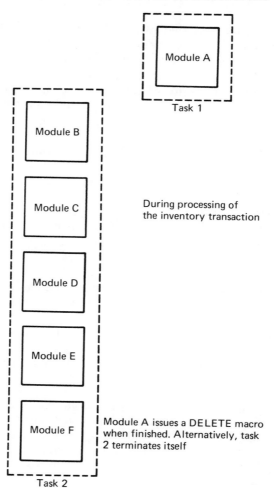

During processing of
the inventory transaction

Module A issues a DELETE macro
when finished. Alternatively, task
2 terminates itself

Fig. H10b Management information system on the IBM System/360
with ATTACH and DELETE macros

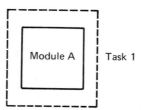

Task 1

After the inventory transaction has been processed,
task 2 has completely disappeared from the system.

Fig. H10c Management information system on the IBM System/360
with the ATTACH and DELETE macros

Alternatively, the system designer could use the WAIT and POST macros to accomplish the same function, with much less interference from the operating system. With this scheme, shown in Figure H11, we would need a common "working storage" area that both Task 1 and Task 2 could share. Task 2 could use a WAIT macro to suspend its operation until Task 1 (which receives input from terminals) turned on a bit to indicate that some input was ready to be processed. Task 2 could be made aware of this by having Task 1 issue a POST macro, which

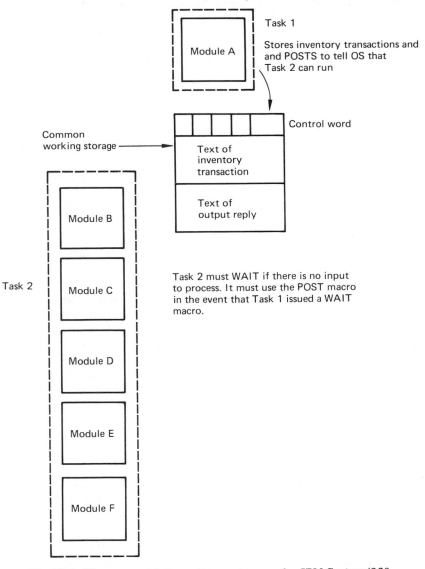

Fig. H11 Management information system on the **IBM System**/360 with the WAIT and POST macros

would tell the operating system that Task 2's wait condition had been satisfied. This decreases the interaction from the operating system considerably, for it eliminates the constant loading, "creating," and "destroying" of tasks. We will discuss this idea at much greater length in Chapter J.

EXAMPLE 6 On the Burroughs B5500 computer system, a large number of application programs are written in the ALGOL language. The machine operates with virtual memory, and the operating system, known as the MCP, is capable of overlaying any BEGIN-END block in the application program. This often results in elaborate schemes on the part of application programmers who, thinking they understand the inner mysteries of the MCP, attempt to build their application programs with segments of an "optimum size." The most common scheme seems to be that of writing a number of very small segments, in the hopes that the MCP will keep the right ones in core as they are needed. However, there are probably only a handful of people in the entire country who know how the MCP's core allocation strategies work, and one really has no way of knowing whether these attempts made by application programmers improve the efficiency of the system as a whole. In fact, a recent study at the University of Virginia[†] shows that most of the ALGOL segments on the B5500 (i.e. the BEGIN-END blocks) are less than 40 words in length, and that there is a great deal of memory fragmentation as a result.

Some Tools for Application Programs

Thus far, we have introduced some of the concepts involved in application programs, and have pointed out some of the major goals that the application programmer should try to keep in mind. We now investigate some of the common mechanisms that the application programmer has at his disposal. One such mechanism is what IBM calls a *job control language*, otherwise known as *control cards*. It is interesting to note that control cards are not usually present in a scientific time-sharing system; they seem to have evolved from the systems that were originally strictly batch systems. The major items that an application programmer can control with these cards, which are submitted to the system at execution time, are:

1   File declarations

2   Core memory estimates

3   Scheduling priority assignments

Depending on the particular system, there may be a number of other cards: assignment of peripheral devices such as magnetic tapes; limits on the amount of CPU time or IO time the job may use; and a specification of actions to be taken in the event that the job terminates abnormally.

The file declaration cards may specify such things as blocking and buffering parameters; access techniques (serial, random, etc.); *save* factors;

[†] Alan Batson, Shy-Ming Ju, and David C. Wood, *Measurements of Segment Size*, Communications of the ACM, Volume 13, Number 3 (March, 1970), pages 155-159

and label equations (i.e. equating a file *label* in the program with an external file name supplied in the control card at execution time). These functions are usually fairly straightforward, albeit tedious to encode on the control card. The application programmer should already know the nature of his file organization and his buffering and blocking requirements—and these are not likely to change dynamically within his program. Thus, while we will have more to say about such things as file organization in Part IV, there is not much to say about file declaration control cards.

However, the control cards that specify core memory and scheduling priority affect the application program itself, and should be used with care. In many cases, these control cards are related to the *job*, rather than to individual tasks within a job. Thus, if the programmer specifies too much core, other jobs in the system may not be able to run efficiently; if he specifies too little, there may be an excessive amount of overlaying and swapping. Similarly, scheduling priority assignments can cause havoc if the programmer does not choose them with care. The situation can become even more complicated if the programmer can include separate control cards with each task within a job.

There are no iron rules that we can give in this area; common sense usually dictates a particular core assignment and scheduling priority. However, there are some common practices which seem to give reasonably good results for most on-line systems of this sort, which the reader is invited to investigate for himself:

1   In an environment where there are background jobs as well as foreground on-line jobs, make sure that the core assignment and scheduling priority assignment clearly favor the latter. Otherwise, the background job, which is usually a very large, processor-bound job, will dominate the machine.

2   If there is any confusion as to how much core should be assigned for a job, try to figure out its maximum requirement—and don't forget such items as buffers and working storage areas. If this causes trouble, *then* an attempt can be made to cut down on the core assignment.

3   The job (or the task within the job) that handles the terminals on the system should have the highest priority. This is important because there will often be peak periods when many transactions arrive in the machine during a short period of time. The teleprocessing job should be able to queue up all of the transactions for eventual processing, and perhaps give the user some kind of response or acknowledgement—so that at least the illusion of quick response may be maintained.

4   If there are many other tasks or jobs that perform the processing of transactions, it is usually best to assign them all the same priority. If necessary, some jobs or tasks might be assigned a higher priority than others, but it is not usually worth the effort to have a very fine gradation of priorities.

Another form of control that may be exerted over an application program comes from the computer operator. On many on-line systems, the operator can dynamically change the priority of jobs, the maximum time allotment, or even the amount of memory assigned to the job. This is usually a fairly reasonable approach on multiprogramming batch systems, since the mix of jobs changes from hour to hour, and the computer operator can be counted on to make a fairly intelligent decision.

It is usually very *undesirable* to allow the computer operator to change priorities or core assignments on an on-line system, unless one has a tremendous amount of confidence in the operator. While it is rare that such activities on the part of the operator actually cause the system to fail, it can drastically alter the throughput of the on-line system, and the response at the terminal. As a result, anywhere from twenty to two hundred users may suddenly find that it takes five minutes to get an intelligent response from their terminals, and *their* response is often both visceral and violent. The application programmer, together with the system designer and the operations manager, should decide on the operating characteristics of the on-line portion of the system, and the computer operator should be instructed to ask for permission before changing the environment of the system.

COMMON MACROS FOR ON-LINE
APPLICATION PROGRAMS

Macros form a large part of the environment in which the programmer writes application programs to run on any system. Consequently, it is important for the programmer to be aware of the various macros that are available on his particular system—although this information can only be obtained by reading rather thick and uninteresting manuals. While every operating system has its own peculiar set of macros, they usually fall into about four distinct categories:

1   *Input/output macros*

There are usually two basic macros for performing input and output on all of the peripheral devices. On the Burroughs B5500, the two macros (actually statements in the ALGOL, FORTRAN, or COBOL languages) are READ and WRITE. On the IBM System/360, the two basic macros are GET and PUT, while on the Digital Equipment Corporation PDP-10, the names .IN and .OUT are used.

The effect of the macro is usually to read a logical record from the specified IO device into the designated memory area, or to write the record from memory to the IO device. Specific information about blocking, buffering, record address (for random access devices), and error conditions may be either:

assumed by the system.

specified in a control card submitted by the programmer at execution time.

specified by the program in a separate IO macro.

specified as part of the READ/WRITE macro.

There are often a large variety of subsidiary IO macros for opening and closing files, rewinding or back-spacing tapes, skipping to top of form on the printer, and so forth.

2   *Memory allocation macros*

These macros are often available only to the assembly language programmer—in the higher-level languages, memory allocation is done by the compiler at compile time, and there is no dynamic allocation of memory at execution time. If such macros are available, there are usually only two: GETMEM and RELMEM, whose purposes are to allocate and release a specified amount of memory.

The GETMEM and RELMEM macros are used on some systems to allocate space for actual programs, but in most cases, the application program issues a GETMEM to allocate working storage space. If there is a convention within the system for allocation of *fixed-size* blocks of core, the overhead incurred in the operating system is usually fairly slight. If, on the other hand, the macro can be used to allocate a variable amount of core, the application programmer should expect a considerable amount of overhead every time he invokes the macro. Some of the techniques for allocation of core are discussed in Part V of this book.

3   *The various forms of the WAIT macro*

On many on-line systems, the application program is automatically suspended as soon as it issues a READ or a WRITE macro, and it is not restarted until the specified IO has finished. However, the application programmer occasionally has the option of starting the IO transfer and continuing the execution of his program. When he decides that he cannot proceed any further, he issues the WAIT macro to tell the operating system to suspend the program.

There are other cases when the application programmer may want to suspend his program temporarily. In an on-line system where there are several concurrently executing tasks or jobs, it may be desirable to make one of those jobs wait for all of the tasks to "catch up," as is illustrated in Figure H12. Also, as we saw in Example 3 above, there are times when different jobs might want to pass control back and forth—and the WAIT macro is very useful in this respect.

There are occasionally some interesting variations to the basic WAIT macro. On the IBM System/360, for example, the POST macro allows a task to inform the operating system that one (of possibly many) conditions for which another task was waiting has now been satisfied. In the Extended ALGOL language on the Burroughs B5500, the DELAY statement allows a program to wait for a specified condition (i.e. until certain masked bits in a specified word have been set to one), and allows the program to *time out* if the condition has not been satisfied within a specified period of time.

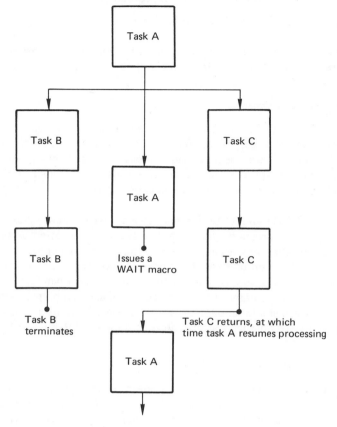

Fig. H12 Use of the WAIT in a multitasking environment

4   *Task linkage macros*

If the on-line system allows individual modules or tasks to be called into the machine, a number of macros are required. If only overlays are to be allowed, we need an OVERLAY or LOAD macro to load a module from disk or drum into core. If the modules wish to pass control back and forth, they may be able to do so with simple assembly language subroutine calls. However, it is possible that the *calling* module might not know the machine address of the *called* module (especially if the LOAD is dynamic—i.e. if it includes an implicit GETMEM), so a CALL and RETURN macro might be provided so that a subroutine call could be made to a module *by name*. Finally, there might be macros to allow parallel tasks—i.e. macros which would allow both the calling and the called modules to continue to process concurrently. The FORK macro in the SDS-940, the ATTACH macro in the IBM System/360, and the ZIP statement in the Burroughs B5500 ALGOL language accomplish this type of activity.

Task linkage almost always involves a large amount of overhead in the operating system. *Any* macro is somewhat costly (on the order of several milliseconds on most current machines) because of the trapping, command decoding, argument fetching, and error checking that takes place; however, the CALL, RETURN, OVERLAY, and ATTACH macros usually require several hundred milliseconds of processing within the operating system, because of all the tables that must be set up.

SOME COMMON PROBLEMS ENCOUNTERED IN APPLICATION PROGRAMS

By now, the reader should have a general feeling for the nature of application programs within an on-line system. In the next chapter, we will compare some of the characteristics of application programs for scientific time-sharing systems and on-line business-oriented systems. We can begin to establish a basis for comparison by outlining the seven major problems faced by the application programmer:

1 *Control of terminals*

The purpose of an application program for an on-line system is to interact with a terminal in a well-defined and useful manner. The purpose of an on-line operating system is to interact with the application program in such a way as to maximize the services provided to the application program while minimizing the overhead. As a result of these two dictums, it turns out that if one application program can control only one terminal, then there must be a separate job for each terminal using the system. This *enormously* magnifies the overhead incurred in the operating system—both in terms of extra space required for tables and extra processing.

The philosophy of "one job = one terminal" is central to the structure of a scientific time-sharing system. The only reason the approach works at all is because each user is normally executing a totally different application program. For dedicated systems where each user is making use of the *same* application, it is a very inefficient approach.

The application programmer also has problems in the way in which he is allowed to use a terminal. On most systems, the application program can generate input/output to teletypewriter terminals one line at a time. This is often very inefficient, since the user must type in several lines of input before the application program can perform any useful work (see Example 4).

There are other terminal problems that might affect the application programmer, too. Some examples are:

The polling and scanning conventions might be awkward for the application programmer.

The character set—e.g. ASCII or EBCDIC—might be difficult for the application programmer to use, especially if he uses an internal 6-bit character code.

Network configuration might be difficult to accomplish from the application program.

Terminal addressing on multi-drop lines can be awkward for the application programmer on many systems.

Detection and correction of data transmission errors is almost impossible for the application programmer on most systems, and the operating system does not always provide this service!

"Paging" on CRTs can be awkward. That is, the application program might have a large amount of data to display on a CRT, so it may decide to break it up into "pages." The user may then want the ability to move the pages forward and backward, which may be difficult for the application programmer to perform.

Faced with these problems, the application programmer should attempt to take advantage of standard vendor-supplied telecommunications packages. BTAM and QTAM are examples of telecommunications packages supplied by IBM for their System/360 computer; other vendors might supply these capabilities as part of the operating system, or as part of the application programming language, or perhaps as a stand-alone applications-oriented package (i.e. a package that can be called from a COBOL or FORTRAN program). As we have already mentioned, it is also a good idea for the application programmer to separate the terminal-handling logic from the rest of his application program.

2   *Sharing of files*

If two or more independent jobs (or tasks) decide to access the same part of the data base at the same time, chaos can result. What few mechanisms do exist to protect against this are usually woefully inadequate. On the one hand, the operating system may not enforce the conventions that it has established for orderly access to the data base, as is the case on the IBM System/360; on the other hand, the operating system might solve the problem by brute force by forcing an application program to "lock" an entire file, even though it only wanted one record.

The problem of simultaneous access to files is illustrated by Figure H13, and is discussed in considerably more detail in Chapter L. Our purpose in this introductory chapter is simply to alert the application programmer to the existence of the problem. As we shall see in the next few chapters, the problem is usually more difficult to control on scientific time-sharing systems than on business-oriented on-line systems.

3   *Overlaying, swapping, and "thrashing"*

Blessed is the application programmer who can place all of his application programs in memory for the duration of his job, for he shall never suffer from the inefficiencies of swapping or overlaying. In all scientific time-sharing systems and a large number of other on-line systems, the application programmer is not so blessed, and he must try to come to terms with these problems. On any *paging* system, the application programmer's main objective should be to fully utilize the pages, as we discussed in Example 2. On systems where the application programmer has control over the paging (with OVER-LAY macros), he must try to achieve Denning's "working set" of modules in core. This is somewhat easy to do if the flow of control from one module to another is fairly well-defined, as illustrated in Figure H14; unfortunately, many application programmers find themselves in the position shown by Figure H15, where there are no clear-cut rules for deciding which module to bring into core.

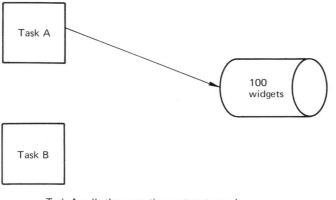

Task A calls the operating system to read
an inventory record. Since it cannot proceed
until the IO has finished, the operating system
turns control over to task B.

Fig. H13a   The problem of simultaneous access

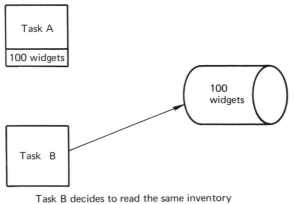

Task B decides to read the same inventory
record. It, too, must wait for the IO to finish.
Since A's IO will finish first, it will receive
control while B is waiting.

Fig. H13b   The problem of simultaneous access

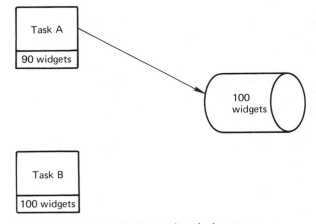

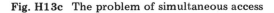

Task A has decided to update the inventory
record by ordering 10 widgets. It updates
the record in core, then calls the operating
system to write it on disk. Meanwhile, task
B has read the original inventory record into
core.

Fig. H13c　The problem of simultaneous access

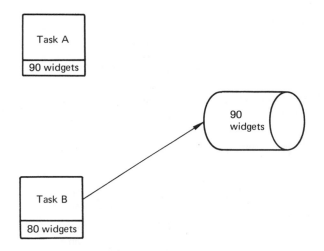

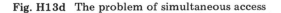

Task B decides to order 20 widgets, so it calls the
operating system to write an updated record. As a
result, the computer's inventory will be 80 widgets;
the *real* inventory should be 70 widgets.

Fig. H13d　The problem of simultaneous access

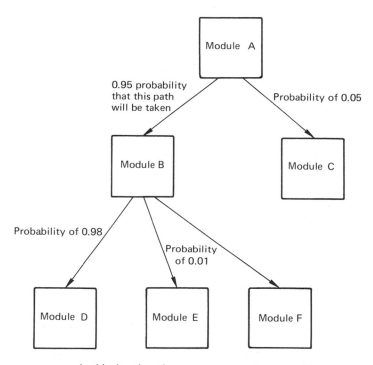

In this situation, the programmer can be reasonably
sure of requiring modules A,B, and D.

Fig. H14   A relatively simple overlaying problem

One of the common suggestions for avoiding this dilemma is to keep
statistics on the behavior of the application modules. If it is determined, as in
Figure H14, that there is a 98% probability that Module B will call Module D,
then there is an argument for loading Module D into core as soon as processing
is begun on a transaction. However, it should be emphasized that statistics
cannot help the analyst solve the problem shown by Figure H15.

A better approach is to allow the application modules a "look-ahead"
capability, as shown in Figure H16. Thus, shortly after Module B has begun its
processing, it should know whether it will need Module C, Module D, or Module
E (or maybe some combination of the three). Then, with the use of a macro
like the SEGLD macro on the IBM System/360, Module B can instruct the
operating system to load the required module(s) into core while processing
continues in Module B. Unfortunately, this type of "look-ahead" capability is
rarely present in current operating systems.

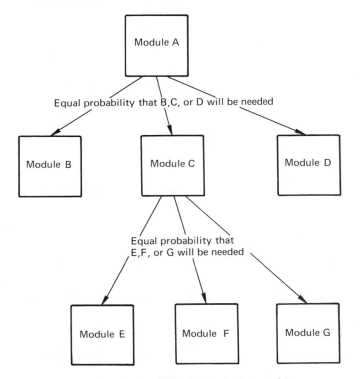

Fig. H15 A more difficult overlaying problem

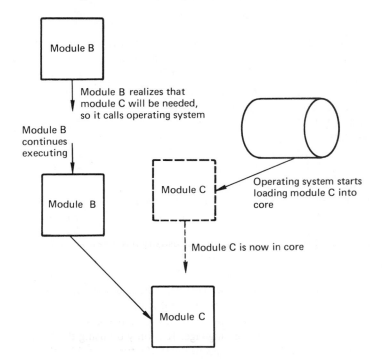

Fig. H16 Look-ahead capability

4   *Segmentation and communication between tasks*

We have already pointed out that effective multiprogramming can be achieved if the application is broken into separate tasks or jobs. The problem is that it is often very difficult for these jobs or tasks to communicate with one another. There are two basic capabilities that must exist before the application programmer can split his program into separate jobs or tasks: the tasks must be able to share common working storage, and the tasks must be able to use a WAIT macro to suspend their operation until a specified event occurs in the other task.

If the application programmer is allowed to have several tasks within the same job, these two mechanisms are usually present. However, if the programmer is forced to resort to separate jobs to accomplish his goal of effective multiprogramming, he will almost always find the problem of communication nearly insurmountable.

5   *Scheduling inequities*

We have noted that the application programmer often has the ability to determine the scheduling priority of his job in an on-line environment. However, there is always the danger that another application program will be submitted with a higher priority—and the on-line application may receive very poor service as a result. This is an even greater danger in systems where the scheduling does not include *time-slicing:* it may be possible for a low-priority job to grab the processor while the on-line job is in a "wait" state, and then never relinquish it.

There is no guarantee that a time-slicing scheduling algorithm will give any better service. If the on-line job temporarily has a slightly excessive amount of computing to do, it may find itself near the bottom of the scheduling queue. This happens quite often in scientific time-sharing systems, where preference is given to jobs that require less than a quarter second of processing time.

The easiest way of eliminating these scheduling inequities is, of course, to *dedicate* the system to the on-line application. This is not possible on scientific time-sharing systems, since each user has his own independent on-line application. It may also not be possible on business-oriented on-line systems because of low utilization of the processor by the on-line application. However, if background jobs are to be included, the application programmer should insist that they truly be *background* jobs—control should be returned to the on-line application as soon as possible after its "wait" condition has been satisfied.

6   *Lack of control with higher-level languages*

The assembly language programmer usually has a vast array of macros and other operating system services upon which to draw. He can control his overlays, initiate parallel tasks, share working storage among tasks, write reentrant modules, allocate buffers and working storage dynamically, and make his entire application as modular as desired. Unfortunately, these mechanisms are often not present in the higher level languages—especially if one is restricted to a "standard" version of the language. It is only by using the "extended" features of the language that each computer manufacturer provides that the programmer can invoke these desirable capabilities—and once the programmer makes use of these extended features, his application is no longer easily transferred to a different machine.

Normally, one finds that COBOL is the most restricted of languages, in terms of these extra "on-line" capabilities. FORTRAN is somewhat more permissive, and languages like ALGOL and PL/I provide almost all of these services to the programmer. On the IBM System/360, only PL/I can allocate storage dynamically, create tasks, and share working storage between tasks; COBOL, FORTRAN, and ALGOL do not have these features at the current time.[†] The application programmer should seriously consider the effect of these restrictions before choosing, say, COBOL, as his application language.

7   *Recovery*

Finally, we should mention that nemesis of on-line systems—the system failure. Application programmers almost never consider the consequences of a system failure in the middle of processing in their program. The most serious problems occur when the application program is in the midst of updating the data base when the system fails. This may result in two problems: the data base may end up in an inconsistent state, and the user may be confused about the status of his last input. The most common solution to the recovery problem is the audit trail approach discussed in Chapter N. However, there may be cases where the application programmer will have to write special recovery routines to "undo" the damage caused by an on-line application program gone berserk. It can be a difficult job trying to imagine all of the cases where the program and/or system could fail and leave the data base and users in a confused state.

[†] *IBM System/360 Operating System: Concepts and Facilities*, Form C23-6535-2, IBM Corporation, Programming Systems Publications, Department D58, Post Office Box 390, Poughkeepsie, New York 12602

Chapter I

A COMPARISON OF SYSTEMS AND LANGUAGES FOR ON-LINE APPLICATIONS

We have now introduced a number of the concepts that are important in the design of application programs for on-line systems. The reader should now be familiar with the notion of a job and a task; he should understand why it is important that his application programs use the concepts of modularity and multiprogramming.

However, the application programmer has only a limited amount of freedom as he designs his system. His design is influenced very greatly by the type of operating system that is provided with his computer, and by the type of application language that he uses. Some operating systems allow a job to interact with only one terminal, for instance, while others allow an application job to access many terminals. Similarly, some application languages allow reentrant programming and dynamic core allocation, while others do not.

Although each computer vendor supplies a different operating system and his own unique features in COBOL or FORTRAN, there are only a few basic *types* of systems and languages that we need examine. Our purpose in this chapter is to discuss the *structure* of application programs for various types of on-line systems. We will then make some comments about the advantages and disadvantages of the common application languages.

APPLICATION PROGRAMS FOR SCIENTIFIC
TIME-SHARING SYSTEMS

The most important characteristic of the scientific time-sharing system is shown in Figure I1: there is a one-to-one relationship between a user, a job, and a terminal. This arrangement is common on university time-sharing systems and mini-computer time-sharing systems, where each person who gains access to the system is considered to be totally independent of all other users.

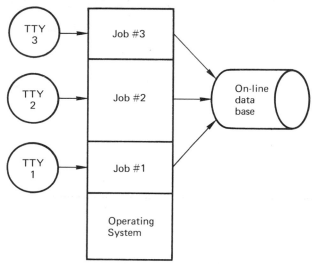

One user = one terminal = one job

Fig. I1   Application programs in a scientific time-sharing system

This independence of users is desirable in a scientific-engineering problem-solving environment. Each user is likely to be creating and executing his own applications, which are likely to be quite different from those of other users. Each user has his own set of files and programs, and does not always want to share them with other users.

The scientific time-sharing structure has tremendous disadvantages if all of the users are involved in the same application. In many business applications, users do *not* create their own application programs at the terminals; instead, they make use of application packages written by the programming department. They do not create their own files and data—instead, they make use of a common data base. Essentially, all of the users are using the same application program, and making use of the same data base.

Thus, the business application is at odds with the true nature of the scientific time-sharing system—which is to treat everyone as an independent user. The worst problems are often associated with the common data base, since each independent time-sharing job has the ability to access the data base by itself. This leads to problems of *simultaneous access* to the data base, which was illustrated in Chapter H. Most time-sharing systems allow a time-sharing program to "lock" a file to prevent other jobs from accessing it at the same time, but as we shall see in Chapter L, this approach is usually inadequate. The "lock" mechanism often allows one job to lock the file for an indefinite period of time, thus seriously reducing the throughput of the system as other jobs wait for the file to be unlocked. Worst of all, it forces the application program to lock an *entire file*, even though the program may have only needed one or two records in the file.

There are other inefficiencies present in the scientific time-sharing approach. The operating system must maintain a number of tables and information about each time-sharing job, and there is usually a fair amount of overhead processing required to keep track of the activities of each application program. Thus, if there are 200 users using the same application package on a scientific time-sharing system, the operating system will be forced to maintain a number of 200-entry tables. It will also be forced to reschedule each time one of the 200 users requires any kind of input/output. On machines without provisions for reentrant programming, each user will also have a separate copy of the same application program.

Thus, the scientific time-sharing structure is to be avoided unless all of the users are likely to be doing independent work. The file accessing problem and the operating system overhead make this approach extremely inefficient for dedicated applications of any kind.

ON-LINE BUSINESS STRUCTURE
WITHOUT MULTITASKING

A second structure for on-line applications is illustrated by Figure I2. The significant difference between this structure and the scientific time-sharing system is that one application program can control *many* terminals instead of just one. However, the application programmer is not allowed to have independent tasks within his job. The reader is reminded that this may be a consequence of the operating system he is using *or* the application language that he is using. Thus, although the operating system on the IBM System/360 allows multitasking, the COBOL language is not able to make use of that capability.

With this approach, we can eliminate the major problem of the scientific time-sharing system: simultaneous access to files. One job can be responsible for updating the data base in some orderly fashion—typically by processing input transactions in a serial fashion. In most cases, there will not even be a need to lock any files, since there will be no competition for the files. This eliminates a little more overhead in the system.

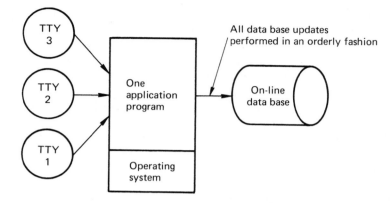

Fig. I2   On-line business structure without multitasking

The major reduction in overhead comes from the fact that the operating system does not have to keep track of so many users. In the scientific time-sharing approach, 200 users would have required 200 jobs; with this approach, we require only one job, and the application program keeps track of the 200 terminals. Scheduling overhead can be reduced, since there is usually no need for time-slicing. Similarly, swapping is often completely eliminated, since all 200 users can share one copy of the application program.

However, effective multiprogramming is often not possible on a system of this type. If the system is dedicated to the on-line application, there may only be one job in the system. Since we have assumed that multitasking is not possible in this structure, we must also assume that the operating system will take control away from the job whenever it must wait for input/output of any kind. Thus, if the application program has to wait for terminal input or disk input, the processor will be temporarily idle. Obviously, we would prefer a structure where we could overlap terminal IO with disk IO and processing of input.

It should be pointed out that this structure is *not* good for the scientific-engineering problem-solving environment. The operating system is often only capable of allowing seven or eight jobs to run concurrently, which, in the scientific time-sharing environment, means seven or eight users. It is interesting that a number of computer manufacturers produced scientific time-sharing systems by simply upgrading their multiprogramming batch systems to allow an application program to interact with a terminal. While this is sufficient for a dedicated application, it is not for a scientific environment, where each user is performing a different application. In some cases, the only remedy was to build a small time-sharing monitor in one of the jobs—a monitor that controlled swapping and scheduling within its own job area, as shown in Figure I3. As one might expect, the overhead associated with this approach is tremendous.

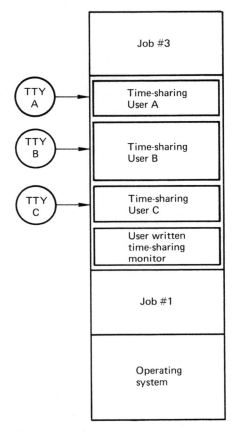

Fig. I3 Time-sharing within an on-line business system

ON-LINE BUSINESS STRUCTURE
WITH MULTITASKING

Still another structure involves the multitasking concept that was introduced in Chapter H. The structure may actually take either of two forms: we have several tasks within one job, or several jobs which can communicate with each other. In either case, the structure is often used in the manner shown by Figure I4.

Communication between the tasks (or jobs) may be somewhat awkward on some systems. As we pointed out in Chapter H, the main thing that the tasks must be able to share is working storage. This is usually more of a problem when separate jobs are involved, as is the case on the Burroughs B5500 computer system. If the operating system allows for multiple tasks within the same job, the awkwardness, if any, is the result of limitations in the higher-level languages.

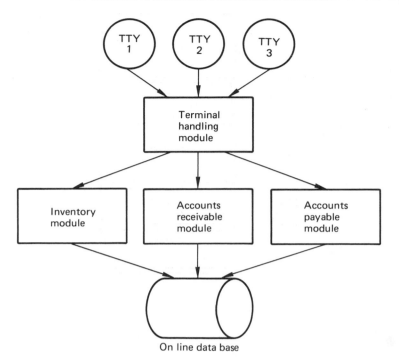

Fig. I4   On-line business structure with multitasking

The task that collects input from terminals may be simplified by software packages provided by the vendor. Thus, with the use of macros, the application programmer may be able to specify polling sequences, buffering conventions, and line control. However, the programmer may still have to provide his own program for such things as queueing of messages, error control, and logging of messages.

The great advantage of the multitasking approach is an increase in the multiprogramming capability of the system. When one task is waiting for IO, the terminal-oriented task can be gathering input or typing output on the terminals. This increase in multiprogramming can, however, be nullified if the tasks are highly segmented and require a high degree of overlaying or paging.

Updating of the data base can still take place in a fairly orderly fashion, as was true in the non-multitasking structure. It may be desirable to have several independent tasks that are capable of updating different parts of the data base in a concurrent fashion. Thus, it might be possible for a management information system to have separate tasks handle inventory transactions, accounts receivable transactions, and accounts payable trans-actions—because each type of transaction involves a different part of the data base.

If there is a possibility of conflict, the application programmer can resolve it by including a "data management" task, as shown in Figure I5.

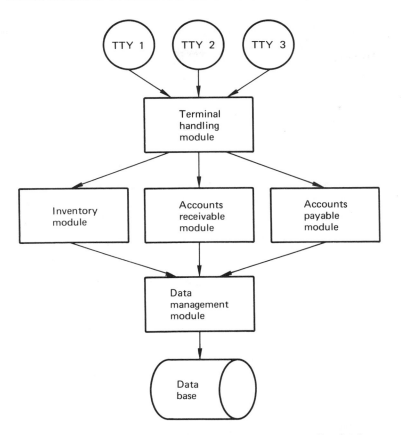

Fig. I5 Handling the simultaneous access problem in an on-line business structure with a data management package

This package would receive updates from the other tasks and perform them in a serial fashion. Alternatively, tasks could avoid conflict by passing *dummy transactions* to each other, as shown in Figure I6.

With the multitasking approach, the system designer still has the freedom to process transactions in a serial fashion. On a system that allows reentrant programming, it is often a great temptation to have multiple incarnations of the same task—thus allowing for concurrent processing of several transactions, as shown by Figure I7. Not only does this practice invoke Yourdon's Paradox by greatly increasing the interaction with the operating system, it also brings back the problem of simultaneous accesses to a common data base.

The application programmer also has the freedom of making his system either "conversational" or "non-conversational." A conversational system is one in which the system responds to each input typed by a user before the user is allowed to type his next transaction. This approach makes scheduling, recovery, buffering, and other problems much easier, though it means that the system cannot be represented with a stochastic mathematical model. A non-conversational system, on the other hand, is one where the user can type in several transactions independent of any processing that may have taken place by the system. While this may make queues longer and recovery more difficult, it has some important advantages:

transactions may be batched to improve the efficiency of file accesses, program overlays, and so forth.

the system becomes amenable to stochastic queueing theory models.

the user does not have to sit at his terminal and wait for a response before typing his next transaction. In fact, he may even be allowed to type all of his transactions and get off the system before any processing is done at all.

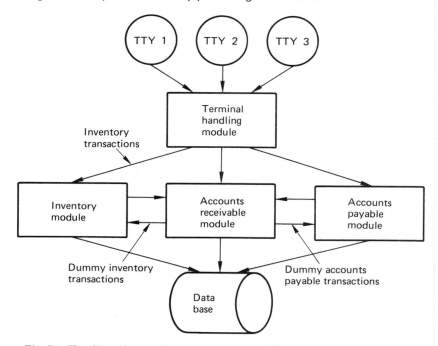

Fig. I6 Handling the simultaneous access problem in an on-line business system with dummy transactions

MANY MODULES VERSUS ONE MODULE

In addition to his decisions on the type of structure for his application programs, the system designer is often forced to choose between two different types of core allocation: one structure in which all (or most) of the application programs are resident in core, and another structure in

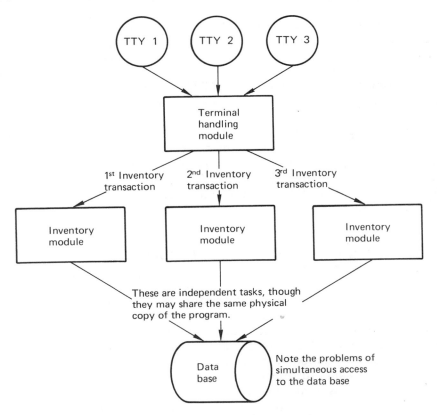

Fig. I7 Concurrent processing with reentrant programs

which the application processing is done by *several* modules, which are called into core as required.

Ideally, the application programmer would like to have all of his modules in core. However, there may be cases where the application programs are so large or numerous that they simply cannot fit in the machine. There may be other cases where the application programmer would be wasting core memory by allocating it to infrequently-used application modules. In other cases, the application programmer may not have control at all in this area: as we discussed in Chapter H, the operating system may invoke paging hardware to minimize the number of application modules that are in core at any moment.

In the event that the application programmer does have the ability to control which of his application modules are in core, he must have two algorithms in his system:

an algorithm to decide when to bring a module into core.

an algorithm to decide when to "throw away" a module—i.e. release the memory that it occupies for use by another module.

The first decision—when to bring a module into core—can be made in a variety of ways. One common approach is to bring the module in *on demand*—i.e. when, and only when, it is actually required for processing. Unless there is a "look-ahead" capability in the system, there can be serious delays waiting for the module to be brought into core. This can be severe if the input requires several application modules during the course of processing.

Another potential weakness of the "many module" approach is that the "bringing-in" part of the system may get into serious conflict with the "throwing-out" part of the system. Modules can get overlayed before they have actually finished their processing. Again, this becomes more and more serious as the number of application modules involved in the processing of a transaction increase.

PROGRAMMING LANGUAGES FOR APPLICATIONS IN AN ON-LINE ENVIRONMENT

Application programs can be written in a variety of programming languages. The choice of one language over another is often based on such factors as company policy, availability of the language on the machine being used, and availability of experienced programmers. From a technical point of view, there are a number of interesting features in each language. We shall restrict our comments to four of the more common languages: FORTRAN, COBOL, PL/I, and assembly language.

FORTRAN has the advantage that it is a relatively straightforward language. Most FORTRAN compilers now generate fairly efficient object code, and it is easy for the application programmer to break his program into several small subroutines. It is fairly common to see reentrant FORTRAN compilers, and it is not too difficult for FORTRAN compilers to generate reentrant object code (though few do at the current time).

For scientific and engineering time-sharing applications, FORTRAN appears to be the most popular language. During the late 1960's, it was estimated that approximately 80% of the time-sharing community used the BASIC programming language, but a growing sophistication among time-sharing users has started a trend back to FORTRAN. On the other hand, BASIC has been "extended" and improved to such an extent that many afficionados claim that it equals FORTRAN in power and versatility.

On one point, however, there is general agreement: FORTRAN-like languages are not well-suited to business applications. Character manipulations and formatting are usually awkward; decimal arithmetic does not exist. As a result, COBOL appears to be the most commonly used application language for on-line systems as well as batch computer systems. This is probably partly due to the abundance of COBOL programmers, and partly due to the business orientation of the language. Another strong argument for the language is the ease with which it may be transferred to another machine.

However, COBOL is usually an inefficient language on most machines (with the exception of Burroughs computers). That is, not only is the compilation process slow, but the object code takes up a tremendous amount of space and tends to execute rather slowly. As a result, many system designers plan on rewriting certain portions of the application in assembly language.

There are usually much worse inefficiencies present in COBOL. As a general rule, COBOL does not permit multiple tasks within one job; nor does it allow for dynamic core allocation during execution of the object code. Also, it is not usually possible to force the COBOL compiler to generate reentrant object code. This means, of course, that multiple executions of the same application will require multiple copies of the application program.

Thus, despite its universality as a programming language, COBOL usually restricts the on-line application programmer severely. The system designer should seriously weigh the advantages of COBOL with the disadvantages (bulkier and slower object code, less modular code, no multi-tasking) before making a decision.

Another fairly popular language, particularly among IBM users, is PL/I. Its main advantage seems to be that it includes the features and capabilities of COBOL, FORTRAN, and assembly language. In addition, some will argue that the language is aesthetically more pleasing than COBOL, though there is equally strong feeling to the contrary. The major disadvantage of PL/I is the fact that it is not as widely accepted as FORTRAN and COBOL. As a result, there are not as many PL/I programmers as COBOL programmers—nor are there as many machines with PL/I compilers as there are machines with COBOL compilers.

Another disadvantage of PL/I is that the object code tends to be relatively inefficient. Procedure calls and other parts of the language tend to have a rather high overhead associated with them. On the other hand, PL/I usually has a number of very powerful features: reentrant code, multiple tasks, dynamic core allocation, and sharing of working storage among tasks. If the system designer can accept the fact that PL/I is not as universal a language as COBOL, he may very well find that these features make it the best of the higher-level application languages.

Finally, we must consider assembly languages as a tool for developing application programs. From a theoretical point of view, assembly language programs are potentially the most efficient. They can be written to run fast, conserve core, execute in a reentrant fashion, and take advantage of whatever capabilities are provided by the operating system. Thus, it should be possible for the application programmer to achieve all of the goals described in Chapter H:

modular execution of programs

good overlap of IO and computation

minimize disk accesses

observe Yourdon's Paradox

On the other hand, assembly language programs tend to be more difficult to test, more difficult to document adequately, and more difficult to maintain. There is not even any *guarantee* that they will be more efficient than a COBOL or PL/I program. A bumbling programmer can easily write a less efficient assembly language program than a talented COBOL programmer, and this may be a serious factor if the system designer is forced to draw upon large numbers of junior programmers or trainees in his on-line projects.

With all of the potential dangers of assembly language programming, it is interesting to note that a number of conservative commercial institutions (banks, insurance companies, and so forth) have decided that the increased efficiency of assembly language more than outweighs the disadvantages of increased testing time and poor documentation.

A SUMMARY OF CONSIDERATIONS FOR CHOOSING A PROGRAMMING LANGUAGE

In this discussion, we have mainly been concerned with the technical features of various programming languages. Because of the demands of an on-line system, it certainly is true that the technical capabilities of a programming language are more important than they were in a batch computer system; however, the system designer should keep in mind *all* of the following considerations before choosing a particular language:

1   *The availability of programmers*

COBOL programmers are in plentiful supply; in fact, at the time this book was written, they were in *extremely* plentiful supply in many major cities of the United States, because of a "mild" economic recession. FORTRAN programmers are also usually fairly easy to find, and it is usually not too difficult to find programmers who are familiar with any of the other popular high-level languages, such as ALGOL, APL, PL/I, BASIC, and so forth.

Assembly language programmers can also be found, but they are not quite so plentiful. Because of the omniscient presence of IBM, one can usually find reasonably competent assembly language programmers on the IBM System/360 and System/370, as well as the older IBM-7094, 7044, 1401, 1620, and 650. Assembly language programmers for Honeywell, GE, RCA, DEC, XDS, and Control Data machines *do* exist, but it might take a few months to build up a decent programming staff of assembly language programmers for these non-IBM machines.

The question of availability of programmers should be kept in mind by the system designer who intends to use an obscure language like LISP, SNOBOL, MAD, SLIP, or JOVIAL; and also by the system designer who intends to develop his own programming language. While it may be desirable to develop a compiler language or a macro language to make better use of the on-line capabilities of the machine, the system designer must count on a complete absence of trained programmers. This may, in turn, set the project back by six months, a delay which may be intolerable to management.

2 *Ability to train programmers in a new programming language*

Another important consideration in the choice of a language is the ability to teach it to the programming staff, assuming that they do not already know it. This consideration is of obvious importance if one is using a new language or an obscure language; it may also be important if one is forced to hire a large number of untrained or inexperienced people for a large computer project.

In this area, one should first examine the languages and try to come to some conclusion about the ease with which they may be taught. There is general agreement that languages like BASIC and JOSS can be taught to a new programmer quickly and easily. Languages like FORTRAN might require a week or more of classroom sessions, while COBOL, ALGOL, and PL/I generally are considered more difficult to teach. If one is willing to begin with a *subset* of the language, then the training period can be speeded up considerably.

One must also consider the quality of the training program within the organization. Some organizations have a large staff of permanent employees whose sole function is to provide in-house data processing training. If they provide regular sessions in FORTRAN, COBOL, or PL/I, then it should not be too much of a burden to train the programming staff. On the other hand, a small organization may not have its own internal training program, and may have to rely on the computer manufacturer, or outside university courses, or perhaps the services of an independent educational firm.

Finally, the ability of the programming staff must be considered before embarking upon an ambitious training program. If the project is to be implemented by a small team of highly experienced professionals, then it is reasonable to expect that they will learn a new programming language on their own, if they are given manuals and other appropriate documentation. However, if the programmers are less experienced (or less competent) and have spent all of their time writing programs in a different language, then there may be serious trouble. It is extremely common to find that a COBOL programmer continues to write COBOL-like programs in FORTRAN; similarly, many FORTRAN and assembly language programmers have great difficulty adapting to COBOL.

If the programming staff is *completely* untrained and inexperienced, then the system designer must use his own judgment in deciding how much training will be necessary. If, for example, the staff has a scientific or engineering background, and if the application involves the same kind of engineering or scientific discipline, then it should be a relatively simple matter to teach them BASIC, FORTRAN, or a subset of PL/I. On the other hand, English majors, truck drivers, and football players may *never* be good programmers, if for no other reason than the fact that their background and training has not prepared them for the type of logical and precise thinking that is supposedly required of computer programmers. Of course, one can never be sure, for some of the *weirdest* people in the world are computer programmers. In any case, the system designer should not expect to see very many good programs from the untrained novice for a period of approximately three to six months.

3 *Ability to use the same language on other computers*

One of the strongest selling points of a language like COBOL or FORTRAN is that it is *universal.* Languages like BASIC, ALGOL, and PL/I are slowly gaining popularity, and it is likely that many of the major computer manufacturers will provide all of these languages on the machines of the 1970's.

However, the system designer must be careful not to trap himself by using "extended" features of a language. FORTRAN is a good example: Figure 18 shows "standard" FORTRAN IV, which is a subset of the version of FORTRAN IV provided by all of the computer manufacturers. This is indeed a dilemma, for the manufacturers can hardly be criticized for their desire to add extra features to the language, and yet the system designer *does* want the ability to move his application programs to a different machine.

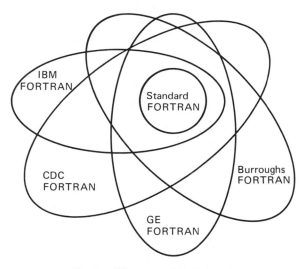

Fig. 18 "Standard" FORTRAN IV

Unfortunately, this problem is usually worse on an on-line system than it is on batch systems. On-line systems make use of *terminals* and *random-access files,* nether of which have been standardized to any great extent. Thus, the COBOL programmer might use an *index-sequential* file on an IBM System/360, and then find that it is incompatible with the file organization scheme on the Burroughs B6500. Similarly, the COBOL programmer might write a teleprocessing package for the GE-635, and then find that it is not compatible with the BTAM and QTAM teleprocessing handlers for the IBM System/360.

Despite these problems, it is generally easier to transfer a program written in a higher level language to a new machine than it is to transfer an assembly language program. If the system designer makes a reasonable effort to avoid the esoteric non-standard features of his vendor's language, he will generally not have too much trouble.

This problem may very well be solved in the 1970's with the advent of microprogramming. It should become easier for the vendors, or perhaps the computer users themselves, to *emulate* different machines on their own processor by using microprogrammed instructions. The IO portion of a program may still have to be reprogrammed, but the logical portion of the program might eventually be transferrable to any machine.

4   *Vendor's support of the language*

Despite the fact that a computer manufacturer offers a programming language on his machine, the language may not be supported very enthusiastically. As a result, the system designer may have a difficult time obtaining manuals and technical assistance from the manufacturer, and it might be better for him simply to avoid using the language.

There are several computer companies, for example, that produce scientific computers with excellent FORTRAN and BASIC languages. They also provide COBOL, but the system designer is likely to find that the documentation is poor, the compiler has bugs, the vendor's technical support staff is not familiar with COBOL, and so forth. The same situation may arise if the programming language has been developed by the vendor's *user group* (e.g. the IBM SHARE group, the Burroughs CUBE group, the Digital Equipment Corporation DECUS group), but is not maintained or warrantied by the vendor himself.

5   *Political considerations*

Unfortunately, political considerations often have more influence than any of the other considerations we have mentioned. There may be standard company policy to use FORTRAN on all computer projects, or a standard policy that all government agencies use COBOL, or a standard policy that all IBM employees use PL/I in an attempt to promote the language.

Many of these administrative policies do allow for exceptions, and if the system designer feels that he has a strong case for using a "non-standard" language, he should certainly try to get approval. Management must be made to realize that COBOL is not necessarily the best language for all applications, nor is FORTRAN or PL/I.

6   *Ability to maintain and document programs written in the language*

From a practical point of view, the system designer should consider the ease with which a program can be maintained and documented. It is generally agreed that assembly language programs are the most difficult to document and maintain, while the higher-level languages are, to some extent, self-documenting and easier to maintain.

This is another area where the system designer must assess the quality of his programming staff. If the staff consists of a small team of competent *professionals*, then it is reasonable to assume that they will document their programs and make them easy to maintain, *regardless of the language they use.* On the other hand, if the staff consists of talented, but undisciplined, "code bums," then assembly language may be a poor choice. Similarly, if one must depend on relatively inexperienced programmers to develop an on-line system, one would generally prefer a higher-level language to assembly language.

7   *Data base features*

For business-oriented applications, the system designer might be interested in taking advantage of *data management* packages provided by the computer manufacturer or independent software companies. Some of these data management packages might be compatible with, or callable by, programs written in a particular programming language; obviously, this might affect the system designer's choice of a language.

An example in this area is General Electric's IDS data management package, which is written as an extension of the COBOL language. The COBOL programmer is required to add some statements in the DATA DIVISION portion of his program to define the type of data structures with which he is dealing; he then calls various IDS functions directly from the PROCEDURE DIVISION of his program. If the system designer wants to use IDS, it is rather obvious that COBOL is the language in which his applications will be written.

8   *Efficiency of the language*

Finally, we should consider the efficiency of the programming language. There are four items of interest here:

compilation speed

object code execution speed

object code memory space

advanced "on-line" features

The compilation speed is usually critical only for environments where a large number of short jobs are expected to be submitted to the system each day. Thus, some remote-batch systems and time-sharing systems might consider the compilation speed to be a critical factor, while the installations that expect to run the same production jobs over and over again are not quite so concerned with this aspect of the language.

There is, of course, universal concern about the *object program*. We are generally interested in the *speed* with which the object program may be expected to execute, as well as the amount of *memory* required by the object program. As we mentioned earlier in this chapter, there is general agreement that assembly language is the most efficient in this respect (assuming that one has a staff of competent programmers!); FORTRAN is generally considered a reasonably efficient language, while COBOL and PL/I are generally rather slow and bulky.

The advanced features of the language will probably become more standard during the next few years. In the meantime, the on-line systems designer should pay a great deal of attention to those languages which permit dynamic memory allocation, multitasking, reentrant programming, and sharable working storage.

Chapter J

AN EXAMPLE —
THE WIDGET CORPORATION OF AMERICA REVISITED

INTRODUCTION

In Chapter F we introduced the Widget Corporation of America, the country's largest manufacturer of widgets. The reader will remember that our hero, Wilbur Goodbody, had persuaded his management not to buy the Aardvark 301 computer, but then decided to leave and start his own company. Undaunted, the Widget Corporation has decided to continue with its plans, and has hired Mortimer Snavely to replace Wilbur Goodbody. If the Widget Corporation is similar to many other large American corporations, we may expect that Snavely will reverse Goodbody's earlier decision, and decide to obtain the Aardvark 301 computer after all.

Our purpose in this chapter, however, is not to delve into the political machinations at the Widget Corporation. We are interested in the design of the application programs that Snavely has produced for the Aardvark 301. We will proceed by first describing the nature of the system, then listing the transactions that a user of the system may type in. Finally, we will describe the application programs that perform the processing.

A GENERAL DESCRIPTION OF THE WIDGET SYSTEM

As we described in Chapter F, the Widget system is intended to help salesmen all over the country place their orders for widgets. From the salesman's point of view, that is all there is to the system: he simply wants to type in the customer's account number, the model, color, and quantity of widgets being ordered. However, if we follow the typical salesman around on a day's selling activities, we find that he needs two other capabilities: the ability to *reserve* a quantity of widgets for a potential order, and the ability to make *inquiries.*

The inquiry capability might be useful for managers as well as salesmen, and might include a number of different options. For example, we would like to allow a salesman to find out how many widgets of a given color are available at a particular warehouse; perhaps he might want to know how many widgets of a specified color were available in all warehouses together. In order to maintain a good relationship with his customers, the salesman will probably want to be able to determine the *status* of any customer's order.

The capability to *reserve* some widgets is also a common capability in most manual systems. In the hope of closing a large order, the salesman might want to hold a specified number of widgets for some period of time—or perhaps until he indicates that the widgets are to be released again.

It is important to note that the salesmen are not the only users of such a system. As we indicated in Chapter F, the processing that takes place when the salesman types in an order basically consists of an *inventory* check and a *credit* check. Thus, the system must receive inputs from the warehouses (where the inventory is maintained) and from the accounting offices. Within the warehouse, the system must provide the capability for indicating the *arrival* of new widgets from the factory, the *transfer* of widgets from one warehouse to another, and the *shipment* of widgets from the warehouse to the customer. The system would become much more complex if we were forced to keep track of "in-process" widgets as well as "finished" widgets, and we will assume that this is not a necessary part of the system. Thus, our on-line system will not be made aware of the existence of a widget until it actually arrives at the warehouse. Because of this restriction, it will not be possible for a salesman to order against non-existent inventory, nor will we have to keep track of the "estimated time to completion" of widgets that are currently being manufactured in the factory.

Our main purpose in this system is to provide a convenient mechanism for the salesman. We are not attempting to provide a production scheduling system for the plant foreman, nor are we attempting to build an on-line accounting system. However, we do want to include some accounting information in the system, so that we will be able to prevent salesmen from selling to customers with a poor credit history. Presumably, the system will be able to make its credit decision based on the amount of money that the customer currently owes Widget, perhaps together with the customer's Dun & Bradstreet rating. Accordingly, the accounting office must have the ability to tell the system of payments that have been *received* from customers, as well as *charges* and *credits* that have been levied against customers.

Everything that we have discussed so far relates to the *on-line* operation of the system. We must also provide some capabilities for *off-line* processing. We must have the ability to add and delete customers from the system, and we must have the ability to add and delete various models and colors of widgets from the system. In neither of these cases is there a requirement for on-line processing; all we need to do is capture the transaction and perform the necessary file updating at night in a batch mode of operation.

Finally, we should recognize the likelihood of growth in the system—growth both in size and scope. If the system succeeds, the Widget management may hire more salesmen, which will increase the number of terminals. The accounting office will realize that most of the relevant accounts receivable information is captured by the system, and will begin to demand various accounting reports. We will certainly have a requirement for sales analysis reports, salesman commission reports, and more on-line inquiry capabilities.

TRANSACTIONS IN THE WIDGET SYSTEM

Table J1 shows the transactions that the system designers have provided in the Widget system. It is anticipated that each transaction will require one line of input from the user, although there may be more than one line of output typed out in reply. We have assumed the existence of six *standard* arguments:

1   *Purchase order number*
    This is probably a simple integer, and is assigned by the system at the time an order is placed. It is used to identify the order if the salesman later decides to cancel the order, or if he wants to know the status of the order. It is also used in the warehouse to identify the order when the widgets are shipped.

2   *Account number*

    We will assume that most of Widget's customers are fairly *steady* customers, for as Widget's president says, "A Widget customer is a *satisfied* customer!" Thus, we can assign account numbers to each of the Widget customers, and refer to each customer by this number. We encounter difficulties only when a salesman unearths a new customer, or when a current customer decides to leave the fold.

3   *Model*

4   *Color*

    As everyone knows, widgets are identified by a model number, and by their color. Afficionados will probably wonder why we have not distinguished between soft widgets and hard widgets, but this was felt to be an unnecessary sophistication.

5 *Warehouse*

A number of the transactions require a specification of the location in which the widgets are kept. The warehouse location is indicated with an alphanumeric string, e.g. CHICAGO, DENVER, or WAREHOUSE3. This is for the convenience of the salesmen, who refuse to associate a numeric code with a warehouse.

6 *Amount*

Most of the inventory-oriented transactions require the salesman to specify the number of widgets involved. Similarly, most of the accounting transactions require the user to specify the amount of money involved, in terms of dollars and cents.

TABLE J1 *Transactions for the Widget Corporation Sales Order Entry System*

Inventory-oriented transactions						
ORDER	P.O.*	Acctno.	Model	Color	(Warehouse)	Amount
RESERVE	P.O.*	Acctno.	Model	Color	(Warehouse)	Amount
CANCEL	P.O.	Acctno.				
ARRIVAL			Model	Color	Warehouse	Amount
SHIPMENT	P.O.	Acctno.				Amount
Accounting-oriented transactions						
PAYMENT	P.O.	Acctno.				Amount
STOPCREDIT		Acctno.				
RESTORECREDIT		Acctno.				
CHARGE		Acctno.				Amount
CREDIT		Acctno.				Amount
Inquiries						
INQA			Model	Color	(Warehouse)	
INQC	(P.O.)	Acctno.				
Batch Transactions						
ADDC		Acctno.				
DELC		Acctno.				
ADDW			Model	Color		
DELW			Model	Color		

* returned by the system as output from the transaction
Items enclosed by parentheses are *optional* arguments.

At this point, the system designers have been able to identify some sixteen transactions for the Widget system. A brief explanation of each transaction follows:

1 *The ORDER transaction*

The ORDER transaction is the one for which the system was designed. It allows the salesman to enter the necessary parameters to describe the sale of some widgets. He must specify the account number of the customer, the model and color of the widgets being sold, and the amount of widgets sold. He may optionally specify the warehouse from which the widgets are to be obtained; if he does not, the system will attempt to allocate widgets from the nearest possible warehouse. When the system receives an ORDER transaction, it types the appropriate information at the warehouse terminal. This enables the men at the warehouse to pick out the specified widgets, and ship them (which *they* confirm with a SHIPMENT transaction).

2   *The RESERVE transaction*

When a salesman merely wants to hold some widgets in the warehouse for a period of time, he can use the RESERVE transaction. It has the same arguments and the same effect as the ORDER transaction, except that the warehouse does not receive any shipping instructions. The system responds to the RESERVE transaction with a purchase order number.

3   *The CANCEL transaction*

The CANCEL transaction allows the salesman to cancel a valid order or a quantity of "reserved" widgets. He is required to type in the purchase order number of the order being cancelled, a number which was furnished to him by the ORDER or RESERVE transaction. If the CANCEL transaction refers to an order which has already been shipped, the system will so indicate; if the CANCEL refers to an order which the warehouse has not yet shipped, the warehouse will receive appropriate instructions. If the CANCEL refers to a "reserved" quantity of widgets, they will be made free and available for other orders.

4   *The ARRIVAL transaction*

The ARRIVAL transaction is not used by the salesmen at all. Instead, the warehouse manager uses the ARRIVAL transaction to indicate the arrival of fresh widgets from the factory. This increases the inventory at the specified warehouse. Obviously, the manager must also specify the model, color, and number of widgets that have arrived.

5   *The SHIPMENT transaction*

The warehouse manager uses the SHIPMENT transaction to indicate the final fulfillment of an order. He is required only to indicate the purchase order number and the account number of the customer whose order is being shipped (both must be specified since one customer may have several orders outstanding). We are assuming that there will be no partial shipments—if the customer orders 10,000 widgets, they all get shipped at once. When the SHIPMENT transaction is processed, it first updates the customer's accounts receivable file, then erases the inventory record.

6   *The PAYMENT transaction*

The PAYMENT transaction is used exclusively by users in the Widget

Corporation accounting office when a customer sends in a payment for a shipment of widgets. The accounting clerk specifies the customer's account number, the purchase order, and the amount of money remitted. The system simply decreases the customer's outstanding accounts receivable record by the amount of money recieved.

7   The STOPCREDIT transaction

The accounting office may occasionally have reason to stop a customer's credit, even though he has not exceeded the computer's credit limit. This may occur if the accounting office learns of the customer's impending bankruptcy, or other outside information. Obviously, the effect of this transaction is to block all future attempts to sell any widgets to this customer.

8   The RESTORECREDIT transaction

In the event that the customer with a STOPCREDIT should become solvent again, the accounting clerk may want to restore his credit with a RESTORE-CREDIT transaction. With both the STOPCREDIT and RESTORECREDIT transactions, it is only necessary to specify the customer's account number.

9   The CHARGE transaction

The CHARGE transaction is used to charge money to a customer's account. In most cases, the SHIPMENT transaction will implicitly issue a CHARGE transaction when widgets are shipped to a customer. However, there may be other cases (extra postage, special delivery or handling, an error on past bills, etc.) when the accounting department will want to issue its own explicit CHARGE transaction to levy additional charges against a customer.

10   The CREDIT transaction

There will also be some cases when monies are credited to a customer—for damaged shipments, overpayments, and so forth. The CREDIT transaction will normally be issued by the accounting department and will specify the account number and the amount of money to be credited.

11   The INQA transaction

The INQA transaction allows the salesman to determine the availability of widgets at a particular warehouse. The salesman is required only to indicate the model number and color of the widgets, and the warehouse in which he is interested. If he omits the warehouse specification, the system will indicate the number of widgets in *all* warehouses. The salesman must remember that the INQA transaction does not reserve any widgets for him. Thus, if he follows the INQA transaction with a RESERVE or an ORDER transaction (or another INQA transaction, for that matter), he may find that the widgets have already been taken by another salesman.

12   The INQC transaction

The INQC transaction allows the salesman to ascertain the status of any of his customer's orders. He is required to specify both the customer's account number and the purchase order number, and the system will respond with either "SHIPPED" or "NOT YET SHIPPED." At the moment, there is no provision for the system giving the salesman an "estimated time until shipment," but this is not felt to be necessary. The major use of this transaction is to *confirm* the shipment of an order of widgets, so that any problems can be blamed on the Post Office.

13   The ADDC transaction

The ADDC transaction is used to add another customer to the system. The transaction is typed in during the day, but no action is taken until an overnight batch run can update the appropriate files. Note that this very primitive scheme assumes that the user supplies the system with an account number, and also that the 24-hour delay will not be too troublesome. This is probably a reasonable assumption whenever a relatively limited system is added as an adjunct to a large, manual system.

14   The DELC transaction

The DELC transaction is the reverse of the ADDC transaction. It is used to permanently remove a customer from the files. Once again, the user merely specifies the customer's account number.

15   The ADDW transaction

The ADDW transaction is used to add another model or color of widget to the product line. This is not expected to occur very often, so it is handled in the same way as the ADDC and DELC transactions: receipt of the transaction is acknowledged at the terminal, but processing is postponed until an evening batch run.

16   The DELW transaction

The DELW transaction is the opposite of the ADDW transaction. It allows the user to permanently remove a particular color or model of widget from the product line.

We should emphasize that the Widget system designers have simplified their system as much as possible, in the hopes of getting something reasonable working as quickly as possible. The astute reader will probably have noticed a number of potential weaknesses or omissions in this simple list of transactions:

1   The system should be able to handle partial shipments, so that the warehouse could send batches of widgets as they became available.

2   There should be a transaction to describe the transfer of widgets from one warehouse to another. The Widget management might decide to shift their inventory around to adjust for uneven loads in different parts of the country.

3   There should be a transaction to allow for *adjustment* of inventory. For

example, when the warehouse manager takes a physical count of his inventory, he will find that it differs from the computer's inventory because of pilferage, spoilage, or bugs in the computer system.

4   There should be some connection between this system and the current Widget accounting system. Since this system is recording all of the sales in the Widget Corporation, it is capturing all of the information necessary for aged accounts receivable reports, etc. By tying in an accounts payable system, it would also be possible to produce profit-and-loss statements.

5   There should be some way for the salesman to indicate the *priority* of his order. In the scheme that has been presented, each order is presumably serviced on a first-come-first-served basis. This may not be sufficient for the important customers who demand a "rush" order.

6   It should be possible for the salesman and/or warehouse manager to indicate *returned* goods. We might want to distinguish between widgets which were returned because they were damaged in transit, and widgets which can be resold.

7   There should be a way for the accounting manager to *change* the credit limit of a particular customer. In the current system, he only has the ability to totally eliminate a customer's credit.

There are probably many other changes and improvements that could be made. However, the Widget system designers have decided that the transactions in Table J1 are sufficient for the first version of the system. Improvements will be added to the second version, after some working experience has been gained.

BASIC DESIGN OF THE SYSTEM

The system designers have decided to structure their system as shown in Figure J1. This is similar to many of the diagrams that we have shown in Chapter I, and seems to allow us to multiprogram effectively, while also achieving a fairly modular execution.

We pointed out in Chapter H that one of the common problems in building application programs for on-line systems was common access to the data base. With the structure shown in Figure J1, we have effectively solved this problem. The inventory module processes the ORDER, RESERVE, CANCEL, ARRIVAL, and SHIPMENT transactions; the accounting module handles the PAYMENT, STOPCREDIT, RESTORECREDIT, CHARGE, and CREDIT transactions; the inquiry module handles the INQA and INQC transactions, while the batch module processes the ADDC, DELC, ADDW, and DELW transactions.

Note that the inventory module only affects the inventory files, while the accounting module only affects the accounting files. The exception to this is the SHIPMENT transaction, which affects *both* the inventory and accounting files. This can be easily handled by having the SHIPMENT transaction send a dummy CHARGE transaction to the accounting module, as we shall see below. The inquiry module and the batch module do not update any files, so there will not be any conflict if they are multi-programmed with the inventory and accounting module.

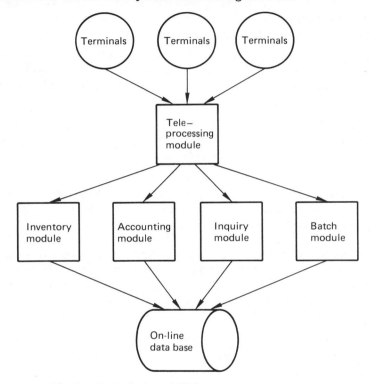

Fig. J1   Basic design of Widget on-line order system

The communication between the various application modules takes place through an area of common working storage, as shown in Figure J2. Four bits are required for control purposes, and the remainder of the common area is used to store the text of input and output messages. The modules use the control bits to indicate to one another when there is work to be done, and use a WAIT macro whenever appropriate. We will describe this communication in more detail below.

THE TELEPROCESSING MODULE

The basic purpose of the teleprocessing module (which we will henceforth refer to as the TP module) is to gather input from terminals,

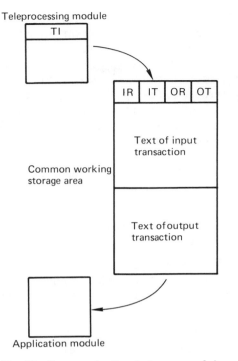

Teleprocessing module

TI

Common working
storage area

IR | IT | OR | OT

Text of input
transaction

Text of output
transaction

Application module

Fig. J2 Communication between modules

decode them, and pass them to the appropriate application module for processing. We are primarily interested here in the decoding and passing of transactions to other modules, so we will make some simplifying assumptions about the mechanisms actually used to gather input. Let us first assume that the TP module is capable of handling many terminals, and that it receives input from the operating system with a macro *that does not automatically place the TP program in a wait state.* For simplicity, we will call this a POLL macro.

The order in which terminals are serviced is unimportant to us in this discussion, and we may assume that the application programmer either specified a particular polling sequence (either with a macro or with a job control card) or that he is willing to allow terminal input to be processed on a first-come-first-served basis. The important point is that the TP module can use the POLL macro to receive input from a terminal, *or to receive an indication from the operating system that there is no input.* This negative indication allows the TP module to proceed with any other processing it may have before placing itself in a WAIT state.

It can be seen that the processing performed by the TP module depends on the setting of the control bits in the common working storage area, and the presence of terminal input, if any. Actually, the TP module can represent the presence or absence of terminal input with a bit which is set to 0 when there is no terminal input, and set to 1 when there is terminal input. Thus, *all* of the TP module's processing depends on the state of various bits—bits which are randomly set and reset by *external* mechanisms.

With this type of system, it is easy for the programmer to construct a straight-forward flowchart that does *not* take into account all of the possible conditions. As an alternative, the application programmer can first identify all of the possible *states* of his program, and then build his program around this state-oriented approach. In the Widget system, the TP module can be in a number of states, depending on the value of the following variables:

TI   Terminal input. If there is terminal input that the operating system has provided, this bit is a 1; otherwise it is a 0.

IR   Input ready. This is one of the four control bits in the common area of working storage, and is set to one when the TP module places a new transaction in the storage area.

IT   Input taken. This bit is set to one when the application module (i.e. the inventory module, accounting module, inquiry module or batch module) has taken the input from the common working storage area and has begun processing it.

OR   Output ready. This bit is set to one by the application module when some output has been placed in the common area.

OT   Output taken. This bit is set to one when the TP module takes the output from the common area and begins giving it to the operating system.

Bits IR and IT are mutually exclusive, and so are OR and OT. That is, if IR = 0, then IT = 1; if IR = 1, then IT = 0. Similarly, if OR = 0, then OT = 1, and if OR = 1, then OT = 0. This is because of the nature of the system—only one thing can happen at any given time. Thus, we *could* describe the input conditions with one bit, instead of using both IR and IT. However, using two bits gives us a better picture of what is actually happening at any time.

As the reader can see, there are a total of two states that IR and IT can be in; similarly, there are a total of two states for OR and OT. Finally, TI can be in either of two states, yielding a total of eight states for the TP module. These eight states are listed in Table J2. By following the teleprocessing module through its eight states, we will better understand the communication between the various modules in the system.

TABLE J2 *States for the Teleprocessing Module*

State	TI	IR	IT	OR	OT	Comments
0	0	0	1	0	1	This is the "idle" state. WAIT until state = 1 or state = 4
1	1	0	1	0	1	Give the input to the appropriate module, change to state = 2

TABLE J2—*cont.*

State	TI	IR	IT	OR	OT	Comments
2	0	1	0	0	1	There is nothing to do here, except to WAIT for state = 0,3,4, or 6
3	1	1	0	0	1	The terminal input must be queued up, and the TP module must WAIT for state = 1 or state = 7
4	0	0	1	1	0	The module's output is taken from the common working storage, and given to the operating system (it may be necessary to WAIT here). Then the state is changed to state = 0
5	1	0	1	1	0	Take output from module, and go to state = 1
6	0	1	0	1	0	Take output from module, and go to state = 2
7	1	1	0	1	0	Take output from module, and go to state = 3

The TP module begins in state = 0, as shown in Figure J3. The control

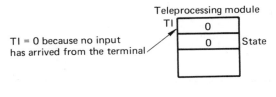

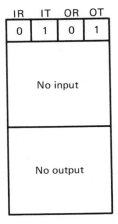

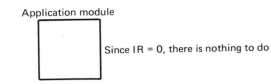

Fig. J3 The TP module in state = 0

bits IT and OT are initialized to one, so that neither the TP module nor the application modules will wait indefinitely for the first input/output. The system remains in state = 0 until some input arrives from a terminal, at which time the TP module changes to state = 1, as shown in Figure J4.

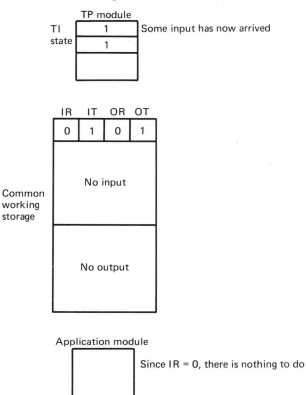

Fig. J4 The TP module in state = 1

State = 1 is only one of four states in which the TP module has some input. However, in this state it sees that the application module has taken its previous input and is ready for new input. Accordingly, the TP module transfers the new transaction into the common working area of storage, as shown in Figure J5, and sets IR = 1, IT = 0, TI = 0. Finally, it changes to state = 2.

State = 2 is the "wait" state. As shown in Figure J6, there is no terminal input to process, and the application module is still working on the current transaction. Since OR = 0, the application module has not produced any terminal output for the TP module. Thus, the TP module must issue a WAIT macro until something happens. There are a number of possible states which may result from eventual action on the part of the application module—states 0, 3, 4, or 6.

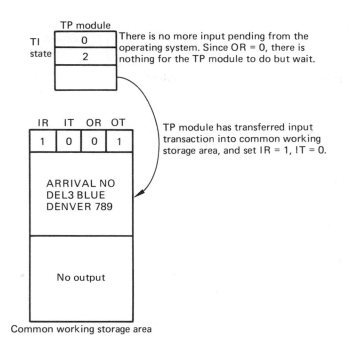

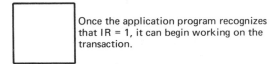

Fig. J5 The TP module in state = 2

State = 3 occurs if the TP module receives input while the application module is still working on a transaction. Since the input cannot be processed immediately, it is queued up. There is nothing more that the TP module can do until the application module causes a change of state.

State = 4 is a result of the application module generating some terminal output. We are assuming, in the Widget system, that only one line of output will be generated for each transaction, although we could allow multiple lines of output with one more control bit. It is important to note that the application module will not place any output in the common working storage area until it sees that OT = 1 (which is the initialized state of OT—see Figure J3). Having done so, the application module sets OT = 0 and OR = 1. This is recognized by the TP module in state = 4, and the output is removed from the common working storage area, as shown in Figure J7. The output is then given to the operating system to begin sending it to the terminal, and the TP module then reverts to state = 1.

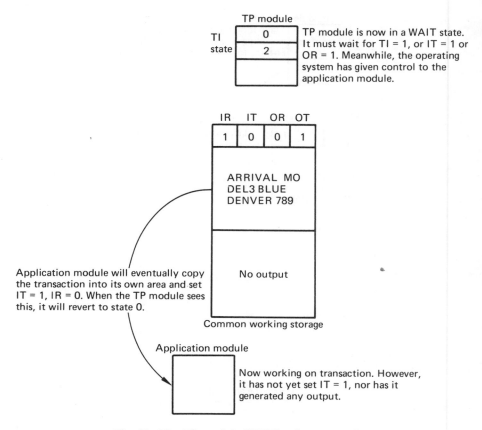

Fig. J6 The TP module WAITing in state = 2

State = 5 is rather complex. As illustrated by Figure J8, it occurs *after* the application module has copied a transaction from the common working storage area into its own working storage, thus permitting the TP module to insert another transaction in the common area. Having copied the transaction, the application module has set IR = 0 and IT = 1, but also generated some output. Meanwhile, some more input has arrived from a terminal, causing TI = 1. In this situation, the TP module takes the output from the common working storage area and changes to state = 1.

States 6 and 7 occur when the application module generates terminal output *after* copying the nth transaction from the common working storage area, and *after* the TP module has inserted the $n + 1$st transaction. In this case, the application module is busily working on the nth transaction, and has set OR = 1 and OT = 0. However, it has not yet accepted the $n + 1$st transaction, so IR = 1 and IT = 0. As Figures J9 and J10 illustrate, state = 6 occurs when this situation takes place with no additional terminal input pending; state = 7 occurs if there *is* additional input pending.

We have somewhat oversimplified our discussion of the teleprocessing module, and the reader may want to extend this state-oriented approach to

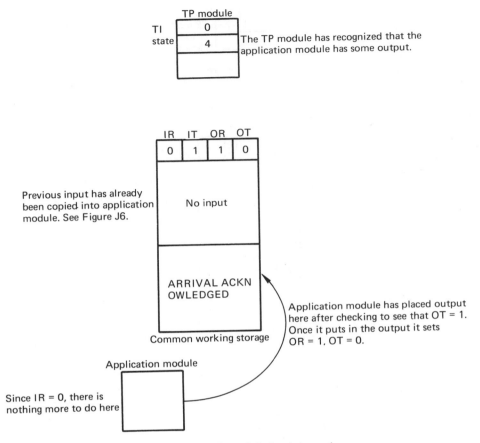

Fig. J7   The TP module in state = 4

make it more sophisticated. As we have already mentioned, it might be desirable to allow the application module to generate more than one line of output. Also, the reader should assure himself that this mechanism works with more than one application module. We have simplified the actual input and output of transactions, and the reader may want to consider the effect of various buffering schemes or terminal IO macros.

In addition, we should make the teleprocessing handler responsible for decoding transactions, and checking for syntax errors. Let us assume for a moment that all users of the system are allowed to use all of the transactions that we listed in Table J1. We can also assume that each parameter in an input transaction is separated by a *blank*. Thus, the following transactions would be legal:

PAYMENT   123456   1234 $35.43
ARRIVAL MODEL3 BLUE DENVER 789
INQA MODEL2 RED HOUSTON

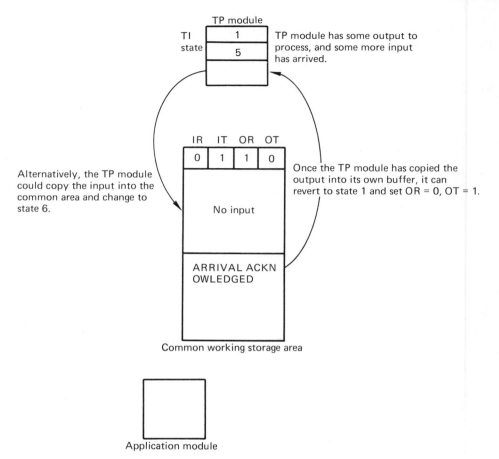

Fig. J8 The TP module in state = 5

Since there are only six standard arguments for the various transactions, we can construct a "matrix," or decision table, shown in Figure J11, to indicate the type of arguments expected for each type of transaction.

With this approach, it becomes fairly simple to write a general "scanning" routine to decode a line of input. We first scan the input line for a *command*, and look it up in a command dictionary, as shown in Figure J12. This tells us which entry to use in the command "matrix," and the routine can then proceed to scan the input line, as shown in Figure J13. Alphanumeric quantities can be looked up in standard "model dictionaries," "color dictionaries," and so forth. The command matrix can also indicate whether a numeric quantity is intended to be converted to an integer or a floating point number.

Again, we have oversimplified to show a general approach. We may want to restrict some users in the Widget system from using some of the transactions, which could be accomplished by having separate tables, dictionaries, and matrices for each user. Alternatively, we could simplify matters by eliminating all of the tables and forcing all input to be numerical in nature—i.e. numerical model numbers, colors represented by numbers, etc.

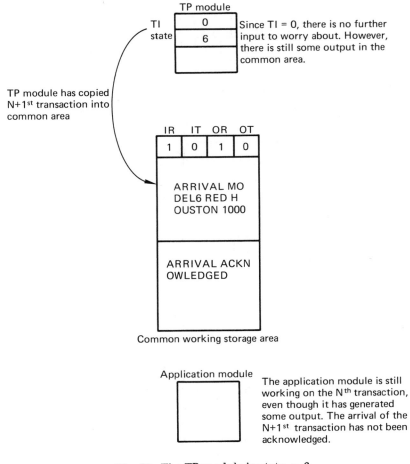

TP module

TI	0
state	6

Since TI = 0, there is no further input to worry about. However, there is still some output in the common area.

TP module has copied N+1st transaction into common area

IR	IT	OR	OT
1	0	1	0

ARRIVAL MO
DEL6 RED H
OUSTON 1000

ARRIVAL ACKN
OWLEDGED

Common working storage area

Application module

The application module is still working on the Nth transaction, even though it has generated some output. The arrival of the N+1st transaction has not been acknowledged.

Fig. J9 The TP module in state = 6

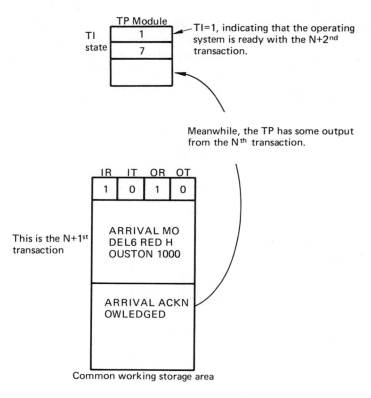

TP Module

TI state

1
7

TI=1, indicating that the operating system is ready with the N+2nd transaction.

Meanwhile, the TP has some output from the Nth transaction.

IR	IT	OR	OT
1	0	1	0

This is the N+1st transaction

ARRIVAL MO DEL6 RED H OUSTON 1000

ARRIVAL ACKN OWLEDGED

Common working storage area

Application module

Still working on the Nth transaction

Fig. J10 The TP module in state = 7

	P.O. #	Acct. No.	Model	Color	W'house	Amt.
ORDER	0	1	3	3	4	2
RESERVE	0	1	3	3	4	2
CANCEL	1	1	0	0	0	0
ARRIVAL	0	0	3	3	3	2
SHIPMENT	1	1	0	0	0	0
PAYMENT	1	1	0	0	0	2
STOPCREDIT	0	1	0	0	0	0
RESTORECREDIT	0	1	0	0	0	0
CHARGE	0	1	0	0	0	2
CREDIT	0	1	0	0	0	2
INQA	0	0	3	3	4	0
INQC	1	1	0	0	0	0
ADDC	0	1	0	0	0	0
DELC	0	1	0	0	0	0
ADDW	0	0	3	3	0	0
DELW	0	0	3	3	0	0

Codes: 0 No argument
        1 Integer argument
        2 Floating point argument
        3 Alphanumeric argument
        4 Optional alphanumeric argument

Fig. J11 Matrix for decoding input transactions

0	ORDER
1	RESERVE
2	CANCEL
3	ARRIVAL
4	SHIPMENT
5	PAYMENT
6	STOPCREDIT
7	RESTORECREDIT
8	CHARGE
9	CREDIT
10	INQA
11	INQC
12	ADDC
13	DELC
14	ADDW
15	DELW

When a command is found in this table, the index tells which
entry in the command matrix will contain information about
the parameters.

Fig. J12 Command dictionary for input decoding

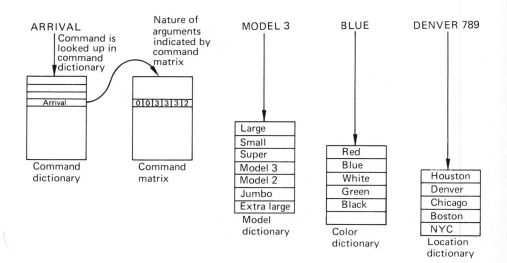

Fig. J13 Input scanning routine

PROCESSING IN THE APPLICATION MODULES

The processing that takes place in the application modules is considerably simpler than that in the TP module. As shown in Table J3, there are only four states that the application module can be in. Basically, the application module waits until input has been placed in the common working storage area, then does its processing. It places its output in the common working storage area unless the OT bit indicates that the TP module has not yet taken the previous line of output.

TABLE J3 *States for the Application Modules in the Widget System*

State	IR	IT	OR	OT	Comments
0	0	1	0	1	This is the "initial" state. The module is also in this state while it is actually processing a transaction (unless there is output or more input pending).
1	0	1	1	0	It is possible to be in this state while the TP module is working on output from the nth transaction and the application module is working on input from the $n + 1$st transaction. If the application module decides to generate *more* output while in this state, it must wait until state = 0 or state = 2.
2	1	0	0	1	This state occurs when the TP module has just placed a transaction in the common working storage area. The application module takes the input and reverts to state = 0.
3	1	0	1	0	This state occurs if the TP module is working on output from the nth transaction, while the application module is working on the $n + 1$st transaction, and the $n + 2$nd transaction has been stored in the common working area.

The application module begins in state = 0. As we mentioned before, the IT and OT bits are initialized to one, so that the TP module will not hesitate to place input in the working storage area and the application module will not hesitate to place output in the working storage area. In state = 0, there is nothing for the application module to do—it must WAIT until state = 2.

When state = 2, the TP module has inserted a transaction in the working storage area. The application module copies the transaction into its own area, as shown in Figure J14, then reverts to state = 0 as it processes the input. At this point, the TP module may decide to place another transaction in the common area, in which case we will reach state = 2 again.

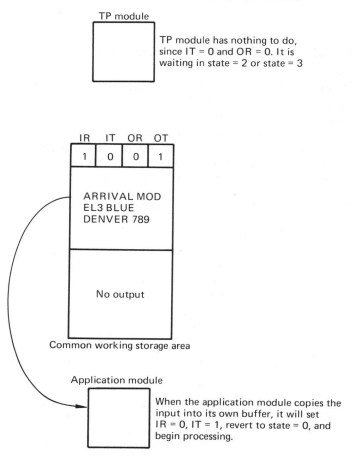

Fig. J14 The application module in state = 2

However, the application module may continue with its processing in state = 2 until it has some output to perform. At that point, it places the output in the common working storage area, and changes to state = 1.

State = 1 can be reached in either of two different ways. If the module receives a transaction and begins working on it, some output may be generated. The output will be placed in the common working storage area, and OR = 1 and OT = 0. Having generated its output, there is presumably nothing more for the application module to do, so it must wait for some more input from the TP module—that is, it must wait for state = 2. However, it is possible that when we reach state = 2, the TP module will still be working on the output in the common working storage area. Thus, the application module will have begun work on the n + 1st transaction while the output from the nth transaction is still in the common working storage area. When the application module gets to the point of producing some output for the n + 1st transaction, we will once again be in state = 1, and the module will have to wait until state = 0 or state = 2.

State = 3 is even more complex. We can reach this state if the TP module is working on output from the nth transaction while the application module is processing the $n + 1$st transaction and the $n + 2$nd transaction has been stored in the common working storage area. This causes no trouble until the application module decides to generate some output for the $n + 1$st transaction, at which time it must WAIT until state = 2.

It should be pointed out that we have not done a complete job here. The application programmer should indicate *all* of the conditions in which each state is reached, and all of the new states that can be attained. In the case of the application module, it may be helpful to add more states to distinguish the cases when the module is *busy* and when it is *idle*. An expanded state table is shown in Table J4, together with some (but probably not all) of the legal transitions of state. Using Table J4, the reader is invited to describe the meaning of the following sequence of state transitions:

$$0,2,4,5,1,3,5,7,6,7,6,2,4,5,1,0$$

TABLE J4   *Expanded State Table for Application Modules*

State	IR	IT	OR	OT	Module Busy *	Can change to states
0	0	1	0	1	0	2
1	0	1	1	0	0	0,3
2	1	0	0	1	0	4
3	1	0	1	0	0	5
4	0	1	0	1	1	5,6
5	0	1	1	0	1	7,1
6	1	0	0	1	1	2,7
7	1	0	1	0	1	4,6,2

* The Module Busy bit is zero if the application module is not currently working on a transaction, and one if it is currently processing a transaction.

A SIMPLER ARRANGEMENT
FOR THE WIDGET SYSTEM

There is one major problem with the system design that we have presented above: it is too complicated. While the reader hopefully was able to understand the mechanics of the multi-tasking arrangement between the TP module and the application modules, it should not surprise us if a junior application programmer would be slightly overwhelmed by our design.

The system is complicated primarily because the TP module is handling several different transactions concurrently. In Figure J10, for example, we saw that it was possible for three different transactions to be in the system, each in a different stage of processing. It is very difficult to visualize all of the possible combinations of conditions that could occur with this scheme, and the reader may have harbored some secret doubts as to whether the system would even work at all (the author certainly did!). In any case, there is no doubt that such an arrangement could be extremely difficult to test, and would be susceptible to various subtle real-time bugs.

The situation would be simplified tremendously if the TP module and the application module worked on only *one* transaction at a time. In this case, we could represent the various activities of the system with three bits:

TI   Terminal input. As before, this bit would be a zero if there was no pending input from a terminal, and would be a one if the operating system had some input from a terminal.

MB   Module busy flag. This flag would be set to zero if the application module was currently idle, and would be set to one if the module was currently working on a transaction.

OB   Output area busy. This flag would be set to zero if there is no output in the common area of working storage, and would be set to one when there is some output to be processed.

To further simplify things, we can assume that the application module has not "finished" processing a transaction until the TP module has processed all output. Thus, we will never have the combination of MB = 0 and OB = 1.

With these assumptions, we can describe the legal states of the TP module very simply, as we see in Table J5. By examining each of these states, it will become evident how much simpler this arrangement really is.

TABLE J5 *State Table for the Teleprocessing Module in the Simplified Widget System*

State	TI	MB	OB	Comments
0	0	0	0	This is the "idle" state. WAIT until state = 4.
1	0	0	1	ILLEGAL. In the simplified system, the module is considered to be "busy" until all output has been taken care of.
2	0	1	0	There is nothing to do here, except wait for a change to state = 6, state = 3, or state = 0.
3	0	1	1	The application module is working on a transaction, and has generated some output. The TP module must process the output, and the state will eventually change to state = 2 or state = 7.
4	1	0	0	Give the input to the appropriate application module, and change to state = 2.

TABLE J5—*cont.*

State	TI	MB	OB	Comments
5	1	0	1	ILLEGAL
6	1	1	0	More input has arrived while the application module is processing the current transaction. The new transaction must be queued, and the state eventually changes to state = 7 or state = 4.
7	1	1	1	The application module is working on the current transaction and has generated some output; meanwhile more input has arrived. At this point, the TP module must queue the new input, process the output, and eventually change to state = 6.

State = 0 is, once again, the idle state. As we see in Figure J15, there is no terminal input for the TP module to process, nor is there any work for

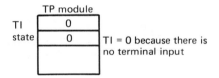

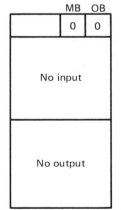

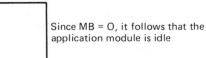

Fig. J15 State = 0 in the simplified TP module

the application module to perform. However, unlike our earlier design, the only legal change of state is to state = 4.

State = 1 is illegal, as we have specified above. To keep our design simple, we are assuming that the application module remains "busy" as long as it has some terminal output pending. This ensures that the application module will never be working on more than one transaction at a time.

State = 2 occurs when the application module has begun working on a transaction, and there is no more input for the TP module to worry about. As we see in Figure J16, the application module has not generated any output, or if it has, the TP module has already processed it, and reset OB to zero. Since there is only one transaction being processed, it should be evident what the legal changes of state might be. First, we might get some more terminal input, in which case TI would be set to one, and we would change to state = 6. Alternatively, the application program might generate some output during the processing of the current transaction, in which case

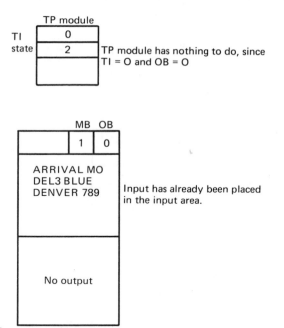

Fig. J16   State = 2 in the simplified TP module

the state changes to state = 3. Finally, it is possible that the application module might finish processing the current transaction, in which case the system would revert to state = 0.

State = 3 occurs if the application module generates some output while processing the current transaction. It places the output in the common area of working storage, as illustrated in Figure J17, and then perhaps continues processing the transaction. If more terminal input arrives while we are in this state, the system will change to state = 7; otherwise, the system will change to state = 2 when the TP module finishes processing the output.

State = 4 occurs when some input arrives from a terminal while the system is idle. Since the application module is idle, the TP module can place the terminal input into the common area of working storage, as shown in Figure J18. The system then changes to state = 2.

State = 5 is illegal, for reasons that we have already discussed.

State = 6 occurs if more terminal input arrives while the application

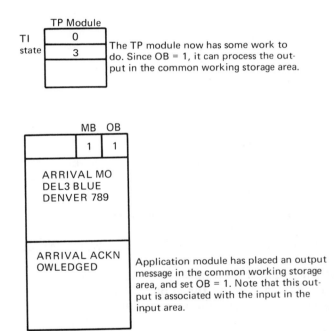

Fig. J17 State = 3 in the simplified TP module

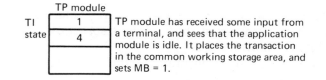

TP module

TI state		
	1	
	4	

TP module has received some input from a terminal, and sees that the application module is idle. It places the transaction in the common working storage area, and sets MB = 1.

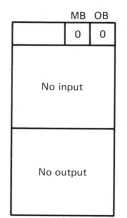

MB OB

	0	0

No input

No output

Common working storage area

Application module

Application program is currently idle

Fig. J18 State = 4 in the simplified TP module

module is busy working on the current transaction. The TP module must queue the terminal input and wait for the application module to do something. If the application module generates some output, the system will change to state = 7; otherwise the application module will eventually finish processing the transaction, and the system will revert to state = 4. This state is illustrated by Figure J19.

State = 7 occurs when the application module is working on the current transaction, and has generated some output. Meanwhile, as shown in Figure J20, more input has arrived from the terminal. At this point, the TP module must queue the new input, since the application module is still busy working on the current transaction (the application module may actually have finished its work, but it must pretend that it is busy until the TP module has taken care of its output). The TP module then proceeds to take care of the output generated by the application module, and eventually changes to state = 6.

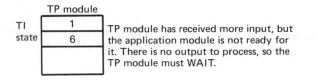

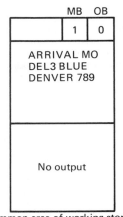

Common area of working storage

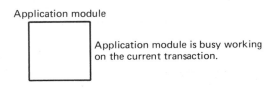

Fig. J19 State = 6 in the simplified TP module

It should be clear that this arrangement is much simpler than the one presented previously. Since only one transaction is being processed by the application module at any one time, there is much less chance for a subtle programming bug to creep into the system—in the previous system, we would almost inevitably have a few cases where the wrong output got sent to the wrong terminal.

On the other hand, this new arrangement seems to make less efficient use of the multiprogramming capabilities of the system. There will be times when the application module is waiting for the TP module to finish processing some output, *and it must remain idle during that period of time.* However, since there are several application modules in the system (i.e. the inventory module, the accounting module, the inquiry module, and the batch module), the operating system should always be able to find at least one executable program.

If there was only one application module in the system, then this simpler arrangement would certainly lead to less overlap of IO and computation. If there were only ten or twenty terminals on the system, this could be tolerated; on the Widget system, though, we are planning 200 terminals, and it is likely that we will need all the efficiency we can get. Thus, if we had only one application module, we would be forced into the more complex type of system that we described earlier in this chapter.

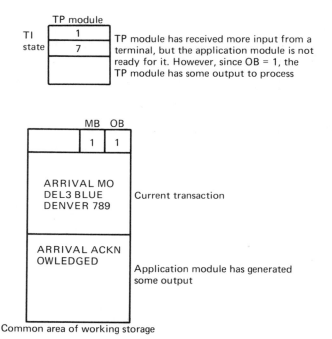

Fig. J20 State = 7 in the simplified TP module

We discussed the general nature of the processing by the application programs when we first introduced the Widget Corporation in Chapter F. A more detailed discussion is not possible until we know more about the organization of the files and records in the Widget system. When Wilbur Goodbody made his design calculations in Chapter F, he assumed that the files would probably be organized as shown by Figures F6 and F7—but this was mostly based on the proposal furnished to him by the Aardvark 301 salesman. Now that we have designed the transactions and the general nature of the application program, we are now in a better position to make a detailed design of the files.

However, we must first make sure that we understand the various types of file organizations for on-line systems. We will need to consider the problem of simultaneous access to the files, though this seems to have been solved with the approach we have taken. We will also have to concern ourselves with file security and file recovery, since our on-line order system deals with the lifeblood of the Widget Corporation. All of these subjects are discussed in Part IV, after which we will return to the design of the Widget system.

FILES AND DATA BASES
FOR ON-LINE SYSTEMS

FILE ORGANIZATION CONCEPTS AND PHILOSOPHIES

INTRODUCTION

The organization of the data base for an on-line computer system is one of the most significant parts of the design work. On-line systems tend to pose much larger problems in this area than batch systems, for a number of reasons. First, the data base is often much larger. While it is true that there are batch systems with large files (such as banks and insurance companies), *most* batch systems get along with fairly moderate files. Most scientific time-sharing systems, on the other hand, have data bases of at least 50-100 million characters. Several organizations are currently planning on-line systems with data bases of two or three billion characters, and by the mid-1970's, we can expect a few systems with data bases of 20-30 billion characters.

Another reason for the importance of the data base in an on-line system is its sensitivity to system failures. Most batch systems update a master file by reading the old master file, reading a "transaction" file, and building a completely new master file. If there is a system failure in the middle of processing, the job may have to be restarted, *but the old master file is intact*. There are occasions when a faulty magnetic tape drive may stretch or crease the old master file, but the cautious data processing manager can avoid catastrophe by keeping a *copy* of the master file in some secure area, and by saving previous versions of the master file, together with the corresponding transaction files. There are a number of well-known procedures in this area, and the result is that it is fairly rare to hear of situations when the data base on a batch system is damaged so badly that information is lost forever.

We are not usually so lucky in an on-line system. There is usually no such thing as updating a master file by passing a transaction file against an old master file. There is only *one* master file (or master data base) in the on-line system, and it is irrevocably *changed* whenever an update occurs. Thus, if there is a system failure, we do not have an intact master file, for it has been changed and altered during the course of processing. As we shall see in Chapter N, there is even a possibility that the system will fail in the *middle* of updating the data base. Thus, there is the danger that the data base will end up in an "inconsistent" state—i.e. with one record updated, and several logically related records *not* updated. The situation may be further confused if the user is not sure whether his last transaction was processed by the system just prior to the failure.

Still another reason for the importance of the data base design in an on-line system is the *dynamic nature* of the data base. As we have already pointed out, the common way of handling a file in a batch system is to read it in a *serial* fashion, updating individual records whenever necessary. In an on-line system, records are read, updated, or deleted in a *random* fashion. The same record may be read and/or written several hundred times during the course of a day, depending on the nature and sequence of transactions that arrive in the system. It is also important to note that *combinations* of records may be read in an on-line system, in order to fulfill complex information retrieval requests from a user. Thus, there is likely to be a tremendous increase in the number of file accesses in an on-line system, as compared with its batch predecessor. As we have already noted several times, this increase in file accessing can be a serious bottleneck in the system. It obviously pays the system designer to plan his data base as carefully as possible in order to minimize this potential problem.

We will be concerned with four major aspects of the data base in this section. In this chapter, we will discuss the file accessing techniques and file organization mechanisms that are available to the application programmer on most on-line systems. In Chapter L, we will discuss the problem of simultaneous access to which we have alluded in previous sections of the book. The problems of file security are discussed in Chapter M, and file recovery is discussed in Chapter N. Finally, we will return to our discussion of the Widget Corporation's on-line order entry system in Chapter O.

To some extent, the type of file organization depends on the computer vendor's operating system. Most third generation operating systems at least allow the application programs to access files in a serial or a random fashion. Some allow more complex declarations on the part of the application programs—such as a file than can be accessed in *either* a serial or a random fashion, or both. It is interesting to note that some operating systems—especially the scientific time-sharing systems—maintain their own file organization on top of the one built by the application programs.

We should emphasize that the file organization and accessing techniques that we will discuss here are fairly simple and straightforward. A great deal of thought has been given to data management techniques, and the reader is invited to browse through some of the papers listed at the end of this chapter. Our purpose here is to examine the usefulness of various file accessing and file organization techniques for on-line systems, using the following criteria:

1 *Minimizing file accesses*

 A file organization that is elegant, but requires many file accesses to retrieve a record, is to be discouraged.

2 *Minimizing the space required by the file*

 There are some popular file accessing techniques that allow the application program to retrieve any record in one access, but they may waste a large portion of the available file space.

3 *Vulnerability to system failure*

 Some of the more complex file organization techniques depend on directories, or linked lists, to locate a specified piece of information. If a portion of the disk becomes unreadable because of parity errors, or if a directory is destroyed, a large portion of the data base may be lost. We will be interested in file organizations that increase our chances of reconstructing the data base after a failure.

4 *Migration*

 Many of the larger on-line systems are built with *hierarchies* of file storage, using a variety of devices such as drums, disks, data cells, and magnetic tapes. Since it is desirable to keep the most frequently accessed information on the fastest storage device, it may be desirable to move records from one device to another as they become more or less "active." Not all file organization techniques allow us to do this easily.

THE CONCEPT OF BUFFERING IN
AN ON-LINE ENVIRONMENT

Before we begin our discussion of file accessing techniques, let us first review some basic concepts, and see how they apply in the on-line environment. The concept of buffering is standard on virtually every third generation computer, and is illustrated in Figure K1. The size and number of buffers associated with a file (or an IO device) may be specified in the job control cards that accompany the programmer's execution deck, or it may be specified when a file is opened with an OPEN macro.

Buffered IO is tremendously useful whenever records are read or written in a serial fashion. Obviously, a large number of IO devices, such as card readers, card punches, high-speed printers, and magnetic tapes, can *only* operate in a serial fashion, and there is good reason to supply two or three buffers for those kinds of devices. We should remember, though, that the

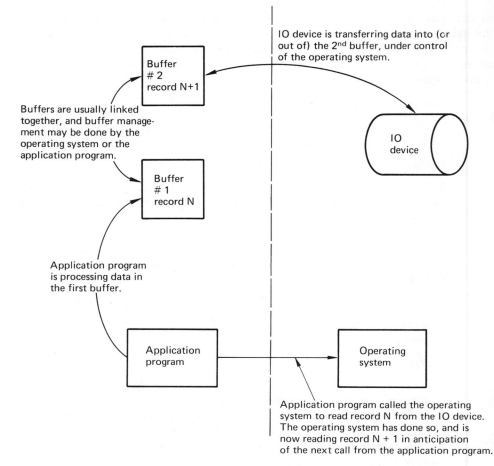

IO device is transferring data into (or out of) the 2nd buffer, under control of the operating system.

Buffer
2
record N+1

Buffers are usually linked together, and buffer management may be done by the operating system or the application program.

Buffer
1
record N

IO
device

Application program is processing data in the first buffer.

Application program

Operating system

Application program called the operating system to read record N from the IO device. The operating system has done so, and is now reading record N + 1 in anticipation of the next call from the application program.

Fig. K1   The concept of buffering

purpose of buffered input/output is to allow the operating system to transfer one buffer of data to or from the IO device while the application program is processing data in another buffer.

When we are talking about data bases for on-line systems, it is questionable whether the concept of buffering is of any use at all. Since records are read in a random fashion, it is impossible for the operating system to predict which record will be required next. Buffered *output* may be more useful, since the application program can be placing the N + 1st random output record in a buffer, while the operating system is transferring the Nth random output record from another buffer to the file storage unit.

There may be some cases when an application program decides to read some records in a serial fashion from a random data base. As shown in Figure K2, the application program may make a *random* access to the Nth record in the data base and may then read the next few consecutive records in a serial fashion. This would seem to be an area where buffering would be useful, but it often turns out that if the programmer has declared the file to be *random*, and if he has indicated, when he opens the file, that he intends to access it in a random fashion, then the operating system may insist on treating all accesses as being unrelated to one another—and it may refuse to buffer any of the records.

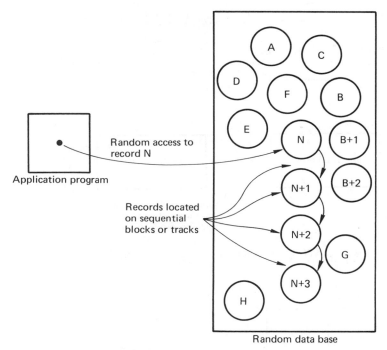

Fig. K2   Sequential accesses in a random data base

We should not completely rule out the concept of buffering for a random-access data base, for there may be some occasions when it can be used. However, the application programmer should carefully investigate the organization of the data base, the nature of his accesses to the data base, and the capabilities provided by the operating system before setting aside any large amounts of core memory for buffers. As we have indicated, buffering may occasionally be useful when the application program is *writing* to the data base, and when the application program decides to read a few records from the data base in a sequential fashion. Buffering may also be useful if the operating system provides a *look-ahead* capability.

A look-ahead capability exists when the application program is allowed to call the operating system to read a record *without being placed in a "wait" state*. As shown in Figure K3, this allows the application program to read record N, and then, while record N is being processed, begin reading record M. When record M is actually required for processing, the application program may have to issue a WAIT macro, but with some luck the operating system may have managed to read it in already—in which case, the

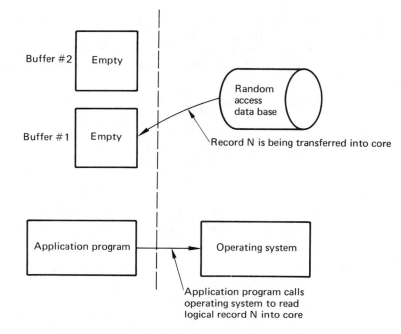

Fig. K3(a) Look-ahead on a random access data base

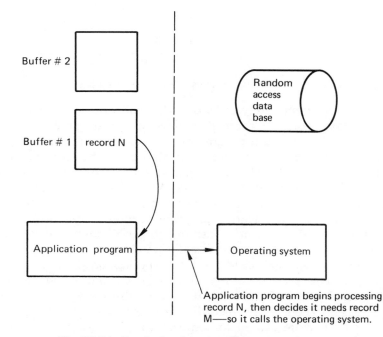

Fig. K3(b) Look-ahead on a random access data base

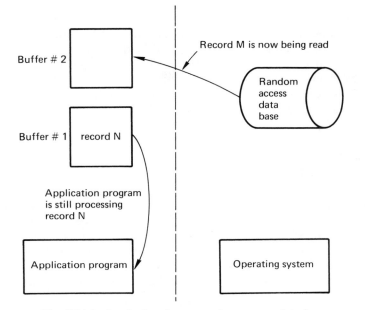

Fig. K3(c) Look-ahead on a random access data base

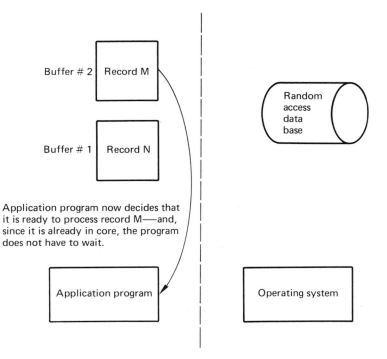

Fig. K3(d) Look-ahead on a random access data base

application program will not have to wait at all. The look-ahead capability is based, of course, on the assumption that the application program knows which record it will need next—in fact, that it knows long enough *in advance* that the operating system can retrieve the record before the application program has finished processing the current record. In an on-line system where the file accesses depend on the nature of the input from the terminals, however, this assumption is usually not valid.

THE CONCEPT OF BLOCKING IN AN ON-LINE ENVIRONMENT

Another concept that is very popular in a batch computer environment is that of *blocking* records in a file. As shown in Figure K4, blocking merely refers to the practice of placing several *logical* records within one *physical* record. This has been a common practice for magnetic tape files, where large physical records can increase the amount of data stored on the tape (because of fewer inter-record gaps), and decrease the IO time (because of fewer starts

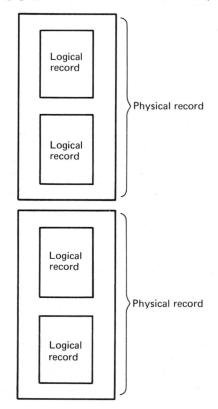

Fig. K4 The concept of blocking

and stops between records). The limiting factor on the size of a block was usually the amount of core memory that the application programmer had available.

The concept of blocking is also used in random-access data bases, but differs from magnetic tape blocking in that there are often some limits placed on the size of both logical and physical blocks. This is because most file storage units are organized in units of *sectors, blocks, tracks, cylinders*, or some other convenient measure. Thus, many of the disk-packs that are currently in use contain 7294 characters (or bytes) per track—and a physical record is often limited by the operating system to integer multiples of tracks. Many other disks (of the non-removable type) are broken into blocks of 144 characters or 240 characters. Thus, the physical records must be a multiple of 144 characters or 240 characters, although logical records may be less than one disk block.

Depending on the type of operating system, there may be further restrictions on the size of the logical records. A common restriction is that the disk block size must be evenly divisible by the logical record size *or* that the logical record size must be an integer multiple of the disk block size. Thus, if we were designing an on-line system with a disk whose block size was 240 characters, the logical record size could be 20, 30, 40, 60, 80, 120, 240, or 480 characters—or any other such size. However, it could not be 160, 180, 200, 300, or 360 characters.

The concept of blocking can be a very powerful tool when combined with some file accessing techniques. The important thing to remember here is that the operating system will read an *entire physical record* into core whenever necessary. Whenever the application program calls for a logical record, the operating system first checks to see if it is already in core—that is, it checks to see if the logical record is part of the physical record that was last read into core.

This, of course, is tremendously helpful if the application program decides to read several "neighboring" records. One of the file accessing techniques we will discuss is that of *linked lists* of logical records, and it pays the application programmer to ensure that a chain of logical records lies within one physical record on the file storage unit, as shown in Figure K5. Note that the only disadvantage of making a "mistake"—i.e. not requiring some of the logical records that have been read in—is some wasted core. Thus, if the disk is organized into 240-character blocks, the operating system *must* read at least 240 characters each time it accesses the disk.

There are some systems that can arrange for less than a full disk block to be transferred from disk to core memory, and there are also cases where a logical record is longer than one disk block. However, even in these two cases, the extra *rotation* time and *transfer* time is much smaller than the *seek* time required to begin reading a disk block. Thus, regardless of the situation, it usually only takes a little more time to read in several logical records than it does to read in only one logical record.

There may be great inefficiencies involved in *updating* a highly blocked

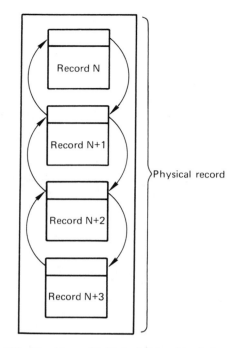

Fig. K5 Blocking with linked lists of logical records

random access file, even though it appears to be more efficient to *read* a blocked file. For example, suppose we decide to read logical record N in an on-line system where we have blocked four logical records per physical record. The unwary application programmer may do some processing and decide to read logical record N + 1, and, as illustrated in Figure K6, the operating system will provide record N + 1 without any additional file accesses. Note, however, that record N has been lost forever.

      Therein lies the problem, for if the application programmer decides to update record N + 1, the operating system will have no alternative but to reread the entire physical record, update logical record N + 1, then write the new physical record back to the disk. There is the possibility that the application programmer might have decided to update logical record N—which was the first one in the physical record. Then, since no records had been "lost" or "forgotten," it would be possible for the operating system to update logical record N in core, and write the physical record back on the disk.

      There is no guarantee that the operating system will perform the necessary bookkeeping to keep track of which logical records are in core, which ones are required for an update, and so forth. Even if the operating system does perform such a service, the application programmer can rest assured that it will involve a fairly large amount of overhead. If blocking is felt to be desirable, and if a large number of updates are likely to be done, it is best for the application programmer to perform his own blocking and deblocking.

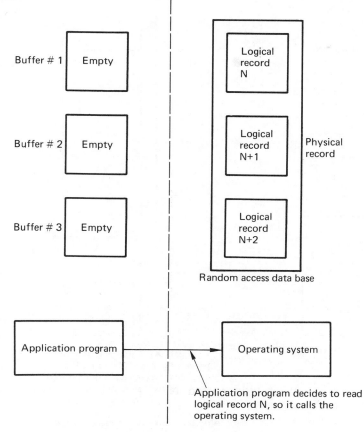

Fig. K6(a)   Updating a blocked random access data base

DIRECT ADDRESSING TECHNIQUES

Now that we have discussed the basic concepts of blocking and buffering, let us examine some of the more common techniques for accessing random files. The simplest is called the *direct addressing approach*, and is illustrated by Figure K7. One of the fields, or keys, of a logical record is itself the logical record number in the file.

For example, in an on-line inventory control system, one of the fields in an inventory item record might be a numeric "part number." The part number could be used as the logical record number, so that an application

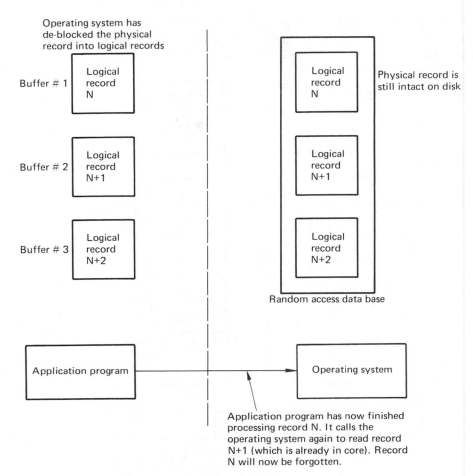

Fig. K6(b) Updating a blocked random access data base

program wanting to retrieve the record on part #1234 could simply issue a macro of the form

READ INVFILE (1234)

As another example, we could design a data base for an on-line management information system with the personnel records containing the employee's Social Security number. The social security number could then be used to *locate* the logical record containing the employee's record. To retrieve the employee record for someone whose social security number was 130-34-9025, we could issue the following sort of macro to the operating system:

READ EMPFILE (130349025)

There is one major advantage to this approach—the minimization of file accesses required to locate a logical record. As long as we know the proper key, or identifying field, there are no computations to be done, no searches,

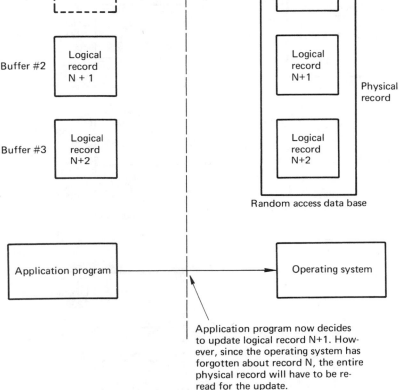
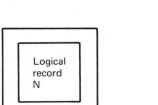

Fig. K6(c) Updating a blocked random access data base

and no "wasted" disk accesses. For on-line systems that require very fast access to the data base, this approach can thus be extremely attractive.

However, we indicated that another criterion to be used in judging various access techniques was the *minimization of disk space.* The direct addressing approach has the unfortunate disadvantage that the available file space is likely to be very poorly utilized unless there is a very dense distribution of keys. For example, our hypothetical management information system above arranged its file in such a way that there is one logical record for each social security number—even though there may only be a few hundred employees in the organization. Similarly, our inventory control system will waste a tremendous amount of space unless the part numbers are assigned sequentially, and there are no gaps or unused numbers.

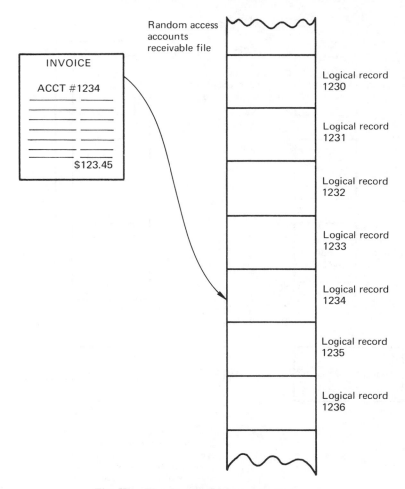

Fig. K7   The direct addressing technique

Thus, in order to make good use of our file space, we must have control over the distribution of keys in our data base. The system designer has no control over the assignment of Social Security numbers, so the direct addressing approach is not likely to be very efficient—unless he chooses a different key, such as an employee number, which he can assign sequentially to each new employee as he is hired. The direct addressing approach might work very well in an inventory control system, assuming that the system designer has control over the assignment of part numbers. On-line systems centered about account numbers, invoice numbers, employee numbers, or other easily assignable numbers might also be candidates for this type of file organization. This point will be illustrated in Chapter O, when we return to our discussion of the Widget Corporation.

Note that we have essentially pushed the file accessing technique away from the computer and into the lap of the user of the system. Thus, we are forcing the user to remember his Social Security number, his employee number, his account number, and so forth. If the numbers are long and difficult to remember, there might be a far greater number of errors on the part of users, partially nullifying the savings in disk accesses. To minimize the chances of faulty numbers provided by our users, we can build check digits into the keys, or ask the user to provide corroborating information along with his key. Thus, a user might be asked to supply his name as well as his employee number—the system would use only the number, but would check the user-supplied employee name against the one found in the record.

Another disadvantage of the direct addressing technique is that it does not allow us to move information around—that is, we cannot easily "migrate" the logical records from one part of the data base (a disk, for example) to another part (a magnetic tape, for example). This is illustrated by Figure K8, in which an employee leaves an organization that has just installed a computerized management information system (we should not be surprised to learn that the installation of the system is precisely *why* he has

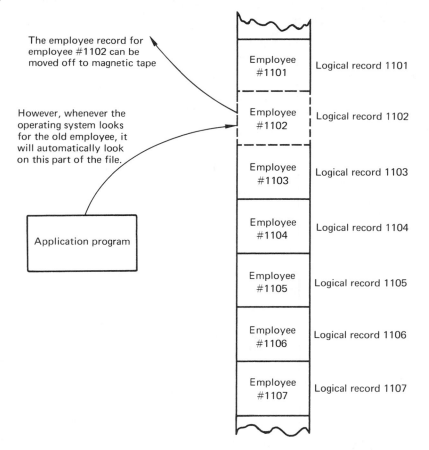

Fig K8 Deleting a record from a direct addressing file

quit!). We would like to keep the ex-employee's file on record for two or three years—in case subsequent employer's ask for references, and to fulfill various government regulations. However, we know that his record is going to be extremely inactive, and it would be convenient if we could remove the record from our on-line disk, and relegate it to magnetic tape, cards, or stone tablets. However, if we *do* have a request for information concerning the employee, we would still like to retrieve it by his old employee number. That means that we cannot re-assign his employee number to a new employee, *and it also means that we cannot assign the logical record on our data base to a new employee.* As long as the key is in use, the corresponding space on the data base will be reserved for it.

Similarly, it may be difficult to *expand* the data base. If we use our management information system to keep track of all of the awards and honors that have been bestowed upon an employee during his tenure with the organization, we may find that some of the employees have so many honors that we cannot fit all of the required information into the allotted space. Our only solution is to create a link to an additional record of information, as shown in Figure K9. This is likely to create more disk

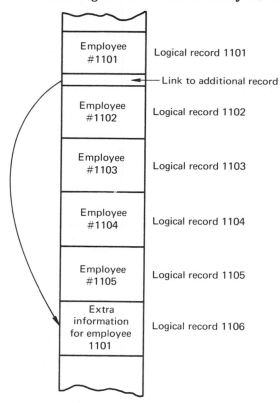

Fig. K9 Link to extra records in the direct addressing approach

accesses, depending on whether the "extra" information is required—and it also eliminates some of the available employee numbers.

In summary, then, the direct addressing technique is extremely fast, but is likely to make poor use of the available disk space unless the system designer can control the assignment of keys. The approach does not allow for "migration" of records, and it makes expansion difficult.

THE ALGORITHM APPROACH

A technique closely associated with the direct addressing approach is the so-called *algorithm approach*. The idea behind the algorithm approach is that the logical record number can be calculated as some algebraic function of a field or key within the record.

For example, an airline reservation system is really just an *inventory system*, with an inventory that changes on a day-by-day basis. We could build the data base in such a way that logical records would be accessed by concatenating the flight number with the date of the flight. Thus, to locate inventory information for Flight 207 on April 30, we would concatenate 207 with 120 (which is the Julian day of the year for April 30), to get a logical record number of 207120.

The major advantage of this technique is the same as the direct addressing approach—a minimization of disk accesses. With a reasonably small amount of processing, we can calculate the logical record number and retrieve it in one disk access. It is important to note that we are *guaranteed* to retrieve the correct record with this technique. To understand this point, let us consider the possibility of organizing our hypothetical management information system on the *last four digits* of the employee's social security number. This certainly seems like an algorithm approach, since we must do some processing, albeit trivial in nature, do reduce a Social Security number of 130-34-9025 to a logical record number of 9025. With this approach, though, we have *not* guaranteed that we will retrieve the right record—for our algorithm approach would also generate a logical record number of 9025 for an employee whose social security number was 345-67-9025, as shown in Figure K10—thus creating a problem. A file accessing technique where we generate a *probable* logical record number is discussed below under *randomizing techniques*.

The disadvantages of the algorithm approach are essentially the same as those of the direct addressing technique. A great deal of wasted file space can result, as we can see from the airline reservation example above. Since there are only 365 days in a year, logical records 207366 through 207999 will never be used. If it turns out that Flight 207 does not fly every day, the situation becomes even worse.

As in the direct addressing approach, we cannot "migrate" records within the data base, nor can we expand the data base with any ease at all.

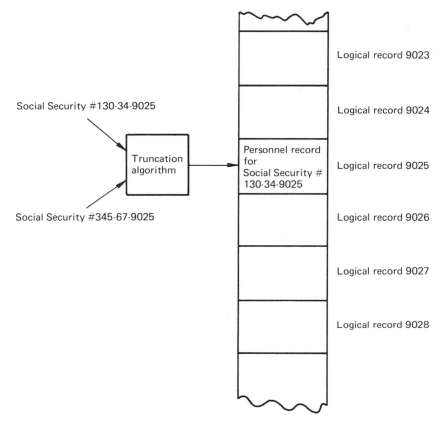

Fig. K10   A failure in the algorithm approach

Thus, we often find the direct addressing approach and the algorithm approach used only in cases where the data base is reasonably *stable*.

One small advantage of the direct addressing and algorithm techniques is their relative invulnerability to *failures*. Thus, if we should have a power failure in the midst of processing input on our hypothetical management information system, we know exactly where the records are after the failure. This is not true in some of the other techniques, which depend on directories, pointers, or links to retrieve a record. However, even though the *location* of a record is invulnerable to system failures with the direct addressing and algorithm approach, we must always be concerned with the vulnerability of the *contents* of the record.

BINARY SEARCH TECHNIQUE

An approach to file organization that is *not* commonly used is the binary search approach. This technique requires keeping the records in some kind of sequential order, as shown in Figure K11. In other words, the

On-line personnel file

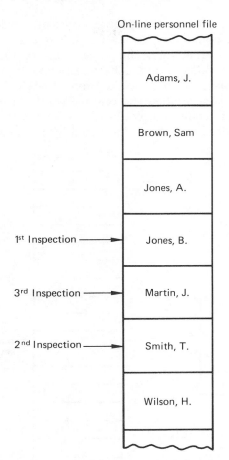

Fig. K11   The binary search technique

records must be sorted on a key—the key which will be used to retrieve the record—when the data base is first constructed.

To locate a record, we read in the "middle" record, from which we determine whether we are too high or too low. The range of the search is continually cut in half, and the total number of disk accesses is proportional to $\log_2$ N, where N is the number of records in the data base. This may seem rather innocent, but the number of disk accesses becomes staggering if the data base is of any appreciable size at all. If the data base consists of 32,768 records, we will require approximately 15 accesses to locate a record; a data base of 262,144 records would require 18 accesses, and so on. Thus, a technique which is excellent for searching tables in core (where the number of items to be searched is rarely more than a few hundred) is prohibitively expensive when searching data bases.

There are some variations of the binary search technique which are occasionally useful. If our logical records are highly blocked (i.e. a large number of logical records per physical record) we might use some other file accessing techniques to locate the proper physical record and bring it into core. A binary search could then be used to locate the correct logical record within that block. Alternatively, the *keys* from every hundredth logical record (or every thousandth, or any other reasonable number) could be kept in core. A binary search in core would then identify which block of one hundred logical records contained the one we want. Another binary search, or perhaps some other technique, could then be used to search through the last group of one hundred records, as indicated by Figure K12.

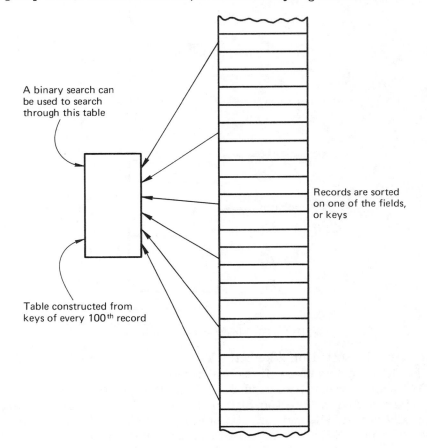

Fig. K12   A variation of the binary search

The nature of the binary search technique is such that it has many of the disadvantages of the previous two techniques we discussed. Since the file must be kept in an ordered fashion, it is difficult to insert new records and delete old ones. We can keep changes of this nature in a separate "transactions" file, but this increases the number of disk accesses required to locate a record, and may also result in wasted disk space. As with the previous two techniques, we cannot easily migrate the records to different parts of our data base. However, we can draw some small consolation from the fact that, as with the other two techniques, the *means of locating* the record with the binary search technique is impervious to system failures.

RANDOMIZING TECHNIQUES

Randomizing techniques—also called "hash codes" or "scramble codes"—differ from the other techniques in that they do not *guarantee* to find the required record on the first file access. The basic approach is to take some identifying key and perform some algebraic or logical manipulation that will generate a *probable* logical record number, as shown in Figure K13.

Consider our management information system once again. If our system is to have a data base of 1000 records (corresponding to an organization with 1000 employees), our randomizing technique might be

(employee's Social Security number) modulo 1000

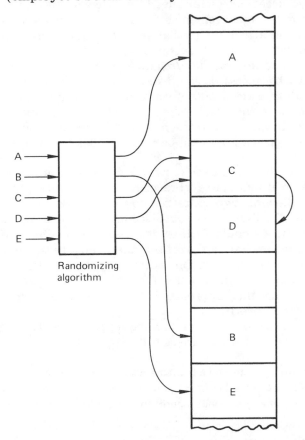

Fig. K13 The randomizing technique

Thus, if we wanted to find the record for the employee whose Social Security number was 130-34-9025, we would first access logical record number 025. Unfortunately, this randomizing technique would generate the same logical record number for an employee whose social security number was 176-67-4025—or for any other employee whose social security number ended in 025.

This problem of "synonyms" or "overflows" is what makes the randomizing technique so tricky. The number of overflows is really a function of the type of keys we use to retrieve the records—if the keys are evenly distributed (or randomly distributed, depending on one's outlook on life), then we can expect a relatively small number of overflows. In most cases, though, experience shows that there will be an unacceptable number of overflows if an attempt is made to pack the data base more than 70-80% full. In our management information system, for example, we might have to reserve 1200 logical records in our data base for our 1000 employees.

The randomizing technique can often be combined with blocking to form an effective accessing technique. If we decide that 1200 records is a reasonable size for our management information system data base, we might use our randomizing algorithm (social security number modulo 1000) in a slightly different way. It might be much more efficient to take the social security number modulo *one hundred*, and use the result as the *physical record number* to be accessed, as illustrated by Figure K14. Our data base would thus be constructed of 100 physical records (which in this context are often referred to as "buckets," "slots," or some other picturesque term) consisting of 12 logical records each. One file access would bring in the physical record which we hope will contain the desired logical record in its midst.

Note that if the employee's Social Security numbers are evenly distributed, there will be ten logical records in use for each physical block of 12 records. By allowing two extra records per block, we allow for some irregularity in the distribution of social security numbers—and by increasing the blocking factor, we could further decrease the possibility of overflows. In the event that we *do* have an overflow, there must be some procedure for determining where to look next. One commonly used approach is to use the next sequential block, though some feel that it may just aggravate the overflow problem; another approach is to reserve one or more dedicated overflow blocks for *all* overflows.

There are a number of common techniques for generating a randomizing code, the most popular of which are as follows:

1 Divide the key by N and take the remainder—where N is the number of elements in the data base. In other words, the logical record number (or the "bucket number," depending on one's approach) is the identifying key modulo N.

2 Use the identifying key modulo P, where P is the greatest prime number less than N. This approach decreases the number of overflows.

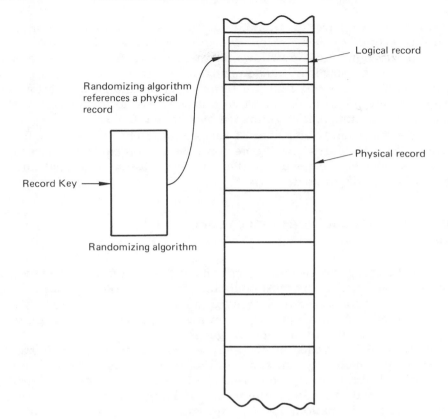

Fig. K14   The randomizing technique with blocking

3 Truncation of the identifying key (i.e. chopping off the low order bits, the high order bits, or perhaps some of the middle bits).

4 Radix conversion of the identifying key.

5 "Folding" — that is, splitting the key into several equal-sized portions, and adding then together.

6 "Squaring" — multiplying the key by itself and taking an appropriate number of bits from the *middle* of the result.

With the right randomizing technique, a reasonable distribution of keys, and a large amount of luck, the application programmer can usually hope to retrieve a record with an average of 1.2-1.5 file accesses. While this is not as good as the direct addressing approach or the algorithm approach, it is obviously better than the binary search technique, and is usually better than the directory-oriented approach we will discuss next. Thus, the randomizing technique, if carefully used, does appear to satisfy our criterion of minimizing disk accesses.

However, we have the same disadvantages that were present in the previous techniques. Some of our file space will have to be wasted if we are to keep the number of overflows down to a reasonable level; we cannot migrate records, since the randomizing algorithm will invoke its overflow technique if it does not find the record in a pre-ordained location. Once again, we take solace in the fact that our ability to locate a record with the randomizing technique is not impaired by a system failure.

Some interesting discussions of hash-coding techniques may be found in Maurer [2] and Morris [3]. Some formulas for probable file accesses are given though they depend on the unrealistic assumption that the keys are uniformly distributed.

DIRECTORY APPROACH (OR "TABLE LOOKUP," OR "INDEX LOOKUP")

The directory approach is perhaps one of the most popular techniques of file organization. It is the *most* common approach to file organization taken by operating systems and other vendor-supplied software systems. It is also used by application programs, either in place of, or as an adjunct to, the file organization provided by the operating system.

Basically, the approach involves having one or more levels, or hierarchies, of tables, in which a record can be "looked up" on a particular key. The directories themselves may be maintained in core, on a high-speed drum, or on the disk itself (along with the record of data). In Figure K15, we see our management information system organized with a three-level directory approach.

Depending on the location of the directories, file accessing may or may not be fast. If, in Figure K15, all three levels of directories are kept on the disk, then it will take *four* disk accesses to retrieve the personnel record of any employee. Obviously, the number of disk accesses decreases as more and more of the directories are kept in core, but it is usually true that *more* file accesses are required with the directory approach than with the other approaches we have discussed. Nevertheless, two or three disk accesses per record is not *too* unreasonable, and if our file accesses are not completely random, we may find that some of the necessary directories have already been brought into core by previous accesses.

What we lose in disk accessing time, though, we gain in disk space. The tremendous advantage of the directory approach is that the files may be densely packed. No space is lost as a result of missing records (contrast this with the direct addressing approach and the algorithm approach!), nor do we have to set aside 20-30% of our disk space for "overflows." On the other hand, some space is taken up by the directories themselves. While this will vary from system to system, a common rule of thumb is to add 10% to the size of the data base to make room for the directories.

Note that we have eliminated another weakness that was present in the previous file accessing techniques—migration. The records themselves can be

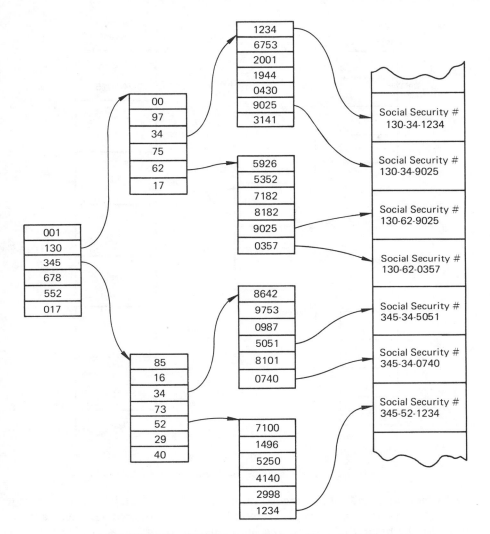

Fig. K15   The directory approach to file organization

moved around from place to place, or from device to device—and all that needs to be done is to change an entry in the appropriate directory. Thus, we can arrange our data base in such a way as to avoid bad spots on a disk, or to take up unused space caused by deleted records; we can also move a "dead" or "dormant" record to magnetic tape if we so desire.

It is a fairly simple matter to build a data base which can be accessed by *multiple keys*, as shown in Figure K16. Thus, we could rearrange our belabored management information system so that a personnel record could be retrieved either by its Social Security number, *or* by its employee number. If the data base is built in this fashion, and if the records themselves are likely to "migrate," then it is desirable to have only *one* directory which

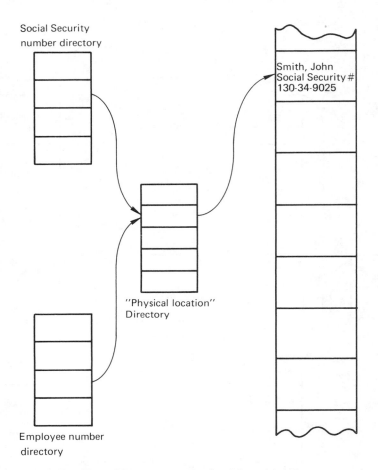

Social Security
number directory

Smith, John
Social Security #
130-34-9025

"Physical location"
Directory

Employee number
directory

Fig. K16   Directory approach with multiple keys

actually contains the logical record number of the record. Thus, if we decide to move the record elsewhere, there will be only one entry to update, and we can avoid the bother of having to search through multitudes of directories to see which ones point to the record we are moving.

Note also that there is no reason for the records to be in any particular *order* on the data base. If we prefer, the entries in the directory may be kept in an ordered fashion so that we can use a binary search, but the records themselves may be scattered all over the disk. While this fact is normally useful only to help fill in "holes" in the data base, the system designer may use it in a different way: the data base could be ordered in such a way that records can be accessed with a binary search on one key, and a directory lookup on another key.

This could prove to be advantageous for systems where we want to make file accessing on one key very fast, and file accessing on other keys not so fast. Thus, we could order the records in our management information system alphabetically by name, as shown in Figure K17, and use a directory approach to access the record by social security number. An employee who remembered his social security number would be able to retrieve his record after only three or four disk accesses, while an employee who remembered only his name (which is about all most of us can remember before our second cup of coffee!) would require about ten disk accesses (since the $\log_2$ 1000 is about 10). Lest the reader become too excited with this idea, we should point out that all of the other techniques conflict with one another. That is, it is not possible (unless by extraordinary good fortune) to arrange a data base so that it can be accessed simultaneously by the direct addressing approach, the algorithm approach, the binary search technique, and the randomizing technique. However, the directory approach *can* coexist with any one of the other four.

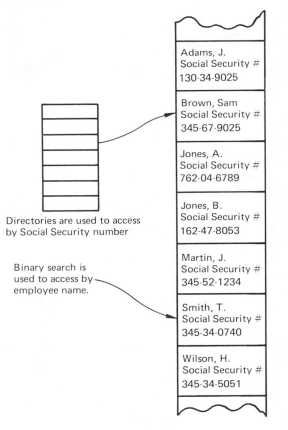

Directories are used to access by Social Security number

Binary search is used to access by employee name.

Adams, J.
Social Security #
130-34-9025

Brown, Sam
Social Security #
345-67-9025

Jones, A.
Social Security #
762-04-6789

Jones, B.
Social Security #
162-47-8053

Martin, J.
Social Security #
345-52-1234

Smith, T.
Social Security #
345-34-0740

Wilson, H.
Social Security #
345-34-5051

Fig. K17   A data base accessed with two techniques

One of the more serious drawbacks to the directory approach is its vulnerability to failures. If a directory is maintained only in core, then a system failure in which core memory is lost may cause the entire data base to be lost. This is basically because the application program cannot *compute* the location of a logical record—it depends on the directory to tell it where to find the record. One approach to this problem is to keep duplicate directories wherever possible—i.e. one in core and one on the disk. Even this is not foolproof, though, because it may turn out that the directory cannot be read from the disk due to parity errors.

The safest solution is to make each record in the data base self-identifying in some way, so that an off-line utility "data base reconstruction" program will know how to rebuild the directories. In order to do this, the utility program must be able to distinguish different *files*—so that it does not intersperse different records from different files. It must also know the blocking characteristics of the file, so that it will be able to tell where a logical record begins and ends.

As we mentioned above, the directories themselves may be searched with the aid of any of the other techniques that we have described before. Thus, we can order the entries in the directory and perform a binary search to locate any particular entry; a randomizing technique could also be used. Even the direct addressing approach is valid here—the key which we use to retrieve the record could be the *index* into the directory, as shown in Figure K18.

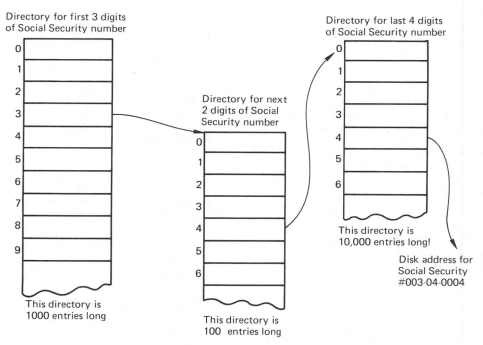

Fig. K18 Direct addressing technique for searching a directory

The directory approach to file organization has one last advantage which we should discuss briefly. Using various hierarchies of directories, it is possible to build a large "computer utility" type of data base, as shown in Figure K19. It is easy to define "public" directories, "semi-public" directories, "library" directories, and "default" directories. This concept is very useful in a large scientific time-sharing environment, where each user is likely to have his own library of files. In this environment, the application program indicates which directory is to be used when accessing a file, and if

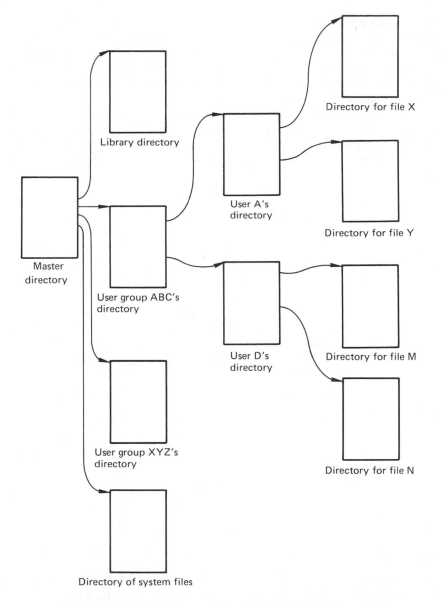

Fig. K19   Directories for an information-sharing environment

it cannot be found, the operating system automatically searches a "default" directory.

LINKED LISTS OF RECORDS IN AN
ON-LINE ENVIRONMENT

At various points in our discussion of file accessing techniques, we have mentioned the concept of *linking* records together. This is often a very handy way of relating a variable number of "similar" quantities. When we link records together, we arrange for *one* of those records to be accessed by a key which is relevant to *all* of the linked records, and then use the links to access all subsequent records in the chain.

Using our management information system as an example again, we might want to link all of the records of employees in the engineering department, as shown in Figure K20. Thus, by accessing the data base by "department number," we would retrieve the personnel record of the first employee in

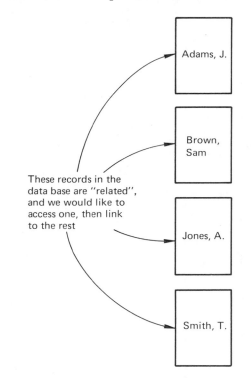

These records in the data base are "related", and we would like to access one, then link to the rest

Fig. K20   Linked records for employees in the engineering department

the department (perhaps the head of the department), which would then contain a link to other members. In a business system, we might want to keep a number of records linked together for one inventory item, as we did in Figure F6 with our Widget system. An on-line accounts receivable system might link together the invoices for each of its customers, while a library information retrieval system would link together records describing books or periodicals on a given topic. We would probably want to build a much more complex arrangement that would allow us to link to "related" topics.

Again, our major purpose here is not to discuss the techniques of data base management. The construction of a data base for as complex a system as a library information retrieval system is beyond the scope of this book, and the reader is referred to the bibliography at the end of this chapter for more information in this area. We are interested here in describing the *usefulness*, the *weaknesses*, and the *problems* of various well-known file organization techniques in an on-line environment. Thus, we will limit our discussion to an investigation of the various linked-list techniques, using the criteria we established at the beginning of the chapter.

LISTS WITH ONE-WAY POINTERS

The simplest type of list structure involves *one-way pointers*. Figure K21(a) shows a typical *forward-pointing* list, while Figure K21(b) shows a typical *backward-pointing* list. The last item in the list is normally indicated

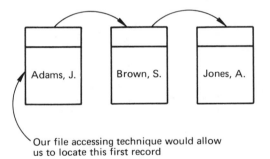

Our file accessing technique would allow us to locate this first record

Fig. K21(a)   Simple forward-pointing list

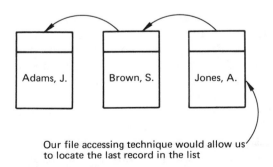

Our file accessing technique would allow us to locate the last record in the list

Fig. K21(b)   Simple backward-pointing list

by a pointer consisting of zero or minus one. The great advantage of this type of list structure is, of course, its simplicity. The overhead required to keep the pointers is small, and the processing required to figure out the location of the next (or previous) item is also rather trivial.

The disadvantage of the one-way pointers is that it is very difficult for the program to remember where it came from. Thus, with the forward-pointing list shown in Figure K21(a), the program can *only* move forward from the Nth item to the $N + 1^{st}$ item; similarly, we can *only* move backward with the backward-pointing list shown in Figure K21(b).

Occasionally, the programmer can arrange his file accessing subroutines so that they remember the "current" item, the "previous" item, and the "next" item in the list, as shown in Figure K22(a). When the program moves forward one record, it updates its pointers, so that the *old* "current" item becomes the *new* "previous" item, the *old* "next" item becomes the *new* "current" item, and the item pointed to by the *new* "current" item becomes the *new* "next" item, as shown in Figure K22(b).

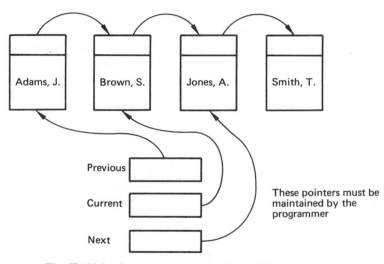

Fig. K22(a) One-way pointers with additional pointers

While this improves the flexibility of the one-way pointer list somewhat, the improvement is rather minor. As we see in Figure K23, a program processing a forward-pointing list can move *backward* only one item, using the extra pointers we described above. While this gives us the ability to delete items from the list with relative ease, it certainly does not allow us to traverse the list freely in either direction.

Inserting a new entry into this type of list structure may or may not be a simple matter. As illustrated by Figure K24, it is trivial to insert a new item at the *beginning* of the list, since we presumably know where the beginning of the list is. However, it can be very cumbersome to insert an item at the

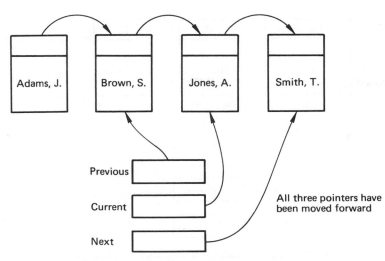

Fig. K22(b) Moving forward with additional pointers

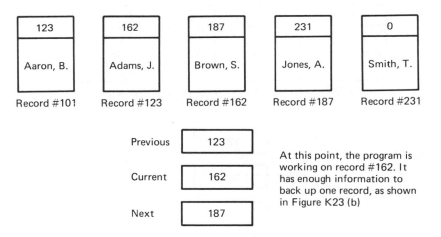

Fig. K23(a) Moving backward with additional pointers

end of the list, as is shown in Figure K25; the program must first start at the beginning of the list, and traverse the entire length of the chain until it comes to the last item. This problem can be remedied by keeping an extra pointer, as shown by Figure K26; this allows us to find the end of the list immediately, at which point a new item can be inserted.

Inserting or deleting an item from the middle of the list can be accomplished efficiently only if we keep the extra "previous," "current," and "next" pointers that we described above. Then, as shown in Figure K27, the program can traverse the list until it finds the point where a new item is to be inserted or an old item is to be deleted.

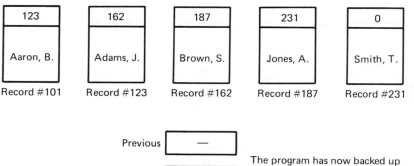

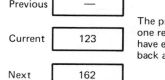

The program has now backed up one record. However, it does not have enough information to move back any more

Fig. K23(b) Moving backward with additional pointers

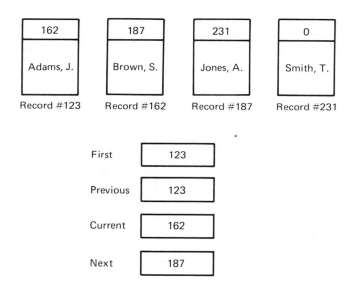

If the program keeps an additional pointer to the beginning of the list (this extra pointer might actually be a directory entry somewhere else), then it becomes a simple matter to insert a new record: the address maintained in First is stored in the pointer field of the new record, and the address of the new record is stored in First. This leads to the structure shown in Figure K24(b).

Fig. K24(a) Inserting a record at the beginning of the list

By this point, the reader should recognize that this simple type of list structure is suitable for only the most straightforward applications. In many business applications, where it is desirable to link together all of the invoices for a particular customer, or all of the inventory records for a particular

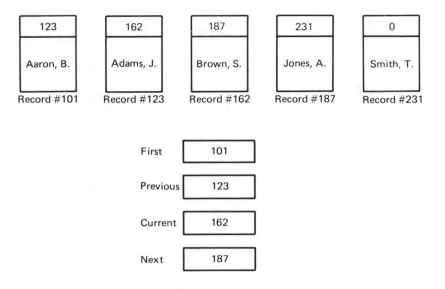

123	162	187	231	0
Aaron, B.	Adams, J.	Brown, S.	Jones, A.	Smith, T.
Record #101	Record #123	Record #162	Record #187	Record #231

First — 101

Previous — 123

Current — 162

Next — 187

The new record has now been inserted.
Note that First has been updated.

Fig. K24(b) Inserting a record at the beginning of the list

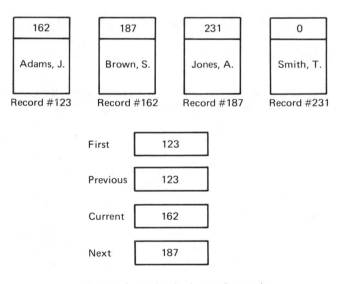

162	187	231	0
Adams, J.	Brown, S.	Jones, A.	Smith, T.
Record #123	Record #162	Record #187	Record #231

First — 123

Previous — 123

Current — 162

Next — 187

With the information in these pointers, the
program has no way of knowing where the
end of the list is. In order to insert a new
item at the end of the list, the program
must start at First and scan forward until
it finds an item with a pointer of zero.

Fig. K25 Inserting a record at the end of the list

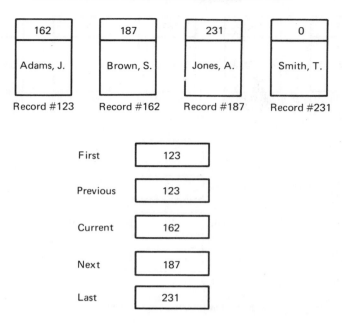

By keeping one extra pointer, it becomes possible for the
program to insert a new item at the end of the list, *or* at
the beginning of the list.

Fig. K26 Inserting a record at the end of the list with extra pointers

item, or all of the open orders for a particular item, this structure is quite
suitable. If, on the other hand, the programmer expects to access and
manipulate the list in a more complex fashion, then the one-way pointer
arrangement will probably not be sufficient.

It should be remembered that the linked-list approach is much more
reasonable when the list is maintained in core memory than it is when the
list is maintained on a disk. In core memory, for example, it is common to
see so-called *percolation* techniques to keep the most active elements at the
front of the list. This technique works by interchanging a list item with the
item in front of it whenever the item is referenced, as shown in Figure K28;
as can be seen, this technique guarantees that the more active elements in the
list gradually "percolate" to the top, while the less active items gradually
settle to the bottom. This is an extremely useful technique when dealing
with lists in core memory, for it tends to minimize the search time for active
list elements; when dealing with lists of disk records, the overhead of
interchanging list items probably makes this technique prohibitively
expensive. Similarly, sophisticated randomizing or binary search techniques
are often suitable for searching lists in core, but would generally not apply to
data base lists.

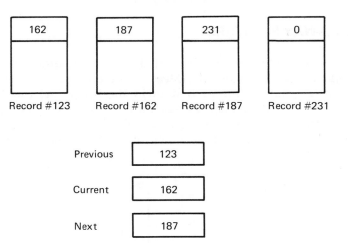

162	187	231	0

Record #123   Record #162   Record #187   Record #231

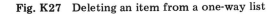

Previous	123
Current	162
Next	187

With these three pointers, it becomes relatively simple to delete the Current item from the list. The deletion is accomplished by taking the address stored in the Next pointer and storing it in the item pointed to by the Previous item. In this example, record #123 would be changed so that it points to record #187.

Fig. K27   Deleting an item from a one-way list

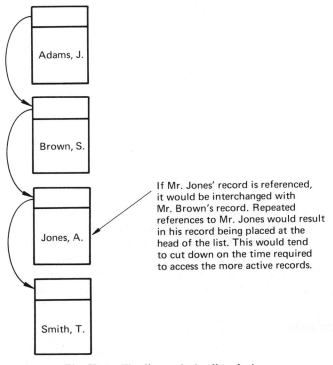

If Mr. Jones' record is referenced, it would be interchanged with Mr. Brown's record. Repeated references to Mr. Jones would result in his record being placed at the head of the list. This would tend to cut down on the time required to access the more active records.

Fig. K28   The "percolation" technique

LISTS OF TWO-WAY POINTERS

We can also construct linked lists of data base records with *two-way pointers,* as illustrated by Figure K29. This represents a major improvement over the one-way pointers, for each item in the list points forward to the next item, *and* backward to the previous item. The two-way pointer lists are usually circular in nature; that is, the first item in the list points backward to the last item in the list, while the last item in the list points forward to the first item in the list.

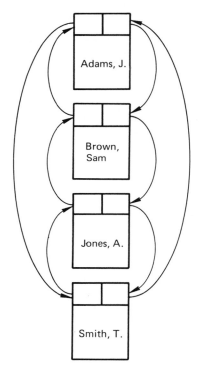

Fig. K29   Linked lists with two-way pointers

The advantage of the doubly-linked list structure is that one can start from any item in the list and move forward or backward with ease. There is enough information contained with each item so that it can be deleted from the list with ease. However, the reader should note that a linked list with two-way pointers requires *five* logical file accesses to delete a record, as is illustrated by Figure K30. It is also rather obvious that more space is required to keep the two pointers than was the case in the previous type of list organization that we discussed.

Thus, the programmer may decide that it would be more efficient to use a simple one-way link to cut down on the number of disk accesses, but he must weigh the possibility of suddenly wanting to reverse direction and start reading records forwards instead of backwards, or backwards instead of forwards.

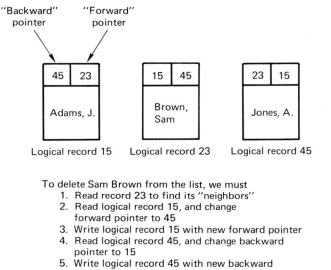

To delete Sam Brown from the list, we must
1. Read record 23 to find its "neighbors"
2. Read logical record 15, and change forward pointer to 45
3. Write logical record 15 with new forward pointer
4. Read logical record 45, and change backward pointer to 15
5. Write logical record 45 with new backward pointer
Thus, there are five logical disk accesses required.

Fig. K30 Deleting a record from a linked list with two-way pointers

There is often an even stronger reason for avoiding the one-way pointers. Since we must always be aware of the possibility of system failures, we should investigate the consequence of a system failure while updating a linked list structure—i.e. while adding or deleting a record. As we see in Figure K31, we may lose a large portion of our file if we have a "crash" while updating a list with one-way pointers. If we have a failure while updating a list with two-way pointers, we can start scanning from the beginning of the chain for a record that points back to the broken part of the chain, as illustrated in Figure K32. The application programmer should bear in mind that the same problem will occur if his application program has a bug in it; if it starts storing "garbage" forward pointers, we can use the backward pointers to reconstruct the file.

Once again, we should point out that this type of list structure is often much more convenient for list structures in core memory than it is for list structures maintained on disk or drum. The main advantages of the doubly-linked list are its flexibility, the ease with which records may be inserted or deleted at any point, and the ease with which a record may be moved to a different place in the list. However, we generally want to avoid as much movement as possible when dealing with a disk-oriented list structure, because of the overhead.

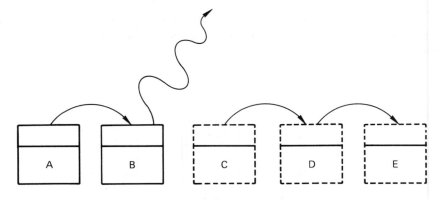

System failed (or there was a program bug) while
we were updating the pointer in record B so as to
delete record C. As a result, records D and E are
also lost.

Fig. K31 System failures with one-way pointers

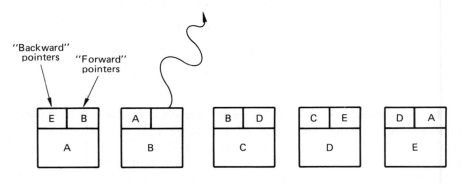

The system failed while we were updating the
forward pointer of record B. However, we can
recover by reading all of the records, looking for
the record whose *backward* pointer is B.

Fig. K32 System failures with two-way pointers

Thus, while the linked lists are a conceptually useful means of
associating similar data base records, they can be extremely inefficient if not
used properly. The application programmer should always attempt to *block*
his linked records, so that an entire chain can be brought into core with one
access. In Figure K33, we see the consequence of *not* blocking the records
together; each time a new link is accessed, we must access the file storage
unit again. This tends to happen fairly often if the records are added and
deleted from the chain during the course of the day.

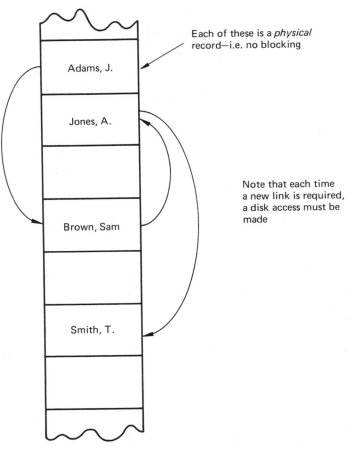

Fig. K33 Linked records without blocking

TREE STRUCTURES AND NETWORK STRUCTURES

Finally, we can organize our data base with a tree structure, as shown in Figures K34(a) and K34(b), or with a network structure, as shown in Figure K35. In the tree structure, there are no interconnections between the branches of the tree, while there may be an arbitrary number of interconnections between the items in a network structure.

The advantage of this type of structure is, of course, that it allows for very complex logical arrangements of data; it is very easy, with these types of structures, to group related subsets of data together. In the network structure, one item can be an element in more than one list, which makes it ideal for some information retrieval applications, and occasionally for some business applications. For example, the network structure would be a

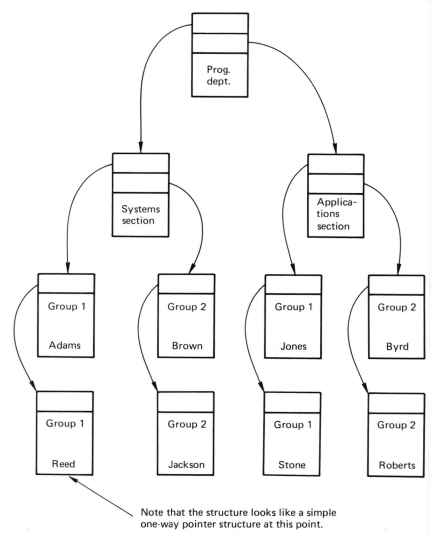

Note that the structure looks like a simple
one-way pointer structure at this point.

Fig. K34(a)   Tree structures

convenient way of representing the combination of customers, open orders
and inventory, as shown in Figure K36.

The disadvantages of the tree structure and network structure should be
rather obvious. There is potentially a tremendous amount of space overhead
required to keep all of the necessary pointers; then, too, there can be a large
amount of processing overhead to search for a particular item in the data
base. Once again, the network structure and tree structure are elegant ways
of representing data, but are rather costly to implement with current types
of random-access file storage units.

Perhaps the largest drawback to the tree structure and network structure

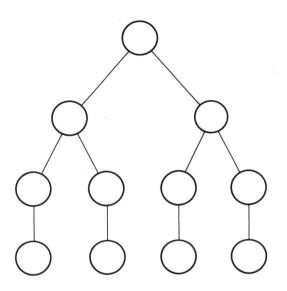

This is just another way of representing the type of structure shown in Figure K34(a). Most such tree structures use one-way pointers, so it is possible to traverse the tree in only one direction.

Fig. K34(b)   Tree structures

is the amount of extra programming required to set up the data base, maintain it, and use it. It is interesting to note that there are a number of languages like LISP and SLIP that allow the programmer to construct complex *core-memory* list structures; there are very few languages, however, that allow the programmer to construct and manipulate disk-oriented list structures. Perhaps the most widely known package at the current time is General Electric's Integrated Data Store package (IDS), which allows the programmer to construct and manipulate network structures of the type shown in Figure K34 and K35 in COBOL. In addition to providing a capability for sequential list accessing, IDS allows the programmer to perform a random-access reference to individual items in the middle of a list.

INVERTED FILES

When we discussed the directory approach to file organization, we mentioned the idea of *multiple directories* to allow us to access a record on more than one key. If we extend this idea to the limit, *each* field in the record will have its own directory (or hierarchy of directories), and we end up with the structure shown in Figure K37. Thus, in our management information system, we could have directories for salary, job title, length of

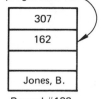

Points to next item in engineer list

162
102
Adams, J.

Record #101

Points to next item in programmer list

307
162
Jones, B.

Record #123

Points to next item in manager list

102
307
Johnson, L.

Record #143

123
192
Brown, S.

Record #162

0
143
Reed, W.

Record #192

76
101
Byrd, H.

Record #307

192
0
Jackson, Q.

Record #76

0
Stone, T.

Record #69

69
76
Wilson, H.

Record #102

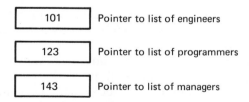

101	Pointer to list of engineers
123	Pointer to list of programmers
143	Pointer to list of managers

Note that some items are members of more than one list.

Fig. K35 Network structures

service, age, and employee name, as well as our original directories of social security number and employee number.

This structure has found great use in *information retrieval* applications. By consulting only our directories, we can fulfill a request for information for "all senior electrical engineers making over $15,000 who have been with the company between five and ten years" *without having to search through our entire data base.* While this is a tremendous feature, the application programmer should remember that it is not *free.*

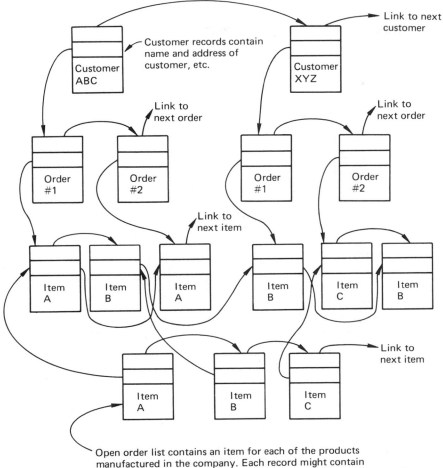

Fig. K36   Network structure for business-oriented on-line system

The inverted list structure combines some of the disadvantages of the directory approach and the linked-list approach. There is likely to be a large number of directories with an inverted list organization, which may take up more than the 10% space overhead that we suggested for the simple directory approach. *Maintenance* of the inverted list structure is also awkward, because *every* directory must be updated whenever a record is added or deleted. There is also a large amount of overhead required to keep track of the directories themselves—which ones are in core, which ones *should* be in core, which ones should be written back to the disk, and so forth.

Because of these disadvantages, the programmer should seriously consider some *compromises* to the inverted list structure. We can construct a *partially inverted* list by keeping directories for only some of the more

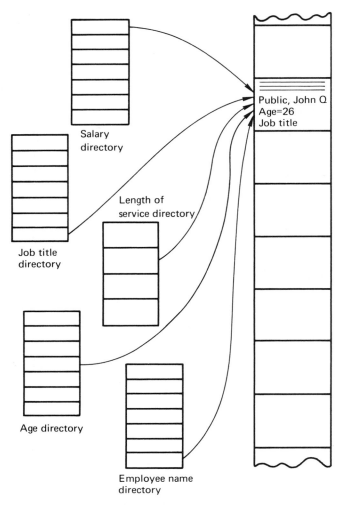

Salary
directory

Length of
service directory

Job title
directory

Age directory

Employee name
directory

Public, John Q
Age=26
Job title

Fig. K37   Inverted list structure

important keys, which is essentially what we were doing in Figure K16. Since the order of records in the data base does not affect the inverted list structure, we could arrange the records so that a randomizing technique or a direct addressing technique could be used to access the data base with one of the keys.

We may even want to make the data base amenable to batch processing. We could still use the inverted list if the records were ordered sequentially, and this might permit more efficient batch processing for applications where we know that every record will be required. Similarly, we might try to arrange for the updating and maintenance of the inverted list structure to be done on an overnight batch basis.

The general characteristics of file organization techniques are summarized in Table K1. From our discussion above, it would appear that

TABLE K1 *Summary of File Accessing Techniques*

Attribute	Direct addressing	Algorithm approach	Binary search	Randomizing technique	Directory approach	Linked lists	Inverted lists
Minimize accesses	Excellent	Excellent	Terrible	Good	Fair to good	Poor to excellent	Excellent
Average number of accesses to retrieve a record	1	1	$\log_2 N$	1.5	1–4	Varies widely	1
Wasted file space	Possibly	Possibly	None	20–30%	10% for directories	None	None
Ability to migrate records	None	None	None	None	Yes	Yes	Yes
Ease of inserting and deleting records	Bad	Bad	Bad	Bad	Good	Good	Good
Vulnerability to failures	Low	Low	Low	Low	High	High	High
Best suited for	Real-time inquiry	Real-time inquiry	Batch, serial data bases	Real-time inquiry	General purpose on-line data bases	Business-oriented systems; information retrieval systems	Information retrieval systems

the direct addressing approach, the algorithm approach, and the randomizing technique are best suited to real-time inquiry systems, where fast accessing is of critical importance. The directory-oriented approach is suitable for general-purpose on-line systems, such as time-sharing systems, remote batch systems, and so forth. The linked list and inverted list file organization schemes are best suited to business-oriented systems and information retrieval systems.

Table K1 also gives a rough estimate of the number of file accesses required to locate a particular record. In order to calculate throughput and response times, it would be desirable to make a more precise estimate, but to do so, *one must have a good knowledge of the type of data that will be maintained in the data base, and the type of accesses that will be made.* One must also make assumptions about the implementation of the data base scheme; for example, we must decide which directories will be maintained in core memory if we are to build a directory-oriented data base, and we must decide on blocking factors for a number of the other file organization schemes. With this extra information, the reader should be able to calculate the number of file accesses that will be required to process a transaction, which, as we discussed in Chapter F, can be used to help calculate the throughput and response time of the system. An illustration of this kind of calculation is discussed in Chapter O, in which we focus our attention once again on the Widget Corporation of America.

REFERENCES

1 James Martin, *Design of Real-Time Computer Systems* (Englewood Cliffs, N.J.: Prentice-Hall, Inc., 1967)

2 W.D. Maurer, *An Improved Hash Code for Scatter Storage*, Communications of the ACM, Volume 11, Number 1 (January, 1968), pages 35-38

3 Robert Morris, *Scatter Storage Techniques*, Communications of the ACM, Volume 11, Number 1 (January, 1968), pages 38-43

4 M.D. McIlroy, *A Variant Method of File Searching*, Communications of the ACM, Volume 6, Number 1 (January, 1963), page 101

5 W.W. Peterson, *Addressing for Random-Access Storage*, IBM Journal of Research and Development, Volume 1 (1957), pages 130-146

6 G. Shay and W.G. Spruth, *Analysis of a File Addressing Method*, Communications of the ACM, Volume 5, Number 8 (August, 1962), pages 459-462

7 L.R. Johnson, *Indirect Chaining Method for Addressing on Secondary Keys*, Communications of the ACM, Volume 4, Number 4 (May, 1961), pages 218-222

8 David Hsiao and Frank Harary, *A Formal System for Information Retrieval from Files*, Communications of the ACM, Volume 13, Number 2 (February, 1970), pages 67-73

9 David Hsiao and N.S. Prywes, *A System to Manage an Information System*, Proceedings of the IFIP Joint Conference on Mechanized Information Storage Retrieval, Rome, Italy, 1967, pages 637-660

10 T.C. Lowe, *The Influence of Data-Base Characteristics and Usage on Direct Access File Organization*, Journal of the ACM, Volume 15, Number 4 (October, 1968), pages 535-548

11 R.L. Wexelblatt and H.A. Freeman, *The MULTILANG On-line Programming System*, Proceedings of the AFIPS 1967 Spring Joint Computer Conference, Volume 30 (Washington, D.C.: Thompson Book Company, 1967), pages 559-569

12 P.R. Weinberg, *A Time-Sharing Chemical Information Retrieval System*, Ph.D. Dissertation, University of Pennsylvania, Philadelphia, Pa., 1968

13 L.D. Martin, *A Model for File Structure Determination for Large On-Line Files*, Proceedings of the FILE 1968 International Seminar on File Organization, Copenhagen, 1968, pages 793-834

14 N.S. Prywes, *Man-Computer Problem Solving with Multilist*, Proceedings of the IEEE, Volume 54, Number 12 (December, 1966), pages 1788-1801

15 A. Shoshani and A.J. Bernstein, *Synchronization in a Parallel-Accessed Data Base*, Communications of the ACM, Volume 12, Number 11 (November, 1969), pages 604-607

16 R.C. Daley and P.G. Newmann, *A General Purpose File System for Secondary Storage*, Proceedings of the AFIPS 1965 Fall Joint Computer Conference, Volume 27, part 1 (New York, N.Y.: Spartan Books), pages 213-229

17 George S. Dodd, *Elements of Data Management Systems*, ACM Computing Surveys, Volume 1, Number 2 (June 1969), pages 117-133

18 D. Lefkowitz, *File Structures for On-Line Systems*, (New York, N.Y.: Spartan Books, 1969)

19 R.E. Bleier, *Treating Hierarchial Data Structures in the SDC Time-Shared Data Management system (TDMS)*, Proceedings of the 1967 ACM National Conference (Washington, D.C.: Thompson Book Company), pages 1-49

20 Donald Knuth, *The Art of Computer Programming, Volume 1* (Reading, Mass.: Addison-Wesley, 1968)

21 W.D. Clemenson, *File Organization and Search Techniques*, Annual Review of Information Science and Technology, Volume 1, Edited by C. Cuadra (New York, N.Y.: John Wiley & Sons, Inc., 1966)

Chapter L

THE PROBLEM OF SIMULTANEOUS ACCESS
TO THE DATA BASE

INTRODUCTION

In many previous chapters of this book, we have alluded to the problem of simultaneous access to an on-line data base. In fact, we even listed it as one of the most significant problems faced by an application programmer (see Chapter H). In this chapter, we will attempt to describe the nature of the problem in more detail, and we will present some of the commonly used solutions to the problem.

THE NATURE OF THE SIMULTANEOUS
ACCESS PROBLEM

One very common problem occurs when one user of an on-line system attempts to interrogate the data base that is in the midst of being updated by another user. A simple form of this problem is shown in Figure L1, where a salesman is attempting to determine the number of widgets in inventory at the same time a warehouse receiving clerk is attempting to update the inventory record to reflect the arrival of some new widgets from the factory.

To some extent, this is simply a more dramatic case of what goes on in many "manual" systems today. A shipment of widgets may arrive in the warehouse, thus increasing the physical inventory level. However, the salesman may be working with yesterday's inventory report, in which case his information is obsolete. All we have done in Figure L1 is *reduce the time*

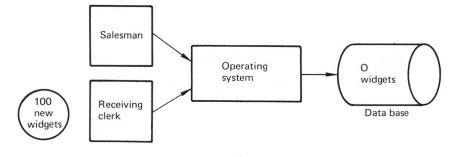

Both the salesman and the receiving clerk type in
transactions at the same time—the salesman's
program wants to read the widget inventory record,
and the receiving clerk's program wants to read the
record so that it can update it. The operating system
decides to honor the salesman's request first.

Fig. L1(a)   A simple form of the simultaneous access problem

scale—that is, we have shortened the period of time during which the
salesman's information is likely to be obsolete.

Note also that there is nothing that the on-line system can really do to
alleviate the problem. We can build in some mechanism to prevent the
salesman and the receiving clerk from accessing the inventory record at the
same time, but that does not really solve the problem. As we see in Figure
L2, it is still possible for the salesman to make an inquiry at 1:16 PM, only
to find that there are no widgets in inventory. The receiving clerk may have
gotten a new shipment of widgets at 1:00 PM, but he may not have bothered
typing in the appropriate transaction until 1:17 PM.

The important thing is that the salesman's inquiry produces information
which is obsolete, but *consistent*. There are other situations, however, where
the salesman may receive *inconsistent* information if he attempts to read the

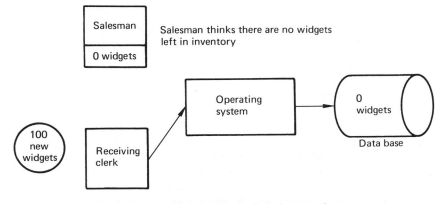

Once the salesman's request is satisfied, the operating
system reads the record for the receiving clerk.

Fig. L1(b)   A simple form of the simultaneous access problem

data base while other users are updating it. This is shown in Figure L3, where a salesman inquires into the status of his customer's order at the same time that a shipping clerk types in a transaction that will update the customer's accounts receivable file and the inventory file. It is possible for the salesman to get *inconsistent* information to the effect that the customer has been billed for merchandise that has not been sent to him.

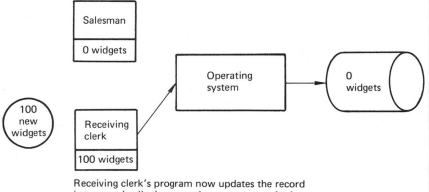

Receiving clerk's program now updates the record in core and calls the operating system to write it back on the disk.

Fig. L1(c)   A simple form of the simultaneous access problem

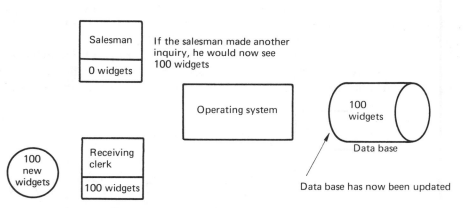

Fig. L1(d)   A simple form of the simultaneous access problem

The example may seem a bit mundane, but it is indicative of a general problem that occurs when one user attempts to read several logically related records while another user is updating them. However, the reader may argue that the situation is not really all that bad, since the salesman would presumably see that the information was inconsistent, and type his transaction in again. From a philosophical point of view, one could argue that this is a very bad way to build a system—for the salesman will very

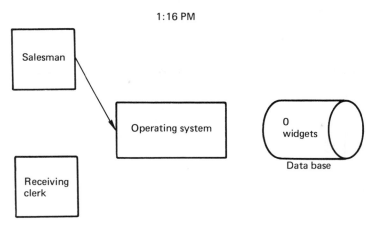

At 1:16 PM, the salesman makes an inquiry and
finds that there are 0 widgets in inventory.

Fig. L2(a)   A variation of the simple simultaneous access problem

correctly view this inconsistent information as a bug in the system. Even
worse, the salesman will begin to lose confidence in the system, thinking that
it is very much like the weather: if he doesn't like the results, all he has to do
is wait a few minutes, and he can get a different answer (and one that might
be more consistent) from the system.

However, there are even worse problems that can occur. In Figure L3,
we saw that the salesman received inconsistent information, but at least the
data base itself was not damaged. The problem becomes much more severe if

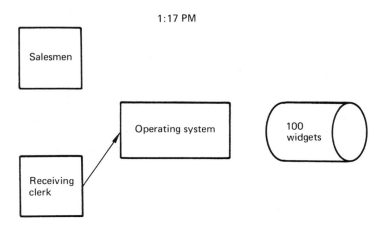

At 1:17 PM, the receiving clerk types in a
transaction to indicate the arrival of 100 widgets.

Fig. L2(b)   A variation of the simple simultaneous access problem

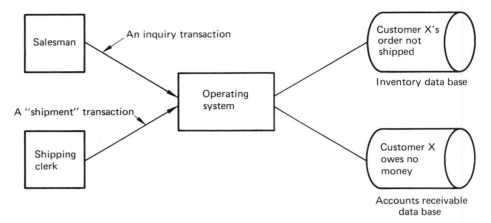

The salesman and the shipping clerk type in their transactions simultaneously. The salesman wants to find out whether a customer's order has been shipped, and how much money he owes. The shipping clerk wants to type in a "shipment" transaction, which will update the inventory data base and will charge the customer for the items shipped, thus updating the accounts receivable data base.

The salesman's program wants to read the inventory data base first, and the accounts receivable data base next. The shipping clerk's program wants to update the accounts receivable data base first and the inventory data base next.

Fig. L3(a) Simultaneous reading and writing of many records

two or more users attempt to update the data base at the same time, as shown in Figure L4. Now we are in a situation in which our salesman is attempting to order some widgets while another salesman is doing the same thing. The result is that the salesman receives information (or an acknowledgement) from the system that is *consistent* (i.e. it makes sense to him), but *wrong*. As we see in Figure L4, we end up with a data base that is incorrect.

This, then, represents the three types of access problems we can encounter with on-line systems. In the simplest case, where one user is attempting to read *one record* while another user is updating that record, we are dealing with a problem that has nothing to do with the on-line nature of the system. However, if one user attempts to read *several records* while another user is updating those records, we have to worry about giving the first user contradictory information. Finally, if two users are attempting to update one or more records at the same time, we can mislead our users and damage our data base.

A SIMPLE SOLUTION—SERIAL PROCESSING
OF TRANSACTIONS

The problems described above arise from a situation in which two or more concurrently executing programs have *independent* access to the data base, as shown in Figure L5. The simplest way of solving the problem is to

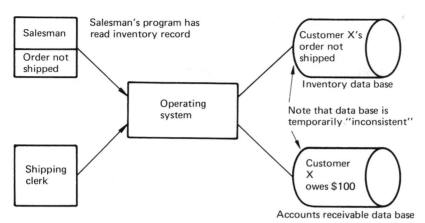

At this point, the salesman's program has read the inventory record, and the shipping clerk's program has updated the accounts receivable file

Now the salesman's program calls the operating system to read the accounts receivable file, and the shipping clerk's program calls the operating system to read and update the inventory file.

(Note that if the system fails at this point, our data base is in a contradictory state. See Chapter N)

Fig. L3(b)   Simultaneous reading and writing of many records

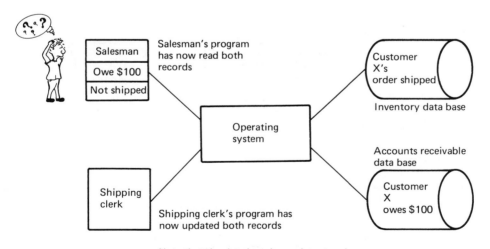

Note that the data base is consistent again.

Fig. L3(c)   Simultaneous reading and writing of many records

avoid it—by having only *one* program receive transactions, as shown in Figure L6.

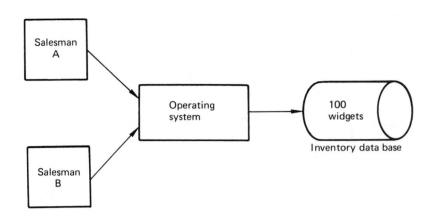

Salesman A and salesman B want to order widgets, and
they type in their transactions at the same time. Their
respective programs call the operating system to read
the widget inventory record. The operating system
decides to do A's request first.

Fig. L4(a)   Simultaneous updates of the data base

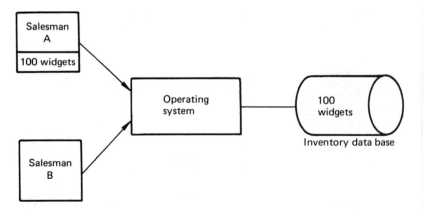

A's program receives the inventory record and begins
doing some calculations. Meanwhile, the operating
system is reading the inventory record for salesman B.

Fig. L4(b)   Simultaneous updates of the data base

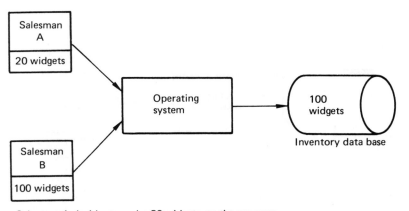

Salesman A decides to order 80 widgets, so the program
updates the record in core, and calls the operating
system to write it out.

Meanwhile, salesman B has received the inventory
record of 100 widgets and is busily doing some
processing.

Fig. L4(c)   Simultaneous updates of the data base

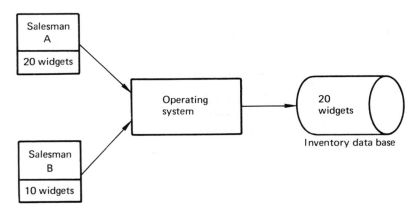

Salesman A has updated the data base and is finished.
Salesman B has decided to order 90 widgets. The program
has updated the record in core and has called the operating
system to write the record on disk.

Fig. L4(d)   Simultaneous updates to the data base

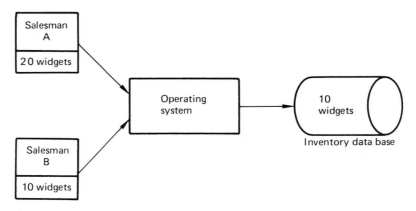

Both programs have now finished. The computer's data
base shows 10 widgets, when it should show −70 widgets

Fig. L4(e)   Simultaneous updates to the data base

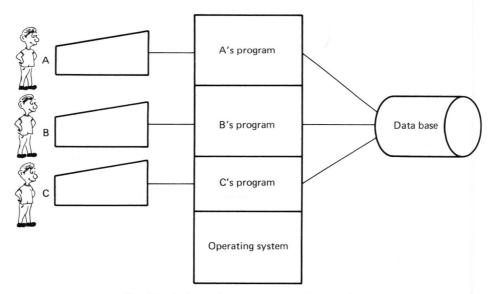

Fig. L5   Independent accesses to the data base

   This was an approach suggested in Chapter I, and it may take several
forms—see, for example, Figures I2, I4, I5, and I6. The important point is
that the data base (or a discrete part of the data base) is affected by only one
program, which queues and processes all reads and writes to the data base.
Thus, the "simultaneous update" problem which was depicted in Figure L4
can be handled in the manner shown by Figure L7.
   We must emphasize that only *one* program can access the data base with
this approach. If the application programmer takes advantage of certain
operating system capabilities, he can make it possible to process several

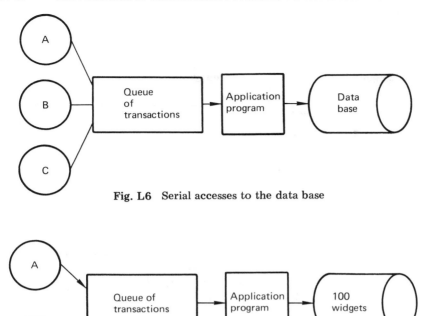

Fig. L6 Serial accesses to the data base

Salesman A and salesman B both type
a transaction to order some widgets

Fig. L7(a) Solution to the simultaneous update problem

transactions concurrently with several "incarnations" of a *reentrant* application program, as shown in Figure L8. This is tempting because it seems to be taking full advantage of the multiprogramming capabilities of the system without greatly increasing the amount of memory, since there is only one copy of the reentrant program. However, so far as the data base is concerned, this situation is *exactly the same* as if we had totally different application programs processing transactions concurrently. In effect, each "incarnation" of the reentrant program is independent of each other incarnation, and they all make their own independent accesses to the data base.

THE CONCEPT OF LOCKING AND UNLOCKING

Many computer vendors supply a rather primitive mechansim for solving the problem of simultaneous access to the data base. With the use of the macros LOCK and UNLOCK, the application program can indicate to the operating system (or perhaps a vendor-supplied data management package) that a specified file is to be reserved for its use until the application program decides to UNLOCK the file.

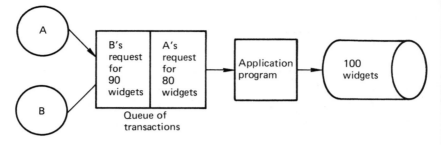

A's request arrived a split second before B's, so it is at the head of the queue.

Fig. L7(b) Solution to the simultaneous update problem

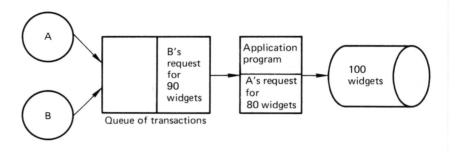

The application program now begins working on
A's request. In the meantime, nothing happens
with B's request.

Fig. L7(c) Solution to the simultaneous update problem

With these macros, the typical sequence that an application program
would use is as follows:

LOCK	fileA
READ	fileA
process	
WRITE	fileA
UNLOCK	fileA

If the application program attempts to LOCK a file that is already being
used by some other program, the operating system will put it into a "wait"
state pending an UNLOCK by the current user of the file. Note that we
could build the same type of LOCK and UNLOCK structure into an
application program in a multitasking environment, as shown in Figure
L9—there is nothing particularly "magic" about the operating system
providing the LOCK and UNLOCK macros.

There are some very large problems with the LOCK-UNLOCK
approach—problems which are often large enough to warrant avoiding it and
using the simpler "serial processing" approach. First of all, the overhead

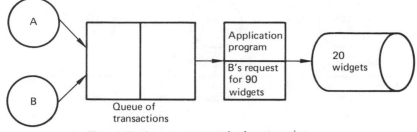

The application program now begins processing
B's request. It sees that the request cannot be
honored, and rejects it.

Fig. L7(d) Solution to the simultaneous update problem

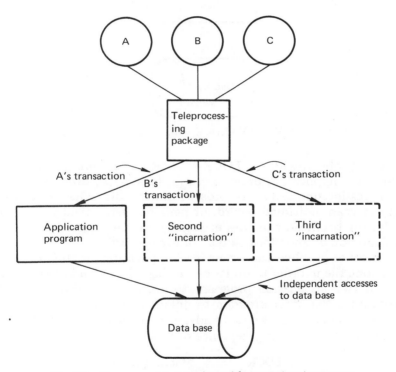

Fig. L8 Concurrent processing with a reentrant program

associated with LOCKing and UNLOCKing is often tremendous. We must
either issue a macro or make a subroutine call to a data management package
each time we want to lock a file or unlock it. If there are many files to be
locked, and/or many application programs competing for use of the file, the
operating system may have to keep tables associated with each file—and
there may be so many tables that they, too, have to be kept on the disk.
Thus, we may require extra disk accesses to open and close a file, which adds
to the overhead of processing a transaction.

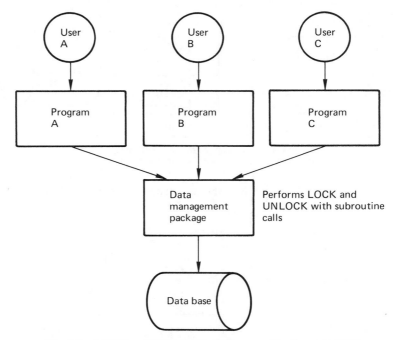

Fig. L9 LOCK and UNLOCK with an application program

Another problem with the LOCK-UNLOCK mechanism is that it usually only allows the application programmer to lock a *file*, even though he may only be accessing one or two records within the file. What is needed is the ability to lock an individual record, or perhaps even a field within a record. Obviously, the overhead becomes even greater if the operating system has to keep information on the "lock status" of each record.

Still another problem can occur if an application program needs to lock more than one file in order to do its processing. As shown in Figure L10, it is possible for two application programs to get into a "deadlock" situation, each waiting for the other program to unlock a file that it needs. Thus, the application program must know in advance which files will be required, so that it can issue the following sequence of instructions:

```
LOCK          fileA,fileB,fileC
READ          fileA
process
READ          fileB
process
WRITE         fileB
READ          fileC
process
WRITE         fileC
WRITE         fileA
UNLOCK        fileA,fileB,fileC
```

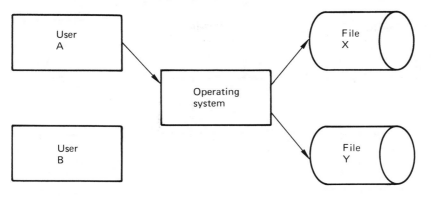

A's program calls the operating system to lock file X

Fig. L10(a)   The "deadlock" problem

It is interesting to note that most operating systems allow an application program to lock only *one* file at a time, in which case we can either get into a "deadlock" situation or we can have the same simultaneous update problem that we illustrated with Figure L4.

The application program must not be allowed to keep the file locked for any undue length of time, or other programs (and users) will be kept waiting too long. This may not be easy to ensure, for we cannot always control the nonsense that application programmers put into their programs. The nightmare of every operating system programmer is the following sequence of code in the application program:

```
LOCK       fileA
READ       teletype
READ       fileA
WRITE      fileA
UNLOCK     fileA
```

Obviously, if the user takes three hours to type in his transaction (which may happen if he has gone off to lunch without disconnecting his terminal), nobody else will be able to access that file. The same thing can occur if there is a bug in the application program of the following sort:

```
LOCK       fileA
READ       fileA
process in an endless loop
WRITE      fileA
UNLOCK     fileA
```

Because of these potential disasters, it has been suggested that the operating system might "time out" an application program that locks a file for too long a period of time. Thus, if the application program kept the file

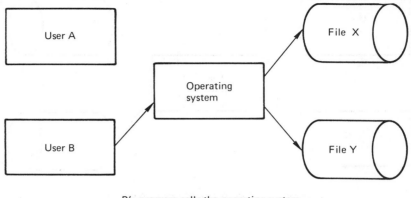

B's program calls the operating system
to lock file Y

Fig. L10(b)   The "deadlock" problem

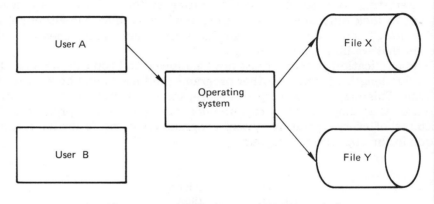

A's program now calls the operating system to lock
file Y. However, since B has already locked it, A's
program must be placed in a "wait" state.

Fig. L10(c)   The "deadlock" problem

locked for more than one minute, the operating system would take control
away and unlock the file. If we do this, though, we must abort the
application program, or it will continue in its endless loop. However, we
must be careful to avoid aborting the program if it is following the sequence
of activities shown below:

                    LOCK   fileA
                    READ   fileA
                    process
                    WRITE   fileA
                    process in an endless loop
                    UNLOCK   fileA

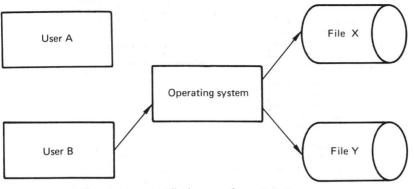

B's program now calls the operating system to
lock file X. However, since A has already locked
it, B must be put into a "wait" state.

A and B will now wait forever in a "deadlock" condition.

Fig. L10(d)   The "deadlock" problem

In this situation, we should act as if the system had failed, and invoke the file recovery procedures that are discussed in Chapter N. This is necessary because aborting the program in the midst of its processing might result in an "inconsistent" data base.

There are often some "philosophical" questions associated with the LOCK-UNLOCK mechanisms. For example, how should we handle the case when an application program wants to LOCK several files, *some* of which are available, and *some* of which have already been locked by another program? We could establish the convention that the currently "available" files will be "reserved" while the program is waiting for the remaining files to become unlocked, but this adds even more overhead to the system.

If the application programmer decides to write his own data management package to perform LOCKs and UNLOCKs, it is suggested that he maintain information on a *program* basis and a *file* basis, as shown in Figure L11. Thus, when file X is unlocked, the file table can be consulted to see which programs have been waiting for permission to lock file X. The program table can then be consulted to see whether there are any additional files, besides file X, that the other application programs were waiting for. If not, one of the application programs can now be given permission to LOCK file X.

In summary, then, the concept of LOCKing and UNLOCKing a file are fraught with problems. It involves a large amount of overhead; it is inefficient in that it forces the application program to lock *entire files* rather than individual records; it is occasionally vulnerable to "deadlock" problems on the part of application programs; and it is vulnerable to an extended "lockout" caused by an endless loop in the application program. The concept is thus useful only in an environment where a user's *natural*

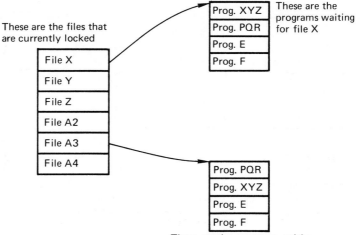

These are the files that
are currently locked

These are the
programs waiting
for file X

These are the programs waiting
for file A3

Fig. L11(a)   File table for file locking

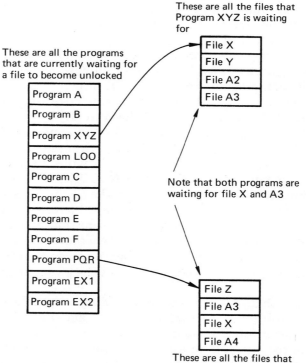

These are all the files that
Program XYZ is waiting
for

These are all the programs
that are currently waiting for
a file to become unlocked

Note that both programs are
waiting for file X and A3

These are all the files that
program PQR is waiting for

Fig. L11(b)   Program table for file locking

tendency is to reserve an entire file at a time, and when other users will not be terribly inconvenienced if they are prevented from accessing the file for some period of time. It is *not* a useful concept if all of the users are sharing a common data base, where an extended delay in their ability to access or update the data base is an intolerable nuisance. In short, then, the concept of locking is useful in a scientific or university time-sharing environment, but is not useful in a centralized information retrieval system, or in most other forms of "dedicated" systems.

Chapter M

FILE SECURITY

FOR ON-LINE COMPUTER SYSTEMS

INTRODUCTION

The advent of on-line computer systems, with their vast data bases, has made the subject of file security much more important than it was with batch systems. Most computer professionals have heard stories of payroll systems that collected fractions of pennies from each paycheck, the lump sum being deposited in the account of the system designer. Banking systems and stock brokerage systems have been the victims of various ingenious schemes invented by men who were high officers in their organization by the time the crime was detected.

The situation is likely to become much more critical with on-line systems, for the potential culprits are not only the *designers* of the system, but the *users* of the system as well. Since the users are remote from the system, it is more difficult to use "physical" security methods—such as guards at the door of the computer room. As long as our on-line systems permit entry via switched communication lines, anyone with a terminal and an acoustic coupler can attempt to gain access to the system.

In fact, the question of security has become much more subtle, for we are no longer simply concerned with people stealing money from a payroll system. In addition to guarding against unauthorized *updates* to the data base (for that is what is really involved in a computerized payroll theft), we are also concerned with unauthorized *reading* of the data base. We are beginning to build systems that contain very privileged and sensitive information, and it is important to ensure that this information is protected from prying eyes. The "computer utility" time-sharing systems of the 1970's will have vast libraries of *programs*, and we may very well want to limit the ability of various users even to *execute* the programs.

LEVELS OF SECURITY

There has been a great deal of discussion and concern lately about the use of computers to gather data banks of information on private citizens. This concern is felt not only by the public, but also by computer professionals and by the Congress of the United States. There is no doubt that our lawmakers have been given a very thorny dilemma: the ability of the computer to gather and disseminate information about individual citizens threatens our privacy to a degree that was never anticipated by the Constitution of the United States. On the other hand, the sheer weight of numbers of 200-250 million people in this country makes it imperative that the government keep more and more information about each one of us—so that it may minister to our needs more efficiently.

It seems likely that we may eventually have to reach a compromise of some sort—we will either have to agree to relinquish some of the privacy that has been our natural right for so many millenia, or we will have to relinquish some of the advantages of our technological society. We have no guarantee that our lawmakers and our citizens will make a wise decision in this area—indeed, some of the possibilities in this area are truly frightening. In fact, the possibilities are probably more frightening to the computer professional than to the well-meaning Congressman because we are so much more aware of the havoc that can be wreaked with our computerized data bases.

Since we, as computer professionals, *are* more aware of the aspects of computerized data bases, we have a responsibility to impart that awareness to those who will eventually decide how to use our computers. We must make sure that everyone understands the *levels* of security that can be provided in an on-line system, and the costs associated with each. We must also see to it that the public is aware that whatever protective mechanisms we computer professionals build into our systems can be undone by someone sufficiently clever and determined.

This last point has been amply demonstrated by the experiences of banks, which have labored for years to build theft-proof vaults and safes. One company went to a great deal of trouble to build a night depository box that was airtight, watertight, and bombproof—presumably to prevent a thief from blasting a hole in the side of the bank and walking off with the box. Unfortunately, one clever thief used the watertight nature of the night depository box to good advantage—he merely filled it up with water and let all the canvas money bags float to the top. Another clever thief had an even simpler scheme—he hung a sign next to the night depository box saying "out of order," and stood nearby in a phony guard's uniform. Unsuspecting depositors, seeing that the night depository box was not working, simply turned over all their money to the thief, thinking that he was a bank guard.

There are similar stories one could tell about on-line computer systems, but the point is that most people will not be so clever, nor go to such lengths to thwart our security measures. We are usually concerned with three different levels of security in our on-line systems:

1 Casual attempts by relatively non-skilled people to gain access to the system.

2 Casual attempts by skilled people (knowledgeable users, programmers, or systems analysts) to gain access to the system.

3 Determined attempts by individuals or groups who stand to gain financially, politically, or in some other fashion.

On some of the larger on-line systems, we might even want to identify another level of security to protect against attempts by well-organized criminals or foreign powers to break into the system.

By a "casual" attempt to break into a computer system, we mean one that is, in a sense, only "half-hearted": if the system makes the illegal entry too difficult or troublesome, the potential criminal will give up. On the other hand, a "determined" attempt may involve electronic eavesdropping, violence, arson, and blackmail. As one might expect, the cost of providing file security in an on-line environment increases as we try to provide higher and higher levels of security.

Basically, there are three parts to the problem of providing an effective security scheme. The first is to *indentify* the users of the system properly; the second is actually to provide the protective mechanisms to prevent illegal entry to the system or access to the files; the third part is to notify the computer operator or some other authority of any *attempts* to break into the system. We shall consider each of these problems separately.

THE PROBLEM OF IDENTIFYING THE USER

Our first job is that of identifying the person who wants to use the on-line system. Most systems identify the user only as an individual; some systems go a step further, and identify the user as a member of a particular group—e.g. the "engineering department," the "systems programming group," the "accounting department group," and so forth.

One way of identifying the user is to make use of various hardware techniques, some of which we mentioned briefly in Chapter C. If the terminal is connected directly to the computer with a direct wire connection, for example, it is very easy to insert some form of identification into the terminal itself. Even on terminals which use public switched communication lines, we could insert in the terminal an identification code which could be interrogated by the computer. However, the terminal may occasionally break down, in which case it may be difficult to switch to another terminal. Also, the hardware identifying mechanism (such as the "answer-back" drum on the Model 33 Teletype terminal) can often be easily tampered with.

Note that this type of hardware identifies only the terminal, and not necessarily the terminal user. This is a sufficient form of security for many business-oriented on-line systems, where we simply want to ensure that the clerks in the shipping department do not inadvertently access files or execute programs that were intended only for the accounting department. It would still be possible for a shipping department clerk to walk into the accounting department, and illegally gain access to the accounting department's files and programs.

We can eliminate this problem by putting hardware into the terminal to help identify the user himself. A common approach here is to give the user a key or a plastic badge that will unlock the terminal; as we mentioned in Chapter C, it would be easy to build a terminal that would "gobble up" an illegal badge, thus discouraging illegal attempts to enter the system. There are a number of variations on this type of hardware, including a terminal where a plastic "chip," inserted by the user, actually dials the telephone number of the system and issues a password unknown to the user.

This type of hardware certainly represents an improvement over the simple "answer-back" mechanism that is built into many current terminals, for it forces the user to participate in the security process. There is always the danger, of course, that the badge or key might be lost, stolen, or forged—but we have probably significantly decreased the possibility of a "casual" attempt to break into the system. For extra security, we might have *two* badges associated with each terminal, each badge being entrusted to a different person.

More sophisticated hardware devices, such as the voiceprint and fingerprint reading devices, are still in the development stage, and will probably not be economically feasible for several years. If these devices ever do become available in large quantities, they will greatly improve the security of the systems, since they cannot easily be circumvented. At the moment, only the badge reader devices are easily obtainable, and they still represent an increase over the cost of a basic terminal. As a result, most of the user identification mechanisms are software-oriented.

The standard software approach to file security at the moment is the notion of a *password*. Most on-line systems require that the user supply the password in addition to a "user name," or "user identification," or "user number." Thus, a common dialogue might be as follows:

> USER NAME?   1034,smith
> PASSWORD?   xanadu

The only problem with this approach is that the password is often printed on the teletypewriter terminal, or displayed on the CRT screen, in full view of any other people who may happen to be in the vicinity.

There are some simple, but fairly effective, techniques for hiding the password from prying eyes. Among these techniques are:

1 Use full-duplex transmission lines between the terminal and the computer. For normal terminal communication, the computer "echoes" each character typed by the user, and thereby causes the character to be printed on the teletypewriter paper. For *passwords*, though, the computer simply does not echo the characters.

2 Allow the password to contain characters which have no printing "graphic." Thus, in the ASCII character set, the "control characters" do not print.

3 Use the "smudge" approach, as illustrated by Figure M1. The computer types several characters in the space where the user is to type his password, then backspaces and types more characters. The result is a black "smudge," on top of which the user can type his password without making it legible to other people.

It should be possible for the user to change his password whenever he wants to, and he should be able to do this from his terminal. Unfortunately, some users have a tendency to forget their password if they change them too often. This can create a problem, since the natural tendency of the user is to call up the computer operator and ask that the password be read over the phone.

There are a few on-line systems that make the password an *algebraic function*, instead of a fixed quantity. Thus, the user might be told that his password consisted of the function $2x + 3y + 4$, and the login procedure might look the following:

> USER NAME?   1034,smith
> X = 4,Y = 2,WHAT IS THE PASSWORD?   18

Obviously, the algebraic function could be made arbitrarily complex, and it would be extremely difficult for someone unfamiliar with the system to supply the right password.

PROVIDING A PROTECTIVE MECHANISM

There are several things we must do to protect the data base of the on-line system, once we have identified the person who wants to use the system. The most important thing is to identify the manner in which the user intends to access the data base; typically, the user might be expected to access the data base in any of the following ways:

executing a program

reading a record or a file in the data base

writing, or *updating,* a record or a file

appending a new record to the end of a file

destroying a file completely, so that no trace of it remains

changing the access privileges

Each of these modes of access may or may not be potentially dangerous, depending on the type of on-line system. On any system where financial transactions are involved, such as payroll, stock transfers, accounts receivables, etc., we might not want to allow arbitrary users to *execute* the program that prints paychecks or stock certificates or credit memos. Similarly, there are a number of situations in which it would be undesirable to allow a user to indiscriminately *read* or *write* records in the data base. We might want to restrict users from *appending* records to payroll files, accounts payable files, and so forth; the power of *destroying* a file is obviously something that we want to restrict. Finally, we want to make sure that only a very limited group of people can *change* the access privileges associated with a file.

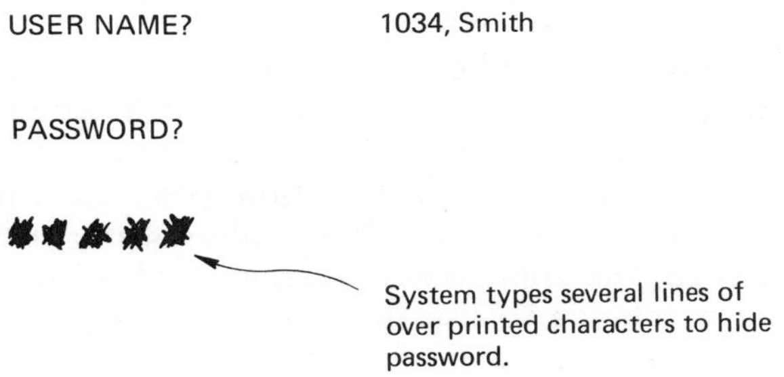

USER NAME?   1034, Smith

PASSWORD?

░▓░▓░ ←

System types several lines of over printed characters to hide password.

Fig. M1   The "smudge" technique for hiding passwords

Our file security mechanism must thus associate these modes of access with users of the on-line system. Actually, we may decide to associate legal modes of access with:

a terminal

an application program

an individual user

a group of users, such as the accounting department

some combination of the above

The most common method of implementing this form of file security is the *access key* shown in Figure M2. The access keys are merely bit-codes which give a "yes" or "no" answer for the combinations of types of users and modes of access.

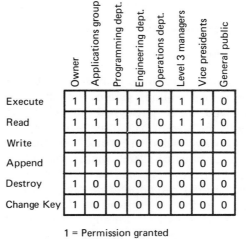

1 = Permission granted
0 = Permission denied

Fig. M2   Access keys for file security

Since the user was forced to identify himself when he logged in to the system, the operating system knows who he is, which terminal he is using, and to which group of users he belongs. When the user types a transaction of some kind from his terminal, an application program will process the transaction and perhaps attempt to access a file. Before being allowed to access the file, though, the application program must inform the operating system as to *how* it intends to use the file, at which time the operating system can check the access key and see whether a legal access is being made. This access checking is usually performed when the application program first *opens* the file; the operating system then has enough information to know whether subsequent calls from the application program to read, write, append, or destroy the file are legal.

We have been talking thus far of providing a security system for *files.* Obviously, the idea can be extended to records, or even fields within records. The only problem, aside from the fact that most vendors do *not* supply operating systems or data management packages with this capability, is that the overhead can become enormous. The overhead consists of extra file space for the access keys, extra disk accesses to read the access keys, and extra computation to check the access keys when the application program calls the operating system for each record access.

This file security software should be considered only a part of the overall problem of security in a computer system. There are three areas where the system designer should make certain that his security procedures are adequate:

1   *The terminal users*

Even with the file security software discussed above, it is important to ensure that the terminal users do not represent a security "leak." For many types of on-line systems, this simply means that the users should avoid hard-copy of sensitive data wherever possible; such information could be displayed on a CRT for a few seconds, and then erased.

On on-line systems where security is a major concern, our terminal users might require even more protection. The terminals could be placed in special rooms to prevent electronic "eavesdropping" by some outside party; special communications lines could be used to minimize the chances of passive or active wire-tapping; special hardware could be added to the terminal to "scramble" or encrypt the transmission to further ensure its integrity.

2   *The file security mechanism*

The system designer should take steps to ensure that the file security mechanism remains intact. He should, for example, have a central authority control the distribution and changing of passwords and access keys; many systems have made it possible for the computer operator and the system programmers to access this information, and the system security suffers as a result. There should be a strong attempt to maintain very tight security on the passwords and access keys, since these represent the major part of the file security mechanism.

To further ensure the integrity of the passwords, the system designer should arrange to have them changed frequently. This must be done in an orderly fashion, so that the users all know when the password has been changed; at the same time, it must be done in a relatively secure fashion, so that the new passwords do not "leak" out. Many organizations, for example, make the mistake of sending a list of new passwords through the inter-office mail.

In some cases, the system designer may even want to establish a "police force" to check continually on the integrity of both the data base and the environment of the system. The police force might have terminals of their own, which they could use to check occasionally on the status and contents of various files; they could also use the terminals to monitor the terminal dialogue of other users on the system. The same approach could be accomplished by making certain users of the system responsible for the security and integrity of specified files in the data base.

3   *The computer center*

While the system designer must give considerable attention to the terminals and the users, he should not neglect the security of the computer center itself. Depending on the sensitivity of the system, he should employ sufficient guards, dogs, alarms, or any other technique necessary to maintain good physical security.

The system designer should also bear in mind that the system programmers might pose a threat to the security of the system. There should be a strong effort to carefully test and inspect the programs, to make sure that there are no obvious attempts to thwart the file security mechanisms. The system designer should see to it that the security of the system is maintained during this testing period; in most cases, this means that a "live" data base should not be used during testing and debugging.

Finally, the system designer should remember that the security of the system can be threatened by the computer operator. The system programmers should not be allowed to operate a sensitive system, for there is no way of knowing whether they are running a slightly "modified" version of the system or not. There should also be tight control maintained over the operation manuals, so that unauthorized personnel will not know how to operate the system improperly for their own benefit.

THE PROBLEM OF REPORTING VIOLATIONS OF THE SECURITY SCHEME

As we mentioned earlier, there will almost always be "casual" attempts to break into an on-line system. Thus, the system designer should attempt to include in his file security mechanism some kind of "alarm" that will be sounded when it appears that the file security system is being tampered with. This "alarm" might take the form of a message on the computer operator's terminal or the security officer's terminal, depending on the nature of the system; the message would result from an illegal attempt to log in to the system, or an illegal attempt to access a file.

In some cases it might be desirable to allow the user a certain number of "mistakes" before sounding the alarm. Thus, the user would be allowed three or four chances to type the correct password when logging in to the system; he might also be allowed one or two incorrect attempts to access a file. In certain very sensitive systems, of course, this approach would not be followed: a security officer could be dispatched to the offending terminal as soon as the first illegal attempt was made. There are a few systems where the culprit is not even immediately aware that his illegal attempt to break into the system has been noticed: an alarm is sounded, and the system then proceeds to give the user false data, while the security officer is dispatched to the scene of the crime.

As we mentioned in Chapter C, illegal attempts to gain access to the system can also be dealt with by the terminal. A terminal that accepts a small, plastic badge, for example, can be modified to "gobble up" the badge if it is incorrect. Alternatively, the terminal could disconnect itself or explode if it decided that the user was illegally trying to enter the system.

Finally, the system designer might want to keep a record of attempts to thwart the security system. By keeping a log of illegal attempts to access a file, he might notice a pattern over a period of time. By keeping a record of illegal attempts to log in to the system, the system designer might be able to find out which terminal is involved. He would also be able to see the techniques employed by the would-be culprits, and perhaps to improve his security scheme.

There is no doubt that a considerable amount of time and money can be spent attempting to protect the integrity of the system. At the current time, most business-oriented on-line systems are only interested in protecting their data from *outside* spies; there does not seem to be much concern about possible snooping and misuse of data by *internal* employees. Time-sharing service bureaus have begun to become more interested in the problem, and the government-oriented information retrieval systems are beginning to come under a large amount of public criticism because of a lack of sufficient security.

SOME UNUSUAL CASES

The mechanisms we described above are sufficient for many applications, for they usually prevent casual accesses to the system by would-be criminals. However, there are a number of situations where the "simple" approach is not sufficient. As an example, consider an on-line military system which keeps track of the location and next refueling date of nuclear ships. We want to allow one level of naval officer to find out the current location of the ship; another level of naval officer is allowed to access information concerning the next refueling date. However, we want to require a much higher level of clearance for access to *both* pieces of information, since the two pieces of information indicate the ship's radius of action. Knowing the ship's radius of action, an enemy could presumably start some trouble just outside of it.

This example transcends the simple access key mechanism because it involves *combinations* of information. Actually, simple cases of this nature *could* be solved with access keys, since we know what kinds of combinations of information are involved, and which users are involved. However, the situation becomes very much more complicated if the combinations and permutations of information increase—and if the system designer is not sure which combinations of records or files will be accessed by users.

Consider, for example, an on-line system that could keep information on all American citizens. We might allow one government agency to obtain information about a citizen's criminal record; we might allow the Internal Revenue Service to access information about a citizen's tax history; other agencies might be allowed to access information relevant to their line of business. However, what do we do if another agency wants information about a citizen's race *and* religion *and* income? If the agency wanted the information only for statistical studies, we might permit the access as long as the citizen's name was not revealed. As we will see below, though, this approach can also lead to trouble.

If we keep one hundred different pieces of information about each citizen, the number of *combinations* of information that might be requested is staggering. To do a complete job, the system designer would have to identify each and every combination of information, and assign the proper security code to each. This is far beyond the capabilities of most on-line computer systems, and the file security will suffer as a result.

There are a number of other file security problems that are far more subtle and difficult to solve. It has been recognized, for example, that an information retrieval system might inadvertently release sensitive information, even though it was programmed to ask the user for all of the appropriate passwords.

Suppose, for example, that we built an information retrieval system that contained various types of personal data about the employees of our company. The system might be programmed in such a way that it would not be easy for the average user to inquire about the criminal record of employees; thus, if we were to ask the system "Has John Smith ever been arrested?", the system would refuse to answer. On the other hand, the system might provide various kinds of *statistical* information, so that we could ask "How many left-handed, blue-eyed, red-haired employees of the corporation have ever had a criminal record?" If the system answered that there was only one such person in the corporation, and if we knew that John Smith was left-handed, had blue eyes and red hair, then we obviously would have acquired the information that the system was trying so valiantly to protect. This is clearly a simple example, but the reader should be able to see that a number of on-line systems suffer the potential weakness of allowing users to discern *correlations* of data.

Another type of subtle file security problem has to do with *patterns* of file accesses. Many of the on-line credit card systems, for example, are programmed to check for suspicious spending patterns: if the program notices that a particular American Express card or Master Charge card is being used for an unusually high number of purchases within a relatively short period of time, it will print a warning report. Other types of on-line systems might have much more difficult types of file accessing patterns to check for: a suspicious number of *executions* of a particular application program, a suspicious number of *read* accesses to a particular file, a suspicious number of new records *appended* to a sensitive file (such as payroll file).

On many systems, it is impossible to tell whether an access to the data base violates the security of the system. At some later time, long after the original access was made, it may become evident that money was stolen, sensitive information was given away, or that valuable files were destroyed. At that point, it becomes very important to have a *log*, or an *audit trail*, of all of the accesses to the data base, together with some identification of the person who made the access. At the time this book was written, there was considerable public controversy over the fact that some on-line systems used by law-enforcement agencies do *not* keep a log of data base accesses, which means that the data base is susceptible to various kinds of misuse.

In summary, we should recognize that the problem of file security is far from being solved. For the simple and straightforward security situations faced by many on-line systems, there are a number of well-known techniques to discourage *casual* misuse of data. For the more complex situations of the type that will be facing us repeatedly during the next few decades in our increasingly computerized society, the simple file security techniques have a number of weaknesses. However, many of these weaknesses have been dealt with by military agencies; it is possible, assuming that we are willing to spend the money, that we may be able to apply their techniques to civilian on-line systems of the future.

Chapter N

FILE RECOVERY FOR ON-LINE SYSTEMS

INTRODUCTION

As we have seen from the previous two chapters, there are many aspects to the design of a data base for an on-line system. We are interested in minimizing the number of file accesses required to retrieve some information; we want to minimize the amount of space taken up by our files and records; and we would also like to be able to "migrate" various records from one storage device to another at various times.

However, an equally large aspect of file design is the *integrity* of the data base. Despite the best efforts of the system designer, the on-line system *will* fail occasionally, and we must be prepared for that eventuality. Since an on-line data base is usually updated on a dynamic, second-by-second basis, it is often more vulnerable to failures than a data base for a batch system. In a batch system, we usually find that the worst consequence of a system failure is that we have to re-run one or two jobs.

In an on-line computer system, there are two different aspects of file recovery. First, we want to be sure that our data base is in a *consistent* state after a failure. As shown in Figure N1, it is quite possible for our system to fail while updating one of several logically related records. If nothing is done to "recover" the data base, we will have a data base that is "contradictory" in nature.

The other important aspect of file recovery for an on-line system is the user of the system. We must make sure that the user is told what his last valid piece of input was, or at least make sure that he has some way of finding out. In many scientific time-sharing systems, the user *can* determine the status of his last input by interrogating his files. Thus, if he was editing his program, he can see whether his last update was actually accepted by the system before it failed.

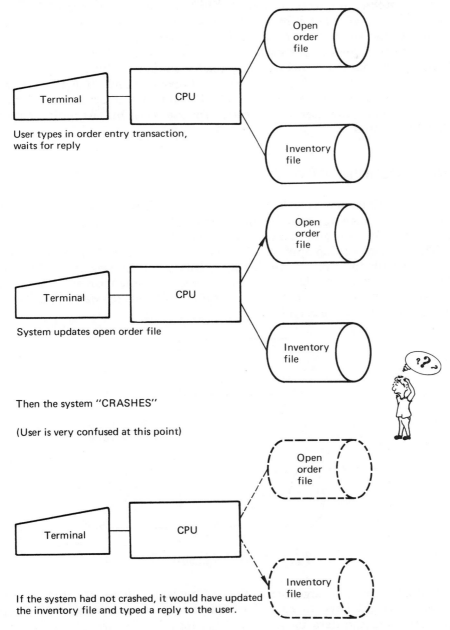

Fig. N1 Example of an "inconsistent" data base

In many cases, though, we do not want to depend on the user's initiative. If our data base contains financial information or medical information, it is critically important to make sure that the user knows what to do after a failure. Thus, we do not want him to *repeat* his last transaction, on the mistaken impression that the system had not processed it before failing; nor do we want him to *omit* his last transaction, on the mistaken impression that the system *did* process it before failing.

There are three or four basic techniques for maintaining a data base, all of which are discussed below. The reader should analyze these different techniques with both of our recovery criteria in mind. If a file recovery approach does not guarantee a "consistent" data base, it is not very useful; if it does not allow the user to determine the status of his last input, it is also somewhat limited.

DUAL RECORDING OF DATA

The basic idea here is to keep the data base on *two* disks, drums, or other types of file storage units, as shown in Figure N2. An update to the data base would thus cause a simultaneous update to both disks.

The dual recording approach is useful if the system failures are mostly associated with the disk. If we develop parity errors on one of the disks, the other one will still contain a valid, consistent, up-to-the-moment copy of the data base. If we have a "head crash," or if an earthquake swallows up one of the disks, our data base is still safe.

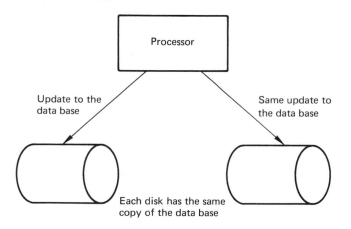

Fig. N2   Dual recording of data

Unfortunately, a large percentage of system failures are due to other causes, as we shall see in Part V of this book. If we have a power failure while updating the data base, *both* disks may be damaged (in a hardware sense, as well as in a software sense). If there is a bug in the application program that updates the data base, both disks will contain garbage.

Thus, the dual recording approach protects the integrity of the data base for only a limited number of types of failures, and at a fairly large cost. We not only require twice the amount of file storage units, but we also place twice the load on the IO channels which transfer information from the processor to the file storage units.

A limited form of the dual recording approach can, however, be useful. As we pointed out in Chapter K, the directory-oriented file organization scheme is extremely vulnerable to system failures, since our only clue to the location of our records is the directory. Thus, we might want to keep a duplicate copy of the critical directories. As shown in Figure N3, we might not keep duplicate copies of *all* of the directories, but only those which represent "libraries" of file names, and so forth. The duplicate copies can be kept on the same disk, in the hope that a disk hardware problem will only render one track, or block, unreadable.

DISK DUMPS

The most common approach to file recovery is the disk dump, which entails copying the entire data base to a magnetic tape (or perhaps to a disk-pack) on some regularly scheduled basis. Most commercial time-sharing service bureaus and a good number of "in-house" on-line systems perform a disk dump at the end of each day's operations.

Despite its simplicity, there are a number of major weaknesses in this approach. The most obvious weakness is its inability to guarantee a "consistent" data base. If we have a system failure at any point during the normal day's operation, we risk losing the entire day's work. There have been attempts to counteract this by performing a disk dump two, three, or even four times a day, but the effect is the same. A catastrophic failure of any type forces us to back up to the last dump, causing all subsequent work to be lost.

A less obvious disadvantage is that the disk dump may take several hours if the data base is very large. One system designer once ruefully admitted that it would take him seventeen days to perform a daily disk dump! To some extent, the length of time required depends on the sophistication of the dump. If the data base is stored on several independent file storage units (disk-packs, for example) it may be possible to make simultaneous dumps of the file storage units onto multiple magnetic tapes. Even on a single file storage unit, a "physical" dump is much faster than a "logical" dump. A physical dump is one in which tracks (or blocks, or cylinders) are dumped in sequential order; a logical dump, on the other hand, is one in which *logical records* are written in sequential order.

Even though the "logical" dump may be slower, it has some advantages. It allows the data base to be rearranged and compacted. It is also a good idea to incorporate some *diagnostic* capability in the disk dump. That is, the dump program could check directories to make sure that the links and pointers are correct, and that the files have not been clobbered. In dedicated systems, it could also check the various fields within each record to make sure that the data have not been damaged. Fields which are supposed to be numeric could be checked, as could fields which are supposed to be alphanumeric. "Reasonableness" checks could be made to see that numeric quantities have not exceeded some level.

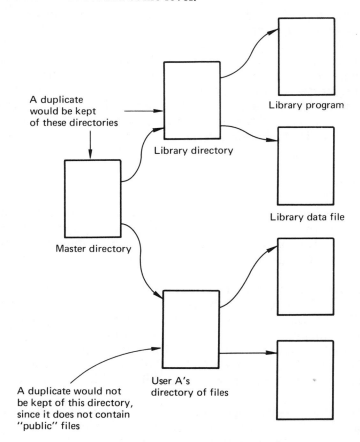

A duplicate would be kept of these directories

Library program

Library directory

Library data file

Master directory

User A's directory of files

A duplicate would not be kept of this directory, since it does not contain "public" files

Fig. N3   Dual recording of directories

With large data bases, a bad record may not be discovered for several days, weeks, or even months. Thus, it is important to keep backup tapes for some time. This must be done in an organized way, or the system designer is likely to find a damaged data base record six months after the damage was done and after all disk dump tapes have been thrown away.

One good approach is to keep seven "daily" disk dump tapes, four "weekly" disk dump tapes, twelve "monthly" disk dump tapes, and one "yearly" tape for each year that the system survives (which, in these days of planned obsolescence, is rarely more than three or four). The following procedure is then used:

1   A disk dump is taken each day.

2   At the end of each week, the most recent daily dump tape replaces the oldest weekly dump tape.

3   At the end of each month, the most recent weekly dump tape replaces the oldest monthly tape.

4   At the end of each year, the most recent monthly tape becomes a yearly tape, which is saved forever.

A variation on the disk dump approach is the so-called *differential disk dump*. With this approach, we keep only a dump tape for those records or files which have changed during the course of the day. Assuming that we have some easy way of keeping track of *which* records have been updated, this can significantly decrease the length of the dumping process. However, the process of piecing together a complete data base may be made a little more difficult, since we must go back to the last complete dump, and then merge in all the differential dumps that have been taken since then. It is suggested that a complete dump be taken at least once a week.

THE AUDIT TRAIL APPROACH

The philosophy behind the audit trail approach is to keep a *history* of the input that has been processed by the system, and the changes that have been made to the data base. In this way, we can easily recover the data base, and reprocess any work that has been lost.

Before discussing the various audit trail techniques, we should first distinguish a "serious" failure from a "trivial" failure—in the context of recovering the data base. We shall consider a serious failure to be one which destroys the data base as it existed at the time of the failure. Thus, a head crash (where the read/write heads of the disk drop suddenly onto the recording surface, scratching the oxide and making most or all of the tracks unreadable) would be considered a serious failure. Similarly, an application program which methodically zeroed out records in the data base during the day would cause a serious system failure when it was finally detected.

A trivial system failure, as the name implies, is one where we do not suspect much damage has been done to the data base. If the computer operator suddenly pushes the STOP button on the console, we may be in the situation depicted in Figure N1, but the major part of the data base is intact. This is the case in a large number of failures—due to program bugs, power failures (that is, power failures which are not sufficiently sudden to cause a head crash), air conditioning failures, and so forth. We may have a few records to "fix up," but, on the whole, the data base is intact after a trivial failure.

With this in mind, let us examine the audit trail techniques. An *audit trail* consists of a record, usually on magnetic tape, of any of the following:

1   The text of an input transaction.

2 The copy of a record *before* it was updated.

3 The copy of a record *after* it was updated.

If we keep only the text of the transaction, the audit trail will take the form shown by Figure N4. Note that while we have a record of all the transactions that have been received by the system, we have no idea of how the data base has been updated. Thus, if we have a system failure, we must assume that the system was in the midst of processing one or more of the most recently arrived transactions—but we do not know how much processing has been done, nor do we know which records have been updated.

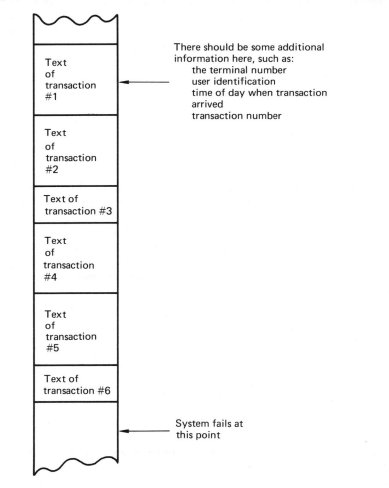

Fig. N4 The audit trail approach with transaction text only

The suggestion is often made that we could write a "recovery program" which would somehow look at the current state of the files and figure out what the application program was doing at the time of the failure. Then, the argument goes, the recovery program could either *finish* the processing that had been begun by the application or *undo* it. This seems an extremely tedious approach, for the recovery program must "mimic" the processing normally done by the application program, checking the data base each time to see whether the update has *already been made* by the application program.

In fact, we can easily show that there are cases when it is *impossible* for the recovery program to tell what the application program was doing at the time of the failure. Consider, for example, a case where the application program merely increments or decrements the contents of a numeric field in a record on the data base. The ARRIVAL transaction in the Widget system discussed in Chapter J is a case in point—the only thing that the application program does is increment the inventory total in the data base. Thus, since the recovery program has no information about the *previous* contents of the inventory record, it has no way of figuring out whether the application program had or had not made the update before the system failed.

This is a very important point: *a recovery program cannot figure out, by computation alone, what the application program was doing at the time of the system failure, in the general case.* Even in special cases where it *is* possible, it would be a tedious and difficult job.

One such special case that deserves brief mention is the idea of reserving one field in each data base record to indicate the transaction number of the last transaction that updated the record. With this extra information, it would be possible to reprocess the last few transactions that entered the system before the failure, using the normal application programs; the data management subroutines, however, would be aware that the system was operating in "recovery mode," and would be able to use the extra information in the data base records to prevent redundant updates during the reprocessing of the transactions.

Thus, if our audit trail scheme consists of keeping only the text of the input transactions, we must reload the last complete dump of our data base, and reprocess all of the transactions that we have recorded on the audit trail tape. This can be very bothersome if any of the following three conditions are true:

1 The data base is large, so that reloading of the last complete dump tape takes a long time.

2 A large number of transactions have been accumulated on the audit trail tape, and/or the transactions require a significant amount of CPU time to re-process.

3 Failures occur frequently, in which case the logistics of reloading the data base and reprocessing the transactions would be rather poor.

It is interesting to note that this form of audit trail scheme works equally well with serious failures and trivial failures, since it does not depend on the current state of the data base.

Another approach is to keep the text of the transaction, and the "before" copy of the data base, as shown in Figure N5. Assuming that the system failure is not serious, our recovery procedure consists of scanning the audit trail tape for all transactions which were not finished, and "undoing" or "restoring" the data base updates caused by those incompletely-processed transactions. This is a very easy thing to do, for our audit trail tape contains the copy of data base records *before* they were updated.

Note that as long as the failure is not serious, we only have to keep track of the transactions that have not been completed. Once the processing of the transaction has been finished, we do not have to keep track of the data base updates or the text of the transaction, for we know that the data base is in a consistent state once the transaction has been finished.

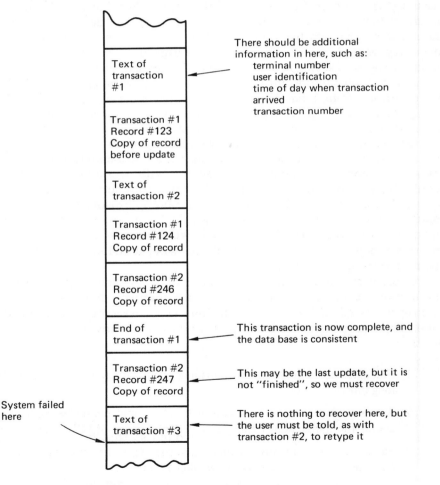

Fig. N5 Audit trail approach with "before" copy of record

However, we cannot always be sure that the application program has processed the transaction properly. If there is a bug in the program, we may not discover it for several minutes or hours, and by throwing away the audit trail records for completed transactions, we lose the ability to recover from these more insidious types of failures.

If the system failure is serious, then we must employ the same technique we described before: the last complete dump of the data base must be reloaded, and all of the input transactions must be reprocessed. In this case, though, we do have the advantage that the data base only has to be reloaded for a serious failure.

If our audit trail tape contains the copy of the data base records *after* they have been updated, our recovery scheme consists of reloading the last dump tape and merging in all of the updates that are associated with *completed* records. This is efficient if the processing of a transaction requires a tremendous amount of computing, but is inefficient if the reloading of the data base takes a long time.

By combining the text of the transaction, the "before" copy of the record *and* the "after" copy of the record, as shown in Figure N6, we can combine all of the advantages that have been described above. If we have a trivial failure, we can use the "before" copy of the records to "unprocess" all of the incomplete transactions. If the system failure was serious enough to destroy the data base, we can reload last night's disk dump, and merge in the "after" copy of records corresponding to *completed* transactions. If we discover that there was a bug in the application program that updated the data base, the "before" copy of the record can be used to undo the damage that was done by the application program. If the damage was so great that the data base was destroyed, we always have the text of the transaction itself.

In all of these techniques, we should point out that the audit trail file must *not* be buffered or blocked, Otherwise, audit trail records might be buffered in core at the time of the system failure. This, too, is an important point, for some system designers feel that if they write out the text of the transaction without blocking, the data base updates (i.e. the "before" and/or "after" copies of the record) *can* be blocked. The point is that unless our audit trail tape is assured of having *all* of the data base updates at the time of the failure, we have no way of recovering the data base other than to reload it.

The audit trail file is normally kept on magnetic tape, mostly because the volume of updates and transactions is such that we would run out of space on the disk. The only problem that one occasionally runs into is that of writing an End-of-File mark on the tape. We must be able to write an End-of-File on the tape before it is rewound so that the recovery program will know where to stop. On most computers, this can be done manually by opening up the tape drive and pushing the proper buttons.

There may be cases where the system designer prefers to keep the audit trail on a disk file. In most cases, magnetic tape is approximately as fast as disk for transferring information in a serial fashion, but the system designer may have a configuration with slow tapes and fast disk. He may also consider the disk to be a more reliable device than the tape, in which case the audit trail should be kept on disk.

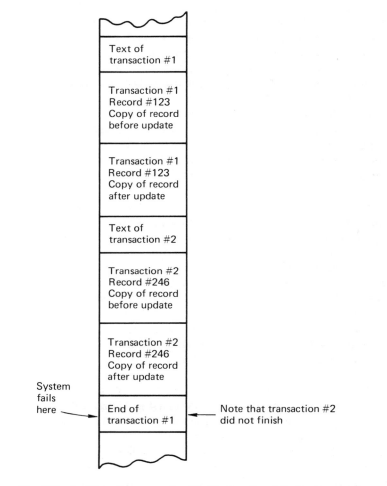

Fig. N6 Audit trail approach with "before" and "after" records

We have not yet discussed the problem of informing the user of the status of his transaction after a failure, but it should be clear that the audit trail gives us the necessary information to do so. We have a record of each transaction received by the system, and it is suggested that the transaction be given a unique *transaction number* when it enters the system. Since we are now considering the *user's* point of view, though, we should remember that the system may have failed *after* he has pressed the "transmit" key (or the carriage return key), but *before* the transaction has been received by the application program (or perhaps even before it has been received by the operating system).

We must thus give a little more thought to the problem of informing the users. It is apparent that we cannot give the user *negative* information when the system becomes operational again—that is, we cannot tell the user about the transactions that were received but not processed, for there may have been some that we do not even know about. We have to give the user some form of *positive* acknowledgement—that is, we should tell him what the last transaction was that we *did* finish processing. The user can then determine whether any transactions were lost at the instant of failure.

Perhaps the best approach is to give the user an acknowledgement at his terminal for *each* transaction that is finished. The acknowledgement can be very simple—perhaps just the letters "OK"—but it should contain the transaction number as a reference in case the system fails. We might thus have the following type of sequence in our on-line system (in the dialogue below, the capitalized items are output from the system, while the lower-case items are input from the user):

> order 1234 model13 blue 75
> OK #31335
> arrival model3 red houston 976
> OK #31347

Notice that the transaction numbers that are typed out by the system are monotonically increasing, but not necessarily sequential. This is because one user's transactions are interspersed with transactions from other users.

If there is a system failure, a recovery program can scan through the audit trail tape, and construct a table of transaction numbers of the last finished transaction for each user who was on the system when it failed. This table could be used when the system was restored to its normal operational state, and could cause the following sort of message to be typed on the user's terminal:

LAST VALID TRANSACTION WAS # 31347 AT 1:28 PM

The user should be carefully trained by the system designer to properly interpret these recovery messages. Note that there are three possibilities:

1 The user has typed in a transaction and has not gotten an acknowledgement at his terminal. Furthermore, the system did not get a chance to process the transaction before the failure. In this case, the LAST VALID TRANSACTION. . . message will refer to a *previous* transaction.

2 The user has typed in a transaction, and has not gotten an acknowledgement at his terminal. However, the system *has* processed the transaction, and it duly recorded on the audit trail tape. In this case, the LAST VALID TRANSACTION. . . message will refer to a transaction number which is *higher* than any the user has seen on his terminal. The user should interpret this as a sign from the omnipotent machine that his last input was actually accepted.

3 The user has typed in a transaction, and *has* gotten an acknowledgement from the system—but he has not gotten around to typing any more transactions yet. In this case, the LAST VALID TRANSACTION. . . message should refer to the

last transaction that the user typed in, and it is, in effect, a "redundant," but psychologically reassuring, confirmation by the recovery program.

When one designs a file recovery scheme, it is important to remember that the system might fail at *any* point during the processing of input. Many on-line systems have gotten into terrible trouble because of the philosophy that "the chances that the system will fail at such-and-such a point (updating some critical directory, for example) are extremely small, so we won't worry about it." When one considers the volume of processing that takes place in most on-line systems, it becomes eminently *probable* that a failure will occur at a critical juncture after a week, two weeks or a month.

With the audit trail scheme, we can show that there is *no* time during the processing of input when we are vulnerable to a system failure. Consider, for example, the processing of a normal application program which accepts a transaction from a terminal, reads and writes several records, then types an acknowledgement on the user's terminal. We have the following steps that are taken during the processing:

1 The user types the transaction on his terminal, and presses the "transmit" key. If the system fails here, we certainly have not damaged the data base with this user's input, for it has not even been seen by the system. Furthermore, we can tell the user that we have not seen his input, by telling him what we *did* see last.

2 The operating system then reads the input from the terminal. As far as the application program is concerned, this is the same as step #1. The application program still has not seen the input, and will so indicate to the user. The data base has obviously not been damaged by this transaction, though it may be damaged by virtue of the system failure itself.

3 The application program then reads the transaction, and immediately writes it on the audit trail, along with such identifying information as the user number, the terminal number, the transaction number and the time of day. At this point, the data base still has not been affected, but the recovery program will now "remember" that the transaction arrived. We can either process the transaction during the recovery procedure, or we can force the user to type the transaction in again.

4 When the application program is ready to process the transaction, it does some computing, and then reads several records from the data base. As far as the recovery program is concerned, things are the same as if we were still in step #3 above.

5 When the application program decides to update a record, it first writes the *current* (or "before") copy of the record to the audit trail. If the system fails at this point, the record has not yet been updated on the data base. However, the recovery program will not know (or care), and will use the copy of the record on the audit trail to restore the data base. Thus, we may have performed a

redundant restoration, but certainly we have not done any harm. Obviously, we are still in a position to be able to tell the user about his transaction.

6 The application program then updates the data base. It is at this point that the audit trail really becomes valuable. If the system fails at this point, the data base will certainly have been damaged, and the recovery program can easily repair the damage.

Steps 5 and 6 are repeated for each record that the application program decides to update. Remember that the application program must write the "before" copy of the record to the audit trail, *and must wait for the completion of that write,* before actually updating the data base.

7 When the application program finishes processing a transaction, it indicates that fact by writing a special record on the audit trail file, as illustrated in Figures N5 and N6. If the system fails *before* this can be done, the recovery program may decide to recover the data base even though the transaction had been finished. Once again, we are faced with a possible redundant recovery, but no harm is done. If the system fails *after* this step has been finished, the recovery program will obviously see that the transaction has been finished, and will recognize that the data base updates do not have to be undone.

8 Finally, an acknowledgement is typed on the user's terminal. At this point, everyone and everything in the system knows that the transaction has been finished.

Chapter O

AN EXAMPLE —

THE WIDGET SYSTEM REVISITED, PART 2

INTRODUCTION

As the reader will remember, we had partially designed an on-line order system for the Widget Corporation of America in Chapter J. The purpose of the system is to allow salesman to type orders from terminals, accounting clerks to input charges and credits from terminals, and warehouse clerks to input inventory transactions from their terminals.

We were forced to abandon our design of the application programs at the end of Chapter J, for we did not know enough about the file organization to proceed any further. Paradoxically, we could not design the files until we had some idea of the nature of the application programs. This is but an example of what we called "circular design" in Chapter D—that is, we design various parts of our system by a series of successive approximations.

Our major accomplishment in Chapter J—from the point of view of being able to design the files—was the definition of the *transactions* of the system, and the *basic structure* of the application programs. To refresh our memory, let us look again at the transactions listed in Table O1, and the basic application structure shown in Figure O1.

Our purpose in this chapter is to continue the design that was begun in Chapter J. Perhaps our most important effort will simply be to identify which files are required. That is, do we need only one massive file with many techniques of accessing it, or would it be better to have several independent files? We will also try to determine which *key* should be used to access the file(s). Do we want to access the information by account number, purchase order number, or some other combination of keys?

TABLE O1   *Transactions for the Widget Corporation Sales Order Entry System*

Inventory-oriented transactions

ORDER	P.O.*	Acctno.	Model	Color	(Warehouse)	Amount
RESERVE	P.O.*	Acctno.	Model	Color	(Warehouse)	Amount
CANCEL	P.O.	Acctno.				
ARRIVAL			Model	Color	Warehouse	Amount
SHIPMENT	P.O.	Acctno.				Amount

Accounting-oriented transactions

PAYMENT	P.O.	Acctno.		Amount
STOPCREDIT		Acctno.		
RESTORECREDIT		Acctno.		
CHARGE		Acctno.		Amount
CREDIT		Acctno.		Amount

Inquiries

INQA			Model	Color	(Warehouse)
INQC	(P.O.)	Acctno.			

Batch transactions

ADDC	Acctno.	
DELC	Acctno.	
ADDW	Model	Color
DELW	Model	Color

* Returned by the system as output from the transaction
Items enclosed by parentheses are *optional.*

We shall also be interested in determining the proper file accessing technique. Our decision to use a direct addressing scheme, a binary search, a randomizing technique or a directory approach will be influenced by the four major criteria we listed in Chapter K:

1 Minimize disk accesses

2 Minimize disk space

3 Allow migration of records

4 Ensure recovery

Since the users of the Widget system will be doing similar things at the same time (i.e. ordering widgets, indicating the shipment or arrival of widgets, and so forth), we shall also have to concern ourselves with the problem of simultaneous access. Finally, we shall consider the problem of file security and file recovery for the Widget system.

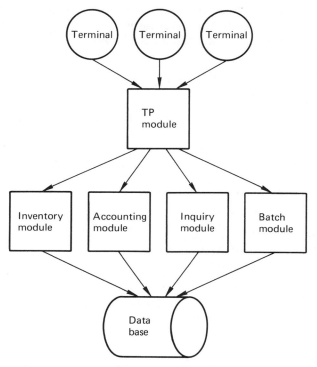

Fig. O1 Basic application structure for Widget system

What Kinds of Files Are Required?

We remember that in Chapter F, when the Widget System was first introduced, we indicated that the Aardvark 301 computer salesman had suggested the file organization shown in Figure O2. At this point, the important thing is not so much that he suggested a directory structure, but that he suggested *two* distinct files: an inventory file and an accounts receivable file. No particular reason was given at the time, and this corresponds to most situations in real life: someone makes an arbitrary decision that there should be one file, two files, or ninety-two files.

If we examine the transactions listed in Table O1, we see that there are really *three* different types of information being maintained by the system: inventory information, accounting information, and "open order" information. This is a very important point: we are not just talking about *one* piece of information which can be accessed in three different ways. We are talking about three separate and distinct *types* of information. The accounting information is quite distinct from the inventory information, and the open order information should also be distinguished from the inventory information.

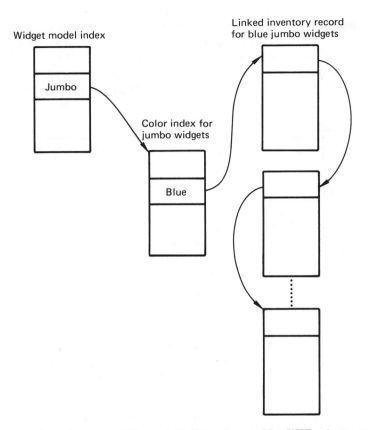

Widget model index

Linked inventory record for blue jumbo widgets

Jumbo

Color index for jumbo widgets

Blue

Fig. O2(a) Inventory file organization suggested by XYZ salesman

If these types of information are really separate and distinct, we should *keep* them separate and distinct in their own files. That is, after all, what a file is supposed to be: a collection of logically related pieces of information.

How Should We Access the Files?

From our comments above, we conclude that there should be an open order file, an inventory file, and an accounting file. Now we must decide how to organize each file, and how to access it.

Let us begin by examining the open order file. An open order is created when the salesman types in an ORDER transaction or a RESERVE transaction, and disappears from the system when the salesman types a CANCEL transaction or the warehouse clerk types a SHIPMENT transaction. Since we assumed in Chapter F that new orders would be arriving from each terminal at the rate of one per minute, the open order file is going to be quite active. It is reasonable to expect that an order for widgets will be filled within two or three days, and if the Widget Corporation is to stay in any kind of equilibrium at all, orders must be shipped at the same average *rate* that they arrive. Thus, if we expect orders to arrive at the average rate of 200 per minute over the course of a year of operation (which works out to one per minute for 200 terminals), then the orders must be filled at the average rate of 200 per minute if the company is to avoid an ever-increasing backlog of orders.

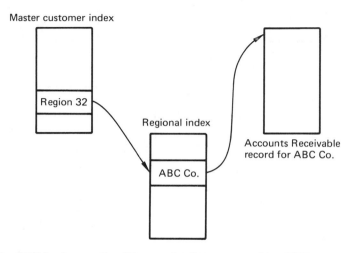

Master customer index

Region 32

Regional index

ABC Co.

Accounts Receivable record for ABC Co.

Fig. O2(b)   Accounting file organization suggested by XYZ salesman

This should prove to be a sobering thought to the systems analyst, for we have suddenly discovered that there are twice as many transactions as we had previously imagined. Obviously, no matter how carefully we had modelled or simulated our system with the techniques discussed in Chapter F, the results would have been worthless because of this omission.

Later in this chapter, we shall investigate the consequences of our new knowledge and more refined assumptions on the design calculations that we made in Chapter F. At this point, though, we are concerned only with the design of the files. We have seen that the open order file will be expanding and contracting rapidly as new orders are created and old ones filled. This almost immediately eliminates the direct addressing approach, the binary search technique, the algorithm approach, and the randomizing technique that we described in Chapter K—for none of these file organization approaches makes it easy to delete records.

Note that we shall want to access the open order file in a number of different ways. When the salesman types in an ORDER or a RESERVE transaction, we only want to create a new open order record and insert it into the file in such a way that we will be able to find it later. We will have to find the record in a random fashion when the warehouse clerk types a SHIPMENT transaction (at which time the record will be deleted from the open order file) or if the salesman types a CANCEL transaction (which will also cause the record to be deleted). We may also have to retrieve the record if the salesman types an INQC transaction to find out what has happened to his customer's order.

By elimination, we have already decided upon a directory approach for the open order file. In this application, the major advantage of the directory approach is the ease with which records can be deleted and added at random, as illustrated in Figure O3. We must now decide what key should be used to access the open order records. The two obvious keys are the *account number* of the customer who ordered the widgets, and the *purchase order number*, which can be assigned by the system when an ORDER or RESERVE transaction is entered. The purchase order number is an obvious choice, for the Widget employees have probably been using purchase order numbers in the batch computers and in earlier manual systems. For psychological reasons and for reasons of control, we want to assign purchase order

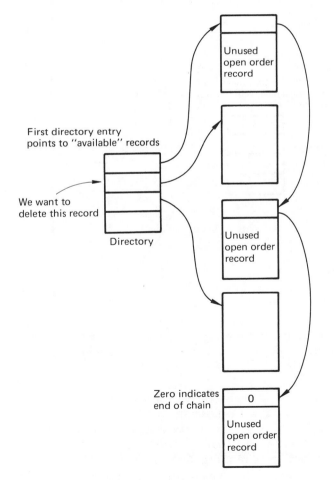

Fig. O3(a)   Deleting a record with the directory approach

numbers in ascending sequence—but we also want to be able to access the open order records in a random fashion.

While the purchase order number should be sufficient, there may be cases when the salesman does not remember the purchase order number. Certainly a *customer* will not tend to remember a purchase order number, and if a salesman's most important customer calls him up to complain about poor service, we should expect that the salesman's first reaction will be to call up the warehouse and ask why that customer's order has not been filled. He may even demand that *all* of the customer's outstanding orders be filled immediately, in which case the warehouse clerk will want to ask the computer system for a list of outstanding orders for the specified account number.

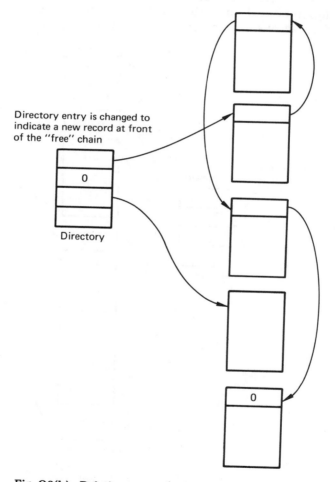

Directory entry is changed to indicate a new record at front of the "free" chain

Directory

Fig. O3(b)   Deleting a record with the directory approach

With this in mind, it is probably reasonable to make the open order file accessible by account number *and* purchase order number. While it is reasonable to assume that most customers will have only one order outstanding at any time, we must recognize that some customers will have several outstanding orders while others have none at all. Thus, we cannot organize the file with a direct addressing scheme by account number, even though we will not be creating or deleting account numbers very often.

We thus conclude that the open order file should be organized as shown in Figure O4—with a set of directories for account numbers and for purchase order numbers. As we see in the diagram, multiple open orders for the same account number are linked together, thus allowing us to retrieve all purchase orders for a specified account.

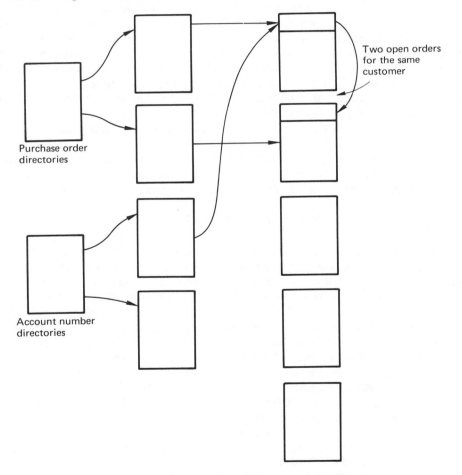

Fig. O4 Organization of the open order file

In Chapter K, we discussed the concept of *blocking*, and pointed out that it can be a useful idea for linked lists of records. Thus, we may want to block the open order file, but only if we are reasonably confident that there will be more than one order per account number, *and* if we are confident that this type of information will be required fairly often. For most of the transactions (i.e. the ORDER, RESERVE, SHIPMENT, and CANCEL transactions) it will not pay to have blocked records, since we know that each such transaction will only involve one record. A reasonable conclusion at this point is to avoid blocking the files, and to gather statistics once the system has begun running. If we then conclude that blocking would be useful, it will be a relatively simple change to the files—and *no* change to the application programs (unless the operating system does not provide blocking features).

Since we have noticed that there will be a tremendous amount of activity in the open order file, we should also decide how to handle the creation of new records and the deletion of old ones. The simplest approach would be to add new records (corresponding to new orders) to the end of the open order file, and not bother to reclaim the space occupied by deleted records. This approach is shown in Figure O5, and obviously involves a tremendous amount of wasted space. On the other hand, it is reasonable to assume that we will be dumping all of our files to magnetic tape at the end of each day's operation, so we can rearrange the files during the dumping process.

Nevertheless, there will be a tremendous amount of wasted space during the course of the day. Since we have assumed that each of the branch offices will be typing in one order per minute, it follows that there will be

$$200 \times 60 \times 8 = 96,000$$

orders typed into the system during the course of an eight-hour day. We have also assumed that it takes two or three days to fill an order, which means that the open order file must have the records for about two or three days' orders in it—which works out to some 200,000-300,000 records. As we pointed out before, we must be filling orders at the same average rate that we are receiving them, so there will be about 96,000 ORDER transactions and 96,000 SHIPMENT transactions during the course of the day. Since each shipment transaction causes an open order record to be deleted, it follows that a policy of *not* reclaiming the space from deleted records means that we are wasting 96,000 records in our data base. Thus, instead of just allowing some 200,000-300,000 records in the open order file, we must allow for about 300,000-400,000 records—an increase of some 33-50%.

Thus, unless we have several million characters of storage to spare, it seems that we should have some way of reclaiming deleted records. One easy way of doing this is suggested by Figure O6, in which one directory entry points to a linked list of "free" records. Thus, when a new open order record is created with the ORDER transaction, the application program can check

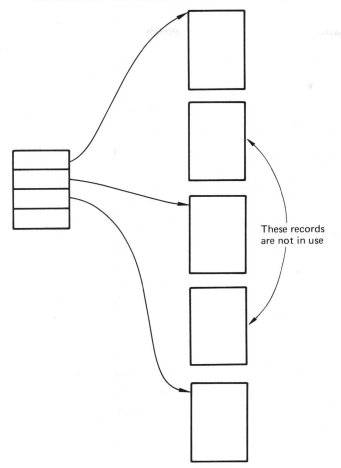

These records
are not in use

Fig. O5 Directory approach without reclaiming deleted records

the directory entry to see if there are any records created by previously deleted open orders. Note that we must have records which are *fixed* in length. With variable length records, we cannot guarantee that we will be able to effectively reuse our storage space.

As for the actual layout of the open order record, we might use the format shown in Figure O7. Naturally, every system and every company will have different requirements for this type of record, *but it is important to minimize the amount of static information* that we keep. For example, we should not keep billing information in this record, for it will be duplicated if there is more than one order per account, and it is probably maintained by the accounting department in its own system. Note that with 300,000 open order records, 60 characters of billing information (bill-to name, address, city, and state) would add about 9 million characters to the data base!

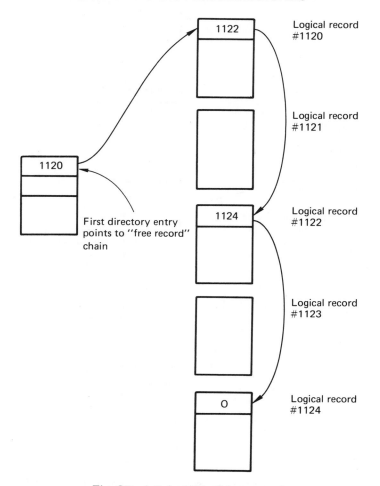

Fig. O6 A linked list of free records

THE ON-LINE INVENTORY FILE

The inventory file is used to keep track of the inventory of widgets in various warehouses around the country. In one sense, it will be very dynamic, since a large number of widgets are changing hands each day. However, the inventory *file* will not change very much, for we will have the same kinds of widgets from day to day—it is only the *amount* of widgets that will change. The only time we expect to see a new kind of widget created is at the beginning of a new season.

We thus see that the inventory file is very different than the open order

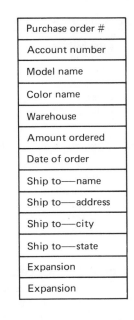

| Purchase order # |
| Account number |
| Model name |
| Color name |
| Warehouse |
| Amount ordered |
| Date of order |
| Ship to—name |
| Ship to—address |
| Ship to—city |
| Ship to—state |
| Expansion |
| Expansion |

For convenience, we have broken the record
into *words* instead of characters

Fig. O7 Layout of the open order record

file, in terms of its behavior. However, we should keep in mind that the
inventory file will be almost as active as the open order file, since it will be
updated by each ORDER transaction and by each ARRIVAL transaction.
Both of these transactions will require a random access to the inventory file,
as will the INQA transaction—which the salesman uses to see how many
widgets are available for him to sell.

In order to decide how the file will be organized, we must first decide
what key will be used to access the file. If we could assign a standard part
number or "widget number" to each different type of widget, the direct
addressing scheme would serve us very well. We would be able to guarantee
that no space would be wasted by assigning the widget numbers sequentially,
and as a result, we would be able to retrieve any record with one disk access.

However, it has long been the tradition at the Widget Corporation of
America that widgets are specified by *model* and by *color*. As part of the
planning that has gone into the Widget system, the management has agreed
on the six standard models shown in Table O2, and the seven standard colors
listed in Table O3. All further efforts to identify the various models of
widget with a number have been rebuffed by management, who feel that it is
the *name* of the widgets (jumbo widgets, family size widgets, and so forth)
that has made them so popular.

TABLE O2 *Standard Widget Models*

Small
Medium
Large
Extra large
Jumbo
Family size

TABLE O3 *Standard Widget Colors*

Blue
Red
Yellow
Green
Orange
White
Purple

In addition to the color and model of widget, we are concerned with the *location* of widgets. The Widget Corporation has a warehouse in each state, and salesmen have been accustomed to referring to the warehouses by the name of the city in which they are located. Thus, one hears references to "the Houston warehouse," "the Denver warehouse," and so on. In many cases, a salesman will order a quantity of widgets from a specific warehouse, to ensure that his customer gets a speedy delivery.

With this information, it seems clear that it will be impractical to attempt imposing some kind of "standard widget number" on the salesmen and employees of the Widget Corporation—even though it would allow us to access our data base more efficiently. However, we can continue to use *model names*, *color names*, and *warehouse names* to form a variation of the algorithm approach that we discussed in Chapter K. To use this approach, we construct a *model name dictionary*, a *color name dictionary*, and a *warehouse name dictionary*, as shown in Figures O8, O9, and O10.

Small	0
Medium	350
Large	700
Extra large	1050
Jumbo	1400
Family size	1750

Fig. O8   Model name dictionary

To obtain the logical record number of a specified type of widget, we must search the three directories and concatenate the values that are obtained, as shown in Figure O11. In this case, concatenation is equivalent to adding together the *value* of the model name, the *value* of the color name,

Blue	0
Red	50
Yellow	100
Green	150
Orange	200
White	250
Purple	300

Fig. O9   Color name dictionary

Houston	0
Denver	1
Chicago	2
NYC	3

Boston	44
Omaha	45
Cleveland	46
Detroit	47
Seattle	48
Jacksonville	49

Fig. O10   Warehouse name dictionary

and the *value* of the warehouse name. These form a logical record number which can be used to retrieve the inventory record with only one access.

It is interesting to note that the model names and color names can all be distinguished by looking at the first letter of the word. As shown in Figure O12, we can look at the "J" in "Jumbo," and the "B" in "Blue" and *dispatch* to the proper entry in the table. The tables are only 26 entries long for the color and model dictionaries, and 50 entries long for the warehouse dictionary. All of the tables can thus be kept in core, and the computation required to calculate the logical record number is fast and convenient.

Note that this approach has the disadvantage that we cannot easily add or delete model names or color names or even warehouses from the system. However, we have assumed that we will not want to do so very often, and have indicated that the ADDW and DELW transactions will not take effect until an overnight batch run can be performed.

The concept of blocking can be very useful for the inventory file, since a salesman is likely to want to obtain widgets from some other warehouse if his own warehouse is empty. Thus, when we read in one inventory record, we would like to also read inventory records for other warehouses, as part of the same physical block. We certainly do not have an easy job here, though, for we assume that the salesman will want, as his alternate warehouse, the one *closest* to his main warehouse. Thus, we should try to arrange the inventory records so that neighboring warehouses are fairly close together in terms of logical record numbers. Then, by blocking five or ten *logical* inventory records (assuming they are relatively short) into one *physical* inventory record, we can be reasonably assured that an access to a neighboring warehouse will not require another disk access.

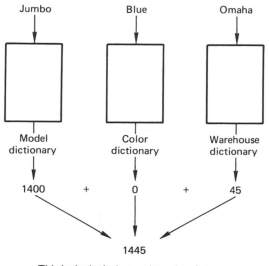

| Jumbo | Blue | Omaha |

Model dictionary   Color dictionary   Warehouse dictionary

1400   +   0   +   45

1445

This is the logical record number for the inventory information for "blue" "jumbo" widgets in the Omaha warehouse

Fig. O11   Calculation of inventory logical record number

THE ACCOUNTING FILE

Finally, we must determine how to arrange the accounting file. We are assuming in this discussion that the Widget system will *not* be the primary source of information for the accounting department, and that its use of accounting information is purely for *credit-checking*. This may seem rather peculiar, but it helps to limit the scope of our discussion—and it is symptomatic of the way many large organizations build their computer systems. On the one hand, the data processing manager for the accounting department can be criticized for refusing to relinquish control of his own

0	−1	Indication of illegal entry
1	−1	
2	−1	
3	−1	
4	1050	Entry for "extra large"
5	1750	Entry for "family size"
6	−1	
7	−1	
8	−1	
9	1400	Entry for "jumbo"
10	−1	
11	700	Entry for "large"
12	350	Entry for "medium"
13	−1	
14	−1	
15	−1	
16	−1	
17	−1	
18	0	Entry for "small"
19	−1	
20	−1	
21	−1	
22	−1	
23	−1	
24	−1	
25	−1	

Fig. O12   A dispatch table for model name dictionary

little empire; on the other hand, he is to be commended for realizing the total chaos that might result from a decision to build a "total" system with accounting, inventory, and "management information" (whatever that is).

Whatever the political reasons may be, we take note of the current decision to separate the current accounting system from our on-line inventory system. However, we should realize that if the inventory system does work, there will eventually be a hue and cry to build in an on-line accounts receivable package. If possible, we should try to build our system in such a way as to make the inclusion of an accounting package *possible*, if not easy.

At the moment, the only purpose of the accounting file is to keep track of the current amount of money owed to the Widget Corporation by each customer. We do not even require that an *aged* list of accounts receivables be kept—i.e. information on how much information has been owed for 30 days, how much for 60 days, and so forth. We have been told by our management that a simple *total* of money owed is sufficient for a credit checking algorithm to make a decision about approving a customer's order. In line with our comments above, we should keep in mind that we will probably be asked, at some later date, to include extra information to help refine the credit-checking algorithm.

As with the inventory file, the accounting file is *dynamic* in the sense that there may be a number of transactions which update the file during the day; and *stable* in the sense that new customers are not added to the file very often, nor are old customers deleted from the file. Thus, we do not have to worry about the problem of adding and deleting records from the file, as we did with the open order file.

We also recognize that we have a handy way of accessing the file—by an account number. The account numbers have already been established by the Accounting Department, and are in increasing sequential order. However, the Accounting Department has had a convention that if a customer stops doing business with the company, his account number remains dormant—it is not given to the next new customer. There is a very good reason for doing this—the records of an old customer have to be kept on file for several years, and the old records are referred to by the account number.

The Accounting Department began its numbering scheme in 1953, when it first obtained EAM equipment. Over the years, there has been a gradual attrition of customers, which has been more than replaced by new customers. Nevertheless, approximately 20% of the account numbers are not in use any more, and this trend is likely to continue over the next few years. Furthermore, the Accounting Department has adamantly refused to begin a new numbering scheme for their account numbers, pointing out that the conversion problem would be tremendous.

With this information, it seems clear that we cannot use the direct addressing approach for the Accounting file, for it would waste about 20% of our available file space. An algorithm approach would have the same problem, for it would be difficult to use any computational scheme to reorder the account numbers in such a way as to eliminate the "random holes" caused by the deletion of old customers.

It seems, then, that the best file accessing technique is the directory approach shown in Figure O13. There will be some additional advantages to this scheme if we are ever called upon to enlarge the scope of the system. We will be able to create multiple accounting records for each account number, and reference them either by account number or by an invoice number. We will be able to change the length of each record to include more information if the Accounting Department so desires.

We may eventually decide to block the file if there are multiple records for each customer, but for the current system, there is no reason to do so. We will never want to access more than one accounting record for each transaction, so there is no need for blocking.

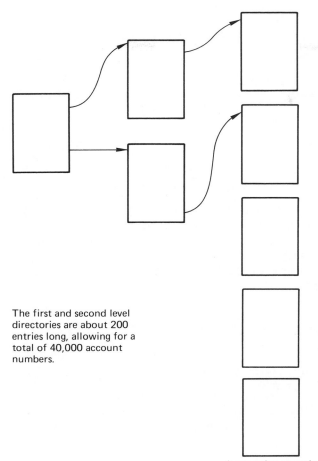

The first and second level directories are about 200 entries long, allowing for a total of 40,000 account numbers.

Accounting records

Fig. O13 File organization for the accounting file

TABLE O4 *Summary of the Important Characteristics of the Widget Files*

	Open order file	*Inventory file*	*Accounting file*
Many accesses to the file during the day?	Yes about 96,000	Yes about 96,000	Yes less than 96,000
Many records created or deleted during the day?	Yes about 96,000 created and 96,000 deleted	No	No

TABLE O4—*cont.*

	Open order file	*Inventory file*	*Accounting file*
Accessing technique	Directory approach	Algorithm approach	Directory
Key used to access the file	Purchase order # account number	Model name & Model color & Warehouse	Account number
Blocking	Perhaps later on, not now	Yes	No

The important characteristics of the file organization are summarized in Table O4. Note that we have postponed a decision on whether to block the open order file, pending later experience with the system. This means that we will eventually have to gather statistics as the system runs, in order to decide if we want to go to the trouble of converting the file to a new blocked format.

THE EFFECT OF THE TRANSACTIONS ON THE FILES

Having determined the basic organization of the files for the Widget system, we are now in a position to examine the effect that each transaction will have on the files. The discussion below essentially amounts to a loose "verbal flowchart" of the application programs required to process each transaction:

1 *The ORDER transaction*

As we see from Table O1, the ORDER transaction requires the customer's account number, as well as a specification of the model, color, and quantity of widgets ordered. The warehouse specification is optional and can be omitted if the salesman is willing to give his customer widgets from the first convenient warehouse that the system finds.

The ORDER program first reads the customer's accounting record to see if his credit rating is in order. This can presumably be done by performing some computation upon information found in the record. If the credit rating is satisfactory, the program then uses the model name and color specification to locate the appropriate inventory record. If the warehouse name is specified, this will be used in the file access computation that we discussed earlier. If there are enough widgets in inventory to fill the order, the inventory record is updated to indicate that some widgets have been allocated. A new open order record is created, along with a new purchase order number. The purchase order number is typed on the salesman's terminal, and the new open order record is linked to any other open orders that the customer may have. Finally, a message is typed on the terminal of the warehouse shipping clerk to inform him of the details of the order.

2 *The RESERVE transaction*

The RESERVE transaction is processed in the same way as the ORDER transaction, except no message is typed on the shipping clerk's terminal. However, an open order record is created and, to avoid confusion, one of the fields in the record is marked to indicate that it is not a real order.

3 *The CANCEL transaction*

The CANCEL transaction may be used to cancel either a true order or a "reserved" order. The user is required to type both the purchase order number and the account number, although only the purchase order number is required.

When a CANCEL transaction is received, the application program uses the purchase order number to locate the correct open order record. The account number in the record is checked against the account number supplied by the salesman to verify that some innocent customer's order is not being deleted. If everything is in order, the record is deleted, and is added to the chain of "free" records.

4 *The ARRIVAL transaction*

The ARRIVAL transaction is used by a warehouse receiving clerk to indicate the arrival of fresh widgets from the factory. When he types his transaction, the clerk must supply the model and color of the widgets, as well as the warehouse location and the amount of widgets.

The program that processes the ARRIVAL transaction uses this input to locate the correct inventory record. The inventory total is updated by the amount specified in the transaction.

5 *The SHIPMENT transaction*

The SHIPMENT transaction is used by the warehouse shipping clerk when an order of widgets is being sent to the customer. The clerk is required to specify the purchase order and the account number, as well as the amount of money which the customer will be charged for the order. We could have included this last parameter as part of the ORDER transaction, but it is convenient to put it in the SHIPMENT transaction so that shipping charges and any other special charges can be included.

The application program that processes the SHIPMENT transaction first locates the open order record and verifies that it is correct by checking the account number supplied by the clerk. The open order record is then deleted in the same manner as in the CANCEL transaction. The program then sends a "dummy" CHARGE transaction to the program that processes the CHARGE transactions, supplying the account number and the amount specified by the shipping clerk. The reason for the dummy transaction is to avoid the simultaneous access problem that we discussed in Chapter L.

6 *The PAYMENT transaction*

The PAYMENT transaction is used by accounting clerks to indicate payments made by widget customers. Since we are not keeping track of the charges for individual orders, it is only necessary for the clerk to specify the account number and the amount of money that was paid. If, at a later time, we are asked to take on more of the functions of the accounting department, the PAYMENT transaction may also require the clerk to specify the purchase order number (this can be accomplished with a simple change to the command matrix that was shown in Figure J11).

The PAYMENT program uses the account number to reference the correct accounting record, and decrements the "outstanding total" field by the amount indicated by the accounting clerk.

7 *The STOPCREDIT transaction*

The STOPCREDIT transaction is used in the event that the accounting department decides to withdraw unilaterally the credit of a customer. The accounting clerk is required only to specify the account number of the unfortunate customer. The STOPCREDIT program reads the appropriate accounting record, and sets a flag to indicate that no further ORDER or RESERVE transactions are to be honored for this customer.

8 *The RESTORECREDIT transaction*

Obviously, the RESTORECREDIT transaction has just the reverse effect of the STOPCREDIT transaction. The accounting clerk indicates the account number of the lucky customer, and the application program resets the flag in the accounting record.

9 *The CHARGE transaction*

The CHARGE transaction is used to indicate any charges levied against a customer. Its main use is to indicate charges made at the time of a SHIPMENT transaction, but it can also be used for any additional charges the accounting department may want to include. It is important to note that only one program performs the file updating associated with the CHARGE transaction.

The action taken by the CHARGE program is very simple. It uses the account number to locate the correct accounting record, then increments the "outstanding total" field in the record.

10 *The CREDIT transaction*

As its name implies, the CREDIT transaction is used to indicate a monetary credit given to a specified customer. Its effect is identical to that of the PAYMENT transaction, but if the system is ever expanded, we can expect that the accounting department will want to distinguish between payments and credits.

The CREDIT program uses the account number to locate the correct accounting record, and decrements the "outstanding total" field by the amount specified by the accounting clerk.

11 *The INQA transaction*

The INQA transaction is used by the salesman to determine the quantity of widgets currently available for sale. He must specify the model and color of widgets, and may optionally specify the warehouse. If he does specify the warehouse, the program will locate the correct inventory record, and type the number of widgets available on the salesman's terminal. Note that this does *not* include the widgets currently allocated to orders and "reserve orders" in the open order file.

If the salesman does not specify a warehouse name, he is indicating that he wants to know the total number of widgets available—in *all* warehouses. On the surface, this may seem like a fairly innocent request, but we have not really provided for it with our current file organization. In order to process this transaction, we must either read all 50 inventory records, or we must keep one more inventory total in our file. While 50 logical record accesses seems terribly high, we should remember that we have decided to block the file. Thus, we may get away with five or ten *physical* disk accesses. On the other hand, if we keep an inventory total for *all* warehouses, we will have to update it for each SHIPMENT and ARRIVAL transaction, regardless of which warehouse is involved. This would add one more disk access to each of these very common transactions, in order to save five or ten accesses for a relatively rare transaction.

The solution seems to be to limit the INQA transaction *without* a warehouse specification to sales managers and others who have a "need to know." For those people, the application program will read each inventory record for the specified model and color and will calculate a grand total of available widgets.

12 *The INQC transaction*

The INQC transaction is used by the salesman to determine the status of a customer's account. He must specify the account number, and may optionally specify the purchase order number of a particular order of widgets. If the purchase order number is supplied, the program will retrieve information about that one order; if no purchase order number is typed by the user, then the program will retrieve information about all outstanding orders for that customer. The program retrieves information by purchase order number, if one is supplied; otherwise, it uses the account number directory to locate an account's orders within the open order file. Since all orders are linked together, it becomes a trivial matter for the program to retrieve all of the information. The application program also uses the account number to reference the appropriate record in the accounting file, so that the salesman may find out how much money the customer owes to the Widget Corporation.

13 *The ADDC transaction*

The ADDC transaction does not cause any on-line processing to take place. It is merely an indication to an off-line batch program that a new record will have to be added to the accounting file.

14 *The DELC transaction*

The DELC transaction, like the ADDC transaction, does not cause any on-line processing. It is an indication to a batch program that a record will have to be deleted from the accounting file.

15 *The ADDW transaction*

The ADDW transaction does not cause any on-line processing. It is an indication that 50 new records (one for each warehouse) will have to be added to the inventory file.

16 *The DELW transaction*

The DELW transaction does not cause any on-line processing to take place. It is an indication to a batch program that 50 records (one for each warehouse) will have to be deleted from the inventory file.

THE PROBLEM OF SIMULTANEOUS ACCESS

As we can see, most of the transactions affect only one or two of our three files. In fact, we have grouped them according to the *type* of transaction. The ORDER, RESERVE, CANCEL, and ARRIVAL transactions affect only the inventory and open order file, while the PAYMENT, STOPCREDIT, RESTORECREDIT, CHARGE, and CREDIT transactions affect only the accounting file. The SHIPMENT transaction, on the other hand, affects the open order file and the accounting file.

Accordingly, we can solve the problem of simultaneous access and update of our files by having one application program handle the inventory-oriented transactions, and another application program handle the accounting-oriented transactions. A third program can handle the inquiry transactions (which, because of multiprogramming, may occasionally deliver obsolete information), and a fourth program can handle the batch-oriented transactions. In this way, we can effectively use the multiprogramming capabilities of the Aardvark 301 without running into any problems with the files. The reader should remember that each program will handle its respective transactions in a serial fashion.

THE PROBLEM OF FILE SECURITY

In Chapter M, we discussed the problems of file security for on-line systems and indicated that the basic technique calls for some way of identifying the user of the system, and some sort of "access key" to prevent unauthorized access to the data base. However, we pointed out that this type of protection can be extremely costly, in terms of overhead, if it is extended to the record level.

In the Widget system, we should note that we have a reasonably controlled environment, since none of the users can create their own programs at the terminal. There are only three files in the system, and a well-defined set of application programs which can access the files. Thus, it seems that the emphasis should be on preventing the wrong people from using the application programs, rather than on preventing the application programs from using the files.

There are actually two areas with which we are concerned. First, we want to make sure that none of the Widget Corporation's competitors can use the system at all. Second, we want to make sure that none of the Widget employees uses the wrong transactions either innocently or maliciously. The warehouse clerks have no reason to be using the accounting transactions, nor have the accounting clerks any reason to be using the SHIPMENT or ARRIVAL transactions. Similarly, the salesmen should be limited to the ORDER, RESERVE, CANCEL, INQA, and INQC transactions.

One way of providing this type of protection is to have a different command matrix, of the type shown in Figure J11, for each user of the system. However, it seems fairly likely that each *terminal* will be dedicated to a particular use: there will be terminals in the warehouses, terminals in the sales offices, and terminals in the accounting offices. Thus, by providing a different command matrix for each terminal, we can prevent the wrong people from using the wrong transactions.

To prevent outsiders (or unauthorized employees) from gaining access to the system, we can provide the password scheme discussed in Chapter M. Once again, it is reasonable to associate the password with the terminal, rather than with individual users, since we are dealing with a dedicated system.

THE PROBLEM OF FILE RECOVERY

Obviously, the Widget system must have a well-designed recovery scheme, for its business depends on the survival of the open order file (note that we could lose the accounting file and survive, since the Accounting Department presumably has its own set of accounting information). Since such a large number of transactions enter the system each day, it is obvious that a simple disk dump will not provide the level of security we need. An audit trail of some form is clearly called for.

It is imperative that the text of each input transaction be maintained, for if the files should be destroyed, we must be able to recreate all of the open order records, and so forth. It is also desirable to be able to keep the "before" copy of the various records, so that the data base can be recovered in the event of a failure. Since each transaction involves such a short amount of actual CPU time, there is no urgent need to keep the "after" copy of each data base update.

As we shall see in Part V of this book, there are many ways in which a system can fail. There are also some standard approaches that one can take to increase the reliability of the system and/or minimize the effects of a failure. At this point in our design, though, it is obvious that if a failure *does* occur, we will want to get the system back into operation again as quickly as possible—for there are several hundred users who cannot do any useful work until the computer is working again. Thus, it is imperative that the file recovery scheme be *fast*, as well as thorough.

Assuming that most of the system failures do not inflict serious damage upon the data base, it should be possible to execute a recovery program to read through the audit trail tape and "recover" the data base within two or three minutes. If the failure is serious, the entire data base will have to be reloaded, which may take anywhere from fifteen minutes to an hour.

A FINAL LOOK AT THE WIDGET SYSTEM

Unfortunately, we do not have space to continue with our discussion of the Widget system. Our purpose has merely been to illustrate some of the concepts of design calculations, application program design and file design for a typical on-line business system. *It is very important to note that we did not have to know anything specific about the nature of the Aardvark 301 computer or its operating system to proceed this far in our design!*

As we mentioned before, our design calculations in Chapter F failed to take into account the fact that accounting clerks and shipping clerks would be typing in transactions at the same rate as the salesmen. Actually, this has only an indirect affect on the calculations: instead of being able to support 200 terminals, we now realize that the system must be able to support 450 terminals (one for each sales office, one for the accounting group located in each sales office, and one for each warehouse). We may actually require another 50 terminals for managers and other miscellaneous functions.

In terms of our basic throughput formula $N = T/P + 1$, we should recognize that the majority of the transactions will be ORDER, SHIPMENT, and PAYMENT transactions. In the case of the ORDER transaction, we have the following file accesses:

3 to read the accounting record

1 to read the inventory record

1 to update the inventory record

2 to read an open order directory, insert a new entry and write it on the disk again

1 to create a new open order record

Similarly, the processing of the SHIPMENT transaction involves the following accesses:

3 to locate the open order record

1 to delete the entry from the directory

1 to delete the open order record from the chain of other open orders for this customer

3 to locate the customer's accounting record

1 to update the accounting record

In each case, it appears that eight or nine file accesses will be required to process most of the transactions (not counting all of the less frequently used transactions). Since we had assumed the Aardvark 301 has a 60-millisecond disk, it follows that 480-540 milliseconds are required for just the file processing part of a transaction. Since we have built a great deal of multiprogramming into our system, it is fairly likely that the file accessing associated with one transaction will be almost completely overlapped with the computation for another transaction. Also, it appears, from our discussion above, that the processing is relatively trivial in nature.

For the sake of argument, then, let us assume that *all* of the processing for a transaction can be done in 600 milliseconds. Our formula then tells us that the system will support

$$N = \frac{60}{0.6} + 1 = 101 \text{ terminals}$$

It is apparent that we have no chance at all of servicing 400-500 terminals if our assumptions are at all correct. However, such common sense calculations have not prevented great countries and large organizations from embarking upon such folly before, and we should not expect any better of the Widget Corporation!

PART

V

OPERATING SYSTEMS FOR
ON-LINE COMPUTER SYSTEMS

Chapter P

THE FUNCTIONS AND STRUCTURE OF

ON-LINE OPERATING SYSTEMS

INTRODUCTION

The purpose of this book has been to present an integrated guideline to the design of on-line computer systems. In so doing, we have attempted to trace the natural sequence of events that most system designers follow either consciously or unconsciously in the development of their own system. Thus, we began by familiarizing ourselves with the nature and characteristics of on-line systems, and looked at some of the common hardware configurations used to develop the systems. We also reviewed some of the important hardware requirements for on-line computer systems.

Following an introductory look at on-line systems, we turned to a discussion of some of the elements of the *design* of the system. We reviewed some of the critical decisions that must be reached during the design process, and suggested a sequence of top-level design actions that should be taken. In this same area, we talked about design calculations, including mathematical modelling, simulation and "common sense" calculations. These, together with *performance measurement*, were felt to be essential to the design of an efficient on-line system.

In Part III and Part IV we discussed the topics of application programs and data bases. Since there is a significant difference between application programs for batch systems and on-line systems, it was necessary to engage in a discussion of *concepts* for on-line application programming. We then suggested several *structures* or *approaches* for on-line application programs in different environments. In the area of files and data bases, we did the same thing. We first examined the various approaches to file organization in an on-line environment, and then discussed the special problems of simultaneous access, file security, and file recovery.

It is interesting to note that many computer professionals who become involved in on-line systems are *only* interested in application programs and data bases. They argue that their on-line systems are built with *existing* computers and *existing* operating systems. Because of the political constraints, discouragement from the computer vendor, lack of time, lack of money, and lack of available talent, the system designer naturally tends to shy away from the development of something as difficult as an operating system. Vendor-supplied operating systems have come to be accepted as widely as the higher-level compiler languages: there are still those who prefer to code in octal and write their own operating systems, but they seem to be an increasingly rare group of social outcasts.

Nevertheless, there are some types of on-line systems where one is almost forced to write one's own operating system. Any type of special-purpose system on experimental hardware falls into this class, as do a number of *small* on-line systems, implemented on mini-computers. Process control systems, data acquisition systems, and various other forms of "control" systems fall into this class. The machines are small, and often have only a limited amount of memory. The system is usually performing a specialized, dedicated function with tight requirements on response and reliability. The operating system provided by many of the vendors of these small machines either lacks the ability to perform real-time work, or cannot interface with the special devices that have been attached to the system, or has some other deficiency. As a result, the system designer is forced to build his own operating system.

From these comments, it would appear that the development of operating systems is almost as specialized as the development of compilers— the only people we would expect to be interested in operating systems would be a few systems programmers employed by the computer manufacturers, and a few other stray people designing their own special-purpose systems. To a large extent, this is true—although the number of people becoming involved in specialized on-line or real-time systems with mini-computers does appear to be growing significantly.

We note, however, that much of our discussion of application programs and data bases was centered about operating systems. The application programmer will certainly admit that he cannot do an effective job unless he is aware of the capabilities provided to him by the operating system. Similarly, we cannot hope to do an effective job of designing the file organization unless we know the types of accessing techniques, blocking, and buffering conventions provided by the operating system. We even went so far as to state *Yourdon's Paradox*, which says that the more one tries to reduce overhead by minimizing the interference between the application programs and the operating system, the more one runs the risk of being outwitted by the operating system.

One can be outwitted by an operating system only if one does not understand it; conversely, one can do an effective job of writing application programs and designing data bases only if one *does* understand what an operating system is and how it works. It is important to remember that an on-line system is, above all, a *system*. A system consists of a number of inter-related parts, and the number of parts in an on-line system is larger than we might expect. In order to implement an on-line system, we must be familiar with the various types of on-line systems; we must understand the concepts and usefulness of mathematical modelling and simulation; we must know how to perform our own "common sense" calculations to test the validity of the simulator results; we must be familiar with testing and debugging routines, effective management principles, and operating systems—in addition to application programs and data bases. In short, we must be *generalists* if we are to succeed in implementing our system. The *specialist* runs the risk of *sub-optimization*—that is, optimizing his part of the system at the expense of the system as a whole.

This section of the book is thus dedicated to the principle that everyone should at least have a working knowledge of operating systems. The computer professional should develop more than just an academic interest in this area, for the effectiveness of his own work rests on the understanding of the limits and capabilities of the operating system with which he works.

For the afficionado, we want to provide a *structure* for developing operating systems, just as we developed structures for application programs. Those structures will be different for different types of on-line systems, but we will see that there is a fair amount of universality.

Our major purpose in this chapter will be to describe the functions of an operating system, and the general structure of a typical operating system. In subsequent chapters, we will investigate the details of some of the major components of typical operating systems. Once again, our emphasis will be on the pragmatic aspects of the design process. Our concern is not so much with the mathematical theories of operating systems (if there are any), but with the *programming* and *implementation* aspects.

FUNCTIONS OF AN ON-LINE OPERATING SYSTEM

Before we can discuss the structure and components of an on-line operating system, we must first agree on the functions which it provides. While the functions of an operating system may vary for specialized systems, there are usually some *general* functions that we can identify.

One of the most obvious functions of an operating system is to perform input/output on all of the peripheral devices. Most of the peripheral devices are available for use by the application program, and the operating system performs IO at the express request of those programs. Thus, it only reads cards from the card reader and records from a magnetic tape when some application program indicates that it wants those cards and records. There are, of course, times when the operating system performs IO for its own purposes—for swapping, overlaying, and reading of library programs into core.

There are a number of things that must be done by the operating system to control the IO devices properly. First, it must be able to receive requests from the application programs (in the form of READ and WRITE macros that we discussed in Chapter H), and place them in a queue of requests to be performed. The operating system must also decide on the order in which requests are to be done (while things are usually done on a first-come-first-serve basis, we may decide to rearrange the order of reads and writes on random-access devices). It must issue the appropriate commands to the IO devices in order to initiate the IO activity. Interrupts must be handled properly, and *quickly* enough to avoid missing data. The operating system must handle any errors that occur during the processing of input/output. We find that most IO errors can be recovered if the operating system retries the operation two or three times. If the IO activity cannot be successfully performed after a reasonable number of retries, there must be some procedure for notifying the application program and/or the computer operator.

The handling of IO is perhaps the most important function of an operating system, and some of the early systems provided nothing but IO services. In many of the second generation systems, and virtually all of the third generation systems, though, additional services came to be expected. *Job management* and *task management* are perhaps chief among these new functions. As we remember from Chapter H, a job is the smallest unit of work in a system for which the operating system maintains accounting information; a task, on the other hand, is the smallest unit of work that can compete for the system's resources. Job management thus consists of a number of functions that are almost administrative in nature: handling of control cards, keeping of accounting statistics, establishment of external scheduling priorities, gathering of performance measurement statistics, and so forth. Job management functions may vary from system to system, as a function of the requirements imposed by the system designers.

Task management is a more interesting function, and in most cases, a much more important one. It is the operating system that provides multi-programming capabilities in the system. In systems where the application programmer is allowed to have *multiple tasks* within his job, the operating system must provide macros such as the CALL, RETURN, ATTACH, DELETE, and WAIT macros to the application programs. The operating system is also called upon to provide time-sharing and time-slicing capabilities if they are required in the system. As we have discussed in earlier chapters, these time-sharing and multiprogramming capabilities are not *necessary* features in an on-line system, but they are very common in all third generation systems.

In our discussion of files and data bases in Part IV of this book, we assumed that the application programs did most of the work when it came to file organization, file accessing, solving of simultaneous access problems, file security, and recovery. In many on-line systems, some of these functions are handled by the operating system. This is especially true in the scientific time-sharing systems, where file protection mechanisms prevent different users from accessing other users' files in an unauthorized manner. Many on-line operating systems also provide standard file accessing techniques which are used either in place of or as an adjunct to the file accessing techniques built into the application programs. Most of these standard file accessing techniques are similar to the *directory structure* that we discussed in Chapter K. The operating system may also provide LOCK and UNLOCK macros to help an application program solve the problem of simultaneous access, and a combination of passwords and access keys to provide the necessary file security.

Although the communications complex may be considered an input/output device, it is common to identify this area as a separate and distinct function of the on-line operating system. This is especially true since many current on-line operating systems have evolved from earlier multiprogramming batch operating systems—which did not have any teleprocessing capability. Depending on the type of system, these activities may be carried out by the operating system in the main computer, or they may be carried out by a separate operating system in a front-end computer.

There is a wide range of activities that must be carried out in the communications area. The operating system must control the initiation of terminal activity, which usually involves the processing of "ring" interrupts when the terminal first attempts to establish contact with the system, and "carrier on" interrupts when the communication link has been fully established. It must then perform actual input or output of terminal messages by polling the terminals, or by receiving interrupts from the terminal on a "contention" basis. Code conversion may be necessary to change from ASCII or EBCDIC code, or perhaps to some internal six-bit character set. The communication routines also check for errors in the transmission of terminal messages, and retransmit the messages if necessary. Editing functions may also be supplied by the operating system to allow the terminal users to "backspace" and delete a character. We also find that the operating system is responsible for *queueing* of messages to be sent to the application programs and to the terminals.

Finally, the operating system is responsible for *error recovery* within the on-line system. In Part IV, we discussed one type of recovery—file recovery—and suggested that it could be handled by the application programs. There are, however, many other types of failures in an on-line systems, and these fall into the domain of the operating system. The operating system controls any attempts that may be made to switch over to a backup processor or backup peripheral devices. When this "switchover" takes place, the operating system is responsible for communicating with the computer operator and the terminal users.

To summarize, the major functions which the operating system must perform include the following:

1   Handling of input/output on peripheral devices

2   Job management, accounting and performance measurement

3   Task management

4   File handling, or data management

5   Handling of the communications complex.

6   Error recovery and switchover

We can describe all of these responsibilities as *allocation of resources*. There are a number of resources that the operating system must worry about: the central processor, memory, IO channels, the peripheral devices, the data base, and so forth. Since the operating system must use such resources as the processor and memory for its own calculations, there are obviously times when it is competing with the application programs for use of the resources. As a result, it is often useful to consider the operating system itself to be a conglomerate of *tasks*, in much the same way that we can break an application program down into separate tasks. Our next job, obviously, is to see what kind of operating system *structure* is necessary for all of these tasks to work together with a minimum of conflict and confusion.

THE BASIC STRUCTURE AND COMPONENTS
OF AN ON-LINE OPERATING SYSTEM

A typical on-line operating system consists of six basic types of modules, which interact with each other in the manner shown by Figure P1. For particular types of systems, some of these modules may not exist or may take different forms. However, this structure seems generally applicable to most existing operating systems.

The most important part of the system is the *priority control program*, which we will discuss at greater length in Chapter Q. Since most of the processing that takes place in the operating system is initiated by input/output interrupts, there is no easy way of predicting the nature or sequence of processing that will be required. A number of IO routines and other tasks may thus be competing for use of the central processor at any one time, and it is the purpose of the priority control program to see to it that the *highest priority* task has control. The priority control program consists of a number of tables and subroutines on computers with fairly simple hardware interrupt structures; alternatively, it may be handled almost entirely by a sophisticated hardware priority interrupt structure.

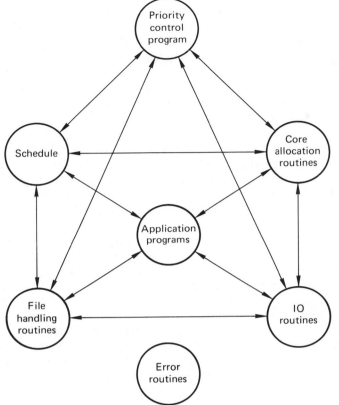

Fig. P1 The structure and components of an on-line operating system

As we see in Figure P1, the priority control program interacts with all of the other components in the operating system, since they must receive permission from the priority control program to do their processing. One of the many tasks over which the priority control program has control is the *scheduler*. The scheduler is concerned with the management of application programs, whereas the priority control program is concerned with the management of all of the operating system tasks. The scheduler may also be called a *task manager* or a *job manager* on some systems, and its main function is to keep track of the current state, or condition, of the application programs that are currently using the system. In this area, it must know which application programs are capable of executing; which ones are waiting for available core memory; which ones are waiting for IO to finish; and so forth. A *scheduling algorithm* may be invoked whenever the currently executing application program becomes non-runnable; it must decide which program is to be allowed to run next, and for how long a period of time.

Both the priority control program and the scheduler are *resource allocators*: the resource that they allocate is the central processor. It is assumed, in most cases, that the tasks in the operating system require *only* the use of the processor—they already have the use of all of the other resources they require, with the possible exception of small amounts of memory. The application programs, on the other hand, are likely to require a number of resources—CPU time, large amounts of memory, access to files, use of IO channels, and peripheral devices. Thus, in addition to scheduling the use of processor time for the application program, the scheduler must also see that all of the other necessary resources have been provided before it tries to turn control over to the program.

It is because of all these other resources that application program scheduling (or task management, as it is sometimes called) is usually kept separate from the scheduling of the operating system's tasks. The extra resources required by the application programs may be specified in control cards or with the use of a job control language; similarly, they may be specified with the use of macros during the execution of the application program.

Another form of allocation involves memory. Again, we often find a difference between the core requirements within the operating system itself, and the core requirements of the application programs. We normally find that the application programs require fairly *large blocks* of memory, which we may allocate in units of 512 words, 1,024 words, 4,096 bytes, or any other convenient unit. The operating system itself, on the other hand, usually only requires core memory for IO buffers, queues, dynamically expanding tables, and so forth. These usually represent demands for fairly small amounts of core, which we might allocate in units of 8 words, 16 words, or 128 words—or some other such small amount.

We obviously require IO routines within the operating system for each of the IO devices, although we may be able to use many common (or even reentrant) subroutines to handle the IO functions. As we shall see in a later chapter, we actually need *two* sets of subroutines for each device, as shown in Figure P2. The first type of subroutine takes requests *out of* a queue, initiates activity on the IO devices, and handles all of the interrupts, timing conditions, errors and so forth. The other subroutine puts requests *into* a queue, after receiving those requests from an application program, or possibly from some other part of the operating system. While each different IO device must have a separate set of IO routines, they all have this structure.

A set of file handling routines may exist in the operating system to keep track of the organization of files on the disk and to provide a minimal file security and file recovery function. The file handling routines may also help the application programs solve the simultaneous access problem with the LOCK and UNLOCK macros. The application programs may use their own file accessing techniques to locate a record within a logical file, and the operating system's file handling routines then convert the logical record number to a physical disk address with the use of a directory scheme.

Finally, we sometimes find a set of error routines in the operating system. The error routines are intended to deal with memory parity errors,

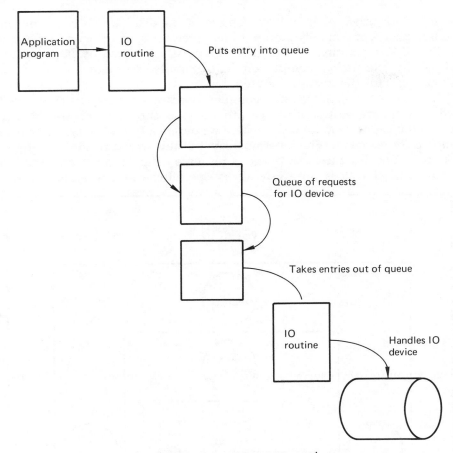

Fig. P2   The two types of IO routines

power failure interrupts, illegal instruction traps and serious IO errors (such as being unable to read a critically important directory). The purpose of the routines is either to bring the system to a "graceful" halt, or to switch control to a backup machine. This is a difficult job, for the error routines must ensure that the computer operator understands what is happening, and that the users are properly informed as to the nature and extent of the error. This subject is discussed in more detail in Chapter U.

ALTERNATIVE STRUCTURES FOR OPERATING SYSTEMS

In summary, we see that an operating system is loosely composed of *resource allocators* and *task managers*. In most cases, as we have seen, the tasks that are part of the operating system require only *one* resource other than the ones already at their disposal: use of the central processor. Thus, the disk IO routines already have control of the disk (which is, of course, a resource itself), and merely require some processor time to figure out how to use the disk. Operating system tasks are mostly initiated by IO interrupts, and usually execute to completion fairly rapidly, so there is no need of a task manager for the operating system tasks.

In a more sophisticated and complex operating system, we may have to have several layers of supervisory programs, as shown in Figure P3. Each level contains one or more tasks, where we define a *task* as an entity that can compete for resources. The innermost layer in this structure contains the one task that allocates the most precious resource of all—the central processor. This innermost task is obviously a very special case, for as a task, it too is

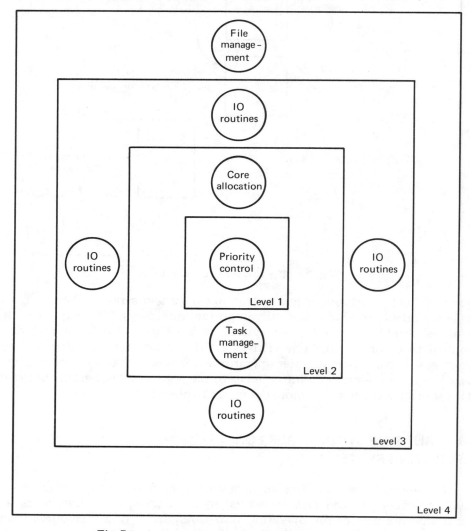

Fig. P3   A more general operating system structure

supposed to compete for use of the central processor—but it is guaranteed to be able to use the central processor whenever it wants to, in order to properly do its job of allocating the central processor to *other* tasks.

Other tasks are put into outer layers of this structure, in a hierarchical fashion. Thus, we find the core allocation task in the second layer, for the only additional resource it requires is the central processor. "Task management" is itself a task, since it must use the central processor in order to keep information about which tasks are waiting for which resources. The IO routines are put into the next layer because they require *both* core memory and use of the central processor. Obviously, the file handling routines belong in an even more remote layer, since they require use of an IO device (such as the disk), use of the central processor, and use of core memory.

In general, then, we can define an operating system to be a series of layers of *resource-allocating tasks*. A task is placed in the Nth level of this structure if the resources it requires are on some lower level M, where N is the smallest integer such that $N > M$. Thus, a task belongs in level 3 if it requires resources in level 2, or if it requires resources in both level 2 and in level 1. A task in level 3 is not allowed to use resources in level 4.

For the purposes of our discussion in subsequent chapters, it is convenient to use the structure shown in Figure P1, since this is more representative of currently existing operating systems. A great deal of work remains to be done in the more general structure discussed above, for we must be careful to define the interfaces between the layers as precisely as possible.

THE PRIORITY CONTROL PROGRAM

INTRODUCTION

Virtually every computer program has a "main loop" that controls the processing performed by the program. In general, this main loop consists of the input of data, the processing of those data, and the output of results, as shown in Figure Q1.

In most non-real-time programs, the processing is initiated by the program itself and progresses in an orderly, well-controlled fashion. Thus, in Figure Q1, the computer program "knows" what it is doing at all steps in the processing: it decides when to read the card, what processing is required and what output should be generated.

This is not the case within the operating system for real-time and on-line computers (or, for that matter, the operating system for a batch system). Processing is usually initiated by *external events*, instead of by the program itself. As we see in Figure Q2, it is sometimes useful to think of the operating system as some sort of helpless amoeba, constantly being "poked" by the outside world. This may be a rather philosophical approach to an operating system, but it helps us see the problems that must be solved within it.

We can see a good illustration of this point by considering the manner in which the operating system performs input/output. As we mentioned briefly in Chapter P (the prelude to a much more detailed discussion in Chapter S), there are two kinds of IO routines associated with each IO device in the operating system. One type of IO routine accepts requests for IO from the

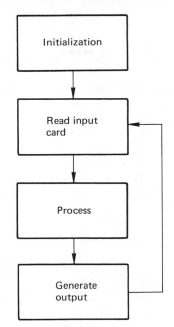

Fig. Q1 Processing in a non-real-time program

application programs, as shown in Figure Q3; the other one takes requests out of the queue, gives it to the IO device, and handles all of the timing, optimization, and error conditions.

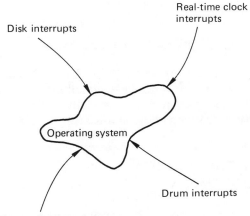

Fig. Q2 Processing in a real-time operating system

While this may seem like an orderly process, there is an important element of randomness and unpredictability to it. The operating system has no way of knowing when the application program will issue a READ or

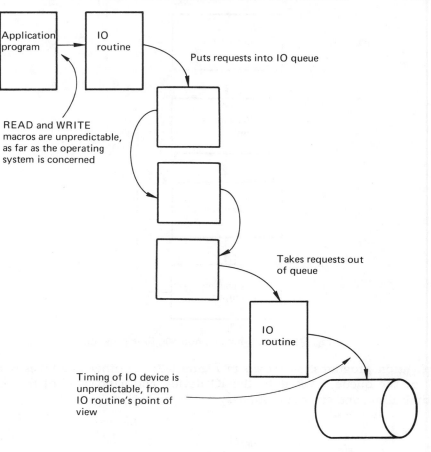

Fig. Q3 Processing performed by the I/O routines

WRITE macro for input or output; similarly, it cannot tell when it will receive interrupts from the IO device signalling the completion of a request. In both cases, it must wait for an essentially unpredictable interrupt (or call from an application program) before initiating a short burst of activity.

FUNCTIONS OF THE PRIORITY CONTROL PROGRAM

From the comments above, it is apparent that we need some mechanism inside the operating system to prevent the random arrival of processing tasks from causing chaos and confusion. The situation is further complicated by the fact that interrupts are likely to arrive when the operating system is in the midst of performing some processing for an earlier interrupt or request from an application program. Thus, we must have some orderly way of starting and stopping processing tasks within the operating system.

The mechanism we will describe in this chapter is a *priority control program*—that is, a *software* approach to the problem. One sometimes has the alternative of using hardware to accomplish the same thing, but the *functions* of this priority control mechanism remain the same. As part of the job of controlling the random arrival of tasks, we must have some way of controlling the priority of activities in the system. Some tasks are inherently more important than others, and should be given preference by the operating system. We certainly need the capability of starting more important tasks first, and perhaps even the capability of *interrupting* less urgent tasks when something critical comes along.

Some tasks within the operating system may be so urgent that we will want to classify them as "emergency," or "crisis-initiated" tasks. Memory parity errors, illegal instructions within the operating system, and power failure interrupts certainly fall into this category, and we may have a number of other external "alarms" that warrant special attention. All new tasks may have to be locked out of the machine as the priority control program tries to bring the system to an orderly pause by finishing all "in-process" tasks.

Finally, the priority control mechanism is often called upon to prevent simultaneous accesses to data within the operating system. This problem is very similar to the file accessing problem we discussed in Chapter L, and exists because many of the subroutines within the operating system are capable of interrupting each other. If the subroutines are accessing common tables or queues, as we saw in Figure Q1, we have the possibility of a conflict.

In summary, then, the priority control mechanism has four major responsibilities. These are as follows:

1 Organize the random arrival of events

2 Control the priority of activities in the system

3 Take care of "emergency" activities

4 Solve simultaneous access problems within the operating system

SOME COMMENTS ON HARDWARE INTERRUPT STRUCTURES

Since, as we have seen in an example or two, much of the processing in an operating system is initiated by IO interrupts, we should first discuss the nature and types of hardware interrupt structures that exist in current computers.

There are many different interrupt structures, but since we are only interested in their *general nature*, we can make some simplifying generalizations. On most current computers, each IO device is capable of "requesting" an interrupt—a request which, if honored, will cause control of the central processor to be abruptly transferred to some specified location in the operating system (usually some location in "lower core"—i.e. the first few hundred memory locations). When the interrupt is honored, the important *registers* (accumulators, index registers, program status words, machine status registers, and all of the other registers that describe the "state of the machine") are saved with the help of hardware and/or software, and the operating system proceeds to carry out the processing required.

The important characteristic of the interrupt structure is the manner in which it gains control of the central processor. On some machines, it is possible for the operating system to "arm" and "disarm" the interrupt structure. If the interrupt structure is *disarmed*, then interrupts will be neither seen nor remembered by the central processor. This is useful if the system wants to ignore totally some types of interrupts (such as floating point underflow and overflow).

When the interrupts are *armed*, they can be either *enabled* or *disabled*. When the interrupts are enabled, they will be recognized (or honored) by the central processor. When the interrupt structure is disabled, interrupts will not be able to gain control of the processor, but will be "remembered" (or, in the terminology of some manufacturers, "queued up" or "stacked up") until such time as the interrupts are enabled again.

We can identify four interesting types of hardware interrupt structures. Type I is the simplest, since it treats all interrupts equally. As we see in Figure Q4, the interrupt structure starts off in the *enabled* state, and then

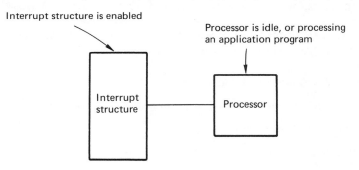

Fig. Q4(a)   Type I interrupt structure

two interrupts arrive simultaneously (or within the same memory cycle). The processor randomly honors one of the interrupts (not necessarily the one with the greatest urgency), *and while the interrupt is being processed, the interrupt structure is completely disabled.* The second interrupt, and any others that may come along during the processing of the first interrupt, are not immediately honored, but are "remembered." When the first interrupt finishes its processing, it *enables* the interrupt structure once again, allowing another interrupt to be honored.

A Type II interrupt structure is slightly more sophisticated. As we see in Figure Q5, if two (or more) interrupts occur *during the same memory cycle*, the interrupt structure will honor the one with the highest priority. The

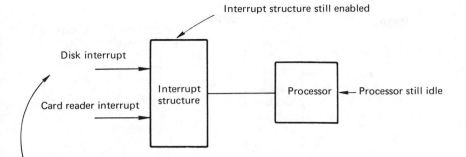

Interrupt structure still enabled

Disk interrupt

Interrupt structure

Card reader interrupt

Processor

Processor still idle

Both of these interrupts arrive at exactly the same time——or during the same memory cycle

Fig. Q4(b)   Type I interrupt structure

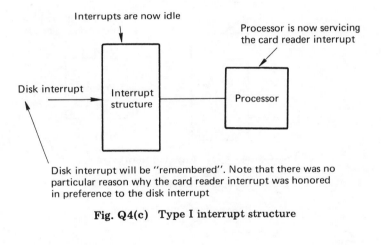

Interrupts are now idle

Processor is now servicing the card reader interrupt

Disk interrupt

Interrupt structure

Processor

Disk interrupt will be "remembered". Note that there was no particular reason why the card reader interrupt was honored in preference to the disk interrupt

Fig. Q4(c)   Type I interrupt structure

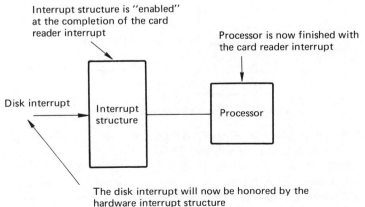

Interrupt structure is "enabled" at the completion of the card reader interrupt

Processor is now finished with the card reader interrupt

Disk interrupt

Interrupt structure

Processor

The disk interrupt will now be honored by the hardware interrupt structure

Fig. Q4(d)   Type I interrupt structure

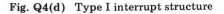
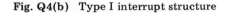

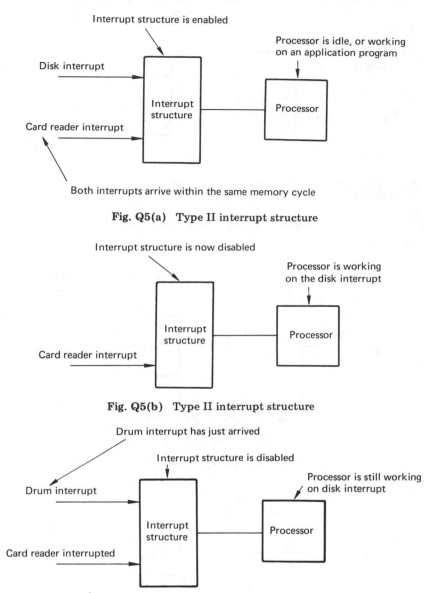

Fig. Q5(a)   Type II interrupt structure

Fig. Q5(b)   Type II interrupt structure

Fig. Q5(c)   Type II interrupt structure

priority of the various interrupts is determined by the computer manufacturer and is wired into the machine. This structure is similar to the Type I interrupt structure in that it is completely disabled while the processing of one interrupt takes place. Thus, as we see in Figure Q5, it is possible for an unimportant interrupt to delay the processing of an important interrupt.

In the Type III interrupt structure, we make some attempt to improve the computer's ability to respond to *critical* interrupts. The "emergency"

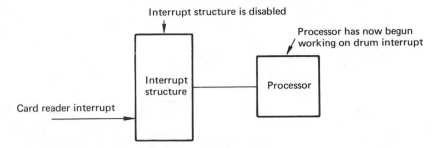

Fig. Q5(d)   Type II interrupt structure

interrupts—memory parity errors, power failure interrupts, illegal instruction interrupts, and so forth—constitute a *level* of interrupts which are allowed to interrupt the processing of the central processor if the interrupt structure is enabled, or if the central processor is processing a "normal" IO interrupt. This is illustrated by Figure Q6, in which we see the computer respond to a memory parity interrupt that occurs during the processing of an IO interrupt.

Finally, we can have the sophisticated interrupt structure shown in Figure Q7. With a Type IV interrupt structure, each IO device and each type of "external" interrupt (power failure, etc.) is assigned (or attached) programmatically to one of N different hardware levels of priority. If an

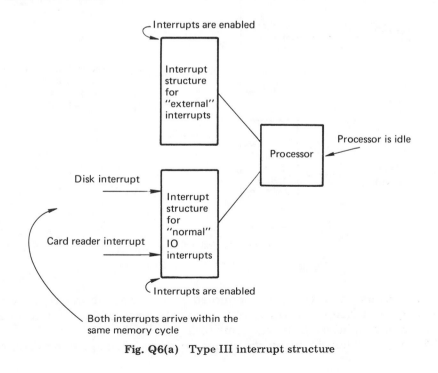

Fig. Q6(a)   Type III interrupt structure

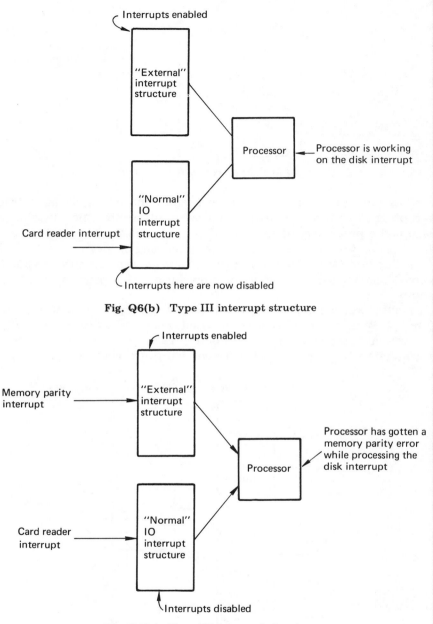

Fig. Q6(b)   Type III interrupt structure

Fig. Q6(c)   Type III interrupt structure

interrupt occurs on level N, it is honored immediately if the computer is processing an interrupt on some lower hardware level, and is not honored if it is processing an interrupt on the same or higher level.

There are obviously many variations on these interrupt structures, but

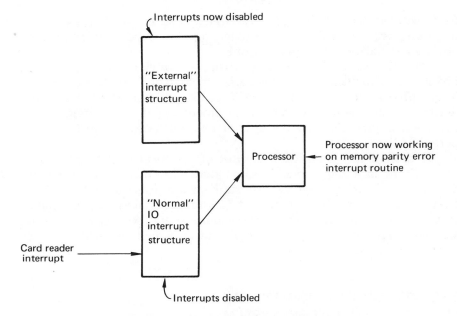

Fig. Q6(d)   Type III interrupt structure

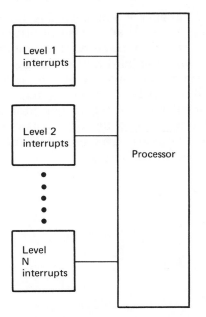

Fig. Q7   Type IV interrupt structure

the important point is whether the processor can *lock out* other interrupts while it is processing one. In the simplest mode of operation, the operating system carries on all of its processing with the hardware interrupts *disabled*.

Even with a Type II or Type III interrupt structure, it is possible for the operating system to delay the processing of a critical interrupt once it has honored a relatively unimportant one.

The disadvantages of this approach are obvious. Timing problems are possible if a high-speed IO device is "locked out" of the processor by an interrupt from a low-speed device. It is also possible to lose data from an IO device, or allow some external environment to get out of control. Thus, this approach is possible only if the interrupt routines execute for a very short period of time.

If there is any significant amount of overhead in the operating system, or if there is a high penalty associated with missing an interrupt, it is desirable to have a Type IV interrupt structure, *or a software equivalent*. Even with a Type IV structure, it is sometimes necessary to include some software to help fulfill the responsibilities that we discussed above. This software scheme is discussed below, after which we will consider some possible alternatives.

THE CONCEPT OF PRIORITY LEVELS
WITHIN THE OPERATING SYSTEM

Unless the system designer is implementing his operating system on a computer with a Type IV hardware interrupt structure, some *software* is required to control the execution of tasks. It is desirable to perform as much processing as possible with the hardware interrupts *enabled*, with a central program determining the relative urgency of various types of interrupts. This program is, of course, the priority control program.

In order to implement the priority control program, we need to define the concept of a *software level of priority*. When the operating system is designed, each task must be assigned a measure of urgency, or priority. Some examples of priority levels are as follows:

real-time clock priority level

drum priority level

disk priority level

magnetic tape priority level

card reader priority level

teletype input priority level

scheduling level

core allocation "clean-up" level

application program level

It is important to realize that these priority levels are represented by *numbers* within the priority control program. Thus, the real time clock might be assigned a priority level of zero; the high-speed drum might be assigned a priority level of one; and so forth, down to the priority level of eight for the application programs.

It is normal to have one priority level for each IO device, plus a few other assorted ones. However, it is possible to have a number of IO routines that execute with different levels of priority. A good example of this is the real-time clock, which might have a high level of priority so that it can respond to "alarm" conditions. In the event that there is no critically urgent processing to be done, though, the real-time clock routines may call for the execution of a *scheduling* program at a much lower level of priority.

There may be cases when a task has to change its priority during execution. This changing of priority is necessary because the task must assume that control can be taken away at any time by the priority control program if a task with a higher priority comes along. Thus, if a task is updating a common table, queue or piece of data, it may want to make itself temporarily "more important," as shown in Figure Q8. When the task has finished its sensitive processing, it can lower its priority to its original level.

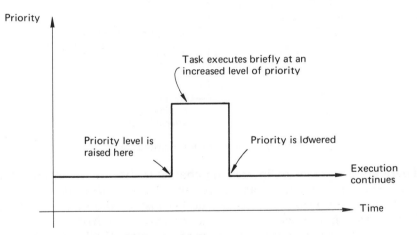

Fig. Q8 Raising and lowering of priority levels

IMPLEMENTATION OF THE PRIORITY CONTROL PROGRAM

Now that we have introduced the notion of priority levels, we can discuss the implementation of the priority control program. The basic premise is that the processing within the operating system takes place with the interrupt structure enabled. Thus, when a new interrupt occurs, it gains control of the processor, and the current processing (which may be an application program or some other part of the operating system) is temporarily suspended. The priority control program is then called with a request to execute a new task at a specified level of priority. Depending on the urgency of the new task, the priority control program will either give permission to the new task to begin its processing, or it will return control to the originally-interrupted program.

This mechanism requires several tables and a few subroutines. The first table that we require is the *list of interrupted tasks*, which we will refer to as the "interrupted list." As we see in Figure Q9, the purpose of this list is to keep track of all tasks which were started, but then interrupted by the priority control program in favor of something more urgent.

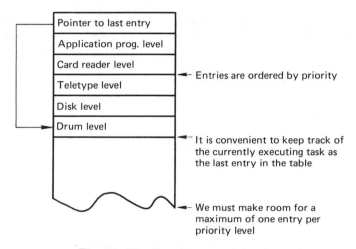

Fig. Q9   The list of interrupted tasks

There are a number of interesting characteristics of the interrupted list. First, we should recognize that entries are placed in the interrupted list *in order of increasing priority*. This is true because of the basic nature of our whole priority scheme—we will not take control away from the current task unless we have a more important task to execute. While this may seem a trivial property of the list, it turns out to be useful: whenever the priority control program wants to determine the most critical of the various *interrupted* tasks, it merely has to look at the end of the list.

We also notice that the list has a maximum length, which is equal to the total number of priority levels that have been defined in the system. Again, this is because of the basic nature of our priority scheme—since we will never interrupt the current task for something of equal or lower priority, there will be a maximum of one entry in the interrupted list for each priority level.

In practice, it is very rare to see more than two or three entries in the table at any one time. Since most of the processing tasks within the operating system require only a few milliseconds to execute, the possibility of multiple interrupts is fairly small. Consider the sequence of events that must have occurred in order for the interrupted list to have ended up in the state shown in Figure Q9:

1 The application program was executing, and there was nothing to do in the operating system. Meanwhile, the interrupt structure was enabled.

2 The card reader caused an interrupt and requested permission from the priority control program to do some processing at the card reader level of priority. Since this is of a higher level than the application program level, the request was granted by the priority control program. An entry for the application program level was made in the interrupted list.

3 In the midst of processing the card reader interrupt, there is an interrupt from a teletype. Since this is of a higher priority than the card reader interrupt, the priority control program takes control away from the card reader IO routine and gives it to the teletype IO routine.

4 Similarly, a disk interrupt arrives while we are in the midst of teletype interrupt processing.

5 Finally, a drum interrupt arrives and gains control of the system with the permission of the priority control program.

As we see in Figure Q9, it is convenient to keep track of the *currently executing task* as the last entry in the interrupted list. It is certainly not *necessary* that it be kept here, but it is convenient in the event that the current task has to be interrupted by some other task.

The priority control program also maintains a *list of waiting tasks*, to which we shall refer as the "waiting list." As shown in Figure Q10, the

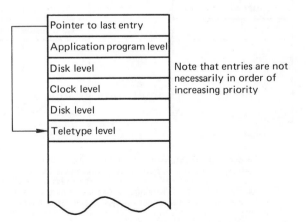

Fig. Q10 The list of waiting tasks

purpose of the waiting list is to keep track of the processing tasks which requested permission to execute, but which have to be delayed temporarily while more urgent tasks are processing.

While this list has the same general structure as the interrupted list, there is no guarantee that the entries will be in any sort of order. As we see in Figure Q11, it is possible for a variety of interrupts to be placed in the waiting list while a high-priority task is executing. Thus, we generally have to search through the list whenever we want to find the waiting task with the highest priority.

The maximum number of entries in the table depends on the manner in which the priority control program and the IO routines work together. If there are a large number of high-priority interrupts, it is possible for a number of lower-priority interrupts to begin piling up in the waiting list, as we see in Figure Q12. However, it is sometimes possible to build the IO

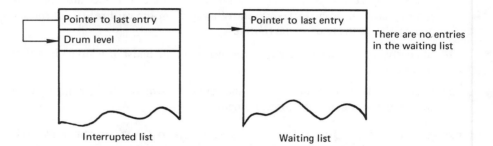

Interrupted list　　　　　　　　　　Waiting list

The drum interrupt routines are currently executing,
and the interrupt structure is enabled.

Fig. Q11(a) Example of entries being placed in the waiting list

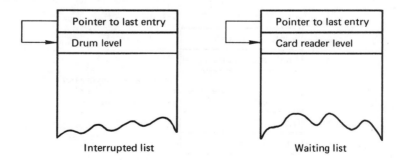

Interrupted list　　　　　　　　　　Waiting list

A card reader interrupt enters the system. The
priority control program does not give permission
to the card reader IO routine to perform its processing
at this point, since it is not as important as the drum
routines. The card reader entry is placed in the waiting
list, and control is immediately returned to the drum
routines.

Fig. Q11(b) Example of entries being placed in the waiting list

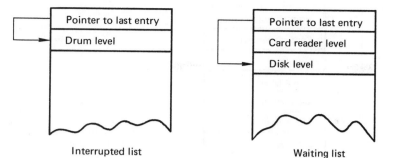

Similarly, a disk interrupt enters the system. It, too, is placed in the waiting list. Processing continues in the drum routines.

Fig. Q11(c) Example of entries being placed in the waiting list

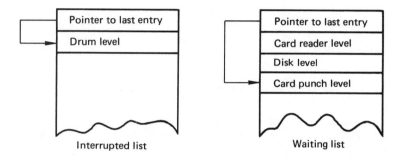

Finally, a card punch interrupt enters the system. Once more, the priority control program places the request in the waiting list. Note that the entries in the waiting list are now in no particular order.

Fig. Q11(d) Example of entries being placed in the waiting list

routines in such a way that the device will go idle (and thus will not generate any more interrupts) if the associated IO routine does not get permission to do its processing.

If there are many entries in the waiting list, it may become inconvenient to search through the entire list to find the most important entry. We may want to have a separate waiting list for each priority level, as shown in Figure Q13, in which requests are serviced in a first-in-first-out fashion on each priority level. While this increases the amount of space required by each level, it certainly cuts down on the amount of processing time required by the priority control program.

Finally, we need a *table of saved live registers*, as shown by Figure Q14, in which to keep the "state of the machine" whenever the priority control program switches from one task to another. Since there can be only one entry in the interrupted list for each priority level, it follows that we need

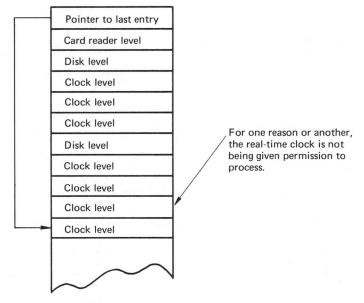

For one reason or another, the real-time clock is not being given permission to process.

Waiting list

Fig. Q12 Multiple entries of the same priority level

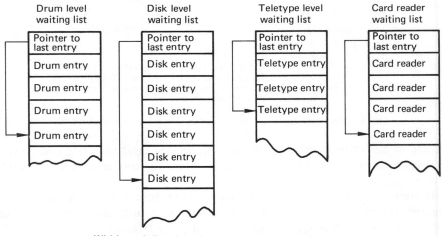

Within each list, the priority control program honors requests on a first-in-first-out basis

Fig. Q13 Multiple waiting lists

one entry in the table of saved live registers for each level. Depending on the type of machine, the following kinds of information may have to be kept in each entry of this table:

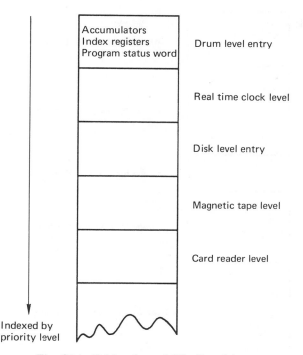

Drum level entry

Real time clock level

Disk level entry

Magnetic tape level

Card reader level

Indexed by
priority level

Fig. Q14   Table of saved "live" registers

accumulators

index registers

program counter

program status words

machine status registers

In addition, it may be convenient to keep a few other memory locations in this table. If, for example, the priority control program always saves and restores memory locations 0-10 (or memory locations 100-200, or any other convenient set of locations), then every operating system task can use that area for temporary storage and variables without worrying about having them destroyed by other high-priority tasks. In effect, this allows us to write *reentrant tasks* within the operating system with a minimum of effort.

There are, of course, much more efficient ways of writing reentrant operating system tasks. A number of the more current computers, such as the PDP-11, provide "push-down" instructions that allow each operating system task to maintain its variables and storage in the manner shown in Figure Q15. This saves a tremendous amount of overhead within the priority control program, since it eliminates the need to copy the contents of

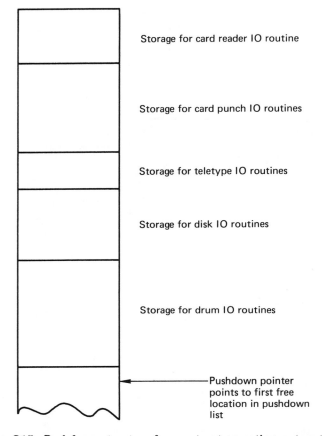

Storage for card reader IO routine

Storage for card punch IO routines

Storage for teletype IO routines

Storage for disk IO routines

Storage for drum IO routines

Pushdown pointer points to first free location in pushdown list

Fig. Q15 Pushdown structure for reentrant operating system tasks

memory locations to and from the table of saved live registers. On the other hand, memory references to the pushdown list are likely to be somewhat slower, since they must be indexed, or relocated, by the pushdown pointer.

SUBROUTINES REQUIRED WITHIN THE PRIORITY CONTROL PROGRAM

As we have seen, we need three tables to keep track of information about all of the tasks that have been interrupted in mid-execution, and all of the tasks that are waiting for permission to begin processing. We also require four priority control subroutines to manipulate these tables, and each of these must execute *with the hardware interrupt disabled*. That is, we cannot afford to have an interrupt take control of the processor while the priority control program itself is executing. In terms of our discussion in Chapter P, the priority control program refuses to *compete* with other operating system tasks for use of the central processor.

The first subroutine is shown in Figure Q16, and is called from the IO interrupt routines, or any other operating system task, to request the execution of a task of a specified priority. As we see in Figure Q16, the subroutine is very simple: it checks to see whether the requested subroutine is more urgent (i.e. of a higher priority) than the task that was executing at the instant of the interrupt. If the requested task is of an equal or lower priority, it is placed in the waiting list, and control is immediately returned to the current task. If the newly requested task is of a higher priority than the current task, it is inserted at the end of the interrupted list. This simple action simultaneously makes the newly requested task the current task, and indicates that the task that was executing at the time of the interrupt has now actually been interrupted. Before transferring control to the new task, the live registers are stored away for the previous task, and initialized (if necessary) for the new task.

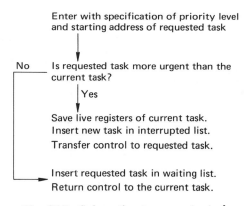

Fig. Q16 Subroutine to request a task

Figure Q17 illustrates the action taken by this subroutine when the newly requested task is of an equal or lower priority than the one executing at the time of the interrupt; Figure Q18 illustrates the case when the newly requested task is of a higher priority than the task that was executing at the time of the interrupt.

We also need a subroutine within the priority control program to which control can be returned when a task has finished its processing. The actions taken by this routine are shown in Figure Q19, and are fairly straightforward. It erases the last entry from the interrupted list to signify that the current task has now finished. Next, it decides whether to *resume* processing of a previously interrupted task or *begin* processing of a task which has not yet had permission to perform its processing.

This decision of "what to do next" requires the routine to look at both the interrupted list *and* the waiting list. As we mentioned earlier, the most important of all the interrupted tasks is guaranteed to be the one at the end of the interrupted list; the most important waiting task, on the other hand, can only be determined by searching through the waiting list. If it discovers

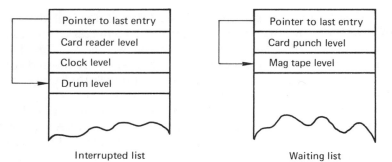

With the interrupted list and waiting list in the above
state, assume that we get a disk interrupt. The disk
IO routines call the priority control program to request
permission to do its processing.

Fig. Q17(a)   Example when the requested task is of a lower priority

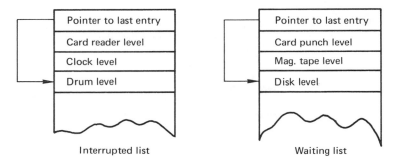

Fig. Q17(b)   Example when the requested task is of a lower priority

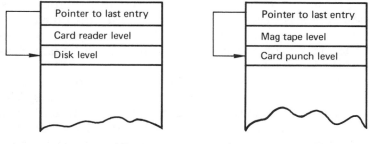

With the interrupted list and waiting list in the above state, assume that
we get a drum interrupt. The drum IO routines call the priority control
program for permission to do their processing.

Fig. Q18(a)   Example when the requested task is of a higher priority

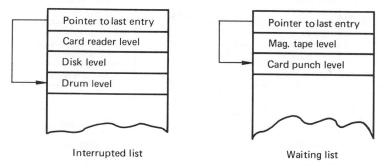

Fig. Q18(b) Example when the requested task is of a higher priority

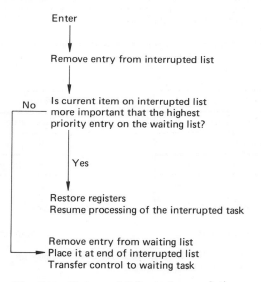

Fig. Q19 Entry point for task completion

that the highest priority task now in the system is a previously interrupted task, it restores the registers for that task and returns control to it. If, however, it discovers that a task from the waiting list is now the highest priority task in the system, it removes that task's entry from the waiting list and places it at the end of the interrupted list. If there is a task of the same priority in *both* the interrupted list *and* the waiting list, the priority control program should first finish the interrupted task.

Figure Q20 illustrates the case where the priority control program decides to resume processing of a previously interrupted task; Figure Q21 illustrates the case where the priority control program decides to begin the execution of a task from the waiting list.

Next, we need a subroutine that will allow the currently executing task to raise its priority. This is a very simple routine, as we see in Figure Q22, for

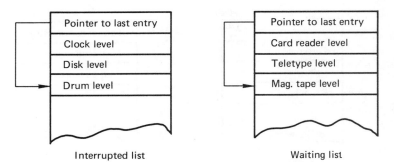

Pointer to last entry		Pointer to last entry
Clock level		Card reader level
Disk level		Teletype level
Drum level		Mag. tape level

Interrupted list   Waiting list

When the drum routines finish processing, the priority control program erases the drum entry from the interrupted list. It then recognizes that the disk routines are now the most important task in the system.

Fig. Q20(a)   Example when the priority control program resumes a previously interrupted task

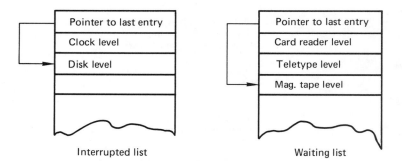

Pointer to last entry		Pointer to last entry
Clock level		Card reader level
Disk level		Teletype level
		Mag. tape level

Interrupted list   Waiting list

Fig. Q20(b)   Example when the priority control program resumes a previously interrupted task

it merely involves changing a number at the end of the interrupted list. In fact, some operating systems do not even force the task to call the priority control program to raise the level—each task is capable of changing the priority level itself by simply changing the entry in the interrupted list. Figure Q23 shows the interrupted list before and after the priority level has been changed.

Finally, we need a call to lower the priority level of the current task. This *must* be a subroutine call to the priority control program, for as we see in Figure Q24, new tasks may have entered the waiting list during the brief period of time that the current task executed at its higher level of priority. Thus, the priority control program behaves almost in the same manner as our first subroutine. As we see in Figure Q25, the routine first checks to see whether the newly-lowered priority level is still the highest priority task in the system. If so, we return control to it; if not, we save its registers, and begin executing a new task.

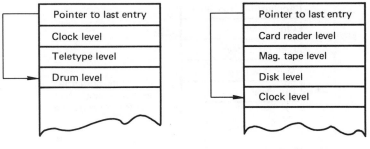

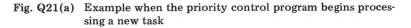

Interrupted list   Waiting list

When the drum routines finish, the priority control
program erases the drum entry from the interrupted
list. It then recognizes that the highest priority task
is the disk routine, which is in the waiting list.

Fig. Q21(a) Example when the priority control program begins processing a new task

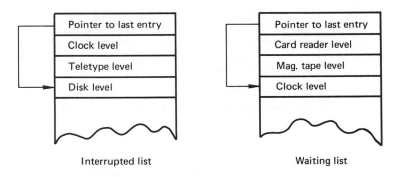

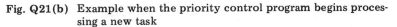

Interrupted list   Waiting list

Fig. Q21(b) Example when the priority control program begins processing a new task

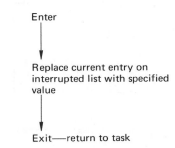

Fig. Q22 Subroutine call to raise priority level

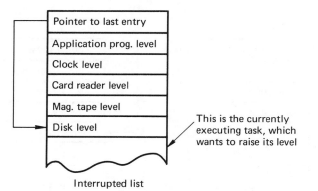

Fig. Q23(a) Interrupted list before the priority level has been raised

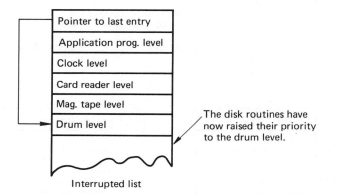

Fig. Q23(b) Interrupted list after the priority level has been raised

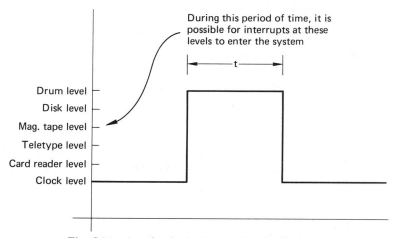

Fig. Q24 A task which lowers its priority level

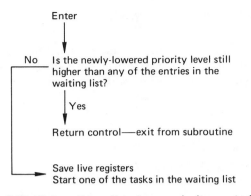

Enter

No   Is the newly-lowered priority level still
       higher than any of the entries in the
       waiting list?

       Yes

       Return control—exit from subroutine

       Save live registers
       Start one of the tasks in the waiting list

Fig. Q25   Subroutine call to lower priority control level

There is a philosophical question about the desirability of allowing a task to lower its level *below its original level*, as we have illustrated in Figure Q26. If we allow this, and if we follow the convention that the current task is kept in the last entry of the interrupted list, then it is possible for the interrupted list no longer to be in order of increasing priority. This is certainly not a difficult problem to fix, but the system designer must be aware of it. The subroutine which lowers the level must check both the interrupted list *and* the waiting list before deciding what to do. If we do not allow a task to lower its priority below the original level, then the situation is much simpler. The following argument can be used:

1   When the task first decided to raise its level, it was *executing,* and was thus the highest priority task in the system.

2   At the time the task decides to lower its level, it is still executing. Thus, it must

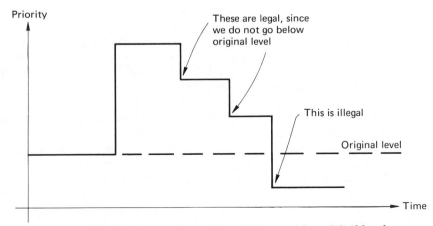

Fig. Q26   Lowering the priority level below the original level

still be the most important task in the system, and it is still more important than the other entries on the interrupted list.

3   Therefore, if the priority level is not lowered below the *original* level, the newly lowered level is still higher than all other entries in the interrupted list. It is only necessary for the priority control program to look in the waiting list to see if any other tasks have entered the system.

ALTERNATIVES AND TRADEOFFS IN THE PRIORITY CONTROL PROGRAM

While the structure we have presented is sufficient to control the activities within the operating system, there is a significant amount of overhead incurred. Most of the overhead is a result of the saving and restoring of registers when the priority control program switches from one task to another, although there may also be a fair amount of overhead required to search through the waiting list each time the priority control program has to start up a new task.

With this in mind, we might ask if it would not be better to perform all of the operating system tasks with the hardware interrupts *disabled*. While this approach would lock out other IO interrupts while the operating system was processing the task, it would certainly eliminate the overhead.

There is certainly a tradeoff to be made here, and it is not easy to state any general rules. When trying to decide whether or not to build in a software priority control mechanism, the system designer should keep in mind that the whole purpose of the program is to prevent the interrupts from being locked out for a lengthy period of time. If none of the operating system tasks require more than a few hundred microseconds of processing time, it may not be needed at all. Similarly, it may turn out that there are no serious consequences of keeping the interrupts locked out for several milliseconds.

Many of the *people-oriented* on-line systems can do without the priority control software, for the operating systems are moderately efficient, and the worst consequence of locking out an interrupt may be a slightly delayed response time. On the other hand, a priority control package makes it easier to optimize IO on disks and drums, which can significantly increase the throughput of the system. We will discuss this at greater length in Chapter S when we talk about the general nature of IO routines.

Perhaps the greatest use of the priority control software is in the process control and data acquisition systems that are implemented on computers with Type I, II, or III interrupt structures. On these systems, there is often a great danger if we do not respond quickly to an interrupt—data may be lost, or a physical process may get out of control. When a critical device causes an interrupt, the system *must* respond immediately, regardless of what it was doing.

A compromise that might be considered is that of eliminating the interrupted list. That is, we can arrange the priority control program in such a way that the operating system tasks perform their processing with the interrupts enabled, but control is not taken away from the task until it has finished. Interrupts that occur during the processing of a task simply get queued up in the waiting list, and then get started up in order of highest priority.

With this approach, we eliminate all of the overhead associated with the interrupting of tasks. We no longer need the table of saved live registers, for the registers no longer have to be saved. The raising and lowering of priority levels are no longer necessary, for a task no longer has to worry about being interrupted by a higher-priority task.

As we have already noted, the software can be almost completely eliminated with a Type IV interrupt structure. It is desirable to have an interrupt structure in which the operating system can programmatically assign various devices to specific hardware priority levels. If the priority levels are hard-wired into the machine, the system designer loses some flexibility: he may have wanted to attach a different priority to various peripherals than the hardware designer did.

Note that the hardware structure works in much the same manner that our software scheme does. When an IO device attempts to cause an interrupt, the hardware checks to see if it is of a higher hardware priority than that of the current task. If so, the interrupt is honored, and the new interrupt routine is faced with the job of saving the state of the machine in a table of saved live registers or in a pushdown list. With even more sophisticated hardware, the state of the machine could be *automatically* saved and restored by the hardware whenever a new interrupt occurred.

The concept of raising and lowering the priority levels is accomplished by masking out, or disabling, selected hardware priority levels. It is also desirable to allow the operating system tasks to "trigger" interrupts themselves: a high-priority IO routine might want to trigger a low-priority clock interrupt to cause rescheduling to take place.

If one has a choice, the machine with the Type IV interrupt structure is a far better vehicle for developing an operating system. This structure is becoming far more common on the newer machines, and should be a "standard" feature within a few years. If one is unfortunate enough to have a computer with Type I, II, or III interrupt structures, the extra overhead of *software* may or may not be worth the effort of writing the software.

Chapter R

THE SCHEDULER PROGRAM

THE BASIC FUNCTIONS OF THE SCHEDULER

In Chapter Q, we discussed a mechanism to keep track of the many tasks within the operating system. One of those tasks is the *scheduler*, whose job it is to keep track of all the application programs in the system. This part of the operating system is usually of great interest to the application programmers, for it has a great deal of control over the service which their program receives.

One of the major functions of the scheduler program is to keep track of the current condition, or state, of each application program (or job, or task, or user, depending on the terminology) that is running on the system. As we will see below, there are two common techniques for keeping this information, and also two techniques for passing the information on to the scheduler when the application program's condition *changes*. Along with the program's condition, the scheduler is also required to keep the application its live registers and all of the information that describes what the program is doing.

The most commonly recognized function of the scheduler is to decide which application program should be allowed to execute next. This scheduling decision is required whenever the current application program is forced to wait for the completion of input/output, and may also be required when the application program has exceeded an allotted "quantum" of time.

Note that control is taken away from an application program in a simple multiprogramming environment only after the program has called for IO. In a time-slicing environment, the scheduler must also decide *how long* the application program is to be allowed to run before control is taken away. The time-slice quantum may be fixed in length for all application programs, or it may be variable.

Finally, the scheduler program must cooperate with the core allocation routines if the application programs can be swapped out of core. Since the core allocation routines decide *which* application programs should be removed from core, it is important that they do not remove a program just before the scheduler decides to execute it.

Keeping Track of the Condition
of Application Programs

As we mentioned above, it is important for the scheduler to keep track of the current condition of each application program in the system. There are basically two approaches to this problem, and both can be used equally well in most operating systems.

The first approach is to identify all of the different states, or conditions, that an application program could be in with a *state code*. Some examples of state codes might be:

state 0 = runnable

state 1 = disk input wait

state 2 = disk output wait

state 3 = teletype input wait

state 4 = teletype output wait

etc.

In general, we would have a state code for each form of input wait and output wait, plus assorted other ones.

The advantage of this approach is that it describes the activities of the application program in a very orderly and well-controlled manner. In addition to describing *all* of the legal states of the application program, we can easily describe all of the legal *changes of state*. Thus, it is legal for an application program to change from state 0 to state 1, and it is equally legal for the program to change from state 1 back to state 0. In a simple on-line system, it appears that an application program can legally change from state 0 to any other IO state, or from some IO state to state 0. However, it does *not* seem reasonable for the application program to change from state 2 to state 3.

A possible disadvantage of this state-oriented approach is that there might be a large number of legal states. Since we are likely to build our scheduler in such a way that we *dispatch* on the state code at various places, much core could be taken up by the dispatch tables. This is especially true if the application program is allowed to perform more than one kind of IO at a time.

If the application program is not forced to "wait" when it has issued an IO macro, it may continue with its processing, or it may decide to issue a macro for some other form of IO. Thus, it is conceivable, on some systems, for the program to be waiting for several different types of IO at the same time. We might thus end up with several hundred different state codes.

Another approach is shown by Figure R1. This *status word* approach maintains a separate bit for each type of "wait" condition in which the

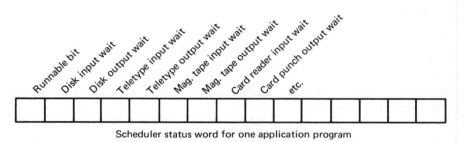

Scheduler status word for one application program

Fig. R1 Status words in the scheduler

application program might find itself. This usually requires more room than the state-code approach, since a total of 20 states requires 20 bits instead of a number that ranges from 0 to 20. However, the extra room is certainly not a major factor, and we are more concerned with the ease with which the approach can be used.

One advantage of the status word approach is that the IO routines can turn the appropriate bits on and off very easily, without affecting the actions of other IO routines. On the other hand, some machines lack the kind of instruction set that makes it easy to set and reset individual bits. Also, it may be possible for contradictory combinations of bits to be turned on. That is, with 20 different status bits, there are 2^{20} different combinations of bits, not all of which may be legal.

All in all, the two approaches are about equal in efficiency and convenience. The state code approach is more compact and less error-prone, but the status word approach seems slightly better suited to the systems with many different "wait" conditions.

Techniques of Informing the Scheduler
of Changes in a Program's Condition

Once we have come up with a technique for keeping information about each application program, we must have a procedure for informing the scheduler of a *change in state*. There are two different approaches here, also, and again they are essentially equal.

The first approach involves *explicitly* calling the scheduler whenever anything happens to the application program. Thus, whenever an IO routine recognizes that a program's IO has been finished, it immediately calls the scheduler and indicates the *new* state. Since the scheduler presumably knows the *old* state, it knows what change is taking place.

The advantage of this approach is that the scheduler can take action immediately (if it wants to) when it learns that a job has become runnable again. Thus, as soon as the IO of a high-priority application program has finished, the scheduler will be able to interrupt the processing of a background job, and resume the processing of the high-priority job.

The disadvantage of this explicit approach is that the scheduler is forced to do a fair amount of processing at high priority levels. Thus, during the high-priority IO processing, the scheduler may be called upon to juggle its scheduling queues and choose a new application program.

The second approach is an *implicit* one—the IO routines and other operating system subroutines change bits in the program's status words and then let the scheduler discover those changes during its regular scheduling time. Thus, if an application program was waiting for some input from the disk, the disk IO routines could, at a high priority level, turn off the "waiting for disk input" status bit (or change the state code)—and the scheduler would discover it at some later time.

The advantage of this scheme is rather obvious: it minimizes the amount of processing required at the IO priority levels. The actual scheduling is left for a lower scheduling priority level, usually triggered by a real-time clock. On the other hand, this approach makes the system less "responsive," since the scheduler will not *immediately* start up a high priority application program when its IO has finished. Also, it forces the scheduler to examine the status words (or state codes) of *all* the application programs to see which ones have changed. If there are 200 application programs running in the system, this could involve a fair amount of overhead.

We see that there are a total of four different approaches to the problems of keeping track of a job's condition, and informing the scheduler when that condition changes:

1 Keeping the information in a state code, and informing the scheduler explicitly when the job changes state.

2 Keeping the information in a status word, and allowing the IO routines to set and reset the bits by themselves.

3 Keeping the information in a state code, and allowing the IO routines to change the state code by themselves.

4 Keeping the information in a status word, and informing the scheduler explicitly when the program's condition changes.

In practice, the first two combinations are the most common, and the second combination is perhaps the most popular of all. Note that the IO routines must *always* call the scheduler explicitly when the current application program is forced to wait for IO, for it is only the scheduler that can determine which program should run next. It is only when the IO *finishes* that the IO routines have the choice of relaying that information to the scheduler implicitly or explicitly.

Although the mechanisms we have described are sufficient for most operating systems, there may be cases when we require more sophistication. If the application program is allowed to issue complex WAIT macros, for instance, the scheduler will have to keep much more than a simple status word. Most of the systems that permit the complex WAIT macros require the application program to specify pairs of *memory locations* and *masks*; the operating system then periodically checks to see if the bits specified by the mask have been turned on in the memory locations. When all of the memory locations have been set in accordance with the masks, the application program is once again placed in a "runnable" status. In order to keep track of this kind of application program, the scheduler would have to keep the kind of table shown in Figure R2.

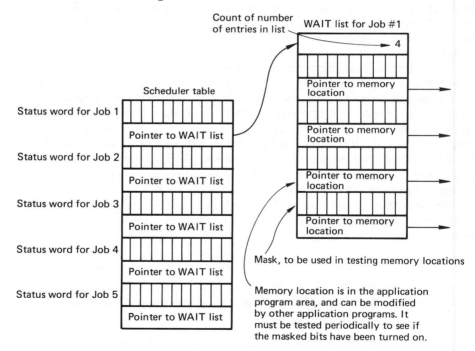

Fig. R2   Scheduler status information for complex WAIT

As a variation on this scheme, the scheduler may keep these memory locations within its own tables. Thus, one application program would have to issue a WAIT macro to specify a mask; other application programs would then have to issue a SETBIT macro to set various bits in these memory locations. Note that this "explicit" approach allows the scheduler to determine immediately when the application program is runnable again, at the cost of the extra overhead of the SETBIT macro. The tables required to keep this information in the scheduler are shown in Figure R3.

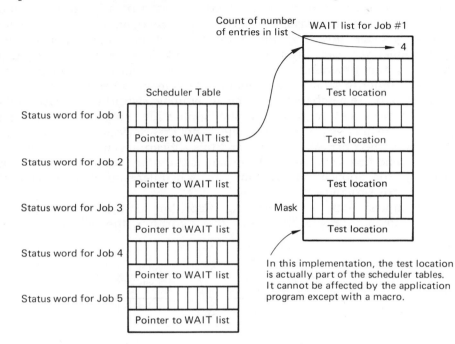

Fig. R3   Alternate solution to complex WAIT

SCHEDULING ALGORITHMS

As we have indicated, there are several ways of informing the scheduler program of changes in the application program's condition. Whenever the currently executing application program becomes non-runnable, the scheduler is called upon to determine which application program should run next. There is a wide variety of scheduling algorithms in existence, and as long as the operating system wants to treat all application programs equally, the scheduling algorithm can be kept fairly simple. If, on the other hand, there is a wide variety of application programs, and if it is desired to give preference to certain types or classes of programs, the scheduling algorithm is usually more complex.

The great problem of all scheduling algorithms is the conflict between *responsiveness* and *throughput*. If we were concerned only with throughput, we would try to arrange for a mixture of application programs that would ensure a proper "balance" of computation and IO, and we would probably process these programs in a simple multiprogrammed batch fashion, with no time-slicing. It is because of the need to give fast response to the users that we engage in time-slicing and swapping. As we will see below, we usually have to pay for this responsiveness with a loss of efficiency and throughput.

In most cases, the application programmer does not have any way of influencing these scheduling decisions—he merely writes his program and hopes that it will receive reasonable service from the operating system. There are some systems, however, where the application programmer or the computer operator can influence the scheduler's decision by assigning *priorities* to the program. Once again, we are usually sacrificing some efficiency in order to satisfy the programmer's demand for responsiveness.

It should be remembered that the scheduling algorithm allocates only one of the resources required by the application program—the central processor. Core memory and use of the peripheral devices are allocated by other parts of the operating system, and this allocation is usually performed on a first-come-first-serve basis. When all of the *other* resources have been supplied to the application program, the scheduler allocates the central processor to the program.

The simplest type of scheduling algorithm is the "round robin" algorithm shown in Figure R4. With this algorithm, the scheduler passes

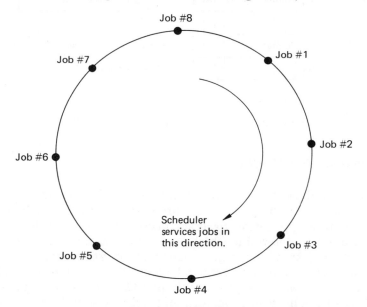

Fig. R4   The round robin scheduling algorithm

regularly from one application program to the next, servicing each in its turn. The round robin algorithm is implemented with the circular queue structure shown in Figure R5, and the scheduler simply looks at the status word (or state code) for each application program.

The round robin approach can be implemented with or without

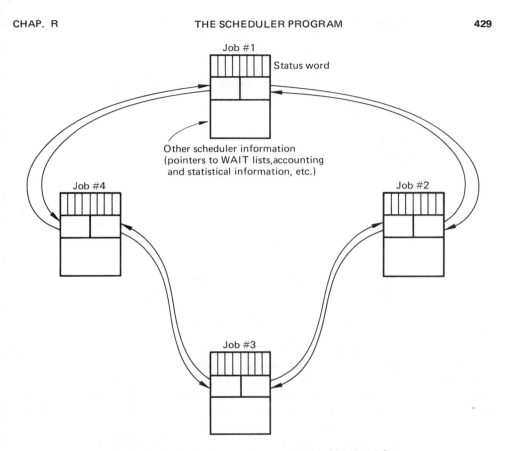

Fig. R5   Implementation of the round robin algorithm

time-slicing. If time-slicing is not involved, the scheduler passes from one
application program to the next only when the current program is forced to
wait for some IO. If time-slicing *is* included, the scheduler takes control
away from the current program if it is forced to wait for input/output, or if
it exceeds its allotted quantum of time. On most operating systems that use
the round robin algorithm with time-slicing, the *size* of the time slice remains
fixed for all application programs. The time slice could be varied from one
program to the next, but it does not seem to be worth the effort.

The important characteristic of the round robin algorithm is that it does
not attempt to give different service to different types of jobs—it merely
passes from one to the next. As a result, it does not give better service to
short jobs, interactive jobs, or any other kind of job. As we see in Figure R6,
it is possible for a short, interactive job to receive very poor service if it is
included in a mix of compute-bound jobs. Even with time-slicing, it is
possible for compute-bound jobs to "hog" the system.

As a result, most schedulers use some form of the *multiple queue*
algorithm shown in Figure R7. The basic purpose of this type of algorithm is
to separate jobs into different *classes*, or *types*, with the "good" jobs rising

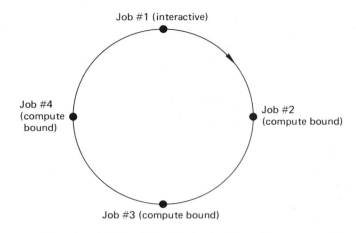

Everytime Job #1 calls for IO, the scheduler will
turn control over to Job 2, 3, and 4 before returning
again to Job #1

Fig. R6   An interactive job in a round robin algorithm

to the top queues, and the "bad" jobs sinking to the lower queues. This
classification of jobs may be based on external information, such as
commands from the computer operator or control cards supplied with the
application program; quite often, though, we find that the scheduler
program separates the application programs into different classes (and hence
different queues) as it learns more about the characteristics of the program.
The longer the program runs, the more it distinguishes itself as a
compute-bound program, or an IO-bound program, or whatever other type
of program the scheduler is interested in discriminating against.

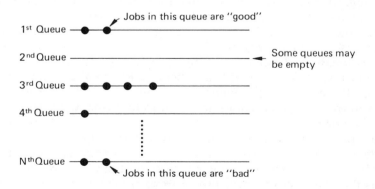

Fig. R7   The multiple queue scheduling algorithm

The multiple queue approach can be implemented in a number of
different ways, the most common of which is shown in Figure R8. With this
implementation, we maintain a number of queues (usually somewhere
between 2 and 7 queues), with forward and backward pointers to link the

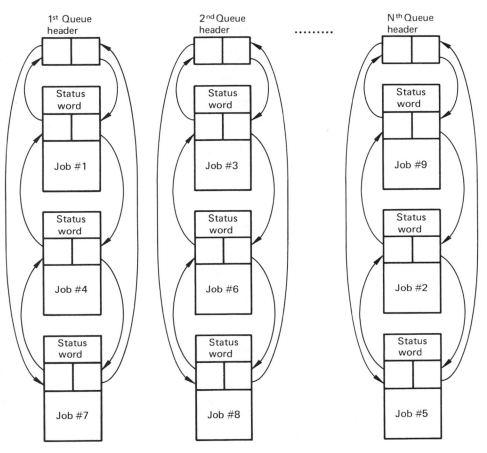

Entries in each queue are linked with forward and backward pointers

Fig. R8 A common implementation of the multiple queue algorithm

various application programs. The scheduler then chooses the application program at the front of the highest non-empty queue, and uses various other rules to remove programs from one queue and insert them at the front or back of other queues.

Another way of implementing the multiple queue approach is shown in Figure R9. Here we keep all of the application programs in one queue, and assign each a *priority number*. The priority numbers usually vary from 0 to 4096 (although the range could just as easily be greater or smaller), which is equivalent to having 4096 different scheduling queues. With this approach, we need some way of determining the highest priority application program, which often means searching through the entire queue. Alternatively, we could keep the queue in an ordered fashion, as shown in Figure R10, but since the application programs are constantly changing their priority, it might be rather cumbersome to maintain the order.

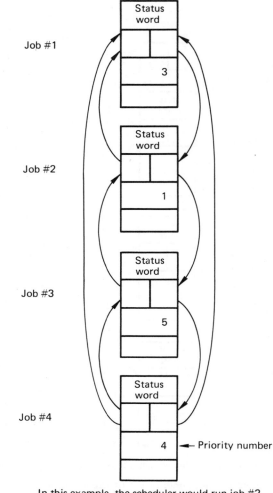

In this example, the scheduler would run job #2,
then job #4, and finally job #3.

Fig. R9   Multiple queue algorithm with priority numbers

Regardless of the implementation technique, there are a number of *decisions* that must be made in the multiple queue scheduling algorithm. The first decision must be made when the application program initially begins its execution: where should it be placed in the queues? There are a number of acceptable choices here:

1   The application programmer can be allowed to specify the priority of the job, which specifies the queue in which it should be placed. This is a very desirable approach in a dedicated environment, where the programmer is likely to know better than the scheduling algorithm which resources are to be optimized. In a

general-purpose on-line system (such as a university time-sharing system), one is likely to find that *all* of the application programmers ask for the highest priority.

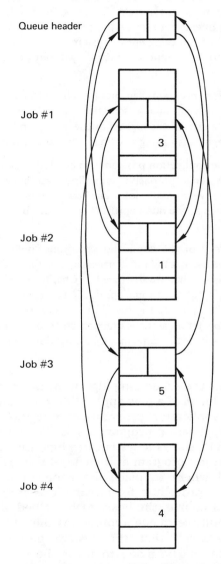

Fig. R10 Multiple queue algorithm with ordered priority numbers

2   The computer operator can be allowed to specify the priority of the job. While this is often a desirable feature in a multiprogrammed *batch* system (where the computer operator is more likely to know the mix of jobs than the application programmer is), it can cause chaos in a multiprogrammed on-line system, unless

carefully controlled. It is normally fairly important for the on-line application programs to receive a high scheduling priority. If the computer operator decides to give a background batch program a high priority, it could seriously degrade the response time of the system. On the other hand, it might be useful to allow the computer operator to *lower* the priority of a background batch program, in order to keep it from tying up the system. In general, this kind of control should not be given to the computer operator without permission from the operations supervisor.

3 The application program can be initially placed on the highest queue. A common practice on many scientific time-sharing systems is to place the program at the *end* of the highest queue, and then let it drift down to the lower queues if it begins displaying any "bad" characteristics.

4 The *size* of the application program can be used to determine where it should be placed initially. This approach is sometimes used in systems where there is a high correlation between *large* jobs and *compute-bound* jobs. Obviously, other parameters, such as the number of files that have been declared, could be used in this same manner.

5 The *past history* of the application program could be used. In order for this approach to be useful at all, it is necessary for the operating system to gather the types of statistics that we discussed in Chapter G. However, the statistics only become meaningful if the same application programs are executed day after day, which is *not* likely to be the case in most scientific time-sharing systems. Thus, we would expect this statistical approach to be useful only in a "production" environment, where the same mix of application programs could be expected on a regular basis.

If we implement the scheduling algorithm as originally shown in Figure R8, the initial placement of a new application program is very simple. Figure R11 shows a new application program entering the scheduling queues in a system where the application programmer is allowed to specify the priority of his job; Figure R12 shows a system in which the scheduler automatically inserts a new application program at the end of the highest queue.

Having decided where to place the application program initially, we must next establish a procedure for moving jobs around from one queue to the next. This is, of course, the heart of the scheduling algorithm, and the advantage of the multiple queue approach is that it can be made to reflect almost any "preference" that the system designer wishes. Thus, the scheduling algorithm can be made to favor the short-compute job, or the terminal-bound job; or it can be made to discriminate against the heavily compute-bound job, or the disk-bound job, or the jobs requiring more than 32,768 bytes of core memory, or jobs belonging to the engineering department.

In practice, this part of the scheduling algorithm tends not to be as complex as it could be. A large number of scheduling algorithms use some procedure for assigning an application program to a queue initially, and then

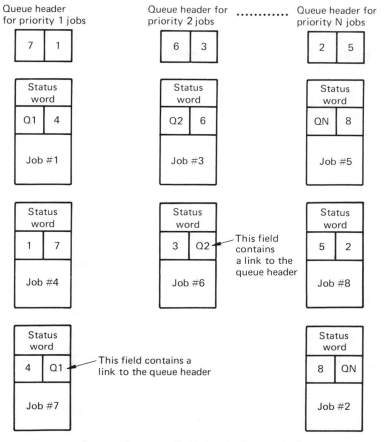

Suppose that an application programmer submits
a job with a priority of 2

Fig. R11(a) Programmer-controlled initial placement of a job

keep the program on that queue. Application programs on each queue are
serviced in a round robin fashion, and if a job must be interrupted, it is
returned to the end of its queue. This is illustrated in Figure R13, in which
the application program is interrupted only when it is forced to wait for IO.

An alternative approach is to allow the scheduling algorithm to move the
application programs from one queue to another, as the program continues
to distinguish itself as a "bad" job or a "good" job. This is illustrated in
Figure R14, which is typical of many scientific time-sharing systems. An
application program begins at the end of the highest queue, and is eventually
given permission to execute. If it executes for more than a pre-specified
amount of time, it is interrupted and placed at the end of the next lower
queue. If it continues to distinguish itself as a compute-bound program, it
eventually finds itself on the very bottom queue.

Regardless of whether the scheduler decides to move an application

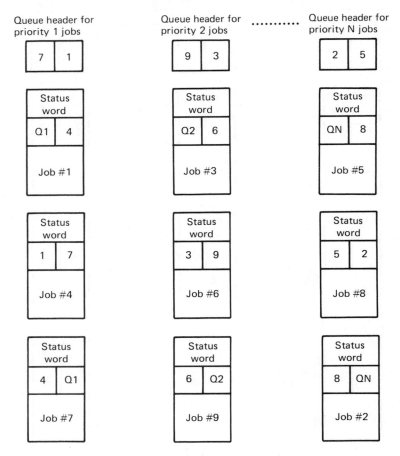

At this point, Job #9 has been inserted at
the end of the second queue

Fig. R11(b) Programmer-controlled initial placement of a job

program around on the queues, it always chooses the program *at the front of
the highest non-empty queue*. If time-slicing is not involved, each application
program so chosen is allowed to execute until it requires IO; in a time-slicing
environment, each application program may be given a *fixed* quantum of
time, or, as we see in Figure R15, we may allow larger time slices for the
lower queues. There are a large number of scientific time-sharing systems
that assign a time quantum of 200-500 milliseconds for jobs on the highest
queue, and then *double* that quantum for jobs on successively lower queues.

  Thus, we might have a system in which jobs on the highest queue receive
1/4 second of CPU time; if the job executes for more than 1/4 of a second, it
is interrupted, and placed at the end of the second queue. When it finally
reaches the front of the second queue, it is given 1/2 second of CPU time
before being placed at the end of the third queue. As we see in Figure R16,

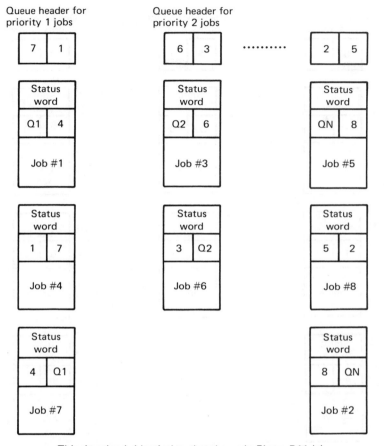

This situation is identical to that shown in Figure R11 (a).
However, in this case, the scheduler will insert a new job
at the end of the first queue.

Fig. R12(a)   Scheduler-controlled initial placement of a job

two compute-bound jobs would sink to the bottom queue, where they
would receive 16 seconds of CPU time before being interrupted. Remember
that the scheduling algorithm will only execute a job on one of the lower
queues if there are no runnable jobs on the higher queues. Thus, although
the jobs on the lower scheduling, queues are given longer time-slices, they are
usually allowed to execute less often.

It should be emphasized that CPU time is not the only parameter that
the scheduler may use to move an application program from one queue to
another. Whenever an application program is forced to wait for IO, we may
decide to move it into a special queue of "waiting" jobs, as shown in Figure
R17. This has the advantage of limiting the rest of our queues to *runnable*
jobs, and means that the scheduler does not have to waste its time examining

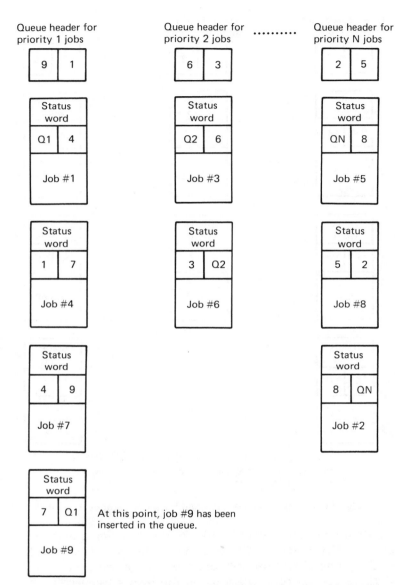

Fig. R12(b)   Scheduler-controlled initial placement of a job

non-runnable jobs. When a job becomes runnable again, we may decide to return it to the end of the queue that it occupied when it became non-runnable, as shown in Figure R18. Alternatively, we may decide to move the job to a higher queue when it becomes runnable, as illustrated in Figure R19. This latter approach is commonly used in scientific time-sharing systems when a job changes from a "teletype input wait" condition to a "runnable" condition.

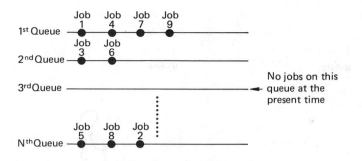

Assume that the scheduling queues are as shown above, and that jobs 1,4,7, and 9 are waiting for IO. In this case, the scheduler will next decide to run job #3. Assume that job #3 executes for some period of time, and then calls for IO. At this point, the scheduler will rearrange the queues in the manner shown in Figure R13 (b).

Fig. R13(a)   Multiple queue algorithm with no movement between queues

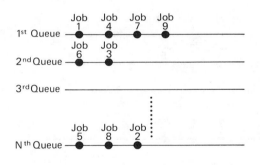

Job #3 has now been placed at the end of the second queue.

Fig. R13(b)   Multiple queue algorithm with no movement between queues

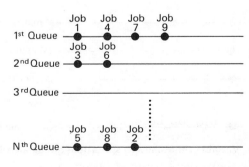

When job #9 first enters the system, it is placed at the end of the highest queue.

Fig. R14(a)   Multiple queue algorithm with movement between queues

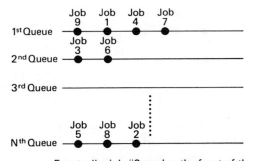

Eventually, job #9 reaches the front of the queue. The scheduler allows the program to run, but only for a limited amount of time. If it is still executing at the end of its time-slice, it is interrupted and moved to the end of the second queue.

Fig. R14(b)   Multiple queue algorithm with movement between queues

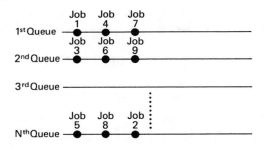

Job #9 will now be executed less often, but will be given a longer time slice.

Fig. R14(c)   Multiple queue algorithm with movement between queues

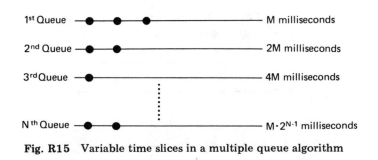

Fig. R15   Variable time slices in a multiple queue algorithm

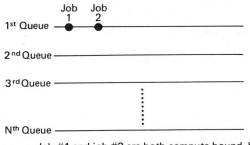

Job #1 and job #2 are both compute bound, but
the scheduler has no *a priori* way of knowing it.
Therefore, it places both jobs in the highest
queue and gives them short time-slices

Fig. R16(a) Compute bound programs in a time-slicing algorithm

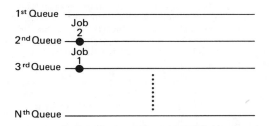

At some later point, job #1 has already
been moved down to the 3rd queue, having
received M milliseconds of CPU time in the
first queue and 2M milliseconds in the 2nd
queue. As we see, job #2 is following close
behind.

Fig. R16(b) Compute bound jobs in a time-slicing algorithm

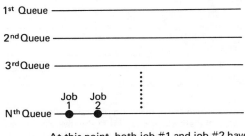

At this point, both job #1 and job #2 have
reached the bottom queue.

Fig. R16(c) Compute bound jobs in a time-slicing environment

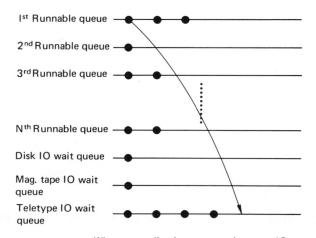

When an application program issues an IO macro,
it is removed from the "runnable" queues, and
placed in the appropriate IO wait queue.

Fig. R17   Queues of waiting jobs

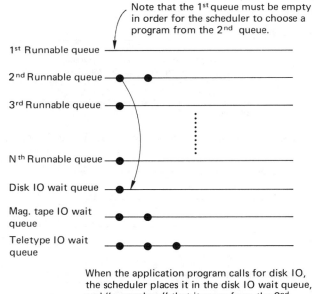

Note that the 1st queue must be empty
in order for the scheduler to choose a
program from the 2nd queue.

When the application program calls for disk IO,
the scheduler places it in the disk IO wait queue,
and "remembers" that it came from the 2nd
runnable queue.

Fig. R18(a)   Returning a waiting job to its original runnable queue

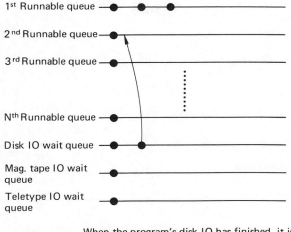

1st Runnable queue

2nd Runnable queue

3rd Runnable queue

Nth Runnable queue

Disk IO wait queue

Mag. tape IO wait queue

Teletype IO wait queue

When the program's disk IO has finished, it is returned to the end of the 2nd queue. This does not guarantee it immediate service, since there may be other jobs on the same or higher queues.

Fig. R18(b)   Returning a waiting job to its original runnable queue

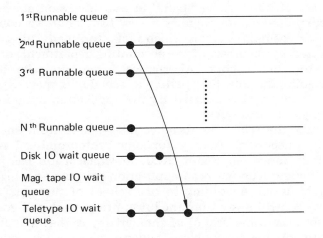

1st Runnable queue

2nd Runnable queue

3rd Runnable queue

Nth Runnable queue

Disk IO wait queue

Mag. tape IO wait queue

Teletype IO wait queue

When an application program calls for teletype IO, it is removed from the runnable queue and placed in the teletype IO wait queue.

Fig. R19(a)   Returning a waiting job to a higher queue

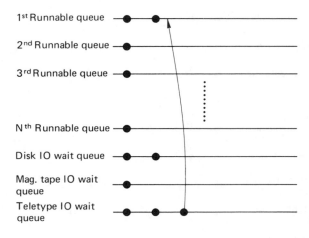

1st Runnable queue

2nd Runnable queue

3rd Runnable queue

Nth Runnable queue

Disk IO wait queue

Mag. tape IO wait queue

Teletype IO wait queue

When the application program is runnable again, it is placed at the end of the highest queue.

Fig. R19(b) Returning a waiting job to a higher queue

In general, we can "tune" the scheduling algorithm to favor any type of application program that we consider "good," and discriminate against any type of program that we consider "bad." In our discussion above, we have assumed that *compute-bound* programs were "bad," but we could just as easily discriminate against programs which make too many file accesses, or programs submitted by members of the accounting department, or programs which occupy too much core. Alternatively, we can take the simple approach of assigning the jobs to a particular scheduling queue, perhaps on the basis of a control card submitted by the application programmer, and then keeping the job on that queue.

If we do allow the scheduler to move jobs around from one queue to another, it is often necessary to allow for some "compromises." A common example of this is shown in Figure R20, in which a job has just begun executing on a lower queue when an application program on a higher queue becomes runnable again. According to one school of thought, we should *immediately* take control away from the lower-priority job and give it to the higher-priority job; the other school of thought argues that we have delayed the lower-priority job for a long time, and we may have incurred a large amount of swapping overhead to get the job into core—so we should allow it to execute for the duration of its long time quantum.

We are faced here with a conflict between "responsiveness" and throughput: to take control away immediately from the lower-priority job is less efficient, but more responsive. As a compromise, we might decide to allow the lower-priority job to execute for *at least as long* as the time quantum of the higher-priority job which is about to interrupt it. Thus, in Figure R21, we see a lower-priority job which has just begun its 8-second quantum of CPU time, when a job reappears on a queue which has been assigned a quantum of 2 seconds. Our compromise algorithm ensures that

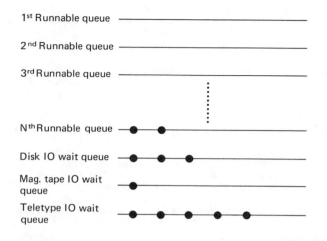

Since there are no application programs on the higher
queues, the scheduler decides to start running the one
at the front of the Nth queue.

Fig. R20(a)   A compute bound job in an interactive environment

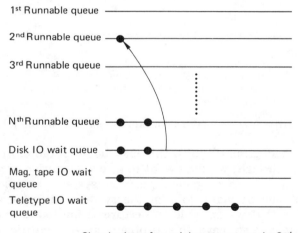

Shortly thereafter, a job reappears on the 2nd queue.
Should the scheduler take control away from the
job that was running on the Nth queue?

Fig. R20(b)   A compute bound job in an interactive environment

the lower-priority job will not be interrupted until it has been allowed to
execute for 2 seconds.

Even with a compromise of this sort, it is apparent that a job on the
lower scheduling queues may receive very poor service. Since the fundamental rule of this type of scheduling algorithm is to run the application
program at the front of the highest non-empty queue, we may *never* get
around to the programs on the bottom queues. If the jobs on these bottom

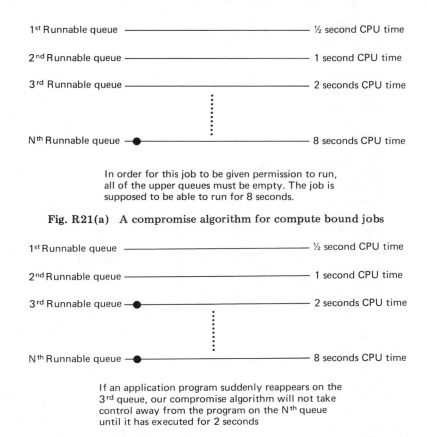

1st Runnable queue ———————————— ½ second CPU time

2nd Runnable queue ———————————— 1 second CPU time

3rd Runnable queue ———————————— 2 seconds CPU time

Nth Runnable queue ●——————————— 8 seconds CPU time

In order for this job to be given permission to run,
all of the upper queues must be empty. The job is
supposed to be able to run for 8 seconds.

Fig. R21(a)   A compromise algorithm for compute bound jobs

1st Runnable queue ———————————— ½ second CPU time

2nd Runnable queue ———————————— 1 second CPU time

3rd Runnable queue ●——————————— 2 seconds CPU time

Nth Runnable queue ●——————————— 8 seconds CPU time

If an application program suddenly reappears on the
3rd queue, our compromise algorithm will not take
control away from the program on the Nth queue
until it has executed for 2 seconds

Fig. R21(b)   A compromise algorithm for compute bound jobs

queues are truly "background" jobs, this may be acceptable. In many types
of on-line systems, though, we may want to give a *guarantee* of *some* service
to the bottom queues. In a general-purpose system where the on-line
application is just one of many jobs in the system, this approach may be
necessary to ensure that we are able to perform a limited amount of batch
throughput. We may also have this problem in a scientific time-sharing
environment, where the users with a 15-minute execution may stay on the
bottom queues for several hours before receiving any service.

There are several methods of ensuring that the background jobs will
receive some service:

1   In a scientific time-sharing environment where the application programs are
    swapped in and out of core, we can ensure that one or two of the lower-priority
    jobs (which are presumably compute-bound) remain in core at all times. This
    cuts down on the amount of memory available for the "interactive" application
    programs, and increases the amount of swapping. As a result, there are liable to
    be significant periods of time when the scheduler will be unable to execute any

interactive jobs, because all of the *runnable* interactive jobs have been swapped out of core. During the time that it is swapping the runnable interactive jobs back into core, the scheduler can execute the resident background job.

2 We could *force* the scheduling algorithm to occasionally run a job from the lower queues. For example, if we had four scheduling queues, we could guarantee that out of 15 passes through the scheduling algorithm, we would choose a job from the first queue eight times, a job from the second queue four times, a job from the third queue twice, and a job from the fourth queue once. To implement this type of algorithm, we could keep a counter in the scheduler, and increment it each time we are forced to reschedule. Our algorithm would then be as follows:

Scheduler counter (modulo 15)	Start looking for an application program in queue number:
0	1
1	2
2	1
3	2
4	1
5	3
6	1
7	4
8	1
9	2
10	1
11	2
12	1
13	3
14	1

3 We could devise an algorithm that would somehow increase the priority of application programs on the lower queues. One way of doing this is to declare a "general amnesty" for all "bad" programs that have been on the bottom queue for a certain length of time, as shown in Figure R22. This would give the job some service, but if it was truly "bad," it would quickly sink down into the nether regions of the scheduling queues again.

A more popular approach is the so-called "limited amnesty," or "parole" technique. As shown in Figure R23, a job which has languished on the bottom queue for a specified period of time is moved to the next higher queue; if it still does not receive service for some period of time, it is moved up again. With this approach, it seems more likely that we will not mix "good" jobs and "bad" jobs in the highest queues, but will still take note of the lack of service for the "bad" jobs. Note that this technique is easier to implement with the *priority number* scheme that we illustrated in Figure R9, since it allows us to pass through all of the application programs periodically and increment the priority numbers.

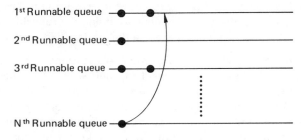
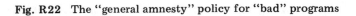

After a program has been on the bottom
queue for some period of time, it is moved
to the end of the highest queue.

Fig. R22 The "general amnesty" policy for "bad" programs

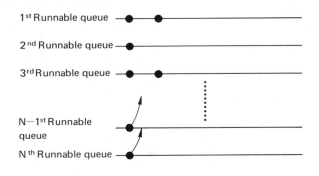
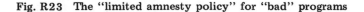

After an application program has remained on the
bottom queue for some period of time, it is moved
to the next higher queue. This same policy is used
for jobs on the N—1st queue, etc.

Fig. R23 The "limited amnesty policy" for "bad" programs

THE INPUT/OUTPUT ROUTINES

INTRODUCTION

In Chapter Q, we indicated the need for a *priority control* mechanism to prevent confusion and chaos within the operating system. Since the input/output routines are the cause of much of this confusion, it is only fitting that we examine them in more detail at this point in our discussion of operating systems.

Unfortunately, our discussion is forced to be somewhat vague and philosophical, because the precise nature of an input/output routine depends on the type of IO device, and the type of computer with which it interfaces. The disk IO routines within the operating system for the IBM System/360 bear little resemblance to the disk routines within the operating system for the NCR Century Series computers, and neither of these bear any resemblance to the card reader IO routines within a Burroughs B5500.

Nevertheless, we can identify the *functions* of an input/output routine in an operating system, and we can attempt to describe a *structure* which seems applicable to almost all IO routines. We will also be concerned with optimization of IO on certain types of devices, and with error recovery on the IO devices.

THE BASIC FUNCTIONS OF THE IO ROUTINES

We will assume throughout this chapter that the IO routines within the operating system have sole control over their respective IO devices. There are a few on-line systems in which the application programs are allowed to execute their own machine-language IO instructions, but this approach has several dangers:

1 When executed in "user mode" or "slave mode," the machine language IO instruction causes a trap to the operating system. The operating system must interpret this as a "legal" IO call, and then reexecute the instruction. All of this takes extra overhead.

2 It is not always possible for the operating system to thoroughly check the application program's IO call for errors. Thus, it is possible for the application program to issue a machine language IO instruction which might destroy files on the disk or cause physical damage to IO devices.

3 The operating system loses the opportunity to optimize the throughput on random access devices, and may lose the opportunity to overlap input/output with computation.

Thus, while this extra capability may be desired by the application programmer, almost all systems limit the access to the IO devices to the operating system itself. Thus, the application programs must call the operating system with a READ or WRITE (or GET and PUT, etc.) macro to specify the type of IO required. This, then, is one of the major functions of the IO routines: to receive requests from the application programs, in the form of a macro, and process them.

It follows that the other major responsibility of the IO routine is to control the IO device. This entails issuing the proper instructions to the device, handling interrupts, and checking for errors. It is this activity that is so unpredictable in nature, since the IO routine can rarely tell exactly how long it will take for the IO device to read or write a record.

Wherever possible, it should also be the responsibility of the IO routines to *maximize the throughput of the IO device*. We will describe some techniques for buffering IO in such a way that the IO device is less likely to go idle; on random-access devices, we can also *rearrange the order of IO requests* in an attempt to maximize the throughput.

Finally, the IO routines are responsible for any errors that may occur during the processing of IO requests for a particular device. In most cases, the error can be rectified by *retrying* the operation, but a serious error may require a more extensive error routine to be invoked.

THE CONCEPT OF OVERLAPPED IO

In the discussions that follow, we shall be attempting to overlap the processing of IO requests with the actual reading or writing of data by the IO device. In order for this to have any meaning, we must have a *queue of requests* for the device, as shown in Figure S1. At any instant of time, there are *three* IO requests in which we are interested: the Nth request, which has been finished by the IO device, and which may require some post-processing; the $N+1^{st}$ request, on which the IO device is currently working; and the $N+2^{nd}$ request, which the IO routines are preparing.

Regardless of any other aspect of optimization or interface with the application programs, the type of overlap shown in Figure S1 is very desirable. Wherever possible, we want to have the IO device and the central processor working at the same time, in order to increase the throughput of the entire system. Thus, when the $N+1^{st}$ activity has been finished on the IO device, we want to have already finished all of the preprocessing and "set-up" work for the $N+2^{nd}$ request, so that it can be started *immediately*.

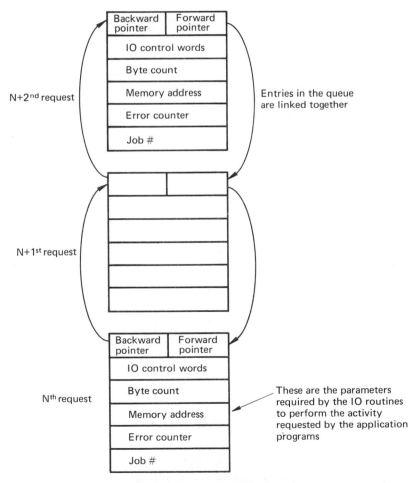

Fig. S1　A queue of IO requests

THE STRUCTURE AND ORGANIZATION
OF THE IO ROUTINES

As we mentioned briefly in Chapter P, there are two types of IO routines: one which puts requests into a queue, and one which takes requests out of the queue and processes them, as shown in Figure S2. For convenience, we will call the first type of IO routine a *trap* routine, and the second type an *interrupt* routine.

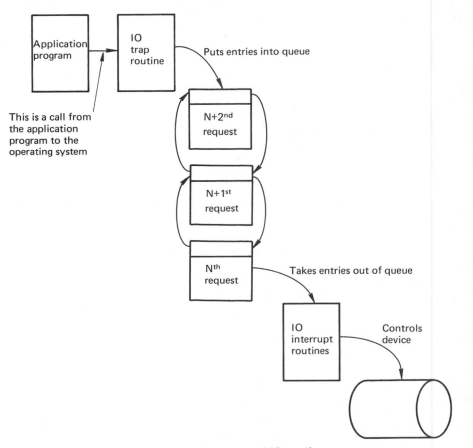

Fig. S2 The two types of IO routines

The trap routines get their name from the fact that they receive calls from the application programs—calls which cause a *trap* to the operating system. When the application program issues a READ or WRITE macro, the operating system gets control, and we assume that the appropriate IO routine processes the request. At this point, the IO trap routine has four duties to perform:

1 The trap routine must check to see that the request is *legal.* In the case of non-sharable devices, such as card readers, card punches, magnetic tape drives, and line printers, we should ensure that the device has been assigned to the application program already. By keeping a *device assignment table,* as shown in Figure S3, the operating system can prevent an application program from making an unauthorized access to another programs's IO device.

It is desirable to force the application program to deal with *logical device numbers,* rather than *physical device numbers.* This can be done on an individual program basis, as shown in Figure S4, or on a system basis, as shown in Figure S5. In either case, it allows the operating system and/or the computer operator to reconfigure the system in case one of the peripheral devices is not working, or has already been assigned by another application program.

In the case of a sharable device, such as a disk, drum, or data cell, it may be necessary to ensure that the application program is making a legal access to a record or a file. A better way of accomplishing this is to force the application program to call a file handling package (either within the operating system or a separate application package).

Drum	In use by system	0
Disk	Shared	1
Card reader	In use by job #3	2
Card punch	Not in use	3
Printer #1	In use by job #1	4
Printer #2	Does not exist on this system	5
Plotter	Not in use	6
Mag. tape #1	In use by system	7
Mag. tape #2	In use by Job #2	10
Mag. tape #3	In use by job #2	11
Mag. tape #4	In use by job #3	12
Mag. tape #5	In use by job #5	13
Mag. tape #6	In use by job #5	14

The index into this table is known as the *physical device number,* and may be a function of the manner in which the peripheral devices are attached to the system.

Fig. S3 Device assignment table

Logical device table for Job #1

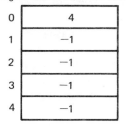

0	4
1	−1
2	−1
3	−1
4	−1

Logical device table for Job #2

0	10
1	11
2	−1
3	−1
4	−1

Logical device table for Job #3

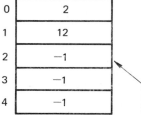

0	2
1	12
2	−1
3	−1
4	−1

An entry of −1 means that the logical device number has not been assigned by the job

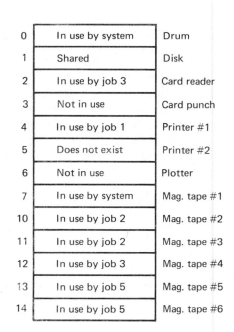

0	In use by system	Drum
1	Shared	Disk
2	In use by job 3	Card reader
3	Not in use	Card punch
4	In use by job 1	Printer #1
5	Does not exist	Printer #2
6	Not in use	Plotter
7	In use by system	Mag. tape #1
10	In use by job 2	Mag. tape #2
11	In use by job 2	Mag. tape #3
12	In use by job 3	Mag. tape #4
13	In use by job 5	Mag. tape #5
14	In use by job 5	Mag. tape #6

Fig. S4   Logical device tables on a program basis

Various other types of error checking may be necessary. The size of the record being transferred to or from the IO device should be checked to see that it is legal; the core address within the application program area should be checked to see that it is within reasonable limits; the *type* of IO might have to be checked (it might be illegal, on some systems, to read a magnetic tape at 1600 BPI density).

2 The second responsibility of the IO routine is to place the request in a queue, from which it will eventually be plucked and processed. In almost all cases, the trap routines place entries in the queue in a first-in-first-out fashion, as we showed in Figure S1. The trap routines could insert entries in the queue according to the scheduler priority of the application program that made the request, as shown in Figure S6, or according to any other reasonable priority classification. It is *preferable* to perform this ordering within the trap routine, since it executes at a very low priority level, whereas re-ordering performed by

The entries in this
table are physical
device numbers, as
listed in Figure S3.

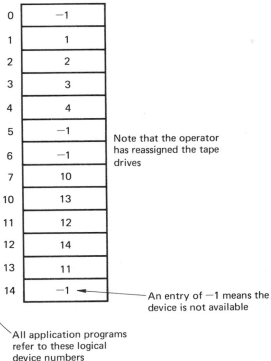

0	−1
1	1
2	2
3	3
4	4
5	−1
6	−1
7	10
10	13
11	12
12	14
13	11
14	−1

Note that the operator
has reassigned the tape
drives

An entry of −1 means the
device is not available

All application programs
refer to these logical
device numbers

Fig. S5   Logical device table on a system basis

the interrupt routine would have to take place at a higher priority level. The trouble is that the priorities are likely to be very dynamic, and may change after the trap routine has inserted the request in the queue. Thus, it is usually better for the trap routine to insert the request in a FIFO fashion and let the interrupt routine choose its next request based on whatever up-to-the-minute information it wants to use.

3 Next, the trap routine must start up the device if it is not currently busy. In most cases, there will be a number of entries in the queue, and the interrupt routine will automatically start working on the next request when it finishes the current one.

4 Finally, the trap routine must call the scheduler with an indication that the application program that made the call is in a "wait" state. The scheduler will then look through its queues for another application program to run. If the system is designed in such a way that the application program is not forced to wait for the completion of IO, the trap routine should return control to the program after completing the activities above.

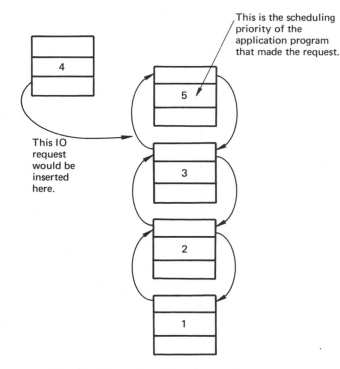

This is the scheduling priority of the application program that made the request.

This IO request would be inserted here.

Fig. S6 IO queue ordered by scheduler priority

The interrupt routines are usually somewhat more complicated than the trap routines. In a small on-line system, it is possible for all of the processing to be performed with the hardware interrupt structure disabled, but this is not desirable in a system where there are high-speed devices that must be serviced quickly, or where optimization of IO is desired. Thus, the interrupt routines often interface with a priority control structure, and execute with the hardware interrupt structure enabled.

In most cases, we can break the interrupt processing into two separate parts. A small amount of processing is done by an *interrupt service routine*, with the hardware interrupt structure disabled; most of the processing is done by an extension of this routine, which we will call the *interrupt extension routine*. The interrupt extension routine runs with the hardware interrupt structure enabled, under the aegis of the priority control program. As we see in Figure S7, it is expected that the interrupt service routine will require no more than 50-100 microseconds of processor time, while the interrupt extension routine may require several milliseconds of CPU time.

The processing performed in the interrupt service routine is shown in Figure S8. It must be remembered that the interrupt service routine is entered when the interrupt actually occurs for a particular device, and takes place with the hardware interrupt structure disabled. The routine first saves any registers that it intends to use—accumulators, index registers, and so

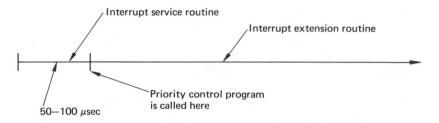

Interrupt service routine

Interrupt extension routine

Priority control program
is called here

50–100 μsec

Fig. S7   Time scale of interrupt service and interrupt extension routines

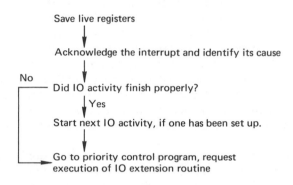

Save live registers

Acknowledge the interrupt and identify its cause

No

Did IO activity finish properly?

Yes

Start next IO activity, if one has been set up.

Go to priority control program, request
execution of IO extension routine

Fig. S8   Processing performed by the interrupt service routine

forth. The registers must be restored at the end of the routine, just prior to the call to the priority control routine. In practice, the IO routine often saves the live registers in the priority control program's area, so as to avoid an extra saving and restoring of the registers.

The next thing that must be done is to identify the cause of the interrupt. On some simple computers (of which the PDP-8 and the NCR Century Series are examples), *all* interrupts cause control to be transferred to one particular location. Thus, the interrupt routine must test various flags to see which IO device caused the interrupt. This becomes a simpler task on more sophisticated machines, where each device has its own interrupt location in the machine.

Having identified the device that caused the interrupt, the interrupt service routine must verify the successful completion of the IO task which it had earlier initiated. It is usually necessary to test various flags or IO status registers to see that there were no errors, or that the IO command was not rejected for some reason. *It is extremely important that the interrupt service routine ensure that the interrupt was, in fact, in response to an earlier command.* Regardless of the brand or type of computer, IO devices will occasionally cause "spurious" interrupts, which can send the IO routines into a frenzy of unpredictable activity. By keeping a flag to indicate whether it is expecting an interrupt, the service routine can tell whether or not to ignore the spurious interrupt.

Assuming that the current IO activity has now been finished, the interrupt service routine should immediately begin the next activity by issuing the appropriate machine instruction. As we mentioned before, our whole purpose in designing the IO routines in this fashion is to ensure the overlapping of IO with computation. Thus, we assume that the $N+1^{st}$ activity (i.e. the next read, or write, or print, or punch request) has already been set up, and is "ready to go."

In some cases, a request from the application program may involve more than one interrupt. If, for example, the program calls the operating system to read a record from disk, the IO routines may get an interrupt at the completion of the "seek," and another interrupt at the completion of the "read" operation. In any event, our major goal at this point is to issue the next command to the IO device as quickly as possible, so as to keep the device busy and so that we can overlap IO with computation.

As we see in Figure S8, the next activity is *not* started in the event of an error. In most cases, we will have to go through some error processing, and this can take place in the interrupt extension routine. In some cases, the interrupt service routine can proceed with the next IO operation, but the system designer must always beware of the read-after-write problem shown in Figure S9.

At this point, the interrupt service routine has performed all of its necessary processing, and hopefully within a very few microseconds. If there is any more processing to be done (which is usually the case), the interrupt service routine calls the priority control program, requesting permission to execute its extension routine, at a specified level of priority. As we saw in Chapter Q, the priority control program will then decide to grant permission to execute the extension routine, or it will decide to return control to the task that was executing at the time of the IO interrupt.

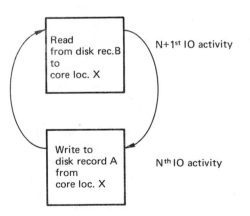

If there is an error in the Nth IO activity,
the interrupt service routine cannot go
on to the $N+1^{st}$ activity, or it will destroy
a record in core.

Fig. S9 The read-after-write problem

The processing performed by the interrupt extension routine is shown in the flowchart in Figure S10. It should be remembered that this routine executes with the hardware interrupts enabled, and is totally under the control of the priority control program.

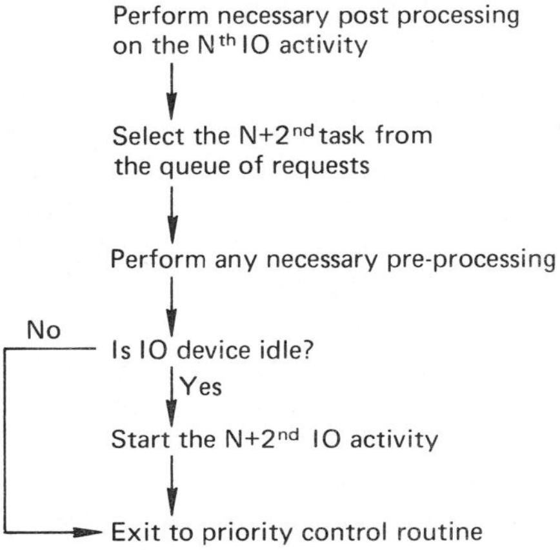

Perform necessary post processing
on the Nth IO activity

Select the N+2nd task from
the queue of requests

Perform any necessary pre-processing

No ─── Is IO device idle?

│Yes

Start the N+2nd IO activity

Exit to priority control routine

Fig. S10 Processing performed by the IO extension routine

The first task of the extension routine is to perform any necessary postprocessing, or clean-up work, for the Nth task—i.e. the one that just finished, and for which we just got an interrupt. The extension routine should check a flag to see whether there was an error associated with the request, in which case some special processing (to be discussed below) may have to be invoked. Assuming that there were no errors, the extension routine should then take steps to "wake up" the application program that was waiting for the completion of the IO. As we discussed in Chapter R, this can be done by having the extension routine reset a "waiting bit" in the application program's status word; alternatively, the extension routine could make a subroutine call to the scheduler to change the state code, or reset the bit in the status word.

Finally, the IO extension routine may have some core memory to "clean up" as part of its postprocessing of the Nth IO activity. As we saw in Figure S1, the queue of requests consists of small blocks of core, in which the details of each request are kept. Now that the Nth activity has been completed, the queue entry is no longer needed, and could be released for other uses. The IO which has just transpired may have involved buffers which can now be released for other uses.

Having finished with the Nth IO activity, the interrupt extension routine must choose the request that will become the $N+2^{nd}$ activity (remember that the IO device is currently working on the $N+1^{st}$ activity while all of this processing is taking place). The $N+2^{nd}$ activity may be chosen from the queue of requests, in a first-in-first-out fashion, or may involve some optimization. Having chosen it, the extension routine then performs any necessary preprocessing, or "set-up" work. It may be necessary to convert from a logical device number to a physical device number, or to calculate the necessary IO status registers or channel command words that will have to be loaded when the activity is to be started. The point here is that we want all necessary calculations to be done at this time, so that when we get the interrupt for the N+1st IO activity, we will be ready to start the N+2nd one immediately.

When all of this processing has been finished, the interrupt extension routine exits to the priority control program, which then decides what to do next. It is possible, of course, that the N+1st activity finished while the interrupt extension routine was performing its postprocessing for the Nth activity and preprocessing for the N+2nd activity. This unhappy set of circumstances may be the result of a delay in the processing of the extension routine because the priority control program felt there were more important things to do, because unusual circumstances increased the processing time required by the extension routine, or because the IO device itself happened to finish very quickly.

At any rate, the consequences are shown in Figure S11. When the N+1st IO activity finishes, it interrupts the extension routine which was in the midst of setting up the N+2nd activity. The interrupt service routine does its limited amount of processing, as we discussed above, *but does not find another request waiting to be started.* The interrupt service routine does not bother checking to see whether this is the result of an empty queue, or because it got ahead of the extension routine—all it cares about is that it has no new request to start up. As a result, the only thing it does is to call the priority control program with a request to execute the extension routine for the N+1st activity. Note that the priority control program will not honor this request immediately, since it is of the same priority level as the extension routine that was executing at the time of the interrupt. Thus, control is returned to the partially processed extension routine, with another request for it in the waiting list. The extension routine finishes its set-up work for the N+2nd task, notices that the IO device is idle, and takes the necessary steps to start it up again (by executing the same subroutine that the trap routine called when it found that the device was idle). It finally exits to the priority control program, which will then notice another request for the same extension routine in the waiting list.

OPTIMIZATION IN THE IO ROUTINES

For serial input/output devices, there is not much that can be done in the way of optimization. If an application program calls the operating system to read cards from the card reader, there is no way for the operating system to rearrange the order in which cards are read; similarly, there is no reasonable way for the input/output routines to rearrange the order in which lines are printed on a high-speed printer.

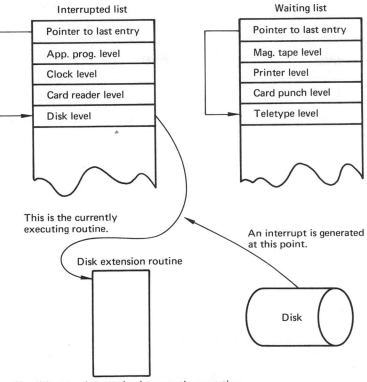

Interrupted list

| Pointer to last entry |
| App. prog. level |
| Clock level |
| Card reader level |
| Disk level |

Waiting list

| Pointer to last entry |
| Mag. tape level |
| Printer level |
| Card punch level |
| Teletype level |

This is the currently
executing routine.

An interrupt is generated
at this point.

Disk extension routine

Disk

The disk extension routine is currently executing
and setting up the N+2nd disk activity when the
disk causes an interrupt.

Fig. S11(a) Timing problems between the interrupt service routine and
the interrupt extension routine

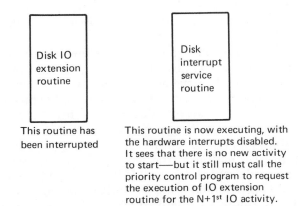

Disk IO
extension
routine

Disk
interrupt
service
routine

This routine has
been interrupted

This routine is now executing, with
the hardware interrupts disabled.
It sees that there is no new activity
to start—but it still must call the
priority control program to request
the execution of IO extension
routine for the N+1st IO activity.

Fig. S11(b) Timing problems between the interrupt service routine and
the interrupt extension routine

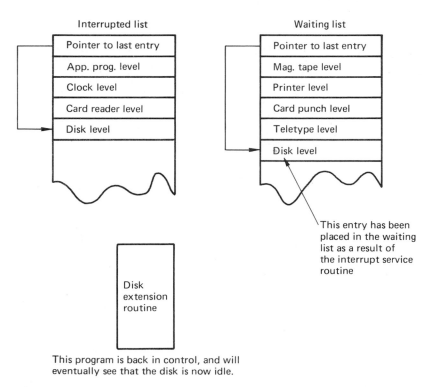

Fig. S11(c)   Timing problems between the interrupt service routine and
the interrupt extension routine

Our interest with optimization is usually associated with *random-access* devices, disks and drums in particular. In addition to being random-access devices, they are *shared* devices. Thus, it is possible that many different application programs may have called the operating system to perform a read or write on a disk, and the operating system is not forced to perform the requests in the order they are received.

We must be very sure that we understand the purpose of optimization on the disk or drum, since it appears to cause a great deal of concern among application programmers. The average application programmer, it must be remembered, is only concerned with *his* program and his disk requests, and is interested in improvement of *system* throughput only if it does not interfere with the service that his own program receives.

In the area of disk and drum optimization, the application programmer's satisfaction is a direct function of the length of time his program must wait for a record to be read from the device. If he took the trouble to keep track of such things, the programmer might notice that his response time was roughly as shown in Figure S12, in a system without optimization. This is a typical *exponential curve*, which shows that the mean response time is one second, with relatively small probabilities that the response time will be

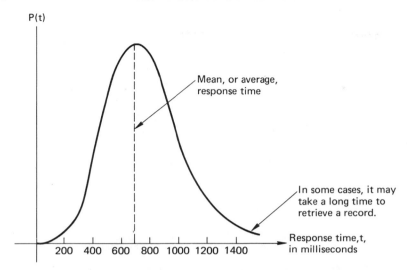

Fig. S12   A programmer's file response time in an unoptimized system

either very short or very long (i.e. the standard deviation is satisfactorily small). The programmer is likely to be fairly *happy* if an optimization scheme can result in a response time graph similar to that shown in Figure S13, for it has reduced his mean response time without significantly affecting the standard deviation. On the other hand, he is likely to be extremely *unhappy* with an optimization scheme that produces the results shown in Figure S14, in which the standard deviation has been significantly increased. In the latter case, the programmer will notice that his READ

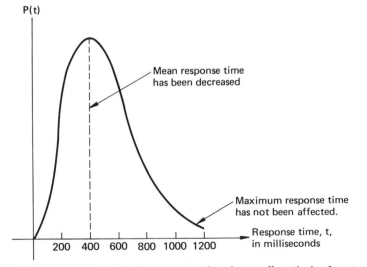

Fig. S13   A programmer's file response time in a well-optimized system

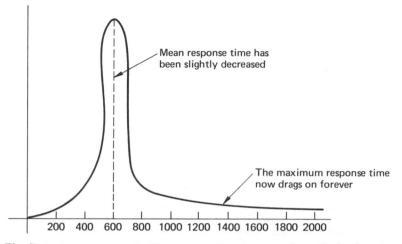

Fig. S14   A programmer's file response time in a **poorly-optimized system**

macro is processed in a period of time that is shorter, *on the average*, than in the non-optimized system—but this shorter response is the result of some *very* short responses, and some *very* long responses. Since the file response time will eventually be felt at the terminal, the user will end up with a very inconsistent response time (i.e. very fast responses to some inputs, and very sluggish responses to other inputs) and will be very unhappy with the system.

This gives us a very important clue as to the type of optimization we want to build into the disk routines or drum routines. The purpose of this optimization is to reduce the mean response time for requests, or, from a throughput point of view, to increase the average number of requests that we can process per minute. At the same time, we do not want the optimization to increase seriously the *maximum* response time felt by any of the application programs.

In the case of fixed head drums, the optimization strategy is very simply stated: the IO routines should always attempt to perform the request that involves the minimum latency time, or, as Denning puts it,† the shortest access time. This is illustrated in Figure S15, and is an intuitively reasonable policy. Using extremely sloppy mathematics (and with apologies to Professor Denning), we can get a feeling for the order of magnitude of improvement with this optimization scheme: if the drum is N sectors in circumference, then N requests will, in the ideal case, require only one revolution of the drum. If those same N requests were performed on a first-come-first-serve basis, each would require an average of 1/2 revolution of the drum, for a total of N/2 revolutions. We thus see that the "shortest access time" policy yields

---

† Peter J. Denning, *Effects of Scheduling on File Memory Operations*, Proceedings of the AFIPS 1967 Spring Joint Computer Conference, Volume 30 (Washington, D.C.: Thompson Book Company, 1967) pages 9-21

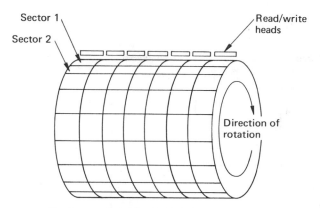

Sector 1

Sector 2

Read/write heads

Direction of rotation

The best optimization is to choose a request
from the sector closest to the read/write heads

Fig. S15 Optimization strategy for a drum

an improvement on the order of N/2 to 1—which can be extremely significant.

The optimization is implemented by having one queue for each sector on the drum, as shown in Figure S16. When an application program calls the operating system, the trap routine places the request in the appropriate queue. The interrupt extension routines simply move from one queue to the next, taking requests from each individual queue in a first-in-first-out basis. This has the extremely important benefit of *not increasing the maximum response time felt by any of the application programs!* Since the drum revolves under the read/write heads independently of the optimization algorithm, the only delay that will be felt by any particular request is due to *other entries in the same queue* (i.e. from the same sector)—but since each queue is handled in a first-in-first-out fashion, the request is not "discriminated" against in any way. At the same time, the *average* response time is significantly decreased.

The only disadvantage with the drum optimization scheme is that the IO routines are forced to issue a read or write for the N+1st sector *very quickly* after the end-of-record interrupt has been received for the Nth sector—often in a matter of a few microseconds. There has been at least one case where the optimization produced *worst case* results (i.e. a *full revolution* of latency time for each request) because the command to read a record from the N+1st sector was issued just after the sector had started passing under the read/write heads. The optimization algorithm can compensate for this problem by reading alternate sectors, if necessary.

On movable head disks, the situation becomes somewhat more complex. In addition to the delay caused by rotation of the disk platters, we have to contend with "seek time" caused by movement of the read/write heads to the proper cylinder of the disk. The shortest-access-time-first policy still yields the greatest reduction in *mean* response time, though the reduction is

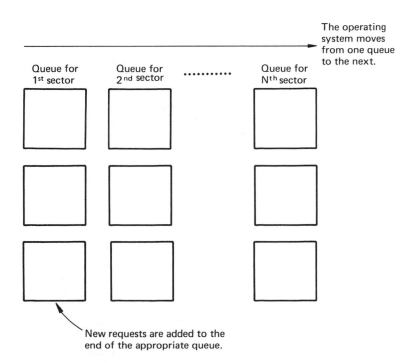

Fig. S16   Implementation of the drum optimization scheme

not so dramatic as it was with the drum. Even worse, the *maximum* response time is greatly increased, for as we see in Figure S17, there is a chance that the read/write heads may always find requests on neighboring cylinders, and may take a long time to decide to move to a request on a distant cylinder. This is somewhat akin to the problem we mentioned in our discussion of scheduling algorithms in Chapter R: a large number of interactive jobs on the upper scheduling queues may effectively prevent the scheduler from ever servicing the jobs on the lower queues.

Just as we found that a "compromise algorithm" was necessary in the scheduler, it is desirable to develop a "compromise optimization algorithm" for the disk. This policy is shown in Figure S18 and consists of "combing" the disk—i.e. moving the disk read/write heads from the outer cylinders of the disk gradually inward, picking up requests in transit. The policy is implemented with the queues shown in Figure S19, and we could improve the optimization by ordering the requests in each cylinder queue in such a way as to minimize the *rotation time* on the cylinder. In any event, the "combing" algorithm yields a *reduced*, but not necessarily *minimized*, mean response time. At the same time, it does not seriously degrade the maximum response time felt by the application program (although it does increase the maximum response time to some extent, contrary to the case with the fixed head drum).

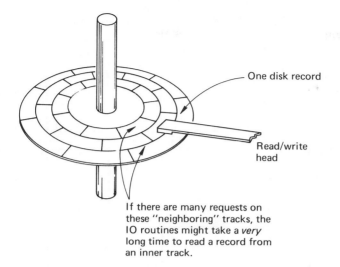

One disk record

Read/write head

If there are many requests on these "neighboring" tracks, the IO routines might take a *very* long time to read a record from an inner track.

Fig. S17　Disadvantages of the shortest-access-time-first policy on the disk

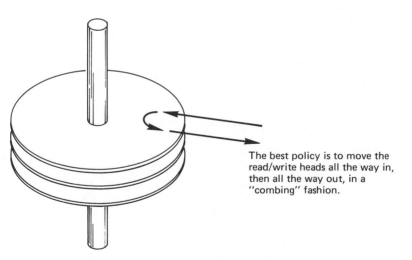

The best policy is to move the read/write heads all the way in, then all the way out, in a "combing" fashion.

Fig. S18　A compromise disk optimization policy

ERROR RETRY AND RECOVERY

Most input/output errors turn out to be "transient" and intermittent. They are more likely to be found in the electromechanical parts of the peripheral device than in the electronic parts, and may be the result of dust, dirt, wear and tear, or poor service.

The most important point about the IO errors is that they can usually be *recovered*. That is, if the IO routines attempt the same read or write *again*,

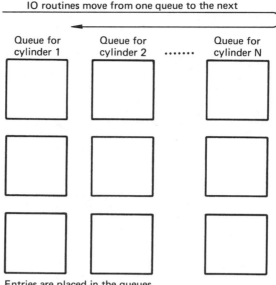

Fig. S19   Implementation of the disk optimization policy

they will often succeed. A common technique for retrying the operation is shown in Figure S20, in which an unsuccessful IO activity is simply requeued and attempted in the normal fashion. For various reasons (the read-after-write problem being the most significant), it is often desirable to force the IO routines to retry the operation immediately on the IO device, without going on to perform other requests on the same device.

There is usually some reasonable limit to the number of times that the read or write should be attempted before giving up. In the case of a *write* operation, it is sometimes important to give up after five or ten attempts, because repeated attempts may *force* the information to be written on a magnetic surface, but it may prove to be unreadable within a few minutes or hours. In the case of *read* operations, a few retries are often sufficient to dislodge a dust particle that may have caused a parity error, and a large number of retries may permanently damage the recording surface. Most on-line operating systems retry the IO activity either three times, five times, or ten times, depending on the whim of the system designer. There is nothing particularly unique about the number three (except for its religious significance, and the fact that it is prime!), or the number five, but these seem to be in the right range.

The important thing is that the rest of the on-line system should not come to a screeching halt while the IO routines are retrying an operation. The advantage of requeueing a faulty request for a disk or drum record is that other application programs can continue to perform their IO without suffering poor response; on other devices, this approach may not be feasible

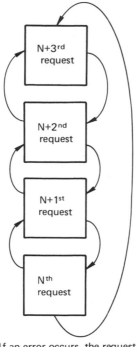

N+3rd request

N+2nd request

N+1st request

Nth request

If an error occurs, the request
is placed at the end of the
queue, and re-tried in the
normal sequence of events.

Fig. S20   Requeueing an IO activity when errors occur

or relevant. In any event, the entire retry operation should be performed within the priority control structure, so that other activities can continue to execute.

In the case of non-recoverable IO errors, more drastic action may have to be taken. Since a great deal of program logic may be involved, it is desirable to incorporate it into a non-resident operating system routine, or perhaps even into an application program. Thus, if an IO routine finds that it cannot read a card from the card reader, it could turn control over to an application routine which would analyze the error and carry on a dialogue with the computer operator—while the rest of the system continued running in its normal fashion. Alternatively, we could pass the error back to the application program that called for the IO in the first place, and let *it* figure out what to do!

All of this assumes that the IO error is not catastrophic. If we find that the magnetic tape containing all of our library routines has been stretched and creased beyond recognition (a calamity which must be suffered by every novice before he can call himself a *real* programmer!) or if the disk directories suddenly become unreadable, the simple procedures described above will not be sufficient. In these cases, it is necessary to invoke the *system* error routines described in Chapter U.

THE CORE ALLOCATION ROUTINES

INTRODUCTION

Aside from the central processor itself, the most valuable resource in an on-line system is memory. On most systems, memory must be allocated in a dynamic fashion, since the *potential* demands far exceed the available amount of memory. As a result, we need subroutines within the operating system to allocate memory properly to the application programs and to other parts of the operating system.

Before describing the types of core allocation, we must first make sure that we understand the various uses of memory within an on-line system. These are as follows:

1 Permanent operating system subroutines, tables and storage.

2 Infrequently used operating system subroutines. These may include error routines for some IO devices, IO routines for infrequently used devices (card punch, X-Y plotter, etc.), console typewriter routines for communication with the console operator, and so forth.

3 Frequently used application programs. In a general-purpose scientific time-sharing system, none of the programs may fall into this category; in a dedicated system, some of the application programs may be so frequently used that they tend to stay in core at all times.

4 Infrequently used application programs.

5 Small blocks of memory for IO buffers, queues, floating tables, and so forth.

On some systems, it is possible to make a *fixed* allocation of memory. That is, we can set aside a fixed area for each of the possible demands on core, and there will never be a need for *allocation* of memory during the processing of the system. This approach works best for small systems that have ample memory, but is not applicable to most on-line systems.

There are many cases, though, where it makes sense to make a fixed allocation of memory for the operating system, as shown in Figure T1. The various IO routines, the scheduler, the priority control program and any other necessary subroutines are assigned to a permanent area of memory, although this arrangement may be changed from one computer installation to another. Through a process known as *system generation*, or *system building*, each installation chooses the necessary operating system subroutines for its particular hardware and software configuration.

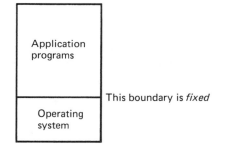

Fig. T1   Fixed allocation of memory for the operating system

Even with this relatively fixed allocation of memory for the operating system, there are liable to be some dynamic requirements. The major contributors to this demand are the input/output routines, which need *buffers* and *queue entries*. As we see in Figure T2, we can take the approach of *dedicating* the necessary IO buffers to each device, but this usually turns out to be extremely wasteful of memory. It is more common to set aside an entire area of memory, as shown in Figure T3, and dynamically allocate small blocks of buffers as they are needed. We elaborate upon this below.

ALLOCATION OF NON-RESIDENT APPLICATION PROGRAMS

The allocation of memory to application programs is usually a more difficult task than that of allocating core to the operating system. Depending on the type of system, there may be any one of the following philosophies used to allocate memory to the application programs:

1   We can have a completely fixed allocation of memory, as we showed in Figure T1. As we pointed out before, this is usually impractical, except on dedicated systems.

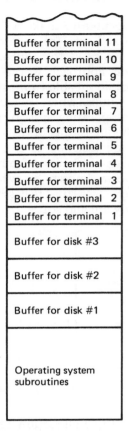

Fig. T2   Dedicated IO buffers in the operating system

2   We can allocate a fixed amount of memory to an application program when it first starts running. The amount of memory required can be specified by the computer operator or the application programmer. If an attempt is made to allocate more core than is currently available, the operating system will refuse to honor it.

3   We can allocate an initial amount of memory to an application program when it first starts running, and then allow it to grow or shrink dynamically. Again, the operating system can refuse to honor any request for core if it is not available.

4   We can allocate either a fixed or dynamic amount of memory to each application program, and use a disk or drum as an extension of memory. For convenience, we will refer to this extension of memory as a drum (although it could be any device), and we will refer to the process of moving an application program from core memory to drum, or from drum to core memory, as *swapping*. This concept allows us to allocate memory to a large number of application programs, though we generally limit each individual program to an amount equal to or less than the area of memory not being used by the

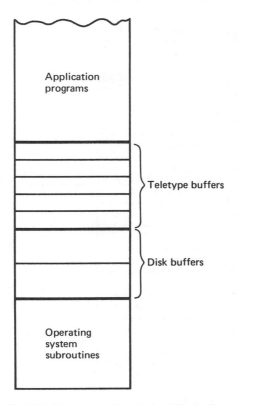

Fig. T3 Dynamic allocation of IO buffers

operating system. With *virtual memory* (or *paging,* as it is sometimes called), we can even remove this limitation: an application program may be allowed to allocate a truly phenomenal amount of memory, even though it exceeds the amount of physical memory on the machine.

Regardless of the philosophy that is chosen, the operating system must keep track of the areas of core memory which are currently available for use. This usually becomes far simpler if we allocate core in fairly large, fixed-size blocks of 512 words, 1,024 words, 4,096 bytes, or some other convenient unit. The size of these blocks, or *pages*, is often dictated by hardware features, such as the relocation registers and protection registers that we described in Chapter C. If 512 words is the smallest amount of memory that the hardware can relocate or protect, then it makes sense to allocate memory in those units.

With this approach, we can describe the availability of memory with a *core map*, as shown in Figure T4. This table has an entry for each block of core and basically describes the manner in which memory is being used. As we see in Figure T4, the high order bit of each entry indicates whether the page is in use or not; the next bit indicates whether the page is "clean," or

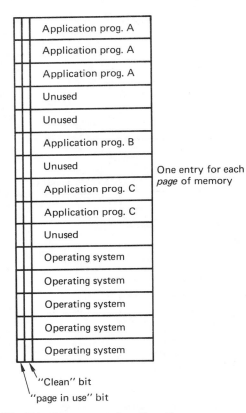

Application prog. A
Application prog. A
Application prog. A
Unused
Unused
Application prog. B
Unused
Application prog. C
Application prog. C
Unused
Operating system
Operating system
Operating system
Operating system
Operating system

One entry for each *page* of memory

"Clean" bit
"page in use" bit

Fig. T4   A core map for allocating core memory

read-only (if so, that area of memory can be reclaimed without swapping, since we presumably have another copy of the page on disk or drum). If the page is in use, we may also want to indicate which application program is using the memory.

When an application program indicates that it needs some core, the operating system can check the core map to see if a sufficient amount of memory is available. If so, the table can be marked to indicate that the core has been allocated. Similarly, when an application program terminates, or when it dynamically releases some memory, the operating system changes the appropriate entries to indicate that the pages are "free" again.

Another approach to this area is to allocate *variable-sized* pages of memory to the application programs. This is certainly a reasonable approach in a system where the hardware protection and relocation registers allow one to work on the word level, as is the situation on machines like the Burroughs B5500 and B6500 computers; it may also be a reasonable approach on any system where core memory is at a premium. In this case, we need two tables, each of which is variable in length. The first table is aptly called a *free list* and contains one entry for each variable-length block of core. As we see in Figure T5(a), it is customary to keep this table ordered by core address,

Beginning
core address   # of words

Beginning core address	# of words
26,771	51,007
24,116	1011
15,476	6037
15,123	234
10,267	4032
10,076	32
10,015	10
7447	201
7260	17
7173	15
7004	46
5735	602
5204	17
5120	3
4076	103

The table is ordered
by core address

This indicates the
number of words
available in the
block

Fig. T5(a)   The free list for variable-sized pages

though Randell [2] suggests that it might also be kept ordered according to
the size of the available memory block, as shown in Figure T5(b). The
second table, as illustrated in Figure T6, is an *occupied list*, and shows the
amount and location of memory being used by the application program.

We could theoretically perform our memory allocation without the
occupied list: all of the memory not represented by the free list could be
assumed to be occupied by some application program. Unfortunately, the
operating system cannot always count on the application programs to behave
reasonably, and we do need some way of reclaiming an application program's
memory in case it aborts abruptly or refuses to give up any of the memory
that it has been hoarding. The value of the occupied list is thus not so much
that it tells us which memory is occupied, but which application program is
using different areas of memory.

When an application program calls for more core memory, we often have
a problem deciding upon the best way to fulfill the request. One approach
would be to search through the free list for the block of memory that is
closest to the size that we need. This approach, known as the "best fit"
technique, requires that we search through the *entire* free list, looking for

Beginning core address	# of words
26,771	51,007
15,476	6037
10,267	4032
24,116	1011
5,735	602
15,123	234
7447	201
4076	103
7004	46
10,076	32
7260	17
5204	17
7173	15
10,015	10
5120	3

Note that this table is ordered by the size of the core
block. This might minimize the amount of time required
to allocate a block of memory, but some overhead would
be required to keep the list ordered.

Fig. T5(b)   An alternate form of the free list

the *smallest* block of available memory that is large enough to fill the request. The best fit technique is illustrated in Figures T7(a) and T7(b).

As we see in Figure T7(b), there is a significant chance that the best-fit approach will lead to *fragmentation*, also referred to as *checker-boarding*, or *fracturing*. Fragmentation is one of the many nightmares that face every operating system designer; it occurs whenever we have large numbers of non-contiguous "pieces" of memory, as shown in Figure T8.

At first glance, it would appear that the amount of fragmentation might be decreased somewhat if the core allocation routines simply took the *first* piece of available memory in the free list, as illustrated in Figures T9(a) and T9(b). Thus, the core allocation routines would begin examining at the low end of the free list, and stop whenever a sufficiently large block of memory was found.

There are a number of interesting characteristics of this "first fit" algorithm, as it has come to be called by Knuth [1] and others. It appears that the core allocation *overhead* is less with this approach than with the "best fit" approach, since the core allocation routines will probably not have to search all the way through the list. With the "best fit" technique, we *always* have to search the *entire* list to find the smallest item, unless we keep the list ordered by block size, as shown in Figure T5(b) (which is not usually

Beginning core address	# words	Program ID
25,770	1,001	Job 13
25,127	641	Job 3
23,535	361	Job 1
15,357	117	Job 4
14,521	402	Job 5
14,321	200	Job 9
10,130	137	Job 2
10,025	51	Job 11
7,650	145	Job 6
7,210	50	Job 14
7,052	121	Job 8
6,537	245	Job 7
5,223	412	Job 10
5,123	61	Job 12
4,201	717	Job 15
0	4,076	Operating system

Note that this table, together with the free list, completely describes the manner in which memory is being used.

Fig. T6   The occupied list for variable sized pages

done, since the overhead of keeping the list ordered is likely to be quite high).

Another interesting feature of the "first fit" core allocation technique is that the fragmentation it produces is not likely to be quite so bad. In Figure T9(b), for example, we notice that the core allocation routines have found an available block of memory, but the resulting "fragment" of memory is still reasonably large. With the "best fit" approach, we are much more likely to keep shaving off *small* fragments of memory, as we saw in Figure T7(b).

The only problem with the "first fit" technique is that it will tend to concentrate its efforts at the low end of the free list, since that is where it begins its search. As a result, we often find that the first several entries in the free list consist of small fragments of memory, while the upper end of the free list has scarcely been touched. This also means that the "first fit" technique is likely to require more overhead as the system runs longer and longer, since it will have to search further and further into the free list before finding a block of the correct size.

To correct this problem, we can make our core allocation routines work in a *cyclic* fashion, as shown in Figure T9(c). This approach, referred to as a "modified" first fit by Knuth, requires the core allocation routines to remember where the last block of storage was found, and then begin the next search from that point. This approach tends to reduce the overhead, and spreads the fragmentation over the entire free list.

Note that fragmentation can also occur in systems where we allocate

Beginning core address	# words
26,771	51,007
24,116	1,011
15,476	6,037
15,123	234
10,267	4,032
10,076	32
10,015	10
7,447	201
7,260	17
7,173	15
7,004	46
5,735	602
5,204	17
5,120	3
4,076	103

Assume that we have a request for 200 words of memory. In this case, though, our core allocation routines search the *entire* free list for a "best fit"

Fig. T7(a)   Scanning the free list for the smallest available block

memory in units of pages. In addition to the problem of not having enough contiguous pages, however, we also have the problem of wasted memory within each page. If, for example, the application program requires 493 words of memory, the operating system allocates 512 words, and everyone conveniently forgets the 19 unused words of memory. In a variable-page system, the operating system allocates *exactly* 493 words, and records the 19 unused words in its free list.

This simple example illustrates a point which is usually true in on-line systems as well as batch systems: the amount of fragmentation is usually a function of the type of memory requests that can be made by the application programs. In a system where the application program is only allowed to allocate memory in units of 1,024 words, we are not likely to have very many "pieces" of memory that are floating around the system, but we are really fooling ourselves, since the application programs are probably not making full use of their 1,024-word pages. In fact, Randell [2] points out that this *internal* fragmentation (i.e. the fragmentation resulting from the application program's inability to make full use of the fixed page size) can easily outweigh the savings in *external* fragmentation (i.e. the fragmentation caused by an insufficient number of contiguous pages).

Beginning
core address   # words

Beginning core address	# words
26,771	51,007
24,116	1,011
15,476	6,037
15,123	234
10,267	4,032
10,076	32
10,015	10
7,647	1
7,260	17
7,173	15
7,004	46
5,735	602
5,204	17
5,120	3
4,076	103

Note that the "best" block of available memory
was found at location 7447. After allocating 200
words, we are left with a block that is only 1
word long.

Fig. T7(b) Scanning the free list for the smallest available block

Fragmentation is one of the many aspects of operating systems that are
not fully understood. As some researchers at the University of Virginia point
out [3], it is difficult to develop any good strategies for avoiding
fragmentation without knowing the types of memory requests that will be
made by the application programs. As one might expect, the manner in
which memory is used differs widely from one system to another: the
statistics reported by the University of Virginia on their B5500 differed
radically from the results found on a time-sharing system at the System
Development Corporation [6]. This is of great concern to the system
designer, for he rarely has any control over the manner in which the
application programmers will allocate memory (an exception being the
Burroughs computers, where most of the memory allocation is essentially
done at the request of the compilers).

On most systems, some form of fragmentation is bound to occur sooner
or later. There is general agreement that the "best fit" technique will cause a
worse kind of fragmentation, and most systems seem to use the "cyclic"
first-fit technique that we illustrated in Figure T9(c). Regardless of the
technique, though, we want to ensure that fragmentation, when it does
occur, does not cripple the system. It is *extremely* desirable to be able to

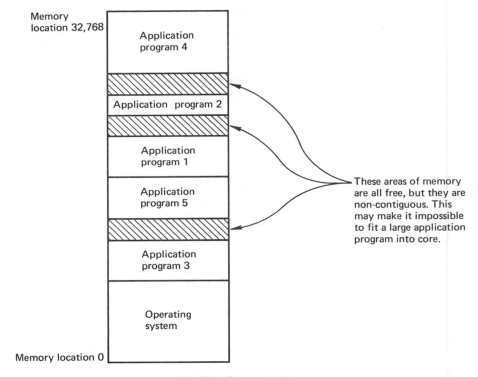

Memory location 32,768

Memory location 0

These areas of memory are all free, but they are non-contiguous. This may make it impossible to fit a large application program into core.

Fig. T8   Fragmentation

move the application programs around in order to consolidate space. On a swapping system, we can do this by swapping a program out of one area of memory, and back into another area, as shown in Figure T10. Even in a non-swapping system, the core allocation routines can occasionally "shuffle" all of the application programs into a more compact arrangement.

There are two different philosophies about the "shuffling" or "garbage collection" activity. It is occasionally suggested that the application programs should be moved as soon as a new block of memory becomes available, as shown in Figure T11. This would have the effect of keeping all of the available memory in a contiguous area, as shown in Figure T11(b). However, it could involve a tremendous amount of overhead if the programs allocate and release memory frequently.

The philosophy that is used more often is to perform "shuffling" or "garbage collection" *only when necessary*. Thus, when an application program releases a block of memory, we can update our free list, but there is no point in moving the application programs around. *As long as new requests for memory can be fulfilled*, there does not seem to be any point in shuffling memory. However, when it appears that memory has become too fragmented to fill any more requests, the operating system can reclaim all of the small fragments of memory with *one* "shuffling" activity.

In order to ensure that the operating system will be able to move the

Beginning core address	# words
26,771	51,007
24,116	1,011
15,476	6,037
15,123	234
10,267	4,032
10,076	32
10,015	10
7,447	201
7,260	17
7,173	15
7,004	46
5,735	602
5,204	17
5,120	3
4,076	103

Suppose we had a request for 200 words, and that we begin looking through the free list from the low end of memory. Since we are looking for the first available block of memory, it will be allocated from the block starting at 5735

Fig. T9(a) Scanning the free list for the first available block

application programs around, it is necessary that they be prevented from calculating any *absolute* machine addresses. If the application program is relocated with a base register or paging registers *that are not accessible* to the application program, the operating system can move it elsewhere by simply changing the contents of the registers. If, however, the application program has been loaded into a *particular* area of memory, or if its relocation is accomplished with index registers or base registers that the application program itself can read, then fragmentation is a certainty.

In some cases, the application program is not to blame for the fragmentation effect. If it calls for IO, the operating system may place the IO buffers in the application program area, and read data directly into (or write data directly from) the application program area. Once the IO has begun, the application program cannot be moved until the transfer of data has been completed. In the case of teletype input, this might be a considerable period of time.

Thus far, the core allocation activities we have described require two subroutines in the operating system: one to *get* memory, and one to *release*

26,771	51,007
24,116	1,011
15,476	6,037
15,123	234
10,267	4,032
10,076	32
10,015	10
7,447	201
7,260	17
7,173	15
7,004	46
6,135	402
5,204	17
5,120	3
4,076	103

 The 200 words of memory was taken from this area.

Note that memory is now more fragmented. If we have a request for 600 words of memory, we will have to search all the way up to 10,267

Fig. T9(b)   Scanning the free list for the first available block

memory. Three different forms of the GETMEM routine are shown in Figures T12(a), T12(b), and T12(c), corresponding to the "best fit," the "first fit," and the cyclic "first fit" techniques we discussed above. The RELMEM routine is shown in Figure T12(d).

If there is not enough room for a new application program or for a program that wants to expand, some algorithm must be invoked to obtain more space (unless, of course, we want to take the simple approach of *refusing* the request). In some systems, it is desirable to allow the application programs to participate in this decision by controlling their own overlays and swapping, in which case we need only provide a few simple macros. In most cases, though, the operating system performs the swapping without the advice and consent of the application program. It is normal for an *entire* application program, or job, to be written out to the swapping drum.

CORE ALLOCATION FOR PAGING MACHINES

The problem of core allocation and swapping is much more subtle on virtual machines, where individual *pages* or *segments* of a program can be removed at will by the operating system. The phenomenon of swapping a page out of memory just before it is needed is very common, and has been

26,771	51,007
24,116	1,011
15,476	6,037
15,123	234
10,267	4,032
10,076	32
10,015	10
7,447	201
7,260	17
7,173	15
7,004	46
6,135	402 ←
5,204	17
5,120	3
4,076	103

Having allocated 200 words of memory in Figure T9(b),
our core allocation routines can keep a pointer to the
free list entry from which the memory was allocated.
On the *next* call to the core allocation routines, we can
begin our search from this point. This tends to spread
the allocated memory more evenly through the free
list.

Fig. T9(c)   A cyclic first fit core allocation technique

affectionately dubbed *thrashing*. In order to understand how thrashing may
be avoided, we must first examine the techniques used by the core allocation
routines in many paging systems.

It is rather difficult to give a general description of the manner in which
operating systems use paging hardware, partly because the paging hardware is
different on every machine. Table T1 lists some of the characteristics of a
few of the more popular third generation paging computers, and it is
apparent that the machines are all radically different. They seem to fall into
three major categories:

1   Machines with a variable page size and a theoretically unlimited virtual memory,
    such as the Burroughs B5500 and B6500.

2   Machines with a virtual memory *smaller* than the physical memory, such as the
    SDS-940 and the GE-485. On these machines, paging was essentially added as an
    afterthought.

3   Machines with a virtual memory *larger* than or *equal* to the physical memory,
    such as the GE-645 and the IBM 360/67.

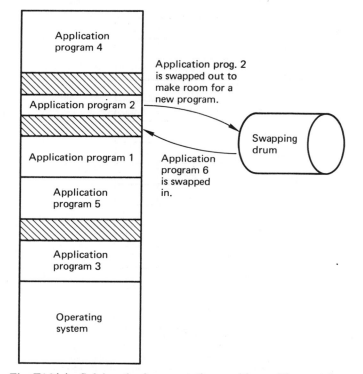

Fig. T10(a)   Solving the fragmentation problem with swapping

TABLE T1   *Paging Characteristics of Some Common Third Generation Computers*

Computer	*Size of pages*	*Amount of memory for application programs*	*Maximum actual memory on the machine*
SDS-940	2048 words	16,384 words	65,536 words
PDP-10	Variable (two relocation registers)	131,072 words	262,144 words
GE-485	512 words	32,768 words	131,072 words
GE-645	64 words and 1024 words	16,777,216 words	262,144 words
Sigma 7	512 words	131,072 words	131,072 words
Burroughs B5500	Variable	Unlimited	32,768 words
Burroughs B6500	Variable	Unlimited	2,000,000 words
IBM 360/67	4096 bytes	16,777,216 bytes (may be made smaller at the whim of the system designer)	16,777,216 bytes

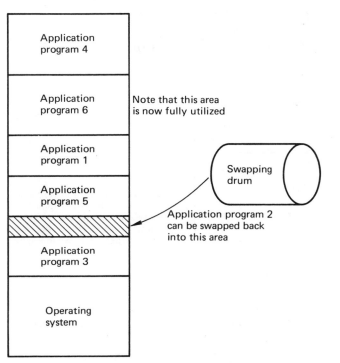

In this simple example, we could have
achieved the same effect by simply
copying Application prog. 2 from
its original area to the new area of
memory.

Fig. T10(b)   Solving the fragmentation problem with swapping

Each of these machines realizes virtual memory in a different way: the Burroughs computers are built around the notion of a Program Reference Table, or PRT [8]; the GE-645 uses a two-level mapping scheme, involving *segment tables* and *page tables* [7]; machines like the SDS-940 and the GE-485 use a hardware "page box." Nevertheless, each of the paging machines faces the same problems, and many of them use the same algorithms and strategies.

We will attempt to describe these common problems and principles in terms of a specific machine, the GE-485. This machine, while not as common as the other ones listed in Table T1, has a paging structure that is sufficiently simple that it can be described easily. The machine has the further advantage of having been used extensively by the author; most of the problems discussed below have been personally, and painfully, experienced by the author.

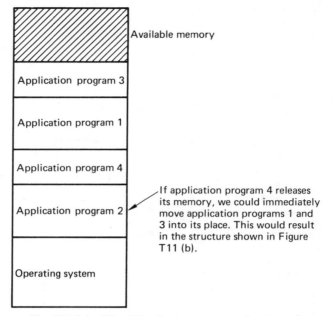

Available memory

Application program 3

Application program 1

Application program 4

Application program 2

If application program 4 releases its memory, we could immediately move application programs 1 and 3 into its place. This would result in the structure shown in Figure T11 (b).

Operating system

Fig. T11(a) "Shuffling" when memory is released

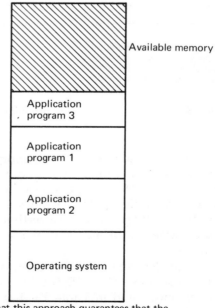

Available memory

Application program 3

Application program 1

Application program 2

Operating system

Note that this approach quarantees that the largest possible contiguous "chunk" of memory is always available. However, it is not really clear that this is necessary.

Fig. T11(b) "Shuffling" when memory is released

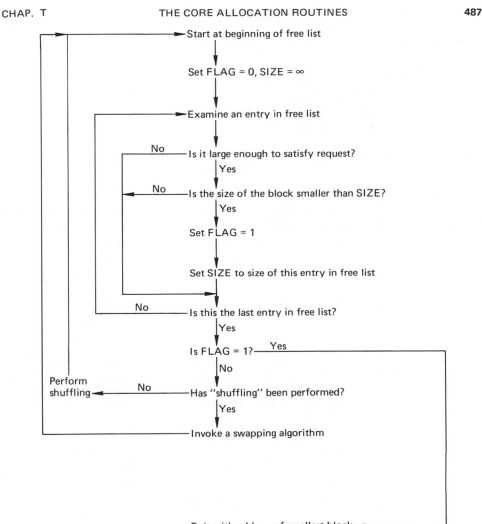

Fig. T12(a) The GETMEM routine for a "best fit" strategy

The GE-485 is a highly modified GE-435, one of General Electric's medium-sized computers. Some of the relevant hardware characteristics of the GE-485 are listed in Table T2, and the instruction format is shown in Figure T13(a). For the purposes of our discussion, we are interested only in the *address field* of the instruction, which is shown in more detail in Figure T13(b). The address field is fifteen bits long, which allows the application programmer to directly address 32,768 words of memory. As Figure T13(b) illustrates, those 32,768 words of memory are divided into 64 *pages* of 512 words each.

TABLE T2 *Relevant Hardware Features of the GE-485 Computer*

24-bit word
2.7 microsecond memory cycle time
32,768 words of virtual memory
131,072 words of physical memory
Type II hardware interrupt structure (see Chapter Q)
Master mode/slave mode capabilities
Real-time clock
Extremely powerful indexing and indirect addressing capabilities
Accumulator maintained in *memory*, rather than in a hardware register

Paging is accomplished with a hardware "page box," shown in Figure T14(a). The page box consists of 64 registers, with one register for each virtual page in the application program's addressing space. As Figure T14(b) illustrates, each page box register consists of an 8-bit *physical page number*, and a number of *control* bits. The individual control bits are listed in Table T3, with a description of their use.

TABLE T3 *Control Bits for the GE-485 Page Box*

Name of control bit	*Meaning*
Use bit	This bit indicates whether the application program is allowed to use the virtual page at all. If the bit is set to zero, *any* access to the page will cause a trap to the operating system; if the bit is set to one, then the application program is at least allowed to read the page. The bit can be set or cleared by the operating system.
Read-only bit	This bit indicates whether the application program is allowed to modify the virtual page. If the bit is set to one, then the page is read-only, and any attempt to store into the page will cause a trap to the operating system. If the bit is set to zero, then the application program will be allowed to store into the page, assuming that the use bit is set to one. The read-only bit can also be set or cleared by the operating system.
"Dirty" bit	The "dirty" bit is set by the hardware whenever a virtual page is modified, or stored into. By checking this bit, the operating system can determine whether the virtual page has been modified during the execution of the application program. The bit can be set or cleared by the operating system.
Program Usage bit	This bit is set whenever the application program makes any kind of reference to the virtual page; that is, it is set on a read or a write instruction. The bit can be interrogated by the operating system, and can thus be used to tell which pages of the application program are active, and which ones are inactive. Again, the operating system can set or clear this bit.
Instruction Usage bit	This bit is cleared at the beginning of every instruction cycle, and then set for each virtual page that is referenced during the effective address calculation and instruction execution. If a page trap occurs in mid-instruction, the operating system can thus tell which pages are required.

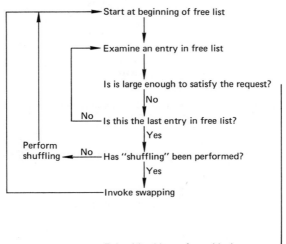

Fig. T12(b) The GETMEM routine for a "first fit" strategy

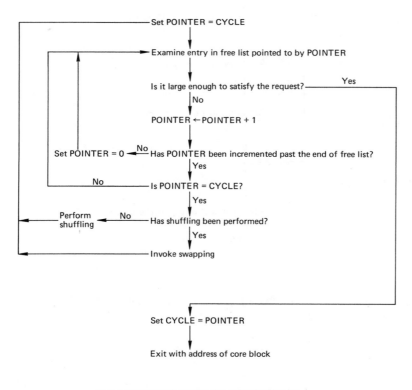

Note that this search starts at the area pointed to by
CYCLE and wraps around the end of the list. When
POINTER reaches CYCLE again, the search has failed.

Fig. T12(c) GETMEM routine for cyclic "first fit" technique

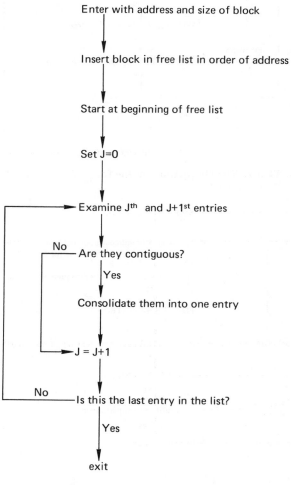

Fig. T12(d)   The RELMEM routine

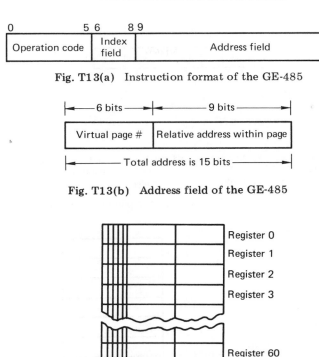

Fig. T13(a)   Instruction format of the GE-485

Fig. T13(b)   Address field of the GE-485

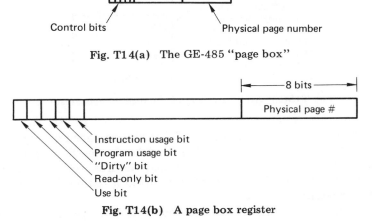

Fig. T14(a)   The GE-485 "page box"

Fig. T14(b)   A page box register

Figure T15 demonstrates how the paging mechanism works on the GE-485. The 15-bit virtual address is broken by the hardware into a 6-bit virtual page number and a 9-bit relative address within a page. The 6-bit

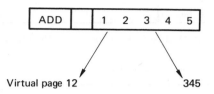

When this instruction is executed, the hardware automatically breaks the 15-bit virtual address into a 6-bit virtual page number and a 9 bit relative address within the page.

Fig. T15(a) An illustration of the paging mechanism

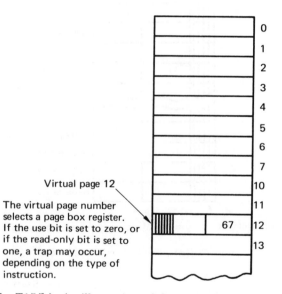

Fig. T15(b) An illustration of the paging mechanism

virtual page number selects one of the 64 hardware page box registers, from which an 8-bit physical page number is taken. The 8-bit physical page number is concatenated with the 9-bit relative address to form a final 17-bit physical address. If one of the control bits listed in Table T3 is set, a trap to the operating system will occur.

Once again, we should emphasize that this kind of paging is radically different from the kind of paging that one finds on machines like the GE-645 or the IBM 360/67. The original GE-435 had a 15-bit address field and no paging; the GE-485 involved the addition of a page box, which resulted in more *physical* memory (131,072 words), but the same amount of *virtual* memory as on the original GE-435. On machines where paging was built into

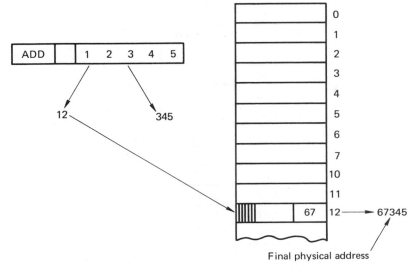

Fig. T15(c)   An illustration of the paging mechanism

the original machine, virtual memory is generally much larger than physical memory, and the hardware realization of paging is usually much different.

On the GE-485, as on many other paging machines, the operating system kept a *page map* for each application program. The page map, shown in Figure T16, contains 64 entries and indicates the manner in which the application program is using its virtual memory; each entry thus describes the manner in which the application program is using the corresponding virtual page. Thus, Figure T16 shows us that the application program is not using very much of its virtual memory space at all; some of it is being used by the actual program, and some of it is being used as working storage or data.

It is interesting to note that the GE-485 operating system did not really distinguish between programs and data; any collection of logically related information was simply referred to as a *segment*, a concept which one finds on a number of current paging systems. Thus, the operating system used the page map shown in Figure T16 to remember *which* pages of *which* segments were being manipulated in *which* virtual pages of the application program's addressing space. Additional information in the page map indicated whether the virtual page was to be considered *read-only* or *read-write*.

Note also that the application program's page map, as shown in Figure T16, does not indicate the *physical* whereabouts of any pages. Since many different application programs may be sharing the same copy of a program or data, the operating system keeps one central table to describe the actual location of pages of a segment; this table is called a *segment table*, and is

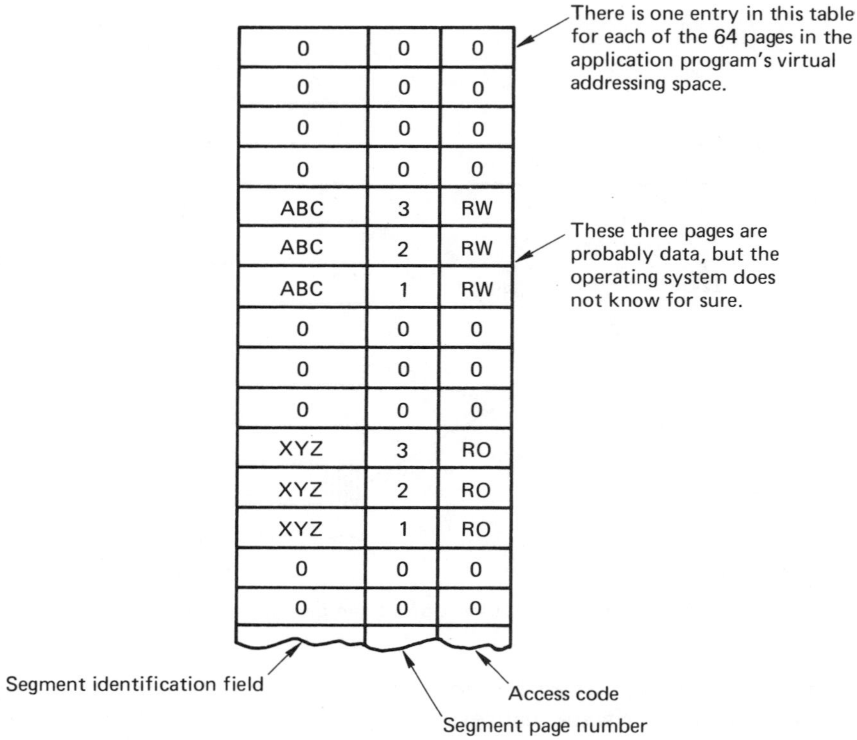

0	0	0
0	0	0
0	0	0
0	0	0
ABC	3	RW
ABC	2	RW
ABC	1	RW
0	0	0
0	0	0
0	0	0
XYZ	3	RO
XYZ	2	RO
XYZ	1	RO
0	0	0
0	0	0

There is one entry in this table for each of the 64 pages in the application program's virtual addressing space.

These three pages are probably data, but the operating system does not know for sure.

Segment identification field

Access code

Segment page number

Fig. T16   Page map for an application program on the GE-485

illustrated in Figure T17. The segment table contains one entry for each page of the segment, and each entry describes the *location* and the *state* of the page.

The state of the page is described by a code that indicates whether the page is currently in core, or on a high-speed swapping drum, or perhaps on a disk. It also indicates whether the page is currently in the process of being swapped into the machine or out of the machine, and whether any application programs are waiting for the page to appear in memory. Table T4 lists all of the legal page states; it should be clear that we can easily determine the legal *transitions* of state from this table.

Finally, the core allocation routines require a *physical core table*, shown in Figure T18. This table is similar to the one shown in Figure T4, in that it contains one entry for each *physical* page in the machine; for the GE-485, there was a maximum of 131,072 words of physical memory, which meant that the physical core table had to be 256 entries long. Instead of describing which application program is using the page, the physical core table indicates the number of application programs sharing the page and the disk or drum address to which the page may be swapped.

Page 0	23124	5
1	146	16
2	23126	5
3	170152	1
4	23130	7
5	102	16
6	67	27
7	34	27
10	123	20
11	71	16
12	114	20

There is one entry in this table for each page in the segment

This field contains a "state code" that describes what is happening to the page. See Table T4 for explanation.

This field contains an *address*. If the page is in core, it is a physical page number; if it is on drum, the field contains a drum address; if it is on disk, the field contains a disk address.

Fig. T17   The segment table

With all of these tables, it is fairly easy for the core allocation routines to "manage" memory. Segment pages are brought into the machine on a "demand" basis, as is shown in the example in Figure T19. When an application program references an area of its virtual memory that is not currently in physical core, a hardware trap (often referred to in the literature as a "page fault") occurs, and the core allocation routines take over. Note that the hardware trap occurred because the operating system set the *use bit* to zero, or the *read-only bit* to one in the page box register that was involved in the application program's last instruction execution.

As we see in Figure T19, the core allocation routines know from the hardware trap which virtual page was referenced. By checking the corresponding entry in the program's page map, we can quickly determine *why* the trap occurred. It may have occurred because of an illegal reference to an area of virtual memory that had never been defined by the application program; in this case, the entry in the page map would contain a zero, and a reference to the page would cause a *use bit trap*. On the other hand, it may have occurred as a result of a perfectly legal reference to a virtual page which is not currently in physical core. In this case, the operating system would have set the use bit to zero in the appropriate page box register so that it would be able to know when the application program really needed the page.

TABLE T4 *Page States for Segment Table Entries*

State	Is page in core?	Is there a copy on drum?	Is there a copy on disk?	Is the page involved in some IO?	How many programs are waiting?
0	No	No	No	No	None
1	No	No	Yes	No	None
2	No	No	Yes	Reading from disk	None
3	No	No	Yes	Reading from disk	One
4	No	No	Yes	Reading from disk	Two or more
5	No	Yes	No	No	None
6	No	Yes	No	Reading from drum	None
7	No	Yes	No	Reading from drum	One
8	No	Yes	No	Reading from drum	Two or more
9	No	Yes	No	Swap from drum to disk	None
10	No	Yes	No	Swap from drum to disk	One
11	No	Yes	No	Swap from drum to disk	Two or more
12	No	Yes	Yes	No	None
13	No	Yes	Yes	Reading from drum	None
14	No	Yes	Yes	Reading from drum	One
15	No	Yes	Yes	Reading from drum	Two or more
16	Yes	No	No	No	None
17	Yes	No	No	Writing to disk	None
18	Yes	No	No	Writing to disk	One
19	Yes	No	No	Writing to disk	Two or more
20	Yes	No	No	Writing to drum	None
21	Yes	No	No	Writing to drum	One
22	Yes	No	No	Writing to drum	Two or more
23	Yes	No	Yes	No	None
24	Yes	No	Yes	Writing to drum	None
25	Yes	No	Yes	Writing to drum	One
26	Yes	No	Yes	Writing to drum	Two or more
27	Yes	Yes	No	No	None
28	Yes	Yes	No	Writing to disk	None
29	Yes	Yes	No	Writing to disk	One
30	Yes	Yes	No	Writing to disk	Two or more
31	Yes	Yes	Yes	No	None

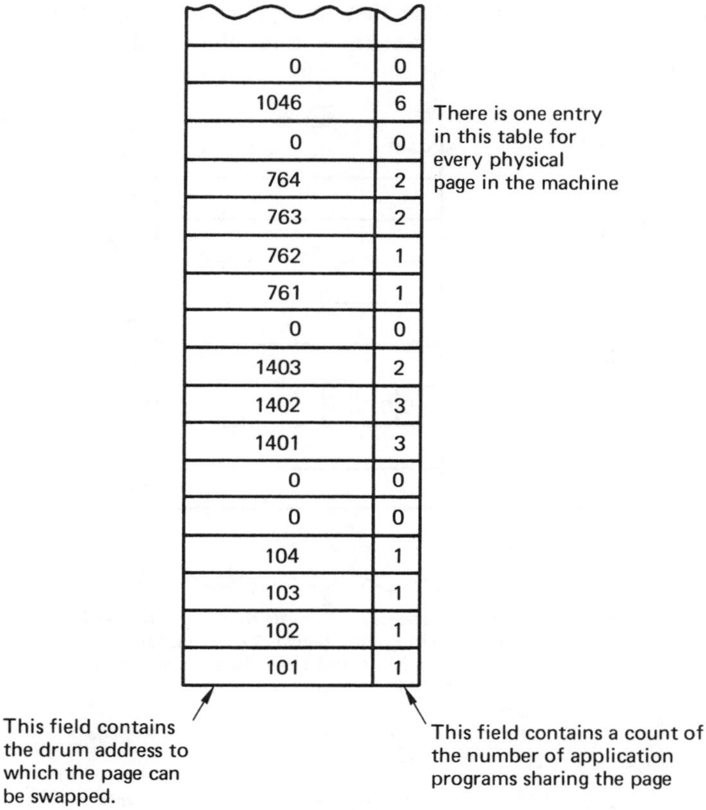

0	0
1046	6
0	0
764	2
763	2
762	1
761	1
0	0
1403	2
1402	3
1401	3
0	0
0	0
104	1
103	1
102	1
101	1

There is one entry in this table for every physical page in the machine

This field contains the drum address to which the page can be swapped.

This field contains a count of the number of application programs sharing the page

Fig. T18   The physical core table

By looking in the page map entry, the core allocation routines can easily see which segment page is being requested. As shown in Figure T19, the appropriate entry in the appropriate segment table is then examined; the *state code* in that entry indicates whether the page is already in physical core, in the process of being swapped in, or on the drum. If the page is resident on the disk or drum, the core allocation routines must perform the following sequence of activities:

1   Allocate a fresh page in physical memory. This will probably involve swapping another segment page *out* of the machine.

2   Call the disk routines or the drum routines to begin reading the application program's page into the newly-allocated physical page.

3   Change the state in the segment table, to indicate that the page is now in the process of being swapped in. Thus, if another application program requests the same page, the core allocation routines will not issue any redundant requests to the drum or disk routines.

4 Call the scheduler to indicate that the application program is not capable of executing until its page has been brought into the machine. In the meantime, the scheduler hopefully will find some other application program to execute.

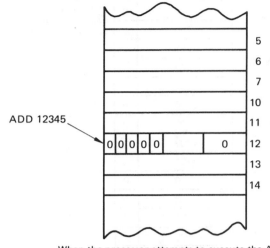

ADD 12345

When the processor attempts to execute the ADD instruction, page box register 12 will be referenced. Since the use bit is set to zero (see Figure T14 (b) and Table T3 for explanation), a trap will occur. The operating system is *explicitly* informed that the trap occurred because of a reference to page box register 12.

Fig. T19(a)   Demand paging in the GE-485 system

When the page finally arrives in memory, the core allocation routines must change the state code in the segment table once again and call the scheduler to indicate that the application program(s) waiting for the page are now runnable again.

On the GE-485 system, "demand" paging was carried to its logical extreme. When an application program was started up, the only page that was guaranteed to be in core was the one pointed to by the program counter. Thus, if the program made *any* references to data or to any other page of instructions, a "page fault" would immediately occur. If the gods happened to be smiling upon the GE-485 at that instant, the core allocation routines might find that the "demanded" pages were already in core; the page box registers would be updated, the *use bit* would be set to one, and the application program would be allowed to continue running. Whenever the operating system decided to interrupt the currently-executing application program, though, the core allocation routines would *forget* which virtual pages were currently being used by the application program; when it was allowed to run again, it would have to go through the page-faulting mechanism all over again to get its page box registers set up properly.

10	0	0	0
11	0	0	0
12	XYZ	3	RO
13	XYZ	2	RO
14	XYZ	1	RO
15	0	0	0
16	0	0	0

Page map

Since the trap occurred on virtual page 12, the core allocation routines examine the 12th entry of the page map. It is apparent that the ADD instruction made a legal reference to the 3rd page of segment XYZ.

Segment table for XYZ

		0
		1
		2
170152	1	3
		4
		5
		6
		7

Since the trap was caused by a reference to page 3 of segment XYZ, the core allocation routines examine this entry. From Table T4, we see that the page is on the disk. The core allocation routines must allocate a page in core, change the state code to 3, and call the disk routines to start reading a page from disk address 170152.

Fig. T19(b)   Demand paging in the GE-485 system

This approach was taken only because it was extremely awkward and inefficient to interrogate and manipulate the page box on the GE-485. On other machines, such as the SDS-940, it is more efficient for the operating system to "remember" which pages are currently being used by the application program. In the case of the SDS-940, the core allocation routines guarantee that whenever an application program is chosen by the scheduler, all of the virtual pages that it is currently using will be brought into physical memory. Thus, an application program on the SDS-940 would never suffer a page fault until it decided that it wanted to rearrange its virtual memory.

There seems to be general agreement among operating system designers that, for a general-purpose time-sharing environment, "demand" paging is the best way to decide which pages should be brought into the machine. However, as we have now seen, there can be several *degrees* of demand paging; the system designer must decide how *much* demand paging the application program will be forced to perform. There are three basic choices here, each with its own advantages and disadvantages:

1   The core allocation routines could be set up so that they "remember" nothing, as was the case in the GE-485. Thus, every time the application program was rescheduled, it would start off with an "empty" page box (i.e. the page box would have all of the *use bits* set to zero, except for the page pointed to by the program counter). This would force the application program to go through the page fault overhead for each new page, but this might be tolerable if the application program spent most of its time in only two or three pages.

2   The core allocation routines could be set up so that they would "remember" *all of the pages that were in physical core.* Thus, when the scheduler decided to run an application program, the core allocation routines could search through the program's page map to see which pages might be required by the program. The appropriate segment tables could then be searched, and the use bit could be set to one for those pages which were already in physical core. However, the core allocation routines would make no attempt to swap in pages that were not currently in core, until such time as the application program began executing and actually referenced them. This approach would obviously cut down on the number of page faults, but would greatly increase the overhead required to start up an application program. On the GE-485, this approach would have required the core allocation routines to examine each entry in the 64-word page map; a segment table would have to be examined for each non-zero entry in the page map, and a page box register would have to be set up for each segment table entry whose state code indicated that it was in physical core. On the GE-485, the overhead for such an approach would have been prohibitively high; on other machines, it might be more efficient.

3   The core allocation routines could be set up so that they would guarantee that whenever the application program is chosen by the scheduler, *all* of its virtual pages would be brought into physical core. This is the approach taken by many SDS-940 systems, and while it minimizes page faults, it also requires a fair amount of overhead. It is a reasonable approach on the SDS-940 because each application program is allowed only *eight* virtual pages; on a machine like the GE-485, whose application programs are allowed 64 virtual pages, the overhead would be horrendous. Another possible disadvantage of this approach is that an application program could bring a virtual page into the machine even when it does not really need the page; the two approaches described above guaranteed that a page would not be brought into the machine unless it was actually referenced by the application program.

What we have discussed thus far is a mechanism for bringing pages *into* the machine. It is obvious that there must also be a strategy for throwing pages *out* of the machine, for the core allocation routines normally find that the physical core table shown in Figure T18 does not have any "unused" entries.

"Page-throwing" strategies have attracted a great deal of attention during the past few years; the reader is referred to an excellent summary of page-throwing strategies by Belady [4]. It is generally the page-throwing part of the core allocation routines that cause "thrashing" to occur: the core allocation routines mistakenly swap a page out of the machine just before it is needed by some application program. Unfortunately, it is *extremely* difficult to develop a good page-throwing strategy: operating systems specialists have reluctantly begun to admit that an application programmer can innocently or maliciously destroy *any* page-throwing strategy with great ease.

Let us first examine the hardware aids that might be used in a page-throwing strategy in the core allocation routines. It has been commonly recognized that the *activity* of a page might be a good criterion for swapping it to the drum or leaving it in core memory; as a result, many paging machines have rather primitive hardware for "measuring" the activity of a page. In the case of the GE-485, each page box register contained a *program usage bit*, which was set by the hardware whenever any reference was made to the virtual page. After allowing the application program to execute for some period of time, the core allocation routines could thus examine the program usage bits of all 64 page box registers to see which pages had been actively referenced.

This kind of hardware mechanism, which has been implemented on a number of other machines, has some serious weaknesses. *First*, it requires a rather large amount of overhead to examine all of the program usage bits; in the case of the GE-485, several milliseconds were required to find out which program usage bits had been turned on. Since the operating system tended to reschedule several times a second, this approach would have led to very high overhead.

Second, this hardware approach does not really give a true measure of the activity of the page. On the GE-485 and on a number of other contemporary paging machines, the program usage bit is turned on whenever *any* reference is made to the page; by looking at the program usage bit, the core allocation routines cannot tell whether the page has been referenced once or a million times. The core allocation routines must consider all of the pages whose program usage bits have been set to be "equally active," which can obviously lead to some poor page-throwing strategies.

Third, the program usage bit and similar hardware techniques only give the core allocation routines information about the *past* activity of the application program. If the application program continues to execute in the future as it did in the past, then the program usage bit might be useful; however, it is obviously possible that a page that has been relatively inactive for the past few seconds might become very active during the next few seconds. Once again, the core allocation routines might be fooled into making some very poor page-throwing decisions.

In addition to the program usage bit, the core allocation routines in the GE-485 computer could make use of the "dirty" bit, which was set whenever a page was modified in core. In many cases, the core allocation routines would read a page from the drum, and set the *page state* in the segment table to 27 (see Table T4); as long as it stayed in state 27, the page-throwing algorithm could reclaim the page in physical core by merely changing the state in the segment table to 5. However, if the application program modified the page, the "dirty" bit would be set, and the core allocation routines would have to change the state of the page to 16; if the page-throwing algorithm wanted to grab the page, it would first have to write it out on the drum.

It is interesting to note that the core allocation routines could easily function *without* the program usage bit and the "dirty" bit. By setting the use bit to zero, the core allocation routines could cause a trap whenever a page was first referenced; as part of the trap routine, the core allocation routines could update *software* information about program activity. Similarly, the core allocation routines could *always* set the read-only bit to one, so that a trap would occur whenever the application program tried to store into a page; assuming that the application program was not acting illegally, the core allocation routines could simply mark the page as "dirty" (by changing the state in the segment table) and return control to the application program. In fact, this approach *was* taken on the GE-485, and it required much less overhead than the alternate approach of interrogating all the program usage bits and "dirty" bits in the page box after each rescheduling of application program.

It would appear that paging hardware could be improved tremendously in this area. For those who would like to use activity as a criterion for page-throwing, it would convenient to have a *count* of the number of times that the page was referenced, rather than a simple program usage bit. In the long run, though, the operating systems specialist really needs the ability to *microprogram* the paging hardware, so that he can build in an arbitrarily complex page-throwing scheme.

In the meantime, current paging computers use *software-oriented* page-throwing strategies, aided by the primitive types of hardware that we have discussed. As Belady points out, a number of the early paging systems used a *first-in-first-out* page-throwing algorithm. On the assumption that most "reasonable" programs proceed in a straight-line fashion, the core allocation routines in machines such as the British ATLAS computer believed that the first page that was brought into the machine should be the first one removed.

A number of contemporary paging systems remove the *least recently used* pages first. The core allocation routines keep a queue of pages, as shown in Figure T20; every time a page is referenced (i.e. every time that the core allocation routines detect that the program usage bit has been turned on), the page's queue entry is interchanged with its next higher neighbor. In this way, the active pages "percolate" to the top of the queue, while the inactive pages gradually sink to the bottom of the queue. Whenever the core allocation routines are forced to remove a page from memory, the entry at the bottom of the queue specifies which page it should be.

As we mentioned above, this type of strategy suffers the weakness of basing its decisions on *past* activity. When implemented with the type of "activity queue" shown in Figure T20, it suffers from another, more subtle, weakness: an application program's pages might gradually drift towards the bottom of the queue because the scheduling algorithm has not yet gotten around to executing the program. Figure T21 shows an extreme case: with a round robin scheduling algorithm, the application program with the least active pages is likely to be the one that will be scheduled next. Thus, the page-throwing algorithm may remove all of the program's pages just before it has a chance to execute—and this is precisely the kind of behavior that leads to "thrashing."

Since it is the scheduler that determines which application programs will be running at any given time, it seems reasonable that the page-throwing algorithm should cooperate with the scheduler. As an example of how this type of page-throwing algorithm works, let us return to the GE-485.

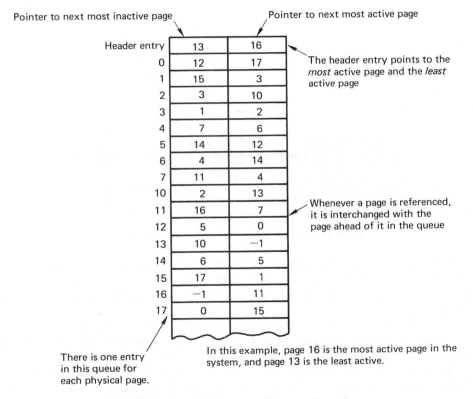

Pointer to next most inactive page

Pointer to next most active page

Header entry	13	16
0	12	17
1	15	3
2	3	10
3	1	2
4	7	6
5	14	12
6	4	14
7	11	4
10	2	13
11	16	7
12	5	0
13	10	−1
14	6	5
15	17	1
16	−1	11
17	0	15

The header entry points to the *most* active page and the *least* active page

Whenever a page is referenced, it is interchanged with the page ahead of it in the queue

There is one entry in this queue for each physical page.

In this example, page 16 is the most active page in the system, and page 13 is the least active.

Fig. T20   An activity queue for page-throwing

The page-throwing subroutine in the GE-485, which was referred to as the "page grabber," was called whenever the number of available physical pages fell below a specified number. The page-throwing routines first called a subroutine in the scheduler to determine the identity of the lowest priority application program in the system. If that application program had already been swapped out of core, the scheduler would be called again. Thus, the page-throwing routines would eventually discover a low-priority application program, some of whose pages were still in physical core.

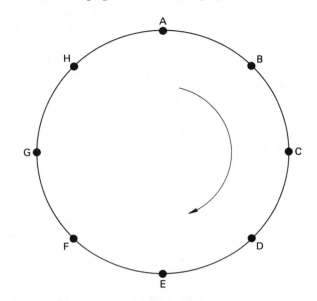

If the scheduler executes application programs on a round-robin basis, then each program's pages will tend to sink toward the bottom of the activity queue when other programs are executing. Thus, while the scheduler is executing program A, program B's pages will be the *least* active in the system, since program B was executed longest ago. Thus, the page-throwing algorithm may remove program B's pages just before they are needed!

Fig. T21   A weakness of the "activity" algorithm

The page map of the unlucky application program was then examined. If any of its pages had been "locked" into core, they would be left alone; this generally occurred only if the page was involved in some IO and could not be moved.

If the page was not locked into core, the page-throwing subroutines checked to make sure that the page had been used at least once; it also checked to make sure that the application program had not been interrupted in mid-execution while using this page to calculate a complex indirect or indexed address. This was done by checking the program usage bit and the instruction usage bit, a copy of which had been saved from the last time the application program was allowed to execute. To prevent thrashing, a page in either of these two states would not be removed; such a page was said to be temporarily "immune" from swapping.

Assuming that the page was not immune from swapping, the page-throwing routines decremented the *usage count* in the appropriate physical core table entry (see Figure T18). If the resulting count was zero, the page would be immediately marked as "available" if there was a copy of the page on disk or drum (i.e. if it was in states 27 or 31, as listed in Table T4). If the page was dirty (i.e. if it was in states 16 or 23), the drum routines would be called to write the page, and the page state would be changed accordingly.

This procedure would be followed for all of the pages associated with the low-priority application program currently under consideration. When all possible pages had been removed, the page-throwing routines would check to see if enough pages had been acquired as a result of its work. If not, it would repeat the entire process by calling the scheduler again to determine the next-lowest application program.

As one might imagine, there is a *tremendous* amount of overhead involved in this kind of page-throwing mechanism; it was tolerable only because five or ten pages would be "grabbed" from some unfortunate application program each time the page-throwing routines were invoked. In fact, evidence from an experimental operating system on the GE-485 suggested that it would be more efficient to swap application programs in their entirety, and avoid *completely* the overhead of the page-throwing mechanism; while there may be more swapping, there would be less operating system overhead, and much less "thrashing."

The type of "demand paging" and "page-throwing" mechanisms we have described are suitable only for general-purpose time-sharing environments, if at all; for a dedicated system where all of the terminal users are sharing the same application programs, the paging strategies could be much more specialized and hopefully much more efficient. In any event, it is *extremely* important that the system designer gather good statistics about the operating of his paging algorithms; the reader is urged to review the types of statistics that were suggested in Chapter G. The system designer should also be prepared to rewrite his paging routines several times, for it is absolutely inevitable that they will require extensive modification and "tuning."

The main purpose of this short discussion of paging has been to leave the reader with an uneasy feeling in the pit of his stomach. Paging is an extremely powerful concept, and in certain limited situations it can greatly improve the efficiency of the on-line computer system. On the other hand, it *can* lead to excessive amounts of overhead in the operating system. At least three ambitious on-line systems have failed because of paging, and several systems designers have been heard to mutter that paging is a Communist plot intended to set the American computer effort back several years.

In all seriousness, paging deserves to be studied very critically over the next few years. There are at least two fundamental questions that must be answered before paging can be considered to be of any lasting value:

1   *Should paging be performed with fixed-size or variable-sized pages?*

Our example above concerned a GE-485 computer with a fixed page size of 512 words. Most of the other popular paging computers also have a fixed page size, ranging from 512 words to 2048 words. The Burroughs B5500 and B6500 computers are the only significant examples of machines with a variable-sized page, and they are so totally unlike the typical IBM and GE machines that it is difficult to draw any comparisons.

There are two very strong drawbacks to the machines with fixed-size pages. As Randell[2] so correctly points out, there is often a great deal of what he calls "internal fragmentation," resulting from the application programmer's inability to make use of *all* of the words in a page. Also, it is often very difficult to arrange programs in such a way that they achieve Denning's notion of a "working set" [15]. As an example, consider the small program loop shown in Figure T22, which happens to be centered about a page boundary. At the very best, this arrangement leads to a poor use of physical core storage, since the operating system must reserve two pages for the small program loop; at worst, thrashing can occur, since the operating system may stubbornly refuse to keep both pages in core.

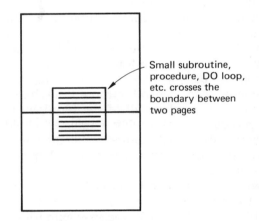

Small subroutine, procedure, DO loop, etc. crosses the boundary between two pages

Fig. T22 A weakness of fixed-size pages

Many of these problems would seem to be eliminated with the type of variable-page structure that exists on the Burroughs computers. With this type of hardware, the operating system could easily arrange for a subroutine to fit into precisely one page; for high-level application programs, we could place an ALGOL procedure or a COBOL paragraph into one page. This would eliminate the artificial boundaries that we find in the fixed-page-size machines, and would presumably eliminate a large amount of overhead.

On the other hand, it is not clear that thrashing is an impossibility on the Burroughs computers. The operating system must still decide which variable-sized pages should be brought into the machine and which ones should be removed in core. Since we are dealing with variable-sized quantities of memory, the operating system must deal with the type of free list structure that we showed in Figure T5; it must still deal with the problem of fragmentation that we discussed earlier in this chapter.

It is the author's personal opinion that the type of paging found on the

Burroughs computers will eventually prove more efficient than the fixed-page-size paging found on other third and fourth generation computers. Unfortunately, this opinion is based on intuition and personal experience, and has yet to be confirmed.

2 *Should paging encompass files and data bases as well as core memory?*

We mentioned that the GE-485 operating system considered any logically related information to be a *segment*; it thus considered programs and data alike. The application programmer referred to information within a file by referencing a specific *page* in a specific *segment* which he had placed in his virtual memory. The application programmer did *not* specifically call the operating system to read or write data base records to disk or drum; he merely called the operating system to move pages in and out of its virtual memory, and let the operating system decide whether those pages should be in core, on the drum, or on the disk.

This type of structure has been attempted or suggested on a few other paging systems, and it is quite appealing. The application program does not perform any direct disk or drum IO, and references only *virtual* quantities; as a result, only the operating system deals with the drum and the disk. The operating system is thus able to consider core, drum, and disk (as well as data cells, magnetic tape, microfilm, cards, stone tablets, and any other form of storage that may be handy) as a *hierarchy* of storage devices; it can decide which items should be kept in core, which ones should remain on the fast drum, and so forth. However, there are two problems which should be considered in this area.

In the case of the GE-485 system, *all* of the segments were broken into 512-word pages. Thus, even if the application program was dealing with 30-character records, the operating system essentially broke all files (i.e. all segments that were being used as data files) into 512-word records. This is potentially extremely inefficient, especially in situations where the application program is making random accesses to widely separated logical records within the paging structure.

The hierarchical storage approach can also make recovery far more difficult, and certainly much less efficient. Since the GE-485 system went to such extreme lengths to eliminate all distinction between programs and data, *it never knew when a data base was being updated.* All it knew was that a page had been modified in core; however, that might have been the result of a non-reentrant program modifying itself as it ran, or the result of a program storing temporary results in a work area, or possibly the result of a data base update. Even if the operating system had been able to distinguish data base updates from other miscellaneous activities in the machine, it would have been forced to write the *entire page* to the audit trail for recovery purposes. Thus, if the application program updated a 30-character data base record, the operating system would have been forced to write 512 words, or 1536 characters, onto magnetic tape!

ALLOCATION OF SMALL BLOCKS OF MEMORY

In addition to allocating fairly large amounts of memory for the application programs, it is necessary for the operating system to allocate *small blocks* of core for IO buffers, queue entries, and floating tables. Most of this allocation is for memory within the operating system's own area of memory, but some of it may be for buffers within the application program's area.

One of the more common techniques for small block allocation is that of chaining a number of fixed length blocks together, as shown in Figure T23. This approach has the advantage that it requires very little overhead to

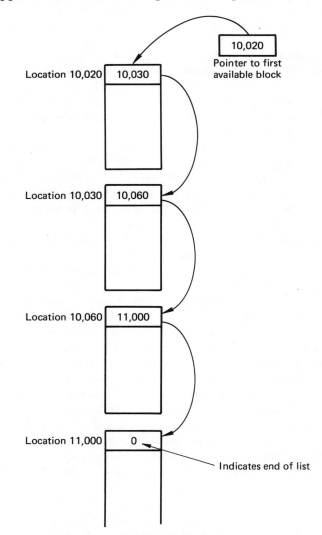

Fig. T23   Allocation with chained blocks

allocate or replace blocks. On the other hand, working with *fixed-size* blocks has some disadvantages. The system designer must choose a block size that seems optimum for his IO buffers, etc., and he may often find that there are requirements for either *more* or *less* core than the block size.

For example, the system designer may construct a list of 40-byte blocks for teletype buffers, on the assumption that very few teletype messages will ever exceed 40 characters. In practice, though, he is likely to find that 90% of the teletype messages are less than 30 characters, which means that the remaining 10 characters will be wasted.

The opposite case is, of course, also possible, and it is a little more difficult to deal with. Thus, the system designer may occasionally find teletype messages that are 50 characters in length, although there is no reasonable way of predicting the message length in advance. In the case of teletype IO, there is a simple solution: the first buffer can be linked to a second buffer, as shown in Figure T24. In many other cases, though, the system designer may require 50 *contiguous* bytes of storage, which cannot be guaranteed with the simple linked list approach.

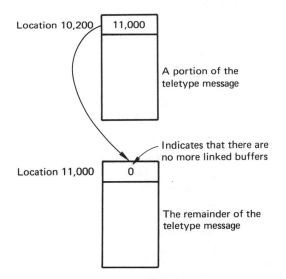

Fig. T24   Linking of teletype IO buffers

To avoid this latter problem, we can keep several lists of fixed-length blocks, as shown in Figure T25. A request for memory is allocated from the list that best fits the request. Thus, a request for 9 bytes of memory would be allocated from the list of 10-byte blocks; a request for 14 bytes of memory would be allocated from the list of 20-byte blocks, and so forth.

It is convenient to make the various block sizes integral multiples of one another, so that a shortage of any particular size of blocks can be remedied by chopping up a larger block. Using the example in Figure T25, we see that a shortage of 10-byte blocks can be remedied by taking a block out of the 20-byte list and chopping it in half. Similarly, a shortage of 20-byte blocks

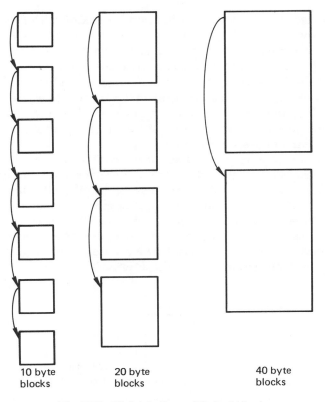

10 byte
blocks

20 byte
blocks

40 byte
blocks

Fig. T25   Multiple lists of linked blocks

can be remedied by allocating a 40-byte block, and chopping it in half. The only disadvantage of this procedure is that we eventually find that all of the blocks are chopped up into the smallest possible size. Thus, all of the blocks in Figure T25 may eventually gravitate towards the 10-byte list, and it may be very difficult to "glue together" the larger blocks.

Finally, we can allocate blocks with a "bit-map" scheme, as shown in Figure T26. We keep track of the availability of fixed-size blocks with a single bit, which is one if the block is available and zero if it is in use. It is possible, with this scheme, to allocate a variable-sized block by allocating a variable number of contiguous fixed-size blocks.

Thus, if our bit-map keeps track of 10-byte blocks, we can allocate 27 bytes by looking for three contiguous "one" bits in the bit-map—for they correspond to three contiguous 10-byte blocks of memory. There can be a significant amount of overhead with this scheme, though the clever programmer can sometimes use a floating point normalize instruction to find the first one bit in the bit-map.

The major problem with the bit-map scheme, aside from its possible high overhead, is the fact that it does not maintain very much information about the blocks that are in use. Thus, it is possible for other operating system

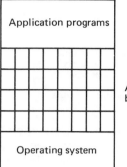

Application programs

Operating system

An entire area of memory is divided into 10-byte blocks (or any other convenient size)

0	0	1	1	1	1	1	0	0	0	1	0	1	0	0	0	0	1	1	1
1	1	1	0	0	1	0	1	1	1	0	0	0	1	0	1	0	0	1	1
0	0	0	0	0	1	1	1	1	1	1	0	0	1	1	0	1	1	1	0

1 = block is available
0 = block is in use

Fig. T26 Bit map approach for core allocation

subroutines to allocate or return blocks of memory erroneously without any way of catching the errors. We shall describe three of the more common forms of core allocation errors.

The first problem is illustrated by Figure T27, and results from a block of storage being returned twice. If the core allocation routines turn on a bit with an arithmetic add instruction, an overflow will result when the block is returned the second time. The problem can be fixed simply by using a logical OR instruction to turn on the bits in the bit-map.

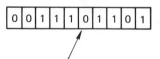

| 0 | 0 | 1 | 1 | 1 | 0 | 1 | 1 | 0 | 1 |

An op. system routine is using this block

Fig. T27(a) Returning the same block twice

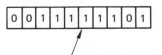

| 0 | 0 | 1 | 1 | 1 | 1 | 1 | 1 | 0 | 1 |

The block has now been released.

Fig. T27(b) Returning the same block twice

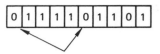

The block has been released a second time.
The original bit is now zero, and a "carry"
has been propagated up to another position.

Fig. T27(c)   Returning the same block twice

However, things become more complicated when an operating system subroutine allocates a block of storage, and then, as we see in Figure T28, decides to return some other block. Since the bit-map does not indicate which program called for the block of storage, there is no way for the core allocation routines to detect the error. As a result, it will mistakenly think that a block of memory is available when it is in use by some other program. The next thing that will occur is another call for a block of storage (from some other innocent operating system subroutine), and we will end up with two routines using the same block of memory—in violation of a basic law of physics!

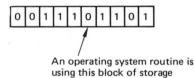

An operating system routine is
using this block of storage

Fig. T28(a)   Returning the wrong block of storage

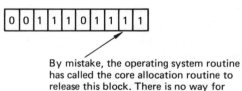

By mistake, the operating system routine
has called the core allocation routine to
release this block. There is no way for
this error to be detected.

Fig. T28(b)   Returning the wrong block of storage

Finally, we can have problems if an operating system routine allocates a block of storage and fails to return it. This does *not* cause a problem when the application programs are the culprit, for as we saw in Figure T4, we always know which program is using which area of memory. Within the operating system, though, it is usually assumed that the various subroutines know what they are doing—so we do not bother keeping information which would be helpful in case of errors. The result of this particular type of error is that available core memory will very quickly disappear.

It should be emphasized that these problems can occur with *any* bit-map allocation scheme. It is fairly common practice to keep track of available storage on disks with the same type of bit-map, and the same problems can occur when records or files are created and destroyed. In the case of a file storage unit, it may take a much longer time for the error to be noticed; in the case of core allocation, an error of the type we discussed above will usually cause the system to fail *very* quickly.

CORE OVERLOADS

Systems overloads tend to show themselves as insatiable demands for core memory. Thus, if too many people begin using an on-line system, or if they begin typing too quickly, we may find that our supply of small blocks of storage runs dangerously low. There are several approaches that can be taken:

1 An ample supply of small blocks of storage can be kept in "reserve" for these overload emergencies. In other words, the system designer can plan ahead for "worst case" contingencies.

2 The application program that initiated the call for more memory can be suspended. Thus, if the application program issues an input/output macro, the operating system will probably have to allocate some blocks of memory for queue entries and buffers. If this core is unavailable, the application program can be put into a "wait" state, and it can be forced to reexecute the macro when core is available at some later time.

3 If an IO device initiates the request for memory, it can be ignored, and the IO activity can be repeated at some later time. Thus, if the disk indicates that it is ready to read a record of data into core, the system might have to allocate some buffer space. If none is available, the disk can be allowed to go idle, and the read can be performed later.

4 If the core allocation routines run out of small blocks of core, they can allocate more space from the area normally reserved for application programs. The major problem here is making sure that this extra core eventually gets returned to the application program when the overload subsides. The system designer must make sure to keep a few small blocks in reserve so that he can swap out an application program when the "extra space" is required.

5 The operating system can come to a screeching halt. This is obviously the least desirable alternative, but it may be necessary if the system designer has not provided any other procedures.

REFERENCES

1 Donald Knuth, *The Art of Computer Programming*, Volume 1: Fundamental Algorithms (Reading, Mass.: Addison-Wesley Publishing Company, Inc., 1968)

2 B. Randell, *A Note on Storage Fragmentation and Program Segmentation*, Communications of the ACM, Volume 12, Number 7 (July, 1969), pages 365-369

3 Alan Batson, Shy-Ming Ju, and David C. Wood, *Measurements of Segment Size*, Communications of the ACM, Volume 13, Number 3 (March, 1970), pages 155-159

4 L.A. Belady, *A Study of Replacement Algorithms for a Virtual-Storage Computer*, IBM Systems Journal, Volume 5, Number 2 (1966), pages 78-101

5 B. Randell and C.J. Kuehner, *Dynamic Storage Allocation Systems*, Communications of the ACM, Volume 11, Number 5 (May, 1968), pages 297-306

6 R.A. Totschek, *An Empirical Investigation into the Behavior of the SDC Time-Sharing System*, Report SP2191, AD622003, System Development Corporation, Santa Monica, California, 1965

7 F.J. Corbato and V.A. Vyssotsky, *Introduction and Overview of the MULTICS system*, Proceedings of the AFIPS 1965 Fall Joint Computer Conference, Volume 27, Part 1 (New York, N.Y.: Spartan Books), pages 619-628

8 *A Narrative Description of the Burroughs B5500 Disk File Master Control Program*, Burroughs Corporation, Detroit, Michigan, Revised October, 1966

9 L.W. Comeau, *A Study of the Effect of User Program Optimization in a Paging System*, ACM Symposium on Operating System Principles, October 1-4, 1967, Gatlinburg, Tennessee

10 G.H. Fine, C.W. Jackson, and P.V. McIsaac, *Dynamic Program Behavior under Paging*, Proceedings of the ACM 21st National Conference (Washington, D.C.: Thompson Book Company, 1966), pages 223-228

11 E.G. Coffman and L.C. Varian, *Further Experimental Data on the Behavior of Programs in a Paging Environment*, Communications of the ACM, Volume 11, Number 7 (July, 1968), pages 471-474

12 John L. Smith, *Multiprogramming under a Page on Demand Strategy*, Communications of the ACM, Volume 10, Number 10 (October, 1967), pages 636-646

13 Paul W. Purdom, Jr., and Stephen M. Stigler, *Statistical Properties of the Buddy System*, Journal of the ACM, Volume 17, Number 4 (October, 1970), pages 683-697

14 Kenneth C. Knowlton, *A Fast Storage Allocator*, Communications of the ACM, Volume 8 (1965) pages 623-625

15 Peter J. Denning, *The Working Set Model for Program Behavior*, Communications of the ACM, Volume 11, Number 5 (May, 1968), pages 323-333

SYSTEM FAILURES AND ERROR RECOVERY FOR ON-LINE SYSTEMS

INTRODUCTION

If there is one universal weakness in new on-line system designers, it is their naiveté. They generally tend to underestimate the number of programmers required to implement the system, the duration of the project, and the amount of money required. These weaknesses basically reflect a lack of *management* experience in the field of on-line systems, and, as such, are beyond the scope of this book.

However, there is another area where the naiveté of system designers leads to catastrophe, and this area *is* within the realm of a technical discussion: system failures and error recovery. It rarely occurs to the programmer or analyst that the central processor might occasionally fail, or that a critical record on the disk might become unreadable. Despite the experiences of the past few years and the gloomy forecasts for the next decade, system designers generally ignore the possibilities of failures in the communications network or the power supply. One generally has to suffer through at least one on-line system before accepting the universality of Murphy's Law: if anything can possibly go wrong, it will. In fact, even if nothing can possibly go wrong, something inevitably will.

Our purpose in this chapter is to demonstrate that there are indeed a number of causes of system failures in an on-line system. Following this, we shall briefly discuss some of the approaches that can be taken to minimize or recover from system failures.

DIFFERENT CONCEPTS OF RELIABILITY

Before we discuss the causes of system failure, we should first recognize that the words "failure" and "reliability" mean different things to different system designers—and as a result, their error recovery procedures take different forms. We can generally identify three different meanings of "reliability":

1 *Prevention of "downtime" of any kind*

There are a number of on-line systems which insist on *continuous* performance. Process control systems, air traffic control systems, on-line medical systems, and some data acquisition systems fall into this category, as do a few business-oriented systems with extremely large numbers of users (such as airline reservation systems).

The important thing here is that *any* failure of *any* duration is catastrophic. A computer that controls the milling and machining of an expensive airplane part cannot be allowed to fail for even a fraction of a second—or the part will be ruined. Similarly, a process control system that is out of service for more than a few seconds may result in an explosion or costly wastage in a manufacturing process.

The standard way of describing the reliability of such a system is by its *mean time between failures*, or MTBF. It is interesting that many control systems are specifying a MTBF of several thousand hours; business-oriented systems are lucky to survive a month (or 8 x 22 = 176 hours) without failures; most time-sharing systems have a failure every day or two.

2 *Prevention of prolonged periods of downtime*

The systems described above require a different kind of reliability than the average business-oriented system. Since the business-oriented system is dealing with human users, it can survive as many as one or two failures a day, *as long as the failures are not prolonged.* A failure in a management information system or an on-line sales order entry system will cause the users to grumble a bit, but the business will not go bankrupt (hopefully).

We must emphasize, however, that this type of system *cannot* tolerate prolonged periods of downtime. If the system requires five minutes to be repaired, a salesman can ask his customer to wait; a manager can chase his secretary around the desk; a clerk can take an extra coffee break. However, if the system is still out of action after half an hour, the salesman will have lost his customer; the manager will have grown tired of chasing his secretary (or will have caught her, perhaps); the clerk will have forgotten which transaction she was working on at the time of the failure.

Note that the "prolonged period" (or Mean Time To Repair—MTTR) to which we refer includes *all* of the time that the system is out of action. It may take the operator five minutes to notice that the system is not functioning (or for the users to convince the operator that the system is not functioning); it may take another five minutes to correct the hardware problem which caused the failure (or to determine that it was caused by software); another ten minutes may be spent running recovery programs to restore the data base; and finally, it may take the operator ten minutes to restart the system and carry on the necessary "initialization dialogue" with the operating system. Meanwhile, the users have spent thirty minutes in a growing state of hysteria, and they may or may not still be around when the system is finally repaired.

3 *Protection of the data base*

Finally, we should mention those systems whose primary concern is the integrity of their data base. There are a number of organizations—especially government agencies—that are beginning to design on-line systems with data bases in excess of ten *billion* characters. In some cases, literally hundreds of magnetic tapes would be required to keep a complete back-up copy of the data base; several *days* would be required to load the back-up copy of the data base from tape to disk. There are other organizations beginning to build data bases which, while not so large, are critically important to the day-to-day operation of the organization. The patient files of an on-line medical system, the financial files of any business system, and the intelligence files of many government agencies fall into this category.

While it may seem an exaggeration, the people in charge of these systems will often state emphatically that they are willing to tolerate a system failure every hour, and that they are willing to let their system stay out of service all day long—as long as their data base remains intact. Similarly, a man in charge of a process control system may feel that MTTR and integrity of the data base are meaningless to him—the only thing he is concerned about is MTBF. Finally, the man in charge of a time-sharing service bureau might admit that MTBF and integrity of the data base are not vitally important; what *is* important to him is MTTR, because his customers may be able to turn to another service bureau.

For many on-line systems, though, it is unrealistic to think that only one of these concepts of reliability is important. For most business-oriented systems of a small or medium size, only the second two types of reliability are important; as long as the MTBF is not horrendously bad, people will live with it. However, as the system grows to include several hundred terminal users who depend on an instant response (again, an airline reservation system is probably the best example), then MTBF becomes increasingly important.

As might be expected, these different concepts of reliability result in different kinds of recovery procedures. If MTBF is the major criterion of reliability, the recovery procedures are likely to involve redundant hardware in a duplexed or dual configuration. This assumes, of course, that virtually all of the failures in the system will be failures in hardware components, and that the software will be able to effect an instantaneous switch-over to the backup component.

When MTTR, or a "safe" data base, is the major criterion of reliability, the recovery procedures are less likely to involve hardware. Instead, the system designer will concentrate on developing software which will facilitate a quick restart, and which will make it easy to restore the data base quickly. Intensive training of the computer operations staff is also important in this area, for the best software cannot always prevent the operator from loading the wrong version of the system, or bungling the recovery procedures.

THE COMMON CAUSES OF FAILURE
IN AN ON-LINE SYSTEM

To the programmer who is being exposed to on-line systems for the first time, the emphasis on system failures may seem rather academic. "There are failures in batch systems, too," he may argue, "and we simply restarted the programs at the beginning, or at a checkpoint. What is so special about failures in on-line systems?"

To some extent, the question is a good one. Most of the causes of failure in an on-line system are the same ones that haunted batch systems—processor errors, program bugs, etc. What has changed, though, is our ability to restart the on-line system. Instead of simply mounting a few tapes and inserting a deck of cards in the card reader to restart a job, we have to go through a very intricate procedure to ensure that the data base is intact (which, in a batch system, consisted of starting the job over with its original input tapes), that the proper application programs are running, and that the many users are aware of the situation.

What makes this procedure even more delicate is that we expect the software to play a major role. In an on-line system, we may require the software to detect various types of errors, and then take the appropriate steps either to correct the error, continue running in some degraded configuration, or shut the system down in a graceful fashion.

Since the computer system itself is expected to play such a major role in the recovery process, it becomes important to identify each of the possible types of system failure to see whether the hardware and/or software will be *capable* of performing the recovery.

To put it another way, it is important for the system designer to be familiar with various types of system failures so that he can plan appropriate preventive or corrective action. He may decide, for example, that it is pointless to install duplexed hardware in an area like New York, where power shortages and air conditioning failures are likely to be the major source of problems.

We can identify eleven major causes for failure in an on-line system:

1 *Processor errors*

There are occasionally situations when the central processor does not execute instructions properly. Because of a "dropped" bit, all instructions referencing a particular accumulator or index register may fail; sometimes a particular BRANCH or SKIP instruction will fail to work properly; sometimes an entire group of instructions, such as the floating point arithmetic instructions, will fail.

In most cases, processor errors are catastrophic. If references to index register 3 suddenly get changed to index register 2, there is very little doubt that the system will go berserk. However, it is even more important to realize that *the software cannot be counted upon to switch to a backup machine, communicate with the operator, or any other intelligent activity.* There have been a few cases in which the floating point or decimal arithmetic instructions failed, but the operating system continued functioning properly—and in such a bizarre situation, it *would* be possible for the operating system to initiate recovery procedures.

It is occasionally suggested that an on-line system could run "diagnostic" programs in its spare time (or in an extra processor) to check constantly on the operation of the machine. While it is a useful concept in special cases, it has serious drawbacks on most systems. First, the diagnostic programs that most vendors provide for their machines will not run well under the control of the on-line operating system (this is especially true of IO diagnostics). Secondly, even the simple diagnostics (such as the ones which test the instruction set of the machine) take up so much memory and processor time that they seriously degrade the performance of the system. For multiprocessing systems, this approach becomes much more reasonable.

2 *Memory parity errors*

Most current computers have a parity bit associated with each word or byte in memory, making it possible to detect almost all memory errors. The parity bit is computed automatically by the hardware whenever a word (or byte) is stored in memory, and checked whenever the word is read from memory. If the hardware detects a dropped bit, it initiates an interrupt, at which time the operating system can take appropriate action.

Fortunately, hardware reliability has improved to the point where memory parity errors and processor errors are extremely rare. When they do occur, they are usually catastrophic, even though memory errors are not *necessarily* fatal. While the ability to recover from a memory error depends very much on the type of hardware, most operating systems make no attempt at all to recover.

To see what type of recovery is possible, we must first see how memory is arranged on the computer. On most machines, memory consists of *modules,* as shown in Figure U1. On some machines, a module, or "bank," of memory may consist of 4096 words, while on others it may be as large as 16,384 words. In the simple case, memory addresses increase monotonically through module zero, module one, and so forth; occasionally, though, memory will be *interleaved,* as shown in Figure U2, to permit the processor to overlap memory accesses.

Let us first consider the simplest kind of recovery from a memory parity error. The operating system can shut the system down as gracefully as possible

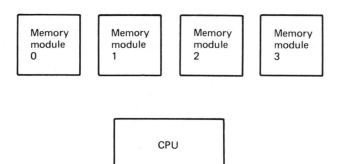

Fig. U1   Memory modules on a typical computer

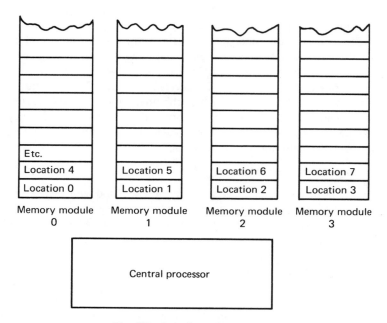

Fig. U2   Interleaved memory

(which it should be able to do, since we assume that the instructions still execute properly). The field engineer can then manually reconfigure the memory modules, as shown in Figure U3, and the system can be restarted.

In order to implement this type of recovery, the system must be able to run with less than its full complement of memory, and it must be able to determine (via a message from the computer operator, or by purposely attempting, during its initialization process, to address non-existent memory) how much memory there is.

A similar approach is simply to make the faulty memory module unavailable, by switching if off-line. As shown in Figure U4, the operating system would then discover, during its initialization, that there was an unusable

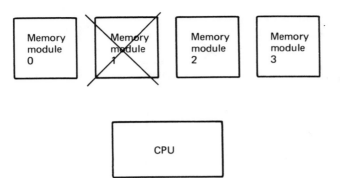

At some point during the operation of the system, it becomes apparent that memory module 1 is inoperable. The field engineer is called in, and by flipping a few switches, he changes the memory configuration as shown in figure U3 (b).

Fig. U3(a)   Reconfiguring memory modules

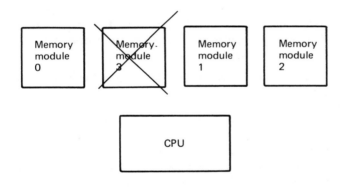

Memory module 3—the bad module—is switched off-line so the system will no longer think it exists.

Fig. U3(b)   Reconfiguring memory modules

"hole" in memory. The page tables and core maps that we discussed in Chapter T could then be marked in such a way that the faulty memory would not be assigned to the application programs.

In theory, recovery from a memory parity error could even take place without shutting the system down. If the operating system detects a memory parity error, it could go through the following sequence of activities:

1 It could stop executing the application program(s) residing in that block of memory.

2 Any necessary file recovery could be performed, in the manner discussed in Chapter N.

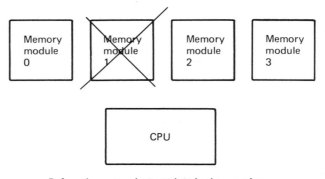

Before the system is started up in the morning,
it is discovered that one of the memory modules
is faulty. Instead of waiting for the field engineer
to reconfigure memory, the computer operator
simple switches the memory module off-line.

Fig. U4(a)   An alternative method of avoiding bad memory

3 If necessary, the user(s) whose program was executing in the faulty module of memory could be requested to retype his last input. If a "front-end" computer was present in the system, it could be requested to retransmit the last transaction.

4 The application program could be reloaded in a different area of memory, and subsequently restarted.

Needless to say, this would be a very delicate operation. Other users on the system might have to be told to wait until the recovery operation was completed; the computer operator would have to be told what was going on. On the other hand, the whole process would probably only take a few seconds, and users would not suffer the chaos and confusion that normally accompanies a full shutdown of the system.

There are two cases when this type of recovery cannot be implemented. If memory is interleaved, then a faulty memory module makes every nth memory cell inaccessible, where n is the number of memory modules on the system. This effectively makes all of the memory modules unusable, and no recovery is possible.

Similarly, a memory parity error in memory module zero, or in any memory module occupied by the resident operating system, will cause serious problems. It is common for the first few hundred locations in the first module of memory to be used as interrupt locations, interval timer counters, program status words, and so forth. Thus, a failure in module zero means that the system will have to be shut down, and the memory modules manually reconfigured. A memory parity error in any other module occupied by the operating system causes the same type of problem, since the operating system is usually not dynamically relocatable.

3 *Failures in the communication network*

Figure U5 shows the parts of the communication network that can fail during

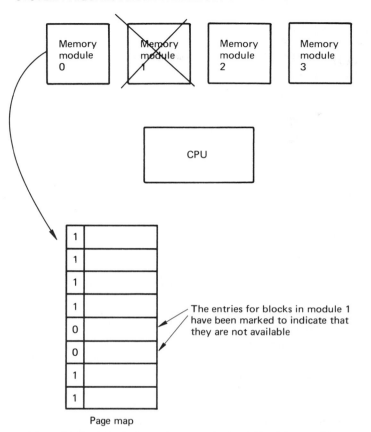

Page map

After initialization, the operating system notes in its page map that some areas of memory are not usable.

Fig. U4(b)   An alternative method of avoiding bad memory

the operation of an on-line system. Note that failures in the terminals, the low-speed communication lines, or their associated modems do not usually cause the *system* to fail; failures in a front-end computer, a multiplexor, a high-speed communication line, or its associated modems, however, are very likely to cause a system failure.

The system designer should examine each part of his communication system to see how it affects the reliability of the system. A faulty terminal may be more dangerous than it appears, if it is being used for some critically important application. If the terminal becomes completely unusable and there are no nearby backup terminals, the entire system may have to shut down as a result.

As an example, consider an order entry-inventory system like the Widget system we discussed in Chapter J. If there is only one warehouse with a terminal to allow the warehouse clerk to input receipts and shipments, then the warehouse terminal is obviously critical to the operation of the system. Even though the salesmen could continue typing orders from their terminals, they

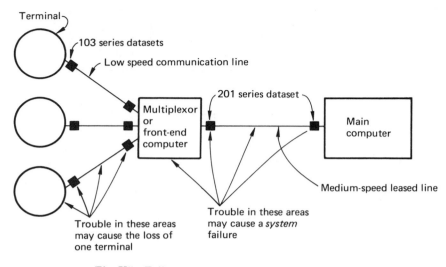

Fig. U5   Failures in the communications network

would be meaningless if the warehouse clerk was unable to indicate the arrival of new goods.

Most of the problems that occur in the communication network are transient, and the system designer will want to ensure that these errors are at least detected, if not automatically corrected. Studies have shown that simple "vertical parity" logic (requiring a parity bit with each character transmitted) will detect only 70% of the errors in the communication lines because a significant number of the errors that occur are due to bursts of noise that obliterate several bits in a character.† Much better results can be obtained with hardware that generates an error-checking code as an algebraic function of an entire message.

This is especially important to the system designer considering the variety of terminals and multiplexors available today. An astonishing number of the teletypewriter terminals rely on the simple vertical parity bit to detect errors. Furthermore, most teletypewriter terminals do not have the ACK-NACK logic necessary to let the terminal indicate erroneous transmission from the computer. If using this type of terminal, the system designer might decide to use full duplex transmission so that the user can detect errors in transmission.

As we have already indicated, errors in the multiplexor (or front-end computer) or high-speed communication line are more likely to be fatal to the system. In the case of a front-end computer, the same type of errors found in the main computer may occur—processor errors, program bugs, memory parity errors, and so forth. There are also a few rare cases when a dataset will start

---

† For a discussion of this interesting statistic, as well as a number of other interesting aspects of error detection, see James Martin, *Teleprocessing Network Organization* (Englewood Cliffs, N.J.: Prentice-Hall Inc., 1970)

generating an infinite number of spurious interrupts, or the multiplexor will somehow get itself into a permanently "busy" state.

In the case of the medium- or high-speed communication line, the system designer should remember that things are much more critical than in the case of low-speed lines. Since most medium- and high-speed lines are leased from the common carriers on an individual basis, it may not be easy to secure another line if the primary line goes bad; if a low-speed switched communication line starts causing trouble, on the other hand, the terminal user can simply redial the computer and have a relatively good chance of getting a different line. While "solid" failures in the medium- and high-speed communication lines are relatively infrequent, the system designer may want to provide a backup line to avoid making his system vulnerable.

4   *Failures in the peripheral devices*

Intermittent, or transient, errors are extremely common in all types of peripheral devices, and are usually due to the electromechanical nature of the device. Specks of dust on a tape, oxide on a read/write head, and scratches on a disk surface are all examples of the kind of problems that plague all computer systems.

There are two reasons why failures in the peripheral devices rarely cause system failures. First, most of the problems with the devices are, as we mentioned above, transient. By retrying the IO operation (as discussed in Chapter S), the error can be circumvented in most cases.

Secondly, on-line systems tend to be less dependent on the standard peripheral devices than their batch predecessors. If a high-speed printer fails or a magnetic tape drive becomes inoperable, the on-line system is not likely to suffer much. One or two tape drives may be necessary for audit trails or libraries, and the other devices may be used occasionally, but the primary IO devices on most on-line systems are the terminals and the mass storage devices.

If there are any IO problems, then, they are likely to occur in the area of the disk and drum. Once again, most of the errors are intermittent: by rereading or rewriting a record, the problem will usually go away. If repeated efforts to write a record to disk or drum are unsuccessful, it can often be written on some other part of the device.

Thus, we are usually only concerned with situations in which a record is definitely unreadable, or when the device suffers extensive physical damage (such as a "head crash," which occurs when the device's read/write heads drop uncontrollably onto the surface, gouging and scratching it beyond repair). We might also include the rare situations when the IO channel fails. One of the more devastating types of failure in this area occurs when an entire record is shifted one character to the left or right; occasionally one also finds situations in which two or three characters in the record are zeroed out as they pass through the IO channel into memory.

In the case of an unreadable record, we can at least console ourselves with the knowledge that the rest of the system is capable of operating. In many cases, the user can be informed that the record he wanted cannot be obtained—and no recovery need be attempted. Alternatively, the user could be told to wait a few minutes, while the computer operator scurries around trying to retrieve the record from a previous dump tape. In either case, the rest of the system can continue to run, and other users can continue typing input.

In the event that a critical directory becomes unreadable, or in the event that the entire device becomes inoperable, all of the users will be affected. On some systems, it may be feasible to maintain a dual copy of the data base on a backup disk, but as we saw in Chapter N, it is generally uneconomical and impractical. Thus, a serious disk or drum failure will probably cause the entire system to shut down, after which the hardware malfunction can be repaired and/or the data base can be reloaded on more reliable parts of the disk.

If an IO channel starts shifting records or dropping characters, it is not always clear that the system will be able to respond intelligently. If the operating system is attempting to read a directory into core, an error of this type (which is *not* accompanied by any error flags or indicators) could be fatal. Even if the error occurs with a record of ordinary data, it could cause the application programs to go into a tailspin; even worse, if the channel error occurs while a record or directory is being written to the mass storage device, it will cause the data base to deteriorate, a fact which may not be noticed for several days.

5 *Operator errors*

Alas, the computer operator is often the weak link in an otherwise reliable system. There is currently a great deal of debate about the type of background and training an on-line computer operator should have, but there is unanimous agreement on at least one point: the computer operator lives in a vastly different environment than he did when he was operating a batch computer system.

In a batch environment, the computer operator could hide his own blunders along with any hardware problems by merely rerunning the job. As long as the job got finished on schedule, the user was not aware of the reliability of the system. In an on-line system, though, a large number of users (or a very sensitive process) are intimately connected to the system, and they are immediately aware of a system failure.

The on-line computer room may or may not be a more hectic place than the batch computer room. With some on-line systems, the computer operator merely has to start the system—from that point on, the system takes care of itself. If a failure occurs, the operator, depending on his natural habits, will either be found in the men's room, at the coffee machine, or asleep in a corner.

In other cases, there may be two or three operators mounting tapes, tending the high-speed printer, and carrying on various conversations with users at their terminals. In such a hectic environment (which is not unusual for some remote batch systems), it is not unusual or surprising that the operators occasionally make mistakes.

There are four broadly-defined areas in which the operator can cause a system failure:

1 Starting up the system

2 Running the system

3 Before, during, and after a failure

4 Shutting down the system at the end of the day.

The first problem area exists for an obvious reason: the procedures for starting up an on-line system are often long and complex. The operator must first check to see that all of the hardware is in correct operating condition (many a system has been out of service for several hours because the operator innocently failed to notice that the field engineer had left a disk or even a memory module in "test" or "off-line" mode). He must then load the proper version of the operating system, the proper data base, and the proper library of application programs into the machine, carry on the proper initialization dialogue, and then take necessary steps to allow users to dial the computer. Each of these activities is fraught with danger: he may load yesterday's version of the operating system with today's application programs and last month's data base (or some other equally disastrous combination), type incorrect information during the initialization dialogure with the system, or fail to "enable" the data sets to allow users to dial the computer.†

Even when the system has been started and is running properly, the operator can be a source of trouble. One organization was plagued by an operator who kept dropping magnetic tapes on the computer console; occasionally the tapes would hit the power-off switch. On other systems, a recalcitrant user will call the operator on the phone and complain that "something is wrong with the system" (when, in fact, the problem was due to bad input, a bug in his application program, or a faulty terminal). The operator, acting on the demands of this one user, will obligingly shut the system down.

In cases where there *is* something wrong with the system, the operator sometimes makes the problem even worse. On many time-sharing systems, for example, it is possible for the operating system to get into a state where it will not accept input from user terminals, but *will* accept input from the console typewriter. Thus, users may complain that the system will not accept their

---

† One of the more humorous examples of operator errors of this type concerns the organization that was trying to think of a foolproof way of preventing the operator from using the experimental version of the system before it was declared operational. The system programmers often spent the night debugging, and when they left at five o'clock in the morning, they would inadvertently leave the "experimental" system tape around, and the operator would innocently mistake it for the "production" version of the system.

The solution was fiendishly simple. The system programmers changed the initialization dialogue in the experimental system to Hebrew, leaving the working version with its original English dialogue. Unfortunately, the experimental version still accepted English input, even though the questions it asked were in Hebrew. Thus, the morning after the change was made, the operator again loaded the experimental version by mistake, and though he didn't understand the Hebrew, he doggedly typed the same input—much to the dismay of the system programmers.

input, but the operator may find that he can still carry on his normal dialogue with the system—and he may refuse to believe that the system is not functioning properly.

As we have already mentioned, the process of shutting a system down and initiating recovery procedures can be an extremely delicate one. The operator's job is made even more difficult at this point because he is under pressure—his shift supervisor and several programmers may have run into the room to look over his shoulder while he goes through his recovery procedures. Users may be calling on the telephone to ask what went wrong, and when the system will be available again. In fact, the clever users may take the opportunity to dial the computer while it is still out of service—knowing that once the system is running again, the computer will "answer the phone," and they will be among the first to get back on the system.

Thus, with scores of datasets ringing in the corner, other users calling on the voice lines, programmers and supervisors dashing about the room with contradictory instructions to the operator, the computer room is often a scene of sheer bedlam. In such situations, operators have been known to hit the "clear memory" switch just prior to dumping memory onto a tape; they may forget to execute a recovery program to restore the data base; they quite often forget, in their haste to get the system running again as quickly as possible, to reset all of the hardware and ensure that it is in proper operating condition.

Finally, the operator can cause problems at the end of the day, when the system is to be shut down. The operator is normally responsible for making sure that the users are gracefully thrown off; he must see to it that the system (including both the hardware and the software) is brought to a graceful stop: he may be required to dump the data base onto tape, or run an accounting program to charge users for the on-line services that have been provided during the day. Obviously, each of these duties can be a source of trouble.

As we mentioned above, there is a great deal of debate about the proper way to select, educate, and train an operator for this new environment. There are many who feel that the complexity of most on-line systems is such that the operator's position should be filled by a junior programmer or systems analyst—someone who understands what is going on inside the machine. Others argue that a programming-oriented operator tends to be less thorough and efficient in some of the more mundane areas of operating the computer: cleaning the tape drives regularly, keeping the machine room as neat and orderly as possible; keeping the equipment running as continuously and efficiently as possible.

At any rate, there are a few things that the system designer should do to minimize the chances of operator error. Perhaps the most important thing is *documentation:* precise, thorough, accurate documentation that will guide the operator through every situation that he can normally be expected to encounter during the day. The vendor's instructions for operation of the hardware or the operating system are not sufficient: the operator should have a manual that tells him such things as when and how to start the system up in the morning; how to recognize the various types of system failures; how to initiate recovery procedures; how to deal with users; and how to shut the system down at the end of the day.

Also, the system itself should provide extensive documentation to show what the operator is doing. For example, the system should print a message at the beginning of the day to indicate which version of the operating system, application program, and data base are being used—so that if problems develop several hours later, the analyst can tell whether the wrong version of the system was loaded. If the operator initiates a "graceful shutdown" of the system, it should be recorded on the console typewriter; when he mounts an audit trail tape and executes a recovery program, that, too, should be recorded. The console typewriter printout should be saved for a reasonable period of time—for a few days, at least.

Finally, the system designer should try to make the system as autonomous as possible. The operator should not be required to make decisions except when absolutely necessary. For example, the operator should not have to tell the system how much memory or which peripheral devices are available: the operating system should be able to determine that for itself. During a shutdown or recovery procedure, the operator should not have to make any decisions, if it can possibly be avoided ("I wonder if I ought to save the disk storage map?").

6 *Program bugs*

There is little that needs to be said about program bugs in an on-line system. There are certainly more of them than in most batch systems; they take longer to find and cause more damage.

We should point out, though, that not all program bugs are the same. Some will cause an instantaneous and total failure of the system: the operating system will halt or zero itself. Other bugs will cause the operating system (or the application programs) to go into an endless loop. On systems with paging hardware, bugs in the page-throwing algorithms can cause the system to slow down gradually to the point where response times become totally unbearable.

7 *Power failures*

Next on our list of common causes of failure is the local utility company. The on-line system may fail from a total power loss, which, though unpleasant, is at least easy to recognize. More difficult to trace are the transient fluctuations of power that may occur at various times of the day. While these may be so brief that the lights in the computer room don't even flicker, they are sufficient to cause trouble for the machine.

Many current computers have "load-levelling" devices that will damp out the ordinary "spikes" and fluctuations in the local power supply. However, there are large areas of the United States (particularly the Boston-Washington corridor) where the power is sufficiently unstable during the summer months that the system designer should be prepared for trouble.

There are a number of approaches that can be taken. If continuous performance is of the utmost importance, it may be necessary to provide the system with its own source of power—such as oil-driven generators. This is usually prohibitively expensive if the generator powers only the computer, but it may prove economically feasible if it is also used to supply electricity for the rest of the computer complex and surrounding offices. Alternatively, a generator could be used strictly as a backup power supply—and, hopefully, the system designer will avoid the mistake of the organization that attached the starter motors for their backup generator to the local power supply. The blunder was not noticed until the Northeast Blackout of 1965.

Still another approach is to use a computer with power on/power off interrupts. The operating system receives an interrupt when the power falls below a certain tolerance, at which point it has twenty milliseconds or so to shut down gracefully. Another interrupt (the power on interrupt) occurs when power has been restored. With this type of equipment, the system designer has the added advantage of being able to identify the cause of the failure—rather than blaming it on a mysterious programming bug.

8 *Environmental failures*

In this category, we include all of the disasters that insurance companies like to avoid. Fire, flood, pestilence, air conditioning failures, electrical noise, student riots, and earthquakes are only a few of the many calamities that have befallen computer systems over the years. Of these, temperature and humidity problems are probably the most common.

9 *Gradual erosion of the data base*

It was mentioned earlier that obscure IO errors can sometimes introduce problems in the data base. This can happen if a disk, drum, or tape drive writes a bad record without any error indication; it can also happen if the IO channel drops some characters or shifts a record.

The data base may also be damaged by subtle bugs in the application programs—bugs which cause an occasional field of data in an occasional record to be destroyed. It is even possible for communication errors and terminal errors to result in a damaged data base: if a user types a "7" at his terminal, it is possible for two bits to be dropped, in which case the vertical parity bit logic will not detect an error.

The larger the on-line data base, the more insidious these problems seem to become. An error might be introduced into the data base, and the affected record may not be referenced for another six months (by which time, all the back-up copies of that record may have been discarded). An accumulation of these errors over a period of time—bad directory pointers, numeric fields where alpha fields were expected, etc.—can eventually cause the system to halt.

Consider, for example, an on-line system written in FORTRAN, using formatted IO statements. On some machines, a number which exceeds the size specified by the format statement is converted into a field of asterisks, with no other error indication. Thus, an application program might unwittingly cause a field of asterisks to be written on the data base, simply because it calculated a number larger than the application programmers had planned for (an event which is presumably rather rare and predictable). If another application program later attempts to read the same record, it will receive asterisks instead of a legitimate number, and its behavior will probably be rather unpredictable.

The reader might suggest, at this point, that the solution to the above dilemma would be to introduce "reasonableness checks" in the application programs to prevent this kind of thing from happening. The point is, however, that subtle bugs like this *do* occur in on-line systems; subtle IO errors or channel errors or transmission errors cause the same kind of damage. If one believes in Murphy's Law, it is inevitable that the data base will eventually contain some "garbage."

The only solution that seems to exist at the moment is a "data base diagnostic" program. A number of organizations have incorporated this diagnostic capability into their disk dump and load programs, so that as each record is read from the disk and written onto tape (or vice versa), it is checked to see that all of the fields contain reasonable information. At the same time, the forward and backward links of a list-structured file can be checked for correctness; directory entries can be checked; disk storage allocation tables, or "bit-maps" can be checked. Many of the errors can be corrected by such a diagnostic program; uncorrectable errors can be brought to the attention of the computer operator or one of the programmers.

The diagnostic program described above is an *off-line* program: it runs either before the system has been started up or after it has shut down (or possibly both). If there are persistent problems with the data base, the system designer might want to add an *on-line* diagnostic program. The ultimate on-line diagnostic is a trace of all accesses to the data base—something which generally costs more in overhead than it is worth. However, it may be very economical to use a sampling approach to examine a few records during idle periods of the system. This would not require very much overhead, and would yield a statistical confidence level for the integrity of the data base.

10 *Saturation*

In some cases, an overloaded system will "hang" or fall into an endless loop if it attempts to handle too many terminals, too many interrupts, or too many transactions, or if it runs out of buffer space, directory space on the disk, or "swapping" areas on the high-speed drum.

In almost all cases, failures of this kind represent an inability of the software to cope with the overload. If the programmer does not plan for such an eventuality, the system failure may be entirely uncontrolled: tables and buffers within the operating system may overflow; input messages from the terminals may be irretrievably lost because interrupts were not serviced quickly enough; the data base may be partially destroyed as files or directories overflow.

If overloads are planned for, the system can respond in a reasonably graceful fashion. If transactions are arriving too rapidly, the terminal users can be asked to wait for a moment while the system "catches up." Since virtually all of the overloads in a business-oriented on-line system are caused, either directly or indirectly, by *users,* the overload can often be handled by simply refusing to process whatever user input caused the overflow. Thus, if a user types a transaction that would cause the system to run out of file space or directory space, the user can be told that it is temporarily impossible to service the request (meanwhile, the system can type an appropriate message to the computer operator or system programmer to have the problem corrected).

11 *"Acts of God"—the unexplained failures*

Unfortunately, a significant number of failures in many on-line systems are never properly categorized, and end up being listed simply as "unexplained." Thus, we have situations when the system suddenly and mysteriously stops, with no error messages, and nothing to indicate whether the problem was due to hardware, software or any of the other sources that we listed above. Even more common are the situations in which the computer operator follows the prescribed procedures after a failure (including a memory dump, a written form that describes the contents of various registers, etc.), but:

1 The memory dump and/or other written documentation concerning the failure gets lost in transit to the system programmer whose duty it is to locate the cause of the failure, or

2 The system programmer finds that the documentation is incomplete or erroneous (e.g. he discovers that the operator cleared memory to zeroes before dumping it onto the high speed printer), or

3 The documentation gives no clue as to the cause of the failure (this is common, for example, in systems that have no power-fail interrupt, and where the power fluctuations are so brief that they are not visibly noticeable), or

4 The system programmer is so overburdened with failure reports that he ignores all that appear to be "random" or "transient," and concerns himself only with the failures that appear to fall into a pattern.

Needless to say, it is extremely important to minimize the number of unexplained failures, so that the *real* causes of failures will become known. If a large number of the failures remain unknown, it obviously becomes very difficult to decide how to go about improving the reliability of the system. Buying a backup processor might prove to be a large waste of money if the unknown failures are caused by power fluctuations. Similarly, it would be tragic to invest large sums of money in a backup power supply, only to learn that the "unknown" failures were caused by operator errors.

SYSTEM FAILURE REPORTS FOR A TYPICAL
SCIENTIFIC TIME-SHARING SYSTEM

Table U1 shows a summary "system failure report" for a composite of several different installations of a particular vendor's scientific time-sharing system. This report illustrates a number of points we have made in this chapter.

First, notice that the total number of failures in each month is rather large, and does not appear to show any significant decline over a 15-month period In fact, since most of the organizations included in this report operated their time-sharing system about 23 days per month, the statistics indicate a MTBF of about four hours (assuming that the system was in operation for eight hours each day). While this is somewhat worse than most scientific time-sharing systems, it is still considered acceptable, which seems to confirm our earlier statement that time-sharing systems are less concerned with MTBF than with MTTR.

Notice also that a large number of failures were caused by problems with the disk. The problems consisted of parity errors that made it impossible to read library programs into core. In some cases, the system might have been able to respond by aborting the job that called for the library program, but the system designers apparently thought it advisable to shut the entire system down. The library programs could then be reloaded on a good part of the disk, and the system could be restarted.

Finally, notice that almost half of the system failures remain unexplained. We have no way of knowing whether they were caused by air conditioning failures, operator errors, bugs in the operating system, power fluctuations, or other causes. The operations manager and programming manager of such an installation are in a quandary, for it is not apparent what they can do to improve the reliability of their system—other than to throw it out and obtain equipment from a different vendor.

TABLE U1 *System Failure Reports for a Typical Time-Sharing System*

Type of failure	4/69	8/69	9/69	10/69	11/69	5/70	6/70	7/70
Insufficient memory	10.2	7.6	5.4	6.6	8.7	7.4	10.3	11.2
Unexpected IO interrupts	1.1	1.2	2.3	2.4	0.8	1.7	1.2	2.0
Disk failures	13.6	5.9	12.3	16.1	14.9	13.2	17.5	14.5
Operating system failures	2.2	2.4	3.1	3.1	3.7	3.7	4.6	3.3
Multiplexor failures	2.3	0.4	0.6	1.8	0.6	1.3	0.2	0.5
Unexplained	19.0	20.6	24.8	28.4	23.2	16.2	19.8	18.0
Total	48.4	38.1	48.5	58.4	51.9	43.5	53.6	49.2

These figures represent failures per month, averaged over approximately ten different installations of the same time-sharing system.

APPROACHES TO ERROR RECOVERY FOR AN ON-LINE SYSTEM

Throughout this chapter, we have implied that there are various approaches that the system designer can take to system failures. Depending on the type of hardware, the type and degree of reliability required, and the type of system being implemented, the system designer may use an extremely simple error recovery philosophy, or he may elect a much more sophisticated one.

There are basically five "philosophies," or approaches, that one can take. The system designer should examine his system and his requirements for reliability, and choose one or more of these philosophies for each of the types of system failures that we described earlier. For some types of failures (such as those involving a disk), it may be necessary for the system designer to use different error recovery philosophies depending on the severity and precise nature of the failure.

Philosophy #1: Bring the System to a Complete Halt

On more than one system, the operating system programmers have written sequences of codes similar to that shown in Figure U6. The "halt" instruction is added half in jest, since it is assumed that the accumulator *must* be either positive, negative, or zero. Unfortunately, the joke sometimes turns sour: the computer somehow manages to get to the halt instruction. The system halts, causing confusion at the terminal (since the users simply find that their terminal no longer responds to their input), in the computer room (since the operator expects to see an error message on the console typewriter if something has gone wrong), and potential damage to the data base.

While this may seem a ludicrous example, it has happened in several on-line installations. The programmers, if not otherwise directed, often adopt an attitude of "if a programming bug or CPU failure is detected by the system, the machine should be halted before further damage is done." It is imperative that the system designer recognize that this type of *unplanned*, or *uncontrolled*, halt has a number of serious disadvantages:

1 It is likely to confuse the computer operator.

2 It is certain to confuse the users.

3 It may cause data or input messages from terminals to be irretrievably lost.

4 It may cause physical damage to the peripheral devices or other external devices under control of the system.

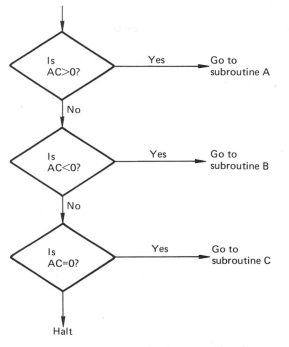

Fig. U6   An example of "dangerous" coding

When properly implemented, Philosophy #1 calls for a *planned, orderly, graceful* system shutdown. Users are politely notified that "due to circumstances beyond our control," the system will have to be shut down for some period of time. The computer operator is given information to let him know *why* the system is shutting down, and what he should do about it. Peripheral devices are brought to a graceful halt, programs are stopped as "gently" as possible, and the system comes to rest with an almost audible sigh of relief.

Looking through the list of possible system failures, the system designer may find several that call for this approach to error recovery: processor failures, memory parity errors, program bugs, power failures, and environmental failures. Notice that in some cases it may be necessary for the computer operator to initiate the "shut-down procedure"—if he sees that the computer room is on fire, for example. In most cases, though, the system itself should initiate the shut down.

The essence of this philosophy is its simplicity and economy. The system designer can avoid the expense and trouble of redundant hardware, complex automatic restart routines, and the like. If a file recovery scheme (such as the audit trail scheme discussed in Chapter N) is implemented, the philosophy of halting the system will often be adequate. On the other hand, if the system failure is at all serious (such as a 30-minute power failure, persistent memory parity errors, a disk "head crash," or some other catastrophe), the system may be out of service for a prolonged period of time. Since, as we indicated earlier, MTTR is just as important, if not more important, than MTBF, the possibility of prolonged periods of system outage may preclude this simple approach to error recovery.

It is economically feasible, in some cases, to provide backup hardware in the event of a serious system failure. The backup equipment might, in rare cases, be idle as long as the primary system is operational; more often, it is used for testing, or for off-line background batch work. If the primary system fails, it can be manually restarted on the backup equipment.

It should be noted that the policy of providing a backup processor, in addition to being rather expensive, does not guarantee a significantly improved reliability. As we discussed earlier, processor errors and memory parity errors are extremely rare in current machines, and these are the only types of failures for which a backup processor will improve the situation with Philosophy #1.

This last point should be emphasized: if the system fails because of a program error or an operator error, it does not matter whether the system is restarted on the primary processor or moved over to a backup processor. The only real advantage to the backup processor is the *speed* with which the system can be restarted: the operator may have the operating system and the appropriate application programs loaded in the backup machine, ready to be manually started in the event of a failure in the primary machine; alternatively, the system designer may arrange for an *automatic switchover* to the backup machine, as discussed in Philosophy #5. In either case, it may be faster than stopping the primary system, reloading the operating system and application programs, and going through the tedious process of initializing and starting the system.

Philosophy #2: Stop Processing the Terminal User or Task That Caused the Error

As we have often indicated, most of the processing carried on by a business-oriented on-line system is initiated by a terminal user. If a serious error occurs during the processing of some user-initiated task, another form of error recovery might be simply to *abort* that processing and type an apologetic note on the user's terminal. This is a perfectly reasonable approach to take in a large number of situations:

1 Transmission errors make it impossible to receive input from a particular terminal. The user is so informed (if possible) and his terminal is disconnected.

2 While executing an on-line program for a terminal user, the system discovers unrecoverable IO errors (i.e. while reading a disk record, punching a card, reading or writing magnetic tape, etc.). The user's application program is stopped, and a message is typed on his terminal to inform him of the difficulty.

3   While processing a transaction in a dedicated system, the application program "blows up"—e.g. it executes an illegal instruction or references beyond its memory area or gets into an endless loop. In this case, the operating system could abort the application program, type a message to the user (asking him not to retype the transaction until the problem has been corrected), restart the application program, and continue processing transactions for other users.

A common criticism of this error recovery philosophy is that it is really just a subtle way of "passing the buck"—that is, the system solves its errors by passing them off to the users. While this is, in a sense, true, many system designers will argue that it is preferable to an approach where *all* of the users are affected by an error that only one user caused. In many cases, there is no other way for the system to respond to the error anyway—if a bug in an application program causes it to "blow up" when it processes a transaction, it will probably blow up *every* time it processes that transaction. Thus, there is no point in restarting the processing of that transaction until the bug has been corrected—but it seems much more equitable to keep only one user waiting, while the rest of the users continue to get their work done.

Philosophy #3: Fall Back to a Less Efficient Mode of Operation

Whenever a hardware failure can be isolated, it may be possible to implement an error recovery philosophy that calls for shutting down only the afflicted part of the system, leaving the remaining hardware elements to run in a degraded mode of operation. There are a number of examples that can be given:

1   If devices such as card punches, tape drives, or high-speed printers fail during the operation of the system, it may be possible to direct the output elsewhere until the error has been corrected. Thus, printer output could be sent to tape or disk; card output could also be sent to tape or disk; a faulty tape drive might result in the system limping along with less than its normal number of tapes.

2   If one memory module becomes unusable because of parity errors, the system could possibly continue running with the remaining memory modules. This might greatly increase swapping and overlaying, thus degrading the response time of the system, but at least the system would continue operating.

3   If the main processor fails, transactions might continue to be accepted and queued by a "front-end" computer. Processing of transactions might have to be delayed for some time, but at least the users would not have been deprived of their ability to input transactions.

4   If the "front-end" computer or the communications network are inoperable, the users might be allowed to prepare their input in an off-line fashion (e.g. on

cards, or paper tape). The input could then be sent to the computer *en masse* when the communications network is repaired, or it could be manually transported to the computer.

5   If part of the data base has been damaged, or if some of the application programs are inoperable, users could be restrained from typing transactions that require the faulty programs or the damaged portion of the data base. Other transactions would still be permissible, and it is conceivable that users could continue to get a reasonable amount of work done.

The most common difficulty with this approach is that of getting the system to recognize that a faulty component has been repaired. The system designer must remember to provide the computer operator with the capability of informing the system that a previously-inoperable component (which may be a hardware unit, a program, or a portion of the data base) is once again capable of being used.

Philosophy #4: Switch to a Stand-By Subsystem

If the system designer is extremely concerned with continuous performance (i.e. high MTBF), it may be desirable to include redundant components in the system. Several years ago, this approach was popular as a method of ensuring data base reliability, but as we discussed in Chapter N, it has proven to be too expensive for most current on-line systems. However, it may be feasible to provide redundant multiplexors, terminals, communication lines, "front-end" communication computers, or other specialized components of the system.

Philosophy #5: Switch to a Stand-by System

This approach requires a complete backup of equipment—processors, data bases, peripheral units, communications equipment, and power supply. It is a reasonable approach only when high MTBF is of the utmost importance, and it can obviously be extremely expensive in terms of extra hardware costs. On the other hand, small process control systems and data acquisition systems may find hardware costs small enough that they can afford to duplicate the mini-computers and other equipment in the configuration.

As we discussed briefly in Chapter A, there are two ways of implementing this approach: either with a *duplexed* system or a *dual* system. In a duplexed system, a backup exists for each component in the system, but it is not used unless there is a failure in the primary component. In a dual system, both the primary and backup component operate in parallel, so that either one will be able to continue operating if the other one fails.

A duplexed system has the advantage that the backup system can be

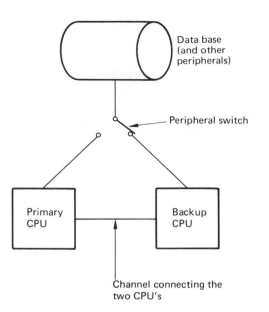

Data base
(and other
peripherals)

Peripheral switch

Primary
CPU

Backup
CPU

Channel connecting the
two CPU's

Fig. U7   Hardware configuration for duplexed system

used for other purposes while the primary system is operational. Thus, such an arrangement is often easier to justify economically than is a dual system, and the duplexed system seems to be the more popular form of this type of error recovery.

A common method of implementing the duplexed approach to error recovery is shown in Figure U7. The processors are connected by a channel that allows them to interrupt each other in much the same way that an IO device can interrupt the processor. The IO devices are arranged in such a way that they can be "switched," under program control, from one processor to another.

So that both machines are constantly aware of the status of the other machine, messages are sent back and forth, as shown in Figure U8. The messages are usually initiated by the primary machine and sent on a regular schedule—e.g. every 1/60 second. The backup machine receives each message, and, as Figure U8 demonstrates, sends back one of its own.

The content of the message is usually something very simple—something which essentially says, "I'm fine, how are you?" This dialogue continues until one of four things happens:

1 The primary machine suddenly stops.

2 The primary machine realizes that it has a failure, and so indicates to the backup machine.

3 The backup machine suddenly stops.

At the beginning of a predetermined "period", the primary
CPU sends a message to the backup CPU. The message
basically says, "I am functioning properly."

Fig. U8(a) Communication between processors in a duplexed system

At the beginning of the next regular period,
the backup machine sends a similar message
back to the primary machine.

Fig. U8(b) Communication between processors in a duplexed system

4 The backup machine realizes that it has a failure and so indicates to the primary machine.

In the first case, the backup machine realizes, after two message "periods," that the primary machine is no longer functioning. It must then abort whatever processing it was carrying on, switch all of the primary on-line peripheral devices to its own control, and take over the operation of the system. This may be a rather difficult task, since the backup machine may not know precisely what the primary machine was doing at the time of the failure.

To rectify this problem, we include in the "I'm fine. . ." message enough information so that the backup machine knows which programs the primary program is executing, which transactions are being processed, and so forth. This information, together with the audit trail that we discussed in Chapter N, is usually sufficient for the backup machine to be able to resume processing.

In the second situation described above, the backup machine must still take over the operation of the system, but the primary machine can shut down gracefully. When it sees, for example, that it has an unrecoverable memory parity error, it can instruct the backup machine to take over—telling it which programs to execute, and so forth.

In the last two situations, the backup machine fails, and is thus not available in the event that the primary machine fails also (an unlikely event, but certainly not an impossible one). Faced with this situation, the primary machine knows that it must choose some other form of error recovery if it has a failure. If at some later time the backup machine indicates that it is

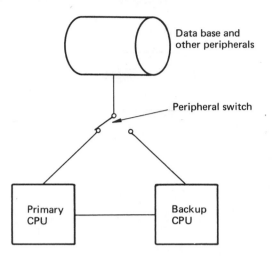

At the point in time when it is supposed to
send a message to the backup CPU, the primary
CPU fails to do so. This may occur because of
a bug in the software, or because the primary
system is busy responding to other interrupts.

Fig. U9(a)   A possible problem with the "switch-over" scheme

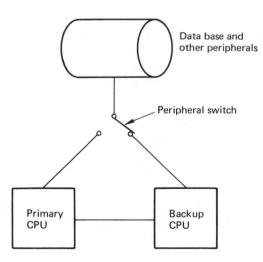

After a reasonable period of time, the backup machine
assumes that the primary machine has failed. Accordingly,
it switches the IO devices to its own control and takes
over the operation of the system.

Fig. U9(b)   A possible problem with the "switch-over" scheme

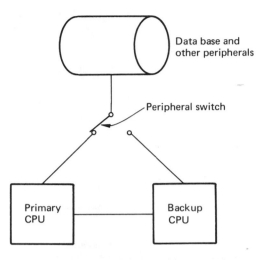

Data base and
other peripherals

Peripheral switch

Primary
CPU

Backup
CPU

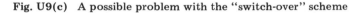

Shortly thereafter, the primary machine gets out
of its loop and resumes its normal activities. Not
knowing (or not caring) that the backup machine
has grabbed the IO devices, it grabs them back.
Chaos reigns supreme . . .

Fig. U9(c)   A possible problem with the "switch-over" scheme

operational again, the primary machine can revert to the more sophisticated
form of recovery.

It should be noted that these "switch-over" schemes are not always
foolproof. On most hardware configurations of this sort, *either* processor can
switch the IO devices to its control. Thus, it is possible for the primary
machine to cause the kind of confusion shown in Figure U9: by getting into
a temporary loop, it does not respond to the ". . . how are you?" message
from the backup machine. The backup machine subsequently decides that
there has been a failure, switches the IO devices, and takes over the
operation of the system. Seconds later, the primary machine gets out of its
loop, and switches the IO devices back to its control again. . . and eventually
both machines, fully convinced that the *other* machine has failed, end up
spending all of their time trying to capture the IO devices.

TESTING AND DEBUGGING FOR
ON-LINE COMPUTER SYSTEMS

Chapter V

TESTING CONCEPTS AND AIDS

In a number of business organizations, "testing" of computer programs has always been a rather nebulous activity. Because of insufficient manpower, insufficient time, or an innocent faith in the abilities of their programmers, many managers are content to let the programmers determine the nature and extent of testing that takes place. As a result, the programmers are often not forced to carry out the kind of thorough testing required of on-line systems, using the excuse that "the best test of the system is the *user.*"

One purpose of this chapter is to demonstrate that such a lackadaisical attitude towards testing will usually cause a large amount of trouble. Most system designers who have suffered through one or more on-line systems will automatically allocate 50% of the total project time to testing and debugging, and at least one system designer has estimated that as much as 80% of the coding generated in an on-line system consists of "off-line" utility routines and test packages.† On smaller systems, one might hope that the testing effort would occupy closer to 1/3 of the total project time, and 33-50% of the total code, but it is still a significant part of the system.

This emphasis on testing may come as a bit of a surprise to the programmer or systems designer whose previous experience involved only batch programs. There are a number of very good reasons, though, for the increased difficulty of testing on-line systems—reasons that the system designer should be familiar with. After we have discussed these reasons, we will turn our attention to some of the testing aids that can be of great assistance in an on-line project.

† T.B. Steel, Jr., *The Development of Very Large Programs*, Proceedings of IFIPS Congress 65, Volume 1

THE VARIABILITY OF ON-LINE SYSTEMS

One of the reasons for increased testing problems is that on-line systems are so much more *variable* than their batch predecessors. Batch computer systems are usually characterized by a fairly well-defined sequence of events, performed in a serial fashion upon a rather limited number of types of input.

In an on-line system, however, the number of permissible inputs may be rather large. The number of input *devices* (e.g. teletypes, CRT's, card readers, etc.) is usually far larger than on batch systems, and the number of different types of transactions is also larger in many cases.

Similarly, the number of possible actions that the system might take is also usually larger than on batch systems. This is especially true in many business-oriented on-line systems, where the action of the system depends on the contents of various records and files, *which change in real time.* To put it another way, the action that the system takes is often a function of the other activities that are going on at the same time—and this obviously leads to highly variable behavior.

This element of variability makes testing of the on-line system much more difficult. A program which was tested successfully on Monday may fail the same test on Tuesday—because it is working with a slightly different data base, or because it is running concurrently with other programs which affect its behavior. It is thus important that a test plan be developed which will ensure that the program will be tested in most, if not all, of the environments in which it will eventually be used. This is not at all easy to do, and is almost impossibly difficult when testing an operating system. For application programs, though, it *is* possible to create a "test environment" which will simulate all of the situations which the program may be expected to encounter.

PROBLEMS AND BUGS TEND TO BE VERY OBSCURE

One of the most frustrating aspects of testing an on-line system is that the bugs are difficult to recreate. Some problems may occur once a day, once a week, or every third Tuesday; other problems may occur only once, to be replaced with other, equally mysterious problems.

From the discussion of system failures in Chapter U, the reader should be able to understand why a number of on-line bugs and problems are so obscure. An IO channel will, on rare, unpredictable occasions, drop one character in the middle of a record; an occasional fluctuation in power, too brief to be seen by the human eye, will cause the system to suddenly halt; an equally obscure program bug will so startle the computer operator that he will forget to gather the necessary data (core dumps, contents of critical registers, etc.) so that the cause of the problem can be ascertained; occasional noise in the communication lines will cause one or two characters to be garbled.

In this area, we should point out that many of the problems of an on-line system are related to an individual user, and the specific nature of his input. The system designer should be prepared for the following kinds of complaints from his users:

I can't get the terminal to do anything.

I can't log in.

I just typed in the XYZ transaction, and the system rejected it.

There must be a bug in the system—my program doesn't work, and it worked fine yesterday.

In order to respond to these complaints, the system designer must know *precisely* what the user typed at his terminal, and what the system did in response. This is not always easy, since users have a tendency to lose the hard-copy output from their terminals, and to forget exactly what they typed.

As we noted above, on-line systems are extremely variable in nature. Thus, it is possible for a user to type the same input day after day with no problems; and then, because of a freak combination of other inputs from other users, an obscure program bug, or a transient hardware failure, he may get an error indication. To find the cause of the problem, it may not be sufficient to recreate the dialogue between that one user and the system-it may be necessary to recreate the entire environment at the time of the problem.

Thus, we see that the system designer has two goals when developing a set of test programs for his on-line system:

1 The test programs should be able to test all, or at least a large fraction, of the environments in which the system will be expected to run.

2 The test programs should allow the system designer to repeat any sequence of events over and over again.

THE COST OF UNTESTED SYSTEMS

As we indicated above, the natural tendency of many programmers is to turn a semi-debugged program over to the customer, using the argument that "the best test of the system is the customer." Even the most responsible programming manager may be forced to adopt this philosophy because of the type of testing problems we have already discussed.

It should be remembered, though, that, by their very nature, on-line systems are beginning to take over functions normally performed by humans. More and more of the functions that were once manually performed are being centralized by an on-line system; more and more of the ledgers, journals, hand-written customer lists, and manually prepared inventory reports are disappearing into a data base that may be thousands of miles away.

As a result, people are often far more dependent on an on-line system than they were on the previous batch or manual system. If the system fails or starts developing serious bugs, the users will often not be able to fall back to "yesterday's report"—simply because there is no report. It may be much more difficult to back up to a manual mode of operation, whereas this was sometimes possible in a batch situation.

This dependency was probably best illustrated by the State of California, which decided to install a centralized on-line reservation system for use of campsites in state parks. The system was discontinued in the summer of 1970 (for reasons which were largely non-technical), and chaos ensued. Officials suddenly remembered that the original manual system had been decentralized: each state park had taken care of its own reservations. As a result, it became extremely difficult (not to mention expensive) to back up to a centralized manual system.

THE PROBLEM OF USER CONFIDENCE

Users of a new on-line system are often not familiar with computers, and may have no technical background at all. The system designer must be aware that it is very easy to lose the user's confidence, and very difficult to regain it. As the user first begins to use a new on-line system, a complex man-machine relationship begins to evolve, in which the following stages are very common:

1 *Impatience*

The clerk or the manager who was told that the system would do "everything" for him will first react with impatience when the machine does not respond as he thought it would. Thus, when he types a transaction that looks "reasonable," but is nevertheless syntactically incorrect, his reaction is likely to be, "C'mon, machine, you know what I mean!"

2 *Cynicism*

After he has learned that the computer is a rather inflexible beast, the user's next reaction will be one of cynicism. If the system designer has spent a great deal of time thinking of a clever acronym for the system (and there are those who argue that this is the first and foremost activity when designing a new system), he will discover that the user has invented new meanings for the acronym. Project MAC, for example, which originally stood for *M*ultiple *A*ccess *C*omputer, was eventually transformed into *M*an *A*gainst *C*omputer.

3 *Distrust*

If the computer continues to misbehave, it may cause extra work for the user. He may have to go to great lengths to regenerate files that were damaged by the system, or he may have to retype several transactions that were lost as a result of a system failure. As a result, the user may start wondering if he is wasting his time by using the computer, and may start thinking of ways of avoiding the use of the system altogether.

4 *Disbelief*

A common superstition among users of on-line systems is, "If the answer comes out wrong, try it again—you'll get a different answer." Other common superstitions are: "Don't type too fast on that terminal—it works better if you type slowly," and "The terminal seems to work better if you kick it a couple of times."

Unfortunately, as with all superstitions, there is often an element of truth in these statements. It is possible that the system might give different answers if the same transaction is repeated—either because of transmission errors or because of real-time file updating considerations. It is possible that rapid typing on a terminal might result in a character being missed by the system. As for the superstition about kicking the terminal—if it works with automobiles, why not with computers?

The important point is that, by this time, the users consider the entire system—machine, system designer, and programmers—as one malevolent entity. They have lost all faith in the ability of the on-line system to make their jobs any easier, and it will be a difficult task to regain that faith.

SOME COMMENTS ON ORGANIZATIONAL REQUIREMENTS FOR TESTING

By now, the reader has hopefully been convinced that thorough testing of an on-line computer system is both a difficult and an important task. Before turning to a discussion of some useful test packages, we should point out that a separate and independent effort is needed for the development of test programs. In a large organization, it is common to find a "Product Test Department" or "Quality Control Department"; even in a small on-line project, it is imperative that a group *other than the implementation group* write the test programs.

There are a number of reasons for this suggestion. The most important is that the people involved with the design and implementation of the system are too busy and too emotionally involved to be able to develop good test programs concurrently. As a result, they will develop their test programs *after* they have developed the system, whereas a separate group of "test programmers" could develop the test programs at the same time the implementation people are developing *their* programs. This kind of *parallel* effort (instead of a serial effort by one group of people) helps ensure that the test programs will be ready when they are needed.

Another reason for delegating the test programs to a separate group is that the *programmers are likely to generate test routines that are trivial in nature.* One programmer, for example, was assigned by his supervisor to write a double precision mathematical library for a new version of FORTRAN IV that was being implemented by the company. The assignment involved writing subroutines that would calculate sines, cosines, square roots, etc. to 18 decimal places—and there were no readily available mathematical handbooks which could be used to check the output of the subroutines to that degree of precision. After a few months of work, the programmer finished writing the subroutines, and in a hurry to move on to his next assignment, made only a few obvious tests: sin 90°, sin 0°, square root of 4, etc. At the time this book was written, some *five years after the programs were "tested,"* nobody really knows whether the programs work—and the programmer, of course, has long since vanished.

While this may be a rather unusual example, it is nevertheless common for the programmer to check only the obvious flow of control through their program. Even the most conscientious programmer is likely to repeat the same logic errors that he made in the program to be tested.

People who are knowledgeable with the system, but not directly involved in the implementation, are likely to do a much more thorough job of testing. One might even argue that there is a certain personality that is ideally suited to the job of testing someone else's programs: the person who derives a kind of malicious satisfaction in finding something wrong with another's work.

TEST PACKAGES FOR ON-LINE SYSTEMS

By now, we have seen that the testing effort in an on-line system is both an important and a difficult one. We have seen that there are a number of reasons for delegating this effort to a separate group of programmers and analysts, the most important of which is the need to ensure *parallel* development of test programs and operational programs.

In order to develop test programs at the same time that the rest of the programs are being developed, the system designer must have a good idea, *at the beginning of the project*, of the type of test packages his system will require. While these will certainly vary from one system to the next, there are a number of packages which have been useful in a large number of systems. A few of these test packages are discussed below.

Simulated Input Package for Application Programs

On-line systems usually have to deal with input from a variety of devices—magnetic tape, card reader, CRT, and so forth. Testing is quite simple with most of these devices, but terminals present a special problem. In general, it is too slow, awkward, and troublesome to generate test input on a terminal by hand. There may be cases where users can be persuaded to assist the testing effort by typing various kinds of input at their terminals, but this is usually a rather inefficient process; also, there may not be a sufficient number of terminals available when the testing takes place.

Hence, it is very desirable to have a test program which will generate simulated input from a terminal. If the application programs are to have the structure shown in Figure V1 (see Chapter H for a more detailed discussion

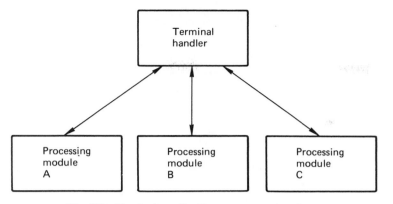

Fig. V1 Typical application program structure

of application program structures), then the simulated input package could be inserted as shown in Figure V2 or as shown in Figure V3. Test input could then be composed on such media as cards or magnetic tape, and fed to the application programs via the test package.

It should be realized that the simulated input package can be as simple or as complex as desired. The system designer might want to arrange to have the program operate in various modes:

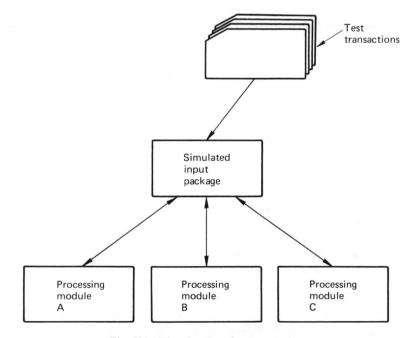

Fig. V2 The simulated input package

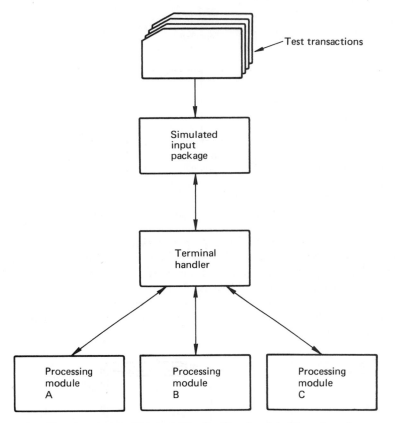

Fig. V3   An alternative structure for the simulated input package

1 *Single terminal mode*

In this mode, the test package would act as if only one terminal were attached to the system. A test transaction would not be passed to the application program until it had finished processing the previous one.

2 *Multiple terminal, serial processing mode*

In this mode, the test package would act as if several terminals were attached to the system. However, it would pass test transactions to the application programs in a serial fashion. This would not test many of the multi-programming features of the system, but it would allow the application programmers to make a thorough test of their individual programs.

3 *Multiple terminal, multiprogramming mode*

In this mode, the test package would pass transactions from several different terminals to the application programs, in such a way that several transactions would be processed concurrently. By controlling the mix of test transactions, the systems designer can test various potential multiprogramming problems: queueing of messages, contention for files, etc.

4 *Multiple terminal, mixed-messages mode*

On systems where a transaction may consist of several lines of input, it may be desirable to have a mode in which the test program sends partial messages from several terminals.

The concept of simulated input is far less useful for testing operating systems, since the IO routines are largely device-dependent. That is, the IO routines in the operating system are written to handle the interrupts, perform the buffering, and otherwise control the particular IO device for which they were written; it is thus not easy to substitute "simulated" input from another device.

If the system's hardware configuration involves a front-end computer, though, as shown in Figure V4, then it may be possible to write a simulated input package to run in the front-end computer. The test program in the front-end machine would read transactions from tape or cards, and then send them to the main computer as if they were normal messages from terminals. The operating system in the main computer would have no way of knowing that they were anything other than ordinary transactions, and could be expected to perform its usual actions upon the transactions.

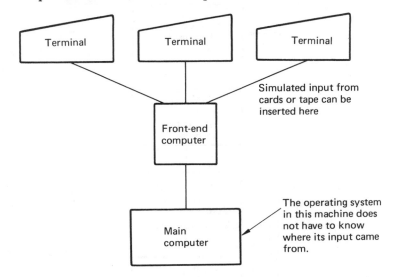

Fig. V4 A typical "front-end" hardware configuration

Finally, we should point out that the simulated input package need not, and indeed should not, be considered an isolated, "stand-alone" test package. As shown in Figure V5, the input package could be combined with a set of statistical routines to gather information about the CPU time and IO time required to process each transaction; Figure V6 shows the input

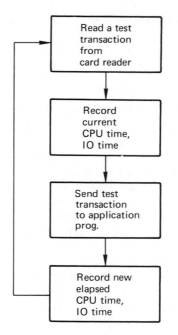

Fig. V5 Simulated input with a statistical package

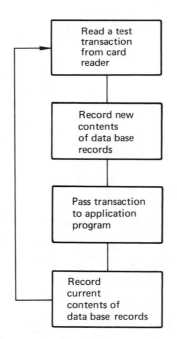

Fig. V6 Simulated input with a data base trace

package combined with a "trace" program to display the contents of critical data base records before and after processing of a transaction.

Test Data Base Generator

Most on-line systems have an extensive set of files which have to be set up prior to any test run. There are several reasons for wanting an artificial test data base instead of a "live" data base:

1   The live data base may not exist at the time the testing is being performed.

2   The live data base may be so large that a great deal of time would be wasted loading it from magnetic tape in preparation for a test run.

3   The live data base may contain classified or "sensitive" information which ought not to be made available to the test programmers.

4   A live data base changes between test runs, making it more difficult for the programmers to check the operation of their program.

As in the case of terminal input, it is extremely awkward and time-consuming to construct a test data base by hand. Instead, it is desirable to have a program that can construct a test data base, given a definition of legal record formats and contents. If a live data base exists and does not contain sensitive information, an alternative procedure might be to construct a test data base from every N^{th} record of the live data base.

A number of auxiliary utility programs might be required to augment this data base generator. It is common to find the following types of data base utility routines:

1   *Data base print routine*

This utility program would print selected records and files, in a suitable format, on a high-speed printer.

2   *Selective dump and load programs*

This program would allow the test programmer to copy selected parts of the data base from disk to tape; conversely, it would retrieve selected records or files from a "tape dump" of a previous test data base and merge them into the current copy of the test data base.

3   *Data base "patch" routine*

This routine would allow the programmer to alter, delete, or add records, or perhaps even fields, within a record. The changes would be indicated in a card deck supplied to the "patch" routine.

Test Output Comparison Package

It is important to realize that the testing of a large on-line system is a task several orders of magnitude more difficult than the testing of any individual program. During the testing and debugging phase of the project, programmers will be changing their subroutines on a daily basis, resulting in the following common phenomena:

1 Bugs that had once been removed from a program will creep back in again. This happens because, over a period of months, an absent-minded programmer may forget why he had originally made certain changes to his program, or, conversely, why he had scrupulously *avoided* making certain changes. This problem also occurs frequently when a new programmer takes over the debugging of another programmer's subroutines.

2 Seemingly innocent changes to a part of the system that is considered "solid," or thoroughly tested, may cause problems. When looking for the new bug, one often tends to overlook the thoroughly tested subroutines. In the words of the programmer, "it couldn't be *that* subroutine—it's always worked, and I only made a teensy-weensy change to it."

3 A change to one part of the system may cause problems in a seemingly unrelated part of the system. Thus, it is often necessary to perform a thorough systems test to see whether a change to one subroutine works properly.

From these observations, it can be seen that it would be useful to have a program that could compare the output from various test runs, listing the discrepancies it found. The output tapes from the test runs might contain such information as the contents of various data base records before and after a transaction was processed; the text of messages generated by the program and sent to the terminal; contents of various queues, buffers, and so forth.

The only problem with this approach is that the system might not process transactions in exactly the same sequence from one test run to the next. Thus, the output from successive test runs might differ significantly, since record contents would be different, queues might be of a different length, and so forth. As a result, it is difficult, if not impossible, for the comparison program to tell whether discrepancies between two test runs are due to the real-time nature of the system or due to new bugs in the system.

In many cases, there simply is no solution to this kind of "timing" problem. In at least two special cases, though, the system designer can continue to make use of the comparison package:

1 On some systems, transactions may be entirely independent of one another—that is, they reference separate parts of the data base, require processing by separate application programs, etc. (a scientific time-sharing system is a good example of this type of system.) In such a case, the system can be expected to perform the same actions from one test run to another, *but in a slightly different order.* If the output tapes are sorted by transaction number, then the comparison program should find no discrepancies.

2 In some cases, the cumulative effect of several transactions may be the same, regardless of the order in which they are processed. Thus, it may be possible to

write a comparison program that will look at record contents before and after a series of transactions have been processed. This approach may not prove to be as thorough a test of the system as one in which the data base is examined before and after *each* transaction is processed.

A Trace of Calls to the Operating System

Another useful testing package is one which records all of the calls from the application programs to the operating system. The trace should record such things as:

the type of call being made—e.g. a READ, WRITE, EXIT, etc.

the arguments of the call—i.e. the parameters being passed to the operating system.

the action taken by the operating system, and any values passed back to the application program.

This type of trace seems to be most useful during the early stages of testing and debugging a system. Its main disadvantage is the tremendous amount of output it generates—there are so many calls to the operating system that it is rather difficult for the trace program to keep up with them.

A Terminal Trace

As we indicated above, a number of the problems in an on-line system are discovered by users who are unable to provide any hard-copy documentation of their dialogue with the system. Also, as we pointed out, it is sometimes necessary to know what *other* users were doing in order to find out why one user was having problems.

Thus, it is often useful to have a trace of all input *and* output messages from the terminals. The trace program should record the terminal number (or user identification) and the time of day, as well as the text of the message. As the reader may have already observed, the trace can be combined with the audit trail that we discussed in Chapter N. If there is no audit trail, the trace can still be maintained on a magnetic tape, or even a high-speed printer.

It may occasionally be desirable to include a utility program which will sort the terminal trace output by terminal number, or user ID. This gives the system designer the ability to see the entire dialogue between a particular user and the system.

Off-Line Data Base Diagnostic Program

In Chapter U, we mentioned that a data base diagnostic program might be useful to prevent failures from "garbage" data bases. Such a program also has value as a testing aid, since it can be executed immediately before and immediately after a test run.

Traditionally, the data base diagnostic programs have checked for damage to the *structure* of the data base. Thus, it can check for bad directory entries, bad links from one record to the next, bad storage allocation maps, and so forth. It should also check to see that two records do not occupy the same physical location on the disk.

In addition to checking the structure of the data base, the diagnostic program can check the validity of the data themselves. Fields which are supposed to be numeric can be checked to ensure that they are numeric; alphabetic fields can be checked to see that they are indeed alphabetic. "Reasonableness" checks can be made to see that numeric fields are within tolerable limits, and so forth.

It must be remembered that a before-and-after trace of data base records which are *supposed* to be affected by an application program does not guarantee that the rest of the data base is safe. It is quite possible for an application program to properly update the records it was supposed to update, and then arbitrarily destroy several other unrelated records. Only by making a periodic check of the *entire* data base can the system designer find bugs of this type.

On-Line Record Usage Trace

If the application programs contain particularly subtle data base bugs, the off-line diagnostic program may not be sufficient. In such a case, the system designer can often make use of an on-line trace of:

> calls to create a new record or file
>
> calls to read a record (not always necessary)
>
> calls to update the data base
>
> calls to delete a record or file

As with the terminal trace, this trace can be combined with the audit trail that was discussed in Chapter N. The only thing that the audit trail might not be expected to contain is a record of calls to *read* a record; for testing purposes, though, this information might be helpful.

Test Transactions

The testing packages described above are useful at various stages of the debugging process. There comes a time, however, when the system works well enough for real users to begin using it (perhaps still on an experimental basis). Problems are still bound to occur, but the system designer will gradually become more and more intent on *keeping the system running* while the problem is being found. It thus becomes less and less desirable to stop the system because of a bug in a critical application program, or a damaged record in the data base.

To be able to continue operation of the system while searching for or attempting to correct problems, we suggest that a number of *test transactions* be added to the system. Presumably, only a select group of users would be allowed to use these transactions, but the point is that they have the same general form as other user transactions. If the application programs are built with the type of structure shown in Figure V1, then the test transactions could be processed by a separate module, as shown in Figure V7.

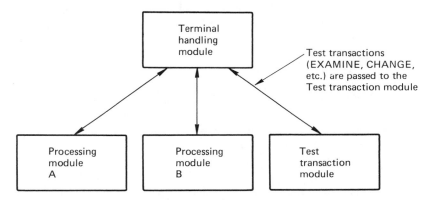

Fig. V7   Application structure for test transactions

Some of the test transactions that might be implemented are as follows:

1 *EXAMINE*

The EXAMINE transaction could be implemented in such a way that a programmer could examine the *current contents* of a specified record in the data base, or a table, a queue, or any other relevant piece of data maintained by the application programs. The programmer would have to bear in mind that the information might be obsolete by the time it was printed on his terminal, since other transactions, being processed concurrently with the EXAMINE transaction, might update the record or data.

2 *CHANGE*

Various forms of the CHANGE transaction might allow the programmer to patch a record, a table entry or any other reasonable piece of data. It should be noted that this practice is an extremely dangerous one, since an error on the part of the programmer might cause the system to fail. Under properly controlled circumstances, though, it can be extremely useful.

3 *KILL*

The KILL transaction would allow the computer operator or the systems programmer to disconnect a specified terminal or a specified user. This can be helpful if it is discovered that the terminal is causing problems (e.g. insisting on using certain programs, transactions, or files that are known to cause problems). A similar transaction, perhaps called INHIBIT, would prevent the terminal (or the user) from dialing the system again for the rest of the day, or until manually overridden.

4 TALK

This transaction would allow a terminal-to-terminal communication between the systems programmer and a user who is having problems with the system. The user would then be able to ask questions about any aspect of the system which, in his humble opinion, does not work properly. The systems programmer would be free to make his usual excuses without suffering a face-to-face confrontation with the user.

5 MONITOR

The MONITOR transaction would allow the systems programmer to spy upon a designated terminal without the terminal being aware of it. All input and output to the terminal would also be sent to the terminal which entered the MONITOR transaction, thus allowing the systems programmer to observe the progress (or lack of same) being made by the user.

6 TRACE

The most difficult transaction to implement would be the TRACE transaction, which could be used to follow the progress of an application program, or to monitor the accesses to a particular part of the data base.

To implement a data base trace requires that all of the application programs access the data base through a common "data base manager." The TRACE transaction would then send a message to the data base manager, telling it which record(s) to trace, and to which terminal the trace output should be sent. The effect of the TRACE transaction is shown schematically in Figure V8.

To implement a program trace is considerably more difficult, since it ordinarily involves modification of the program to be traced—and the modification is normally performed at compilation time. Inserting a trace in the middle of a *running* program is a very delicate procedure, and is discussed in more detail in Chapter W. In a simple case, though, it might be possible to trace all entries to a subroutine, or all calls from one application module to another. It could be accomplished, however, only if all subroutine calls and inter-module transfers took place through a common "control" module; this would make the situation analagous to the data base trace described above.

It must be emphasized that these test transactions are *dynamic* in nature; that is, they are used at the whim of the programmer *while the system is running.* The other traces and testing aids described earlier in this chapter required explicit instructions at the time the system was started up; or special test runs; or analysis of the system after it had finished running.

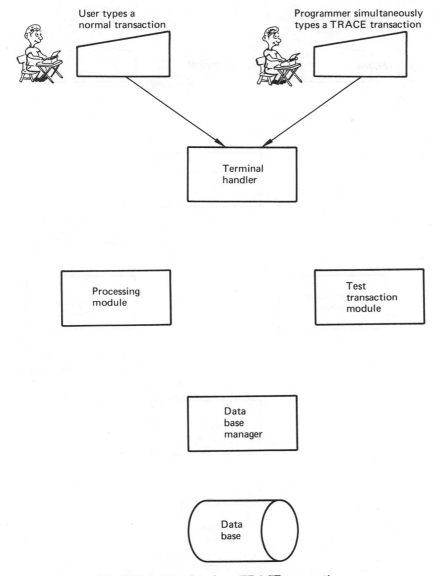

Fig. V8(a) The data base TRACE transaction

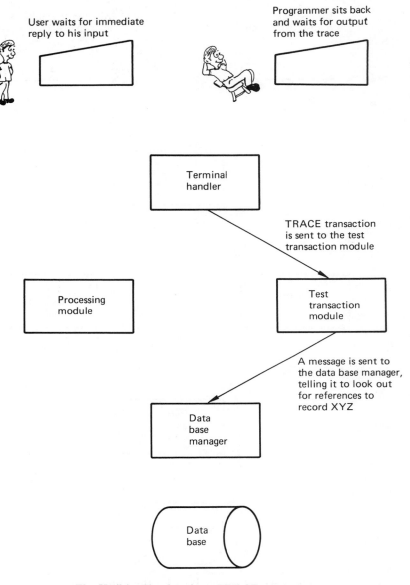

Fig. V8(b)   The data base TRACE transaction

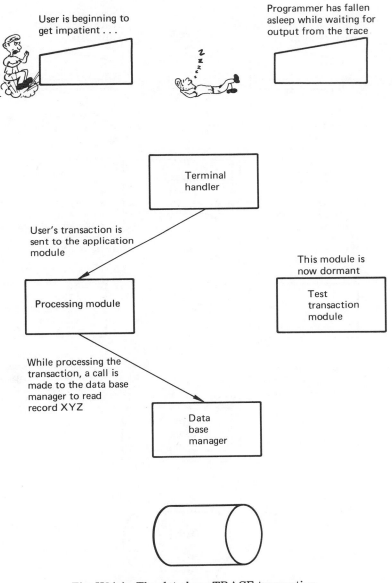

Fig. V8(c) The data base TRACE transaction

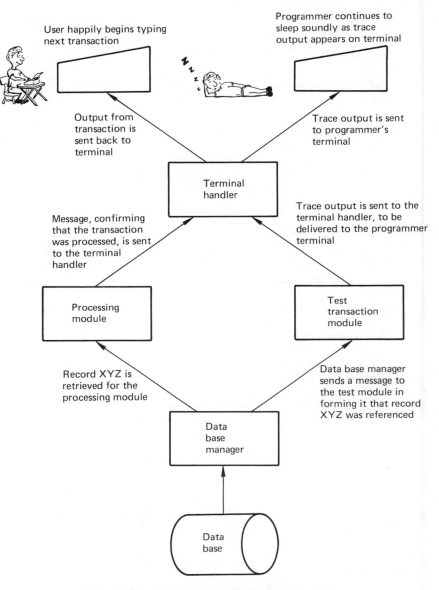

Fig. V8(d)   The data base TRACE transaction

THE DDT DEBUGGING PROGRAM

In many on-line computer projects, it is possible to distinguish between the activity of *testing* and the activity of *debugging*. While this may seem a rather subtle exercise in semantics, it is useful to think of *testing* as *an activity which documents the presence or absence of errors in the system.* Thus, many of the testing aids discussed in Chapter V constituted a kind of "quality assurance" for the system: test transactions to ensure that the system behaved properly, various types of traces to allow the programmer to make a step-by-step check of the system's behavior, off-line data base diagnostic programs to see whether the system had damaged the data base, and so forth. As we have mentioned, many programming organizations have a separate group of people dedicated to this kind of activity; and it is usually the case that when the Quality Assurance Department (or the Product Test Department, or whatever other name it may have) has found a problem with the system, they turn it over to the programmers.

This leads us to the activity of *debugging*. As the above comments imply, *debugging refers to the practice of finding and removing bugs in a program or system*, bugs which were brought to light by the Quality Assurance Department. The debugging aids used by the programmer are often the same as those used by the testing group—e.g. traces, snapshots, core dumps, and so forth. However, it is important to realize that it is an entirely different activity. It is one thing to discover that something is wrong with a program, and quite another thing to locate the source of the problem and correct it.

Probably the most agonizing task a programmer faces is the elimination of bugs from his program. The simple bugs may be found by extensive desk-checking, but the more obscure bugs have traditionally required the use of test programs, selective traces and dumps, and other procedures which attempt to catch a program in the act of performing some incorrect action.

While the testing aids discussed in Chapter V are often sufficient to *debug* (as opposed to *test*) an on-line system, there are many situations where they are simply inadequate. First of all, many bugs are caused by timing problems, as we have noted several times. In a situation analagous to that of the atomic physicist, the programmer often finds that by attempting to observe the phenomenon, he changes the very nature of the phenomenon. For example, a selective trace that displays the contents of certain variables or data base records on a high speed printer often slows the system down to such an extent that the timing problem never occurs.

As we also noted in Chapter V, a number of obscure bugs may linger on past the point where the system begins to be used in a "production" mode. It has been estimated, for example, that there are over 250,000,000 different paths that the programs in the American Airlines SABRE system may take, and it is entirely possible that some of them are executed as infrequently as once a day or once a week; timing problems, if they exist in any of these 250,000,000 program paths, may not be noticed for several months. In such cases it would be unreasonable to expect that a trace, which would generate ream upon ream of printer output, could be used to find the bug.

Finally, we should point out that the testing aids described in Chapter V do not give the programmer any control over the execution of the programs. He may use a post-mortem dump, or perhaps the off-line data base diagnostic program, to examine various aspects of his program *after* it has executed; he may use various traces and "snapshots" to glean information about the program as it runs. However, he can *not* suddenly say to himself, *while his program is executing*, "Gee, if my program ever gets into subroutine A, I'd like to stop and see what subroutine B is doing. . . and maybe I should check and see whether subroutine C updated the XYZ table properly. . ."

Instead, the programmer must insert various statements (such as the PAUSE statement in FORTRAN, or the MONITOR statement in the Burroughs ALGOL language) into his program *at compilation time*, and then proceed to run his program. If the PAUSE statement is reached, he usually has a little flexibility in determining what to do next; if he changes his mind about the portion of his program that should be monitored, he must ordinarily recompile his program.

Note that our comments thus far have been concerned with application programmers, i.e. programmers writing code in a higher-level language to run under the control of an existing operating system. For the programmer attempting to debug a process control system or data acquisition system, however, the situation is entirely different. As we pointed out in Chapter B, almost all of the code for such systems is written in assembly language. There are rarely any programs that one would consider an "application" program; all of the programs form part of the operating system or monitor. Furthermore, as Chapter B indicated, most of these systems are implemented on small mini-computers, whose vendors do not provide much in the way of traces, snapshots, and dumps.

For these programmers, debugging often takes a very primitive form. Sitting at the console of the mini-computer, the programmer must watch the console lights, and occasionally press the "halt" button to "single-step" the program through its execution. It is usually very difficult to determine the status of variables, buffers, queues or data within the machine, and the programmer often feels that he is debugging "blind."

We must conclude, then, that for programmers of process control systems and data acquisition systems, and for application programmers of business-oriented on-line systems, there is a need for a more adequate debugging aid than those presented in Chapter V. Before we discuss such a debugging aid, let us first review the debugging needs of the on-line programmer.

THE DEBUGGING NEEDS OF AN ON-LINE PROGRAMMER

There are five basic capabilities desired by the programmer, all of which he should be able to employ *while his program is running:*

1 *The ability to determine the contents of any memory location*

As his program executes, the programmer may want to examine the contents of accumulators, index registers, or other machine status registers; he may want to examine various tables, arrays, buffers, queues, or other data being manipulated by his program. In fact, he may even want to examine the program itself, to see whether subroutine-return addresses have been properly set up.

In effect, we are saying that the programmer should have the capability of *tracing* any part of his program, *or any other piece of data in the machine.* In addition, he should be able to decide, on a dynamic basis, *which* memory locations he wants to examine.

2 *Ability to change program parameters while the system is running*

After examining various parts of his program, the programmer may want to change instructions, constants, or data. This amounts to on-line patching of the program as it runs.

There may be other cases when the programmer wants to change program parameters just to see what effect it will have on the system. Thus, he may want to change scheduling algorithm parameters, overload alarms, buffering parameters, and so forth. This is much more convenient than forcing the programmer to insert patch cards in a load deck, or forcing him to recompile his program.

3 *The ability to determine the status of the data base*

Just as the programmer may want to examine programs or variables within the machine, he may want to examine records within the data base. For a complex data base structure, the programmer may want to see what other records are linked to the one at which he is looking.

4   *The ability to change the data base as the system runs*

This capability is similar to the capability of patching the program while the system is running. The programmer may want the ability to change an entire record, or perhaps just a field within a record.

5   *The ability to "stop the action" and then proceed*

This is perhaps the most important capability that the programmer requires when debugging an on-line program. The programmer needs the ability, while the system is running, to somehow say, "If my program ever reaches location X, I want to *stop.*" If his program does reach the designated "breakpoint," as it is usually called, he then wants the ability to examine various parts of his program, insert any necessary patches, *and then allow his program to proceed.* This is the essence of *dynamic debugging;* the programmer does not know, when he sits down at his terminal to begin debugging, exactly where he wants to start looking. When he issues instruction to have his program stopped at location X, he often has no idea of what he would do if he actually got there. Everything proceeds on a dynamic, experimental basis.

A DESCRIPTION OF THE DDT DEBUGGING AID

The concept of a *dynamic debugging technique*—or a DDT program, as it is more commonly called—is certainly not new, and, in fact, has enjoyed great popularity on some mini-computers and some scientific time-sharing systems; a variety of such programs have been described in the literature. The major purpose of this chapter is to describe the features common to almost all DDT programs, both to enlighten the reader who is unfamiliar with such debugging aids, and to establish the terminology for a later discussion on the implementation of a simple version of DDT.

The purpose of DDT is to allow the programmer to maintain control over the execution of his program from a terminal. There are three general forms of DDT, which may be distinguished by the manner in which they handle terminal input:

1   *Stand-Alone DDT*

This is the simplest form of DDT, and is often used to debug non-real-time programs on mini-computers. As its name implies, Stand-Alone DDT does not depend on an operating system, and does not run concurrently with any real-time system; it truly "stands alone."

The distinguishing characteristic of Stand-Alone DDT is that it handles its own terminal IO; that is, it receives terminal input from the programmer without the aid of any operating system, and it is equally adept at sending terminal output back to the user. Furthermore, it does not allow any processing to take place while it is waiting for input from the programmer. This is a very important point: *the machine sits in an "idle" loop while waiting for input from the programmer.* This implies rather inefficient use of the available machine time, since the programmer is likely to stare at the ceiling for long periods of time while trying to decide what to do next. However, such a practice is often acceptable when debugging a real-time system on a mini-computer, because there are no other programmers waiting to use the machine, and because the only alternative to a DDT program is to debug with the console switches; this latter argument is sometimes valid when debugging an operating system on a larger on-line system, also.

The important point that we want to emphasize here, though, is not that a Stand-Alone DDT makes inefficient use of the machine, but rather that it does not allow the programmer to examine and modify his program while it is actually running. Either DDT or his program may be running at any one time; it is not possible for the two to be running concurrently.

2 *User DDT, or "application program" DDT*

The second form of DDT differs from Stand-Alone DDT only in that it receives terminal input by calling the operating system, and executes, along with the program being debugged, under the control of the operating system.

This means that the operating system can perform other functions while it is waiting for the programmer to provide terminal input to the User DDT program. This arrangement is very common in scientific time-sharing systems, where several programmers can be debugging their programs concurrently, each with his own copy of DDT (or perhaps sharing one reentrant copy).

A side benefit of User DDT is that it runs under the protection features of the operating system. Thus, if the user's program goes berserk, the operating system will prevent it from executing illegal instructions or referencing an illegal area of memory. Note that as far as the applications programmer is concerned, the User DDT program does *not* run concurrently with his own program; once again, either his program is executing, or the User DDT program is executing, but not both concurrently. The multiprogramming features of the system, which are usually present in the operations system, affect *other* users, other jobs, and other application programs.

3 *Exec DDT, or "supervisor" DDT, or "operating system" DDT*

The most complex form of DDT is the one that allows other programs to execute while it is waiting for input from the programmer's terminal. While it is possible to build such a DDT for the application programmers, using the *multitasking* concepts discussed in Chapters H and I, it is extremely uncommon. If one were to construct a multitasking application programmer's DDT, it would have the same type of capabilities as the *test transactions* discussed in Chapter V, and would have the structure shown in Figure V7.

Exec DDT, as its name implies, is usually designed to help debug *Executive programs*, or operating systems. As we have indicated, the different forms of DDT are distinguished by the different forms of terminal input/output which they use. In the case of Exec DDT, the terminal is usually the *console typewriter,* which is located beside the computer console and connected directly to the machine; Exec DDT serves as an IO handler (of the general nature discussed in Chapter S) for the console typewriter.

Thus, while the programmer is sitting idle at the terminal, the rest of the system is free to run unhindered. When he types some input, an interrupt is generated, and the Exec DDT program gains control of the processor with the aid of a hardware priority interrupt structure, or with the type of software priority control program discussed in Chapter Q. After it has processed the programmer's request to examine memory, change memory, etc., it releases the hardware interrupt (or exits to the priority control program), and the rest of the system continues to run.

In the discussion that follows, we shall be describing *universal* features of DDT; when necessary, we will show how the features differ in Stand-Alone DDT, User DDT, and Exec DDT.

We will assume that the program being debugged by DDT is an *assembly language program*, since most currently available versions of DDT allow only assembly language debugging. It is possible to build a DDT-like debugging aid for the higher-level languages, but for some reason, they have never been popular with the computer vendors.

In general, DDT is loaded into the machine along with the program(s) to be debugged. This leads to a core layout as shown in Figure W1, or perhaps

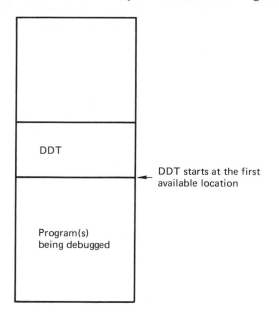

Fig. W1 Core layout with DDT

as shown in Figure W2. For User DDT programs running in machines with virtual memory, it is sometimes possible to make DDT "invisible." That is, when the DDT program is executing, the application program's virtual

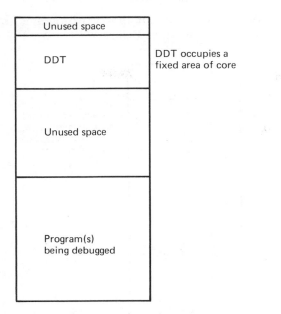

Fig. W2   An alternative core layout with DDT

memory may be similar to that shown in Figure W2; when the application program is executing, User DDT would cause itself to disappear from virtual memory (but not necessarily from physical memory), as shown in Figure W3. In fact, since User DDT and the application program are not operating

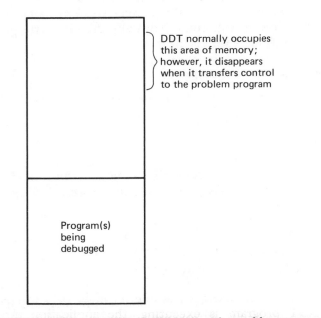

Fig. W3   User DDT in a virtual machine when the problem program is in control

concurrently, it is even possible for the two programs to occupy the same area of virtual memory, as shown in Figure W4.

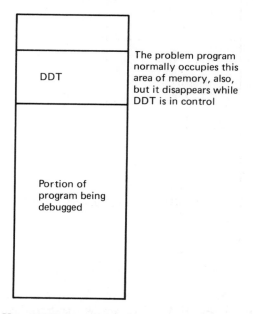

Fig. W4(a)   User DDT occupying common virtual memory with a problem program

The DDT program communicates with the programmer at his terminal in one or more standard *modes*. In the simpler versions of DDT, there may be only one mode allowed, e.g. octal. Normally, however, the programmer has the option of specifying a variety of modes:

symbolic, or assembly language mode

numeric mode, in some specified radix (octal, decimal, hexadecimal)

text mode (ASCII, EBCDIC, etc.)

floating point mode

The mode is specified as a separate command, and DDT operates in a standard mode (usually octal or symbolic) unless specifically instructed otherwise.

BASIC DDT COMMANDS—OPENING OR EXAMINING A MEMORY LOCATION

A feature that is present in even the most primitive of DDT programs is the ability to examine and change any memory location accessible to the programmer. The memory location to be examined is indicated as an octal

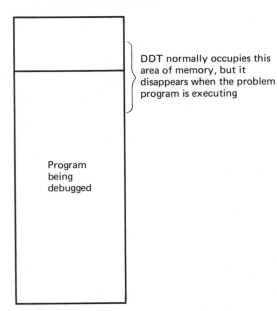

Fig. W4(b)   User DDT occupying common virtual memory with a problem program

parameter in some versions of DDT, while other versions make use of the symbol tables generated by the assembler to allow the programmer to specify the memory location as a symbolic expression.

The command which instructs DDT to examine a memory location is the *slash character*, i.e. "/" character, in almost all versions of DDT. Thus, to examine location 234, the programmer would type

234/

on his terminal. In a version of DDT that permits symbolic input, the programmer might type

XYZ+3/

to examine the third location following the one symbolically defined as "XYZ" in his program. Lest the reader think that there is something magic about the use of the slash character, we should note that some versions of DDT use the "E" character to indicate the "examine" command. Thus, the programmer might type

234E

to examine location 234.

When it receives a command to examine a memory location, DDT responds by typing the current contents of the memory location. Thus, when the programmer asks to examine location 234, the following dialogue takes place (output from DDT is underlined to distinguish it from programmer input):

234/1234

In a more sophisticated version of DDT, the dialogue might appear as follows:

XYZ+3/<u>ADD ABC+1</u>

In both cases, the programmer is asking for the same type of information; however, in the second case, the DDT program prints out the contents of the memory location in symbolic assembly language format.

Note that two successive "examine" commands for the same memory locations will yield the same output, if Stand-Alone DDT or User DDT are used. That is, it is possible for the following dialogue to take place between the programmer and DDT:

234/<u>1234</u>

234/<u>1234</u>

Since DDT and the problem program do not multiprogram with each other, the program cannot execute while DDT is waiting for input from the programmer. Thus, location 234 must, by necessity, have the same contents.

When using Exec DDT, on the other hand, it *is* possible for the contents of a memory location to change suddenly; the reason, as we explained above, is that the rest of the system continues to run while Exec DDT is waiting for input. Thus, the following type of dialogue is possible with Exec DDT:

234/<u>1234</u>

234/<u>1235</u>

234/<u>1236</u>

Once DDT has typed the contents of a memory location, it is said to be *open*, or subject to modification by the programmer. At this time, he can either make a change to the memory location, or indicate that he is satisfied with the current contents. To change memory location 234, for example, the programmer might carry on the following dialogue:

234/<u>1234</u> 4231 (CR)

where (CR) is the notation for a "carriage return" character. With a more sophisticated version of DDT, the programmer might type the following dialogue:

XYZ+3/<u>ADD ABC+1</u> SUB ABC+1 (CR)

If he is satisfied with the current contents of the memory location, the programmer might so indicate with a (CR) , leading to the following type of dialogue:

234/<u>1234</u> (CR)

or

XYZ+3/<u>ADD ABC+1</u> (CR)

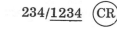

Once the programmer has typed one of the above commands (either changing a memory location or leaving it unchanged), the memory location is said to be *closed*, i.e. no longer subject to modification.

The ability to change and examine memory locations is certainly the most universal one found in different versions of DDT; there are, however, an almost endless number of variations. Among the commands that supplement the basic "open" and "close" commands are:

a command to open a memory location without typing its current contents. This type of command is useful when changing large sections of a program.

a command to close the current memory location (with or without changes) and simultaneously open the next sequential location.

a command to close the current memory location and simultaneously open the previous memory location

a command to close the current memory location and simultaneously open the memory location pointed to by the effective address of the current memory location

a command to type the contents of memory locations within a specified range (e.g. memory locations 100-200), but without allowing modification. This command is useful for quickly examining a number of memory locations.

THE BREAKPOINT AND PROCEED COMMANDS

As we indicated earlier, it is extremely desirable to allow the programmer to stop his program in mid-execution, if it reaches a specified location. This is implemented in DDT with the *breakpoint* command, which the programmer issues prior to turning control over to his program. Thus, he might type the command

456B

to tell DDT to stop his program if control ever reaches location 456. In a more sophisticated version of DDT, of course, the programmer might be able to type a command of the following type:

XYZ—3$B

(The $ character is necessary to distinguish the breakpoint command from other symbolic input.)

On some versions of DDT, the programmer has access to as many as 16 different breakpoints, which he can reference by number. Thus, he might say, "Insert the first breakpoint at location 203" by typing the command

203$1B

Similarly, he might say, "Insert the second breakpoint at location 765" by typing the command

765$2B

If he does not care which breakpoint is used, the programmer might say "Insert the next available breakpoint at location 404" by typing

404$B

The facility for multiple breakpoints is an extremely powerful one, if used properly by the programmer. Faced with the situation shown in Figure W5, he can insert breakpoints at the beginning of subroutine A *and* subroutine B *and* subroutine C; one of the breakpoints is certain to be reached. Even when the DDT program only allows one breakpoint, it can be a powerful debugging tool. Faced with a section of code that is known to harbor a bug within it, the programmer can use the breakpoint facility to perform a "binary search for bugs," as shown in Figure W6.

With breakpoints inserted, the programmer normally instructs DDT to transfer control to his program. If, during execution, his program reaches any of the specified breakpoint locations, control is returned to DDT *before the execution of that instruction*, and an appropriate message is typed for the benefit of the programmer. Thus, the following message might appear if the breakpoint at location 765 were reached:

$$\underline{\$2B\ AT\ LOC\ 765}$$

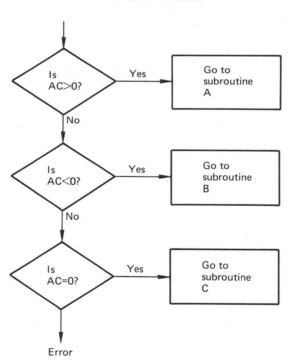

Fig. W5 A possible debugging situation

The message, though somewhat cryptic, is sufficient to tell the programmer that control reached the second breakpoint he had inserted, and that his program had been stopped just prior to executing the instruction at location 765. On some versions of DDT, the contents of the accumulator and/or the program instruction at the breakpoint location are automatically typed out when the breakpoint is reached.

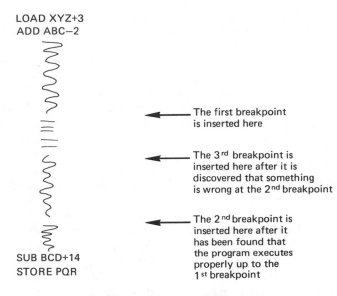

LOAD XYZ+3
ADD ABC−2

◄────── The first breakpoint
is inserted here

◄────── The 3rd breakpoint is
inserted here after it is
discovered that something
is wrong at the 2nd breakpoint

◄────── The 2nd breakpoint is
inserted here after it
has been found that
the program executes
properly up to the
1st breakpoint

SUB BCD+14
STORE PQR

Fig. W6 A binary search for bugs

Once a breakpoint has been reached, the programmer uses DDT to examine pertinent locations, make any necessary patches, and, in general, evaluate the progress of his program up to that point. Having satisfied himself that the program is running properly, he usually wishes to proceed with the execution of his program. This capability is provided by the *proceed* command in DDT; it is indicated when the programmer types the command

P

At this point, DDT resumes the execution of the program at the point of the last breakpoint.

With some versions of DDT, it is possible to construct so-called "conditional" proceed commands. The most common form of conditional proceed instructs DDT not to stop at the current breakpoint again until control has passed through it a specified number of times. To give an example, let us suppose that a programmer is attempting to debug a section of his program that goes through a loop 100 times. He might want to insert a breakpoint to see whether the program is executing properly on the initial pass through the loop; he would then like to stop the program again on the last pass through the loop. When the breakpoint has been reached for the first time, he might type

98P

to tell DDT not to stop at the breakpoint until it has passed through an additional 98 times. On the 99th pass through the loop (which is actually the 100th, counting the initial pass), DDT will stop at the breakpoint and return control to the programmer.

With an extremely sophisticated version of DDT, the conditional proceed command is analagous to a *selective trace*. That is, the programmer might be allowed to specify that a breakpoint should be by-passed until the accumulator is zero, memory location 45 contains the number 4567, and index register 3 contains a −7. This kind of sophistication is almost unheard of, though it would not be too difficult to implement.

The breakpoint commands function similarly in Stand-Alone DDT and User DDT, but can be rather tricky in Exec DDT. Again, we remind the reader that while the programmer is communicating with Stand-Alone DDT or User DDT, his program is not executing. Only when he specifically instructs DDT to transfer control to his program (which is done with the "go" command described below) does his program actually begin to execute. Thus, while he is communicating with DDT, he can insert a breakpoint, then change his mind and move it elsewhere; similarly, when the breakpoint is reached, his program is suspended and DDT regains control.

With Exec DDT, we must remember that the rest of the system is running while the programmer is communicating with DDT. Thus, it is possible that while the programmer is typing the command to insert a breakpoint in a particular program, that program is executing. Furthermore, it is possible that the breakpoint might be reached an instant after DDT has inserted it; thus, the programmer might type a breakpoint command, and immediately receive a message to the effect that the breakpoint was reached.

It is not always clear what actions Exec DDT should take when a breakpoint is reached. On the one hand, Exec DDT is supposed to allow the rest of the system to run while it is communicating with the programmer; on the other hand, the purpose of the breakpoint, from the programmer's point of view, is to *stop everything* when the breakpoint is reached. This implies that Exec DDT should immediately disable all other hardware interrupts (or establish itself as the highest priority task in the system) when a breakpoint is reached. When the programmer types a proceed command, Exec DDT could once again enable the interrupts (or establish its original software priority level).

Immediately after the breakpoint has been reached, the system is supposed to be "frozen," or in a "state of suspended animation." When this is feasible, it is a tremendously useful feature, for it allows the programmer to see exactly what the system was doing, in a real-time sense, at the time of the breakpoint. Unfortunately, it is not always feasible. In a process control system, such a breakpoint might result in an explosion; in a data acquisition system, it might result in lost data; in a time-sharing system, users would immediately begin complaining that their terminals had broken down (in such a situation, one time-sharing user actually demolished his terminal!).

It may have occurred to the reader that the programmer will occasionally want to remove one or more of his breakpoints. In a simple version of DDT, where only one breakpoint is allowed, the command would be sufficient to remove the breakpoint; in a more sophisticated version of DDT, the programmer would type the command

$3B

to remove the third breakpoint, and

$B

to remove *all* breakpoints.

Finally, we should point out that the breakpoint facility does not allow the programmer the kind of "address stop" feature available as a console switch on some computers. That is, on some computers, the programmer can, by manipulating switches on the computer console, instruct the machine to stop if a specified location is referenced as the effective address of any instruction. This capability can be implemented in DDT only if the program to be debugged is executed interpretively.

THE GO COMMAND

To transfer control from DDT to his program, the programmer types the following command:

567G

or

START+3$G

THE SEARCH COMMANDS

While other DDT features are somewhat optional, many are quite common in different implementations and have been found to be quite convenient. Among the most convenient features are the *word-search* capabilities found in many DDT programs. While debugging his program, the programmer often wants to find all references to a specific subroutine, all instances of a certain instruction, all references to a particular index register, or all instances of a certain constant. These may be accomplished with the *word search*, the *not-word search*, and the *effective address search*.

Let us begin by describing a simple example. Suppose the programmer wanted to search through his program for all instances of the constant 4567. To cause DDT to perform this search, he would type the command

1000,2000,4567W

This command would instruct DDT to search from location 1000 to location 2000, printing out all locations whose contents are 4567. Thus, DDT might print the following information as a result of the above command:

1234/4567

1456/4567

1457/4567

1776/4567

With a more sophisticated version of DDT, the programmer might type a symbolic command of the following form:

START,END,CAT + DOG$W

Once again, the three parameters are the same: the lower and upper bounds of the search, and the item being searched for.

Suppose now that the programmer wants to search a table for all non-zero entries. In this case, he is not searching *for* a particular quantity; instead, he is searching for the *absence* of a particular quantity, namely the absence of zero. To effect this search, the programmer would type

1000,2000,0N

This would instruct DDT to search from location 1000 to location 2000 for all memory locations whose contents are not equal to zero. As a result, it might print the following information:

1234/4567

1324/7654

1605/7777

1776/0001

Finally, the programmer might want to search through his program for all references to a specified location. This capability is sometimes provided with assembly cross-reference listings, but DDT provides a full effective address calculation (i.e. including indirect addressing, indexing, and so forth), which the assembler cannot do.

Suppose, for example, that the programmer wanted to find all instructions that referenced location XYZ + 3. With a sophisticated version of DDT, he could type the following command:

START,END,XYZ+3$E

The following type of printout would result:

START+4/ADD XYZ+3

LOOP+1/SUB XYZ+3

LOOP+6/STORE XYZ,3   (a reference involving indexing)

ABC+14/LOAD* PNTR   (a reference involving indirect addressing)

In many versions of DDT, there is a *mask* associated with the various search commands. When it looks at a word in memory to see if it satisfies the search condition, DDT only looks at those bits specified by the mask. Unless directed otherwise, DDT sets the mask to all ones, thus effecting a full-word search or not-search. By setting the mask with a separate command to DDT, the programmer can look for any combination of bits in a word.

Suppose, for example, that the programmer wanted to find all references to index register 3. For the purposes of this example, let us assume that the programmer is working with a 24-bit machine, in which the index register field is specified by bits 6-8 of the instruction. Thus, the programmer would set the mask as follows:

00700000M

This would tell DDT to disregard everything but bits 6,7, and 8 when making a comparison for a word search. The search itself would be accomplished with the following command:

1000,2000,11311111W

Obviously, the following command would serve the same purpose:

1000,2000,55355555W

IMPLEMENTATION OF A SIMPLE VERSION OF DDT

To complete our discussion of DDT, we provide here the flowcharts for a very simple version of DDT. This DDT is intended for a word-oriented machine, and will accept only octal input. Furthermore, it allows only one breakpoint to be inserted. However, this simplicity can have advantages: a DDT of this nature can be implemented in as little as 200 (octal) locations on a mini-computer, and it can be coded in a matter of a few hours.

Input to this simple version of DDT consists of an octal number, followed by a command character; alternatively, the command might consist of a command character alone. Thus, legal input to DDT might consist of the following:

1234/

1234G

4321B

B

P

As the reader may have guessed, the DDT program works by simply accumulating an octal number until it recognizes a command character; it then performs the action specified by the command character.

The easiest way of describing the implementation of DDT is to describe the subroutines shown in Figures W7-W16.

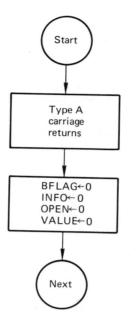

Fig. W7   The DDT initialization routine

THE DDT INITIALIZATION ROUTINE
(see Figure W7)

The initialization routine is quite simple in nature. It first types a carriage return (or any other suitable message that might be desired) to let the programmer know that it has been started and is waiting for input. Three flags and an internal working register are then intialized: BFLAG, INFO, OPEN, and VALUE.

BFLAG is a flag which tells DDT whether the programmer has typed in a breakpoint command. If BFLAG = 0, then there is no breakpoint; if BFLAG = 1, then there is a breakpoint. BFLAG is initialized to zero when DDT begins; it is set to one, or reset to zero, when the programmer types a "B" command, shown in Figure W13.

INFO is a flag which tells DDT whether it has seen any numeric input when it is accepting a command. INFO is set to zero when DDT begins, and is reset to zero whenever DDT begins looking for a new command; it is set to one whenever DDT receives an octal digit, as shown in Figure W9. Thus, if the programmer types the command

1234B

then INFO will have been set to one by the time that DDT sees the "B" character. If, on the other hand, the programmer has typed the command

B

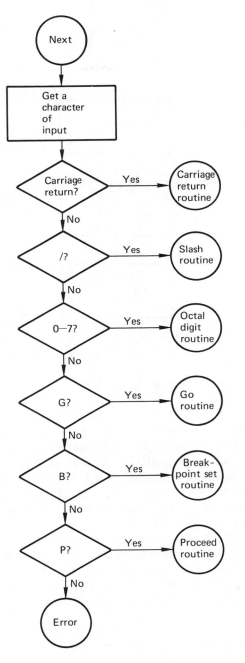

Fig. W8   Main input sequence

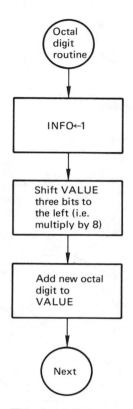

Fig. W9   Octal digit processor

then INFO will be zero when the "B" character is recognized by DDT.

OPEN is a flag which tells DDT whether there is an "open" register. If OPEN = 0, there is no open register; if OPEN = 1, the memory location pointed to by LOC is open, and subject to modification. OPEN is set to zero in the initialization routine, and is set to one by the routine which processes the *slash* character (see Figure W10).

Finally, VALUE is an internal working register that accumulates the value of octal input as it is typed in. VALUE is initialized to zero, and is reset to zero whenever DDT begins looking for new input.

Having performed its initialization, DDT then goes to its main input sequence, shown in Figure W8 and described below.

THE MAIN INPUT SEQUENCE *(see Figure W8)*

The purpose of the main input routine is to accept one character of input from the programmer's terminal and decide what to do with it. As we

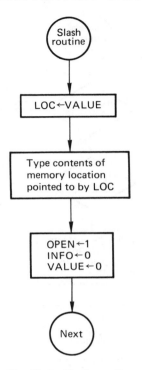

Fig. W10 Slash routine

discussed earlier, the "get a character of input" subroutine is what distinguishes Stand-Alone DDT from User DDT and Exec DDT.

Once a character of input has been received, DDT then checks to see whether it is a legal input character: an octal digit, a slash character, a carriage return, a "G," a "B," or a "P." If it is, DDT proceeds to a routine which will process the input depending on its type; if it is not a legal character, DDT proceeds to an error routine.

THE OCTAL DIGIT PROCESSOR *(see Figure W9)*

The purpose of this routine is to accept one octal digit and accumulate it into the current VALUE. As Figure W9 shows, it also sets the INFO flag to one, so that DDT will later be able to remember whether a command was accompanied by octal input.

To see how the subroutine works, let us assume that we are working with a 12-bit machine, and that the programmer has typed the command

1234G

When DDT first begins looking at this command, VALUE has been initialized to zero. The octal digit processor is entered when the digit "1" is seen, and at the end of the routine, VALUE has been set to

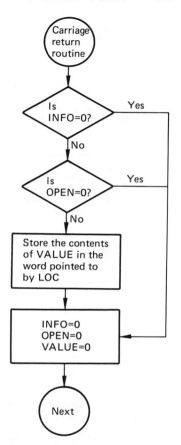

Fig. W11 The carriage return processor

VALUE/0001

When the octal digit processor is entered again to process the digit "2," VALUE still contains 0001. The routine first shifts VALUE three bits left, which results in the following:

VALUE/0010

The digit "2" is then added to VALUE, resulting in

VALUE/0012

Similarly, after the digit "3" has been processed, VALUE appears as

VALUE/0123

and after the digit "4" has been processed, VALUE appears as

VALUE/1234

Note that this is a very primitive octal input routine. If the programmer types too large a number, VALUE simply overflows and no error indication

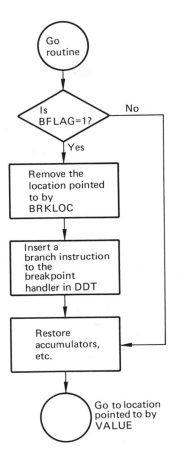

Fig. W12   The GO routine

is given. It is an easy process to add such an error check to the routine; similarly, the routine may be easily modified to allow decimal input or hexadecimal input.

THE SLASH ROUTINE *(see Figure W10)*

As we saw in Figure W8, the slash routine is entered when the main input routine finds a "/" character. At this point, it is aparent that the programmer must have typed something like

1234/

and it is the duty of the slash routine to display the contents of memory location 1234.

First, though, DDT must save the current contents of VALUE. Once it types the contents of the specified memory location, DDT will go back to the main input routine to await more instructions; consequently, VALUE

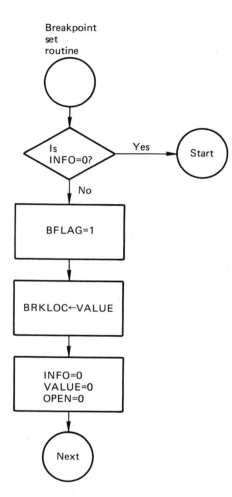

Fig. W13 Breakpoint set routine

will have to be reset to zero. Thus, the current contents of VALUE, which is the address of the memory location to be examined, are saved in LOC.

Next, DDT types the current contents of the memory location, formatting its output so that it will be legible:

$$1234/\underline{7654}$$

At this point, DDT does not know whether the programmer will make a change to the location or not; consequently, the location is considered to be open, and DDT waits for more input from the programmer.

Before returning to the main input routine, DDT sets the OPEN flag to one, so that it will remember the open memory location; INFO is set to zero, so that DDT will be able to know whether the *next* command contained any octal input; and VALUE is reset to zero.

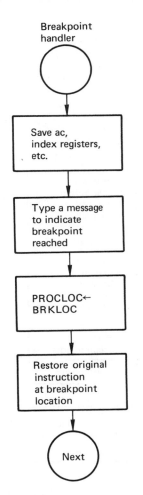

Fig. W14   The breakpoint handler

THE CARRIAGE RETURN PROCESSOR
(see Figure W11)

The main purpose of the carriage return is to *close* an open memory location. In so doing, it may or may not have to make a change to the current contents of that location.

The carriage return routine first checks the status of the INFO flag. If it is zero, then the programmer must have typed the following kind of command:

1234/7654

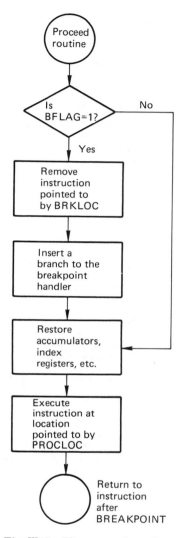

Fig. W15 The proceed routine

That is, if the INFO flag is zero, there was no octal input immediately preceding the carriage return character. This indicates that the programmer did not want to make any changes to the memory location; DDT then resets the OPEN flag and the VALUE register, and returns for more input.

IF the INFO flag is set to one, it is an indication that the programmer must have typed a command of the following sort:

$$1234/\underline{7654}\ 4567\ \textcircled{CR}$$

That is, if the INFO flag is one, it indicates that there *was* octal input immediately preceding the carriage return character. This octal input has

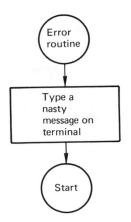

Fig. W16   The error routine

been accumulated in VALUE by the octal digit routine, and it represents the *change* that the programmer wants to make to the memory location pointed to by LOC.

Before making the specified change, though, DDT checks to see that the OPEN flag is set to one. This prevents the programmer from typing a command like

1234 (CR)

That is, it prevents him from modifying a memory location without first examining it. Similar kinds of error-checking are often built into the other DDT routines, but it is critical here; an error on the part of the programmer can cause part of his program or data to be destroyed.

If everything is proper, DDT changes the memory location as instructed by the programmer. It then clears the INFO flag, the OPEN flag, and the VALUE register; finally, it returns to the main input routine.

THE GO ROUTINE *(see Figure W12)*

The purpose of the GO routine is to transfer control from DDT to the program being debugged. The address to which control is transferred is specified by the programmer in his command:

1234G

To be safe, the GO routine should first check the INFO flag, to make sure that the programmer has not simply typed

G

For simplicity, this is avoided in our description, and such a programmer error would cause DDT to transfer control to location zero. With this philosophy, it might be better to make DDT's initial message to the programmer, "Caveat emptor."

DDT's major job is to see whether the programmer had previously inserted a breakpoint. As we see in Figure W12, this is done by checking the BFLAG. If it is set to one, DDT removes the contents of the memory location at which the programmer had requested a breakpoint; it then inserts a special instruction to cause a program branch to the breakpoint handler (see Figure W14).

Any accumulators, index registers, or other status words which the problem program expects to be set up are then restored by the DDT program. Finally, control is transferred to the location specified by the programmer; as usual, it is contained in VALUE.

THE BREAKPOINT SET ROUTINE *(see Figure W13)*

This routine does not do very much; its main function is to *remember* that the programmer requested a breakpoint, so that it can later be inserted when the "go" command is processed.

The routine first checks the INFO flag to see whether the command was of the form

1234B

or simply

B

As with the past routines, if INFO = 0, then the "B" character was not preceded by any octal input; if INFO = 1, the breakpoint routine knows that the command consisted of an octal number, followed by the "B" character.

If the programmer typed just the "B" character, it is assumed that he wants to remove his breakpoint. This is easily accomplished by having DDT transfer back to the beginning of the initialization routine, at which time all of the flags, including BFLAG, are reset.

If INFO = 1, then the programmer is requesting that a breakpoint be placed at a specified location. At this point, DDT simply sets BFLAG to one, so that it will remember that a breakpoint exists, and saves the location of the breakpoint (which, as usual, has been accumulated in VALUE) in BRKLOC. It then clears the INFO flag and the OPEN flag, resets VALUE, and returns to the main input routine.

At this point, the reader may wonder why DDT does not insert its special branch instruction as soon as the breakpoint command is issued by the programmer. The reason may be seen by looking at a typical sequence of commands by the programmer:

1234B
1234/<u>7654</u>
1235B

In this example, the programmer decided to insert a breakpoint at location 1234. After thinking about the situation for a moment, though, he was not sure that he had put his breakpoint in the correct place, so he asked to examine location 1234. If DDT had immediately inserted its branch instruction at location 1234, the programmer would see *that* instead of his original instruction—and he would be understandably confused.

As a result, DDT's policy is to insert the breakpoint only at the instant it transfers control to the program, i.e. when a "G" or a "P" command is processed.

THE BREAKPOINT HANDLER *(see Figure W14)*

The breakpoint handler is entered when the problem program reaches a previously specified breakpoint. Instead of executing the instruction that the programmer thinks is in that location, the program executes a branch to the breakpoint handler in DDT.

DDT's first task is to save all of the accumulators, index registers, and other live registers, so that the program will never know that it has been interrupted. The registers are restored whenever a "G" or "P" command is processed.

The breakpoint handler then types a message to the programmer to let him know that the breakpoint was reached. The breakpoint message can be trivial in this version of DDT, since there is only one breakpoint.

Next, DDT must remember the fact that the problem program has been interrupted at the breakpoint location. As we saw in Figure W13, the breakpoint location was saved in BRKLOC; the contents of BRKLOC are now saved in PROCLOC. This is necessary because the programmer might type the following sequence of commands:

> 1234B
> 4321G
> [breakpoint message]
> 2003B
> P

That is, after the breakpoint has been reached, the programmer might decide to move his breakpoint to a different location. Thus, BRKLOC may receive a *new value, but DDT wants to remember to proceed from the old breakpoint.*

DDT then restores the instruction that had previously been in the breakpoint location. Once again, this allows the programmer to examine his program without finding any of DDT's special branch instructions.

THE PROCEED ROUTINE

This routine is very similar to the "go" routine that was shown in Figure W12. It first checks to see whether a breakpoint exists, and if so, inserts the special branch instruction and saves the problem program's original instruction. It then restores the accumulators, index registers, etc. that had existed at the time of the last breakpoint.

Finally, DDT wants to return control to the program. There is a potential problem, though, because DDT may have a breakpoint at the location to which it wants to return. For example, suppose the programmer had typed the following sequence of instructions:

```
1234B
4321G
[breakpoint message]
P
```

The breakpoint was reached just prior to executing the instruction at location 1234, because DDT had inserted, without the programmer's knowledge, its own instruction in location 1234. When the programmer types "P," he assumes that that his own instruction at location 1234 will now be executed, and that the program will continue until it proceeds *up to* location 1234 again, at which time the breakpoint will be invoked.

This means that DDT must execute the instruction that the programmer originally had in location 1234, and then transfer control to location 1235. In this fashion, it manages to keep its own special branch instruction in location 1234. This is fairly easy to perform on any machine with an "execute" instruction; the sequence of code at the end of DDT's proceed routine might look like the following:

```
EXC        SAVLOC
BRANCH     1235
BRANCH     1236
```

If the programmer's original instruction (which is presumed to be saved in SAVLOC) is a simple instruction, like an ADD, then the instruction following the EXC instruction will be reached; that is, the BRANCH 1235 instruction will be executed. If the instruction in SAVLOC is a *skip* instruction of some type, then the BRANCH 1236 instruction will be executed; if the instruction in SAVLOC is a branch or subroutine call instruction, neither of these instructions will be executed, and the problem program will regain control by itself.

Note that the breakpoint situation can be rather complicated. If the machine has no "execute" instruction, DDT will have to store the original instruction right in its own sequence of code; that is, the proceed routine will look something like this:

```
SAVLOC        **
BRANCH        1235
BRANCH        1236
```

Also, if the programmer places a breakpoint at a subroutine calling instruction in his problem program, things might go awry; the execution of the subroutine calling instruction will generate a return address *within DDT* instead of within the program itself. Finally, if the programmer inserts a breakpoint in a location that is modified by his program, pandemonium will result.

THE ERROR ROUTINE *(see Figure W16)*

The error routine simply types a nasty message on the programmer's terminal, and returns to the beginning of DDT. On most versions of DDT, the error message consists of the "?" character, or perhaps the cryptic comment, "eh?"

SUMMARY

It should be apparent that a DDT debugging program can be implemented quite simply; the ambitious reader may have noticed a number of areas where improvements could be made quite easily.

On the other hand, one might argue that it would be a waste of time to implement DDT. If all of the suggestions, warnings, guidelines, and innuendoes of the previous chapters are followed, the system designer might well produce an on-line system without any bugs; hence there will be no need for a debugging program. Amen.

REFERENCES

1 Edward Yourdon, editor, *Real-Time Systems Design* (Cambridge, Mass.: Information & Systems Press, 1967)

2 Sheldon Boilen, et al., *A Time-Sharing Debugging System for a Small Computer*, Proceedings, Spring Joint Computer Conference, 1963

3 T.G. Evans and D.L. Darley, *DEBUG — An Extension to Current On-Line Debugging Techniques*, Communications of the ACM, Volume 8, Number 5 (May, 1965)

4 R.L. ver Steeg, *Talk — a high level source language debugging technique*, Communications of the ACM, Volume 7, Number 7 (July, 1964)

INDEX